Oregon Painters

The First Hundred Years (1859-1959)

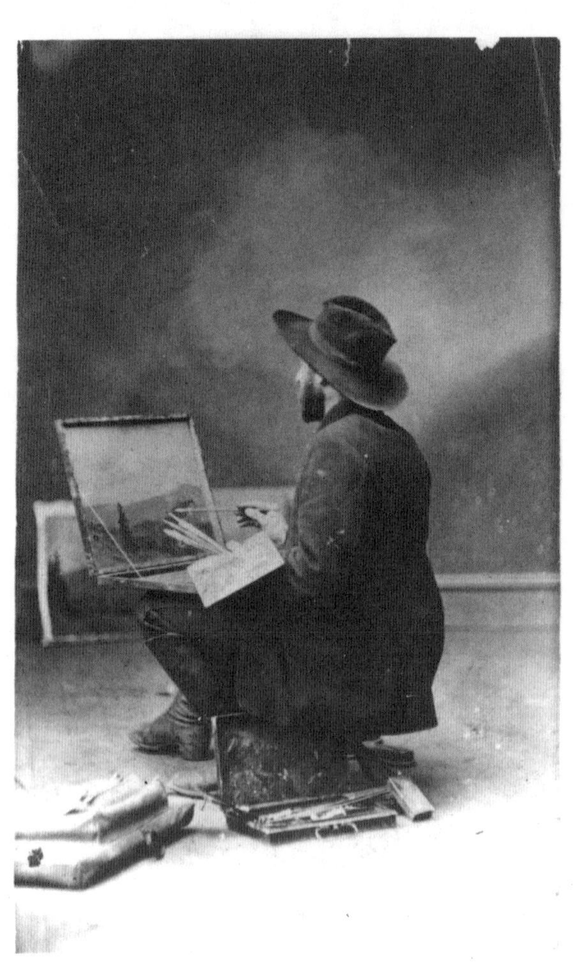

Oregon Painters

The First Hundred Years (1859-1959)

INDEX AND BIOGRAPHICAL DICTIONARY

GINNY ALLEN AND JODY KLEVIT

Introduction by J. D. Cleaver

OREGON HISTORICAL SOCIETY PRESS,

PORTLAND, OREGON

Frontispiece: The artist J.E. Stuart as photographed by Peter Britt in Jacksonville in 1882. J.E. Stuart was the grandson of the renowned painter Gilbert Stuart. He made his first trip to the Northwest in 1876. In the early 1880s he had a studio in Ashland, Oregon. See his entry on p.294. OHS neg. 63544

Oregon Historical Society
1200 SW Park
Portland, Oregon 97205
www.ohs.org

Designed and produced by the Oregon Historical Society Press.

Library of Congress Cataloging-in Publication Data

Allen, Ginny
Oregon painters: the first hundred years (1859-1959): index and biographical dictionary / Ginny Allen and Jody Klevit; introduction by J.D. Cleaver
cm.
Includes bibliographical references
ISBN 0-87595-271-2
Artists-Oregon Biography Dictionary. I. Klevit, Jody, 1933- . II. Oregon Historical Society. III. Title. IV. Title: Index and biographical dictionary.
N6530.O7A55 1999
759.195-dc21
[B] 99-23461
CIP

Printed in the United States of America.
The paper used in this publication meets the minimum requirements of American National Standard for Information Sciences—Permanence of Paper for Printed Library Materials, ANSI Z39.48-1984.

The publication of this volume is made possible by
generous gifts from the
Harold & Arlene Schnitzer CARE Foundation
and from the
Jordan & Mina Schnitzer Foundation

To the men and women whose vision of
Oregon lives on through their art.

CONTENTS

ILLUSTRATION LIST

See color plates, where the paintings are listed alphabetically

Augusta Marshall,
Columbia Slough

Anne Kutka McCosh,
House on Patterson

David McCosh,
Gangster's Funeral

Charles C. McKim,
Mt. Hood from a Marsh

Jack McLarty,
The Bystander

Charlotte Roberta Mish,
Visitor from London

Carl Morris,
Light and Rock

William S. Parrott, *Mt. Hood*

Albert Patecky,
Abstraction (Composition) #51

Conrad Pedersen,
Looking West from the Steel Bridge

C.S. Price,
By the River

Ed Quigley,
Yellow Slicker

Lucy Dodd Ramberg,
Richard Frederick Scholz

Regina Dorland Robinson,
Woman With Umbrella

Cleveland Rockwell,
Early Salmon Canneries, Mid-Columbia River Near Crown Point

Albert C. Runquist,
View of Multnomah Hotel, Portland

Arthur Runquist,
Lunch

Myna Russell,
Lilacs

Michele Russo,
Girl With Daisies

Nels Sandgren,
Upper Forest Fantasy

Alfred Schroff,
Summer Landscape

Edward Sewall,
Death of A House

Howard Sewall,
Seated Baby

Peter Sheffers,
Foggy Morning on the Coast

Eva Cline Smith,
Hollyhocks on Garden Gate

Amanda Snyder,
Price's Work Table

Nellie Starr,
Mt. Hood

Clara Jane Stephens,
New Bridge at Oregon City

Thelma Johnson Streat,
Black Virgin

James Everett Stuart,
Indians on The Bank of the Columbia River

Jefferson Tester,
Arlington Church, Oregon

John Trullinger,
Woman with Parasol

Andrew Vincent,
Coast Cottage

Charles Voorhies,
East of Hood

John Waddingham,
Whistle Stop

Maude Wanker, *Skidmore Fountain, Winter*

Harry Wentz, *Sullivan's Gulch Bridge*

Harry Widman, *Horse and Rider*

Myra Albert Wiggins,
Metals With Glass and Porcelain

Lucia Wiley, *Winter on Beaver Creek*

Jack Wilkinson,
Carnival Dancers

Milton Wilson,
Untitled

Melville T. Wire,
Steens Mountain/ Alvord Ranch

Vernon Witham,
Sunlit Studio Interior

C.E.S. Wood,
Eastern Oregon Desert

PREFACE

During our years as docents at the Portland Art Museum, we were unable to find a practical, concise guide to historic Oregon painters of the first one hundred years: pioneer days to the Centennial. We decided to respond to the need for such a publication by developing this dictionary, a resource we hope will benefit all who enjoy and study the art of Oregon.

While compiling our data, we worked with the following people in mind: docents and museum-goers, art students and scholars, gallery owners and browsers, tourists and history buffs, antique lovers and collectors, as well as auction and estate sale patrons. We were forced, by sheer volume of work, to focus our research on just one medium in order that the artists may be given a thorough historical treatment. Painters made up the largest portion of artists during the formative first one hundred years and were therefore our subject of choice.

While there were painters present in Oregon prior to 1859, we have chosen to emphasize the ensuing one hundred years from statehood to the Centennial. This was a time when artists established residence and contributed significantly to the cultural life of the region. This period of artistic development culminated in the 1959 Centennial, which was marked by a statewide series of exhibitions and celebrations.

The history of Oregon art prior to the time frame of this book is very intriguing, and we are thankful that Jack Cleaver has contributed his essay, "Introduction to Oregon Art History," to this volume. We urge the reader to look to this retrospective for insights into the time period prior to 1859.

For the purposes of classification, the term "painter" refers to those who used oil and watercolor primarily; where the artist was adept in other media it is noted (exhibitions and other information are excluded where the media is uncertain). While the book's time frame ends with 1959, many artists continued to produce important paintings beyond that date. We have included selected exhibitions that occurred after 1959, which featured painters of historical significance.

Most of the painters in this book created a major portion of their work while residing in Oregon. However, the state attracted artists from afar who made important contributions as well. The criteria for inclusion in this book are based on time spent in the area, volume of work, public exhibitions, and/or the significance of their legacy.

Our original database, drawn from the criteria above, consisted of more than three thousand names. We have selected in excess of five hundred artists from that source to constitute the Biographical Dictionary of this book. The database includes research from newspapers, magazines, libraries, colleges, universities, historical societies, and personal contacts.

We welcome inquiries and invite readers to share additional information about Oregon painters. Please contact us online in care of The Oregon Historical Society Press at orhist@ohs.org citing *Oregon Painters* in the subject line.

FOREWORD

Oregon's art history is an emerging story, still incomplete, being told in parts and from a variety of perspectives. The publication of *Oregon Painters, The First Hundred Years* sets the stage for an integrated and balanced telling of the major chapter of this story concerning Oregon's painters from pioneer days to just past the middle of the twentieth century. As Ginny Allen and Jody Klevit's important new book goes to press in 1999, forty years after the volume's cut-off date of 1959 (the year Oregon celebrated its centennial), many of the artists discussed in it are still living and active. For them, in particular, this publication is a validation of the careers they chose to conduct out here on the edge of things. While those artists were far from the art centers of the world, it turns out they were in the midst of a tradition of art-making more complex and extensive than, without the aid of this book, most of us would have realized.

Although *Oregon Painters* is built around more than five hundred brief and factual individual biographical entries, it provides a more comprehensive view of the history of Oregon art than its subtitle "Index and Biographical Dictionary" might suggest. The introduction describing the four periods of Oregon art history, written by Jack Cleaver, the Vasari of Oregon art, sets the stage for understanding individual biographies in the dictionary. So do Robert Joki's account of the exhibitions organized on the occasion of the Lewis and Clark Exposition in Portland in 1905, the chronology of important dates in Oregon art history, the list of Oregon Centennial exhibitions held throughout the state in 1959, and the list and description of arts organizations active in Oregon during the period 1859–1959.

The cross-referencing that occurs within and throughout the five hundred individual entries also begins to tell a comprehensive story of Oregon painting. It is difficult to look up just *one* entry in this book; the one will lead you to a second and third as the interconnections between artists and groups become clear. *Oregon Painters* sets the stage for understanding the comprehensive art history of Oregon while also providing curators, teachers, researchers, students, collectors, and dealers with a concise, well-written guide to the lives and work of individual artists active within the hundred-year period.

This is not the first reference book on Oregon painters/artists. The Oregon section of Marion Appleton's *Who's Who in Northwest Art* was published in 1941. *The Oregon Artists Sourcebook Circa 1941*, published in 1979 by Roger Colman, updated Appleton and, until now, served as the only such volume to focus solely on Oregon art. Allen and Klevit have created the first reference book devoted exclusively to Oregon painters. It is therefore more comprehensive in selection and thorough in discussion than has been possible in earlier sources. It incorporates much new research on both well-known and recently rediscovered artists (including a surprisingly large number who created art here in the nineteenth century). Allen and Klevit's research is supplemented with information compiled by Jack Cleaver in his decades of patient work at the Oregon Historical Society. The authors have selected their five hundred entries from a database they compiled of some three thousand Oregon painters; the names they include represent the largest possible scope of artists of all periods and regions appropriate to their study.

By presenting famous names along with those that are less familiar, the book confirms a legacy while also setting the stage for further research. This book also reminds us of the statewide basis of Oregon's art history; while Portland became the art center, other towns and regions—Salem, Eugene, the coast and southern, central, and eastern Oregon—all had remarkably active artists and artist groups from the earliest days of settlement forward. This book reminds us, too, that despite isolation, Oregon art did not get made in a vacuum. Entries on Albert Bierstadt, Childe Hassam, Frank Vincent DuMond, and others make clear some of the links that early visitors to the state helped establish between Oregon and the broader American art scene.

Finally, comparing *Oregon Painters* to a standard survey of American art makes clear another point: Beginning with Nancy Thornton and Marie Craig LeGall, Oregon has been a state of women artists as well as men. The general accounts of American art are male-dominated in the extreme. In Oregon (and one suspects in many other regions, as well), women have been numerous and active from the beginning as artists and artist-educators. This book lets that fact emerge and speak for itself. What Allen and Klevit do in this volume is set forth accurate information in a variety of forms, made ready for statistical and interpretive uses in the many contexts of study that will lead to the creation of the definitive art history of Oregon. Without this book, the next step would be difficult if not virtually impossible. *Oregon Painters, The First Hundred Years* is an invaluable contribution to the cultural studies of Oregon.

Roger Hull
Professor of Art History
Willamette University

INTRODUCTION TO OREGON ART HISTORY

by
J. D. Cleaver
Curator of Collections, retired
Oregon Historical Society

At last, a directory of Oregon artists that can be trusted! One that goes a long way in presenting the true roots of Oregon's art heritage. It covers painters for the period 1859–1959, and in doing so encompasses the early development of Oregon's art community.

For too long art in Oregon has been regarded as an activity with vague historical roots, something that "sort of happened" once in a while, but didn't really exist until the 1890s. Many references to Oregon's artistic past have been spur of the moment, insufficiently researched, drawn from fuzzy memory, or based on a variety of undocumented or non-existent sources.

By imposing modern conceptions of what art *should* have been, Oregon's art history of the nineteenth and early twentieth centuries has largely been ignored, losing the continuum from then to now. Lost is the fact that the foundations for today's artist organizations, art exhibits, museums and galleries, educational institutions, and collecting were *all* created in the nineteenth century.

Responding to this void, Ginny Allen and Jody Klevit have scrounged resources, checked and rechecked dates, and conducted countless interviews in order to come up with a worthwhile memorial to more than five hundred of Oregon's painters.

Although they are here, this book is not just a directory of the region's best artists, a number of whom achieved national and international notice. It is a record of aesthetic traditions from a frontier environment to a growing appreciation of art—good, bad, or indifferent. Art did not mystically swing into play in 1892 when a group of civic leaders met and established the first art association in the Pacific Northwest. That moment had been slowly nurtured for over forty years by those and other individuals—all influential pioneers in establishing Oregon's first artistic, educational, and other cultural institutions.

Oregon art history essentially can be divided into four periods. Its earliest phase, 1839–1859, is rooted in exploration—a heritage tied to the early sea expeditions of reconnaissance and trade in the Pacific Northwest during the late eighteenth and early nineteenth centuries.

The second period dates roughly from Oregon statehood to shortly after the 1905 Lewis and Clark Centennial Exposition in Portland. It encompasses the establishment of art institutions in Oregon, a subject covered in this introduction. The third period begins in 1907 with the formation of the Portland Arts and Crafts Society and School. It ends with the statehood centennial in 1959.

The fourth period, since 1960, has yet to be compiled. It will include not just additional artist names, but an explosion of artist organizations, art education, public art, and new definitions of art. Nearly ten thousand entries from 1839 through 1989 are in the Oregon Historical Society records. These document not only painters but graphic artists, sculptors, crafts people, illustrators, art photographers, assorted other artists, and organizations deserving of at least a mention in Oregon art history. Probably two-thirds of those entries date past the 1959 time frame of this book. Hopefully this will not be the only book of its kind and others will follow to continue the history of Oregon painters and also to acknowledge other art fields.

The compilers of this dictionary have selected 1859 as the chronological beginning for Oregon art. It is well chosen, reflecting the arrival of Nancy M. Thornton*.[1] Not only was she, in 1847, the first artist known to make a home in Oregon, but she was also the first art teacher. In 1859, she was also one of the first of three artists to be recorded with an exhibit award in the

[1] * Indicates that the artist is listed in the Biographical Dictionary of this book.

Pacific Northwest. Mrs. Thornton, however, was not the first artist in Oregon. The heritage of art in the Oregon Country begins much earlier.

Those first artists of Oregon Country came by sea. In the late eighteenth and nineteenth centuries they voyaged along the Pacific Coast from Baja to Unalaska, assisting in the mapping of uncharted waters and shoreline. Among the officers and crew of the American, British, Russian, Spanish, and occasionally French ships were some academically trained artists. Those who possessed the greatest skill were part of officially sanctioned expeditions into this unknown territory.

Public awareness of expedition artwork was minimal. A few journals kept during these voyages—sometimes edited and published in small number—often included engravings from the original artist's sketches. Even more limiting, much of the art from these expeditions was not ever engraved or published and would not become publicly known for decades, a century, or more. This artwork, largely pencil or pen and ink drawings and watercolor sketches, languished in government archives; some passed into public institutions or private hands. Only in recent times, for example, have some of the illustrations from these explorations become available for research in Spanish and Russian archives.[2]

Many of the expedition leaders became heroic legends or left their name on geographic features (e.g. James Cook, George Vancouver, and Vitus Bering). One of Cook's officers, William Bligh, was not only quite proficient at sketching shore profiles but would be remembered more often than his leader when his name became infamously associated with the word *mutiny*. Primarily known by scholars, the names of the artists of these expeditions range from the talented and trained artist, John Webber, of the Cook expedition to the less-skilled George Davidson, who signed on as ship's "painter" on the *Columbia Rediviva*. Davidson sketched several events during his voyage with Robert Gray, although not the most significant—the "discovery" by Gray of the Columbia River in 1792.

During that year the only inland view of Oregon Country was rendered

[2] A good introduction to these artists from the sea can be found in such books as *Early Maritime Artists of the Pacific Northwest Coast, 1741–1841* by John Frazier Henry (Seattle/London, 1984).

from afar by John Sykes, *Mt. Rainier from Admiralty Inlet.* It later appeared as an engraving in the report of the 1792 sea expedition of George Vancouver. While many of the artists, such as Sykes, were ship officers who were well-trained in draftsmanship, others were crewmen, such as the artistically talented José Cardero, who began as a cabin boy with the 1791–1792 Malaspina expedition.

Actual documentation from the interior of Oregon Country would not come until the next century. This region was vast, left to be defined by Meriwether Lewis and William Clark. Extending from the upper left-hand corner of the Louisiana Purchase, on some maps Oregon Country encompassed the territory between the Pacific shore and the Continental Divide in the Rockies, and from northern California to near the present-day Alaska border. Lewis and Clark brought no professional artists along on their arduous 1804–1806 journey to the Pacific mouth of the Columbia and back. They returned with crude, but poignant, journals and even rougher sketches tucked away in their field notes.

A hiatus of several years would transpire before artists ventured inland. After Lewis and Clark, trappers and traders moved in producing maps and charts. Gabriel Franchère, employee of the Pacific Fur Company, published his memoirs of Fort Astor. This journal included the earliest-known illustration of what is now within the state of Oregon—a view of Fort Astor, by an unknown artist, published in Montreal in 1820. A few artists, such as Alfred Miller, had sketched and painted to the eastern boundary of the Oregon Country. Their work was exhibited to a select few back east, but for most people the introduction to any sort of art from the Far West had been, and would come, from published reports.

Interior Oregon was barely known to explorers, much less artists, in 1839. This was the year that Louis Jacques Mande Daguerre in Paris and William Henry Fox Talbot in London were demonstrating a new photographic process that would eventually transform the way artists viewed the world. As Talbot described it to the Royal Society, this was "the process by which natural objects may be made to delineate themselves without the aid of the artist's pencil."

While the 1843 expedition of John Charles Fremont carried daguerrotype equipment into Oregon (with unsuccessful result), the daguerrotype was not available to record the moment in 1839 when Captain Edward Belcher crossed the Columbia bar and anchored his ship near old Fort Astor (now Fort George). Belcher was in command of a British survey of the Pacific Coast. He is credited with sketching the Fort, a drawing that would later appear as one of several engravings in the published journal of Belcher's voyage. This report also included four drawings of Indian subjects in the chapter on the Columbia River. The sketch was not simply the artist's rendition of local scenery; Belcher was particularly interested in the Fort's defenses. During the next half dozen years in this far away corner of the world, Great Britain and the United States would react to political events by sending naval and ground forces into the region to show the flag and to survey fortifications in the event of conflict over the question of who would control the region. Although credit for the first illustration within the boundaries of what is now Oregon appeared in Franchère's memoirs, it was Edward Belcher, in 1839, who was the first known artist.

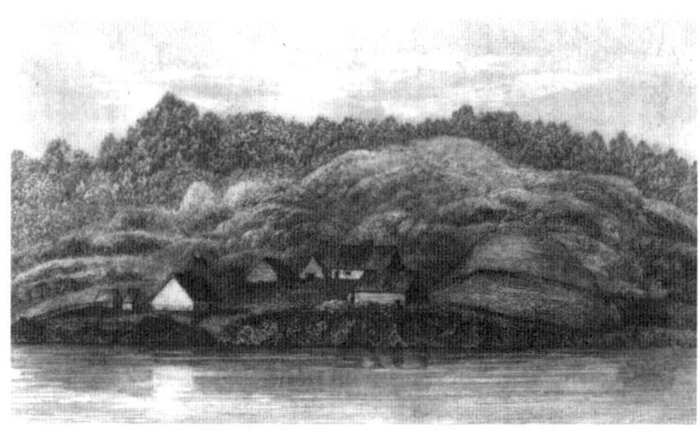

Captain Edmund Belcher's view of Fort George (Astoria), 1839. From Belcher's Narrative of a Voyage Around the World. *OHS neg. CN 8350*

In 1840 Captain Belcher and U.S. Navy Lieutenant Charles Wilkes, going in opposite directions, met in the vast Pacific off the Fiji Islands. Belcher had departed from the Pacific Northwest the previous year and Wilkes would be heading there after wintering at the Sandwich (Hawaiian) Islands. Wilkes and Belcher, wary of each other, did have one thing in common besides being expedition commanders; both were able artists and contributed to the illustration of the Oregon Country.

The U.S. Exploring Expedition, commanded by Wilkes, would leave the first indelible, artistic impression of Oregon. Joseph Drayton and Alfred T. Agate were the assigned artists with the Wilkes expedition. The campaign also included artistically talented naturalists James Henry Dana and Titian Ramsey Peale, the youngest son of the famed artistic family of Charles Willson Peale. In addition, a number of other scientists and officers, including Wilkes himself, were adept at sketching when necessity or mood suggested it.

From May through September in 1841, exploring parties sent out by Wilkes had scurried throughout the Northwest—south from Puget Sound to the Oregon-California border and east to Chimikain and Fort Walla Walla. The scientists, engineers, naval officers, and artists participated in the description and collection of specimens as well as the mapping and illustration of rivers, streams, mountains and valleys, lakes, and other scenic grandeur. They also recorded the location of scattered settlements of trappers, missionaries, and Indians.

From the standpoint of both the scientific and artistic record, the Wilkes expedition brought more specimens and sketches out of the Pacific Northwest than any previous and most later expeditions. There would have been even more surviving sketches if Peale had not lost his sketchbook, drawing instruments, and journal during a mishap in southern Oregon. The record of the expedition was published in 1844 as five hefty, profusely illustrated volumes of narrative written by Wilkes from daily journals and reports of expedition members. In addition, twelve of nineteen projected scientific reports were officially published, eleven by 1856 and the last in 1873. These volumes and seven supplemental atlases were filled with illustrations by Agate, Drayton, Dana, Peale, Wilkes, and many others.

Four years after Wilkes, the Royal Engineers Henry J. Warre and Marvin Vavasour came disguised as tourists. The primary purpose of this British military reconnaissance was to investigate the region's defenses in case of conflict over the boundary issue. Lieutenant Warre, also an artist, sketched prodigiously during the trip. Twelve of his sketches were later made into colored engravings for his 1848 *Sketches in North America and the Oregon Territory* folio book published in London.

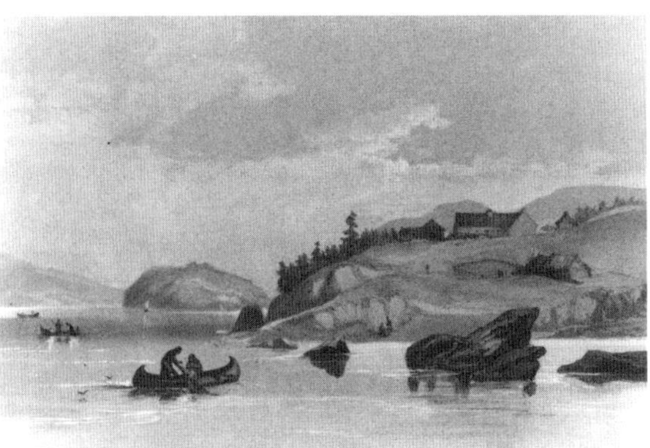

Henry Warre's view of Fort George (Astoria). OHS neg. 35111

About the time that Warre was transporting his sketches and reports back to Montreal, two free-spirited artist adventurers were making their way to Oregon, both of a mind to do a lot of sketching of the Native Americans. Canadian Paul Kane was first to arrive, reaching Fort Vancouver in December of 1846 and visiting what is now Oregon the following year. His adventure produced a number of artworks and a book, *Wanderings of an Artist* (London, 1859), with only a few of his nearly four hundred field sketches included as engravings.

John Mix Stanley* came from the South. His arrival was announced by the *Oregon Spectator* in the July 8, 1847 issue: "We are pleased to announce the arrival among us of a young American artist, Mr. J.M. Stanley, who visits our territory for the purpose of transferring to canvas some portions of the beautiful and sublime scenery with which our country abounds." The following year Stanley would be on his way to Waiilatpu to visit the Whitman Mission when he was informed that Indians had killed Marcus and Narcissa Whitman and several others at the mission. According to Stanley, he had to elude Indians on his way to Walla Walla lest he suffer a similar fate. Upon his return to New York in 1850, Stanley displayed 134 of his works from eight years of travel in what was called *Stanley's North American Indian Gallery.* Many of his Pacific Northwest paintings were among the 151 works deposited and exhibited with the six-year old Smithsonian Institution from 1851 to 1852. A disastrous fire at the Institution in 1865 destroyed most of that collection. Stanley would return to the Pacific Northwest as an artist with the Isaac Stevens railway survey from 1853 to 1855.

Partly in response to the Whitman mission tragedy, the U.S.

Government planned the outfitting of a military regiment to provide defense. Not until 1849 did it arrive. Historically, the march of the Mounted Riflemen regiment is significant in being the first military unit to completely cross the Oregon Trail, from Fort Leavenworth to Oregon City, May 21–October 5, 1849. The report of the expedition by Major Osbourne Cross was accompanied by thirty-six engraved plates, beginning with a view of Fort Laramie and ending with *Commencement of the Cascade or Great Falls on the Columbia River.*

Controversy surrounds the origination of these plates. The expedition was accompanied by two artists, William Henry Tappan* and George Gibbs; most authorities consider Tappan the artist for most of the original sketches. Tappan assisted in laying out the town of St. Helens, Oregon in 1851. There he also served as postmaster and possibly did a sketch of the town that appeared as an engraving in *Gleason's* pictorial magazine. He moved north across the Columbia River, to serve as a commissioner of the newly-established Washington Territory in 1854. He resigned that same year to accept an appointment as a special Indian agent and participated in the 1855 Indian treaty negotiations. Tappan was in Portland when one of his paintings was awarded first premium at the 1862 Oregon State Fair. He probably returned permanently to his Massachusetts home shortly thereafter.

On an 1855 jaunt north from California, a party commanded by Lieutenants R.S. Williamson and Henry Larcom Abbot explored Oregon for the railroad survey. John Young was the staff artist and topographical engineer. Credited to Young are a number of lithographs in Abbot's report and at least five of the lithographs of indigenous trees in the botanical reports.

Also taking place during the last half of the nineteenth century were the surveys of the Pacific Northwest by the United States Coast and Geodetic Survey. William B. McMurtrie and James Madison Alden were the earliest of the survey artists in Oregon and the last was Captain Cleveland Rockwell*. Eventually Rockwell would retire and settle in Portland, becoming one of Oregon's most highly regarded painters of his time.

A few other less significant expeditions entered the Oregon interior during the period before and shortly after statehood. The expeditions came and tarried awhile, moving up and down the rivers and streams by boat and into the hinterlands by horse and by foot. Then they were gone.

What does all of this expedition stuff have to do with art history? Nothing, if we reject the continuum of history as having little, if anything, to do with the present. The purpose of the expedition artist was not to interpret the environment imaginatively, but to provide a record—a precise documentation of a view, event, or specimen. Nevertheless, expedition art, when published, was the first pictorial glimpse of the Oregon Country for many, including would-be immigrants. This was Oregon's first public art.

An example that this pictorial art was influential can be seen in a painting exhibited by Anna Josephine Waldo at the 1864 Oregon State Fair. It was probably copied in class at St. Mary's Academy, after the engraving, *Coeur d'Alene Mission St. Ignatius River*, delineated by Stanley*. His rendition had appeared in the published report of the railroad surveys.

The second period of Oregon art history encompasses significant progress in the development of art, beginning roughly with Oregon statehood. Art education was well established in several of Oregon's early private schools. It had been, in fact, since 1847 when Nancy M. Thornton* introduced art classes at her Female School for the Instruction of Young Ladies and Misses in Oregon City as part of its rounded curriculum for the "young girl of refinement." To be sure, art was aimed at young, "refined" girls in these early drawing and painting classes in the 1850s and 1860s.

It is not known whether Susan Belle Walker Cooke* included art in her early teaching that began, shortly after her overland arrival, at the Oregon Institute in 1851–1852. It is recorded that after 1864 she conducted a private school in Salem that emphasized music and art. She garnered a number of art awards at Oregon State Fairs and was also an accomplished poet. Perhaps her most famous pupil was her son, Clyde*, who won his first art award in 1865 at age five. He would later become one of Oregon's first artists to travel to Europe to study art, after which he would give art lessons to his mother.

Cyrus A. Reed* may also have taught early art classes. He is described as doing so in 1874 by Samuel Clarke ("Oregon Letter" to *Sacramento Union*, October 26, 1874), recounting a State Fair exhibit:

> "In the front Pavilion were hung pictures, some of them paintings made by the pupils of C.A. Reed of this city. Several of these display talent at copying, and as the artists are quite young in some instances, they might possibly develop talent if it was sufficiently cultivated. In this vicinity the ladies take precedence as art students, as quite a class of them have taken to painting."

After arriving in Oregon in 1849, Reed supported himself as a sign and house painter, operated a sawmill, and became one of the founders and directors of the Willamette Woolen Mills. He served as Colonel Reed, the first adjutant general. As an artist, his most memorable work should be easy to spot, if it still exists. It measured three feet by seven feet, depicting a river view of several miles complete with steamboats, the Falls, Oregon City built in a canyon, and the Canemah Indian village—all seen from an elevated view along a "rough and inhospitable" western shore. This may have been Reed's *Panorama of Oregon*, which hung in the U.S. Centennial exhibit in Philadelphia, France, and Germany.

After the artist-explorer came another kind of visiting artist, the itinerant and the rover. This would include such artists as George Catlin (noted painter of Indians), Frederick A. Butman (up from California), and Danish itinerant Peter Tofft*. Perhaps the visit that sparked the most interest was that of artist Albert Bierstadt* and journalist Fitz Hugh Ludlow in 1863. Judge Matthew Deady reported Bierstadt to be a "gentlemanly Teuton of the brush and easel," but found Ludlow to be unbearably obnoxious. Ludlow returned to the East to write about his travels with Bierstadt, published in a series of *Atlantic Monthly* articles in 1864. It is these articles that prompted local criticism.

Ludlow's visit would eventually pass into obscurity while Bierstadt's* paintings of Mt. Hood would leave a lasting impression and controversy for many years. Oregonians would follow his success back east and local art would be compared favorably or unfavorably with his work. His painting did not receive universal applause in Oregon. The Portland *Evening Bulletin* in its July 8, 1869 issue announced the arrival of a California visitor, landscape artist William Keith*, and compared his Mt. Hood with that of Bierstadt: "Instead of painting Oregon scenery in its most unpleasant and forbidding aspect (as his last predecessor *attempted* to do) he has snatched this beautiful gem of mountain scenery from its setting in the wilderness to place it on canvas."

Ludlow in 1863 commented that, while on a boat trip from Portland to Fort Vancouver, he began to recognize "our return from rudimentary society to civilized surroundings and a civilized interest in art and literature." Had Bierstadt* and Ludlow stayed in Oregon long enough to visit Salem that fall, they would have noted definite signs of a society taking a "civilized interest in art and literature" at the third annual State Fair. This might have been considered Oregon's first public art gallery.

Louise Rasmussen, who compiled Oregon art history in the early 1940s, noted many instances of art appreciation in Oregon Country prior to statehood. At first the closest some early settlers got to art was looking at engravings in published reports and periodicals. In the 1850s, a few of Oregon's first county fairs mounted art exhibits. It was at the 1859 Benton County Fair that Nancy Thornton* received her award. The first State Fair, in 1861, included not only painting, but also considered the new technology of photography (sun pictures) as art.

While a lot of the art exhibited at the State Fair might be regarded as mediocre, it should also be noted that some of Oregon's finest painters received their early exposure at these annual events. Appearing at the State Fair early in their careers were Clyde Cooke* (recipient of nearly forty awards), William S. Parrott*, and his noted follower Eliza R. Barchus*. It was at the State Fair that friendly neighbors Myra Albert Wiggins* and Helen Plummer Gatch* competed in all departments as artists and photographers, garnering nearly two hundred State Fair awards between them from 1885 to 1909. Both became noted photographers on national and international levels. Later artists such as Maude I. Kerns* and Rockwell W. Carey* achieved their first successes at the State Fair. From 1861 through 1878 the State Fair remained the sole location for artists statewide to gather on an annual basis. Only occasionally would selected artists have their work appear in art goods stores and various businesses in Salem, Portland, and elsewhere.

The establishment of two institutions in Portland would change all of that. First came *The West Shore* magazine (1875) and then the Mechanics Fair

(1878). Both would have an impact on the direction of Oregon art for several years, as Portland became the center for artistic endeavor and the arbiter of artistic taste. The first issue of Leopold Samuel's magazine, *The West Shore*, appeared in August 1875 and thereafter for the next sixteen years, attaining a peak of fifteen thousand copies for a regular issue. Samuel's declared intention was to publish "a family paper, devoted to Literature, Science, Art and the Resources of the Pacific Northwest." In the following years Samuel gathered a corps of artists and lithographers to produce the finest illustrated magazine in the West. Samuel's illustrators ranged far and wide throughout the region and beyond to help cram *The West Shore* full of engravings. Among them were Alfred Burr*, William H. Byrnes, Henry Epting*, Clarence Smith*, and Junius F. Whiting, all of whom exhibited on the side as painters.

The Portland Mechanics Fair was an annual event which lasted under various guises until shortly after the turn of the century. While it primarily centered on industry and business, it also showcased a variety of other exhibits and demonstrations. Its art exhibit featured not only local talent vying for awards, but also works by internationally-known artists acquired by Oregon—mostly Portland—citizens. An examination of this artwork, which hung in proximity to local endeavor, often reveals discriminating and astute taste by the collectors. Besides French, Italian, and Spanish art, locals were acquiring such American artists of the period as George DeForest Brush, William Merritt Chase, George Inness, and James McNeil

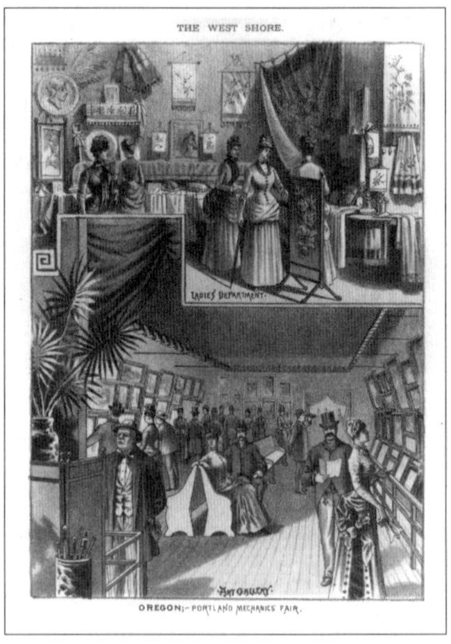

The Ladies' Department and the Art Gallery at the Portland Mechanics Fair. From an 1886 The West Shore *magazine. OHS neg. OrHi 77867*

Whistler. Collectors included such names as Henry W. Corbett, Henry Waldo Coe, Henry F. Failing, William M. Ladd, S.G. Skidmore, D.P. Thompson, Holt C. Wilson, and Charles Erskine Scott Wood* (who also painted). Those were the tastemakers of yesterday, laying the foundations not only for today's art institutions, but for Oregon's first literary, musical, and cultural institutions as well.

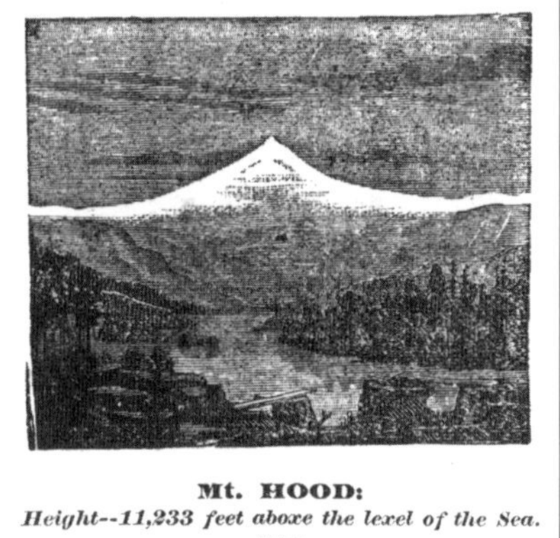

Ad for the Shanahan Art Gallery from 1888 The West Shore *magazine. OHS neg. OrHi 84832*

Represented as part of the art exhibit at the first and subsequent Portland Mechanics fairs were two galleries: the Shanahan Gallery, owned by William T. Shanahan and C.C. Morse's Palace of Art. Both included Oregon artists in their exhibits. Shanahan opened his music store in 1864 and by 1867 had added an art gallery. He was probably the first art dealer in the Pacific Northwest. Morse also operated a combination music store and art gallery.

Special exhibits at the Portland Mechanics Fairs (later known as the Industrial Expositions) acknowledged the art of Oregon students. St. Helen's Hall for girls and Bishop Scott for boys, both Episcopal schools in Portland, had established art courses by 1871. The services of visiting artist, Edmund Thomas Coleman (a.k.a. Edward T. Coleman, an Englishman who had exhibited at the Royal Academy) were acquired to teach the first year. In later years St. Helen's Hall scoured east coast colleges and art schools for young, unmarried teachers, all of whom would teach but a few years and then vanish, marrying or returning east. Among those teachers were Elizabeth Fullick*, "a lady of English birth," graduate of Vassar College and trained in some of the "best art schools" in the East; Rachel Taylor, trained at the New

York Art Students League; and Bonnie King McLeary, who studied at the Académie Julian in Paris. The Bishop Scott course consisted only of drawing until 1888, when Norwegian immigrant and painter Nielsen "Nels" Hagerup* was hired as drawing and painting instructor. While here, Hagerup became a charter member of the Oregon Art Association. Portland Public Schools established art courses in 1877 and student work was exhibited. Soon art courses would begin appearing in schools around the state.

The first Oregon institution of higher learning to offer continuous, full-fledged art programs was Willamette University. The University had provided short-lived painting and drawing courses as early as 1860, but not until the Women's College (established in 1880) included an art department did art become a main part of the curriculum. Marie G. Craig LeGall*, who taught at Willamette University from 1885 to 1908, would become perhaps the most influential Oregon art educator in the nineteenth century—certainly the busiest, developing an accredited two-year art program. Craig LeGall had studied at the Philadelphia School of Design and the Pennsylvania Academy of Fine Arts. Among Willamette University's several hundred art students were Mamie Parvin Brown*, Margaret Gill*, Clyde Leon Keller*, Myra Albert Wiggins*, and Melville T. Wire*.

Pacific University inaugurated an art department in 1883; Emma Blum* and Clyde Cooke* were the first two art teachers. Cooke later spent one year heading the art department at Willamette University. By the turn of the century art was being taught in some fashion at many Oregon colleges and schools.

Another arts advocate was Henry C. Corbett, who sought a gallery space for the exhibition of local art. He arranged the use of a room in the First National Bank Building, thus allowing the Portland Art Club (founded in December 1885) to meet for "mutual improvement by association, for the encouragement of art in the city, and for social pleasure." It would be the first art organization in the Pacific Northwest. Corbett's efforts were rewarded with the presidency. Cleveland Rockwell* was chosen vice-president, Edward L. Espey* (recently returned from study in Paris) was secretary—these were two of Portland's most popular artists. Grafton Tyler Brown*, painter and also the only known black American lithographer, was elected treasurer. Among better-known artist members of the club were Clyde Benton Cooke*, Elbridge W. Moore* (also a successful photographer), James T. Pickett*, James E. Stuart*, and four of *The West Shore* magazine art staff: Alfred Burr*, William H. Byrnes, Henry Epting*, and Clarence Smith*. In addition, there was the young sign painter, Louis B. Akin* along with James Norman Biles*, one of the first graduates of Portland high school's new art program. Other members included railroad engineer and painter, Richard P. Habersham* and artist and photographer, Arthur R. Stringer.

The Portland Art Club met on Monday nights to sketch from models. Every second Friday there was a contest with members presenting a composition relating to a subject previously assigned. The three artworks receiving the greatest number of votes for merit of conception and execution became the property of the club. "The walls of the club room are decorated with the prize sketches of these various themes," reported *The West Shore* (May 1886). It is not known what happened to these artworks, more than sixty in all. By 1889 the Club was spoken of in past tense as former artist members served as pallbearers for the young Espey*. Another young artist, Pickett*, also died that year. By that time, Stuart* and Habersham* had moved on. Soon Biles*, Brown*, and Cooke* would follow. Sign painter Akin* would also leave, first to the New York Art Students League and then to Arizona, where he became a noted painter of southwest Indians. Despite the disbandment of the Portland Art Club, there was still a gallery in Corbett's

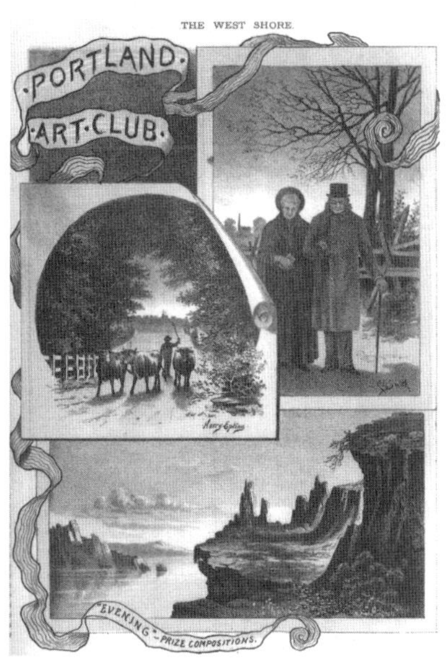

Portland Art Club competition winners shown in 1886 The West Shore *magazine. OHS neg. OrHi 84833*

future. By 1892 the Portland Art Association was organized and would open the region's first art museum in 1895.

Noticeably missing from the more than twenty Portland Art Club members were women. This was rectified in 1895 with two new art organizations, the Portland Sketch Club and the Oregon Art Association, both of which admitted women artists. Two of these ladies would carve careers with the Portland Art Museum. Anna Belle Crocker*, after study at the New York Art Students League and a tour of European art centers, became curator of the Museum and was instrumental in establishing the Museum Art School in 1909, holding the position until 1926. Clara Jane Stephens* studied under William Merritt Chase in Italy, at the Museum Art School, and the New York Art Students League. Although she gained some international attention as a painter in the 1920s, she would spend her time primarily as a teacher, first with the Sketch Club, then Allen Preparatory School, Portland Academy and, closing out her career, with the Museum Art School.

Rising local interest in the arts attracted more visitors. After the expeditions, after Kane and Stanley*, after Bierstadt* and Keith*, the visitors continued to come, many leaving an immeasurable influence—a model to which many Oregon artists could aspire. A number were immigrants or travelers from other countries, including Meyer Straus from Bavaria, L.E. Jardon* from Paris, Howard T. Campion* of Great Britain, Olof Grafstrom* from Sweden, and Carl Henrik Jonnevald from Norway. Many came up from San Francisco, where they were based. Some would linger in Oregon for awhile, especially in Portland, where several took the time to exhibit at the Mechanics Fairs. German-born itinerant Christian Eisele* traveled throughout the West, making a number of appearances in Oregon, during which time he exhibited at the Portland Mechanics Fair. Horace Duesbury*, born in England, remained in Portland long enough to open a portrait studio and win art medals at Portland Fairs. Peter Baumgras*, from Bavaria, was a portrait artist who also found many commissions in Oregon. There were also the English-born brothers, Thomas and Edward Hill*, who visited the Pacific Northwest several times. Edward lived in Hood River for several years before his death. In the early 1880s, Edward Rufus Hill*, son of

Thomas, resided in Portland, where he exhibited at the fair.

Among American-born visitors were Gilbert Munger, itinerant John Joseph Englehardt*, William Cogswell*, and James E. Stuart*. Stuart opened his first studio in Portland, exhibited at the 1883 Mechanics Fair, and joined the Portland Art Club. One influential visitor was Raymond Dabb Yelland*, who taught Stuart in San Francisco. He created dramatic landscapes and scenes along the Columbia in the early 1880s. Yelland and his colleagues, Virgil Williams and William Keith*, taught at the School of Design in San Francisco. Their names would appear as teachers in the biographies of several Oregon artists.

By the turn of the century many Oregon artists had studied in the major European centers of Dusseldorf, Munich, and Paris. Among the first to travel were Clyde Cooke*, Mary Bridges Watson*, Edward Espey*, Katherine Lucy Trevett*, and Virginia Walker. Toward the end of the nineteenth century and into the next, art education centers in New York, Chicago, Philadelphia, and San Francisco drew Oregon artists.

In 1886 gallery owner William T. Shanahan had advocated the establishment of a professional school specializing in music and art. A dozen years later Warren E. Rollins*, artist member and instructor at the Portland Sketch Club, echoed Shanahan's dream for a professional art school. The dreams were achieved fragmentally. A good attempt was made in 1897 when Z.M. Parvin, former director of the Conservatory of Music at Willamette University, and his daughter, artist and musician Mamie Parvin Brown*, opened such a school in Salem. Later moving to Portland, the school survived until 1921. By then only music remained in the curriculum, probably because of the more successful Museum Art School.

Frank V. DuMond*, instructor at the New York Art Students League, and his Oregon-born wife, artist Helen Savier DuMond*, visited Portland in the late 1890s and established a studio at St. Helen's Hall. DuMond lectured twice a week at the Portland Sketch Club. The DuMonds would return in 1905, when Frank was chosen director of the Fine Arts exhibits at the Lewis and Clark Centennial Exposition. DuMond brought together masterworks from throughout the world, emphasizing the Barbizon and Impressionist schools.

A supplemental exhibit to the Exposition was located at the new Portland Art Museum building. It included Portland artists Helen Savier DuMond, Clara J. Stephens*, Harry F, Wentz*, and Charles Erskine Scott Wood*. In a separate exhibit, Eliza R. Barchus* was awarded a gold medal for her landscape paintings; Josephine T. Hayne*, Annabelle Hutchinson-Parrish, Caroline K. Sweetser*, Alice Aubrey Weister*, and china painter George Jeffery* also received awards.

The influence of DuMond during his brief stays cannot be measured, but it was significant in several ways. He introduced many Worlds' Fair visitors to an exceptional caliber of art, the like of which they had never been exposed. Furthermore, he had a major affect on Oregon's promising artists. As a result of his teaching and contact, there would follow over the next couple of decades a steady exodus of Oregon artists to the New York Art Students League.

Three women members of the Portland Sketch Club were especially influenced by DuMond: Anna Belle Crocker*, Clara Jane Stephens*, and Lilian Pherne Bain*. Bain, who was an instructor at Pacific University, would study at the New York Art Students League and become DuMond's assistant for several years. Upon returning to Oregon, she was appointed to the Portland Art Commission, which was established in 1923.

The third period of Oregon art history begins in 1907 with the establishment of the Arts and Crafts Society and School and ends with the statehood centennial in 1959. These fifty years saw dramatic changes in Oregon art communities. Numerous, but usually brief, groups of artists came and went. Between 1911 and 1915 the Circle A Club, Society of Oregon Artists, and the Mutual Art Association introduced such artists as Rockwell W. Carey*, Aimee Spencer Gorham*, Edward Hill*, Clyde Leon Keller*, Charles C. McKim*, Clara Jane Stephens*, and Carl Walters*. Harry Wentz*, an active member of the earlier Sketch Club and a member of some of the later art groups, joined the teaching staff at the Portland Art Museum School in 1910. He was perhaps Oregon's most influential teacher until he retired in 1941. Many of these talented artists would influence the direction of the art community for several decades.

In 1926 came the more permanent Oregon Society of Artists, which included in its membership most of the art educators from the Portland Art Museum and the University of Oregon School of Architecture and Allied Arts, established in 1914.

So-called "modern" art arrived in Portland with the 1913 exhibition of the painting, *Nude Descending the Staircase.* The artist, Marcel Duchamp, was born in 1887, two years *after* the first organization of artists in the Pacific Northwest had been founded. True to the impact it had wherever it was shown, the appearance of the Duchamp painting at the Portland Art Museum set off a controversy in the Oregon community of artists that continues today. It was the first of many exhibits at the Portland museum that would introduce the "modern" art of a given moment, including a 1922 *Futurism* exhibit that featured Matisse and Picasso, among others.

In spite of the Depression, 1930 to 1939 was a robust decade for Oregon art. In 1930 two chapters of the American Artists Professional League were established for Portland and Oregon state at large. In 1933 these chapters created *Art Week*, a statewide event that presented artistic, literary, educational, and other cultural lectures to the public. The program included open studios by many artists. The *Art Week* idea, inspired by Florence Marsh*, spread nationally and internationally.

1933 was also the year that the Public Works of Art Projects were created for the employment of artists, followed two years later by additional government-sponsored art programs under the Works Progress Administration. Through these commissions, murals and other paintings were placed in government buildings, schools, libraries, museums, and other public venues. In 1937 the Salem Art Center opened its doors. As one of fifty-two community art centers opened across the nation by the WPA, it offered classes, lectures, and exhibits. The heirloom of the Oregon WPA projects was Timberline Lodge, which included artwork by painters Darrel Austin*, Martina Gangle Curl*, Virginia Darce*, Dora Erikson*, Karl Feurer*, Aimee Spencer Gorham*, Charles Heaney*, Erich Lamade*, Douglas Lynch*, Clayton S. Price*, and Howard Sewall*. In 1935 Darce and Phyllis Muirden Ryder* organized the cooperative Skidmore Fountain Artists Association.

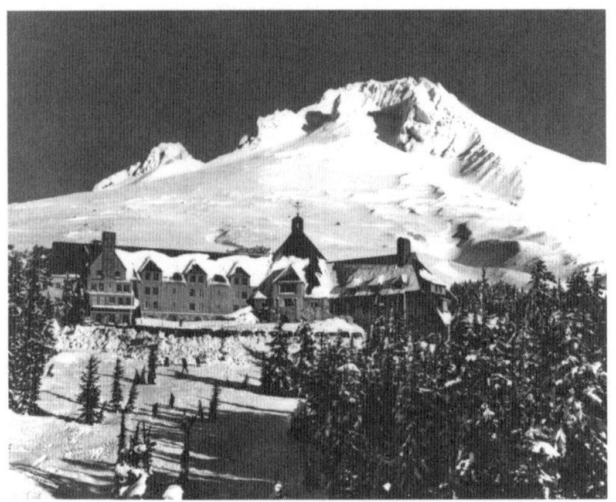

Timberline Lodge on Mt. Hood. OHS neg. CN 23388-a

During the 1930s and 1940s, the Depression and ensuing war notwithstanding, art programs were expanded at major institutions. The Museum Art School added painters Louis Bunce*, William T. Givler*, Douglas Lynch*, Jack McLarty*, Michele Russo*, Charles Voorhies*, and Lucia Wiley* to its staff. At the University of Oregon's School of Architecture and Allied Arts, David McCosh*, Andrew McDuffie Vincent*, and Jack Wilkinson* joined a faculty that already included Eyler Brown*, Maude I. Kerns*, Alfred Schroff*, and Nowland B. Zane*.

Constance E. Fowler* resurrected the art department at Willamette University in 1935 and was replaced by Carl A. Hall* a decade later. After the war, Nelson Sandgren* joined a strengthened art course at Oregon State College (now University). In 1944 Ruth Halvorsen*, longtime high school art instructor, replaced her former teacher, Esther Wuest* as Portland Public Schools superintendent of art. She later became president of the National Art Education Association. A former officer in the American Artists Professional League, she was a strong supporter of the Oregon Ceramic Studio and the Portland Art Museum. As artists, many of these new educators were exploring abstraction, expressionism, and other new art movements. As educators they would be influencing students throughout the 1940s and 1950s—decades of conflict for both the established and the emerging art forms.

World War II raged on both eastern and western fronts, drawing a number of Oregon artists into the fray. One was Robert Ashley Russell*, a descendent of an artistic family that included Grace Russell Fountain* and

Mabel Russell Lowther. He was the promising product of the Portland Public Schools art program and had been studying under a scholarship at the Portland Museum Art School when he was drafted. He was killed by a sniper in France a few weeks after D-Day.

Those artists who returned to the home front discovered a culture war simmering below the surface of the Oregon art community. Many of the state's finest artists were experimenting with the new modern ideas of art. Among them were adherents of what would be called Northwest Mysticism, a style influenced by Japanese sumi painting. It was characterized by monochromatic colors, stark contrasts, and calligraphic brushstrokes. In the 1930s, Seattle artists Mark Tobey and Oregon-born Morris Graves were leaders in the Northwest School movement. One of their disciples was Carl Morris*, who brought the style to Portland.

While some artists experimented with modern forms, others were content to remain traditional. Much that has been written about the new art of the 1930s through the 1950s lacked comment on the expanding rift between artistic conservatism and innovation.[3] Representational artists contended, often in bitter confrontation at community fairs and in art museums, with the followers of modern art.

A growing schism between the Oregon Society of Artists and the Portland Art Museum typified this controversy. These two entities had maintained close ties during most of the 1930s. The Museum presented one of the two Oregon Society of Artists' annual exhibits (the other was held at the Meier and Frank Gallery). Likewise, the Society had sponsored the first exhibit of C.S. Price*, who was regarded as an Oregon pioneer of modern trends. In fact, most of the Museum Art School faculty were or had been members of the Society during the 1930s. Thus, initially the Museum's annual exhibits displayed both traditional and modern art. It seemed, however, that the Museum's tastes were beginning to lean dramatically toward the newer art forms. Soon annual exhibits began to be tailored to a group of favored

[3] *Art of the Thirties: The Pacific Northwest* and *Art of the Pacific Northwest from the 1930s to the Present* (Portland Art Museum, May–June 1972 and 1974) are fine accounts of the emerging modern art of the period, but do not chronicle all the art activity throughout the state.

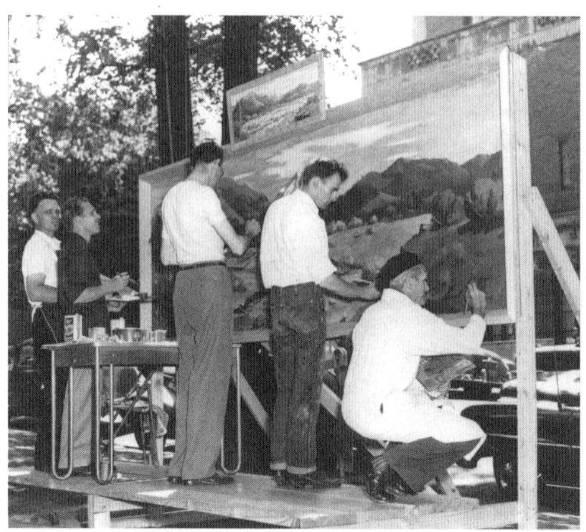

Five artists worked five hours to complete a mural at the Oregon Society of Artists Fair in 1951. Photograph by Al Monner. Oregon Journal *Collection, OHS neg. CN007314*

artists.[4] As these exhibits showcased more and more of the modernists, Society artists appeared to respond by becoming increasingly traditional. In the end, most of the Museum's ties with the Oregon Society of Artists were severed, including the annual as well as other exhibits for members.

Granting that some of the art that had been exhibited by OSA members in the early annuals was marginal, the new exhibit policy appeared to penalize many highly regarded artists who found themselves blocked at the Museum's biennial All-Oregon exhibit. In 1954 the Society constructed its own building, obviating the necessity to find space for its exhibits.

Meanwhile, artists such as Edward Sewall* were dismayed to find their work no longer acceptable in the Museum. Sewall was the first winner of the Museum Art School's prestigious Carey Prize and had enjoyed many local and national successes in the 1930s. Sewall thus abandoned art and took up photography.

Some well-respected and largely conservative artists were not so troubled. Maude Wanker* established the Lincoln County Art Center in 1941. Wanker's Gallery by the Sea in DeLake became a coastal haven for some of Oregon's outstanding traditional artists. In 1958 Wanker was also instrumental in founding the Master Watercolor Society of Oregon, another fair-

[4] Leonard Kimbrell* defined the favored group of previous years as the "annointed" in his "Portland Art: the Old Order Changeth" (*Oregonian: Northwest Magazine*, Feb. 15, 1981). Kimbrell brought the controversy forward into the 1970s, beyond just conservative versus modern, during which time many good artists of varying styles were still being stifled by elite groups.

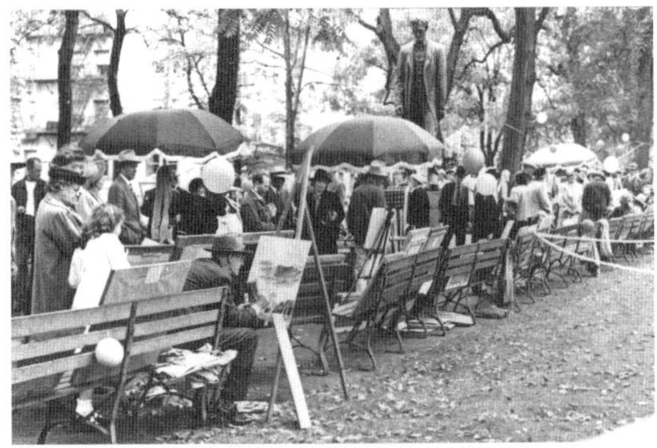

A 1949 crowd watches painters in action at the Oregon Society of Artists Annual Fair in the South Park blocks of Portland. Oregon Journal *Collection, OHS neg.CN 007025*

ly conservative group.

Western artist Ed Quigley*, longtime member and supporter of the Oregon Society of Artists, also found he was denied exhibit space at the Art Museum. However, he found opportunities elsewhere. Besides the Gallery by the Sea, conservative artists were exhibited at such private galleries as the Cascade in DeLake, the Dekum Gallery in Portland, the Elfstrom Gallery in Salem, and sometimes the 12th Avenue Gallery in Eugene. Quigley gained a national reputation, was inducted into the Cowboy Hall of Fame, and received a prestigious Oregon Governor's Art Award in 1982, a few years before his death.

The Governor's Art Award, created in 1977 by the Oregon Arts Commission to honor exceptional contributions to Oregon art development, has included other prominent painters whose successful careers began before 1959: Michele Russo*, LaVerne Krause*, Carl* and Hilda Morris*, Sally Haley*, and George Johannson*.

Another influential artist of the period was James Haseltine*, who helped organize both the Oregon Art Alliance in 1950 and a chapter of Artists Equity, which supplanted the American Artists Professional League in Oregon. Haseltine's next big challenge was to organize *The Oregon Scene*, the invitational exhibition of Oregon paintings and sculpture for the 1959 Oregon Centennial. The job was somewhat hindered by the continuing discord between traditional and modern artists. The controversy regarding selection committees and judges spilled over into the newspapers. Nevertheless, an exhibit representing ninety-two of the state's best conservative and modern painters brought the two groups together, if only temporarily. A suitable date and place for ending this book, it is perhaps the final major event where traditional and abstract art would reside in the same exhibit for many years.

An exception to the dissentions of the 1940s was the late Albert Patecky*. Patecky, a representational artist in between terms as Oregon Society of Artists president, was admitted to study at the New York Art Students League. While there, he was won over by the new abstract artforms, especially the work of Vasily Kandinsky. Along with Maude Kerns*, he was an Oregon pioneer in the non-objective art movement and exhibited at the Museum of Non-Objective Art (now the Solomon R. Guggenheim Museum) in New York, and in Paris and Rome. He also developed new techniques for monoprints. Both ventures provided him with exhibit space at the Portland Art Museum, but even he fell out of favor in the 1950s. Patecky, nevertheless, sympathized with his fellow members of the Oregon Society of Artists, lamenting that artists of all persuasions were now selected on the basis of form rather than solely by their talent and quality of work.

The brief Patecky Gallery (1948–1949) attempted to bridge the faction by representing such diverse artists as Sidney Bell*, Ed Quigley*, Mildred Warner*, Louis Bunce*, Charles Heaney*, C.S. Price*, Howard Sewall*, and Amanda Synder*. From 1949 to 1955 Louis Bunce* and his wife Eda operated the Kharouba Gallery, representing primarily the emerging abstract art of the period. The self-defined New Gallery of Contemporary Art was organized in 1958 by Ronald and Norma Peterson*, featuring sculptors Marlene Gabel and Lee Kelly, and painters Byron J. Gardner* and Duane Zaloudek*. Today, so many art programs, galleries, and other exhibit sites exist that it would seem implausible that any talented, serious artist would be neglected—whatever his style or school of thought. That situation, however, was not prevalent in 1959.

It is well to keep in mind that when Oregon became a state in 1859 no art museums or galleries were in existence, nor were they plentiful in the rest of the West. Vincent van Gogh was only six years old and it was twenty-two years before the birth of Picasso. There was no such thing as "impressionism" much less the later modern art forms. Artistic merit and endeavor was measured by the traditional and established European forms, adopted or modified in American centers of art, such as New York and (later) San Francisco. Other than the occasional artist hired for an official government survey or other project, there was no government support for artists.

Thus it is a mistake for today's many art critics to apply their values of the present to the past, ignoring the principles of the time in which the art appeared and the reasons for which it was created. This can unfortunately produce inaccuracies and inadequate, even irresponsible, history. It would not seem necessary to even state that point if it were not for the view of one recent authority who decided, without evidence, that the "fine arts community in the Pacific Northwest is a comparatively youthful one, having developed, in the main, during this century." He then summarily dismisses over a half century of earlier art in the region as "traversed by artist explorers during the first half of the nineteenth century. . . followed later by itinerant painter-signpainters and a few hardy photographers who made the gold and timber boom towns their homes."[5] This unfortunate view, apparently not grounded in any extensive research of Pacific Northwest art history, ironically overlooks the fact that probably not a half dozen of several hundred competent Oregon artists before 1900 fit his description of signpainter. Those artists who did begin as signpainters would include Louis B. Akin*, Paul Kane, and John Mix Stanley*—all of whom established national reputations.

The history of Oregon art is not a list of hand-picked examples created from current taste and happenstance scholarship. It is a record of how each generation views its art within the framework of its values, traditions, and institutions. It is not a public duty to appreciate art. It is the artist's task, if he seeks approbation, to create art that is appreciated. Most important, art history is about continuity, a view expressed well by artist William Cumming:

> "Contemporariness has become so engulfed in trendy waves of fad and fashion and hype, trumpeted in the shrill jingle of media jargon, that art before 1948 has become pretty much terra incognita unless it can be mortised into the modern fast sell. . . . The his-

[5] *50 Northwest Artists* by Bruce Guenther (San Francisco Chronicle Books, 1983).

> tory of art like the history of everything else is served up in little slices of chic with no sense of continuity or development."[6]

It is hoped that this book—devoted to Oregon painters—will be more than just another slice of "chic" and will inspire more exploration of Oregon's neglected artists and art development.

[6] *A Memoir of the 1930's and the Northwest School* by William Cumming (Seattle/London, 1984).

VISITING ARTISTS, NINETEENTH CENTURY

The names below are not in the Index and Biographical Dictionary section of this book. They are included here because of the historical significance of their contributions to the early development of art in nineteenth-century Oregon. Further information about these artists can be found at the Oregon Historical Society. The parenthetical dates indicate known life span; the dates in italics indicate time spent in Oregon.

Alfred T. Agate (1812–1846): Official artist, U.S. Exploring Expedition. *1841*

James Madison Alden (1834–1922): Artist for U.S. Coast and Geodetic Survey. *1854–1857*. Northwestern Boundary Survey. *1858–1860*

Addie L. Ballou (1837–1916): California suffragist, artist, lecturer, poet, and essayist made at least two visits to Oregon, receiving a first premium for an oil portrait at the 1878 Oregon State Fair. *1870s*

Frederick A. Butman (1820–1871): Railroad survey artist, completed *1000 Miles of the Columbia River* (sketches and paintings). *1860–1865*

George Catlin (1796–1872): Noted painter of Indians, visited Oregon and Pacific Northwest. *1854*

William Lindsay Challoner (1852–1901): Artistic sea captain, painted Yaquina Bay. *ca. 1890*

Edmund Thomas Coleman, a.k.a. Edward T. (1823–1892): English visitor, taught at St. Helen's Hall and Bishop Scott Academy in 1871. *early 1870s*

Alexis T. Coughlin: Completed historic painting, *View of Newport, Oregon. ca. 1870s–1880s*

Joseph Drayton (? – 1856): Official artist, U.S. Exploring Expedition. *1841*

Edward de Girardin: French visitor, sketched several landscapes and Indian portraits while serving as topographer with various survey groups in the Pacific Northwest. *ca. 1855–1860*

George Gibbs (1815–1873): Accompanied Mounted Rifle Regiment to Oregon, sketched Oregon and Pacific Northwest, one known painting. *1849–1852*

Robert Swain Gifford (1840–1905): Illustrator, painted Mt. Hood and views of Columbia River for William Cullen Bryant's *Picturesque America. 1869*

Dr. Hewitson: Presumed English, signature appears on one known drawing and two engravings of Oregon and Washington. *ca. 1841–1844*

Thomas Hill (1829–1908): Precise times of Hill's visits to Oregon are uncertain. He may have at various times visited with his brother, Edward Hill* or his son, Edward Rufus Hill*, both of whom were in Oregon from the 1880s to the early twentieth century. Portland's Pittock

Mansion owns a Mt. Hood painting by Thomas Hill.

Carl Henrik Jonnevald (1856–ca. 1930): Completed trips from San Francisco to the Pacific Northwest. *mid 1880s*

Paul Kane (1810–1871): Canadian artist visited Pacific Northwest. *1846–1847*

Edward Meyer Kern (1823–1863): Survey artist and watercolorist with John C. Fremont's third expedition and other expeditions into the Pacific Northwest. Kern's engravings appear in Fremont's memoirs. *1845–1846*

William Birch McMurtrie (1816–1872): Completed six Oregon views while working for the U.S. Coast and Geodetic Survey. *ca. 1849*

Gilbert Munger (1837–1903): Frequent visitor to Oregon, completed views of Mt. Hood. *before 1875*

Titian Ramsey Peale (1799–1885): Naturalist, U.S. Exploring Expedition, only a few drawings and paintings of Oregon flora and fauna survived a mishap on the Umpqua river. *1841*

Francis Marion Pebbles (1839–1928): San Francisco portrait artist had several Oregon commissions. *1870s*

Father Nicholas Point (1799–1868): Catholic missionary and artist did a sketch of St. Paul mission complex. *ca. 1844*

Charles Preuss (1803–1854): While not a painter, he nevertheless is historically significant as a mapmaker/illustrator with the Frémont Expedition of 1842–1843.

Julian Walbridge Rix (1850–1903): Visited Oregon from California. *1870s–1880s*

Frederick Ferdinand Schafer (1839–1927): German painter, settled in San Francisco, painted Pacific Northwest landscapes and Indians. *1880s*

Meyer Straus (1831–1905): From Bavaria, traveled north from San Francisco to paint in the Pacific Northwest. *late 1870s–1880s*

Alfred Sully (1820–1879): Son of artist Thomas Sully. Amateur artist and Brigadier General in command of Ft. Vancouver; completed at least two paintings of the Fort and may have painted or sketched Oregon subjects. *1874–1879*

Henry Warre (1819–1898): British Royal Engineer, painted in Pacific Northwest. *1845–1846*

Junius F. Whiting: Traveling artist for *The West Shore* magazine. *ca. 1882–1885*

Charles Wilkes (1798–1877): Commanded U.S. Exploring Expedition, contributed several Pacific Northwest drawings for engravings in the final report. *1841*

James Wise: Portrait, miniature painter, and photographer from San Francisco, exhibited at the first Oregon State Fair. *1861*

John Young (1830–1879): Artist with Williamson-Abbott railroad survey into Oregon. *1855*

IMPORTANT DATES IN OREGON ART HISTORY

1847 .... Nancy M. Thornton* teaches the region's first art classes in Oregon City.

1856 .... Washington County Agricultural Society sponsors the region's first exhibition with award categories for art.

1859 .... Benton and Linn County Fairs begin recording exhibit award recipients, leaving the earliest record of artists' names.

1860 .... Willamette University offers the first college art classes in the Pacific Northwest.

1861 .... State Agricultural Society sponsors the first Oregon State Fair. This fair provided early opportunities for public art and photography exhibitions, awards, and recognition.

1863 .... *Portland City Directories* begin publishing artist listings.

1867 .... William T. Shanahan, thought to be the first art dealer in the Pacific Northwest, opens The Shanahan Gallery.

1874 .... Thaddeus Welch* travels to Europe to study, making him the first Oregon artist to study art abroad.

1875–91 *The West Shore* magazine begins publication with a staff of professional artists.

1877 .... Portland public schools offer first art courses.

1878-88 The Portland Mechanics Fair is established. This fair not only featured local artwork, but also included internationally-known artists. It later became:

- **1889** North Pacific Industrial Exposition, which became:
- **1891** Portland Industrial Exposition, which became:
- **1895–99** Oregon Industrial Exposition

1885 .... The Portland Art Club is established, forming the first organization of artists in the Pacific Northwest.

1886 .... The Portland Library Association acquires Edward Espey's* *Repose*. It is the first work of an Oregon artist to be purchased by an Oregon civic organization. *Repose* is currently housed in the Central Library.

1888 .... The Skidmore Fountain, by Olin Warner, is Oregon's first public art. The fountain sits at SW 1st and SW Ankeny in Portland.

1889 .... The Eastern Oregon District Agricultural Society holds its first fair in Baker City.

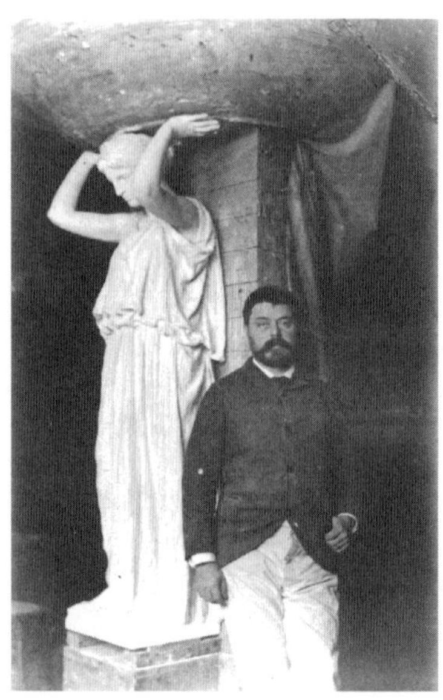

An 1888 studio shot of sculptor Olin Warner with his work for the Skidmore Fountain. OHS neg. 1503

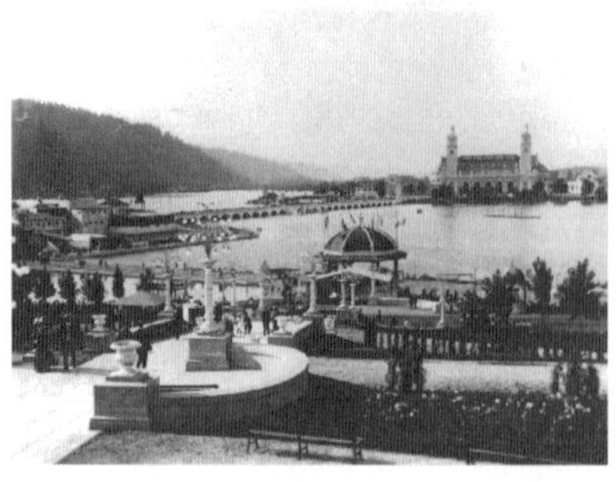

A lake view of the 1905 Lewis and Clark Centennial Exposition. OHS neg. 28137

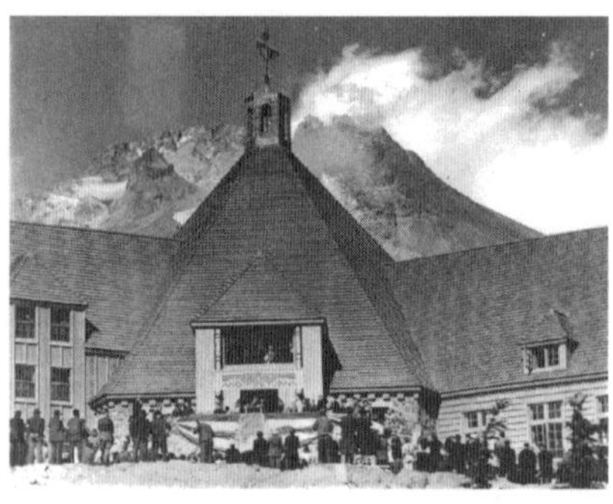

Timberline Lodge dedication ceremonies, September 28, 1937. OHS neg. OrHi 50187

1889....... The *Oregonian* (established as a daily newspaper in 1860) employs artist/photographer Edgar Felloes as its full-time staff illustrator.

1890....... The first Southern Oregon Agricultural Fair is held in Central Point.

1892....... The Portland Art Association is founded.

1895....... The Portland Art Museum opens its doors, becoming the first art museum in the Pacific Northwest.

1895....... The Portland Sketch Club is founded. It later became:

1906 The Oregon Art Students League

1895....... The Oregon Art Association is formed. It later merged with:

1898 The Portland Sketch Club

1898....... *Pacific Monthly*, a magazine highlighting art and literature, is established. It later merged with:

1911 *Sunset* magazine

1905....... The Lewis and Clark Centennial and American Pacific Exposition and Oriental Fair (hereafter referred to as the Lewis and Clark Centennial Exposition) is held in Portland. The Fine Arts Exhibit at this World's Fair introduced the public to international masterwork paintings of Barbizon, Impressionist, and other schools.

1907....... The Arts and Crafts Society and School in Portland is founded by Julia Hoffman*.

1907–41 The *Spectator* magazine is established in Portland. The *Spectator* regularly reviewed Oregon artists.

1908....... The Portland Art Association purchases its first oil painting, *Afternoon Sky, Harney Desert*, by Childe Hassam*.

1911....... The Circle A Art Club is founded.

1912....... The Society of Oregon Artists is formed.

1913....... Selections from the New York Armory Show are featured at the Portland Art Museum. This exhibit included Duchamp's *Nude Descending A Staircase.*

1913–14 The School of Architecture and Allied Art is established at University of Oregon.

1914....... The Mutual Art Association is established.

1915....... The Panama-Pacific International Exposition, which featured an exhibit of Oregon Painters in the Art Room of the Oregon Building, is held in San Francisco.

1919....... The Salem Art League is founded.

1923....... The *Futurism* exhibit at the Portland Art Museum is organized by Sally Lewis. This show featured works by Picasso, Matisse, and other important examples of modern art.

1923....... The Portland Art Commission is established.

1925–70 The Attic Club is formed.

1926....... The Oregon Society of Artists is established; First annual exhibit is held in 1927.

1930....... The American Artists Professional League establishes Portland and Oregon chapters.

1930....... The University of Oregon in Eugene establishes its Museum of Art.

1932....... The Portland Art Museum Building, designed by Pietro Belluschi, opens to the public.

1933....... The American Artists Professional League sponsors *American Art Week* in Portland. This later became a statewide, and then national, event.

1933....... The Public Works of Art Project begins in Oregon.

1935....... The Works Progress Administration creates the Federal Art Project (FAP) in Oregon.

1935....... The Skidmore Fountain Artists Association is established.

1935....... Fire destroys the State Capitol building in Salem, including the artwork inside.

1935....... Southern Oregon Art Association is established in Medford.

1936....... The Skidmore Fountain Artists Center, Inc. is established in Portland.

1937....... The Oregon Ceramics Studio is established in Portland. It later merged with the Contemporary Crafts Gallery.

1937....... Timberline Lodge opens to the public, featuring the work of Oregon artists. The lodge is a WPA project, situated near the top of Mt. Hood.

1941....... The Lincoln County Art Center is established at DeLake (later incorporated into Lincoln City).

1944....... The Oregon Guild of Painters and Sculptors is formed.

1949....... The Eugene Arts Center opens. This later became the Maude Kerns Art Center.

1950....... The Coos Artists League is founded. This group later established the Coos Art Museum.

1951....... The Oregon Art Alliance is established in Portland.

1951....... The Oregon chapter of Artists Equity is formed.

1957....... The Master Watercolor Society of Oregon is formed.

1958–62 The New Gallery of Contemporary Art opens in Portland.

1959....... The Rental Sales Gallery opens in the Portland Art Museum.

1959....... Oregon's Centennial is celebrated with statewide art exhibitions and gallery shows.

Please see sections on Arts Organizations and Art Education for additional information.

THE ART OF THE FAIR

The Lewis and Clark Centennial Exposition, 1905

by Robert L. Joki, Director, The Sovereign Collection

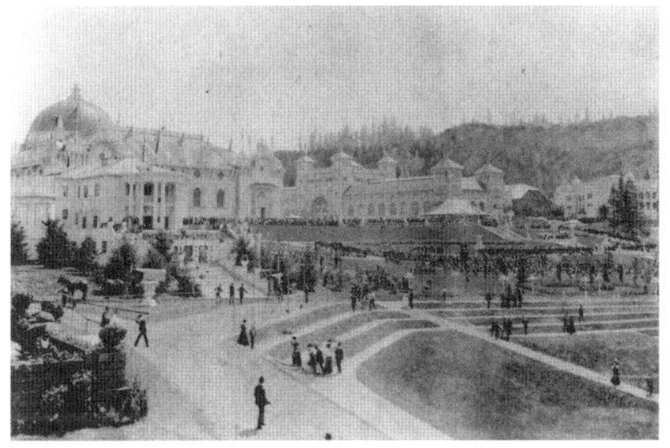

Opening Day of the Lewis and Clark Exposition, June 1, 1905. OHS neg. OrHi 100851

The Lewis and Clark Centennial was the first major exposition west of the Rocky Mountains. The Fine Arts Exhibit of this 1905 Fair served as a catalyst for Oregon's maturing artistic community by introducing them to a new standard of international aesthetics. Following in the footsteps of the 1904 St. Louis Exposition, the Portland World's Fair was final confirmation that civilization and culture now extended all the way to the Pacific Coast.

In its original intention, the Fine Arts Exhibit of the Fair was to be a "re-hanging" of the art exhibits from St. Louis the year before. This would have been a simple and predictable solution to the problem of organizing and transporting a major exhibit so far from the art centers of the East. However, that plan would change with the hiring of the young Frank Vincent DuMond* as chief of the Fine Arts Department.

DuMond began his teaching career at the Art Students League of New York City in 1892. His marriage to Helen Savier* of Portland in 1895 resulted in regular visits and art lectures at the Portland Sketch Club and the Portland Art Association. These presentations were attended by many of Portland's early talents, including Harry Wentz*, Clara Jane Stephens*, and Anna Belle Crocker*. DuMond found Portland to be fertile recruiting grounds for the Art Students League as well as for his summer school in Old Lyme, Connecticut. As a result, the pathway between America's "art center" and Portland's art world was opened; allowing Oregon artists, for the first time, direct access to the newest trends in American art.

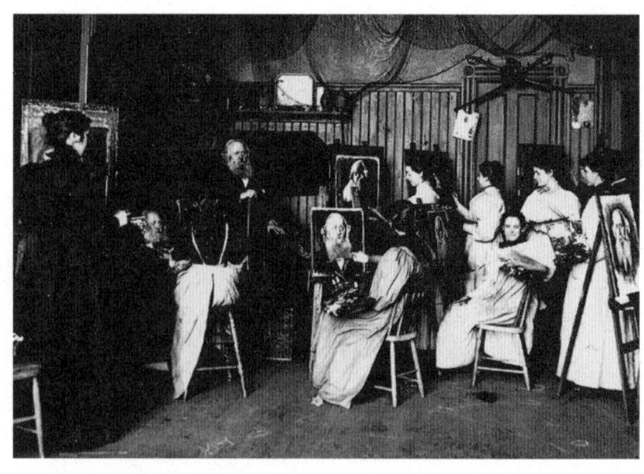

Frank DuMond, teaching and modeling in this photograph taken by Julia Hoffman in her studio at 714 Everett, prior to 1896. Oregon College of Art and Craft

DuMond's vision for the Fair went far beyond the typical format of arranging an international contemporary art exhibit, as was held in Chicago in 1893, Buffalo in 1901, and St. Louis in 1904. The educational possibilities of a more historic and comprehensive exhibit would require selection by periods, schools, movements, transitions, and influences, rather than solely by countries of origin. The need to secure valuable pieces by "great masters" put a strain on insurance and transportation budgets. The willingness of the Crocker family in nearby Sacramento, California to loan their superb art collection to the Fair assured the feasibility of this approach.

Chronologically the exhibit covered nearly two hundred years of art history, beginning with important early Dutch, French, and English masterpieces and extending to the most important contemporary artists of the day. The Barbizon and Impressionist schools were represented by numerous, well-

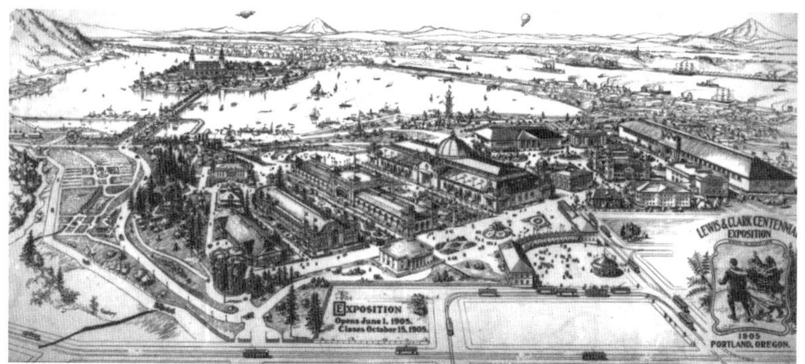

Bird's eye view of the Lewis and Clark Exposition. OHS neg. OrHi 36787

chosen examples, such as works by Corot, Monet, Cassatt, Sisley, and Pisarro. Whenever possible each artist was represented by two to six examples of their work. This allowed for a more thorough study of each artist's work.

DuMond's reputation and connections at New York's National Academy guaranteed that the highest-quality contemporary American paintings would be sent to the exhibition. Virtually every American painter of note was eager to be included. DuMond's demanding curatorial selections made (and lost) him many friends. An artist's reputation alone was no guarantee of inclusion. Throughout the selection process, DuMond kept complete control. His goal was to create an exhibit of a quality that would clearly surpass anything that had appeared in previous world's fair exhibits.

The fireproof cement and brick Fine Arts Building provided over ten thousand square feet of gallery space. Over six hundred paintings were hung, for the most part three high, on burlap-covered walls. An additional fifty-eight pieces of sculpture extended down the center aisle of the "L" shaped building. Exhibits of miniatures and photographs were included as well. Modern electric lights illuminated virtually every item in the exhibit.

The Portland Art Association planned completion of their new museum building at Fifth and Taylor in downtown Portland to coincide with the opening of the Fair. This would allow DuMond the opportunity for twice the space and two separate exhibits. The Portland Art Museum's inaugural exhibition, *Section B of The Fine Arts Department Exibition*, consisted of nearly four hundred watercolors, pastels, original illustrations, and sketches from nature. Helen Savier DuMond*, Clara Jane Stephens*, Harry Wentz*, and C.E.S. Wood* were Oregon artists who exhibited in *Section B.*[1]

The art of the Fair was met with critical acclaim from all corners of the world. With over one thousand individually selected "world class" paintings and sculpture spread between the two exhibit buildings, Frank Vincent DuMond had exceeded the hopes and expectations of the Lewis and Clark Fair Committee and the international art community as well. This exhibit would stand as one of the greatest accomplishments in DuMond's career and serve as a milestone that may never be surpassed in Portland.

[1] In addition to the fine arts sections, other Oregon artists participated in the Lewis and Clark Centennial Exposition in a variety of venues.

OREGON CENTENNIAL, 1959

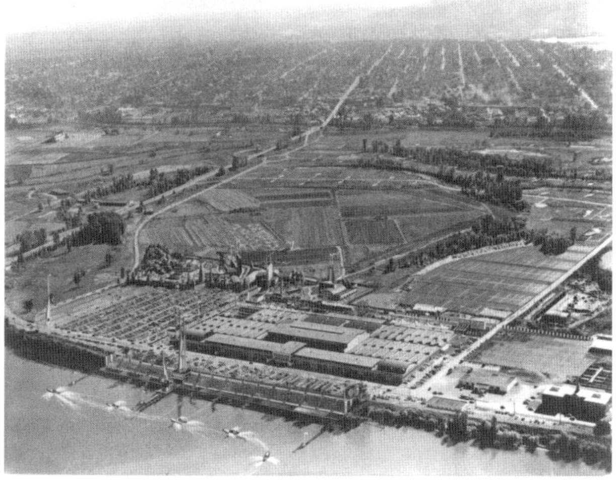

Oregon Centennial Grounds at Expo Center in North Portland, with the air-brushed additions of a boat review stand and an amusement park. OHS neg. OrHi 100850

The 1959 Oregon Centennial was marked by statewide celebrations of every kind. A major art exhibition was held at the Centennial Exposition Center in Portland, featuring artists who were selected from regional competitions. The Portland Art Museum held at least five special exhibitions: One-person shows by foremost Oregon artists C.S. Price* and Charles Heaney* in addition to three other shows that featured Oregon art. Collegiate sites also participated: Portland State University hosted a watercolor exhibit and the University of Oregon in Eugene held an exhibit entitled *Art of the Oregon Territory*. Arts organizations such as the Oregon Society of Artists and the Oregon Society of China Painters sponsored their own celebrations. Even community service organizations, such as the Rose Festival Society and private industry, such as the General Motors Company, participated by presenting Oregon artists. Following is a partial list of these sites and their respective exhibitions:

CENTENNIAL EXPOSITION CENTER, Portland

A major arts event was held at the Centennial Exposition Center on north Marine Drive. Dr. James Hart chaired the advisory committee, assisted by Carl Hall*, James McGarrell*, and Dr. Francis Newton. Rachael Griffin* chaired the visual arts section.

The Centennial Building, one of several on the grounds, housed a five hundred foot mural "suggesting topography of the land, coast, cities, byways, fields, streams and people." Richard James Norwood* designed the panorama and, with the assistance of Byron Gardner* and Duane Zaloudek*, completed it in forty-two days. The following exhibitions were held in the Centennial Building:

> *The Oregon Scene* (see References C6): James Haseltine* chaired the committee and jury, Dr. Francis Newton served as curator. The exhibition was a major, cataloged invitational of Oregon paintings and sculpture selected from regional competitions in Corvallis, Coos Bay, Medford, DeLake (Lincoln City), and La Grande.
>
> An *Architectural Exhibition* featured a pool at the main entrance containing a fifteen-foot welded sculpture by Manuel Isquierdo. The exhibit showed the Oregon architectural past and present, with introductory panels by Arvid Orbeck.
>
> The *Oregon Crafts Exhibit*, featuring arts and crafts, was held in the Centennial building.
>
> The *Printmakers Fair* featured a different printmaker each day and artists demonstrated the techniques used in their work.

The International Garden of Tomorrow was located on the exposition grounds and featured sculpture by Oregon artists. Charles Voorhies* was the curator.

The Hall of Religious History housed eight-by-ten-foot paintings completed by Carl Morris*.

The Horticulture Building contained a thirty-two-foot mural rendered by Louis Bunce*. He sought to convey "something of a garden feeling with a sense of light that emanates from a colorful garden."

The Forest Products Pavilion contained untitled work by Oregon artists. Phil Gilmore completed a three dimensional collage presenting the regions' best-known woods.

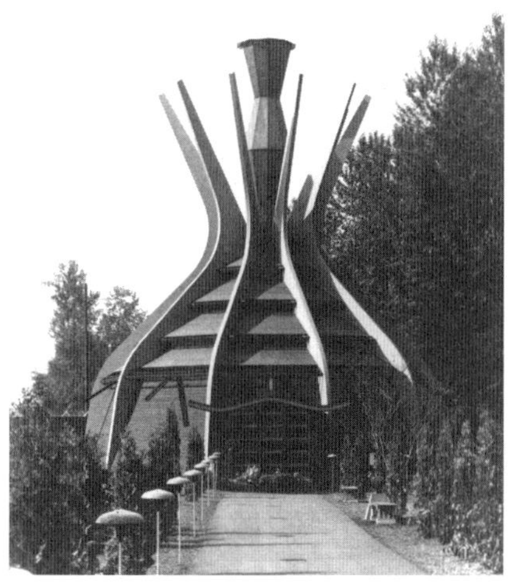

The Hall of Religious History at the Oregon Centennial which contained paintings by Carl Morris. OHS neg. OrHi 46695

PORTLAND ART MUSEUM

During the centennial year, the Portland Art Museum hosted several major exhibitions. The calendar year began in 1958 and there were three main shows celebrating the centennial season:

Calligraphy: Golden Age of Modern Revival, Fall of 1958

Van Gogh, October 1958–April 1959

Paintings and Sculpture of the Pacific Northwest Oregon, Washington and British Columbia, June 13, 1959–August 9, 1959 (See Reference A4).

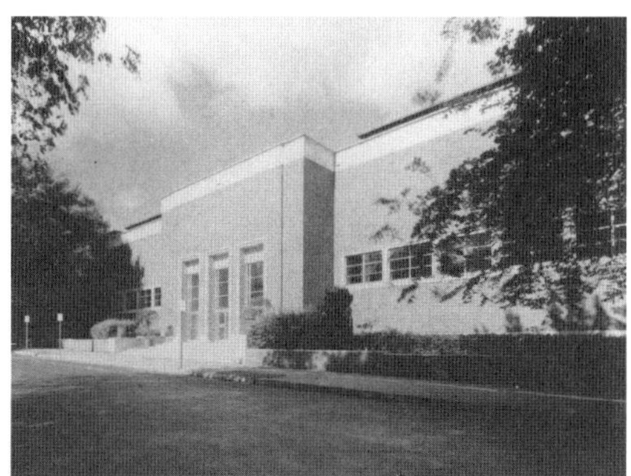

Portland Art Museum OHS neg. 43184a

This exhibition featured fifty-nine artists from the Pacific Northwest: Vancouver, British Columbia to the Willamette Valley. The main theme was the Pacific Northwest with an emphasis on Oregon.

Early Days in the Pacific Northwest: The Collection of Dr. and Mrs. Franz Stenzel, Portland Art Museum, September 23–October 25, 1959. (See Reference C16). Included drawings by James G. Swan.

C.S. Price—Paintings, Drawings and Models

Oregon Territory, 28 Lithographs from the Library of Congress

Charles Heaney, one-person show

OREGON SOCIETY OF ARTISTS, Portland

This group held a *100 Day Celebration* beginning in June at their Oregon Society of Artists Gallery on Southwest Park Place. The celebration included:

A group show featuring members: Colista Dowling*, Thayne Logan*, Chester Murphy*, Ed Quigley*, Jack Rudfelt, Arthur Selander*, and John Waddingham*.

A two-person show featuring William Drake* and Clyde Archibald*.

PORTLAND STATE COLLEGE

Oregon Art Alliance sponsored *27 Watercolors by 27 Artists.* The exhibit was held at Portland State College (now University), juried by Frederick Heidel*. The exhibit circulated for one year through the department of statewide services of the Oregon system of higher education. The participating painters were:

Wes Baxter*, Joyce Britton*, Louis Bunce*, Max Buhman*, Bonnie Butler*, Craig Cheshire*, Robert Colescott*, Patricia Dodd*, Byron Gardner*, Howard Hall*, Ruth Halvorsen*, Charles Heaney*, Frederick Heidel*, Anne M. Johnson*, Willard Johnson*, LaVerne Krause*, Don Kunz*, Percy Manser*, Claude McGraw*, Jack McLarty*, Richard Newstrum*, Albert Patecky*,

Richard Prasch*, Florence Saltzman*, Virginia Saward*, Charles Voorhies*, and John Waddingham*.

UNIVERSITY OF OREGON, Eugene

Art of the Oregon Territory (see Reference C12). This exhibit featured works from the collection of Dr. and Mrs. Franz Stenzel. It was hosted by the Museum of Art at the University of Oregon.

ROSE FESTIVAL ART EXHIBITION, Portland

This annual art exhibit was held on the Southwest Park blocks in Portland. In addition to various organizations and groups working in fine arts and crafts, twenty-five artists were represented for the first time.

OREGON PHOTOGRAPHY, Portland

This Land, This Oregon featured the work of Oregon photographers. Charles Politz was the designer of this exhibit, which portrayed the theme, Monumental Oregon. Nationally-recognized photographer, Minor White returned to Portland to teach a photographic workshop for the Oregon Centennial Arts Commission, July 20–29.

HARVEY WELCH GALLERY, Portland

Harvey Welch, an interior designer, routinely held exhibitions at his store on Southwest Yamhill street. During the centennial year, the featured artist for June and July was Catherine MacKenzie*, who showed her drawings and paintings.

OREGON CERAMIC STUDIO, Portland

The Oregon Ceramic Studio (now merged with Contemporary Crafts Gallery in SW Portland) sponsored an invitational exhibit based on regional and centennial themes. It featured sculpture, pottery, weaving, woodwork (including furniture), and other decorative arts.

OREGON SOCIETY OF CHINA PAINTERS, Portland

This active group celebrated the Centennial by hosting an exhibition of watercolors and painted china by member Jeanne Stewart. Demonstrations of china painting were held at the Meier and Frank Co.

GENERAL MOTORS EXHIBIT, Portland

Portland artist Ed Quigley* painted and carved two four-by-twelve-foot panels for the General Motors Company. The subjects were the contrast of heavy machinery and logging with an ox team; strip mining and panning for gold; dam construction and the Indians at Celilo Falls.

BRIEF HISTORY OF THE PORTLAND ART MUSEUM

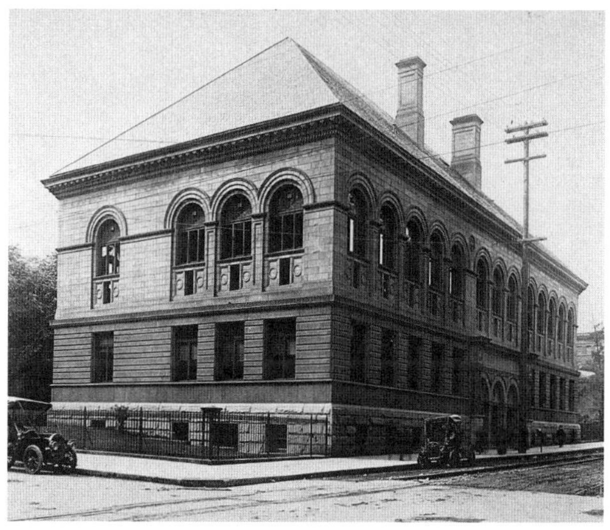

The first home of the Portland Art Association, the "new" library building on Southwest Stark. OHS neg. 81081

Portland businessman, Henry Winslow Corbett, organized the Portland Art Club in 1885. It was founded "for the encouragement of art in the city . . ." and was the first organization of artists in the Pacific Northwest. The following year the Library Association, again with the active participation of Corbett, purchased the painting *Repose* by Portland artist Edward Espey*. *Repose* had received recognition at the Paris Salon the year before. In January 1892, a loan exhibition of paintings and sculpture was held at Marquam Hall in Portland. Corbett and a group of citizens demonstrated their interest in art by contributing to this important exhibition.

On December 12, 1892, Henry Corbett was joined by Winslow B. Ayer, Rev. Thomas L. Eliot, Henry Failing, William M. Ladd, Dr. Holt C.

Wilson, and C.E.S. Wood* to establish the Portland Art Association. The founders believed in the power of art to create enlightened citizens and dedicated themselves to providing a "first-class museum."

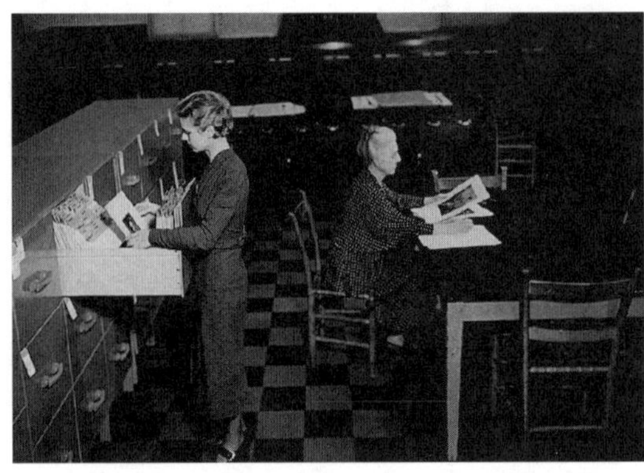

Henrietta Failing seated in library, 1936. Portland Art Museum

In 1895 the upper hall of the new library building—on Southwest Stark between Broadway and Park—housed the first collection of this group. It consisted of plaster casts of Greek and Roman sculpture, which were purchased through the generosity of Henry Corbett. The presentation of loan exhibitions began in 1902, often drawing from the collections of founders C.E.S. Wood*, Henry Corbett, Henry Failing, and William Ladd. The Museum's first curator was Henrietta Failing, who served until 1909.

By 1905 the Portland Art Association succeeded in constructing a new museum building at Southwest Fifth and Taylor. It was opened in time to present *Section B of the Fine Arts Department Exhibition* of the Lewis and Clark Centennial Exposition. In 1908, Childe Hassam's* *Afternoon Sky, Harney Desert* became the first painting to be purchased for the Museum's collections. Museum exhibitions occurred more frequently throughout the next two decades with the introduction of regional annuals and one-person shows in addition to the continued loan shows.

In 1932, Pietro Belluschi, an architect in A.E. Doyle's firm in Portland, won the heated competition to design the new museum building located at Southwest Park and Jefferson. It was a significant architectural approach because it was "neither derivative nor modern." The Solomon and Josephine Hirsch wings were completed in 1939, allowing more space for permanent collections and traveling exhibitions. Finally, in 1969, construction began on the Hoffman Wing, which provided classroom and studio space in addition to a sculpture mall and a new vault for the collections. Plans in 1999 call for yet another expansion and major renovation.

MUSEUM ART SCHOOL (1909)

The Museum Art School had its beginnings in the early Portland Sketch Club (founded in 1895), which later acquired the membership of the Oregon Art Association in 1898. This group of artists then reorganized as the Oregon Art Students League in 1906, becoming the Museum Art School in 1909. Anna Belle Crocker* held the simultaneous positions of school principal and museum curator until her retirement in 1936. The first class, under the instruction of Kate Cameron Simmons* and Harry Wentz*, graduated in 1910. Among the members of that class were Norma Bassett Hall*, George Bingham*, Edna Cranston Breyman*, Rockwell Carey*, Isabelle Trullinger Geer*, Lute Pease*, Nell Pease*, Clara Jane Stephens*, and Esther Wuest*.

Many prominent Oregon artists were alumni of the Museum Art School. The institution provided scholarships to worthy students, even in its early years. In 1929 a group of students, under faculty guidance, established the Arts Guild. Their purpose was to mount exhibitions "that would create a favorable atmosphere for creative effort and attainment." The Arts Guild presented the work of both former and current students.

The Museum Art School achieved accreditation under Dean William Givler in 1962. Twenty years later the school's name changed to The Pacific Northwest College of Art.

The Museum Art School provided a faculty of nationally-recognized artistic stature. Among the instructors through 1959 were:

Wallace Baldinger*, W.L. Barnes, Edward Barnhart, Mary Taylor Barrier*, Sidney Bell*, Louis Bunce*, Anna Belle Crocker*, Robert Tyler Davis, Henrietta Failing, Byron Ferris, William Givler*, Walter Gordon, Rachael Smith Griffin*, Paula Grum, Annemarie Henle, Clementine Hoff, John Jackson, Irwin Jalliver,

Eunice Jensen*, Melvin Keegan, Leta Kennedy*, Frederic Littman, Douglas Lynch*, Don MacGregor, Irwin McFadden, Jack McLarty*, Austin Mecklem, Hilda Morris*, Helen Putnam, Lloyd Reynolds, Robert Reynolds, Thomas Robertson, Michele Russo*, John Ryder, Edmund Schildknecht, Kate Cameron Simmons*, Clara Jane Stephens*, Charles Voorhies*, Mary Hortense Webster*, Bennett Welsh, Henry Wentz*, Margaret DeVal White, Lucia Wiley*, Duane Zaloudek*.

MUSEUM EXHIBITION HIGHLIGHTS

Invitational of Oregon Artists: 1911

Series of Regional Annuals (Portland and Vicinity, Pacific Coast, Pacific Northwest): 1912–15, 17, 19–22, 32

Works from the New York Armory Show: 1913

"Futurist" exhibition, curated by Sally Lewis: 1923

Works from Der Blaue Reiter (The Blue Rider School): 1927

Arts Guild (sponsored by students of the Museum Art School): 1930, 33

Contemporary Paintings and Sculpture (juried): 1933–39, annually

All Oregon Paintings and Sculpture (non-juried): 1940, 42, 44, 46, 48

Artists of Oregon (juried): 1949–58, annually

Walter P. Chrysler Collection: 1956 (This exhibit marked the beginning of the present Docent Program.)

Van Gogh Exhibition: 1959

Oregon Centennial Exhibits: 1959

MUSEUM COLLECTIONS AND BEQUESTS

Greek and Roman Casts: Henry W. Corbett

Greek and Roman antiquities and ceramics: Sally Lewis

Japanese prints: Mary Andrews Ladd

French Impressionist: Winslow B. Ayer

Asian: Margery Hoffman Smith*

French: C.F. Adams

Native American (Axel Rasmussen collection, purchased through public contributions)

Pre-Columbian: William Sargent Ladd

English Silver: Alice B. Nunn

FEDERAL ART PROJECTS IN OREGON

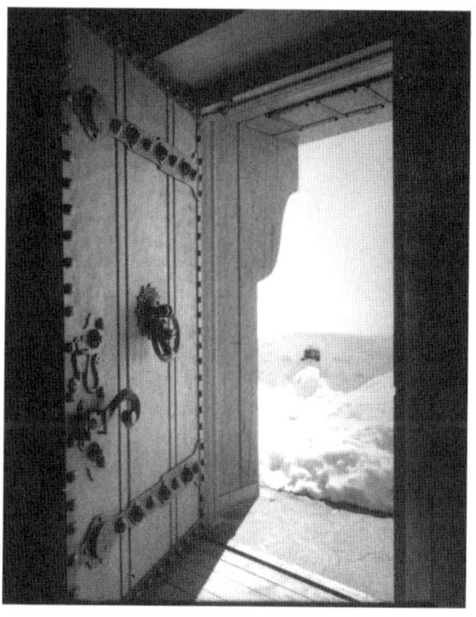

The front door to Timberline Lodge. OHS neg. 42806

During the Great Depression, the Federal Government created several programs that benefited artists. In December 1933 the U.S. Treasury Department sponsored a short-lived program called the Public Works of Art Project (PWAP). It was administered at a federal level with the country being divided into regions; Oregon was in Region 16, along with Washington, Idaho, and Montana. The goal of the PWAP was to bring about a wider recognition of artists' worth by providing contracts to established artists to create works that stressed the "American Scene." The process required bids and proposals for specific projects. The PWAP ended in June 1934. In Oregon, most of the work that had been created was displayed at the Portland Art Museum in *The Exhibition of Work Done in Oregon Under the Public*

Works of Art Project, May 1934. After the exhibition, the work was distributed to universities, colleges, high schools, libraries, hospitals, federal, county, city, and other buildings which were supported wholly or in part by taxes. In many cases it was the first time significant artwork had been placed in these buildings, thereby giving the public an opportunity to view the art on a permanent basis.

Eleven months after the PWAP ended, the Works Progress Administration (WPA) was created. This federal program became the official government-sponsored relief program of the time. Arts projects operated under a branch of the WPA known as "Federal One." It was responsible for the Federal Art Project (FAP) in addition to the Federal Theatre Project, the Federal Music Project, and the Federal Writers Project. The director of the FAP was Holger Cahill, former Director of Exhibitions at the Museum of Modern Art in New York City. However, there were two main differences between the newly formed FAP and the earlier PWAP. Projects were now administered at state and regional levels and artists were supported based upon need. Artists were paid salaries for teaching, creating specific pieces, or for working on projects they deemed appropriate. For the next several years, money was made available to hundreds of artists in Oregon, who then were able to make a living producing art. The FAP also sponsored community art centers for classes, lectures, and displays. It created the *Index of American Design*, to record the wealth of American folk design and indigenous products. In addition to offering employment to artists, Cahill's bigger goal was to create art for the larger community. Where art had once been exclusively enjoyed by the upper class, Cahill sought to make it available to everyone.

On the state level, Burt Brown Baker oversaw Region 16 (Oregon, Washington, Idaho, and Montana). He was assisted by Marjorie Hoffman Smith*, who later became the state director for the FAP in Oregon. Smith also supervised the interior decoration of Timberline Lodge, another WPA accomplishment.

Timberline Lodge is located sixty miles east of Portland at the six thousand-foot level of the south slope of Mt. Hood. The booklet, *Timberline Lodge: A Guided Tour*, explains:

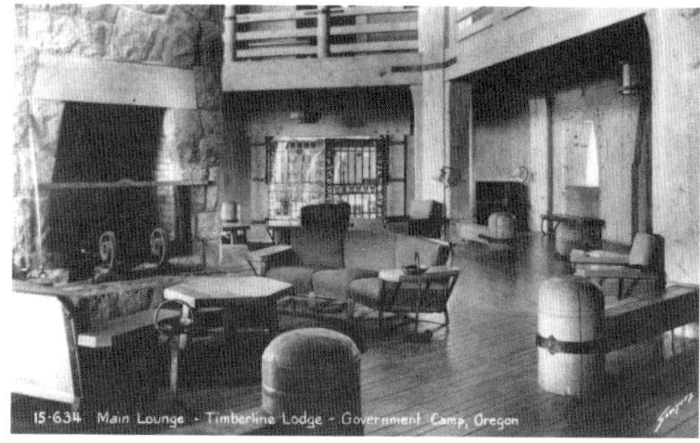

Interior of the Main Lodge at Timberline showing examples of the craftmanship that went into the lodge. In later years, WPA-period paintings were hung on the walls as well. OHS neg. OrHi 71455

> "It is the only twentieth-century public building of its size constructed and furnished entirely by hand with original craft work in wood (both carved and inlaid marquetry), wrought iron, weaving, applique, painting, mosaic, carved linoleum and stained glass. The Lodge is an inn, but it is also a museum in the sense that it houses a permanent catalogued exhibition of American design, painting, and craft work of the 1930's, created under extraordinary circumstances for a special purpose: to furnish and decorate a mountain lodge for skiers, hikers and nature lovers."

Timberline Lodge is an example of Cascadian architecture, built under the auspices of the WPA during the Great Depression. Its construction employed hundreds of master craftsmen. Holger Cahill wanted Timberline Lodge to be a shrine for the best of the Federal Art Project art.

In 1939 the government stopped funding the federal projects and the FAP was placed under state control. In Oregon it became the Oregon Arts Program. By 1943, when the federally sponsored WPA ended, the government placed thousands of works produced by the FAP on indefinite loan to museums, educational institutions, government facilities, and public areas throughout the country. The Portland Art Museum's allocation included several hundred prints, photographs, and paintings.

FEDERAL ART PROJECT PAINTERS, WORKS, AND ORIGINAL LOCATIONS

□ - The artist participated in the *Exhibition of Work Done in Oregon Under the Public Works of Art Project* at the Portland Art Museum, May 1934 (See Reference C10 p.95)

△ - The artist was awarded a government-sponsored commission under the Federal Art Project after July 1935.

○ - Artwork is presently housed in the Long-term Loan of Federal Art Project Works in the Portland Art Museum.

* - The artist is listed in the Biographical Dictionary of this book.

The following is a list of painters, works, and the original location of the artwork, if known. It was compiled from a variety of sources and is in no way comprehensive.

Ackley*, Herbert □

Anderson*, Anna M. □

Austin*, Darrel □ △ ○
Evolution of Medical Education (1936), University of Oregon Medical School, Portland; *Musicians, Dishwashers, The Skier* (1937) and *Woodcutters* (1938), Timberline Lodge; *Fish Story* (1937), Tongue Point Naval Air Station, Astoria; Doernbecher Memorial Hospital, Portland

Ballator*, John △
Development of St. Johns (1936) Louis Bunce and Erich Lamade, assistants, St. Johns Post Office, Portland; Franklin High School, Portland

Barber*, Olivia Shepard □

Barchus*, Eliza □

Barto*, Vivian □

Becquet, Marion □

Bell*, Sidney (Sydney) □

Bendixen*, George □

Biles, Stuart □

Bohlman*, Herman T. □

Bunce*, Louis □ △ ○
Rogue River Indians (1938), Grants Pass Post Office; (1937–38), Bush Elementary School, Salem, assisted by Clifford Gleason; assisted John Ballator, *Development of St. Johns* (1936), St. Johns Post Office, Portland

Carey*, Rockwell □ △
Early Mail Carriers of the West (1937), Newberg Post Office; Gresham High School; Federal Courthouse, Portland; Capitol Building, Salem; Treasury Building, Washington D.C.

Clark, Florence □

Curl*, Martina Gangle □ △
Columbia River Settlement and *Pioneers Sailing by Raft down the Columbia* (1940), Rose City Park School, Portland; wildflower watercolors, Timberline Lodge; assisted Arthur Runquist, *Early Oregon* (1941), Pendleton High School

Darce*, Virginia □ △ ○
The Harvesters (1937), Library, Oregon City; sketches for Blue Ox Bar, Timberline Lodge; Doern-

becher Memorial Hospital (1936), Portland

Day*, Rosamund Stricker □

DeNoyer, Nelva □

Dowling*, Colista □

Elmer*, Clementine □

Erikson*, Dora □ △
Open Air Concert (1936); wildflower watercolors, Timberline Lodge

Fabrick*, Anton Piers □

Feurer*, Karl □ △
Plant and wildflower watercolors (1941), Timberline Lodge

Field*, Marian □

Fiske, John △
Mural Map of Oregon (1941), Portland Chamber of Commerce

Fitzgerald, Edmond J. △
Trail to Oregon (1938), Ontario

Flaherty, Kathryn □

Flavelle, Alan △ ○
Community Sports (1942)

Fulton*, C.J. □ △
YWCA, Salem; YWCA, Eugene; Chamber of Commerce, Eugene; Leaburg Power Station, Leaburg

Gibbs, Howard S. △
Parachute mural, Astoria Harbor map (1942), Tongue Point Naval Air Station, Astoria

Gilbert, Louise □

Gilmore, Wesley H. □

Givler*, William □

Gleason*, Clifford △
Bush Elementary School, Salem, assisted by Louis Bunce

Gordon*, C.S. □

Gorham*, Aimee S. □

Gould, Corrine □

Graves, Orie △
Fisher Folk and *Navy Smoker* (1941), Tongue Point Naval Station, Astoria

Grellert*, Paul △
Post Rider (1936), East Portland Post Office

Griffin*, Rachael □ △
George Himes, Oregon Historical Society

Gustafson*, Vesta Wells □ △
Farm Scene, Medford High School

Hart*, Lance △
Snohomish Post Office, Washington

Hayes*, William P. □

Heaney*, Charles △ ○
The Mountain, Timberline Lodge; *Junction City* (1937), *A Portland Street* (1937), *Village* (1938), *Columbia River* (1938), *Cow Creek Canyon* (1938), *The Marshal* (1938), *Cliff*, *Columbia* (1938), *North Portland* (1938), *Winter* (1938), *The Mountain* (1938), *Washoe Mountains* (1938), *Landscape With Figures* (1938), *Ft. Stevens* (1938), *View of Seattle* (1938), *Tree Study* (1939), and *Road to Madras* (1939), Tongue Point Naval Station, Astoria

□ - The artist participated in the *Exhibition of Work Done in Oregon Under the Public Works of Art Project* at the Portland Art Museum, May 1934 (See Reference C10)
△ - The artist was awarded a government-sponsored commission under the Federal Art Project after July 1935.
○ - Artwork is presently housed in the Long-term Loan of Federal Art Project Works in the Portland Art Museum.
* - The artist is listed in the Biographical Dictionary of this book.

Hedrick*, Mary □

Helser*, Margot □ △
Fairy Tale Series (1937) and *Christ Child*, Doernbecher Memorial Hospital, Portland

Hetrovo*, Nicolai S. □
Watercolor cityscape, Oregon Historical Society

Heywood*, Herbert □

Hollister*, Maude □

Hudson, Harlow □

Hult, Esther □

Jeffery*, George □

Johnson*, Jeannette □

Johnson, Mabel □

Johnson*, Halley Philip □ △
Forestry (1941), University of Oregon, Eugene

Kafoury*, Eleanor Patten □

Keller*, Clyde Leon □

Kellogg, Anita □ △
Drawing, Oregon Historical Society

Krause*, LaVerne □

Lamade*, Erich □ △
Early and Contemporary Industries (1938) and *Mountain* (1939), Tongue Point Naval Station, Astoria; assisted John Ballator, *Development of St. Johns* (1936), St. Johns Post Office; Grants Pass Post Office; *Oregon History* (1940), Abernathy School, Portland; watercolor (1932), Timberline Lodge

Latta, Henrietta □

Lavare, Gabriel △
Magellan (1938), Washington High School, Portland

Leavstrand*, Pete □

Loomis, Birdie □

Lynch*, Douglas □ △
Wall panels, Barlow Room, Timberline Lodge

Lyon, Cathryn □

MacKenzie, Catherine* □

Manser*, Percy □ △ ○
Murals for Hood River High School, Courthouse, Hospital and Elks Hall; The Dalles High School

Marsh*, Harold D. □

McKim*, C.C. □

Mish*, Charlotte △
Leading Cargo (1941), *Freighter* (1941), *Ancient Record* (1941), *Plane Carrier* (1942), and *Ship Launching* (1942), Tongue Point Naval Air Station, Astoria; *Map of Wasco County* (1941), Finance Department, Portland City Hall; *General Pershing in Dry Dock* (1936) and *Steamer "Portland"* (1936), Port of Portland; *Oregon Flora Map* (1941), Oregon State University Library; *Thumbelina No.1, No.2 and No.3* (1939), Highland School

Morris*, Carl △ ○
Willamette Valley Lumber, Farming and Husbandry (1943), Eugene Post Office, Eugene

O'Hara, Eleanor □

□ - The artist participated in the *Exhibition of Work Done in Oregon Under the Public Works of Art Project* at the Portland Art Museum, May 1934 (See Reference C10)
△ - The artist was awarded a government-sponsored commission under the Federal Art Project after July 1935.
○ - Artwork is presently housed in the Long-term Loan of Federal Art Project Works in the Portland Art Museum.
* - The artist is listed in the Biographical Dictionary of this book.

Pedersen*, Conrad G. □

Price*, C.S. □ △ ○
Agriculture (1937), Pendleton Junior High School; *Pioneers* (1936), Gold Beach School, Gold Beach; *Sawing Wood* and *Mountain Landscapes* (1937), U.S. Forestry Service; *Huckleberry Pickers* (1940), *Pack Train* (1940), *The Team* (1940), *Plowing* (1940), and untitled landscape, Timberline Lodge; *Indians* and *Pioneers*, Multnomah County Library, Portland

Pritchard, Walter △
Baseball Pitcher (1936), University of Oregon, Eugene

Quigley*, Ed △
Settling of the West, Irvington School, Portland

Ricen*, Stanley □

Runquist*, Albert □ △
Tree of Knowledge (1938), University of Oregon Library, Eugene; Sedro Wooley Post Office, Washington

Runquist*, Arthur □ △ ○
Tree of Knowledge (1938), University of Oregon Library, Eugene; *Early Oregon* (1941), Martina Gangle Curl, assistant, Pendleton High School; *Powder Monkey* (1938), 29th Engine Battalion

Serebrennikov, Maria □

Sewall*, Edward □

Sewall*, Howard △
Wood (1938), *Metal* (1938), *Three Figures* (1938), *Builders of the Lodge* (1937), Timberline Lodge; *The Theatre* (1936) and *Pioneers* (1935), Oregon City High School

Sewell*, Alice □

Sibley, Frank □

Sisson*, Nellie □

Skinner*, Charlotte □

Smith*, Margery H. △
Supervised interior decoration of Timberline Lodge

Snodgrass, Ella △
Circus Horses (1940)

Sweetser*, Carolyn K. △
Watercolor wildflowers, Timberline Lodge

Trullinger*, John □

Utter, Louise △
Cougar and Cub (1937), University of Oregon, Eugene

Van Scoy, Myrtle □

Van Zandt, Rosalie □

Vincent*, Andrew M. △
Builders of Salem (1942), Salem Post Office, (now the State Executive Office Conference Room); Eugene City Hall

Von Schmidt, Fritz □

Wanker*, Maude □

Wells, Donald □

Wiley*, Lucia △
Captain Gray Entering Tillamook

□ - The artist participated in the *Exhibition of Work Done in Oregon Under the Public Works of Art Project* at the Portland Art Museum, May 1934 (See Reference C10)
△ - The artist was awarded a government-sponsored commission under the Federal Art Project after July 1935.
○ - Artwork is presently housed in the Long-term Loan of Federal Art Project Works in the Portland Art Museum.
* - The artist is listed in the Biographical Dictionary of this book.

Bay (1943), Tillamook City Hall; Tillamook Courthouse

Wilkinson*, Jack □

Cattle Roundup (1941), Burns Post Office, later moved to County Courthouse

Wiseman, Josephine □

York, Rhoen □

□ - The artist participated in the *Exhibition of Work Done in Oregon Under the Public Works of Art Project* at the Portland Art Museum, May 1934 (See Reference C10)

△ - The artist was awarded a government-sponsored commission under the Federal Art Project after July 1935.

○ - Artwork is presently housed in the Long-term Loan of Federal Art Project Works in the Portland Art Museum.

* - The artist is listed in the Biographical Dictionary of this book.

COMMERCIAL ART GALLERIES AND EXHIBITION SPACES

1860–1900

The Art Gallery, Portland
B.B. Rich Concessions, Portland Hotel and 274 Morrison, Portland
Bernstein's Art Store, Alexander Bernstein, Jr. (ca. 1890), Portland
Eastman, Gilman L. Photography and Art Gallery (ca. 1880), Portland
Felloes Art School, Washington Building, Portland
Gray's Music Store (ca. 1870), Portland
Gump's Gallery (ca. 1880), Portland (branch of the San Francisco store)
Hillman and Co. Music and Art Gallery (ca. 1870), Portland
J.K. Gill Stationers (ca. 1870), Portland
McNary Gallery, Anna L. and Mattie C. McNary (ca. 1890), Salem
McQuillan Gallery of Art (ca. 1870), Portland
Mrs. Robinson's Art Rooms, 290 Morrison, Portland
New Art Gallery, John Hansen (ca. 1880), Salem
Palace of Art, C.C. Morse (ca. 1870), 163 1st Street, Portland
Robbins and Yates, 1st between Salmon and Main, Portland
Sanford, Vail and Co. (ca. 1880), 170 1st Street Portland (branch of San Francisco company)
Shanahan Gallery, W.T. Shanahan (est. 1867), 3rd and Alder, Portland
Snow and Roos (ca. 1870), Portland (branch of San Francisco store)
Steel, George A. (ca. 1870), Portland
Volney, Victor, Art Supply and Framing Shop (ca. 1870), Portland

1900–1930

Adele's Restaurant, Portland
Allen Eaton Art Supply and Gallery (ca. 1900), Eugene
Artcraft and Curio Shop, SW Morrison Street, Portland
Art Man, Clyde Leon Keller* (1907–36), SW Washington Street, Portland
Atiyeh Brothers (ca. 1912), Portland (traveling exhibits, not regional)
Burlington House Galleries, Meier and Frank Co., Portland
Christiansen Art Company and Gallery, George C. Christiansen (1906–22), 375 Stark Street, Portland
Gilbert Gallery, Roman Monroe Gilbert* (ca.1920), Salem
Hood River Gallery, Hood River
Hostess House Gallery, *The Oregonian*, Portland
Little Art Shop (Ye Old Art Shop, ca. 1906), Portland
Little Gallery, Lipman Wolfe department store, Portland
Portland Commercial Club, Morgan Building, Portland
Rose City Art Store, George Bingham* (ca. 1900), Portland

Shop of Fine Arts and Industry (est. 1909), sponsored by Arts and Crafts Society, predecessor to the current Hoffman Gallery, Oregon College of Arts and Crafts, Portland

Western Picture Frame Co. (ca. 1914), succeeds Sanford, Vail and Co., Portland

YWCA Parlors (ca. 1900), Portland

1930–1959

The Art Gallery, 16 Selling-Hirsch Building, Portland

Art Shop Gallery, Bertel and Minnie Wonsmos, 407 Broadway, Seaside

Brass Lantern Gallery (Restaurant), Portland

Cafe Espresso Gallery, SW 6th, Portland

Cascade Art Gallery, DeLake (Lincoln City)

Clifford Gleason's* Studio and Art Gallery, 162 South Commercial, Salem

Creative Art Gallery, Olivia F. Barber* (est. 1932), Portland

Dark Horse Gallery, Viktor von Pribosic* (est. 1953), Beaverton

Dekum Gallery, Gordon Jones, 3rd and Washington, Portland

Elfstrom Company Gallery (ca. 1946), Salem

Florence Knowlton Art Gallery, Portland

Fole-Myers Galleries, 535 NW 23rd, Portland

Friendship House, 3310 N. Williams, Portland

Gallery 720, Eugene

Harvey Welch Gallery, 1013 SW Yamhill, Portland

Kharouba Gallery, Louis* and Eda Bunce (1949–55), 1016 SW Morrison, Portland

Lincoln County Arts Center, also known as Gallery by the Sea, Maude Wanker* (est. 1949), DeLake (Lincoln City)

Lloyd Furniture Stores, Portland

Louver Gallery, Lloyd Center, Portland

Margaret's Studio, Margaret Merritt (1950–1990), Bend

McCarthy Gallery, Albany

Meyer Gallery, Harriet Meyer*, SW Summit Drive, Portland

Morrison Street Gallery, Don Sorenson*, Portland

New Gallery of Contemporary Art, Ron and Norma* Peterson (1958–62), 2405 SW 5th, Portland

O'Mansky's Dance Studio, Portland

Old Heathman Hotel, Portland

Olds, Wortman and King, 10th and Morrison, Portland

Oregon Ceramics Studio, merged with Contemporary Crafts Gallery, Portland

Paint Box Gallery, Maude Wanker* (est. 1945), Wecoma Beach

Patecky Studio Gallery, Albert Patecky* (1948–49), Selling Hirsch Building, SW 10th and Washington, Portland

Patecky-von Pribosic Studios, Albert Patecky* and Viktor von

Pribosic* (est. 1953), 1329 SW Broadway, Portland
Peebles Gallery, Portland
Rorick's, 17 NW 23rd Place, Portland
Ruthermore Gallery, J.G. Gilmore (1950–56), 1434 SW Mill St., Portland (later opened in San Francisco)
Shannon Company, Portland
Siebert's Furniture Store, Portland
Sloan Tamkin Gallery, Portland
Thelma Pearson* Gallery, Lincoln City
Town Art Gallery, Robert Huffman*, NW 23rd, Portland
12th Avenue Gallery, Thyrza Anderson, Eugene
Washington Hotel, Portland
West Coast Picture Company, Portland
West Shore Gallery, Portland
The Wildwood Art Gallery (ca. 1940), Milton-Freewater
Window Gallery, Salem
Woodstock Community Center, Portland

Schools, universities, and libraries also dedicated space for art exhibitions. Some of these institutions operated full-time galleries.

ART ORGANIZATIONS AND CENTERS

AMERICAN ARTISTS PROFESSIONAL LEAGUE (1930)

CHARTER OFFICERS: Stuart Biles, Evelyn Clogston*, Ruth Halvorsen*

Portland and Oregon branches of the American Artists Professional League were established in 1930. In 1933, Portland's *American Art Week* was started under Florence Marsh*, President of the Oregon chapter and State Chairman of the national organization. The event featured art, literature, and other cultural events, an idea that was copied nationally and internationally. The American Artists Professional League held exhibitions from 1932 to 1939.

ARTISTS EQUITY ASSOCIATION, INC. (1951)

CHARTER MEMBERS: Mary Taylor Barrier*, Robert Colescott*, Frank Elliot*, Robert Feasley*, Anson Frohman*, James Haseltine*, LaVerne Krause*, Ray Levra*, Albert Patecky*, Michele Russo*, Jack Wilkinson*

The Oregon branch of the Artists Equity was one of four West Coast chapters to belong to the national organization, along with Washington, Northern California, and Southern California. According to the membership application, "Artists Equity Association is a national, non-political, aesthetically non-partisan organization representing the professional fine artists of America. It was formed to further the economic interests of artists and give strength and effectiveness to their united professional aims."

ART LEAGUE OF GRANTS PASS

ATTIC CLUB (1925–1970)

CHARTER MEMBERS: Leslie Beaton, Harold Detje, Hal Grandy, Paul Keller*, Taylor Poore, Will Pierce, Errol Proctor, Ernest Richardson*, Jefferson Tester*, Rene Weaver.

The Attic Club was originally established by ten newspaper and commercial artists who wanted to keep their skills sharp by sketching from live models. Commercial work was banned from discussion. The group chose the spider and web as their emblem because it symbolized a maker of fine things in poor surroundings. They initially met in the Commonwealth Building and limited their membership to ten. They were later called the Attic Sketch Club, with Stanley C. Ricen* as their manager.

They exhibited as a group at the Multnomah County Fairs and at occasional public exhibits. The club was known as the Attic Studio from 1930 to 1967 and offered life drawing classes. From 1939 until its demise it was managed by Clyde Archibald*.

CASCADE ARTISTS GROUP (1952)

ORGANIZER: Ruth Grover*

MEMBERS: Constance Cole*, Jim Colley, Lois Goodfellow, Dean Larson, Earl Nelson, Martha Kay Renfroe, Herbert Rydell, John Ulrich

This cooperative group of coast artists met at Ruth Grover's home at Road's End and at their gallery, Cascade Artists Gallery, in the Lincoln Bookshop in Nelscott. They organized exhibitions of members' works that traveled to community art centers up and down the West Coast. The group gradually dissolved in the 1970s. Records for the Cascade Artists Group are housed at the Hallie Ford Museum of Art archives at Willamette University.

CIRCLE A ART CLUB (1911–12)

ORGANIZER: Fred Routledge*

CHARTER OFFICERS: Val Deveraux (president), Lute Pease*, Harry Wentz* (vice presidents), W. H. Blevins* (secretary-treasurer)

MEMBERS: E.D. Fowle*, C. J. Fulton*, Percy Manser*, C.C. McKim*

According to a November 4, 1911 article in the *Spectator* magazine, "The club was originally organized by Fred Routledge and a few other men actively engaged in occupations which require a knowledge of art. The charter members include architects, newspaper and magazine illustrators, commercial artists, and decorators and designers. . . The club met two evenings a week for inside work from life figures and one afternoon for landscape work. The club has no instructor; the club members study and criticize each other's work." There is no record of the club after 1911. It may have been a forerunner of the Society of Oregon Artists, which was founded in 1912.

COOS ARTISTS LEAGUE (1950)

ORGANIZER: Janice Scott

PAST PRESIDENTS: Lucilla Germain, Mabel Hansen, Florence Harlan, Charles Hoffman, Margaret Law, Howard Peck, Janice Scott

CHARTER MEMBERS: Gladys Duffield, Jack Grace, Mabel Hansen, JoAnne Lowery, Dorothee Moore, Howard Peck, Edith Peterson, Mrs. T.T. Phillips, Florence Hall Smith, Art Snyder, Blaine Snyder, Clare Wehrle

Comprised largely of local artists, the Coos Artists League was responsible for initially housing the Coos Art Museum in the Carnegie Public Library. They held meetings to encourage work and criticism, classes, and exhibitions of local and traveling artwork. To facilitate this last goal they joined the Oregon Art Alliance sometime after 1950.

COQUILLE VALLEY ART ASSOCIATION/ ART CENTER

CORVALLIS ART GUILD

CORVALLIS ARTS CENTER

CREATIVE ART GUILD (1959)

THE DALLES ART CLUB (1955)

ORGANIZER: Percy Manser*

OFFICER: Gini Smith (secretary)

MEMBERS: Charlotte Addisson, Laura Ashbrenner*, Anne Chambers, Gayle Fenton, Betty Hartman, Ray Hotka*, Minnie Kenney, Carl Kramer, Iva McLeod, Lloyd McLeod, Dora Pizzalato, Roscoe Sexton, Dorothy Tenneson
INSTRUCTORS: Ray Hotka*

This group met to paint together and host visiting instructors such as Arthur Selander* and Phil Tyler*. In addition to the classes, members donated paintings for art auctions that were open to the community. They met at the community center on 4th Street and later moved into the vacated Carnegie Library building. Incorporated in 1959 as the Dalles Art Club, Inc., they are still in existence.

EUGENE ART CENTER (1951)

ORGANIZER: Maude Kerns*
DIRECTOR: Margaret Karl*
INSTRUCTORS: Howard Hall*, Margaret Kemp*, Anne Kutka McCosh*

When it was formed in 1951, the original mission of the Eugene Art Center was to provide classes and exhibition space for area artists. The Center eventually outgrew its location. Maude Kerns*, a founding member and frequent exhibitor, was convinced of the need for a community-based art center separate from the University, so in 1957 she purchased a small house and donated its use to the Center.

The Center continued to thrive, and by 1962 it was obvious that, once again, they would need to find a larger facility. A former local Presbyterian Church, built in 1896, was selected as a fitting place for relocation. Maude Kerns agreed to the sale of the previous building and the use of those funds for the purchase of the church. She also donated funds for the remodeling that was required to turn the church into an Art Center. The new facility was named the Maude Kerns Art Center in her honor.

HARNEY COUNTY ART ASSOCIATION

The Harney County Art Association is located in Burns.

JUNIPER ART GUILD

INSTRUCTORS: Earl Hazelle, Percy Manser*, Chester Glenn Murphy*, Arthur Selander*

The Juniper Art Guild was located in Crook County and offered art classes to the public.

KLAMATH ART ASSOCIATION

OFFICERS: Lorraine De Young Johnson* (president) and Barbara Sampson Kensler*

The Klamath Art Association was located in Klamath Falls.

LINCOLN COUNTY ART CENTER (1941)

ORGANIZER: Maude Wanker*

Maude Wanker*, of Wecoma Beach, gathered a group of artists whose purpose was the promotion of art in all its forms. The Center, located in DeLake (Lincoln City), was a community project in which all citizens and children were welcome to participate. Teachers donated their time and membership fees were nominal. "Friends of the Center", a support group, created a show place for paintings called The Gallery By the Sea.

MASTER WATERCOLOR SOCIETY OF OREGON (1958)

CHARTER OFFICERS: Maude Wanker* (president)

CHARTER MEMBERS: Betty Allen*, Betty Allyn*, Margaret Carr*, Mae Cronant*, Ruth Grover*, Carl Hall*, Ruth Halvorsen*, Robert Huck*, Demetrios Jameson*, Ray Levra*, Percy Manser*, Immanuel Piladakis*, Nelson Sandgren*, Menalkas Selander*, John Waddingham*, Mildred Warner*

The Master Watercolor Society of Oregon held their first exhibit at Lincoln County Art Center in DeLake (Lincoln City) in 1958. They joined with The Oregon Amateur Watercolor Society to form the Watercolor Society of Oregon in 1966. In addition to exhibitions, they invited guest speakers and teachers to learn more about watercolor techniques. This group also painted together and conducted critique sessions.

MUTUAL ART ASSOCIATION (1914–15)

CHARTER MEMBERS: Eliza Barchus*, Arne Berger*, George Bingham*, Clarice Bruhn*, E.D. Morgan Fowle,* George Fowler*, Aimee Spencer Gorham*, Myra Helm*, Edward Hill*, Clyde Leon Keller*, W.L.E. Knowles*, Paul Lauritz*, Adelaide Lowden*, Robert Miller*, Charles Post*, Lucy Ramberg*, Alice Weister*, Melville Wire*

Located in Portland, this group was dedicated to the encouragement of art in Oregon. They held at least two annual exhibitions at the Public Library. Though short-lived, membership included some of the foremost artists of the day.

OREGON AMATEUR WATERCOLOR SOCIETY (1957)

MEMBERS: M. Akers, Betty Allen*, Betty Allyn*, Constance Cole*, Lois Goodfellow, Ruth Grover*, Mabel Hanson, Maude Wanker*

This group of watercolor artists held juried exhibitions and provided educational lectures and classes on technique. They merged with the Master Watercolor Society of Oregon in 1966 to form the Watercolor Society of Oregon.

OREGON ART ALLIANCE (1950)

ORGANIZER: James Haseltine*

MEMBERS: William Givler*, LaVerne Krause*, Jack McLarty*, Jeanne Moment*, Albert Patecky*

This group was formed in early 1950 by representatives of various art organizations who met at the Portland Art Museum at the invitation of its director. They took action to survey the art resources of the state, the art needs of Oregon communities, and to discover how these needs could best be met. The preamble to their bylaws states their mission: "To promote the exchange of facilities, material, and knowledge and to present a unified voice and purpose toward the desirable end of the growth and development of the arts of Oregon." The Art Museum served as secretary-treasurer of the group.

OREGON ART ASSOCIATION (1895–98)

OFFICERS: Cleveland Rockwell* (president); Eva Woolfolk* and Lionel Deane (vice presidents), Lucy Bower* (secretary), Amanda Smith* (treasurer) CHARTER MEMBERS: James A. Anderson*, Alfred Burr*, Mrs. Burr, Anna B. Crocker*, Kate Gibbs*, Mrs. Gowdy, Jennie M. Griswold*, John Grover*, Nels Hagerup*, Mrs. Robert Haydn, Josephine Hayne*, Agnes Jamieson*, Mary Kollock*, Warren Rollins*, Mrs. Rollins, Eva Ford Cline Smith*, Bertha Stuart, Katherine U. Taft*, Alice Weister*, C.E.S. Wood*, Jennie Wright*

The Oregon Art Association held their first annual exhibition in 1896 to benefit the Library. They merged with the Portland Sketch Club in 1898. The club later reorganized in 1906 as the Oregon Art Students League.

OREGON GUILD OF PAINTERS AND SCULPTORS (1944)

MEMBERS: Herbert Ackley*, Mary Barrier*, Louis Bunce*, Rockwell Carey*, Martina Curl*, Bernard Geiser*, William Givler*, Clifford Gleason*, Ruth Halvorsen*, Ruth Hart*, Maude Kerns*, Anne Kutka McCosh*, David McCosh*, Jack McLarty*, Carl Morris*, Albert Runquist*, Arthur Runquist*, Edward Sewall*, Andrew Vincent*, Charles Voorhies*, Harry Wentz*, Lucia Wiley*, Jack Wilkinson*

The purpose of the Guild was to stimulate public appreciation of the members' work and benefit area artists by showing continuous exhibitions of art.

OREGON SOCIETY OF ARTISTS (1926)

CHARTER OFFICERS: William Gray Purcell (president), Clyde Leon Keller* (vice president), Sally Hart* (secretary)

CHARTER MEMBERS: Sidney Bell*, Pietro Belluschi, Graziella Boucher, D.W. Bowman, Clarice Bruhn*, Milles Bruhn, Elvira Bump*, Walter Church*, Edna Clark, J.M. Coleman*, Lillian Cram, Anna Belle Crocker*, Edyth Ellsworth*, William Ensign, J. Leo Fairbanks*, Kyuzo Furuya*, Aimee Spencer Gorham*, Vesta Wells Gustafson*, Edith Hazen, Charles Heaney*, Georgia Heckbert*, Mary Hedrick*, Margot Helser*, Alda Jourdan*, Yasuo Kamei*, Leta Kennedy*, Maude Kerns*, Bird LeFever*, Adelaide Lowden*, Catherine MacKenzie*, Percy Manser*, R.O. Marks, William McIlwraith*, Charlotte Mish*, Lena Ross Mitchell, Sadao Mizuno*, Charles Modeer, H. Osterhoff, Doris Pewtherer, Maude Hoover Portwood, Kate Cordon Raymond*, Arthur Runquist*, Fred Sandstrom, Alice Sewell*, Mrs. C.L. Smith*, Marjorie Hoffman Smith*, Clara Jane Stephens*, Ethel Stevens, Charles Stout, Ray Strong*, Louise Thomson*, Helen Kreps Trayle*, Harry Wentz*, Dorothy Gilbert Wilson*, Melville Wire*, N.B. Zane*
INCORPORATED IN 1929 WITH NEW OFFICERS: William Gray Purcell, Clyde Leon Keller*, Mrs. Harold Dickson Marsh*, Colista Dowling*, W.H. Drake*, Herman T. Bohlman*, Katherine McRae
PAST PRESIDENTS: E.D. Morgan Fowle*, Albert Gerlach*, Clyde Keller*, Clyde Leon Keller, Jr., Ben Larsen*, Thayne Logan*, George McBride*, Harold McMahon*, Albert Patecky*, William Gray Purcell, Menalkas Selander*, Arthur Selander*, Henry Tomlinson*

The Oregon Society of Artists started within the Portland Art Museum. Their first exhibition was held at the Museum and subsequent shows took place in a variety of venues. The first meetings were held at Clyde Keller*'s studio, but in 1954 they moved into their own building at 2185 SW Park Place (designed by member Thayne Logan*). Originally called the Society of Oregon Artists, they changed to their present name in 1929. Over time they have developed a conservative, representational approach to art.

PACIFIC ART GUILD (1956)

The Pacific Art Guild was located in Astoria.

PELICAN BAY ARTS ASSOCIATION

The Pelican Bay Arts Association was located in Brookings.

PORTLAND ART CLUB (1885)

ORGANIZER: Henry Winslow Corbett

CHARTER OFFICERS: Harry Winslow Corbett (president), Cleveland Rockwell* (vice president), Edward Espey* (secretary), Grafton Tyler Brown* (treasurer)

CHARTER MEMBERS: Louis Akin*, Arne Berger, J. Norman Biles*, Alfred Burr*, William H. Byrnes, Clyde Cooke*, Henry Epting*, John Gill*, Lou Goldsmith, Alfred Greenbaum, Richard P. Habersham*, C.C. Maring, Elbridge W. Moore*, James Pickett*, Arthur E. Powell, Walter S. Rogers, L. Samuel, C.L. Smith*, Arthur R. Stringer, James E. Stuart*, and Jesse Waddell

Founded "for the benefit to be derived from mutual improvement by association, for the encouragement of art in the city, and for social pleasure." They held weekly meetings in the former First National Bank Building and held semi-annual exhibitions.

PORTLAND SKETCH CLUB (1895)

MEMBERS: Lilian Bain*, J. Rita Bell*, Anna Belle Crocker*, Caroline Dilly, John Gill*, Josephine Hayne*, Warren Rollins*, Eva Ford Cline Smith*, Clara Jane Stephens*, Harry Wentz*, Eva Woolfolk*

INSTRUCTOR: Frank Vincent DuMond* (1898, 1905)

While originally an all-male architect's club, female membership was added in 1896. The Portland Sketch Club held its first exhibition in 1896. They absorbed the Oregon Art Association in 1898. It was reorganized in 1906 as the Oregon Art Students League.

REMBRANDT ARTISTS GUILD (1938)

MEMBERS: Ralph Gilbert*, Ella Hathaway*, Lillian Laughlin*

The Rembrandt Artists Guild was located in Salem.

ROGUE VALLEY ART ASSOCIATION (1959)

ORGANIZER: Eugene Bennett*

The Rogue Valley Art Association began meeting in Eugene Bennett's studio with a nucleus of professional artists and art teachers who wanted to establish a gallery in Medford. Their intention was to bring in fine art exhibitions, showcasing work from outside the valley that would not otherwise be available to the community. The Association was formed in April of 1959 and the gallery was opened in April of 1960. The name was later changed to Rogue Valley Art Center and art education was offered.

SAGE BRUSHERS ART SOCIETY (1952)

CHARTER PRESIDENT: Irene Cothrell

CHARTER MEMBERS: Pat Bells, Eileen Duffy, Betty Keith, Margaret Meritt*, Lee Paul, Claudia Russell, Barbara Steinhauser, Helen Well, Pat Winters

The Sage Brushers was originally founded by a group of Central Oregon artists who wanted to promote the appreciation of art in the community. They met for many years at the old Richardson School on the Burns Highway in Bend. In 1962 the Sage Brushers Art Society acquired their own gallery at 851 Roosevelt Avenue in Bend. Members exhibited in shows, fairs, and festivals throughout the Northwest. They held art sales and also provided paintings for many offices and businesses in Central Oregon. Through the years many well-known artists have given lessons at their gallery.

SALEM ART ASSOCIATION (1941)

In 1941 the Salem Art Center became the Salem Art Association and acquired non-profit status. In 1953 the Bush House (built by Oregon statesman

Asahel Bush in 1877–78) was turned over to the Association. Originally the House included a first floor museum and a second floor gallery with class space; the old barn served as a storage area for the Parks Department. After a fire, the barn was remodeled to house classrooms, a gallery, and a rental sales area. It is known today as the Bush Barn. The original house has continued to serve as the Bush House Museum. Bush Pasture Park is the setting for this complex.

SALEM FEDERAL ART CENTER (1937)

INSTRUCTORS: Helen Blumensteil*, Louis Bunce*, Erich Lamade*, Charles Lemery

In 1937 during the WPA era, a group of civic-minded people encouraged the state director of the Federal Art Project to open a branch in Salem. It became one of the fifty-two art centers in the country established to benefit the local community. The Salem Federal Art Center was open daily with free classes and exhibits that changed frequently; the first exhibit was held in 1938. There was an influx of East Coast painters who came to work at the Center and then remained in the area.

SALEM ART LEAGUE (1919)

ORGANIZER: Roman Monroe Gilbert*

The League had modest beginnings in study groups and guilds around the turn of the century. In 1919 the Salem Art League was officially formed for the purpose of working together to share knowledge and enthusiasm for the arts.

SKIDMORE FOUNTAIN ARTISTS ASSOCIATION (1935)

ORGANIZERS: Virginia Darce* and Phyllis Muirden Ryder*

Members of the Skidmore Artists Association were primarily artists and writers. Many members, which included Harold McMahon*, moved into the old New Market Building facing the Fountain to live and work.

SKIDMORE FOUNTAIN ART CENTER, INC. (1936)

ORGANIZER: Florence Marsh*

OFFICERS: Florence Marsh* (president), H. Elmer House* (vice president), Evelyn Clogston* (secretary)
MEMBERS: Aimee Gorham*, Charles Lemery, Maude Wanker*

Representatives of various civic, art, music, literary, and architecture groups were appointed to represent their respective organizations on the council of the Art Center.

SNAKE RIVER VALLEY ART ASSOCIATION

SOCIETY OF OREGON ARTISTS (1912–13)

CHARTER OFFICERS: C.C. McKim* (president), Adelaide Magner* (vice president), G.C. Christiansen (secretary), Harry Wentz* (treasurer)
CHARTER MEMBERS: George Bingham*, Wade H. Blevins*, Rockwell Carey*, John M. Crook*, George H. Fowler*, Cyrus J. Fulton*, Genevieve Haley, Myra Helm*, Mrs. A. Jackson, Clyde L. Keller*, W.L.E. Knowles*, L.C. Miles, Robert A. Miller*, Ellen Ravenscroft*, Fred Routledge*, Jeanne Stewart, Fred Watrin

The Society of Oregon Artists, not to be confused with the Oregon Society of Artists (established in 1926), was formed with a desire to promote and stimulate both fine and applied art in Portland. According to an article in the *Spectator*, April 6, 1912, their group contained both honorary and associate members who were "to seek to interest buyers of works of art in the productions of Oregonians and to encourage the work of artists (and to) endeavor to promote harmony among artists and bring into prominence latent talent." Their first meetings were held at the art gallery and studio of George Christiansen, 375 Stark Street. Other meetings were held at the public library. The group sponsored at least four exhibits during their one-year tenure.

SOUTHERN OREGON ART ASSOCIATION (1935)

ORGANIZER: Elizabeth Edmondson*
CHARTER MEMBERS: Vivian Barto*, Stephen Bayless*, Dorothy Milbank*, Margaret Ossenbrugge*

Elizabeth Edmondson* gathered the few artists that lived in Medford in 1935 and started the Southern Oregon Art Association. The group organized large-scale art exhibits, which featured displays from Paris, New York, and San Francisco. Medford residents could view the art without charge.

SOUTHERN OREGON SOCIETY OF ARTISTS (1951)

ORGANIZER: Clifford Platz*
CHARTER MEMBERS: John Ahern, Hal Bishop*, Eugene Ferrel, Mrs. Ralph Fitzgerald, Mrs. A.V. Hardy, Mrs. Kenneth McLarty, Colista Moore, Iva Reeds, Maccine Titues, Daniel Tesch
HONORARY MEMBERS: Mrs. F.W. Clogston and Elizabeth Edmundson*

Founded in Medford in 1951, the purpose of the Society was to encourage the progress of each artist member as well as to promote an interest in and better understanding of art by the general public.

SPRINGFIELD ART LEAGUE

MEMBER: Ida Bessie Pruit*

WESTERN CENTRAL OREGON ART ASSOCIATION

The Western Central Oregon Art Association was located in Sweet Home.

YAQUINA ART ASSOCIATION

Membership lists are not always complete and end at 1959.

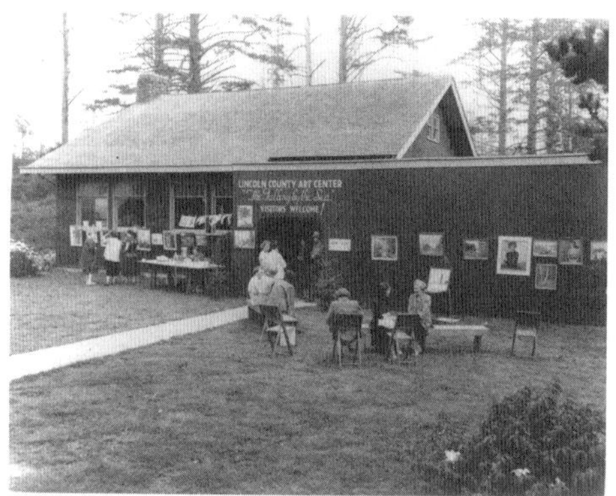

Lincoln County Art Center, DeLake (later Lincoln City), Oregon. OHS neg. OrHi 100849

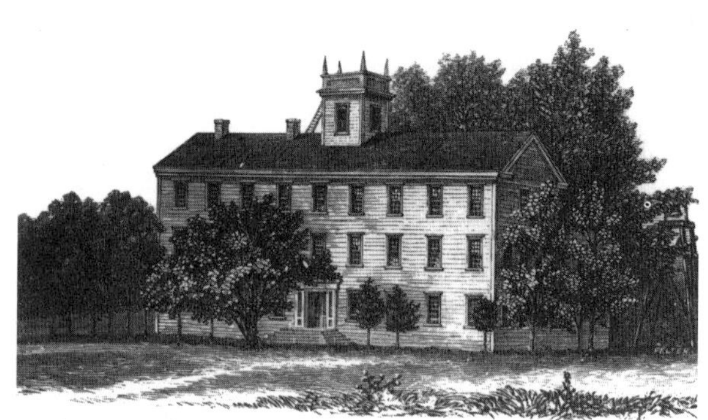

Oregon Institute, later Willamette University in Salem. OHS neg. OrHi 564, 565

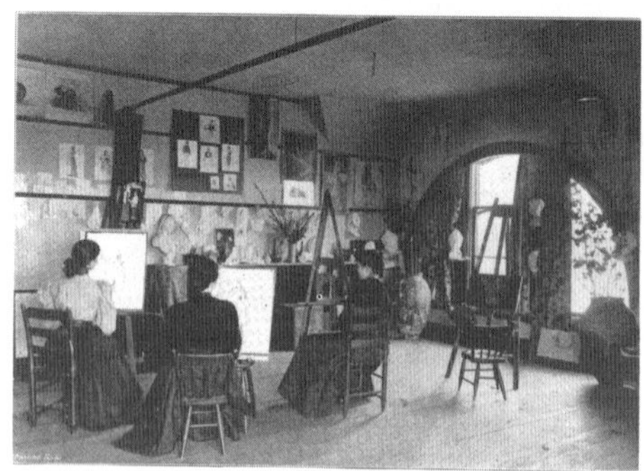

THE STUDIO

St. Helen's Hall, art studio. From an 1899-1900 catalog for the school. OHS neg OrHi 77872

ART EDUCATION IN OREGON

Selected List of Early Institutions and Art Teachers

HIGHER EDUCATION

1842

Oregon Institute–Willamette University, Salem
1853 **Willamette University**
Lucia A.N. Jordan (1860)
Mattie G. Rounds (1869–71)
Susan Belle Walker Cooke* (1873)
1880 Art Department is established
Harriet S. Curtis (1880–81)
Della Quivey (1881–83)
Mary Bridges Watson* (1882–87)
Marie Craig LeGall* (1885–1908)
Clyde Cooke* (1889–90)
Margaret Gill* (1910–12)
Ardella Fuller (1911–12)
Adelaide Magner* (1912–13)
Constance Fowler* (1935–47)
Carl Hall* (1947–86)

1848

Tualatin (Tuality) Academy–Pacific University, Forest Grove
1854 **Tualatin Academy and Pacific University**
Sylvia M. Keeler (1853)
1883 Art Department added to Pacific University
Emma Cornelius Blum* (1883–85)
Clyde Cooke* (1886–89)
Martha Frazier (1891–92)
Lilian Bain* (1904–10)
1923 **Pacific University**
Daye Marshall Hulin (1944–48)
Bernard Perry (1949–50)
Dorothy Yezerski* (1958–62)

1853

Albany Academy, Albany–Lewis and Clark College, Portland
1867 **Albany Collegiate Institute**
Mrs. W.R. Butcher (1871–72)
1905 **Albany College**
1934 **Albany College at Portland**
1938 **Albany College**
1942 **Lewis and Clark College**
Bernard Hinshaw* (1942) became department head (1946)

1855

McMinnville Academy–Linfield College, McMinnville
1857 **Baptist College at McMinnville**
Clara B. Martin (1887)
Virginia Watson (1897)
1922 **Linfield College**
Mrs. Walter Pritchard (1937)
Helen Blumensteil* (1946–47, 53–65)

1856

Monmouth University–Western Oregon State University, Monmouth
1865 **Christian College**
Miss E. McFadden (1882–85)
Eugenia J. Zieber (1887)
Lena Bosworth (1887–89)
Bessie Gibson (1889–91)
1891 **Oregon State Normal School**
Ella Smith (1891–93)
Rosa Bassett (1895–96)

Grace A. Higgins (1901–02)
Dorothea Nash (1905)
1910 **Oregon Normal School**
Alabama Brenton (1912–33)
1923 Art Department established
1939 **Oregon College of Education**
1997 **Western Oregon State University**

1858

Corvallis College–Oregon State University, Corvallis
Ida Burnett (1882–84)
1885 **State Agricultural College**
1888 **Oregon Agricultural College**
Dorothea Nash (1897–1900)
Farley D. McLouth (1898–1924)
J. Leo Fairbanks* (1923–46)
Ida Martha Matsen* (1927–48)
Marian Field* (1942–44)
Gordon Gilkey (1946–78)
Paul J. Gunn* (1948–80)
became department head (1964–72)
Wirth V. McCoy* (1948–53)
Nelson Sandgren* (1948–86)
Demetrios G. Jameson* (1950–82)
1953 **Oregon State College**
Shepard Levine* (1954–89)
Robert Huck* (1955–61)
Imamuel Piladakis* (1959–62)
1961 **Oregon State University**

1859

St. Mary's Academy, Portland–Marylhurst, West Linn
Sister Mary of Mercy
1893 **St. Mary's Academy and College**
1931 **Marylhurst, West Linn**
Sisters Mary Editha
Mary Alexina
Mary Rosina* (1924–77)
Mary Telesphore
Mary Edina* (1930)

1867

Philomath College, Philomath
Belle Gray (1882–86)
W.S. Gilbert (1891–92)
Jessie Allen (1897)

1872

Ashland College, also known as **Ashland Academy–Southern Oregon College, Ashland**
1879 **Ashland College and Normal School**
1887 **Ashland State Normal School**
Emma Tolman (1887–92)
1895 **Southern Oregon State Normal School**
Angie L. Engle (1895–17)
1917 **Southern Oregon Normal School**
Elizabeth Ady (1932–33)
Marion Ady (1937)
1939 **Southern Oregon College of Education**
1956 **Southern Oregon College**
Stephen Bayless*
1997 **Southern Oregon University**

1876

University of Oregon, Eugene
Nellie Meacham (1877)
1914 School of Architecture and Allied Arts
Alfred Schroff* (1915)
became chairman (1923–27)
Esther Wuest* (extension 1916–22)
Arthur Runquist* (1918–20)
Eyler Brown* (1921–61)
Maude Kerns* (1921–47)
Nowland Zane* (1924–46)
Louise Schroff* (1927–40)
Michael Mueller*
department head (1928–31)

Andrew Vincent* (1928)
became department head (1931–68)
Lance Hart* (1931–42)
David McCosh* (1934–72)
Jack Wilkinson* (1941–68)
Frederick Heidel* (1948–54)
Richard Prasch* (1949–51)
Charles Ryan* (1951–89)
Shep Levine* (1953)
Harry Widman* (extension 1956–60)

1879

Drain Academy–Central Oregon State Normal School, Drain
1885 **Drain Academy and Normal School**
Belle Dodge
Myrtle Russell (1887–88)
Mrs. G.T. Russell (1889–90)
Mrs. F.L. Russell (1891–96)
1899–1908 **Central Oregon State Normal School**

1884–1925

Eastern Oregon Normal School–Eastern Oregon State Normal School, Weston
Phronia Ketchum (1891–93)
1893 **Eastern Oregon State Normal School**
Julia B. Washburn (1899–1900)

1885

Friends Pacific Academy–George Fox University, Newberg
1891 **Pacific College**
Ella L. Hartley (1891–92)
Elma Brown (1893)
1949 **George Fox College**
1996 **George Fox University**

1887

Mt. Angel College and Seminary, Mt. Angel
1891 Drawing and painting classes
Anselm Weissenborn (1893–94)

1891–1900

Portland University
Katherine Upson Taft* (1891–98)
Alice Aubrey Weister* (1894–1900)

1897–1914

Lafayette Seminary and Dallas College, Lafayette
Etta Weaver Carter

1901

Columbia University–University of Portland
1923 Art Department established
Emil Jacques*, department head (1923–29)
1935 **University of Portland**

1909

Museum Art School–Pacific Northwest College of Art, Portland
Kate Cameron Simmons* (1909–10)
Harry Wentz* (1910–41)
Mary Hortense Webster* (1911–14)
Sidney Bell* (1914–15)
Helen Putnam (1914–18)
Clara Jane Stephens* (1917–38)
Leta Kennedy* (1922–71)
William Givler* (1931)
became dean (1941–73)
Charles Voorhies* (1939–57)
Lucia Wiley* (1947–55)
Mary Taylor Barrier* (1946–49)
Louis Bunce* (1946–72)
Jack McLarty* (1946–81)
Albert Runquist* (1946–47)
Michele Russo* (1948–74)
George Johanson* (1955–80)

1982 **Pacific Northwest College of Art**

1909

Reed College, Portland

1928 Joint Reed College/Museum Art School degree program is established

Robert Bruce Horsefall*

1927

Eastern Oregon Normal School–Eastern Oregon State College, La Grande

Thelma Irene Whaley (1932–33)

1939 **Eastern Oregon College of Education**

1956 **Eastern Oregon State College**

George Nightingale, depart ment head

1948

Vanport Extension Center, Vancouver, Washington–Portland State University, Portland

Vivian Pesola (1948)

Frederick Heidel*, joint appointment with University of Oregon (1951)

1954 **Portland Extension Center**

Frederick Heidel*

1955 **Portland State College**

Frederick Heidel* department head (1955–80)

Richard Prasch* (1955–83)

Robert Colescott* (1957–66)

Richard Muller* (1959)

1969 **Portland State University**

SECONDARY SCHOOLS

1847

Female School for the Instruction of Young Ladies and Misses, Oregon City

Nancy Thornton* (1847–48)

1849 **Clackamas County Female Seminary**

1856 **Oregon City Seminary**

1862 became part of the Public School System

1851–78 **Portland Academy and Female Seminary, Portland**

Mrs. E. A. Kingsley (1851–1855)

1851

Portland Public Schools

Ellen (Nellie) Turner (1877–91)

Esther Wuest* (1907–44)

Ruth Halvorsen* (1944–62)

1854–88

Umpqua Academy, also known as **Wilbur Academy, Wilbur**

Mrs. M. A. Royal (1856)

Mrs. C. W. Todd (1873–74)

1856

Trinity School, Oswego–Bishop Scott Academy, Portland

1870 **Bishop Scott Grammar and Divinity School**

Edward T. Coleman (1871)

1887 **Bishop Scott Academy**

Nels Hagerup* (1888–92)

1856

Young Ladies' High School, Portland

Mrs. Hill

1861

Spencer Hall–St. Helen's Hall–Oregon Episcopal School, Milwaukie

Esther Robbins Hurgren* (1864)

1869 **St. Helen's Hall**

Edward T. Coleman (1871)

Elizabeth Fullick* (1882–84)

Mary Norton* (1886–96)

Alice Porter (1893–95)

Mary Kollock* (1895–97)

Rachel Taylor (1895–98)

Georgina Burns (1903–04)

Ellen Ravenscroft* (1911–14)

Louise Thomson* (1921–31)

1973 **Oregon Episcopal School**

1869–85
Baker City Academy, Baker City
Painting class (1870)

1871
Salem Public Schools
Anna L. McNary (1891)
Ada M. Andrews

1881–93
Wasco Independent Academy, The Dalles
Elizabeth M. Folsom (1888–91)
1890–93 **The Dalles Normal School**

1889–1916
Portland Academy
Katherine Trevett* (1890–1912)
Clara Jane Stephens* (1904–16)

1893
Miss D'Arcy Select School, Portland
Teresa D'Arcy*

1904–16
Allen Preparatory School
Clara Jane Stephens* (1904–16)

OTHER SCHOOLS

1886
Art School
Miss Morgan
Mrs. E. W. Caswell

1890–97
Portland Art School
Amanda J. Smith*
Lottie C. Young

1897–1904
Northwest Normal College, also known as **Capitol Normal School, Salem**
Mamie Parvin Brown* (1897–1904)

1902–04
Pfeil and Lewis Art School, Portland
Lili Pfeil (1903–04)
Jacoba Pfeil (1904)
Anna M. Lewis

1905–10
Pease School of Illustration, Portland
Lute Pease*
Nell Pease*

1909
Pacific School of Arts and Crafts, Portland
Ada Elder*

1912–21
Northwest Normal School of Music and Art, Portland
Mamie Parvin Brown*

1927–84
Advertising Art School, Portland
Alan J. Mekelberg

1927–38
Neville's School of Applied Arts, Portland
Paul P. Neville

1929–31
Portland Academy of Art
Paul J. Keller*

1930–38
National Art University, Portland

1933–51
National Institute of Music and Arts, Portland

1934–38
Nelson School of Art, Portland
Victor L. Nelson

PORTRAITS OF VARIOUS ARTISTS

The selection of portraits found on the following pages are from the Photographic Archives of the Oregon Historical Society. Many of the photographs originally ran in the now defunct, Portland-based *Oregon Journal.*

Eliza Barchus, seated among the Oregon landscapes in her studio, working on two canvases. OHS neg. CN 000466

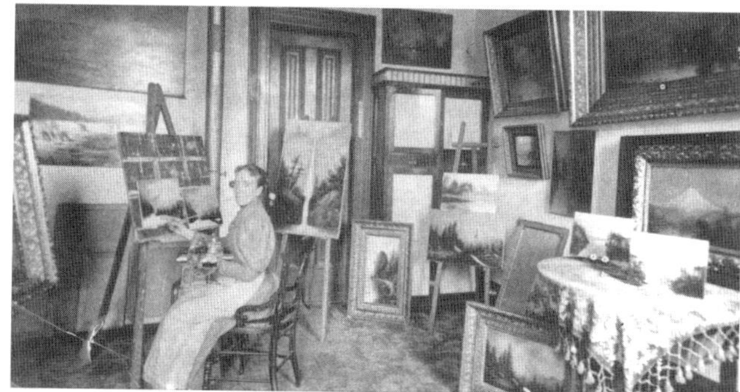

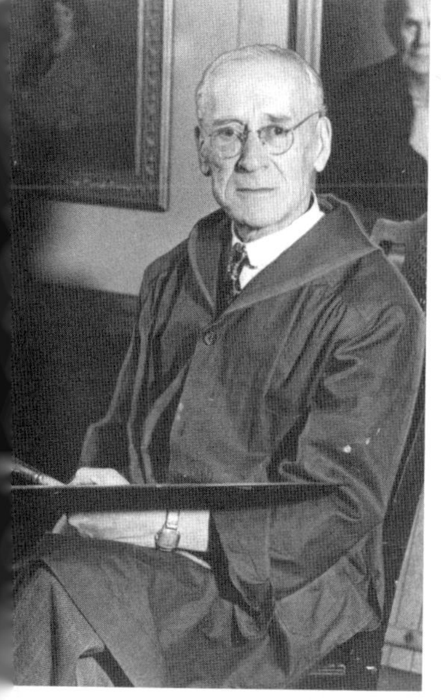

he portrait painter Sidney Bell in 952 with two of his works in the ckground. Oregon Journal *ollection, OHS neg. 00716*

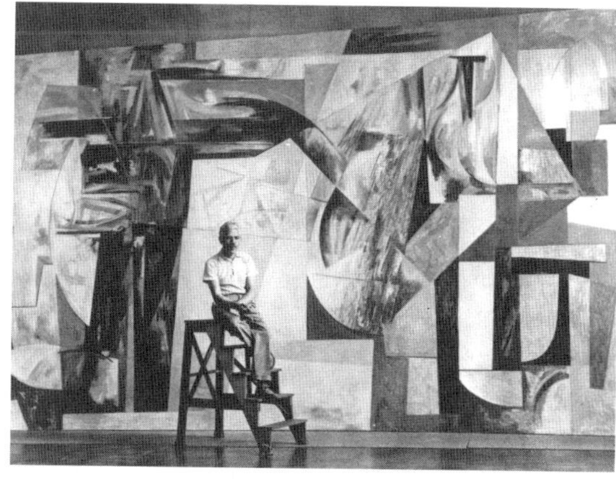

Louis Bunce in front of his 1958 revised mural for the Portland International Airport. The original piece was considered to be too abstract for a public art project. OHS neg. OrHi 72917

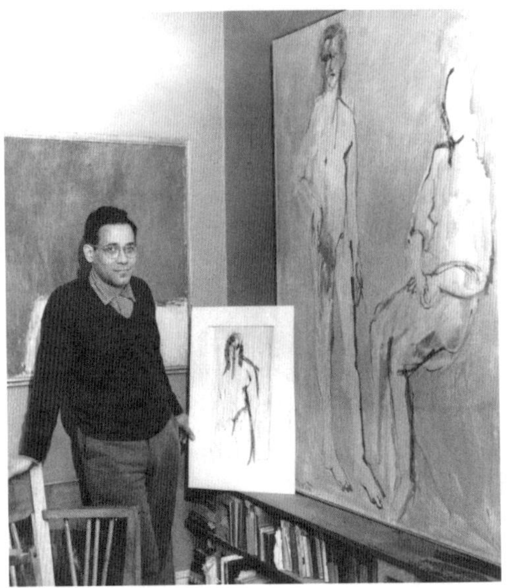

Robert Colescott, in 1958, a painter who would later gain international renown. At the time he was teaching at Portland State University and preparing work for an upcoming show at a Seattle art gallery. Photograph by Al Monner. Oregon Journal *Collection, OHS neg. CN001390*

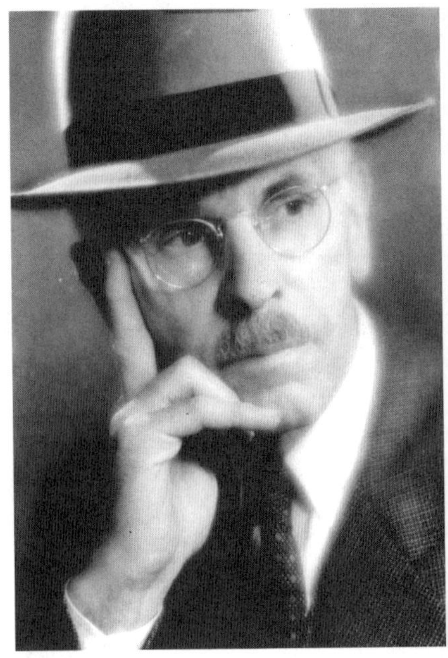

Cyrus J. Fulton in 1937. He came to art via his profession of haberdashery. He liked the artistic aspects of his work so well (sign lettering, window trimming, and ad writing) that he set up a home studio and art shop. It was not until 1935 (when he was sixty-two) that he was able to devote himself full time to his painting. OHS neg. CN011345

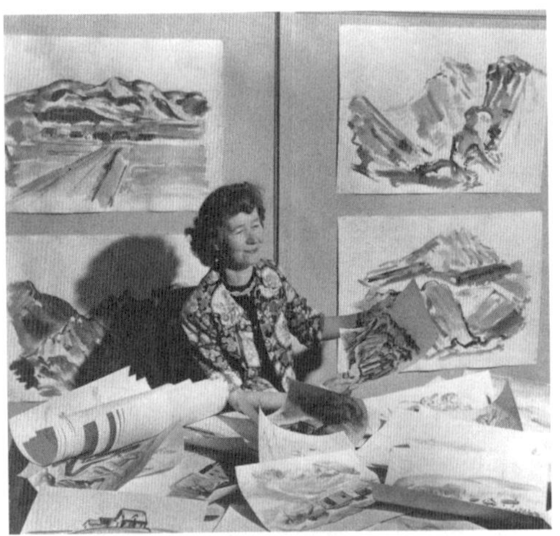

This 1949 photo of artist and art educator Ruth Halvorsen shows her surrounded by a series of seven-minute works she created while on a transcontinental train trip. Oregon Journal *Collection, OHS neg. CN011059*

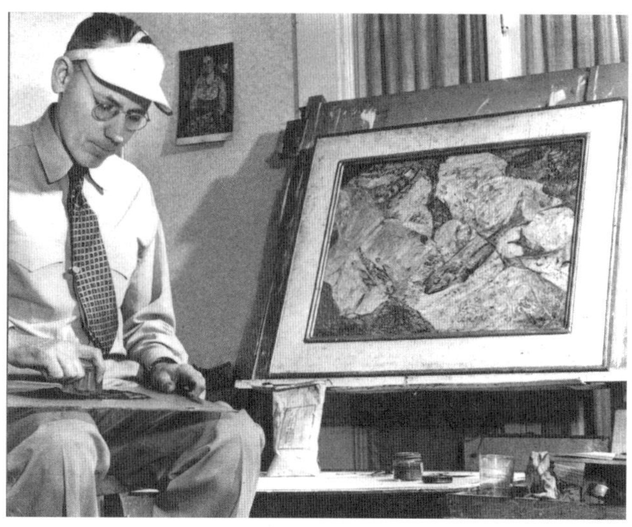

Charles Heaney grinding tempera paint at his home studio in 1948, a fossil painting to his right. OHS neg. CN010802

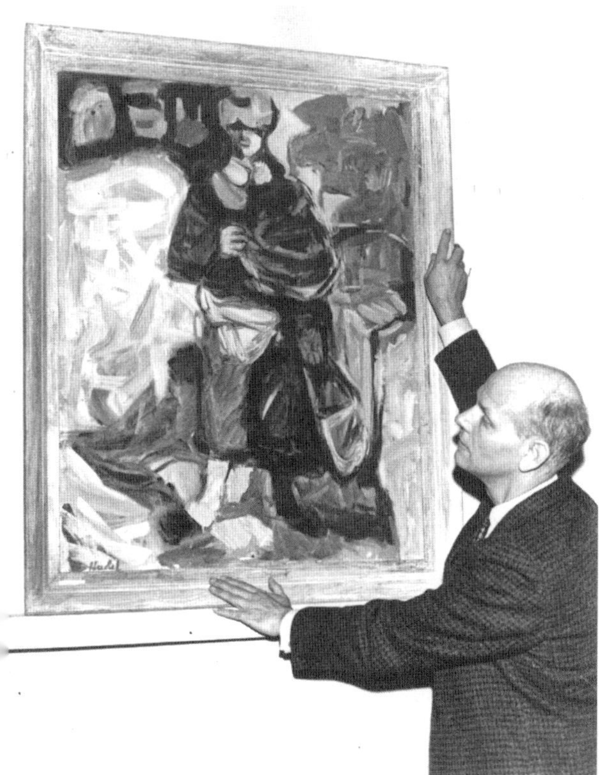

Frederick Heidel, head of the Portland State University Art Department with one of his paintings in 1963. Oregon Journal *Collection, OHS neg. CN 010848*

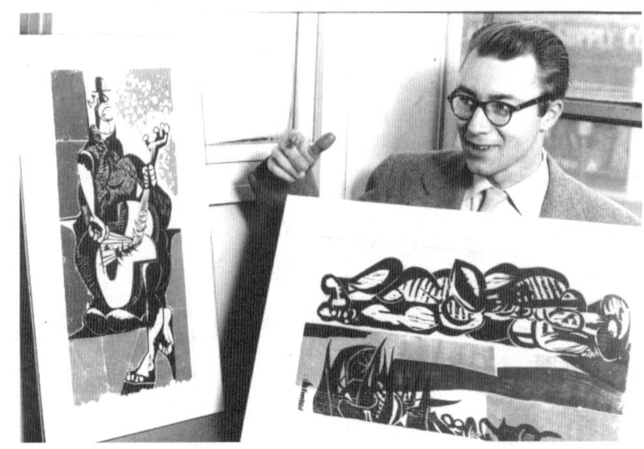

George Johanson, longtime instructor at the Museum Art School, works in a range of media. This 1956 photo shows him with two of his woodcut prints. OHS neg. CN01260

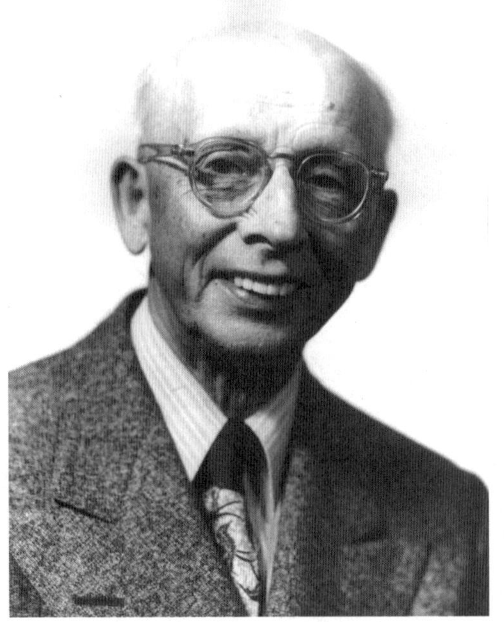

In 1884, Clyde Leon Keller enrolled in art classes at Willamette University at the age of 12. He was a prolific painter and ran an art and framing shop in Portland from 1907-1936. The sign outside his shop read "The Art Man" and he was known by that title for many years. OHS neg. 012059

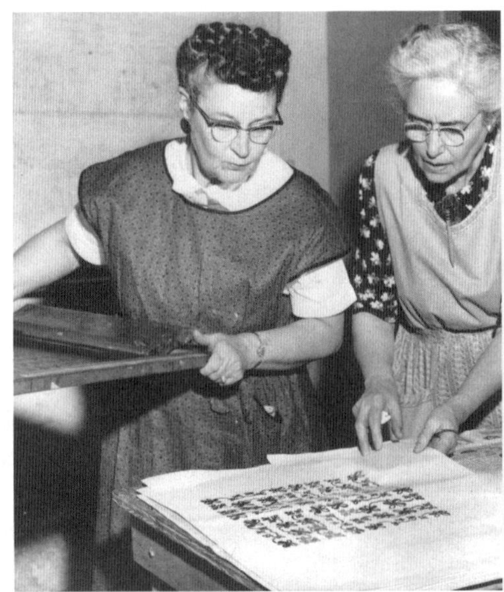

Leta Kennedy (right), artist and art educator at the Museum Art School, looks on as her student, Mrs. Piazza lifts a silkscreen to check her proofsheet in this 1957 photo. OHS neg. CN 013642

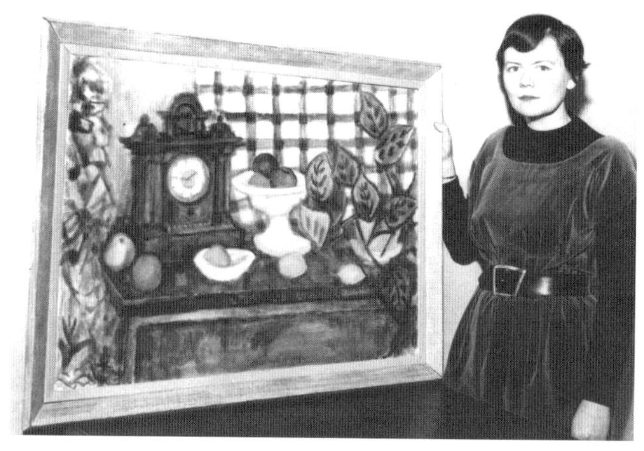

LaVerne Krause with one of her still life paintings in 1957. Photograph by Al Monner. Oregon Journal *Collection, OHS neg. CN012399*

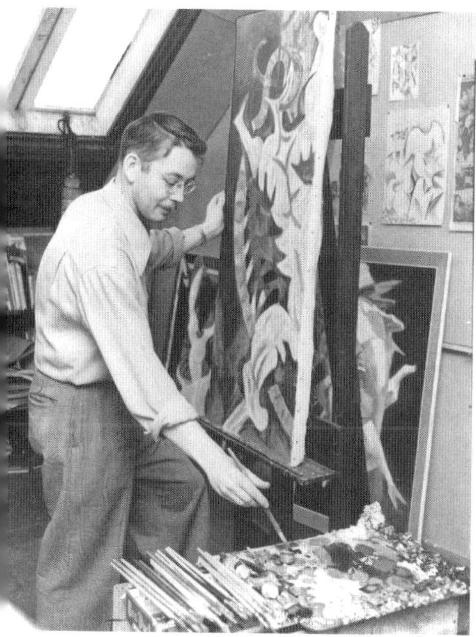

long-time teacher of painting at the Museum Art ·hool, this photo shows Jack McLarty working in s attic studio. Oregon Journal *Collection, OHS ·g. CN012451*

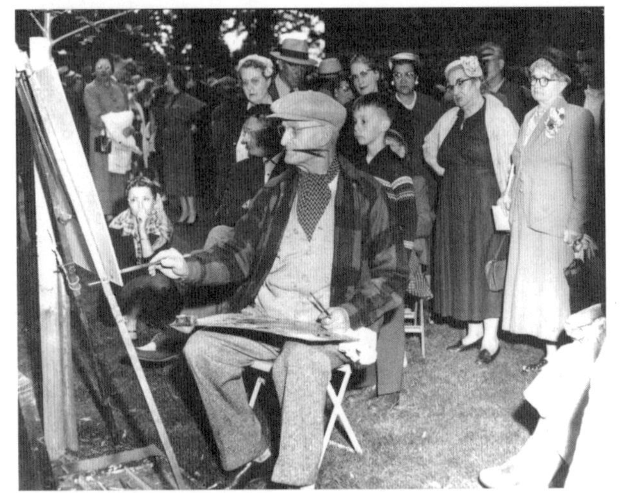

Percy Manser, an artist from Hood River, paints intently as a rapt audience looks on in the South Park blocks at the Greenwich Fair in 1955. The Fair was an annual event for the Oregon Society of Artists. Oregon Journal *Collection, OHS neg. CN 013175*

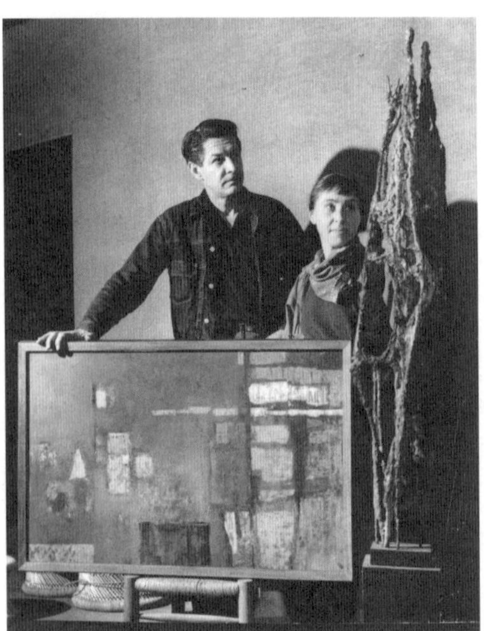

Carl and Hilda Morris, in their home with artwork they had recently sold. Photograph by Edmund Y. Lee, Oregon Journal *Collection, OHS neg. CN013207*

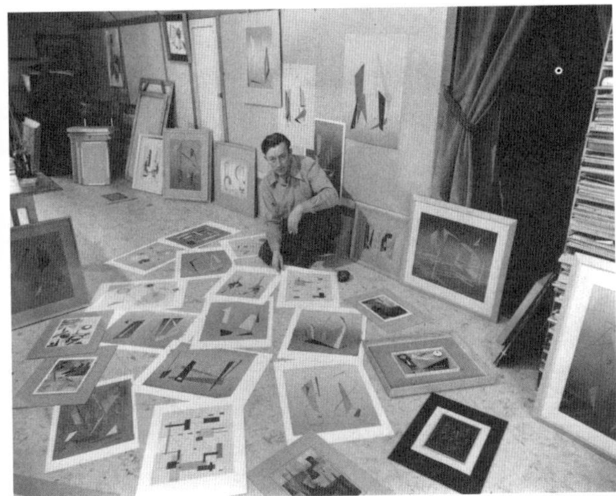

Albert Patecky in his home studio making selections for an upcoming show in 1951. Photograph by William Grand, Oregon Journal *Collection, OHS neg. CN013364*

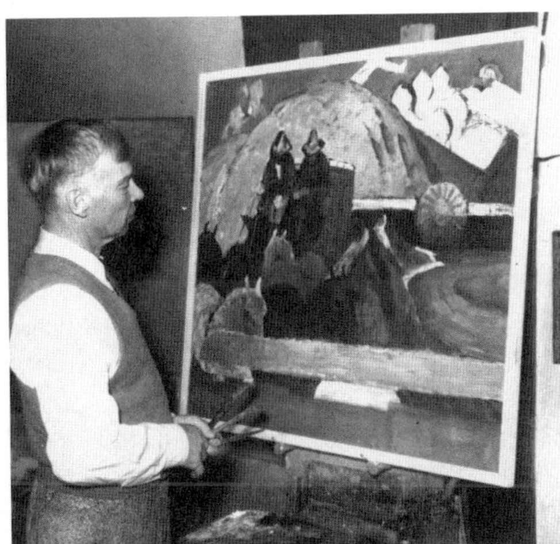

C.S. Price works on one of his paintings. Oregon Journal *Collection, OHS neg. CN024110*

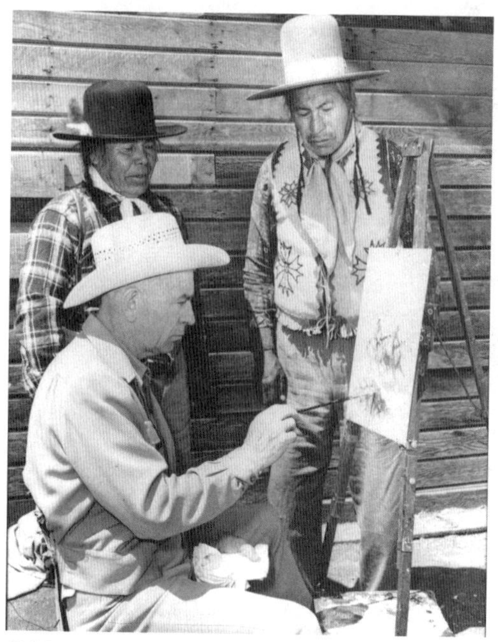

Ed Quigley working on one of his western scenes in 1956 at Priest Rapids, Washington while two unidentified Wanapum men look on. Photograph by James Rayner. Oregon Journal *Collection, OHS neg. CN014455*

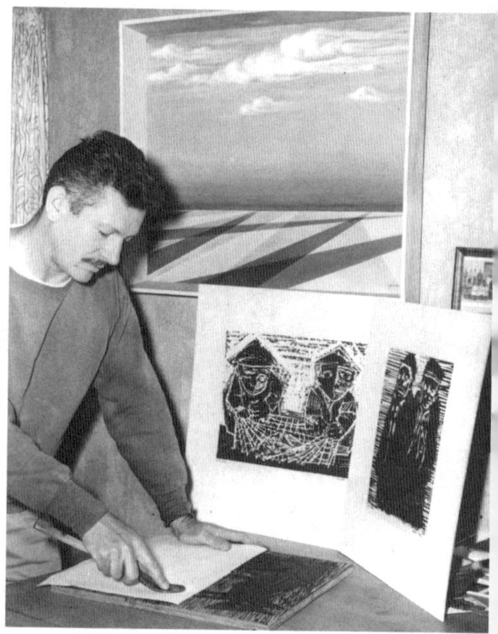

Michele Russo demonstrates his technique for woodcut printing in this 1952 photo. The painting on the wall is by Sally Haley, his wife. Oregon Journal *Collection, OHS neg. CN014430*

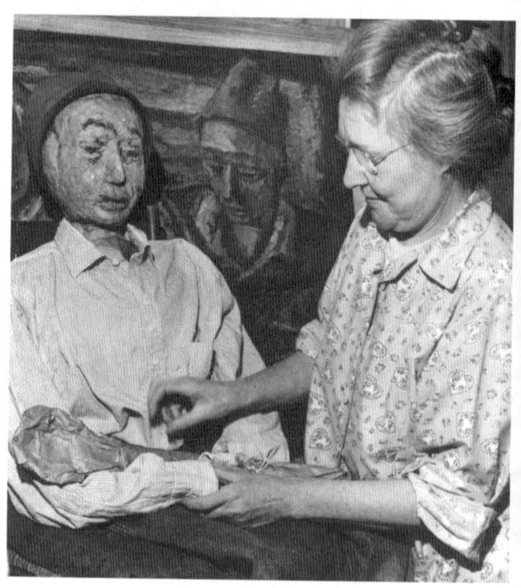

Amanda Snyder posing one of the papier mâché models to be used for her paintings in this 1953 photo. Oregon Journal *Collection, OHS neg. CN014620*

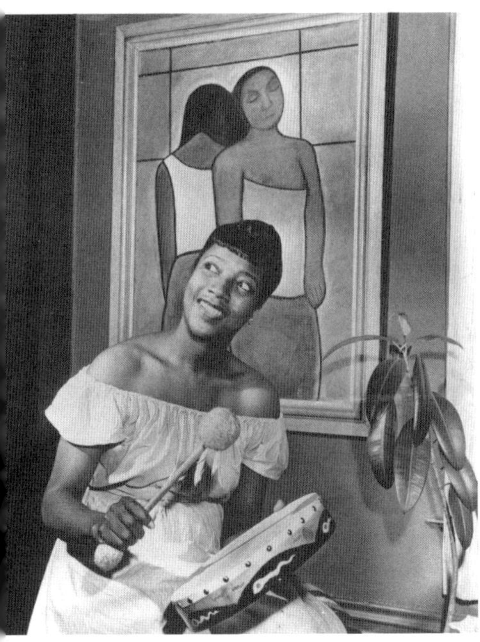

'helma Johnson Streat shown with her artwork in '948. In addition to her work as an artist, she was singer and dancer. Photograph by Mel Junghans.)regon Journal *Collection, OHS neg. CN012004*

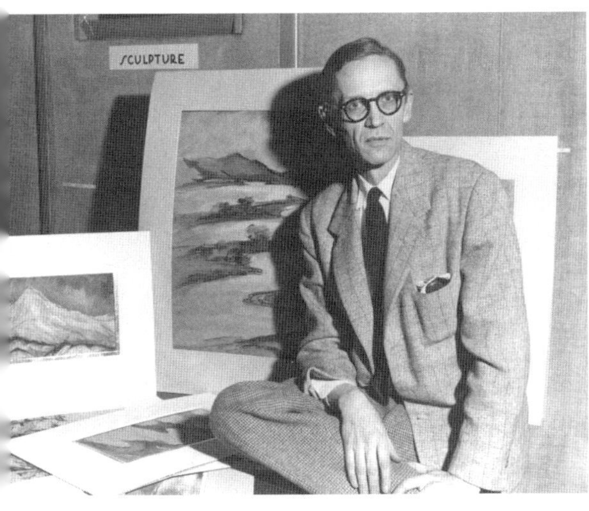

Charles Voorhies at the Kharouba Gallery in Portland, prior to hanging a 1952 show. Oregon Journal *Collection, OHS neg. CN018226*

USER'S GUIDE

The Dictionary is arranged in alphabetical order by last name. For each category of information there is a standardized format with biographical data and references. A complete list of References and Abbreviations follow this Guide.

SAMPLE ENTRY:

The following is a fictitious entry to assist the reader in interpreting the tabulated information:

(1) **ARTHUR, Sarah J.**
(2) ***b.*** 1872 Salem, OR
d. Portland, OR
(3) ***Education:*** Willamette University—Salem: *M. LeGall** (1892); Museum Art School: *H. Wentz** (1912); *S. Bell** (16)
(4) ***Membership:*** Arts and Crafts Society; Oregon Society of Artists; Attic Club; Arts Guild
(5) ***Awards:*** Oregon State Fairs (1917, 19–20, 24); Oregon Society of Artists (27–30, 32, 34–36)
(6) ***Collections:*** Powell Collection; Oregon Historical Society
(7) ***Exhibits:*** Oregon State Fairs (1917, 19–24); Oregon Society of Artists; Portland Art Museum; Clatsop County Historical Society (94)
(8) ***References:*** COL; WWN; A2 (1940); A5 (30, 33); C3 (27–36); C11; C27; ARTC; CD (27–34); M2
(9) ***Media:*** Oil, watercolor, pastel, prints
(10) ***Specialty:*** Portraits, landscapes
Sarah Arthur developed an interest in painting while in grade school. Her teachers . . .

INFORMATION CATEGORIES:

The time frame for this book is 1859-1959. When a date first appears in each category it is written as a full century date; where the century changes, the full date is written again.

(1) ***Artist's name***

(2) ***Birth* and *death* year and place are listed, if known.**

(3) ***Education:* Institution and/or location with teacher and years of attendance or graduation are listed, if known. * Asterisk indicates the artist is listed in Index.**

The artist was educated at Willamette University, studying under Marie Craig LeGall* (who is also listed in this Index) with attendance or graduation in 1892. She then attended the Museum Art School in Portland, studying under Harry Wentz* with attendance or graduation in 1912. She also studied independently with Sidney Bell* in 1916.

④ *Membership:* **All known art affiliations are included.**

The artist was a member of the Arts and Crafts Society, the Oregon Society of Artists, the Attic Club, and the Arts Guild at the Portland Art Museum.

⑤ *Awards:* **All exhibit awards are listed chronologically, where known, with the year. This category may not include awards received after 1959.**

The artist received awards at the Oregon State Fairs in 1917, 1919–20, and 1924 (dates for Oregon State Fair awards after 1909 appear in this category and in Exhibits, where known; Oregon State Fair awards prior to 1910 appear in the References category because the documentation comes from premium lists for award winners). Arthur also received awards from the Oregon Society of Artists in 1927–30, 1932, and 1934–36.

⑥ *Collections:* **A selected list of unalphabetized public and private painting collections (holdings subject to change). See Private Collections, p. 96 for further collection information.**

The Powell Collection and the Oregon Historical Society.

⑦ *Exhibits:* **Artist's selected exhibit history is listed chronologically, where known. Exhibition dates are not noted if the exhibit catalog is listed in the References category.**

The artist exhibited at the Oregon State Fairs in 1917 and 1919–24. The dates for her exhibitions at the Oregon Society of Artists C3 (1927–36) and the Portland Art Museum A2 (1940), A5 (1930 and 1933), and C27 (1974) are found below in the References category. Her work was also featured in a posthumous exhibit at the Clatsop County Historical Society in 1994.

⑧ *References:* **Sources are abbreviated. Complete information can be found under Reference Abbreviations, Catalogs, or Manuscripts.**

COL: Colman's *Oregon Artist's Source Book*; WWN: *Who's Who in Northwest Art*; A2 (1940): the Portland Art Museum exhibition in 1940; A5 (30, 33): the Portland Art Museum's Arts Guild exhibitions in 1930 and 1933; C3 (27–36): Oregon Society of Artists exhibits from 1927 through 1936; C11: *Oregon Artists Collection* at Clatsop County Historical Society in 1994; C27: *Art of the Pacific Northwest from the 1930's to the Present* exhibit held at the Portland Art Museum in 1974; ARTC: stands for art clubs with specific name found in Membership category, such as Attic Club; CD (27–34): stands for Portland City Directory artist listings from 1927 to 1934; M2: refers to J.D. Cleaver manuscript, *100 Significant Oregon Women Artists 1845–1945*.

⑨ *Media:* **Listed in order of frequency, where known.**

Oil, watercolor, pastel, prints

⑩ *Specialty:* **Specific subject matter, themes.**

Portraits, landscapes

The text of each entry may provide additional biographical data as available.

REFERENCE ABBREVIATIONS

1PS.......... 1 Person show. Also listed as 2, 3, or 4 person shows. More than five artists in an exhibition is a group show.

ALM....... Brooks, J.E., ed. 1961. *Oregon Almanac and Book of Facts.* Portland: Binford and Mort.

AM.......... Artist Membership.

ARTC..... Art Clubs: AC (Attic Club); CAC (Circle A Club); MAA (Mutual Art Association); OAA (Oregon Art Alliance); PAC (Portland Art Club); PSC (Portland Sketch Club); SOA (Society of Oregon Artists).

BEN....... Benezit, E. 1976. *Dictionnaire des Peintres, Sculpteurs, Dessinateurs & Gravures.* Nouvelle édition. Paris: Librairie Grund.

BI............ 1976. *Directory to Bicentennial Inventory of American Paintings Executed Before 1914.* Smithsonian Institution: Arno Press.

BIN......... Binheim, Max. 1928. *Women of the West.* Los Angeles: Publishers Press.

CD......... Portland City Directories. Artist listing (1863–1959).

COL....... Colman, Roger. 1979. *Oregon Artists Source Book Circa 1941.* Portland: Portland State University.

DAV....... Davenport, R.J. 1996–97. *Davenport's Art Reference and Price Guide.* Marceline, Missouri: Walsworth Publishing.

DAW...... Dawdy, Doris Ostrander. Volume I, 1974, Volume II, 1981, Volume III, 1985. *Artists of the American West, A Biographical Dictionary.* Chicago: Swallow Press.

FAP........ Federal Art Project.

FI............ Fink, Lois Marie. 1990. *American Art of the 19th Century Paris Salons.* Cambridge: Cambridge University Press.

FIE......... Fielding, Mantle. 1986. *Mantle Fielding's Dictionary of American Painters Sculptors and Engravers.* Poughkeepsie, New York: Apollo.

FSO (Year) First Southern Oregon District Agricultural Fair, premium lists (1896, 98, 99).

GER....... Gerdts, William H. 1990. *Art Across America: Two Centuries of Regional Painting 1710–1920.* New York: Abbeville Press.

GW........ Groce, George C. and David H. Wallace. 1957. *New York*

Historical Society's Dictionary of Artists in America 1564–1860. New Haven, Connecticut: Yale University Press.

HAV....... Havlice, Patricia P. Volumes I and II, 1973, Supplement, 1981. *Index to Artistic Biography*. Metuchen, New Jersey: Scarecrow Press.

HOW..... Howes, Durwood, ed. 1939. *American Women: The Standard Biographical Dictionary of Notable Women, Volume III (1939–40)*. Los Angeles: American Publications, Inc.

HUG...... Hughes, Eden M. second edition, 1989. *Artists in California 1786–1940*. San Francisco, California: Hughes Publishing, Co.

KOV ...... Kovinick, Phil and Marian Yoshiki–Kovinick. 1998. *An Encyclopedia of Women Artists of the American West*. Austin, Texas: University of Texas Press.

MAL ...... Mallett, Daniel T. 1935. *Mallet's Index of Artists, International-Biographical*. New York: Peter Smith, The Bomber Co.

MAL SUP Mallett, Daniel T. 1948. *Supplement to Mallet's Index of Artists, International-Biographical*. New York: Peter Smith, The Bomber Co.

MYH...... *West to the Oregon Territory*. (unpublished exhibit information). Maryhill Museum. Goldendale, Washington (March–November, 1993).

OET....... Corning, Howard McKinley. 1951. *Oregon, End of the Trail*. Portland: Binford and Mort.

OHS....... Oregon Historical Society. Portland, Oregon.

OR .... Oregon Recommendation (outside of Portland) from: Historical Societies, Art Associations and Groups, WPA, FAP lists and others.

OSF........ Oregon State Fair, premium lists (1861–81, 83, 1885–1904, 06–09).

PET .... Petteys, Chris. 1985. *Dictionary of Women Artists: An International Dictionary of Women Artists Born Before 1900*. Boston: C.K. Hall and Co.

PS........... Paris Salon(s).

SA........... Marlor, Clark. 1991. *Salons of America 1922–1936*. Madison Connecticut: Sound View Press.

SAM....... Samuels, Peggy and Harold. 1976. *Samuels' Illustrated and Biographical Encyclopedia of the American West*. Garden City, New Jersey: Doubleday.

SEO (year) Second Eastern Oregon District Agricultural Fair, premium lists (1891–98).

SIA......... Marlor, Chris. 1984. *Society of Independent Artists Exhibition Record 1914–1944*. Park Ridge, New Jersey: Noyes Press.

SM.......... Smith, Ralph C. 1930. *A Biographical Index of American Artists.* Baltimore, Maryland: The Williams & Wilkins Co.

SO (Year) Southern Oregon Agricultural Fair, premium lists (1890, 92).

SOCF (Year) Southern Oregon County Fair, premium lists (1898, 99).

THI........ Thieme, Ulrich and Felix Becker. 1976. *Allgemeines Lexicon Der Bildenden Künstler.* Leipzig: E.A. Seemann.

VOL....... Vollmer, Hans. 1972. *Allgemeines Lexicon der Bildenden Künstler: Des XX Jahrhundreds 1953–1962.* Leipzig: E.A. Seemann.

WPA ...... Works Progress Administration.

WWAA.. Gilbert, Dorothy B., ed. 1959. *Who's Who in American Art.* New York: R.R. Bowker Co.

WWN.... Appleton, Marion Beymner, ed. 1941. *Who's Who in Northwest Art.* Seattle: Frank McCaffery.

WWW... Falk, Peter, ed. 1985. *Who Was Who in American Art.* Madison, Connecticut: Sound View Press.

YNG ...... Young, William. 1968. *Dictionary of American Artists, Sculptors and Engravers from the Beginnings Through the Twentieth Century.* Cambridge, Massachussetts: W. Young.

CATALOGS

A1 (Year) Portland Art Association loan exhibits (1902, 06, 08, 09, 20, 24, 33, 53).

A2 (Year) Portland Art Museum non-juried exhibits (1911–15, 16, 17, 19–22, 32–34, 40, 42, 44, 46, 48).

A3 (Year) Portland Art Museum juried exhibits (1935–39, 49–58).

A4 (Year) Portland Art Museum group exhibits (1911, 14, 29, 41, 46, 52, 55, 59, 72).

A5 (Year) Arts Guild exhibits held at the Portland Art Museum (1930, 33).

C1 .... *Art: USA: 58*, Artists Equity and American Federation of Arts, New York (1958).

C2 (Year) Portland Industrial Expositions: North Pacific Industrial Exposition (1889, 90), Portland Industrial Exposition (1891–93), Oregon Industrial Exposition (1895, 96, 99).

C3 (Year) Oregon Society of Artists exhibits (1927–36, 45–51).

C4 (Year) Portland Mechanics Fairs (1878–88).

C5 .... Art Room in the Oregon Building, Panama Pacific International Exposition, San Francisco (1915).

C6 .... *The Oregon Scene*, Centennial Building, Portland (June–September, 1959).

C7 (Year) *Exhibition of Northwest Artists*, Seattle Art Museum (1914, 15, 17–23, 25–28, 28a, 29–32, 34–59).

C8 .... *Oregon Artists*, San Francisco Museum of Art (February, 1943).

C9 .... *Contributing Artist: The Oregon Art Community 1839–1989*, Oregon Historical Society, Portland (February–August, 1990).

C10 .... *Exhibition of Work Done in Oregon Under the Public Works of Art Project, May 1934*, Portland Art Museum (1934).

C11 .... *Oregon Artists Collection: First half of the Twentieth Century*, Clatsop County Historical Society, Astoria (April–October 1994).

C12 .... *Art of the Oregon Territory*, University of Oregon, Eugene (1959).

C13 (Year) *Oregon Professional Artists*, R.F. Elstrom Gallery, Salem (1946–48).

C14 .... *6th Anniversary Exhibition featuring Oregon Artists*, Lincoln County Art Center, DeLake (January–February, 1948).

C15 (Year) *Selected Work by Western Painters*, Western Association of Art Museum Directors, Portland Art Museum (1922–23); Western Washington Fair, Puyallup (1946).

C16 .... *Early Days in the Pacific Northwest: The Collection of Dr. and Mrs. Franz Stenzel*, Portland Art Museum (September–October 1959).

C17 .... *Watercolors by Oregon Artists*, Portland Art Museum (1953).

C18 .... *Art of the Thirties: The Pacific Northwest*, Portland Art Museum (May–June, 1972).

C19 .... *Paintings of the American Scene: WPA in Oregon*, Portland Art Museum (September–December, 1987).

C20 .... *2nd Pacific Coast Biennial*, Santa Barbara Museum of Art, Portland Art Museum (September–March, 1957–58).

C21 .... *Department of Fine Arts*, Lewis and Clark Exposition, Portland (1905).

C22 .... *A Gift of Love*, University of Oregon, Eugene (November–December, 1975).

C23 .... *Independent Spirits: Women Painters of the American West*, Autry Museum, Los Angeles (1995).

C24 .... *Snowy Mountains*, Washington State Capitol Museum, Olympia (1988).

C25 (Year) Annual Exhibition of University Alumni Art League, University of Oregon, Portland Art Museum (1935, 36).

C26 (Year) Southern Oregon Art Exhibit, American Association of University Women, Grants Pass (1953–56, 58–59).

C27 .... *Art of the Pacific Northwest from 1930's to the Present*, Portland Art Museum (1974).

C28 .... *Northwest Classics: Early Paintings of the Pacific Northwest*, Washington State Historical Society, Tacoma (1985).

C29 (Year) Northwest Watercolor Society Exhibitions, Seattle (1947, 48, 52–57); New York (1948).

C30 (Year) Western Washington State Fair, Puyallup (1940, 41, 46, 48–52, 58, 59).

MANUSCRIPTS

M1.......... Rasmussen, L., *Art and Artists in Oregon 1500–1900*, (1940).

M2.......... Cleaver, J. D., *100 Significant Oregon Women Artists 1845–1945.*

M3.......... Cleaver, J. D., *Oregon Women Artists 1845–1945.*

PRIVATE COLLECTIONS

Baldwin Saloon Collection, The Dalles

Booth Collection: Brian and Gwyneth Booth, Portland

Breithaupt Collection: Henry and Mary Breithaupt, Portland

Cofield Collection: Brooks and Dorothy Cofield, Portland

Counting Eagles Collection: William S. Stallings and Diane V. Cazalet, Portland

Gerber Collection: Mr. and Mrs. Matthew Gerber, Lake Oswego

Goodman Collection: Doug and Lila Goodman, Portland

Humpal Collection: Mark Humpal, Portland

Huntington Collection: Wallace K. Huntington, Portland

Hurst Collection: Peter and Lannie Hurst, Portland

Lundberg Collection: Robert Lundberg, Portland

Marquard Collection: Jim and Elizabeth Marquard, Portland

Martin-Zambito Collection: David Martin and Dominic Zambito, Seattle

Miranda Collection, Portland

Painting Restoration Studio Collection: Steve Maker and Harvey Freer, Portland

Parsons Collection: Michael Parsons and Marte Lamb, Portland

Pathways/O.I. Collection: Ron Ennis, Portland

Powell Collection: Alice and Michael Powell, Portland

Riley Collection: Marge Riley, Portland

Arlene and Harold Schnitzer Collection, Portland

Slippery Slope Historical Collection, Salem

Stenzel Collection: Franz Stenzel, sold as collection, June, 1980

Witham Collection: Vernon Witham, Santa Fe, New Mexico

OTHERS

Kaiser Permanente Collection: Kaiser Foundation Health Plan of the Northwest, Portland

Multnomah Athletic Club Collection, limited access, Portland

Timberline Lodge Collection: U.S. Forest Service, Mount Hood National Forest

A

AARIS, Hamilton Peter

b. 1906 Portland, OR
d. 1973 Eagle Creek, OR
Education: University of Oregon; University of Portland: *E. Jacques**; *S. Bell**
Membership: American Artists Professional League; Arts and Crafts Society; Oregon Society of Artists; Attic Club
Awards: American Artists Professional League (1939); Oregon State Fairs (35, 36, 38, 39); Oregon Society of Artists (35–39, 52)
Collections: Powell Collection; Oregon Historical Society; Parsons Collection
Exhibits: Oregon State Fairs (1935, 36, 38, 39); Multnomah County Fairs (36–39); Oregon Society of Artists (39); Portland Art Museum; Clatsop County Historical Society (94)
References: COL; WWN; A2 (1940); C3 (35–38, 52); C11; C27; CD (40, 55–59)
Media: Oil, watercolor, pastel, prints
Specialty: Portraits, landscapes
See artwork in color section

Hamilton Aaris had over seventy-four one-person shows in Oregon and other states, garnered more than 150 awards, and sold over one thousand works of art during his career. Aaris was a private art teacher as well as an arts reporter in Portland for the *Spectator*, the *Oregonian*, and the *Oregon Journal*. He maintained a studio in Portland at 3022 NE Broadway and later at 2381 NW Flanders from the 1940s to 1971. In addition to painting, Aaris produced ceramics and sculpture. He retired to Palm Springs, California in 1971.

ABBOTT, Prudence Jernberg

b. 1888
d. 1957 Alameda, CA
Education: Art Institute of Chicago
Membership: American Artists Professional League; Oregon Society of Artists
Exhibits: Oregon Society of Artists (1930); American Artists Professional League (32)
References: DAV; HUG; CD (1921–22, 24)
Media: Oil
Specialty: Still life

Prudence Abbott, best known as an interior decorator, had a studio in the Public Service Building and was an arts reporter for the *Spectator*. She was noted for her decorative arts and crafts, especially hand-painted lampshades. Abbott lived in Portland from 1921 to 1932, then moved to the San Francisco area, where she remained until her death.

ACKLEY, Herbert Mayhew

b. 1905 Chicago, IL
d. 1944
Education: Museum Art School (1927–30)
Membership: American Artists' Congress; American Artists Professional League; Oregon Guild of Painters and Sculptors; Arts Guild
Awards: Seattle Art Museum (1936)
Exhibits: Portland Art Museum (3PS 1936; 1PS 1947); Arts Guild; Creative Art Gallery (33); San Francisco Museum of Art (35); Seattle Art Museum (33–36); American Artists' Congress (37); American Artists Professional League (37–38); Oregon

Guild of Painters and Sculptors (48)
References: COL; DAV; HAV; MAL SUP; WWN; WWW; A2 (1932–34, 40, 46); A3 (35–38); A4 (46); A5 (33); C7 (34, 36, 39); C10
Media: Watercolor, oil, tempera
Specialty: Landscapes

Herbert Ackley was a graduate of Portland's Museum Art School and a member of the American Artists' Congress, the American Artists Professional League, the Oregon Guild of Painters and Sculptors, and the Arts Guild of the Portland Art Museum. He exhibited with those groups during the 1930s and 1940s. He was a WPA artist who also exhibited in Seattle and San Francisco. Ackley had a studio on SW Canyon Road in Portland.

ADAMS, Derroll Lewis

b. 1925 Portland, OR ***d.***
Education: Reed College/Museum Art School
Exhibits: Portland Art Museum; Seattle Art Museum
References: A2 (1946, 48); C7 (47)
Media: Oil
Specialty: Still life

Derroll Adams joined the U.S. Navy when he was a teenager. He said the experience had a profound effect on his life and work. After his military service, he returned to Portland to attend the Reed College/Museum Art School joint program. He exhibited at the Portland and Seattle Art Museums from 1946 to 1948. During that time he taught himself to play the banjo and, in addition to his painting, became a song writer, musician, and singer. He sang with Woody Guthrie and other folk singers. Adams went to Europe to travel and perform. He then settled in Belgium.

ADAMS, Rhoda Gantenbein

b. 1909 Portland, OR
d. 1977 Portland, OR
Education: Museum Art School; Art Students League
Membership: Oregon Society of Artists; Arts Guild
Exhibits: Portland Art Museum; Seattle Art Museum; Oregon Society of Artists; Creative Art Gallery (1933); Arts Guild
References: COL; WWN; A2 (1932, 33); A4 (36); A5 (33); C3 (30)
Media: Watercolor, tempera, pastel, oil
Specialty: Landscapes

Rhoda Adams was educated at Portland's Museum Art School and New York's Art Students League. She was a member of the Oregon Society of Artists and the Arts Guild and exhibited with both groups in the 1930s. She was active in the formation of Portland's Oregon Ceramic Studio (now the Contemporary Crafts Gallery) in 1937.

AKIN, Louis Benton

b. 1868 Portland, OR
d. 1913 Flagstaff, AZ
Education: New York: *Chase, F. DuMond**
Membership: Portland Art Club
Collections: American Museum of Natural History—New York; Gilcrease Museum—Oklahoma
Exhibits: Portland Art Club
References: BEN; BI; DAV; DAW; FIE; OET; MAL; SAM; WWW; YNG; ARTC; CD (1896)
Media: Oil
Specialty: Southwest themes, especially Indians

Louis Akin's grandparents came west on the Oregon Trail in 1852. The family settled in Oregon, where Akin began his career as a signpainter during the 1880s and 1890s. He was a charter member of the Portland Art Club and won awards at the Portland Mechanics Fairs of 1886, 1889, and 1891 with his sign displays.

He left Oregon in the late 1890s to

study art in New York City. In 1903 Akin arrived in Oraibi, Arizona, where he rented a room in the pueblo and began painting desert scenery and the Indians. By 1904 he completed a series of Hopi paintings, some of which were sold and reproduced for the tourist trade. Because of his interest in the Indians of the region Akin was honored with initiation into a Hopi secret society. Critics agreed that Akin's masterpiece is an unsigned painting of the Grand Canyon last seen in 1929, hanging in Verkamp's Curio Store on the Grand Canyon's rim.

ALBERT, Mary Elizabeth Holman

b. 1844 Salem, OR
d. 1905 Salem, OR
Awards: Oregon State Fairs
Exhibits: Oregon State Fairs
References: OSF (1864–67, 73, 74, 79)
Media: Oil
Specialty: Landscapes

Mary Albert was the second generation of her family to exhibit in the Oregon State Fairs. Her mother, Almira Holman, exhibited at the Fair in 1864 as did her daughter, Myra Albert Wiggins*, years later.

ALBERT, Myra. *See* WIGGINS, Myra

ALISKY, Charles William

b. 1866 San Francisco, CA
d. 1946 San Francisco, CA
Education: Munich; Dresden (1890–91)
Awards: Portland Mechanics Fair (1885)
Exhibits: Portland Mechanics Fair
References: DAV; HUG; C4 (1885)
Media: Watercolor
Specialty: China painting

Although born in California, Charles Alisky grew up in Portland. He was one of the earliest Oregon artists to study abroad. He married Charlotte Duncan, also an artist, in Munich where they were both studying. They returned to Portland and opened a studio, where Charles became well known for his china painting. After a few years in Portland the Aliskys divorced and he left for California in 1898.

ALLEN, Betty M.

b. 1923 Long Beach, CA
d. 1982 Medford, OR
Education: Fresno State College
Membership: Oregon Amateur Watercolor Society; Southern Oregon Society of Artists; Master Watercolor Society of Oregon; Portland Art Museum (Artist Membership)
Exhibits: Southern Oregon Society of Artists (1957, 58); Master Watercolor Society of Oregon (58); Maude Kerns Art Center; Oregon Centennial (59)
References: C26 (1958)
Media: Watercolor

While Betty Allen's primary medium was watercolor, she also produced sculpture, some of which was shown at the Portland Art Museum in 1958. She was a member of the Oregon Amateur Watercolor Society, the Master Watercolor Society of Oregon, and the Southern Oregon Society of Artists. She lived and exhibited in the Medford area.

ALLEN, Mary

b. d.
Awards: Oregon State Fairs
Exhibits: Oregon State Fairs
References: OSF (1890–92, 94); CD (1905)
Media: Oil
Specialty: Portraits, still life, natural history

Mary Allen lived in Salem during the time she exhibited at the Oregon State Fairs. Her name was sometimes spelled Allin.

ALLYN, Betty Swain

b. d.

Education: University of Oregon (1960)
Membership: Oregon Amateur Watercolor Society; Master Watercolor Society of Oregon; Portland Art Museum (Artist Membership)
Exhibits: Portland Art Museum; Master Watercolor Society of Oregon (1958)
References: A3 (1955, 57, 58)
Media: Watercolor, oil
Specialty: Landscapes (coastal scenes)

Betty Allyn made her home in Depoe Bay and Lebanon. She was a member of two watercolor societies and exhibited in the 1955, 1957, and 1958 juried shows at the Portland Art Museum.

ALTERMATT, Archer Robert

b. 1886 Springfield, MN
d. 1945 Portland, OR
Membership: Oregon Society of Artists
Collections: Wasco County Courthouse, Old Fort Dalles Museum, and Wasco County Library—The Dalles; Oregon Historical Society; Slippery Slope Historical Collection
Exhibits: Portland Art Museum; Oregon Society of Artists
References: A2 (1940, 44, 46); C3 (28)
Media: Watercolor, oil, charcoal, pastel

A member of a pioneer Oregon family, Archer Altermatt moved to Shaniko in 1910 and worked as a signpainter and bank cashier. He lived a short time in Berkeley, California with his brother John, then returned to the Eastern Oregon Banking Company in Shaniko. When the bank failed during the Depression, he moved to a sheep ranch near the John Day River at The Dalles. Altermatt came to Portland in 1943. He sketched constantly but seldom painted from life. In 1945, while preparing for a show at the Portland Art Museum, he died suddenly of a heart attack. The view of Mt. Hood from Lost Lake was a favorite subject, as were Multnomah Falls, Yosemite, and scenes of western life. He signed his works *A.R. Altermatt* or *A.R.A.*

AMES, John

b. d.

Exhibits: Portland Art Museum
References: A2 (1932, 33, 40, 44, 48); CD (50)
Media: Oil, watercolor
Specialty: Landscapes, genre

John Ames was married to artist Lorette Ames* and lived in Portland. He exhibited oil and watercolor paintings in five shows at the Portland Art Museum.

AMES, Lorette

b. d.

Membership: Oregon Society of Artists; Arts Guild
Awards: Oregon Society of Artists (1942, 43)
Exhibits: Portland Art Museum; Arts Guild; Oregon Society of Artists
References: A2 (1933, 40, 42, 44); A5 (33); C3 (42, 43)
Media: Watercolor
Specialty: Florals, genre

Lorette Ames lived with her husband, artist John Ames*, in Portland. She was a member of the Oregon Society of Artists and the Arts Guild, exhibiting with both groups from the 1930s through the 1940s.

ANDERSON, Anna Maud

b. 1885 Marshalltown, IA
d. 1968 Portland, OR
Education: *C. Keller**; *M. Wanker**; *Pelton*
Membership: Oregon Society of Artists; American Artists Professional League

Collections: Eastern Oregon College
Exhibits: Corcoran Gallery of Art—Washington, D.C.; Oregon Society of Artists; Portland Art Museum; YWCA—Salem
References: COL; DAV; DAW; WWN; A2 (1940, 44); C3 (29–31, 33–36, 47); C10; M2; M3
Media: Oil, watercolor
Specialty: Landscapes

Anna Anderson was a WPA artist who lived and taught art in the Portland area. She exhibited at the Portland Art Museum, the Salem YWCA, the Corcoran Gallery in Washington, D.C., and with the Oregon Society of Artists.

ANDERSON, C. Bryce

b. 1911 Redmond, OR ***d.***
Education: Museum Art School: *A. Gerlach*; S. Bell**
Exhibits: Portland Art Museum
References: COL; WWN; A2 (1932, 33, 40, 42)
Media: Watercolor, pastel
Specialty: Landscapes

Bryce Anderson, a friend of C.S. Price* and Edward Quigley*, created watercolor designs as well as pastel non-objective and abstract works. He was well known for his stained glass art and was a member of the Stained Glass Association of America.

ANDERSON, James A.

b. 1847 MO
d. 1908 Portland, OR
Membership: Oregon Art Association; Portland Sketch Club
Collections: Oregon Historical Society; University of California Davis; Washington State Historical Society—Tacoma
Exhibits: Oregon Art Association (1896); Portland Mechanics Fair; Oregon Historical Society (1990)
References: DAV; HUG; C4 (1896); C9; ARTC; CD (92–93)
Media: Watercolor
Specialty: Landscapes, genre, architectural renderings

In 1890 James Anderson lived at the Tacoma Hotel in Tacoma, Washington. A Portland resident from 1892 to 1897, he lived in San Francisco from 1897 to 1900 and then returned to Portland. Anderson produced magazine illustrations as well as paintings. Following his death from typhoid fever, the Portland Architectural Club held a posthumous exhibition of his work in 1909. His probable death date is 1908 in the Portland area but there is some uncertainty. There has long been some confusion between James A. Anderson and another artist, John Q. Anderson.

ANDERSON, Patricia Mae

b. 1927 Seattle, WA ***d.***
Education: Cornish College of the Arts—Seattle; Art Institute of Chicago (1949); Museum Art School: *C. Voorhies**
Membership: Oregon Society of Artists; Portland Art Museum (Artist Membership)
Awards: Oregon State Fairs (1951–54)
Exhibits: Art Institute of Chicago (1949); Oregon Society of Artists; Oregon State Fairs (51–54); Portland Art Museum (AM, 54); Hostess House Gallery (53, 54)
References: A3 (1953); C3 (51)
Media: Watercolor

Patricia Anderson attended the Cornish College of the Arts in Seattle, the Art Institute of Chicago, and Portland's Museum Art School. She exhibited her watercolors at the Art Institute, the Portland Art Museum, the Oregon State Fairs, and the Oregon Society of Artists. In 1953 and 1954 Anderson displayed her work at the Hostess House Gallery in Portland.

ANDREWS, Cora May

b. 1860 Oneida Castle, NY
d. 1954 Lane Co., OR
Education: Iowa
Membership: Oregon Society of Artists
Exhibits: Oregon Society of Artists
References: COL; DAV; DAW; WWN; C3 (1933); M2; M3
Media: Watercolor, oil, pastel
Specialty: Landscape

Most of Cora Andrews' paintings were of the Coburg Hills—the area surrounding her home—near Eugene. She was a member of the Oregon Society of Artists and claimed to be largely self-taught. Andrews signed her paintings *CMA*.

ARCHIBALD, James Clyde

b. 1903 Albany, OR
d. 1997 Portland, OR
Education: Oregon State University: *J. Fairbanks** (1925)
Membership: Attic Club; Oregon Society of Artists
Collections: Oregon Historical Society
Exhibits: Oregon Society of Artists; Oregon Centennial (1959); Oregon Historical Society
References: C3 (1947–51); ARTC
Media: Oil, pastel
Specialty: Portraits, figure studies

Clyde Archibald was referred to as a "child prodigy" in a newspaper article describing his sculpture at age ten. He continued to sculpt and added painting to his creative output. Archibald's work was influenced by newspaper illustrator Mahlon Blaine.

Archibald was a civil engineer with the U.S. Army Corps of Engineers in Portland and worked on plans for the Bonneville Dam, among other projects. He managed the Attic Studio from 1939 until it closed in 1970. For twenty-five years he made weekly visits to Doernbecher Children's Hospital patients to paint their portraits; he was once honored as "Hero of the Week" for this project. Archibald counted artists Ed Quigley*, Clyde Keller*, Albert Patecky*, John Waddingham*, and Thayne Logan* among his friends. In 1959, as part of the Oregon Centennial Celebration, he held a two-person show with William Drake* at the Oregon Society of Artists center.

ASHBRENNER, Laura

b. 1914 Battleground ,WA ***d.***
Education: Clark College; Lincoln County Art Center; Seattle; Mexico: *Acker*
Membership: Oregon Amateur Watercolor Society, The Dalles Art Club
Awards: Wasco County Fairs
Exhibits: Portland; Hood River Gallery; The Dalles; Sisters
Media: Watercolor, oil, acrylic, pastel

Laura Ashbrenner was twelve years old when she began drawing. By the age of fourteen she progressed to oils. Ashbrenner says she is mainly a self-taught artist. She has won awards at the Wasco County Fairs and received a fifteen-year merit award from the Watercolor Society of Oregon. Ashbrenner's paintings have been placed in Switzerland, Australia, Brazil, Texas, and Spokane, Washington. She has lived in The Dalles for many years.

ASMAR, Alice

b. 1929 Flint, MI
d. 1976 Burbank, CA
Education: Lewis and Clark College: *B. Hinshaw** (1949); University of Washington: *Archipenko* (51); Ecole des Beaux Arts—Paris (58)
Membership: Artists Equity; Portland Art Museum (Artist Membership)
Awards: Seattle Art Museum (1952); Oregon State Fairs (55–57); Southern California Exposition Memorial
Collections: Seattle Art Museum;

Franklin Mint—Pennsylvania; Smithsonian Institution
Exhibits: Portland Art Museum; Lewis and Clark College (1PS 1949); Seattle Art Museum (52, 54); Fole-Myers Gallery (53); Peebles Gallery (54, 55, 57); Oakland Museum (54); Western Washington Fair; Oregon State Fairs (55–57); Reed College (57); Artists Equity (58); Bush House Museum—Salem (58); Paris (59); Oregon Centennial (59)
References: DAV; FIE; HAV; KOV; SAM; THI; A2 (1948); A3 (55, 56); C1; C7 (52, 54); C30 (54)
Media: Oil, acrylic, casein, india ink
Specialty: Genre, portraits, landscapes, animals

Alice Asmar grew up in Portland and, by age ten, gained local recognition for designing and painting a "cathedral" window for her elementary school. At sixteen she won a four-year scholarship to Lewis and Clark College, graduated in 1949, then continued her training at the University of Washington and in Paris. She was the director of the Uitti Gallery in Seattle prior to 1955, when she accepted a position as an art teacher at Lewis and Clark College, Portland. She moved to California in 1960. Asmar exhibited throughout the United States, Canada, and Europe, where she continued to win numerous awards. Asmar's work is a combination of realism and expressionism. Some of her favorite subjects were the Native American people of the Southwest.

AUBREY, Alice. *See* WEISTER, Alice

AULERICH, Glen

b. d.
Membership: Portland Art Museum (Artist Membership)
Exhibits: Portland Art Museum
References: A3 (1954, 55, 58)
Media: Oil

Glen Aulerich exhibited oil paintings at the Portland Art Museum during the juried shows of the 1950s.

AUSTIN, Darrel

b. 1907 Raymond, WA ***d.***
Education: University of Portland: *E. Jacques**; University of Oregon; University of Notre Dame
Membership: American Artists Professional League
Awards: American Artists Professional League; Pennsylvania Academy of Fine Art—Philadelphia (1950)
Collections: Portland Art Museum; Timberline Lodge Collection; Metropolitan Museum of Art; Museum of Modern Art; Pennsylvania Academy of Fine Art—Philadelphia; Los Angeles County Museum of Art; Detroit Institute of the Arts; Boston Museum of Fine Arts; Parsons Collection; Oregon Historical Society
Exhibits: American Artists Professional League (1933); Portland Art Museum; Putzel Gallery—Los Angeles (1PS 38); New York (1PS 40, 45, 47, 48, 50, 53, 55, 57); Pennsylvania Academy of Fine Art—Philadelphia (50)
References: ALM; BEN; DAV; HAV; OET; WWW; A3 (1949); A5; C10
Media: Oil
Specialty: Landscapes, genre, fantasy, murals
See artwork in color section

Darrel Austin was two years old when his family moved to Portland. In 1927 he joined Kleeb Art Service, beginning his career as a commercial artist. During this time he won the Chamber of Commerce prize for best poster. While attending classes at Emil Jacques'* studio he met Charles Heaney* and C.S. Price*, who greatly influenced his work. He assisted Jacques with a mural commission for St. Mary's Cathedral of

Portland, following him to South Bend, Indiana to complete the job.

Austin married artist Margot Helser* in 1933. He painted a mural for the University of Oregon Medical School in 1936 entitled *The Evolution of Medical Education*, done in four six-by-eight foot panels, representing ignorance, doubt, revolt, and triumph. They were painted in the style of Mexican murals—bold and daring—and were controversial from the start. The murals hung for sixteen years, never liked or appreciated. During a 1952 remodeling they were removed from the walls and have since disappeared. It appears that Austin was ahead of his time for the public taste. In 1976 the Smithsonian Institution requested permission to include the murals in the National Collection of Fine Arts. A search was mounted but the murals were never found. As a WPA artist he painted a mural entitled *Fish Story* for the Tongue Point Naval Station near Astoria. In 1937 Austin produced eight paintings for the WPA; among them are *Dishwashers*, *Musicians*, *Woodcutters*, and *The Skier*, which can be found at Timberline Lodge on Mt. Hood.

The Austins moved to Los Angeles, where his 1938 one-person show at the Putzel Gallery was extremely successful. His subjects were women and girls in green orchards. One critic compared his "rhythmic riots of color" to Van Gogh. His work had a unique, sensitive imagery and a sense of mysticism about it. This marked the beginning of his highly personal style of painting—an introverted observation of images created in his soul. His 1940 one-person show in New York brought great critical and popular acclaim. He was featured in art publications as well as popular magazines. *Life*, *Time*, *Esquire*, and *Fortune* carried stories on this artist who had captured the popular imagination.

B

BABBITT, Hal

b. 1909 Kellogg, ID
d. 1981 Telapa, Mexico
Education: Oregon State University: *J. Fairbanks**; Museum Art School; *Lavare*
Collections: Henry J. Kaiser Co.
Exhibits: Portland Art Museum
References: WWN; A2 (1944); A3 (35–37)
Media: Watercolor, oil
Specialty: Landscapes (river scenes)

Among other works, Hal Babbitt did a series of four paintings of the Bonneville Dam.

BABCOCK, Ida Pratt

b. 1851 RI
d. 1939 Salem, OR
Education: Willamette University
Awards: Oregon State Fairs
Exhibits: Oregon State Fairs
References: OSF (1885, 86)
Media: Oil
Specialty: Landscapes

Ida Babcock came to Oregon as a child in 1857. She lived in the Salem area, attended Willamette University, and became a teacher. Her paintings were entered in early Oregon State Fairs.

BAIN, Lilian Pherne

b. 1873 Salem, OR
d. 1949 Portland, OR
Education: Art Students League: *F. DuMond**, *Pennell, Walcott, Rose* (1900–05)
Membership: American Artists Professional League; Oregon Society of Artists; Portland Sketch Club
Awards: American Artists Professional League (1936, 37, 39); Oregon Society of Artists (37)
Collections: Pacific University; Parsons Collection
Exhibits: Portland Sketch Club (1896, 1900); Art Students League; Salons of America (22, 23); National Academy of Design (23, 24, 27); Portland Art Museum (1PS 35); American Artists Professional League (35–37); J.K. Gill Gallery (36); Oregon Society of Artists
References: ALM; COL; DAV; DAW; FIE; HAV; KOV; MAL; PET; SA; WWN; WWW; A2 (1940); A3 (35–37); ARTC; CD (1897, 98, 1938); M2
Media: Prints (etching), oil
Specialty: Landscapes, portraits, seascapes

Lilian Pherne Bain was a sculptor as well as a painter. She studied at the Art Students League in New York City, where she assisted instructor Frank DuMond* for more than ten years. She also taught children's classes at the Metropolitan Museum of Art in that city. After returning to Portland, she taught at Pacific University (which was founded by her great, great grandmother, Tabitha Brown) from 1904 to 1910. She was one of the early women members of the Portland Sketch Club. Years later she served on the Portland Art Commission from 1940 to 1946. Her style was impressionistic. Both Kovinick and Petteys (see Ref. KOV, PET) list activity in Ogonquit, Maine. Bain's first name was spelled both Lilian and Lillian.

BALDINGER, Wallace Spencer

b. 1905 Springdale, PA
d. 1993 Eugene, OR
Education: Oberlin (1928, 32); Pennsylvania Academy of Fine Art—Philadelphia (28–30); University of Paris (32, 33); University of Chicago (38)
Exhibits: Mulvane Art Museum—Topeka, Kansas (1936)
References: ALM; DAV; HAV; WWW
Media: Oil, pen and ink

A magazine illustrator in the 1920s, Wallace Baldinger began his teaching career in the Midwest. He received a Ph.d. in art history from the University of Chicago. In 1944 he moved with his wife to Oregon. An instructor at the Museum Art School in 1944 and 1945, Wallace Baldinger left to teach at the University of Oregon School of Architecture and Allied Arts in Eugene. There he became curator of the Art Museum for two years before serving as its director from 1955 to 1970. During that period the museum grew to include Northwest art, visiting art exhibits, and an expanded Asian art collection. Baldinger traveled the world as a visiting lecturer, art historian, scholar, and art appraiser. He was author of a book titled, *The Visual Arts*. He also wrote numerous articles, catalogs, and chapters on American and Asian art in books and encyclopedias.

BALLATOR, John R.

b. 1909 Portland, OR
d. 1967 Roanoke, VA
Education: Museum Art School; University of Oregon (1928); Yale University: *Hudson, Camden, Taylor* (29, 34)
Membership: American Artists' Congress; University Alumni Art League, University of Oregon
Collections: Portland Art Museum; University of Portland; Smithsonian Institution
Exhibits: Creative Art Gallery (1933); Seattle Art Museum; University Alumni Art League, University of Oregon; American Artists' Congress (37); Golden Gate International Exposition—San Francisco (39–40); Hollins College, Randolph Macon Womens College, Washington and Lee University, University of Virginia—Virginia
References: ALM; COL; DAV; HAV; MAL SUP; OET; WWN; WWW; C7 (1934, 35); C25 (35)
Media: Oil, tempera
Specialty: Portraits, frescoes, murals

John Ballator was an artist with the WPA. He was awarded the commission to paint a mural for the St. Johns Post Office in Portland, and hired Louis Bunce* and Eric Lamade* to assist him with the project. He also created murals for Portland's Franklin High School in 1934 and the Department of Justice Building in Washington, D.C. He was an art teacher at Hollins College in Virginia for thirty-one years, where he became the chairman of the art department in 1951. He founded the Roanoke, Virginia Fine Arts Center. Ballator frequently returned to Portland for the summer.

BALLINGER, Thomas O.

b. 1911 Chicago, IL *d.*
Education: Art Institute of Chicago; Universidad de Nacional—Mexico; University of New Mexico
Collections: University of New Mexico; University of Oregon
Exhibits: University of New Mexico (1949); University of Oregon (54, 55)
Media: Oil, watercolor, mixed media

Thomas Ballinger was professor and chairman of the art education department at the University of Oregon. He had a great interest in Asian art and was a member of the Pacific Arts Association, an art education organization.

BARBER, Olivia Failing Shepard

b. 1906 Portland, OR
d. Sonoma County, CA
Education: Museum Art School (1919–28); Art Students League
Membership: American Artists' Congress; Arts Guild
Exhibits: Portland Art Museum (3PS 1936); Seattle Art Museum; Creative Art Gallery (33); Arts Guild; American Artists' Congress (37)
References: COL; WWN; A2 (1932, 33, 40, 42); A3 (35, 36, 38); A5 (30, 33); C10; CD (34, 39, 41); M2; M3
Media: Tempera
Specialty: Landscapes

Olivia Shepard was a scholarship student at Portland's Museum Art School. She was one of the organizers of the Creative Art Gallery in Portland in 1932, a cooperative venture with other artists. As a WPA artist and professionally during the 1940s, she used the names Olivia Shepard and Olivia Barber interchangeably. Barber's paintings appeared in many Portland Art Museum shows during the 1930s and 1940s. She began working as a clerk for the Portland Art Museum in 1939, and in 1941 became the Museum librarian. She moved to Berkeley, California with her husband, Roger, in 1952.

BARBER, Ralph Shaw

b. 1913 Manchester, England
d. 1995 Marion County, OR
Education: Willamette University; *P. Manser**
Membership: Oregon Society of Artists
Awards: Oregon Society of Artists (1946)
Exhibits: Oregon Society of Artists; Portland Art Museum; Hood River; Spokane
References: A2 (1942, 44); C3 (45, 46, 48–50)
Media: Oil
Specialty: Landscapes

Ralph Barber was a practicing attorney who lived in White Salmon, Washington in the 1940s. He produced oil landscapes which were exhibited in Hood River, Spokane, the Portland Art Museum, and with the Oregon Society of Artists.

BARCHUS, Eliza Rosanna Lamb

b. 1857 Salt Lake City, UT
d. 1959 Portland, OR
Education: *W. Parrott**
Membership: Mutual Art Association
Awards: Portland Mechanics Fairs (1887, 88); North Pacific Industrial Exposition (89, 90); National Academy of Design (90); Portland Industrial Exposition (99); Oregon State Fair; Lewis and Clark Centennial Exposition (1905)
Collections: Portland Art Museum; Oregon Historical Society; Powell Collection; Painting Restoration Studio Collection; Miranda Collection; Gerber Collection; Counting Eagles Collection; Bancroft Library—University of California Berkeley; Chicago Historical Society; Washington State Capitol Museum; Sunnyside Congregational Church, now the Staub Memorial—Portland; Pittock Mansion Collection; Crater Lake National Park; President Woodrow Wilson; President Theodore Roosevelt; William Jennings Bryant
Exhibits: Portland Mechanics Fairs; North Pacific Industrial Exposition (1889, 90); National Academy of Design (90); Oregon Industrial Exposition (99); Oregon State Fair; Pan American Exposition—Buffalo, New York (1901); Lewis and Clark Centennial Exposition (05); Mutual

Art Association (14); Pacific International Livestock Exposition—Portland (1PS 31); Portland Art Museum; Washington State Capitol Museum (88); Oregon Historical Society (90); Clatsop County Historical Society (94)

References: ALM; BI; COL; DAV; DAW; GER; HUG; KOV; PET; SAM; WWN; WWW; A2 (1940, 42); A3 (53); C2 (1889, 90, 99); C4 (83, 85–89); C9; C10; C11; C24; ARTC; CD (86–92, 96, 97, 1899–1902, 11, 15, 16, 25, 27, 28); OSF (1900); M1; M2

Media: Oil

Specialty: Landscape (mountains), western scenery

See artwork in color section

See photograph of artist on p. 81

In 1880 Eliza Barchus and her husband came to Portland from Utah. She took lessons from William Parrott* in 1884 by observing him paint, and began her artistic career in 1885. Her first sale was a work entitled *Mt. Rainier*, bought by someone who paid $1 and promptly retitled it *Mt. Tacoma* (the mountain's original name). Early awards from the Portland Mechanics Fairs encouraged her to continue her painting in earnest. In 1899 she became a widow with a family to support, and soon learned how to market the romantic scenes that she remembered or imagined. Her landscapes—particularly her mountain views of Hood, Rainier, and Shasta—spread the beauty of the West to the rest of the country and even to the world. In 1890 her *Mt. Hood* was exhibited at the National Academy of Design in New York. The work impressed viewers not only because of its subject but because of the gender of its painter, a rarity for the time. In the early years she worked at home, then moved to a studio at Third and Yamhill. She eventually moved to Fifth and Yamhill, now the Corbett Building. In 1905 she was awarded a gold medal for her painting at the Lewis and Clark Centennial Exposition; it was also here that her entrepreneurial skills surfaced. She introduced color postcards to Portland, featuring six scenes, which continue to be popular with collectors. She also produced a catalogue offering 8x10 paintings, "nicely framed for 75 cents," receiving orders from across the country.

Financial pressure forced her to produce thousands of works. Although she received criticism for her assembly-line style, she displayed considerable ability. Her larger works revealed a talent that was lacking in some of her smaller paintings. Her style was very realistic. Her favorite story was that of a friend's released canary, which hopefully batted its wings against the water pictured in one of her paintings. During her most prolific period, from the late 1880s to about 1920, she sold many works through the B. B. Rich cigar and tobacco concession at the Portland Hotel.

In 1935 failing eyesight and arthritis combined to bring her painting career to an end; she died twenty-four years later in 1959 at the age of 102. In 1957, on her one hundredth birthday, she was the subject of nostalgic newspaper articles and interviews, including one in "My Day", the nationally syndicated column by Eleanor Roosevelt. Fifteen years later, largely through the efforts of her daughter Agnes, the Oregon Legislature named Eliza Barchus "The Oregon Artist." Agnes also wrote a biography of her mother, *Eliza R. Barchus: The Oregon Artist*, published by Binford & Mort in 1974. Even today, Barchus continues to grow in popularity and her work is very collectable.

BARRIER, Mary Taylor

b. 1919 Portland, OR ***d.***

Education: Reed College; Museum Art

School; New York: *Hartwell*
Membership: Oregon Guild of Painters and Sculptors; Portland Art Museum (Artist Membership)
Exhibits: Portland Art Museum (1PS 1947); Oregon Guild of Painters and Sculptors (48); Santa Barbara Museum of Art
References: OET; A2 (1942, 44, 46); A3 (38); A4 (59)
Media: Oil
Specialty: Landscapes, genre

A graduate of the Museum Art School, Mary Barrier went to New York for further instruction. She returned to Portland and became a Museum Art School faculty member from 1946 to 1949. She exhibited her landscape and genre oil paintings in Oregon and at the Santa Barbara Museum of Art in California.

BARTLETT, Dana

b. 1882 Ionia, MI
d. 1957 Los Angeles, CA
Education: Art Students League: *Chase, Eaton*; Paris (1924)
Membership: Mutual Art Association; California Watercolor Society
Collections: Los Angeles County Museum of Art; Huntington Library
Exhibits: Portland Art Museum; Mutual Art Association (1914, 15); Los Angeles County Museum of Art (21–24, 26–28); Salons of America (26)
References: BEN; BI; DAV; DAW; FIE; HUG; MAL; SA; SAM; SM; WWW; A2 (1914); C15 (46); ARTC
Media: Watercolor, prints (etching)
Specialty: Landscape

Dana Bartlett worked as an illustrator, private art teacher, and commercial artist for Foster Kleiser of Portland. A member of the Mutual Art Association, he exhibited with them in 1914 and 1915 and in that year moved to California, where he continued to display his watercolors and prints. He was in a WPA exhibit organized in California late in the 1930s. While most references list his birth year as 1882, the Bicentennial Inventory lists it as 1878.

BARTO, Vivian Norman

b. Logan, IA ***d.***
Education: Pratt Institute—Ashland; Seattle: *Forkner*
Membership: Southern Oregon Art Association
Collections: Portland Post Office
Exhibits: Portland Art Museum; Corcoran Gallery of Art—Washington D.C.
References: COL; WWN; C10
Media: Oil, watercolor, pastel, pen and ink

Vivian Barto, a WPA artist, lived in Central Point. She studied at the Pratt Institute campus in Ashland and was a member of the Southern Oregon Art Association. She was interested in crafts as well as painting. Barto later taught art in Seattle.

BASSETT, Norma. *See* HALL, Norma

BAUMGRAS, Peter

b. 1827 Bavaria, Germany
d. 1903 Chicago, IL
Education: Royal Academy of Arts—Munich
Collections: Oregon Historical Society; Stenzel Collection
Exhibits: Washington, D.C. (1859); National Academy of Design (68); San Francisco (72, 77)
References: BEN; BI; DAV; DAW; FIE; GER; GW; HUG; MAL; THI; YNG; M1
Media: Oil
Specialty: Portraits, landscapes

Peter Baumgras was educated in Munich before his arrival in the United

States in 1853. He moved to San Francisco in 1869, arrived in Portland in 1872, and became an art instructor at the University of Illinois from 1877 to 1879. He moved to Washington D.C., where he was the founder of the Washington Art Club in 1887.

BAXTER, Wesley E.

b. 1920 Corvallis, OR ***d.***
Education: Museum Art School: *L. Kennedy**, *C. Voorhies**, *H. Wentz**; California School of Fine Arts; Académie de la Grande Chaumière
Membership: Portland Art Museum (Artist Membership)
Exhibits: Portland Art Museum; London (1955); Oregon Centennial (59)
References: A2 (1940, 48); A3 (58)
Media: Watercolor, oil
Specialty: Nature, genre

Wesley Baxter attended Portland's Museum Art School, the California School of Fine Arts, and the Académie de la Grande Chaumière in Paris. From 1953 to 1957 Baxter studied, traveled, and exhibited in Europe. He was also an art teacher.

BAYLESS, Stephen

b. 1926 ***d.***
Education: Eastern Oregon College: *Kollmeyer*; University of Oregon: *A. Vincent**, *D. McCosh** (1948); Washington State University (51)
Membership: Southern Oregon Art Association; Portland Art Museum (Artist Membership)
Exhibits: Portland Art Museum (AM, 1954); Southern Oregon Art Exhibit
References: A3 (1953); C17; C26 (56, 58)
Media: Watercolor

Stephen Bayless was educated at Eastern Oregon College, University of Oregon, and Washington State University. He was an art teacher for the Medford Public Schools, Southern Oregon College, and a member of the Southern Oregon Art Association. Bayless was an exhibitor in the Oregon Annual of 1953 as well as the group watercolor shows of 1953 and 1954 at the Portland Art Museum.

BAYLOR, Elwood (Edward)

b. d.
Exhibits: Portland Industrial Exposition (1893); Oregon Industrial Exposition (99)
References: C2 (1893, 99); CD (99, 1900)
Media: Oil
Specialty: Landscapes, marines, character studies

Elwood Baylor exhibited in several Portland Industrial Expositions in the 1890s.

BEATON, Pattie. *See* DODD, Pattie

BECQUET, Gabriel A.

b. 1909 Roseland, KS ***d.***
Education: Museum Art School (1930s)
Exhibits: Portland Art Museum; Seattle Art Museum
References: A2 (1932, 33, 40); A3 (36); C7 (39); CD (39–41)
Media: Oil
Specialty: Portraits, still life

Gabriel Becquet attended Portland's Museum Art School in the 1930s. He exhibited portraits and still lifes at the Portland and Seattle Art Museums. A 1936 article in Portland's *Spectator* spelled Gabriel Becquet's name "Bequest." He had a studio at 206 SW Washington Street in the 1940s.

BELL, Rita

b. d. 1908 Salem, OR
Membership: Portland Sketch Club
Awards: Oregon State Fair
Exhibits: Oregon State Fair; Portland Sketch Club (1900)
References: ARTC; OSF (1889); M2; M3

Media: Oil
Specialty: Landscapes
Rita Bell exhibited in the 1889 Oregon State Fair and was a member of the originally all-male Portland Sketch Club. She was an illustrator of books and magazines, including *The Pacific Monthly*, forerunner of *Sunset* magazine.

BELL, Sidney

b. 1888 London, England
d. 1964 Coos Bay, OR
Education: Royal College of Art—London
Membership: American Artists Professional League; Oregon Society of Artists
Awards: Oregon Society of Artists (1931); American Artists Professional League (34)
Collections: Powell Collection; Oregon Historical Society; Cofield Collection; Painting Restoration Studio Collection; University of Oregon; Capitol Collection—Salem
Exhibits: Portland Art Museum (1PS 1920); Seattle Art Museum; San Francisco Art Society (22); Portland Woman's Club (26); Oregon Society of Artists; American Artists Professional League (33, 34, 36, 37, 39); University of Oregon; Oregon Historical Society (90); Clatsop County Historical Society (94)
References: ALM; COL; DAV; DAW; MAL; OET; WWN; WWW; A1 (1920); A2 (15, 17, 19–22); A4 (29); C3 (27, 28, 31, 35, 49); C7 (22); C9; C10; C11; C15 (22); CD (16–18, 20–41, 43–4, 50, 52)
Media: Oil, watercolor, pastel
Specialty: Portraits, miniatures
See artwork in color section
See photograph of artist on p. 81
Successful careers as an art professor in Cheltenham, England, a cartoonist for *Vanity Fair*, and a portrait painter for the nobility were left behind when Sidney Bell was persuaded to move to Portland by art patrons Mr. and Mrs. J. G. Edwards. After his arrival he continued to achieve recognition as a portrait artist, with many prominent Portland families as his patrons. He was acclaimed as the "dean of regional portrait painters."

Bell taught briefly at the Museum Art School and established private studio classes in the Commonwealth, Labbe, and Dekum Buildings as well as the Edwards Hotel until 1952. Among his students were Hamilton Aaris*, Frank Binns*, Albert Patecky*, Amanda Snyder*, and Jefferson Tester*. He was also an artist for the WPA.

His portraits were said to have hung in New York, Boston, Washington, D.C., the University of Oregon, the State Capitol in Salem, and many private collections. His most acclaimed portrait, *Charlotte*, was still being reproduced and sold nationally when Bell died. He may have signed his paintings *Sydney Bell.*

BENDIXEN, George

b. 1883 Oslo, Norway
d. 1936
Education: New York: *Henri*
Membership: American Artists Professional League; Oregon Society of Artists
Exhibits: Buffalo Fine Arts Academy; Oregon Society of Artists; Portland Art Museum; American Artists Professional League (1936)
References: ALM; COL; DAV; DAW; WWN; A2 (1946); C3 (28); C10
Media: Oil
Specialty: Landscapes, still life
A WPA painter, George Bendixen's murals decorated Oregon City, West Linn, and Milwaukie High Schools (*Navigation at Milwaukie*), as well as the Multnomah County Courthouse in Portland. He was a member of the Ore-

gon Society of Artists and the American Artists Professional League. His landscapes were used to illustrate the book, *Land of the Free*, by H. Agar.

BENJAMIN, Ida

b. 1914 Portland, OR ***d.***
Education: Reed College; Museum Art School (1944–50)
Membership: Portland Art Museum (Artist Membership)
Exhibits: Portland Art Museum; Reed College (1954)
References: A2 (1946, 48); A3 (55)
Media: Oil
Specialty: Landscapes, cityscapes

Ida Benjamin was a graduate of Reed College and the Museum Art School in Portland. She was a social worker and taught Saturday children's classes at the Museum Art School for several years. She exhibited her paintings and sculpture at the Portland Art Museum and at Northwest fairs and festivals.

BENNER, Anna

b. 1880 ***d.***
Education: *P. Britt**
Awards: Oregon State Fair
Exhibits: Oregon State Fair; San Francisco Art Association (1885)
References: DAV; HUG; OSF (1880)
Media: Oil
Specialty: Portraits

Anna Benner lived in Jacksonville and studied with Peter Britt*. She then moved to Portland where she shared a studio with artist May Thornton. The Oregon Historical Society has one of her portrait drawings in their collection. She exhibited at the Oregon State Fair in 1880. After Benner moved to California, she exhibited with the San Francisco Art Association in 1885.

BENNETT, Eugene Peart

b. 1921 Central Point, OR ***d.***
Education: University of Oregon (1940–43); Art Institute of Chicago (47–54)
Membership: Southern Oregon Society of Artists; Rogue Valley Art Association; Portland Art Museum (Artist Membership)
Awards: Art Institute of Chicago (1956); Navy Pier—Chicago (57); Southern Oregon Society of Artists (59); Oregon Centennial (59)
Collections: Salishan Lodge Collection; Museum of Modern Art; University of Oregon; Haseltine Collection; Pacific Power and Light Collection; First Interstate Bank; U.S. Bank—Medford
Exhibits: Portland Art Museum (1PS 1950); Brooklyn Art Museum (51); Art Institute of Chicago (54, 56, 57); Navy Pier—Chicago (57); Artists Equity (58); New York (58); Southern Oregon Society of Artists (59); Oregon State Fair (59); Southern Oregon College (1PS 59); Oregon Centennial (59); University of Oregon (75)
References: A2 (1948); A3 (49, 50, 56); C1; C6; C22
Media: Oil, watercolor, ink, collage, prints
Specialty: Landscapes, cityscapes
See artwork in color section

Eugene Bennett and his family lived briefly in Medford before settling in a rural area near Prospect. It was here he developed an affinity for nature that would manifest itself in his work. During his high school years in Medford he was strongly influenced by painter and piano teacher, John Reisacher. After studying the work of Cézanne, he began to analyze the forms of nature. In 1940 Bennett enrolled as a music student at the University of Oregon. Although he was not formally studying art, he continued to roam the hills, painting and drawing with friends. Bennett left school to serve in the Navy during World War II. While stationed in various places in the United States, he was able to attend art classes and began to appreciate and produce his own abstract art. Bennett decided to devote himself to the visual arts while on assignment in Hawaii. During this period the work of Raoul Dufy became a major influence. As a result, Bennett's work—saturated with color—became more simplified, and his own style began to emerge.

Following discharge from the Navy, Bennett attended the Art Institute of Chicago in 1947. He exhibited frequently while in Chicago and received critical acclaim for his work. After earning his MFA in 1954, Bennett left for Europe, where he traveled, worked, and experimented with his art. The effect of stained glass cathedral windows reinforced his use of grid-like structures in his compositions. He returned to Chicago in 1955 with many paintings, drawings, and studies, which he exhibited and sold. He continued teaching at the Art Institute and elsewhere. He frequently taught summer art school in southern Oregon, and in 1958 returned there permanently.

Bennett taught private art classes in Medford and, later, Jacksonville, where he concentrated on painting, incorporating the natural environment, and introducing the Rogue Valley landscape into his work. In the mid-1950s there were few opportunities to see or study art in the Rogue Valley. With the encouragement of his students and others, Bennett helped plan and organize the Rogue Valley Art Association in November, 1959. The next year the Association sponsored the opening of the Rogue Gallery.

His early representational style of the mid-1940s gave way to a new Chicago style—almost non-objective, geometrical cityscapes, with a stained-glass, European influence. In Oregon, Bennett's paintings showed the influence of the literal representation of natural forces and the non-objective lessons he learned in Europe. He has continued to exhibit his work nationally, with critical acclaim.

BERGER, Arne K.

b. d.

Membership: Mutual Art Association; Portland Art Club

Awards: Oregon State Fair

Collections: Slippery Slope Historical Collection; University of Oregon

Exhibits: Oregon State Fair; Mutual Art Association (1914)

References: ARTC; OSF (1908); CD (10, 11, 13–18)

Media: Oil

Specialty: Portraits

Arne Berger was a member of the early Mutual Art Association and the Portland Art Club. One of his charcoal portraits is housed in the collection of the Oregon Historical Society. The Bicentennial Inventory lists an A. Kron Berger, who may be the same artist.

BERZEVIZY, Julius

b. 1875 Hormonna, Hungary ***d.***

Education: Museum Art School (1913–14)

Membership: Society of Oregon Artists

Exhibits: Society of Oregon Artists (1913); Portland Art Museum

References: BI; DAV; FIE; HAV; MAL; WWW; A2 (1913, 14); ARTC

Julius Berzevizy attended Portland's Museum Art School in 1913 and 1914. He was a member of the early Society of Oregon Artists and participated in their exhibitions. His work was also displayed at the Portland Art Museum. Berzevizy lived only a few years in Oregon before moving to New York State.

BEST, Arthur William

b. 1859 Petersboro, Canada

d. 1935 Oakland, CA
Awards: Oregon State Fair
Collections: University of Oregon; Mark Hopkins Institute; Oakland Museum; Counting Eagles Collection
Exhibits: Oregon State Fair
References: BEN; BI; DAV; DAW; HUG; SAM; WWW; OSF (1891)
Media: Oil
Specialty: Portraits, landscapes, marines

Arthur Best and his brother Harry* came to Oregon as band musicians—Arthur played clarinet and Harry, violin. They arrived in Portland in 1887, became enamored with the magnificent scenery, and began painting. Best spent some time in Salem, where he was listed in the 1891 City Directory. He also briefly lived in Silverton before moving to San Francisco in 1897. He worked for the *San Francisco Examiner* and later established and taught at the Best Art School. He is known as the "painter of the Grand Canyon" because of the spectacular views he produced there. The Bicentennial Inventory and Dawdy (see Ref. DAW) list his birthdate as 1859; but *Who's Was Who in American Art* and Samuels (see Ref. SAM) give a birthdate of 1865.

BEST, Harry (Henry) Cassie

b. 1863 Petersboro, Canada
d. 1936 San Francisco, CA
Membership: San Francisco Art Association
Collections: Yosemite National Park; Counting Eagles Collection
References: BEN; BI; DAV; DAW; HAV; HUG; MAL; SAM; WWW
Media: Oil
Specialty: Landscapes

Harry Best arrived in Oregon in 1887 with his brother Arthur.* It was said that his first sight of Mt. Hood inspired him to become an artist. After he sold a painting of Mt. Hood for one hundred dollars he gave up life as a musician. He moved to Silverton in 1891 before heading to San Francisco in 1895. It was in San Francisco that he met artist Thaddeus Welch* and sketched with him in Yosemite Park in 1900. Best took up residence in the park for a while, operating a summer studio there. His San Francisco studio later became the studio of photographer Ansel Adams, who married Best's daughter, Virginia. In the 1990s the Ansel Adams Gallery at Yosemite held a retrospective of Best's work.

BEST, Nellie Grace

b. 1905 Sterling, WA
d. 1990 Eugene, OR
Education: University of Oregon (1923–30)
Membership: American Artists Professional League; Oregon Society of Artists; University Alumni Art League, University of Oregon
Awards: American Artists Professional League (1932)
Exhibits: Oregon Society of Artists; Portland Art Museum; American Artists Professional League (1932, 33); University Alumni Art League; Minnesota Institute of Art (38); Corcoran Gallery of Art—Washington, D.C. (39); Los Angeles County Museum of Art (42); Cincinnati Art Museum (52)
References: DAV; HAV; HUG; MAL SUP; WWN; WWW; A2 (1932); C3 (31); C25 (35, 36)
Media: Oil
Specialty: Portraits, murals

Nellie Best attended the University of Oregon and was a member of both the Oregon Society of Artists and the American Artists Professional League. She exhibited locally and nationally in Cincinnati, Minneapolis, and Washington, D.C. In addition to painting, Nellie

Best created sculpture and crafts. She painted murals for the Post Office in Ontario, California and the Section of Fine Arts in the Public Buildings Administration, Washington, D.C.

BIERSTADT, Albert

b. 1830 Solingen, Germany
d. 1902 New York, NY
Education: Dusseldorf (1853); Rome (57)
Collections: Metropolitan Museum of Art; Corcoran Gallery of Art—Washington, D.C.; Hermitage Museum; Portland Art Museum; Painting Restoration Studio Collection; Stenzel Collection
Exhibits: Washington Art Association—Washington, D.C. (1859); Paris Salons; Portland Mechanics Fair; Portland Industrial Exposition (92); University of Oregon (1959); Oregon Historical Society (90)
References: BEN; BI; DAV; DAW; FI (1869, 75, 79, 80, 82, 89); FIE; GER; GW; HAV; HUG; MAL; THI; WWW; C2 (92); C4 (83); C9; C12; MYH
Media: Oil
Specialty: Landscapes

Albert Bierstadt arrived in New Bedford, Massachusetts with his family in 1832, and became a U.S. citizen in 1853. From 1853 to 1857 he studied in Europe, where he learned to create realistic, theatrical landscapes based on numerous sketches from nature.

He traveled west on sketching trips through the Rockies and first visited Oregon in 1859, returning in 1863 and later. With writer Fitz Hugh Ludlow, Bierstadt left San Francisco for the Oregon Territory in September, 1863. They came north to the Columbia River then east to The Dalles and Celilo before returning to San Francisco by steamer. His *Mount Hood* of 1869, housed in the collection of the Portland Art Museum, is typical of his working method and style. Painted on a grand scale in his studio in New York from small studies created while in Oregon, it employs dramatic lighting and a juxtaposition of elements to create a romanticized scene. Mount Hood, Multnomah Falls, and Lone Rock have been unnaturally aligned for artistic effect; in fact, the mountain is not visible from the ostensible vantage point of the painting. Everything is in focus, from foreground to background. The detailed foreground elements were added to indicate scale and add interest. At the high point of his career, paintings like this made Bierstadt the highest paid artist in America. His works are found in major collections world-wide.

BILES, James Norman

b. 1865 Portland, OR
d. 1914 Portland, OR
Education: *Turner*; Art Students League (1904); Académie Julian (09)
Membership: Portland Art Club
Collections: Oregon Historical Society; Slippery Slope Historical Collection
Exhibits: Portland Mechanics Fairs; Portland Art Club (1886); North Pacific Industrial Exposition (90); Portland Industrial Expositions (91, 92); Oregon Industrial Exposition (95); Portland Art Museum; Oregon Historical Society (1990)
References: DAV; HUG; A2 (1913, 14); C2 (1890–92, 95); C4 (83, 85); C9; ARTC; CD (90); M1
Media: Oil, crayon
Specialty: Landscapes, genre, portraits

J. N. Biles created his first art work in 1879. From 1887 to 1892, he was one of the first students to attend Ellen Turner's art classes in the Portland Public Schools. During that time he received awards and recognition for work entered in student exhibits at the Portland Mechanics Fairs. In 1885, at age twenty, Biles painted a black on white oil painting, *Portland Insane Asylum*, which became, in 1900, the first art object acquired by the Oregon Historical Society.

In 1896 Biles moved to California, where he worked as a commercial artist and an illustrator for the *San Francisco Examiner* and *San Francisco Chronicle*. He left for New York in 1904 and then moved to Paris in 1909. He returned to Portland in 1913 to establish a commercial art business, only to die a year later. Biles was the uncle of artist Stuart Biles. He signed his work *J. Norman Biles* or *J. N. Biles*.

BINGHAM, George E.

b. 1884 MA
d. 1957 Multnomah Co., OR
Education: Art Students League; Museum Art School (1910)
Membership: Society of Oregon Artists; Mutual Art Association
Collections: Oregon Historical Society
Exhibits: Portland Art Museum; Mutual Art Association (1914, 15)
References: A2 (1912); ARTC; CD (13, 14, 16, 17)
Media: Oil, watercolor
Specialty: Landscape

George Bingham, a student in the first class of the Portland Museum Art School in 1910, also attended the Art Students League in New York City. He was a member of two early art groups in Portland: the Society of Oregon Artists and the Mutual Art Association, with whom he exhibited. In the early 1900s George Bingham owned both the Rose City Art Store and Gallery and the Western Art School in Portland, where he taught life drawing. He was also an art instructor at the YWCA in 1910.

BINNS, Frank E.

b. 1912 Seattle, WA ***d.***
Education: University of Oregon: *D. McCosh*, A. Vincent*, L. Hart*, N. Zane*; C. Keller*; S. Bell**
Membership: Oregon Society of Artists
Collections: Powell Collection; Alderwood, Glendoveer Country Clubs—Portland
Exhibits: Oregon Society of Artists; Oregon State Fair (1938); Portland Art Museum; Clatsop County Historical Society (94)
References: ALM; COL; WWN; A2 (1940, 44, 46, 48); A3 (52); C3 (37–39); C11; CD (39)
Media: Oil
Specialty: Landscapes

Frank Binns received his art education at the University of Oregon. He also took private art instruction from Clyde Keller* and Sidney Bell*. He was a member of the Oregon Society of Artists, and participated in their exhibitions. His work was also shown at the Portland Art Museum. Binns often painted small coastal villages and ports. He and his wife Lorette, also an artist, lived in Newport in the 1940s.

BISHOP, Flora Melissa

b. Minneapolis, MN ***d.***
Education: California School of Fine Arts; University of Oregon; *C. Keller**
Membership: Oregon Society of Artists; Southern Oregon Society of Artists
Exhibits: Oregon Society of Artists; Portland Art Museum
References: DAV; HUG; MAL; WWW; A2 (1934); C3 (29–31)
Media: Oil
Specialty: Marines

Flora Bishop studied at the California School of Fine Arts, the University of Oregon, and privately with Clyde Keller*. Her husband, Hal*, was also an artist. Together they owned an art supply store in Medford from the 1940s into the 1960s. She was a member of the Oregon

Society of Artists and the Southern Oregon Society of Artists, which she and her husband helped establish.

BISHOP, Hal E.

b. d.

Membership: Oregon Society of Artists; Southern Oregon Society of Artists

Collections: Southern Oregon Historical Society

Exhibits: Portland Art Museum; Oregon Society of Artists

References: OET; A2 (1948); C3 (49, 50)

Media: Oil

Specialty: Landscapes, figurative, murals

From the 1940s to the 1960s, Hal Bishop created murals for buildings in Medford. Many of those structures have been razed, leaving only a few surviving murals on canvas. Some of his smaller paintings can still be found. His large paintings depicted scenes from Oregon history and the area surrounding Medford. Art restoration and framing supplemented his painting career. He and his wife, Flora*, have been credited with creating a greater awareness of art in the Rogue Valley. They worked together to help establish the Southern Oregon Society of Artists.

BLEVINS, Wade H.

b. d. 1943 Portland, OR

Membership: Circle A Club; Society of Oregon Artists; American Artists Professional League

Awards: Lewis and Clark Centennial Exposition (1905)

Exhibits: Lewis and Clark Centennial Exposition (1905); Portland Art Museum; American Artists Professional League (34)

References: A2 (1912, 13); ARTC

Wade Blevins was a member of several early art clubs before the 1920s. He was also a member of the American Artists Professional League. He exhibited at the Lewis and Clark Exposition and the Portland Art Museum.

BLUM, Emma Cornelius

b. 1854 Cornelius Prairie, WA

d. 1926 Los Angeles, CA

Exhibits: Portland Mechanics Fairs

References: C4 (1882, 83); CD (83, 87, 92, 93); M2; M3

Media: Oil, watercolor

Specialty: Landscapes, still life, florals, portraits

Emma Blum was an art teacher at Pacific University from 1883 to 1885. She exhibited in the Portland Mechanics Fairs of 1882 and 1883. Blum had an art studio in Portland from the late 1880s to the early 1890s. Her sister, Tillie Cornelius, and husband, Isaac Blum, were also artists.

BLUMENSTEIL, Helen Alpiner

b. 1899 Rochester, NY

d. 1975 Eola Hills, OR

Education: University of Rochester: *Trautman* (1918–22); Grand Central School of Art: *Gorky*, *Williams* (27); Ecole des Beaux Arts—Fontainebleau (29–30); University of Oregon (50–51); New York: *Hofmann* (51)

Membership: Portland Art Museum (Artists Membership); Society of Independent Artists—New York

Awards: Memorial Art Gallery—Rochester, New York (1922, 28, 29)

Exhibits: Memorial Art Gallery—Rochester, New York (1922, 28, 29); Society of Independent Artists—New York (35); National Academy of Design (37); Portland Art Museum; Seattle Art Museum; Willamette University; Tacoma Art Museum; Linfield College (59); Bush Barn—Salem, retrospective (76)

References: ALM; DAV; DAW; HAV; MAL SUP; PET; WWW; A3 (1951); C7 (52); M2; M3
Media: Oil, prints (lithograph, wood-cuts)
Specialty: Landscapes, still life

Helen Blumensteil studied at the Ecole des Beaux Arts in Fontainebleau, France from 1929 to 1930, then continued her art training in Paris for four months. She returned home to New York and became a magazine illustrator in the early 1930s. As part of the WPA in 1937, Blumensteil came to Oregon to teach at the Salem Federal Art Center. Two years later when the WPA project ended, she spent some time at the Brooklyn Children's Museum working on dioramas. In 1943 Blumensteil bought a small farm in Oregon and, from that point on, was tied to the land. She lived simply and found inspiration for her art in the land. She taught in the Linfield College art department in 1946, then left to pursue other interests. She returned to head the department from 1952 to 1965. Blumensteil occasionally gave private lessons in her studio. Her work was exhibited at the Portland and Seattle Art Museums as well as Linfield College. The Bush Barn in Salem presented a retrospective of her work in 1976.

BOHLMAN, Edgar LeMoine

b. 1902 Cottage Grove, OR *d.*
Education: Museum Art School; University of Oregon (1926); New York; Paris
Membership: Arts Guild; University Alumni Art League, University of Oregon
Awards: Honolulu, Hawaii
Collections: University of Oregon; California Palace of the Legion of Honor
Exhibits: Detroit Institute of the Arts; Casablanca; Lisbon; Arts Guild; Portland Art Museum; Galeria Mona Lisa—Paris (1PS 1934); University Alumni Art League; Marie Sterner Gallery—New York City (35); Meier and Frank Co. (1PS 47); University of Oregon (75)
References: ALM; DAV; HAV; MAL; OET; WWW; A2 (1932, 48); A5 (30); C22; C25 (35)
Media: Watercolor, oil
Specialty: Genre, murals

Edgar Bohlman was a decorator, illustrator, costume and set designer, and artist for a scientific expedition to North Africa in 1932. He left Portland in 1926 and lived in Morocco and New York. There he designed costumes, sets, and scenery for New York opera productions. Bohlman also illustrated articles for *Studio Magazine* and *Town and Country*. After returning to Portland, he was a set designer for the Portland Civic Theatre in 1947 and 1948. He exhibited at the Portland Art Museum and in a one-person show at the Meier and Frank Co.

His work was recognized for its exactness of color, line, and delicacy of sentiment. Bohlman's exhibitions were well attended and his work sold quickly. He was the son of artist Herman Bohlman*.

BOHLMAN, Herman Theodore

b. 1872 Portland, OR
d. 1943 Portland, OR
Education: *C. Keller**
Membership: American Artists Professional League; Oregon Society of Artists
Awards: American Artists Professional League (1932, 33); Oregon Society of Artists (33)
Collections: Powell Collection; Portland City Hall; Parsons Collection
Exhibits: Audubon Society (1922); Oregon Society of Artists; Portland Art Museum; American Artists Profes-

sional League (32, 33); Clatsop County Historical Society (94)
References: COL; DAV; DAW HAV; MAL; WWN; WWW; A2 (1932, 33); A3 (52); C3 (27–30, 32–36); C10; C11
Media: Oil, watercolor
Specialty: Nature (birds), genre, landscapes

Herman Bohlman worked with his partner, W.L. Finley, as a naturalist and photographer of birds. Their work appeared in national and international magazines. In 1900 he was a charter member of the John Burroughs Society, the forerunner of the Audubon Society. His entries in the Audubon Exhibit of 1920 and the Panama Pacific International Exhibit of 1915 (Oregon Room) were photographs, however he displayed paintings in many exhibits. Herman Bohlman won thirty-eight awards in Multnomah County Fairs and also worked as a WPA artist in the 1930s. His son, Edgar Bohlman*, was also an artist. Bohlman sometimes signed his work with a monogram.

BONBRIGHT, Millicent C.

b. 1869
d. 1970 Berkeley, CA
Membership: American Artists Professional League; Oregon Society of Artists
Awards: Oregon Society of Artists (1933, 35, 36, 39, 42, 43)
Exhibits: Portland Art Museum; Oregon Society of Artists (1939); American Artists Professional League (32–34, 36, 37); Lincoln County Art Center (48)
References: A2 (1922, 32, 40, 42, 44, 46, 48); A3 (35); C3 (29, 30, 32–37, 42, 43, 45, 46, 48–50); C14; M3
Media: Watercolor, oil
Specialty: Landscapes, florals

Millicent Bonbright was a member of the Oregon Society of Artists and the American Artists Professional League. She exhibited with both of these art groups and at the Portland Art Museum from 1920 to 1950. Bonbright participated in the 1948 exhibition at the Lincoln County Arts Center featuring Oregon artists. She moved to California, died there, but was buried in Portland.

BOULIER, F. Loren

b. Dysert, IA ***d.***
Education: University of Nebraska
Membership: Oregon Society of Artists; Northwest Watercolor Society
Awards: Oregon Society of Artists (1947)
Exhibits: California Watercolor Society (1940); Portland Art Museum; Oregon Society of Artists; J. K. Gill Gallery (46); Elfstrom Gallery; Seattle Art Museum (47); Northwest Watercolor Society; Lincoln County Art Center (48, 49); Rhode Island School of Design; M. H. DeYoung Museum—San Francisco; California Palace of the Legion of Honor—San Francisco
References: A2 (1944); C3 (46–49); C13 (46–48); C14; C29 (47, 48)
Media: Watercolor
Specialty: Landscapes, seascapes

Loren Boulier exhibited with the California Watercolor Society in 1940 at the Riverside Museum in New York City. He was an artist in the Marine Corps during World War II, later becoming the director of the Elfstrom Art Gallery in Salem for three years. He was a member of the Northwest Watercolor Society and Oregon Society of Artists, exhibiting with both. Boulier's work was shown at the Rhode Island School of Design, the De Young Museum, the California Palace of the Legion of Honor, and the Seattle and Portland Art Museums. In 1949 he moved to the

Oregon Coast and became the director of an art gallery at Wecoma beach.

BOWER, Lucy Scott

b. 1864 Rochester, IA
d. 1934 Paris, France
Education: Pennsylvania Academy of Fine Art—Philadelphia; New York School of Art; Académie Julian: *Fleury*, *Lefebre*; *Simon*; *Menard*
Membership: Oregon Art Association; National Association of Women Artists, Inc.; Pen and Brush Club; Society of Independent Artists—New York
Awards: "Arc en Ciel"—Paris (1917)
Collections: Oregon Historical Society; Pen and Brush Club; Lundberg Collection
Exhibits: North Pacific Industrial Exposition (1889); Oregon Art Association (96); Paris Salons—Artists Français (1912, 21), d'Automne (19, 20, 24); Society of Independent Artists—New York (26); London
References: BEN; BI; DAV; FIE; HAV; MAL; OET; PET; WWW; YNG; C2 (1889); ARTC; CD (90–96, 98, 99); M2
Media: Oil, watercolor, pastel, crayon
Specialty: Portraits, landscapes
See artwork in color section

Around the turn of the century, Lucy Bower advertised in the local papers as one of Portland's leading portrait painters. While best known for her portraits, she also painted landscapes and worked in a variety of media—oil, watercolor, pastel, and crayon. Her works were influenced by the French Impressionists. She and husband John Monroe Bower were active in Portland's social scene until his death in 1912. Bower then began to travel and exhibited in New York, London, and Paris. It was in Paris that she lived and worked until her accidental death from gas poisoning in 1934. Also a poet of some repute, she published *In a Mirror Vein* in 1913. The Oregon Historical Society owns her chalk on canvas portrait, *B.C. Duniway*.

BREWSTER, William L.

b. d.
Education: Museum Art School
Membership: Arts Guild
Exhibits: Arts Guild; Portland Art Museum
References: A2 (1942, 44, 46, 48); A5 (33)
Media: Watercolor, oil, pastel
Specialty: Cityscapes

William Brewster was a member of the Arts Guild. He exhibited at the Portland Art Museum during the 1940s.

BREYMAN, Ada

b. d.
Education: Willamette University (1863–66, 72, 82–85)
Awards: Oregon State Fairs
Exhibits: Oregon State Fairs
References: OSF (1888–94)
Media: Oil, watercolor

Ada Breyman was living in Salem when she exhibited paintings, china painting, and painted fire screens in the State Fairs.

BREYMAN, Edna Cranston

b. 1881 Prineville, OR
d. 1918 Portland, OR
Education: Museum Art School (1910); Art Students League: *F. DuMond**; New York City: *Chase*, *Dow*
Membership: Society of Oregon Artists; Mutual Art Association; Oregon Society of Artists
Collections: Parsons Collection
Exhibits: Art Students League (1910); Portland Art Museum; Society of Oregon Artists (13); Mutual Art Association (14); Panama Pacific International Exposition—San Fran-

cisco (15); Oregon Society of Artists
References: DAV; DAW; PET; WWW; A2 (1911, 12, 14, 15, 17, 18); A4 (11); C5; ARTC; CD (17, 18); M2; M3
Media: Oil
Specialty: Portraits, seascapes, landscapes
See artwork in color section

A graduate of the Portland Academy, Edna Breyman went to Smith College in Northhampton, Massachusetts. Later she was a member of the first class of the Portland Museum Art School. She also studied in New York at the Art Students League with Frank DuMond* and privately under Chase and Dow. She was a member of the early Society of Oregon Artists, the Mutual Art Association, and the Oregon Society of Artists, exhibiting with those groups and at the Portland Art Museum. She was part of the Oregon Room exhibit at the Panama Pacific International Exposition in San Francisco in 1915. Breyman used vivid color and an impressionistic style to produce landscapes filled with light. Her career was cut short when she died of peritonitis at age thirty-seven.

BRIDGES, Mary. *See* WATSON, Mary

BRITT, Peter

b. 1819 Obstalden, Switzerland
d. 1905
Education: Switzerland
Collections: Oregon Historical Society; Southern Oregon Historical Society
Exhibits: Oregon Historical Society
References: SI; YNG; M1
Media: Oil
Specialty: Portraits, landscapes

Peter Britt came to America in 1845 and settled in Illinois. Even though he had studied portrait painting in Switzerland, he decided to open a daguerreotype studio in Highland, Illinois in 1847. In the spring of 1852 Britt heard that gold had been discovered in Southern Oregon. He loaded his equipment into a covered wagon and headed west. He ended his journey in Jacksonville, where he opened a photography studio in 1852. He built a log house, started a gallery, and taught art students at his studio. The Peter Britt Music Festival was established in Jacksonville in his honor.

BRITTON, Joyce Maybelle

b. d.
Membership: Portland Art Museum (Artists Membership)
Exhibits: Portland Art Museum; New Gallery of Contemporary Art (1959); Oregon Centennial (59)
References: A3 (1956–58)
Media: Watercolor, oil, enamel

Joyce Britton exhibited in Portland at the New Gallery of Contemporary Art and the Portland Art Museum during the late 1950s.

BROWN, Eyler

b. 1895 Waynesville, OH
d. 1966 Eugene, OR
Education: University of Oregon (1916); MIT; Belgium; Royal Academy of Arts—London
Membership: Oregon Society of Artists; American Artists Professional League; University Alumni Art League, University of Oregon
Collections: Lundberg Collection
Exhibits: Seattle Art Museum; Oregon Society of Artists; University Alumni Art League; Portland Art Museum
References: ALM; BEN; COL; DAV; DAW; OET; WWN; A2 (1940); C3 (31, 34); C7 (30, 38); C25 (35, 36)
Media: Watercolor, tempera, prints (etching)
Specialty: Genre

Eyler Brown pursued his art education in Belgium and at the Royal Academy of Art in London. He was assistant professor of architecture at the University of Oregon from 1921 to 1961. He was also a member of the University Alumni Art League, the Oregon Society of Artists, and the American Artists Professional League. Brown exhibited at the Portland and Seattle Art Museums.

BROWN, Grafton Tyler

b. 1841 Harrisburg, PA
d. 1918 St. Peter, MN
Membership: Portland Art Club
Awards: Portland Art Club
Collections: Smithsonian Institution; Oakland Museum; Evansville Museum of Arts and Sciences—Indiana; Oregon Historical Society; Washington State Historical Society—Tacoma; Stenzel Collection; Painting Restoration Studio Collection; Counting Eagles Collection
Exhibits: Victoria, B.C. (1883); Portland Art Club (86); Washington State Capitol Museum (1988)
References: DAW; GER; GW; HAV; HUG; MAL SUP; SAM; WWW; YNG; C24; ARTC; CD (1887–89); M1
Media: Oil, prints (lithograph)
Specialty: Landscapes, portraits

Grafton Tyler Brown, an early black artist, migrated to California during the Civil War period. By 1861 he had worked for a lithography firm, first as a draftsman and then as a lithographer. After the owner died, Brown remained as manager until 1867 when he opened his own shop. In the 1880s he traveled in the Pacific Northwest, living and working in Victoria, B.C. He finally arrived in Portland in 1886, where he became Treasurer of the Portland Art Club. *The West Shore* magazine published lithographs of his British Columbia paintings in 1886 or 1887. He left Portland in 1890 to work with the U.S. Army Corps of Engineers, spending the last twenty-five years of his life in St. Peter, Minnesota.

Although primarily known as a lithographer, Brown produced many paintings of Yellowstone Park, British Columbia, and San Francisco. He was an exacting realist and paid great attention to detail. His 1886 oil, *Cliff House Beach*, showed fine details of shadow and the effects of water on sand. His work has been compared to the luminist work of the artist John F. Kensett.

BROWN, Mary (Mamie) Parvin

b. 1867 Bardolph, IL
d. 1932 Portland, OR
Education: Willamette University: *M. LeGall** (1882–88); *M. Watson**; *C. Cooke**
Membership: Oregon Society of Artists
Awards: Oregon State Fairs
Collections: Oregon Historical Society; Painting Restoration Studio Collection
Exhibits: Oregon State Fairs; Heppner; Hillsboro; Oregon Society of Artists (1930)
References: C3 (1930); CD (04, 06–13, 20, 25, 28–32); OSF (1891, 94, 1900, 02); M2; M3
Media: Oil, pastel, watercolor
Specialty: Landscapes, seascapes, still life, animals
See artwork in color section

Mary Parvin Brown attended Willamette University, studying under Marie Craig LeGall*. She later worked at Northwest Normal College, also known as the Capitol Normal School, founded by her father in Salem in 1897. She served as the school's principal and also taught china painting, fine art, and music. Brown moved to Portland around the turn of the century and opened the Northwest Normal School of Music and Art. She exhibited with the Oregon Society of Artists and in Oregon State Fairs. Brown had a studio in Portland on NW Thurman Street. She was also known as Mrs. James Brown.

BROWN, Virginia White

b. Minneapolis, MN
d. Klamath Falls, OR
Education: Minneapolis School of Art
Membership: American Artists Professional League; Oregon Society of Artists
Awards: Oregon Society of Artists (1946)
Exhibits: American Artists Professional League (1938); Portland Art Museum; Oregon Society of Artists
References: COL; WWN; A2 (1940, 42, 44, 46); A3 (53); C3 (46–49, 51)
Media: Watercolor, oil
Specialty: landscapes (houses)

Virginia Brown was a member of the American Artists Professional League and the Oregon Society of Artists. She exhibited with both of these groups and at the Portland Art Museum. Brown painted a variety of subjects, including baskets and houses. She lived in Klamath Falls from 1940 to 1946.

BRUHN, Clarice M.

b. 1873 Davenport, IA
d. 1952 Portland, OR
Education: Art Institute of Chicago
Membership: Mutual Art Association; Oregon Society of Artists; American Artists Professional League
Collections: Oregon Historical Society
Exhibits: Mutual Art Association (1914); Portland Art Museum; Oregon Society of Artists; American Artists Professional League (32); American School of Miniature Painting
References: ALM; BI; A4 (1914); C3 (27, 28); ARTC; CD (32, 39)
Media: Watercolor, oil, pastel
Specialty: Portraits

Clarice Bruhn lived in Tacoma, Washington before moving with her husband to Portland in 1897. She was a member of, and exhibited with, the Mutual Art Association, the Oregon Society of Artists, and American Artists Professional League. She was well known for her miniature portraits in watercolor painted on ivory. Many Portlanders sat for her large oil portraits. Bruhn also exhibited with the Portland Park and Garden Club.

BUHMANN, Max William

b. 1905 Ayden, NC
d. 1985 Portland, OR
Education: National Academy of Design; Art Students League; Reed College
Membership: Artists Equity; Portland Art Museum (Artist Membership)
Exhibits: Portland Art Museum; Seattle Art Museum (1955); Oregon Centennial (59)
References: A3 (1953, 55, 57); C6; CD (55–59)
Media: Watercolor, prints

Max Buhmann attended Reed College in Portland and both the Art Students League and the National Academy of Design in New York City. In addition to painting, Max Buhmann created sculpture, mostly in metal. He served as registrar for the Portland Art Museum from 1949 to 1953. His work was shown at the Seattle and Portland Art Museums.

BUMP, Elvira

b. 1856 Portage, WI
d. 1946 North Howell, OR
Education: New York City: *Gunn*
Membership: Oregon Society of Artists
Exhibits: Oregon Society of Artists
References: COL; DAV; DAW; WWN; C3 (1927, 28, 34, 35)
Media: Oil, pastel
Specialty: Landscapes (river scenes)

Elvira Bump studied in New York City, lived in South Dakota, and then moved to Portland after the death of her husband. She exhibited with the Oregon Society of Artists in the late 1920s and early 1930s.

BUNCE, Louis Demott

b. 1907 Lander, WY
d. 1983 Portland, OR
Education: Museum Art School (1925–26); Art Students League: *Robinson, Weber* (27–31)
Membership: Artists Equity; American Artists Professional League; Oregon Guild of Painters and Sculptors; American Artists' Congress; Arts Guild; Portland Art Museum (Artist Membership)
Awards: Seattle Art Museum (1934); Oregon Centennial (59)
Collections: American Academy of Arts and Letters; Metropolitan Museum of Art; National Museum of American Art; Portland Art Museum; Oregon Historical Society; Multnomah Athletic Club Collection; Powell Collection; Goodman Collection; Booth Collection; Tonkon Torp Collection; Seattle Art Museum; Whitney Museum of Art; Reed College; University of Washington; Hollins College—Virginia; Philadelphia Art Museum; University of Oregon; Hallie Ford Museum of Art—Willamette University; Capitol Collection—Salem; Pacific Northwest Bank of Washington; Springfield Art Museum—Missouri; Arlene and Harold Schnitzer Collection; Huntington Collection; Pacific University
Exhibits: Art Institute of Chicago; Metropolitan Museum of Art; Pennsylvania Academy of Fine Art—Philadelphia; Colorado Springs Fine Arts Center; Corcoran Gallery of Art—Washington, D.C.; M.H. DeYoung Museum—San Francisco; Portland Art Museum (1PS 45, 47, 55, 56; 3PS 36); Creative Art Gallery (33); American Artists Professional League (33, 37); Arts Guild; Seattle Art Museum (34–36, 1PS 36, 53, 4PS 53); San Francisco Museum of Art (35); Lipman Little Gallery (36); American Artists' Congress (37); New York World's Fair (39); Western Washington Fair; Golden Gate International Exposition—San Francisco (39–40); Hollins College—Virginia (1PS 41, 58); Reed College (47, 51); Harvey Welch Gallery (47); Willamette University (48); Oregon Guild of Painters and Sculptors (48); Kharouba Gallery (50, 1PS 52); Museum of Modern Art (1PS 50–51); Henry Art Gallery—University of Washington (51); Whitney Museum of Art (51, 53–54, 59); Kraushaar Galleries—New York (52); Sao Paulo Biennial III—Brazil (55); Santa Barbara Museum of Art (57); Artists Equity (58); Portland State University (58); Ruthermore Gallery—San Francisco (59); Oregon Centennial (59); Weltzer Gallery—New York (1959); New Gallery of Contemporary Art (59); University of Oregon (75); Oregon Historical Society (90)
References: ALM; COL; DAV; HAV; MAL; OET; WWN; WWW; A2 (1932, 33, 42, 46, 48); A3 (35, 36, 39, 49–53, 55–59); A4 (52, 59); A5 (33); C1; C6; C7 (34, 35, 36, 39, 45, 51, 55, 57, 58); C9; C10; C11; C15; C18; C20; C22; C27; C30 (46); CD (38)
Media: Oil, gouache, pencil, prints (serigraph)
Specialty: Landscapes, murals
See artwork in color section
See photograph of artist on p. 81

Louis Bunce came to Portland with his parents in 1913. He attended high school and the Museum Art School before leaving for the Art Students League in New York. There he established a New York connection that began when he first attended classes in 1927 and continued over the years with frequent visits. He became friends with many promising artists, including Jackson Pollock and David Smith. In 1939 he worked for the WPA Easel Project in New York. By the time he returned to Portland he was an established artist on the East Coast. He worked at the WPA Art Center in Salem as an instructor and assistant director. His work included murals, two of which are in the Post Offices in Grants Pass and St. Johns. Their subjects, mining and orchard farming, are the respective industries of each region. "I have always been visually drawn to the landscape, at first the desert and mountain regions of Wyoming; then the lush and gentle color of the Pacific Northwest and the urban landscape of New York." From 1942 to 1945 he worked as an illustrator, a tool designer, and in assembly for the Oregon Shipbuilding Corporation.

After World War II, Bunce joined the faculty of the Museum Art School in Portland, where he had been a student. He taught there until his retirement in 1972. He excelled at producing serigraphs and introduced this technique to Oregon. While maintaining a national reputation as a painter throughout the 1950s and 1960s, some of New York's most prestigious galleries represented him. Theater buffs will remember his murals and portraits for the Portland Civic Theater's 1938 production of *Pride and Prejudice*.

In a career that made him one of the most recognized names in Oregon's art history, Bunce had many styles: cubism, expressionism, surrealism, and abstractionism. His 1958 mural in the Portland International Airport presents this abstract style: "whirling propellers and shadows of the concourse as seen from above." It was controversial at the time, considered too abstract for a public art project. Bunce and his wife, Eda, opened a full-time art gallery in Portland in 1949, called the Kharouba. Located first at 1016 SE Morrison, then at SW 11th and Alder, the gallery represented many of the leading artists of the day: Josephine Cameron*, William Givler*, Clifford Gleason*, Jack Hammack*, Charles Heaney*, Frederick Heidel*, George Johanson*, Jack McLarty*, Rick Norwood*, C.S. Price*, Arthur Runquist*, Jolan Torok*, Charles Voorhies*, Milton Wilson*, and Duane Zaloudek* among others.

BURGESS, Bess. *See* WIRE, Bess

BURR, Alfred B.

b. 1854 Compo, CT
d. 1942 San Francisco, CA
Membership: Oregon Art Association; Portland Art Club
Awards: Lewis and Clark Centennial Exposition (1905)
Exhibits: Portland Art Club (1886); North Pacific Industrial Exposition (89); Oregon Industrial Exposition (93, 95); Oregon Art Association (96); Lewis and Clark Centennial Exposition (1905); Seattle Art Museum
References: C2 (1889, 93, 95); C7 (1922); ARTC; CD (1883, 85, 86, 89, 90, 92); M1
Media: Oil, prints (lithograph, engraving)
Specialty: Landscapes, genre, portraits

Alfred Burr, descendant of Aaron Burr (third Vice President of the U.S.), was an artist and lithographer for *The West Shore* magazine and illustrator for the *Oregonian*. He was head of the *Oregonian* art department from 1901 to 1918. Burr was one of the group of newspaper cartoonists whose work was published by E. A. Thomson in 1906 under the title *As We See 'Em*. He was a member of, and exhibited with, the Portland Art Club and the Oregon Artists Association. Burr's wife, Hattie, was also an artist and member of the Oregon Art Association, exhibiting with them in 1896. He showed in the Portland Industrial Expositions, Lewis and Clark Exposition, and the Seattle Art Museum.

BURRILL, Virginia Stone

b. d.

Membership: Oregon Society of Artists; Artists Equity

Exhibits: Portland Art Museum; Oregon Society of Artists; Elfstrom Gallery; Lincoln County Art Center (1948)

References: A2 (1944, 46, 48); C3 (45–51); C13 (47); C14

Media: Oil

Specialty: Still life

Virginia Burrill, a member of Artists Equity and the Oregon Artists Society was active in Oregon in the 1940s and 1950s. She exhibited at the Elfstrom Gallery in Salem, and the Lincoln County Art Center in Lincoln City.

BUTLER, Bonnie. *See* CHESHIRE, Bonnie Butler

C

CAMERON, Josephine (Jo) Elaine

b. 1925 Portland, OR ***d.***

Education: Marylhurst College (1944); Museum Art School (46–50); Seattle: *Tobey* (48); *W. Givler** (53)

Membership: Artists Equity; Portland Art Museum (Artist Membership)

Awards: Fur Rendezvous Art Show—Alaska (1957–58)

Collections: University of Oregon; Oregon Historical Society; Henry Art Gallery—University of Washington

Exhibits: Mt. Angel College; Portland Art Museum (1PS 1954); Seattle Art Museum (48); Henry Art Gallery—University of Washington (48–58); Reed College (55); Kharouba Gallery (1PS); Vancouver Art Gallery (1PS); University of Portland (1PS); Little Gallery (1PS); Anchorage Studio One (1PS)

References: HAV; MAL SUP; WWAA; A2 (1948); A3 (53, 55, 58)

Media: Oil, prints (engraving, woodcut, etching)

Specialty: Nature, animals, murals

Jo Cameron won a scholarship for her first year at Portland's Museum Art School. She painted a mural for the Sandy High School Library and had one-person shows at the Kharouba Gallery, the University of Portland, and the Vancouver Art Gallery. She taught adult and children's art classes at the YWCA. She often portrayed the world of nature and its creatures.

CAMPBELL, Agnes Dorothy

b. d.

Exhibits: Portland Art Museum

References: A2 (1916, 17, 20, 21)

Agnes Campbell lived in Monmouth. She exhibited at the Portland Art Museum.

CAMPION, Howard T.S.

b. England ***d.***

Education: Royal Academy of Arts—London

Awards: London (1909)

Collections: Oregon Historical Society

Exhibits: Portland Mechanics Fair; Royal Academy of Arts—London (1876–83)

References: BEN; DAV; GER; HUG; CD (1874, 75); M1

Media: Oil

Specialty: Landscapes, portraits, still life

Howard Campion was a London landscapist who visited Oregon from 1873 to 1876. During his stay he also painted portraits, including an oil of General Canby which was later presented to the General's widow.

CAREY, Rockwell W.

b. 1882 Waldo Hills, OR

d. 1954 Portland, OR

Education: Museum Art School (1910)

Membership: American Artists Professional League; Society of Oregon Artists; Oregon Society of Artists; Oregon Guild of Painters and Sculptors

Awards: Oregon Society of Artists (1930); American Artists Professional League (34, 36, 37, 38); Oregon State Fair

Collections: Powell Collection; Portland Courthouse; Capitol Collection—

Salem; Oregon Historical Society; University of Oregon; Parsons Collection; Lundberg Collection; Slippery Slope Historical Collection

Exhibits: Oregon State Fair; Society of Oregon Artists (1912, 13); Portland Art Museum; Panama Pacific International Exposition—San Francisco (15); Oregon Society of Artists; American Artists Professional League (33–38); Grumbacher traveling exhibition (36); J.K. Gill Gallery (36, 1PS 45); National Academy of Design (43, 46); Library of Congress (45); Oregon Historical Society (90)

References: ALM; COL; DAV; DAW; HAV; MAL SUP; OET; WWN; WWW; A2 (1912–15, 32, 33, 40, 42); A3 (52); C3 (29–31); C5; C9; C10; C11; ARTC; OSF (08); CD (31)

Media: Watercolor, oil, prints (lithograph)

Specialty: Marines, landscapes, murals

See artwork in color section

Largely self-taught, fifteen-year-old Rockwell Carey won a prize for drawing at the Oregon State Fair in 1897. He continued to enjoy success with his watercolors at the Society of Oregon Artists in 1912 and 1913. Carey attended the Museum Art School and was a member of its first graduating class. As a participant in the U.S. Treasury's Public Works of Art program, which preceded the WPA by several months, he produced a mural, *Early Mail Carriers of the West*, for the Newberg Post Office. Carey also won a prize in the American Artists Professional League show of 1937, where his painting was voted the most popular. The next year he won the grand prize for *The White House*. Although his early work was impressionistic, he was later known for his expressionist-style marines and landscapes. He was also a lithographer. Carey was living in Santa Barbara by 1949, but died in Portland while on a visit in 1954.

CARLBERG, Wolfgang

b. 1907 Hamburg, Germany ***d.***

Education: California School of Fine Arts: *Pool, Oldfield* (1934); Museum Art School (40)

Awards: Chicago International Exhibition (1937); San Francisco Museum of Art (38)

Exhibits: San Francisco Museum of Art (1935, 38, 41); Art Institute of Chicago (36); San Francisco Art Association (36, 39); Chicago International Exhibit (37); Portland Art Museum

References: DAV; HAV; HUG; MAL SUP; WWW; A2 (1940, 48)

Media: Oil, watercolor, prints

Specialty: Portraits, florals, genre

Wolfgang Carlberg was born in Germany and became a U.S. citizen in California. He won awards from the Chicago International Exhibition in 1937 and the San Francisco Museum of Art in 1938. He came to Portland in 1940 and worked as a custodian at the Portland Art Museum, taking art classes at night. Carlberg worked in the shipyards during World War II. He eventually became a teacher at Molalla High School, continuing to paint in his leisure time. In his later years he remained in Molalla as a rancher and, to his regret, produced very little work during that time.

CARPENTER, Marie (Mae) Dinah Rogers

b. 1830

d. 1911

Awards: Oregon State Fairs

Collections: Coos County Historical Society

Exhibits: Oregon State Fairs

References: OSF (1894, 95)

Media: Watercolor, pastel

Specialty: Florals

Mae Carpenter lived on the Coos River in Oregon. She exhibited in Oregon State Fairs during the mid 1890s. Her work is represented in the Coos County Historical Society collection.

CARR, Margaret

b. d.
Membership: American Artists Professional League; Oregon Society of Artists
Exhibits: Portland Art Museum; American Artists Professional League (1937)
References: A2 (1933, 34, 40, 42, 48)
Media: Oil
Specialty: Landscapes, florals

Margaret Carr exhibited in Portland at the Art Museum during the 1930s and 40s. She was a member of the American Artists Professional League and the Oregon Society of Artists.

CARTER, Pearl

b. d.
Awards: Oregon State Fairs
Exhibits: Oregon State Fairs
References: OSF (1896–1900)
Media: Oil, watercolor
Specialty: Landscapes, florals, portraits

Pearl Carter lived in Salem when she exhibited at Oregon State Fairs from 1896 to1900.

CHAPMAN, M. N., Mrs.

b. d.
Awards: Oregon State Fairs
Exhibits: Oregon State Fairs
References: OSF (1893, 96, 98, 99, 1904, 06)
Media: Oil
Specialty: Landscapes, florals, still life

Mrs. M. N. Chapman lived in Salem during the years she exhibited at the State Fairs.

CHASE, Althea

b. 1870 Iowa
d. 1959 Portland, OR
Exhibits: Portland Art Museum; Seattle Art Museum
References: A2 (1913–15, 40); C7 (15); CD (13, 14, 16–20, 23)
Media: Watercolor
Specialty: Landscapes

Althea Chase exhibited at the Portland and Seattle Art Museums. An 'Althea Chase' is listed in *Who Was Who*, Benezit, Kovinick and Petteys (see Ref. BEN, KOV, PET) and may be the same person. Petteys indicates that she studied at the Art Institute of Chicago under Mucha and Whistler and with Merson in Paris.

CHESHIRE, Bonnie Butler

b. 1934 Astoria, OR
d. 1994 Portland, OR
Education: University of Oregon (1954–60)
Membership: Portland Art Museum (Artist Membership)
Exhibits: Portland Art Museum; Oregon Centennial (1959)
References: A3 (1958)
Media: Watercolor

Bonnie Cheshire was educated at the University of Oregon. She exhibited at the Portland Art Museum, the Oregon Centennial, and in many exhibitions after 1959. She was married to artist Craig Cheshire*.

CHESHIRE, Craig Gifford

b. 1936 Portland, OR ***d.***
Education: UCLA (1954–55); University of Oregon: *D. McCosh** (58, 61); Lewis and Clark College
Membership: Portland Art Museum (Artist Membership)
Collections: Kaiser Permanente Collection; U.S. Bank; University of Oregon; Eastern Oregon College
Exhibits: Portland Art Museum; Seattle Art Museum (1958); Smithsonian Institution Traveling Exhibits (59); Oregon Centennial (59)

References: A3 (1958); C6; C7 (58)
Media: Watercolor, oil
Specialty: Landscapes

Craig Cheshire was just beginning his career in the late 1950s and has had many exhibitions in the years that followed. He taught at Portland's Museum Art School and at Portland State University. Cheshire says painting is a way of observing, and strives to render equivalents on canvas for images of the environment that attract him. His wife, Bonnie Butler Cheshire* was also an Oregon artist.

CHILSTROM, Gladys E. Keenan

b. 1897 Portland, OR
d. 1988 Portland, OR
Education: Museum Art School
Membership: Oregon Society of Artists; Portland Art Museum (Artist Membership)
Awards: Oregon Society of Artists (1947)
Exhibits: Oregon Society of Artists; Portland Art Museum
References: A2 (1944, 48); A3 (55); C3 (31, 35, 43, 44, 46–51); CD (40, 41, 43–44)
Media: Watercolor, oil
Specialty: Landscapes, florals

Gladys Chilstrom was a commercial artist in Portland and a charter member of the Oregon Society of Artists in 1927. She exhibited her watercolors and oils at the Portland Art Museum and the Oregon Society of Artists. She was the mother of artist Raymond Chilstrom*.

CHILSTROM, Hazel Hanson

b. 1919 Portland, OR *d.*
Education: Atelier 17—New York City; Museum Art School (1952); Instituto Allende—Guanajuato, Mexico (53); Brooklyn Art Museum (54)
Membership: Artists Equity; Portland Art Museum (Artist Membership)
Exhibits: Portland Art Museum (1PS 1952; AM, 3PS 52); Seattle Art Museum; Library of Congress; Oregon Centennial (59)
References: A2 (1948); A3 (51, 55–57); C6; C7 (51, 52)
Media: Oil, watercolor, prints (wood block, lithograph, lino-cut)
Specialty: Portraits

Hazel Chilstrom attended Portland's Museum Art School, the Instituto Allende in Mexico, the Brooklyn Art Museum, and Atelier 17 in New York City. Her major interest was printmaking, although she exhibited oils and watercolors at the Portland and Seattle Art Museums, the Library of Congress, and the Oregon Centennial. She received the National Tiffany Award for printmaking in 1951. She worked as an instructor in the Portland Art Museum Children's Art Program. Chilstrom was also a playwright, whose work was produced in the Los Angeles area. Her husband, Raymond Chilstrom*, was also an artist.

CHILSTROM, Raymond L.

b. 1925 Portland, OR
d. 1999 Portland, OR
Education: Museum Art School
Membership: Artists Equity; Portland Art Museum (Artist Membership)
Collections: University of Oregon
Exhibits: Portland Art Museum; Seattle Art Museum; Henry Art Gallery—University of Washington; Bush House Museum—Salem (1958)
References: A2 (1948); A3 (51, 55); A4 (59); C7 (51, 52, 54, 57)
Media: Oil, watercolor
Specialty: Genre

Raymond Chilstrom was a graduate of Portland's Museum Art School. He exhibited in Portland and Seattle during the 1940s and 50s. He and his wife, artist Hazel Chilstrom*, moved to California where they co-founded a theater;

she wrote and acted and he painted theater sets. They returned to their native Portland in 1984. His mother, Gladys Chilstrom*, was also an artist.

CHRISTENSEN, Ted, Jr.

b. 1911 Vancouver, WA ***d.***
Education: Museum Art School: *W. Givler*, L. Bunce*; M. Helm*; C. McKim*; C. Keller**; Otis Art Institute
Membership: Oregon Society of Artists
Awards: Multnomah County Fair (1937-38); Oregon Society of Artists (1943, 47)
Collections: Ford Motor Company Collection—Dearborn, Michigan
Exhibits: Multnomah County Fair; Portland Art Museum; Oregon Society of Artists
References: DAV; WWN; A2 (1940, 42, 44, 48); C3 (43, 46, 47, 49); CD (43–4)
Media: Oil, watercolor, acrylic
Specialty: Landscapes

Ted Christensen attended Portland's Museum Art School. He studied privately with Myra Helm*, C.C. McKim*, Clyde Keller* and, in California, at the Otis Art Institute. He worked in an impressionistic style with oil, watercolor, and acrylic. He won prizes at the Multnomah County Fairs of 1937 and 1938. He also showed at the Portland Art Museum and with the Oregon Society of Artists. Christensen moved to California in 1949 and taught art at the College of Marin from 1952 to 1960.

CHURCH, Fay Hoffman

b. 1897 Milwaukee, WI
d. 1974 Colorado Springs, CO
Education: Syracuse University (1918); Académie de la Grande Chaumière; Académie de Colarossi (22)
Membership: Oregon Society of Artists; Portland Art Museum (Artist Membership)
Exhibits: Oregon Society of Artists; Portland Art Museum; Boston Museum of Fine Arts; Elfstrom Gallery; Artists Equity (1958); Oregon Centennial (59)
References: A3 (1955); C3 (45–48, 50, 51); C1; C6
Media: Oil
Specialty: Portraits

Fay Church, a WPA artist, was a member of, and exhibited with, the Oregon Society of Artists. She also exhibited at the Portland Art Museum, Salem's Elfstrom Gallery, the Oregon Centennial Exhibition, and the Boston Museum of Fine Arts.

CHURCH, Stuart Hoffman

b. 1932 Cambridge, MA ***d.***
Education: Boston Museum of Fine Arts; Accademia di Belle Arti—Florence, Italy; *F. Church*; A. Patecky**
Membership: Portland Art Museum (Artist Membership)
Exhibits: Portland Art Museum (AM, 3PS 1952); J.K. Gill Gallery (48); Elfstrom Gallery (50); Harvey Welch Gallery (50, 51); Gallery by the Sea—Lincoln City (50, 51); Milan, Italy (58)
References: A2 (1946); A3 (51, 53)
Media: Oil

Stuart Church showed oil paintings at the Portland Art Museum, the J.K.Gill Gallery, the Harvey Welch Gallery, Salem's Elfstrom Gallery, and Lincoln City's Gallery by the Sea. He studied and exhibited in Italy in 1958.

CHURCH, Walter E.

b. 1893 Boston, MA
d. 1974 Arch Cape, OR
Education: MIT (1921); University of Oregon
Membership: Oregon Society of Artists; American Artists Professional League; University Alumni Art

League, University of Oregon
Exhibits: Oregon Society of Artists; Portland Art Museum; American Artists Professional League (1933); University Alumni Art League
References: A2 (1932, 33); C3 (27–29, 31); C25 (35, 36)
Media: Watercolor
Specialty: Landscapes

Walter Church attended the Massachusetts Institute of Technology and the University of Oregon. He was a member of, and exhibited watercolors with, the Oregon Society of Artists, the American Artists Professional League, and the University Alumni Art League. Church was a practicing architect with the firm of Whitehouse, Stanton and Church, who designed many of the buildings on the Capitol Mall in Salem. Temple Beth Israel in Portland was among his many commissions. He was with an architectural firm in Portland until his retirement in 1972 to Arch Cape on the Oregon Coast. Church served in World War I and World War II.

CLARE, Miriam. *See* MURPHY, Miriam

CLEAVER, Mabel

b. 1878 Wauwatosa, WI *d.*
Education: California College of Arts and Crafts; *M. Wanker**
Membership: American Artists Professional League; Oregon Society of Artists
Awards: American Artists Professional League (1936)
Collections: Cofield Collection
Exhibits: American Artists Professional League (1935, 36); Oregon Society of Artists; Portland Art Museum; Lincoln County Art Center (48)
References: COL; DAW; HUG; WWN; A2 (1940, 42, 44); A3 (52); C14; M2; M3
Media: Watercolor, oil
Specialty: Landscapes, still life

Mabel Cleaver attended the California College of Arts and Crafts and studied privately with Maude Wanker* in Oregon. She exhibited her watercolors and oils at the Portland Art Museum and the Lincoln County Art Center. She was a member of, and exhibited with, the American Artists Professional League and the Oregon Society of Artists. While living in La Grande in the 1940s, Mabel Cleaver exhibited her work at the Union County Fair.

CLINE, Eva Ford. *See* SMITH, Eva Ford Cline

CLOGSTON, Evelyn. *See* WATSON, Evelyn

COGSWELL, William F.

b. 1819 Fabius, NY
d. 1903 South Pasadena, CA
Collections: White House, Capitol, National Gallery of Art—Washington, D.C; Multnomah County Library Collection; Oregon Historical Society; Bush House Museum—Salem; Parsons Collection
Exhibits: National Academy of Design; Oregon Historical Society (1990)
References: BI; DAV; DAW; FIE; GER; GW; HUG; MAL; YNG; C9; M1
Media: Oil
Specialty: Portraits, genre

In 1873 William Cogswell settled in Pasadena and became a California resident. He came to Portland to paint portraits as early as 1875. His painting, *John McLoughlin* was lost in the fire at the Oregon State Capitol in 1935. The Multnomah County Library Collection contains four of his portraits. The Bush House Museum in Salem displays his portrait of Asahel Bush in the library, painted when Mr. Bush was fifty-six years old. Cogswell's portrait, *Lincoln,* was placed in the White House; his

General Grant hung in the U.S. Capitol; and his *President Grant and Family* was displayed in the National Gallery of Art.

COLE, Constance I.

b. 1900 Denver, CO
d. 1985 Portland, OR
Education: University of Oregon: *N. Zane** (1922)
Membership: University Alumni Art League, University of Oregon; Oregon Amateur Watercolor Society; Cascade Artists Group
Collections: Oregon Historical Society
Exhibits: University Alumni Art League; Cascade Artists Group
References: C25 (1935, 36); CD (28–31, 32)
Media: Watercolor, oil

Constance Cole was a painter, illustrator, sculptor, and costume and stage designer. Although never legally adopted, she lived with the Henry Van Duzer family from about 1920 until her death. Up to 1950 she is intermitently listed in City Directories as an artist. It has been said that she was a member of the Oregon Society of Artists and the American Artists Professional League, although no records can be found to support this, nor did she exhibit with these groups. She was a member of the Cascade Artists Group, exhibiting in their gallery. Cole was a friend of Ruth Grover*. She had a studio in the Worcester Building in Portland.

COLEMAN, J.M.

b. d.
Membership: Oregon Society of Artists; American Artists Professional League
Collections: University of Oregon
Exhibits: Portland Art Museum; Oregon Society of Artists; American Artists Professional League (1933)
References: A2 (1917, 20, 22); C3 (27–33)

J. M. Coleman lived in Astoria and exhibited at the Portland Art Museum and with the Oregon Society of Artists and the American Artists Professional League. *The Bicentennial Inventory* lists a 'J.M. Coleman' who is possibly the same person.

COLESCOTT, Robert

b. 1925 Oakland, CA ***d.***
Education: University of California Berkeley (1949, 52); Paris: *Léger* (49–50)
Membership: Northwest Watercolor Society; Portland Art Museum (Artist Membership)
Awards: Seattle Art Museum (1952); Henry Art Gallery—University of Washington; Northwest Watercolor Society (55)
Collections: Portland Art Museum; Goodman Collection; University of Oregon; Reed College; Seattle Art Museum; Arlene and Harold Schnitzer Collection; Catlin Gabel School Collection
Exhibits: Oakland Museum (1949, 51); Paris Salon—de Mai (50); California Palace of the Legion of Honor (51); Seattle Art Museum (52); Western Washington Fair; Northwest Watercolor Society; Henry Art Gallery—University of Washington (56; 3PS 59); Portland Art Museum (AM, 1PS 58); Reed College (IPS 58; 59); Portland State University (58); Dusanne Gallery—Seattle (58); Ruthermore Gallery—San Francisco (59); Oregon Centennial (59); University of Oregon (75)
References: DAV; A3 (1957); A4 (59); C22; C29 (55); C30 (54)
Media: Oil
Specialty: Still life, genre
See photograph of artist on p. 82

Robert Colescott was educated at the University of California Berkeley and studied for a year with Fernand Léger in Paris. From 1957 to 1966 Colescott was professor of art at Portland State College (now Portland State University). In 1959 the Henry Gallery at the University of Washington held a three-person show for Colescott, Robert McGarrell*, and Michele Russo*. The paintings he produced while living in Oregon were still lifes and abstracts, which explored paint and texture with simple, but elegant, compositions. These form the basis of his later work—pieces that addressed racial stereotypes—for which he achieved fame. In these paintings his use of fantasy left reality askew. He produced large, painterly canvases that exploit the power of emptiness. Colescott achieved international stature in later years.

COLVIG, Helen

b. d.

Exhibits: First Southern Oregon District Agricultural Fair; Southern Oregon County Fair

References: FSO (1898); SOCF (99)

Media: Watercolor

Helen Colvig lived in Sams Valley in southern Oregon. She exhibited her watercolors at the First Southern Oregon District Agricultural Fair of 1898 and the Southern Oregon County Fair of 1899.

CONFER, Nancie Stamps

b. d.

Education: Chouinard Art Institute; *M. Warner**

Membership: Oregon Society of Artists; Northwest Watercolor Society

Awards: Oregon Society of Artists (1943, 47)

Exhibits: Portland Art Museum; Oregon Society of Artists; Seattle Art Museum (1947); Elfstrom Gallery (2PS 47); Santa Paula, California (47); Bellevue, Washington (47); Northwest Watercolor Society

References: A2 (1940, 42, 44, 46); C3 (43, 45, 46–48, 49); C29 (47, 48, 52)

Media: Watercolor

Specialty: Landscape, portraits

Although Nancie Stamps spent most of her active professional life in Washington, she was a member of the Oregon Society of Artists and exhibited with them at the Portland Art Museum in the 1940s. Salem's Elfstrom Gallery featured her work in a two-person show with Bernice Huber.*

COOKE, Clyde Benton

b. 1860 Salem, OR

d. 1933 Berkeley, CA

Education: Willamette Academy: *S. Cooke** (1872–73); Royal Academy of Arts—Munich (80–85)

Membership: Portland Art Club

Awards: Oregon State Fairs; Portland Mechanics Fair (1885)

Collections: Oregon Historical Society

Exhibits: Oregon State Fairs; Portland Mechanics Fairs; Portland Art Club (1885–87); Portland Industrial Exposition (93); Mark Hopkins Institute (98, 1900, 02); Oregon Historical Society (90)

References: COL; DAV; GER; HUG; C2 (1893); C4 (79, 83, 85, 86); C9; ARTC; CD (80, 87); OSF (75–79, 81, 88–90, 92); M1

Media: Oil, watercolor, pencil, pen and ink

Specialty: Landscapes, seascapes

See artwork in color section

Clyde Cooke won a drawing award at the Oregon State Fair at the age of five. He studied at Willamette Academy with his mother, artist Susan Belle Walker Cooke*, then became one of the first Oregon artists to study abroad. He remained a student in Munich for five years. Then he returned home to win awards at the Portland Mechanics Fair in 1885. He continued exhibiting at the State Fairs and the Industrial Fairs for many years. He joined the Portland Art Club and exhibited with them from 1885 to 1887. Cooke began his teaching career at Pacific University in 1886, then returned to Willamette University to head the art department in 1889. Shortly after, he moved to San Francisco to continue his work and study. Unfortunately, he lost much of his personal artwork in the earthquake of 1906. In later years he worked in the art department of the *San Francisco Chronicle.*

COOKE, Susan Belle Walker

b. ca. 1834 Meriden, CT
d. 1918 Newberg, OR
Education: *C. Cooke**
Awards: Oregon State Fairs
Collections: Oregon Historical Society
Exhibits: Oregon State Fairs; University of California Berkeley, retrospective (1931)
References: OSF (1865–83); M2; M3
Media: Oil, pastel
Specialty: Landscapes

Susan Cooke came to Oregon with a pioneer family in 1851 and remained until 1896. She taught at the Oregon Institute in Salem and, later, at Willamette University. She also founded and taught at a private school in her home, emphasizing music and art. Cooke was a published poet (*Tears and Victory,* 1871) and was also a correspondent for the *Oregonian.* She served as the first woman clerk in the Oregon legislature. Cooke moved to San Francisco after 1900 to be with her son, Clyde Cooke*, and gained some recognition there as an artist. She returned to Oregon late in her life, where she died. In 1931 the University of California Berkeley held a retrospective exhibit of her work.

CORNFORD, Elaine. *See* MARSH, Elaine

COUSE, Eanger Irving (E.I.)

b. 1866 Saginaw, MI
d. 1936 Taos, NM
Education: Art Institute of Chicago (1882); National Academy of Design (83–85); Ecole des Beaux Arts; Académie Julian: *Bougereau, Fleury* (86–91)
Membership: Salmagundi Club; American Watercolor Society; Lotos Club
Awards: Académie Julian (1887, 90); Salmagundi Club (99); National Academy of Design—Hallgarten (1900, 01, 02, 11, 13); Carnegie (12, 16, 21); Paris International Exposition (1900); Pan American Exposition—Buffalo (01); St. Louis Universal Exposition; Lotos Club (10); Panama Pacific International Exposition—San Francisco (15); Pennsylvania Academy of Fine Art—Philadelphia (21)
Collections: Brooklyn Art Museum; Metropolitan Museum of Art; National Gallery of Art; Colorado Springs Fine Arts Center; Stenzel Collection; University of Oregon; Portland Art Museum; Dallas Art Museum; Santa Barbara Museum of Art; Toledo Museum of Art; Detroit Art Museum; Smith College—Northampton, Massachusetts; Portland Courthouse
Exhibits: Paris Salons; Paris International Exposition (1889, 1900); North Pacific Industrial Exposition (1889); home of T. B. Trevett—Portland (1PS 91); Marquam Hill—Portland (92); Portland Industrial Exposition (92); World Columbian Exposition—Chicago (93); Pan American Exposition—Buffalo (1901); Portland Art Museum (1PS 04); St. Louis Universal Exposition (04); Lewis and Clark Centennial Exposition (05); Alaska-Yukon Pacific Exposition (09); Panama Pacific International Exposition—San Francisco (15); Santa Fe Museum, memo-

rial (36); University of Oregon (59)
References: BEN; BI; DAV; DAW; FI (1888–96, 98, 99); FIE; GER; HAV; MAL; SAM; SM; THI; WWW; YNG; A1 (99, 1902, 06; 08); C2 (1889, 90); C16; C21; MYH
Media: Oil
Specialty: Indians, portraits, western scenery, marines

Although E.I. Couse lived in Oregon for only brief periods, his legacy to the state is an interesting one. In Paris he met and married Oregon artist, Virginia Walker. After finishing their art training, the Couses returned to Oregon in 1891. Couse's portrait, *Judge Matthew Deady* has been on view at the Portland Federal Courthouse. He also painted his first Native American subject, *Captive*, presaging his lifelong interest in Indians. During these years, Couse taught an art class in Portland. His work was shown at the Marquam Hill loan exhibition in 1892.

Escaping the gray and rainy Northwest days, the Couses moved to Normandy, France where he was very successful. They continued to return to the Walker family ranch in Washington for summer visits. Couse established a studio in New York in 1898 and joined the Salamagundi Club, a prestigious private club that held exhibitions and awarded prizes. On invitation from Ernest Blumenschein and other friends who were establishing homes in Taos, New Mexico, he began to visit there. He returned, however, to New York, which was still the center of the art world. After the Santa Fe Railway used one of Couse's paintings on their calendar in 1914, his images became recognizable in all regions of the country. This collaboration with the Railway continued for many years.

Couse finally settled in Taos in 1928, where he became an active participant in the art community. He remained there until his death. A prolific and talented artist, he produced over fifteen hundred paintings in his lifetime. Samuels' reference book (see Ref. SAM) says of Couse, "He has come as close to the spirit of the Indian as the white man ever can."

CRAIG, Marie. *See* LeGALL, Marie

CROCKER, Anna Belle

b. 1868 Milwaukee, WI
d. 1961 Portland, OR
Education: Art Students League: *F. DuMond*, Dow*
Membership: Portland Sketch Club; Oregon Art Association; Oregon Society of Artists; American Artists' Congress
Collections: Portland Art Museum
Exhibits: Portland Mechanics Fair; Oregon Art Association (1896); Portland Sketch Club (1900); Portland Art Museum; Seattle Art Museum; Panama Pacific International Exposition—San Francisco (15); Oregon Society of Artists; American Artists' Congress (37); Autry Museum—Los Angeles (95)
References: ALM; GER; A2 (1913–15, 17, 20, 34); A3 (36, 37); C3 (27, 28); C4 (1886); C5; C7 (1915); C23; ARTC; M2
Media: Oil
Specialty: Portraits, florals

Anna Belle Crocker came to Portland with her parents in 1878. Their home was on the site of the present Benson Hotel. After she graduated from the Art Students League in New York, William Ladd, one of the founders of the Portland Art Museum, appointed her to a dual position of museum curator and school principal, replacing Henrietta Failing on her retirement. To prepare for this position she immediately embarked for Europe to study museums. She remained curator and, in effect, the director for twenty-seven years. Her own artistic specialty was portrait painting.

Crocker's enthusiasm for helping others realize their artistic potential gained her the respect and admiration of those with whom she had contact. She traveled widely and often in order to keep abreast of new directions in the art world. She lectured frequently both at the school and in a memorable series of twelve lectures on the understanding of painting and sculpture. She also wrote the book, *It Goes Deeper Than You Think.* Crocker was one of the few women allowed entry to the Portland Sketch Club in 1896.

CRONANT, Mae

b. 1902 SD
d. 1994 Tillamook, OR
Education: Oregon State University; *C. Mulvey**
Membership: Master Watercolor Society of Oregon
Collections: Oregon Historical Society; Tillamook County Pioneer Museum
References: OR (Tillamook County Historical Society)
Media: Watercolor, oil
Specialty: Landscapes (South Dakota snow scenes)

Mae Cronant taught oil and watercolor classes in Tillamook and did touch-up work in her family's photography studio. In 1965 Cronant was a founding member of the Watercolor Society of Oregon. During her artistic career, she received more than forty Watercolor Society of Oregon awards. She was also a member of the Tillamook Art Association, for which she served as president and secretary.

CROOK, John Marion

b. 1867
d. 1924 Portland, OR
Education: Art Institute of Chicago; *Elkins; Robstusky; Von Haefliger*
Membership: Society of Oregon Artists
Collections: Oregon Historical Society; Miranda Collection; Parsons Collection; Gerber Collection
Exhibits: Portland Art Museum; Society of Oregon Artists (1913); Seattle Art Museum; Portland Woman's Club (26); Pacific Art League; Oakland Art Gallery, posthumous (29); Oregon Historical Society (90)
References: DAV; HUG; A2 (1912, 15, 20–22); C7 (17, 21); C9; ARTC; CD (03, 04, 16, 20)
Media: Watercolor, oil
Specialty: Landscapes (western scenery, Mexico to Canada)
See artwork in color section

John Crook taught art privately in Chicago for ten years before moving to Portland, where he continued to teach and exhibit. He became treasurer of the early Society of Oregon Artists.

His specialty was atmospheric mist, fog, and the opalescent hues of hazy mornings and late afternoons. Living the last fifteen years of his life on the coast near Astoria, he had many opportunities to observe and refine this technique. Crook's work was recognized as an outstanding development in watercolor as it applied to the interpretation of scenic beauty. The Pacific Art League sponsored exhibitions of his work in Portland and Seattle. In 1925, he was featured posthumously in a national exhibition entitled *Painters of the Pacific Northwest* and in 1929 in a posthumous show at the Oakland Art Gallery.

CROWELL, Pers

b. 1910 Pasco, WA ***d.*** 1990
Membership: Attic Club; American Artists Professional League; Oregon Society of Artists
Awards: Oregon Society of Artists (1935); American Artists Professional League (37)

Exhibits: First National Bank (1PS 1935); American Artists Professional League (35–37); Portland Art Museum

References: ALM; OET; A2 (1940); C3 (35); ARTC

Media: Oil

Specialty: Western art (horses, frontiersmen, Indians, cowboys, trappers)

Pers Crowell was an illustrator, commercial artist, and author as well as a painter. He illustrated *Cavalcade of American Horses*, published in 1951. He was a member of the Attic Club, the American Artists Professional League, and the Oregon Society of Artists. He exhibited with those groups, at the Portland Art Museum, and had a one-person show at First National Bank of Oregon. A review of his work stated that, "he painted the excitement of a time gone by." Crowell had a studio in Beaverton.

CUMMING, Shannah. *See* WHEELER, Shannah

CURL, Martina Gangl(e)

b. 1906 Woodland, WA

d. 1994 Portland, OR

Education: Museum Art School; Western Oregon State College

Membership: American Artists' Congress; Oregon Guild of Painters and Sculptors; Arts Guild

Collections: Oregon Society of Artists; Portland Art Museum; Timberline Lodge Collection; Booth Collection; University of Oregon; Parsons Collection; Huntington Collection; Pathways Collection

Exhibits: Portland Art Museum; Arts Guild; New York World's Fair (1939); Oregon Guild of Painters and Sculptors (48)

References: COL; DAV; HAV; KOV; OET; WWN; WWW; A2 (1932, 33, 40, 42); A3 (35); A5 (33); C10; CD (40); M2

Media: Oil, tempera, watercolor, prints (etching, lino-cut)

Specialty: Landscapes (shipyards), wildflowers, murals

One of seven children, Martina Gangle went to work at age eight to help her mother support the family. After graduating from the Museum Art School, she joined the WPA. Her favorite subjects were working people: shipyard laborers she knew when she worked as a welder during World War II, or migrants she had worked among as a young girl. *The Columbia River Pioneer Migration* is the title for her series of murals in Portland's Rose City Grade School. Curl's wildflower paintings and woodcuts are part of the WPA Timberline Lodge collection.

This life-long empathy for the common man involved Curl in many social issues, where her activism resulted in more than one protest arrest. She was secretary for the Workers Alliance in Oregon, which fought for the rights of the unemployed. She joined the Communist Party in the 1930s and remained a Communist until her death in 1994. The paper, *People's Weekly World*, says, "She believed socialism bridged the gap between the Christian ideals she had been taught as a child and the reality of capitalism." After a trip to Europe she deleted the *e* from Gangle to reflect a more European spelling. Her signature appears both ways. In later years she returned to the shipyards every week with her long-time comrade and husband, Hank Curl, to distribute the *People's Weekly World*.

Propagandist themes, coupled with a fantasy world inhabited with earth-mothers and children, dominated her artistic output. Curl also achieved some fame as a wood carver.

D

D'ARCY, Teresa E.

b. d.
Awards: Oregon State Fairs
Exhibits: Oregon State Fairs
References: OSF (1883–86)
Media: Watercolor

Teresa D'Arcy lived in Oregon in the 1880s and 1890s, during which time she exhibited at Oregon State Fairs. She also operated Miss D'Arcy's Select School in Portland in 1893.

DARCE, Virginia Chism

b. 1910 Portland, OR
d. 1985 Los Angeles, CA
Education: University of Oregon: *Steinhof*
Membership: Oregon Society of Artists; American Artists Professional League; American Artists' Congress
Collections: Portland Art Museum
Exhibits: Portland Art Museum; Oregon Society of Artists; American Artists Professional League (1937); American Artists' Congress (37); Skidmore Fountain Art Association (38); California Palace of the Legion of Honor—San Francisco (39); Seattle Art Museum
References: COL; DAV; HAV; KOV; OET; WWN; WWW; A2 (1932, 42); C7 (44); C10; CD (38, 40); M2
Media: Watercolor
Specialty: Cityscapes, murals, scenes of Washington and Oregon

Virginia Darce painted murals, was an illustrator, designer, and writer. She wrote art criticism for the *Spectator* in the 1930s and the *Spokane Review* during World War II. She worked as a stained glass artist for the W.P. Fuller Glass Co. and produced stained glass designs for the WPA that were used for the Blue Ox Bar of Timberline Lodge. Darce also created a seventy-foot mural for the Oregon City Post Office. During her time in Portland she was manager for the Skidmore Fountain Artist Association. She left Oregon in the 1940s and was active in Spokane and Los Angeles.

DAVIES, Clive

b. 1915 Swansea,Wales ***d.***
Education: Art Institute of Pittsburgh—Pennsylvania (1934–37)
Membership: Portland Art Museum (Artist Membership)
Exhibits: Delgado Museum—New Orleans (1945); Harvey Welch Gallery (49); Portland Art Museum; Oakland Art Gallery (52); Oregon Centennial (59)
References: A3 (1950–53, 55); C6; C17
Media: Watercolor, acrylic, prints (silkscreen)
Specialty: Landscapes, seascapes

Clive Davies served in the U.S. Army during World War II, where he produced silkscreen posters. He visited Oregon in 1946 and decided to remain. He exhibited at the Portland Art Museum, the Harvey Welch Gallery, the Delgado Museum in New Orleans, the Oakland Art Gallery, and the Oregon Centennial. Davies was the art director for McCann-Erickson advertising firm in Portland. Following his retirement, he moved to the Tillamook area on the Oregon Coast, where he continued his drawing and painting. The Portland Art Museum's Rental Sales Gallery represented his work.

DAVIS, Mary Huntington

b. 1907 Pittsburgh, PA
d. 1989 Portland, OR
Education: Museum Art School: *L. Bunce*, M. Russo*, W. Givler** (1952–56); *M. Wanker** (39); *H. and C. Morris** (52–57); *L. Wiley**
Membership: Portland Art Museum (Artist Membership)
Collections: Portland Art Museum; Goodman Collection; U.S. Bank; Pacific Power and Light Collection; University of Oregon; Hilton Hotel; First National Bank; Pacific Northwest Bank of Washington; Arlene and Harold Schnitzer Collection
Exhibits: Portland Art Museum; Seattle Art Museum; Morrison Street Gallery; Lipman Little Gallery (1959); Ruthermore Gallery—San Francisco (59); Harvey Welch Gallery (1PS); San Francisco Museum of Art; University of Oregon (75); M.H. DeYoung Museum—San Francisco
References: A2 (1948); A3 (53, 55, 56, 58); C7 (55, 58); C22
Media: Oil, casein, acrylic, collage
Specialty: Nature

Mary Davis attended Portland's Museum Art School and studied privately with Maude Wanker*, Lucia Wiley*, and Hilda and Carl Morris*. She exhibited at the Portland and Seattle Art Museums and in many local galleries as well as the San Francisco Museum of Art and the California Palace of the Legion of Honor. The paintings of Mary Davis have either literal or abstract references to nature. These are subtle works that evoke haunting and mystical images. Mother of artist Richard Davis*, she was also known as Mrs. Clyde Davis.

DAVIS, Richard H.

b. 1931 Portland, OR *d.*
Education: Museum Art School (1949); Brooklyn Art Museum
Membership: Portland Art Museum (Artist Membership)
Collections: Portland Art Museum; Goodman Collection; Hilton Hotel; University of Oregon; U.S. Bank; Haseltine Collection; Pacific Northwest Bank of Washington; Multnomah Athletic Club Collection; Arlene and Harold Schnitzer Collection; Hurst Collection
Exhibits: Portland Art Museum; Oregon Society of Artists; M.H. DeYoung Museum—San Francisco (1952); Brooklyn Art Museum (1PS 53); Seattle Art Museum (54); Harvey Welch Gallery (54); Reed College (1PS 57); University of Puget Sound (58); California Palace of the Legion of Honor—San Francisco (1PS 59); Ruthermore Gallery—San Francisco (59); Oregon Centennial (59); University of Oregon (75)
References: A2 (1948); A3 (52–55, 58); C3 (50); C6; C7 (55, 58, 59); C22
Media: Oil, casein
Specialty: Nature

Richard Davis studied at the Museum Art School and at the school of the Brooklyn Art Museum, where he had a one-person show in 1953. He exhibited in Oregon, Washington, and California. Davis commented that it was not important if art was representational or not, but it had to be creative, dispensing with what is superficial or merely fad. He felt the true artist must have imagination balanced with reason, a will to search and discover, to understand what is momentary and what is timeless. Davis said the artist must have strong convictions, knowledge, and purpose, and be acutely sensitive to life, always growing. He hoped his art reflected these tenets.

Prior to 1959, Davis's paintings were generally small, monochromatic, evocative works, which were closely related to nature. His later works show brilliant color and a more decisive move toward abstraction. He is the son of artist Mary Davis*.

DAWSON, Alfred J.

b. d.
Membership: Oregon Society of Artists; Attic Club
Exhibits: Oregon Society of Artists; Portland Art Museum; Medford (1PS 1948)
References: A2 (1948); C3 (48–50); ARTC
Media: Oil
Specialty: Still life

Alfred Dawson was a member of, and exhibited with, the Attic Club and the Oregon Society of Artists. The Oregon Historical Society lists a portrait sketch by Alfred Dawson, produced at the Attic Club, in their collection.

DAY, Rosamund Stricker

b. 1910 Grants Pass, OR ***d.***
Education: Museum Art School
Membership: American Artists' Congress; Arts Guild
Exhibits: Portland Art Museum; Arts Guild; Creative Art Gallery (1933); American Artists' Congress (37); San Francisco Art Association (38)
References: HUG; A2 (1930, 32, 33); A3 (35, 36); A4 (36, 59); A5 (30, 33)
Media: Oil, watercolor, tempera
Specialty: Landscape

Rosamund Stricker, a 1929 scholarship student of the Museum Art School, was a member of the Arts Guild and the American Artists' Congress. She exhibited locally and was a WPA artist. She moved to San Francisco in 1938, returned to Oregon the next year and, in 1941, married and took up residence in San Rafael, California. She signed her early works *Rosamund Stricker*.

DEWERT, Mae Winterrowd

b. d.
Exhibits: Portland Art Museum
References: A2 (1913, 16, 17)

Mae Dewert exhibited at the Portland Art Museum from 1913 to 1917.

DE YOUNG, Lorraine. *See* JOHNSON, Lorraine

DODD, Patricia Beaton

b. 1929 Ajo, AZ ***d.***
Education: University of Oregon (1945–49); Museum Art School (50); *H. and C. Morris**
Membership: Artists Equity; Portland Art Museum (Artist Membership)
Collections: Kaiser Permanente Collection; First National Bank; U.S. Bank
Exhibits: Portland Art Museum (AM, 1954; 4PS 59); Morrison Street Gallery; Oregon Centennial (59)
References: A3 (1953–58); A4 (52); C6
Media: Watercolor, oil, prints (woodcuts), mixed media
Specialty: Semi-abstract

Patricia Dodd exhibited with Leonard Kimbrell*, Nelson Sandgren*, and Richard Newstrum* in a four-person show at the Portland Art Museum in 1959, sponsored by the Artist Membership. She has said she thinks the ideal, both in life and painting, is to produce those things that have longevity and the gift of life. Dodd produced drawings and sculptures in addition to her paintings. The Portland Art Museum's Rental Sales Gallery has represented her work.

DODGE, Harriet

b. d.
Collections: Douglas County Museum
References: OR (Douglas County Museum)
Media: Oil
Specialty: Landscapes, still life

Harriet Dodge was a painter who

worked in the Roseburg area in the 1870s. Two of her oils are housed in the Douglas County Museum.

DOLPH, Marie Dorothy

b. 1884 Baraboo, WI
d. 1979 Post Falls, ID
Education: University of Minnesota (1901–03); Milwaukee Art Institute (06–08); Art Institute of Chicago: *Mucha* (08)
Membership: Oregon Society of Artists
Collections: Capitol Collection—Salem; University of Wyoming—Cheyenne, Wyoming; Buffalo Bill Historical Center—Cody, Wyoming
Exhibits: National Exhibition of American Art (36); Wyoming: Fine Arts Club—Casper (1PS 1937, 41), Cheyenne, Laramie; Oregon Society of Artists; John Herron Art Institute—Indianapolis;
References: COL; DAW; KOV; MAL SUP; PET; WWN; C3 (1945–48)
Media: Oil, prints (drypoint)
Specialty: Landscape, western scenes

Marie Dolph taught near Madison, Wisconsin until 1912. She married in 1913 and moved to Wyoming. While there she exhibited in group shows at the University of Wyoming for several years. She was also a WPA artist and appeared in WPA-sponsored shows. Her work was shown at the National Exhibition of American Art in 1936 at the Rockefeller Center. Dolph lived in Hood River in the 1940s and became a member of the Oregon Society of Artists. She lived in California until 1966 and then in Idaho for the rest of her life. She signed her work *M.D. Dolph.*

DOMINIQUE, John August(us)

b. 1893 Virserum, Sweden
d. 1994 Ojai, CA
Education: California School of Design; Museum Art School (1913); Otis Art Institute; San Francisco Institute of Art (15–16); Santa Barbara School of Art (21, 27–29); *Hansen; Borg; Cooper*
Membership: Oregon Society of Artists; American Artists Professional League
Awards: Oregon Society of Artists; Oregon State Fairs (1936–38, 40,41)
Collections: University of Virginia; Canby Library; Miranda Collection; Lundberg Collection; Cofield Collection
Exhibits: Art Club—Santa Barbara (1924); Chicago Society of Artists (26); Oakland Museum (28–31); Egan Gallery—Los Angeles (1PS 33); Mission Art Store (1PS 34), Chamber of Commerce (34)—Santa Barbara; Oregon State Fairs (36–38, 40, 41); Oregon Society of Artists; Portland Art Museum; Salem Federal Art Center (1PS 38); Oakland Art Gallery (41); Los Angeles County Museum of Art (44)
References: COL; DAV; DAW; HAV; HUG; WWN; WWW; A2 (1940); A3 (36); C3 (35–38)
Media: Oil, watercolor, prints (etching), pastel
Specialty: Oregon and California scenery

John Dominique came to the United States in 1898 from his native Sweden. He spent his youth in Oregon, where he studied at the Museum Art School. He later worked as a typesetter and cartoonist for a small newspaper. A 1938 Salem *Statesman* review of his show at the Salem Art Center indicated that his work was not as enthusiastically accepted locally as it was in the East and in California. His career took him from Canby, Oregon to California, where he opened a studio in Santa Barbara in the 1930s. However, he frequently returned to Oregon to paint.

His early works were impressionistic

oils and watercolors, but later his style became more expressionistic and abstract. He always worked from nature in the *plein air* tradition. Characteristics of his works are vibrant colors: ochres, blues, greens, and purples and a spiritual sense of place that came from an emphasis on atmosphere. Though blind in later life, Dominique was still painting into his seventies. He sometimes signed his work *Dominique*.

DOUD, Delia A.

b. 1837 Gainesville, NY
d. 1926 Portland, OR
Awards: Oregon State Fair
Collections: Oregon Historical Society
Exhibits: Oregon State Fair; Portland Mechanics Fair; Portland Woman's Club (1926); Oregon Historical Society (90)
References: KOV; C4 (1879); C9; OSF (77); M2; M3
Media: Oil
Specialty: Portraits, landscapes

Delia Doud graduated from Lima College, New York in 1860. Her brother, William Wallace Thayer, was Governor of Oregon from 1878 to 1882. She was active as an artist in New York before moving to Portland. Doud's 1887 prize-winning oil, *View of Portland*, is in the collection of the Oregon Historical Society. This painting was sent to the Long Beach, California Museum of Art for an exhibition in 1984. The Portland Woman's Club, of which she was a member, has a dedication to her in their building on SW Taylor Street.

DOWLING, Colista Murray

b. 1881 Coffey County, KS
d. 1968 Portland, OR
Education: Museum Art School; Art Students League; Pennsylvania Academy of Fine Art—Philadelphia; Oregon State University; University of Oregon; Drexel Institute—Philadelphia; Columbia University; *Luks; Donaldson*
Membership: Society of Oregon Artists; Oregon Society of Artists; American Artists Professional League
Awards: Oregon Society of Artists (1932, 38, 39, 43)
Collections: Oregon Historical Society; Painting Restoration Studio Collection; Parsons Collection; Lundberg Collection; Huntington Collection; Slippery Slope Historical Collection
Exhibits: Society of Oregon Artists (1912, 13); Portland Art Museum; Portland Woman's Club (26); Seattle Art Museum; Oregon Society of Artists (1PS 38, 39); American Artists Professional League (33); Oregon Historical Society (90); Clatsop County Historical Society (94)
References: ALM; COL; DAV; HAV; KOV; MAL; OET; WWN; WWW; A2 (1913–15, 17, 19, 20, 32–34, 40, 42, 44, 46, 48); A4 (29); C3 (27, 28, 32–36, 38, 43, 45–51); C7 (28, 28a, 35); C9; C10; C11; ARTC; CD (09–14, 16, 18, 50, 52); M2
Media: Watercolor, oil, pen and ink, pencil
Specialty: Landscapes (lakes, rivers), portraits, city-scenes, murals, caricatures, posters

Classically trained at the Art Students League in New York and the Pennsylvania Academy of Fine Arts, Colista Dowling was considered one of the leading watercolorists in the Northwest. She painted charming, small city scenes, and many large murals for local clubs, hotels, and churches, such as St. Paul's Lutheran Church of Portland. She was a member of the Portland Woman's Club and completed murals to decorate their dining room walls and the backdrop for their theater. The Woman's Club building still stands at 1220 SW Taylor

Street. Dowling was known for her portraits: *John McLoughlin* is in the Milton High School Collection in Milton-Freewater and *William J. Standley, the Philosopher* was owned by the Portland Public Schools.

Dowling was a charter member of the Oregon Society of Artists and retained a close association with them as an exhibitor and officer for most of her career. She was also a well-known illustrator for *The Pacific Monthly* and several books, among them pen drawings for *Ox Bows and Bear Feet* by John R. Leach in 1952. She contributed to the popular caricature book, *As We See 'Em* in 1906. Her 1914 Rose Festival poster won that event's competition. Dowling was a very successful commercial artist for sixty years.

DRAKE, William H.

b. 1890 Souix City, IA
d. 1967 Portland, OR
Membership: Oregon Society of Artists
Exhibits: Oregon Society of Artists (2PS 1959); Oregon Centennial (59)
References: C3 (1927–30, 32–34, 47)
Specialty: Still life, cityscapes

William Drake was a veteran of World War I. While he was living in California he became a charter member of the Oregon Society of Artists. He retired to Portland in 1952. Drake exhibited with Clyde Archibald* in a two-person show sponsored by the Oregon Society of Artists during the Oregon Centennial in 1959.

DRENNER, Robert S.

b. KS
d. 1971 MT
Exhibits: Portland Art Museum
References: A2 (1942); OR (Cottage Grove Museum)
Media: Oil, watercolor
Specialty: Nature

Robert Drenner arrived in Oregon in 1934 to settle in Cottage Grove. He was a painter as well as a conservationist and poet. He produced a series of 110 bird paintings and two murals for the Cottage Grove High School Library. He lived for a time in Culp Creek, Oregon. Drenner died in Montana while on a fishing trip.

DRISCOLL, Norma. *See* GILMORE, Norma

DUESBURY, Horace A.

b. 1851 Sheffield, England
d. 1904 Alameda, CA
Education: England; Australia; San Francisco
Awards: Portland Mechanics Fairs (1881–83)
Collections: M.H. DeYoung Museum—San Francisco; Oregon Historical Society; Multnomah County Library Collection
Exhibits: Portland Mechanics Fairs; Oregon Historical Society (1990)
References: BI; DAV; GER; HUG; C4 (1879–83); C9; CD (80–83, 85)
Media: Oil
Specialty: Portraits

Horace Duesbury moved from England to Australia, then to San Francisco in 1876. Three years later he came to Portland, where he established a reputation as a portrait artist. Duesbury painted a portrait of Father Blanchet, the first Oregon Archbishop, in 1881. This painting is still owned by the Catholic Diocese. He exhibited at the Portland Mechanics Fairs from 1879 to 1883, where he won several awards. He returned to San Francisco in 1886.

DUFF, Aimee L. Pernot Stewart

b. 1898 Corvallis, OR
d. 1978 Coos County, OR
Education: Museum Art School (1919); Oregon State University: *McLouth*
Membership: American Artists Profes-

sional League; Oregon Society of Artists
Awards: American Artists Professional League (1935–37)
Collections: Washington State University; Lundberg Collection
Exhibits: Oregon State University (1PS); Portland Art Museum; Oregon Society of Artists; Oregon State Fair; American Artists Professional League (1935–37); Grumbacher traveling exhibition (35); J.K. Gill Gallery (36); Egan Gallery—Los Angeles
References: COL; DAV; DAW; WWN; A2 (1933, 34, 42)
Media: Oil, watercolor, pen and ink
Specialty: Seascapes, landscapes

In 1918 while attending Jefferson High School in Portland, Aimee Pernot won a scholarship to study art. She also received instruction in watercolor at St. Helen's Hall and the Museum Art School before attending Oregon State University, where her father, Emile Pernot, was a professor.

Duff lived in Waldport and Port Orford and maintained a studio on the Oregon Coast, where she was frequently seen sketching along the beach. She received many awards for her paintings and exhibited in the Grumbacher show in New York. She also wrote and illustrated stories for children.

Duff was active in arranging American Artists Professional League Art Week exhibitions throughout the state. She exhibited in group shows in New York City, Los Angeles, and Salem, Oregon. She signed her paintings *P. Stewart* or *Duff.*

DuMOND, Frank Vincent

b. 1865 Rochester, NY
d. 1951 New York City, NY
Education: Art Students League: *Beckwith, Sartain;* Académie Julian: *Boulanger, Lefebre, Constant*
Awards: Paris Salon (1890); Pan American Exposition—Buffalo (1901); St. Louis Universal Exposition (04)
Collections: First Interstate Bank; Art Students League; Portland Art Museum; Painting Restoration Studio Collection; Parsons Collection
Exhibits: Paris Salons; Portland Industrial Exposition (1892); World Columbian Exposition—Chicago (93); Bernstein's Art Gallery (98); Portland Art Museum; St. Louis Universal Exposition (1904); Lewis and Clark Centennial Exposition (05); Alaska-Yukon Pacific Exposition (09); Oregon Historical Society (90)
References: BEN; BI; DAV; DAW; FI (1889–92, 96–98); FIE; GER; HAV; MAL; WWW; YNG; A1 (1902, 05, 06, 09, 33); A2 (14, 32); A4 (14); C2 (1892); C9; C21; ARTC
Media: Oil, watercolor
Specialty: Landscapes, portraits

There are many who feel that Frank DuMond's impact on Oregon art has never been fully appreciated. His contribution was important—as an artist, as a teacher, and as an influence on the art community. His career started, oddly enough, at the funeral of New York Governor, Samuel J. Tilden in 1886. Young DuMond sketched the proceedings from behind a curtain. This so impressed the staff at *Harper's Weekly* that they employed him as illustrator. Shortly thereafter, he began his art studies in earnest in Paris at the Académie Julian, gaining recognition and medals at the Paris Salon. Upon his return to the United States he began instructing at the Art Students League in New York, where he remained for fifty-nine years until his death, except for his Oregon residence from 1895 to 1900. He was the League's oldest teacher and the one with the longest term of service.

His connection to Oregon resulted

from his marriage to one of his promising students, Helen Savier* of Portland. Their presence in Portland in the late 1890s gave him the opportunity to instruct at the newly formed Portland Sketch Club. At this time he also began teaching at St. Helen's Hall, where he set up a studio. A display of DuMond's paintings in Portland's Bernstein's Gallery prompted artist W. E. Rollins* to raise the question of need for a permanent art gallery where art of this caliber could be exhibited.

In 1905 DuMond curated the department of fine arts for the Lewis and Clark Centennial Exposition. This exposition brought the artwork of world-renowned artists, including many famous French Impressionists, to Portland for the first time. Inspired by the Exposition, a group of art patrons founded and opened the Portland Art Museum in time to exhibit 'Section B' of the Fair's art exhibit.

By the turn of the century, the DuMonds had returned to New York, but they continued to summer in Portland, where he taught classes at the Museum Art School. In later years, he did likewise in France, Italy, and eventually Old Lyme, Connecticut, where he, his wife, and family finally settled. Frank DuMond was the brother of Frederick Melville DuMond, a respected California artist who specialized in Southwest scenes.

Frank DuMond's approach to painting was an academic one. Classically trained in Europe, he employed physics to analyze how light reflects from surfaces. His earlier work contained muted, figural landscapes that later changed to a lighter *plein air* style, yielding almost impressionistic interpretations with an emphasis on atmospheric effects. Noted artist John Marin said he had many masters, but among teachers, DuMond was the only one.

DuMOND, Helen Savier

b. 1872 Portland, OR

d. 1968 Alhambra, CA

Education: Art Students League: *Brandege, DuMond**; Paris: *Colin, Merson*

Membership: National Arts Club (life member)

Exhibits: Paris Salons; Lewis and Clark Centennial Exposition (1905); Portland Art Museum

References: BI; DAV; DAW; FI (1897, 98); FIE; GER; HAV; MAL; PET; WWW; YNG; A1 (1905); C21

Specialty: Miniatures

Helen DuMond, a member of an old Portland family, studied at the Art Students League in New York City and privately in Paris with Colin and Merson. She exhibited at the Paris Salon of 1897 and 1898 and in Portland at the Lewis and Clark Centennial Exposition of 1905. She painted under the name *Savier* before her marriage to Frank DuMond.* The DuMonds returned to spend many summers in Portland with her family.

E

EASTMAN, Lizzie S.

b. d.
Membership: Mutual Art Association
Exhibits: Portland Art Museum; Mutual Art Association (1914, 15)
References: A2 (1913); ARTC; CD (13, 14, 17)

Lizzie Eastman was active in Portland from 1913 to 1917. She was a member of, and exhibited with, the Mutual Art Association and the Portland Art Museum.

EDINA, Sister Mary (Isabel Theresa Springer)

b. 1885 Kansas City, MO
d. 1950 Marylhurst, OR
Education: St. Mary's Academy
Membership: American Artists Professional League
Awards: American Artists Professional League (1938)
Exhibits: Bernstein's Art Shop; Portland Art Museum; American Artists Professional League (1938)
References: A2 (1940); A3 (36, 37)
Media: Watercolor
Specialty: Still life

Isabel Springer attended St. Mary's Academy in Portland. In 1902 she won a prize in a contest sponsored by an art shop on Alder Street. In 1906 she became a Sister of the Holy Name and taught in their schools in Jacksonville, Astoria, Medford, and elsewhere. She returned to St. Mary's as an art teacher and, in 1930, when Marylhurst College opened, was appointed director of school art in the elementary education department.

EDMONDSON, Elizabeth

b. 1874 Plymouth, IN
d. 1955 Medford, OR
Education: Valparaiso, Indiana; Pratt Institute
Membership: Oregon Society of Artists; American Artists Professional League; Southern Oregon Art Association; Southern Oregon Society of Artists
Awards: Oregon State Fair
Collections: Southern Oregon Historical Society
Exhibits: Mercury Gallery—New York City (1918); American Artists Professional League (33); Art Institute of Chicago (35); Cincinnati Art Museum (36); Corcoran Gallery of Art—Washington, D.C. (37, 39); Oregon Society of Artists; Denver Art Museum (37); Portland Art Museum; Oregon State Fair
References: ALM; COL; WWN; A2 (1940); C3 (36)
Media: Watercolor, oil, pastel, charcoal, tempera
Specialty: Nature (wildflowers, animals), portraits, landscapes, seascapes

Elizabeth Edmondson started art school at age twelve, working at her easel from morning until evening. She taught school in Wisconsin. Then, following the death of her husband in 1902, she homesteaded with her daughter near McLeod. After the death of her second husband, William Lee, Edmondson taught school in Oregon and Washington. She moved to Medford in 1920 and continued teaching school and private art classes from her home, working with as many as one hundred students at one time. Edmondson exhibited nationally at the Art Institute of Chicago, the Denver Art Museum, and the Corcoran Gallery, Washington, D.C. She was instrumental in forming the Southern Oregon Art Association. Edmondson painted over one hundred varieties of Oregon wildflowers. Her son, William Edmondson, was a sculptor.

EISELE, Christian A.

b. 1847 Essling, Germany
d. 1917 Lincoln, NE
Membership: Society of Utah Artists
Awards: Utah State Fair (1909)
Collections: Denver Public Library; Oregon Historical Society; Stenzel Collection; Mormon Temple—Logan, Utah; Painting Restoration Studio Collection; Counting Eagles Collection
Exhibits: Portland Mechanics Fair (1888); North Pacific Industrial Exposition (89, 90); Portland Industrial Exposition (93); World Columbian Exposition—Chicago (93); Utah State Fair (1909); Wyoming State Museum; Oregon Historical Society (90)
References: BI; DAV; DAW; GER; WWW; C2 (1889, 90, 93); C4 (88); C9; CD (90, 91, 1912, 13)
Media: Oil
Specialty: Landscapes

Christian Eisele was an itinerant painter who first appeared in Oregon in 1888. His oil paintings were shown at the Portland Mechanics Fair and the Industrial Expositions. He operated the Omaha Exchange Saloon in Portland from 1890 to 1891. He reappeared in Oregon in 1903, 1905, and 1906 and again from 1911 to 1913. He was also known as *Carl* or *Charles M. Eisele.*

ELDER, Ada Francis

b. d. 1935 Portland, OR
Membership: Oregon Society of Artists
Exhibits: Portland Art Museum; Oregon Society of Artists
References: A2 (1917); C3 (28); CD (07–08, 09, 11–14, 16–18, 20, 23, 24)

According to a 1909 advertisement, Ada Elder was the owner of, and taught at, the Pacific School of Arts and Crafts. She exhibited with the Oregon Society of Artists and at the Portland Art Museum.

ELLIOTT, Frank Sanje

b. 1933 Centralia, WA ***d.***
Education: Lewis and Clark College: *B. Hinshaw** (1954); Museum Art School: *L. Bunce**, *M. Russo**, *W. Givler** (55–56); Accademia di Belle Arti —Florence, Italy (56–8); *Kokoschka* (58)
Membership: Portland Art Museum (Artist Membership); Artists Equity
Awards: Florence, Italy (1957)
Collections: Portland Art Museum; Kaiser Permanente Collection; Portland Civic Auditorium; Parsons Collection
Exhibits: Portland Art Museum; Lewis and Clark College (1PS 1954, 55); Hood River (1PS 56); Jewish Community Center—Portland (1PS 56); Rome (1PS 57), Florence (1PS 57), Livorno (57)
References: A3 (1953, 56)
Media: Encaustic, oil, watercolor, collage
Specialty: Landscapes, figures,

Frank Elliott went to school in Portland before going to Europe for additional art training. Following his study in Italy, he lived in Munich from 1958 to 1961. He returned to Portland in 1963. Elliott held one-person shows in Rome and Florence and exhibited in Livorno, Italy, all in 1957. One of Elliott's drawings is in the collection of the Uffizzi Gallery of Florence, Italy.

ELLSWORTH, Edyth Glover

b. 1879 Portland, OR
d. 1954 Portland, OR
Education: Art Institute of Chicago: *Bridgeman;* Chicago Academy of Fine Arts: *Khoerner;* University of Minnesota: *Snow;* Museum Art School: *H. Wentz*, C. Stephens*;* Oregon State University Extension: *B. Hinshaw*, A. Fairbanks*
Membership: Oregon Society of Artists; American Artists Professional League
Awards: Oregon Society of Artists (1933, 35, 42, 43)
Collections: Oregon Historical Society; Lundberg Collection
Exhibits: Oregon Society of Artists; American Artists Professional League (1932, 38); Portland Art Museum; Lincoln County Art Center; Oregon Historical Society (90); Clatsop County Historical Society (94)
References: ALM; COL; DAV; DAW; KOV; WWN; A2 (1932, 40, 42, 44, 46, 48); C3 (27–36, 42, 43, 45–47, 49); C9; C11; CD (30, 39, 50); M2; M3
Media: Oil, watercolor, pastel
Specialty: Portraits, landscapes, seascapes, florals, murals

Edyth Ellsworth lived in Tacoma and Seattle before moving to Portland with her husband in 1918. She was a commercial artist for the Portland department store, Lipman and Wolfe. For a brief time she shared a studio with artist Mabel Haines Oster*. Eventually she became a free-lance artist, painting murals in private homes during the 1920s and exhibiting frequently during the 1930s and 1940s. Her painting, *Summer Pastures,* was in the Portland Woman's Club collection. In addition to her work on canvas, Ellsworth created sculpture. She was a charter member of the Oregon Society of Artists in 1927. During World War II, she produced small oil portraits for servicemen to send home to their families. She taught privately and at the Lincoln County Art Center in Lincoln City on the Oregon Coast.

ELMER, Clementine Catlin

b. 1879
d. 1957 Multnomah County, OR
Exhibits: Portland Art Museum; Creative Art Gallery (1933); Seattle Art Museum
References: COL; WWN; A2 (1932, 33, 40); A3 (35); C7 (36); C10; CD (34)
Media: Oil
Specialty: Cityscapes

Clementine Elmer was a WPA artist who exhibited oil paintings at the Portland and Seattle Art Museums. She was the supervisor of children's art classes at the Museum Art School from 1942 to 1946. In later years she became best known for her sculpture.

ENGLAND, Olive Stanton

b. 1851 Salem, OR ***d.***
Awards: Oregon State Fairs
Exhibits: Portland Mechanics Fair; Oregon State Fairs
References: C4 (1885); OSF (87–93, 97, 98); M2
Media: Oil
Specialty: Landscapes, portraits, nature

Olive England was awarded many prizes for her art work, including china painting. She exhibited at the Portland Mechanics Fair and the Oregon State Fairs. In 1903 Mrs. England remarried and was known as Mrs. John Enright.

ENGLEHART, John Joseph

b. 1867 Chicago, IL
d. 1915 Oakland, CA
Awards: New York City (1909)
Collections: Washington State Historical Society—Tacoma; Portland Woman's

Club; Oregon Historical Society; Coos Art Museum; Oakland Museum; Sherman County Historical Society; Tillamook County Pioneer Museum; Baldwin Saloon Collection; Clark County Historical Society; Painting Restoration Studio Collection; Counting Eagles Collection

Exhibits: New York City (1909); Washington State Historical Society—Tacoma (85); Washington State Capitol Museum (88); Oregon Historical Society (90);

References: BI; DAV; DAW; HUG; C9; C24; C28

Media: Oil

Specialty: Landscapes (especially mountains), Indians

John Englehart lived in Oregon, Washington, and California and scenes from these states abound in his paintings. Englehart had a studio listing in Portland from 1902 to 1904. Although it has been said that he exhibited at the Lewis and Clark Exposition, no evidence has yet been found to substantiate this claim. He exhibited in St. Louis and Europe.

It is alleged that Englehart sometimes bartered his work for food and drink. He may have been an alcoholic, which could have contributed to the variable quality of his work. There are a variety of signatures found on his paintings, the most common being *J. Englehart*, but he also used *J. J. Englehart* and, more rarely, *J. Englehardt.*

EPTING, Henry

b. Germany

d. 1911 Portland, OR

Membership: Portland Art Club

Exhibits: Portland Art Club (1886)

References: DAV; GER; HUG; ARTC; M1

Media: Oil

Specialty: Landscapes

Henry Epting was an illustrator for *The West Shore* and the *Oregonian*. He later spent time in California, but returned to Portland melancholy and depressed. He was known as a great colorist and panoramist. His last painting was of the Columbia River, a view from Hood River toward Portland. In 1911 he committed suicide in Council Crest Park in Portland.

ERICKSON, LaVerne. *See* KRAUSE, LaVerne

ERIKSON, Dora

b. 1905 Orange, ME ***d.***

Education: Museum Art School: *H. Wentz*, W. Givler**; Art Students League

Collections: Portland Art Museum; Timberline Lodge Collection; Pacific Northwest College of Art

Exhibits: Portland Art Museum

References: A2 (1933); A4 (59); C10

Media: Oil, watercolor

Specialty: Florals

Dora Erikson was a scholarship student at Portland's Museum Art School and continued her art training at the Art Students League in New York City. As a WPA artist, Erikson produced a group of wildflower paintings and an oil, *Open Air Concert*, for Timberline Lodge. She was best known for her sculpture, which she showed at the Creative Art Gallery in Portland in 1933. Her name is sometimes spelled Erickson.

ESPEY, Edward Lincoln

b. 1860 Champaign City, IL

d. 1889 Portland, OR

Education: San Francisco: *Williams, R. Yelland**; Académie Julian: *Bourgereau, Constant*

Membership: Portland Art Club

Awards: Oregon State Fair; Portland Mechanics Fair (1888)

Collections: Multnomah County Library

Collection; Maryhill Museum—Goldendale, Washington; Painting Restoration Studio Collection

Exhibits: Portland Mechanics Fairs; Paris Salon; Oregon State Fair; Portland Art Club (1886); North Pacific Industrial Exposition (89); Portland Art Museum; Panama Pacific International Exposition—San Francisco (1915); Oregon Historical Society (90)

References: BI; DAV; GER; HUG; FI (1885); OET; A1 (1902); C2 (1889); C4 (80, 81, 83, 85–8); C5; C9; ARTC; CD (82, 84, 86); OSF (85); M1

Media: Oil

Specialty: Landscapes, still life

See artwork in color section

Edward Espey first came to the attention of the Portland public at the 1880 Mechanic's Fair with an entry of sketches and a painting of Mt. Hood. A Portland newspaper stated that he sailed for France in 1881 and exhibited a large oil in the Paris Salon that year, but there is no reference in Fink (see Ref. FI) that this happened. His reputation was achieved from the works he produced abroad, many of which were exhibited in the Portland area between 1883 and 1892. His 1885 Paris Salon oil, *Repose*, a view of the graves of sailors on the coast of Brittany, was the first work purchased by the Portland Library Association in 1886. A subscription of one thousand dollars, a substantial sum in those days, was raised for the purchase. This was the largest amount paid to an Oregon artist by an Oregon institution to that date.

The *Oregonian*, in an 1887 article on Espey, stated that "another marine was accepted by the Paris Salon"; there was no listing, however, in Fink's book (see Ref. FI) on the Salons indicating this was so.

Edward Espey lived for a time in Oysterville, Washington, where members of his family homesteaded and continued to live. He died at age twenty-nine of tuberculosis. His name is sometimes spelled Espy.

EUWER, Anthony Henderson

b. 1877 Allegheny, PA

d. 1955 La Jolla, CA

Education: Princeton University; Art Students League

Membership: American Artists Professional League

Awards: Oregon Society of Artists (1928); American Artists Professional League (32)

Collections: Powell Collection; Miranda Collection; Oregon Historical Society

Exhibits: Portland Art Museum; Multnomah Hotel (22, 24, 26); Portland Woman's Club (1926); Oregon Society of Artists (1PS 30); American Artists Professional League (32); Clatsop County Historical Society (94)

References: ALM; BI; DAV; DAW; FIE; MAL; OET; WWW; YNG; A2 (1920, 22); C3 (27, 28, 35); C11

Media: Watercolor, pastel, oil

Specialty: Landscapes (forest, woodlands), bookplates

See artwork in color section

An *Oregon Journal* editorial that eulogized Anthony Euwer began: "The coming generation now has the interesting and delightful task of discovering Anthony Euwer as he really was ... it was hard for his contemporaries really to discover him, for the confusing reason that there were so many of him." This talented man loved life and humanity and was able to express feelings in many ways. He received his art education at the Art Students League in New York. He published his first book, *Christopher Cricket on Cats*, in 1910 and received invitations to publicly read his humorous poems. He was also an illustrator whose cartoons appeared regularly in the *New York Times, Colliers, Punch, and Harpers.*

He first became acquainted with Portland in 1911, while visiting his brother Eugene, who had purchased property in Hood River Valley. Euwer decided to stay and help his brother farm. He fought brush fires by night and sketched by day. His second volume, *Rhymes of Our Valley*, was published in 1916. It revealed Euwer's transformation from a New York humorist to a farmer with sensitivity for the land. His paintings, too, reflected this change. Painting in a small studio that stood beside the big log house on the Euwer ranch in Hood River, he produced works which showed drama and color, mirroring the majesty of his new environment. Euwer married a Portland woman, Ruby Page Ferguson, in the early 1920s. Over the course of the next two decades he became an important part of the local art and entertainment world. He contributed a weekly picture and poetry page to the *Oregon Journal*. He continued to write books of verse, which often appeared first in the paper. His style was to paint large canvases with bold strokes, and small ones with fine workmanship. A 1926 exhibit at the Multnomah Hotel featured examples of both techniques. Many saw a mystical, almost oriental quality in his paintings. This exhibit also included bookplates, decorative designs, and original color drawings.

After his divorce in 1931, Euwer traveled to Japan and the islands of the Pacific. On his return he settled in Seattle, where he daily broadcasted *Philosopher of the Crossroads*. He then moved to Corvallis and continued his radio work. Eventually he moved to Los Angeles, where health problems forced an early retirement. Euwer was known equally for his poetry, illustrations, paintings, and his role as humorist. His work strongly reflected a fascination for the Oregon Country during the two decades he lived there.

EYERLY, Raymond Leslie

b. 1894 Canton, IL
d. 1980 Sisters, OR
Education: Canton, Illinois
Exhibits: Southern Oregon Art Exhibit
References: C26 (1956); OR
Media: Oil, watercolor, pen and ink
Specialty: Western scenes, Indians

Ray Eyerly worked as a janitor to earn his art school tuition in Canton, Illinois. He had about eighteen months of formal art training. When he was fifteen his family moved to Montana, where he began to absorb the essence of western life and scenery that would permeate his work. He worked on cattle ranches and wheat farms and, during that time, had the opportunity to meet Charlie Russell, the famous western artist. Eyerly was working for Billy Karrel, a good friend of Russell, when he showed Russell a painting of a horse. The cowboy artist took an interest in the twenty-year old and showed him how to proportion a horse. Eyerly recalled it as the "lesson I never forgot." He always used Russell's method of proportioning subjects throughout his long career. Eyerly sold his first painting at age fifteen for five dollars and his next work two years later for twenty-five dollars. Since ranch hands only received thirty dollars per month, Eyerly began to think more seriously about painting.

During World War I Eyerly served in the Signal Corps. In 1919 he moved to Salem, where he worked for the Highway Department. Through his assignments in the high country of eastern Oregon, he developed a great love for the landscape. He lived in Lakeview and there began producing works featuring cowboys, the open range, and the Klamath and Warm Springs native people. His style was that of the traditional western painter. In 1955 he stopped all outside employment in order to devote himself completely to his painting. He sold paintings to a calendar company to use for reproductions, keeping the original canvas himself. Although he chose not to exhibit in museums and large galleries, he developed a large and loyal following. The demand for his work far outstripped his ability to produce sufficient paintings to satisfy his collectors. The Oregon Historical Society has four lithographs of his work in their collection.

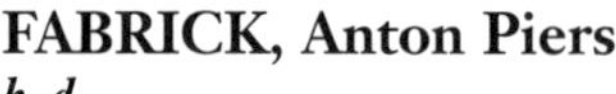

FABRICK, Anton Piers

b. d.

Membership: American Artists Professional League

Exhibits: Portland Art Museum; American Artists Professional League (1932, 34)

References: A2 (1932); C10; CD (32, 34, 35)

Anton Fabrick was a member of the American Artists Professional League. He was a WPA painter who exhibited at the Portland Art Museum. He moved to Montana in the 1940s. Fabrick often signed his work *Anton Piers.*

FAIRBANKS, John Leo

b. 1880 Payson, UT

d. 1946 Corvallis, OR

Education: Columbia University; Académie Julian; Académie de Colarossi

Membership: Oregon Society of Artists; American Artists Professional League; American Federation of Arts

Awards: Oregon Society of Artists (1932, 37); American Artists Professional League (32)

Collections: Parsons Collection; Oregon State University

Exhibits: Oregon Society of Artists; Portland Art Museum; American Artists Professional League (1932, 37, 38); Art Institute of Chicago; Oakland Art Gallery

References: ALM; BEN; BI; COL; DAV; DAW; FIE; HAV; MAL; SAM; WWN; YNG; A2 (1932, 40); A4 (29); C3 (27–29, 31, 32, 34)

Media: Oil, prints (etchings)

Specialty: Landscapes (Washington, Oregon), portraits, murals

After working as director of art for the Salt Lake City Public Schools, J. Leo Fairbanks came to Oregon State College (now Oregon State University) first as a teacher, then as head of the art department from 1923 to 1948. He turned to sculpture in his later years; one of these pieces is in the collection of the Oregon Historical Society. Even his murals have a sculptural quality, such as those in the Oregon State University Library and the Mormon Church in Portland. Fairbanks was a member of the New York Architectural League. He was the brother of Avard Fairbanks, a teacher and sculptor at the University of Oregon. He signed his work *J. Leo Fairbanks.*

FANCHER, Reid

b. d.

Education: Museum Art School (1942); California School of Fine Arts

Exhibits: Portland Art Museum (1PS 1948); Harvey Welch Gallery (48)

References: DAV; A2 (1944, 46); A4 (46, 59)

Media: Watercolor, gouache

Specialty: Still life, landscapes

Reid Fancher joined the U.S. Army Air Corps after graduating from the Museum Art School. Following his tour of duty he worked as the registrar for the Portland Art Museum into the 1950s. He exhibited at the Portland Art Museum and the Harvey Welch Gallery. Fancher listed a San Francisco address in the catalog for the 1959 Portland Art Museum exhibit.

FEASLEY, Robert

b. 1926 Downers Grove, IL *d.*
Education: University of Oregon (1949–51); Mills College—Oakland: *Beckmann* (58); Académie de la Grande Chaumière (52–53)
Membership: Portland Art Museum (Artist Membership); Artists Equity
Awards: Seattle Art Museum (1951, 53, 57); Tacoma Art Museum (57, 58); Spokane (57, 59); Oregon Centennial (59)
Collections: Portland Art Museum; Seattle Art Museum; University of Oregon; Haseltine Collection; Multnomah Athletic Club Collection
Exhibits: Portland Art Museum (AM, 1PS 1955); Harvey Welch Gallery (1PS 52); Seattle Art Museum (4PS 55); Andover, Massachusetts (55); Tacoma Art Museum (57, 58); Denver Art Museum (58); Oregon Centennial (59); University of Oregon (75)
References: A3 (1951, 54, 55, 58); C6; C7 (51–59); C22
Media: Oil

Robert Feasley was selected to represent the University of Oregon in the 1955 exhibit, *Art Schools USA*, in Andover, Massachusetts. This show later traveled throughout the eastern United States. Feasley exhibited in Oregon Annuals and had a one-person show at the Portland Art Museum in 1955. He lived in Roseburg, Oregon before leaving to pursue an active career as an artist and member of the art faculty of Washington State University.

FEE, Chester Anders

b. 1893 Pendleton, OR
d. 1951 Portland, OR
Education: Museum Art School
Membership: Oregon Society of Artists
Exhibits: Oregon Society of Artists; Portland Art Museum
References: ALM; BI; COL; DAV; DAW; WWN; A2 (1940, 44); C3 (38)
Media: Oil, watercolor, pen and ink
Specialty: Landscapes

Chester Fee attended the Museum Art School He was a member of the Oregon Society of Artists. Fee became an English professor at the University of Oregon after he gave up wheat and pea farming. He was the editor of several newspapers and the author of poems and biographies.

FEURER, Karl

b. Portland, OR
d. 1945 Portland, OR
Education: Dresden Academy—Bavaria
Awards: Seattle Art Museum (1921)
Collections: Timberline Lodge Collection
Exhibits: Portland Art Museum; Seattle Art Museum
References: DAV; DAW; OET; A2 (1940); C7 (21–23); C10; CD (40, 41)
Media: Watercolor, oil, prints (lithograph)
Specialty: Florals, landscapes

After studying in Europe for seven years, Karl Feurer lived in Seattle from 1921 to 1925. While there he exhibited at the Seattle Art Museum. He returned to Portland in 1927 and, as a WPA artist, completed a collection of watercolor wildflowers for Timberline Lodge. Some references indicate a European birthplace for Feurer; his obituary states Portland, Oregon.

FIELD, Marian

b. 1885 ND *d.*
Education: Cincinnati Art School; Minneapolis School of Art; University of Oregon; University of California Berkeley
Membership: University Alumni Art League, University of Oregon

Exhibits: Portland Art Museum; University Alumni Art League; Salem; Eugene; Corvallis
References: COL; DAV; DAW; WWN; WWW; A2 (1946); C10; C25 (35, 36)
Media: Watercolor, oil, graphite
Specialty: Botanicals

A WPA artist, Marian Field was head of the Salem Art Center in 1941. She painted dioramas for the Museum of Natural History at the University of Oregon. Field taught at Oregon State Agricultural College (now Oregon State University) from 1942 to 1944.

FONG, Wylog

b. ca. 1900 San Francisco, CA ***d.***
Education: Museum Art School
Exhibits: Portland Art Museum
References: DAV; HUG; OET; WWW; A2 (1920, 22); A4 (59); CD (18)
Media: Oil, pastel
Specialty: Chinese figures

Wylog Fong was born about 1900. He attended high school in Portland and later studied at the Museum Art School. There he met Clyde Rice, who mentions their association in his book, *A Heaven in the Eye.* Fong exhibited oils and pastels at the Portland Art Museum. He listed a Los Angeles address in 1959.

FOSTER, J.O.

b. d.
Membership: Portland Sketch Club
Exhibits: Portland Industrial Exposition (1893); Oregon Industrial Exposition (95); Portland Sketch Club (96)
References: C2 (1893, 95); ARTC
Specialty: Cityscapes

An early Oregon artist, J.O. Foster lived in Portland. He exhibited in the Oregon Industrial Fairs of 1893 and 1895 and with the Portland Sketch Club.

FOUNTAIN, Grace Russell

b. 1858 Yreka, CA
d. 1942 Oakland, CA
Education: *W. Parrott**
Collections: Oregon Historical Society; Oakland Museum; Southern Pacific Railroad Company
Exhibits: First Southern Oregon District Agricultural Fair; National Gallery of Art (1917); San Francisco Art Association (18); California Palace of the Legion of Honor—San Francisco (21); Oakland Art Gallery (28)
References: BI; DAV; HUG; KOV; PET; CD (1901–03); FSO (1898); M1; M2; M3
Media: Oil
Specialty: Landscapes
See artwork in color section

Raised in Ashland, Grace Fountain was active in Oregon as an art teacher and painter from 1880 to 1905. She lived in Klamath Falls for a time and exhibited in the First Southern Oregon District Agricultural Fair of 1898. She studied with William Parrott*. She painted many views of Crater Lake, Mt. Hood, and the Columbia River. One of her Crater Lake paintings was used by the Southern Pacific Railroad Company in one of its publications. It later hung in the National Gallery of Art in Washington D.C. Fountain had a studio in Portland in the early 1900s, which she shared with her artist sister, Mabel Russell Lowther. In 1904 Fountain produced illustrations for an article in the September issue of the *Pacific Monthly* magazine. She and her husband, James, moved to Oakland, California in 1907.

FOWLE, Edwin Denison Morgan

b. 1875 Washington, DC
d. 1941 Manzanita, OR
Education: Corcoran Gallery of Art School—Washington, D.C.
Membership: Mutual Art Association; Society of Oregon Artists; Circle A

Club; Oregon Society of Artists; American Artists Professional League

Awards: Oregon Society of Artists (1935); Seattle Art Museum (42, 44)

Collections: Powell Collection; Humpal Collection; Oregon Historical Society; Lundberg Collection

Exhibits: Society of Oregon Artists (1913); Mutual Art Association (14, 15); Portland Art Museum; American Artists Professional League (34); Oregon Society of Artists; Seattle Art Museum (42, 44); Clatsop County Historical Society (94)

References: A2 (1914, 16, 17, 19, 20); C3 (35, 36); C11; ARTC

Media: Oil, watercolor

Specialty: Landscapes

See artwork in color section

Edwin Fowle was a founding member of the first Society of Oregon Artists and a member of the Mutual Art Association, the Circle A Club, and the American Artists Professional League. He was president of the later Oregon Society of Artists in 1935.

Fowle worked in the impressionistic manner, and he produced many scenic views of the Manzanita and Neahkahnie areas on the Oregon Coast. He had a one-person show at the Seattle Art Museum and was represented in group shows at the Portland and Seattle Art Museums. Fowle signed his work, *EDM Fowle.*

FOWLER, Constance Edith

b. 1907 International Falls, MN

d. 1996 Oregon City, OR

Education: Washington State University: *McDermitt* (1929); University of Washington (30); University of Oregon: *Wilcox, A. Vincent** (40); Columbia University

Membership: American Artists Professional League; Oregon Society of Artists

Awards: Oregon Society of Artists (1934); American Artists Professional League (36–38); Seattle Art Museum (40, 42, 43, 44)

Collections: Oregon Historical Society; Portland Art Museum; Seattle Art Museum; Civic Center, Public Library, Mission Mill Museum, Capitol Collection—Salem; Hallie Ford Museum of Art—Willamette University; Washington State University

Exhibits: Oregon Society of Artists; Salem Library (1934); American Artists Professional League (34–38); Portland Art Museum (1PS 45); Seattle Art Museum; Willamette University (1PS 37, 39); Oregon State Fair (39); San Francisco Museum of Art (39, 43); Salem Federal Art Center (1PS 42); Bush Barn—Salem (45); Western Washington Fair; Oakland Museum; Coos Art Museum; Linfield College (59)

References: COL; KOV; WWN; A2 (1934, 40, 42, 44, 46); A3 (36–39); C3 (34); C7 (36–40, 42– 46); C8; C15 (46); C30 (46); M2; M3

Media: Watercolor, oil, prints (woodblock)

Specialty: Landscapes, seascapes, old houses

See artwork in color section

In 1923 the Fowler family moved to Pullman, Washington so that Constance and her younger sister, Margaret, could attend Washington State College (now Washington State University). Later, after a year at the University of Washington in Seattle, she moved with her family to California and then to a farm outside of Salem, Oregon, where she taught art privately. In 1935 she was hired to teach at Willamette University, where she rescued the art department and remained as chair until 1947. Fowler taught at Albion College in Michigan from 1947 to 1966. She also taught summer classes at Central Washington State College in 1949 and 1950. She was the recipient of three Carnegie Scholarships at the University of Oregon during the summers between 1936 and 1938.

Fowler's painted designs on lampshades brought her favorable attention in the Salem area. She exhibited woodblock prints of *Twenty Landmarks In and Around Salem* at the 1939 New York World's Fair. These were later published in a book entitled, *The Old Days: In and Near Salem.* The original woodblocks for these prints are in the collection of the Oregon Historical Society.

Constance Fowler was a well-recognized artist on the Northwest scene from 1936 to 1946. Her work was shown in major West Coast exhibitions and her canvases were acquired for collections throughout the Pacific Northwest. At that time Fowler's landscapes exhibited a subtle sense of color harmony and textural quality. A feeling of movement was evident through her expressive application of thick layers of paint. An article by Roger Hull in *Artifact* (November/December 1996) states, "she was rightly recognized as an artist genuinely expressive of the mood and poetry of the Northwest. More than most others, she sensed and expressed the turbulence and darkness of nature, as well." Fowler found the post-war art trends a challenge. She spent the latter part of her career experimenting with abstract, non-representational painting while continuing to implement the expressionism of her earlier works. She retired in 1965 and moved to Seal Rock, Oregon, where the ocean continued to inspire the abstract images she produced and exhibited there. Her papers are housed at the Hallie Ford Museum of Art at Willamette University.

FOWLER, George H.

b. d.

Membership: Mutual Art Association; Society of Oregon Artists

Collections: Hallie Ford Museum of Art—Willamette University

Exhibits: Portland Art Museum; Mutual Art Association (1914, 15)

References: A2 (1912); ARTC; CD (10, 12)

George Fowler, a member of the Mutual Art Association, exhibited in Portland from 1910 to 1915.

FOX, Nelly

b. d.

Exhibits: North Pacific Industrial Exposition (1889); Portland Art Museum

References: A2 (1913); C2 (1889)

Nelly Fox exhibited in the 1889 Industrial Exposition and at the Portland Art Museum.

FRIED, Otto

b. 1922 Koblenz, Germany ***d.***

Education: University of Oregon: *D. McCosh*, A. Vincent*, J. Wilkinson** (1949); France: *Léger* (49–51)

Collections: Metropolitan Museum of Art; University of Oregon; Portland Art Museum; Centre National d'Art et de Culture Georges Pompidou—Paris; Goodman Collection; Pacific Power and Light Collection; Tonkon Torp Collection; Arlene and Harold Schnitzer Collection; Hallie Ford Museum of Art—Willamette University

Exhibits: Kharouba Gallery (1949); Paris Salons—d'Automne (50), de Mai (51), de l'Armée (51); Reed College (1PS 52); Oregon Journal Building (1PS 52); University of Oregon (53, 75); Center Gallery—New York (55); Dayton Art Institute (56); Portland Art Museum (99)

References: C22

Media: Oil

Specialty: Landscapes, figures

After escaping from Nazi Germany as a child, Otto Fried grew up in Portland. In the initial twenty years of his artistic life he depicted first realistic, then abstract figures. When he turned to landscape painting, he used Oregon scenes. From 1951 to 1959 Fried exhibited in three Paris Salons and had seven solo shows. He created cubist works, then moved further into abstraction. Maintaining studios in Paris and New York, Fried continued his internationally acclaimed career.

FROHMAN, Anson (Hans) S.

b. 1888 Portland, OR
d. 1976 Portland, OR
Education: Museum Art School; *H. and C. Morris** (1953–55)
Membership: Portland Art Museum (Artist Membership); Artists Equity
Exhibits: Portland Art Museum; Oregon Centennial (1959)
References: A3 (1955, 58); C6
Media: Oil

An insurance agent, Anson Frohman was an enthusiastic amateur painter. He studied at the Museum Art School and with Hilda and Carl Morris*. He wrote about the joys of painting in an article for the Museum Art School Journal of September, 1954. He also served the Museum as a long-time board member.

FULLICK, Elizabeth

b. England *d.*
Education: Vassar College—Massachusetts
Exhibits: Portland Mechanics Fair
References: C4 (1883); M2
Media: Oil, watercolor, crayon, charcoal, pen and ink, pencil
Specialty: Landscapes, florals, genre

Elizabeth Fullick studied in eastern United States studios. She came to teach art at Portland's St. Helen's Hall in 1882.

FULTON, Cyrus James

*b.*1873 Pueblo, CO
d. 1949 Eugene, OR
Education: Museum Art School: *H. Wentz**; University of Oregon: *A. Schroff**
Membership: Circle A Club; Society of Oregon Artists; American Artists Professional League; Oregon Society of Artists
Awards: Oregon Society of Artists (1934, 35); American Artists Professional League (37, 38)
Collections: Powell Collection; Chamber of Commerce—Eugene; YWCA—Salem; YWCA—Eugene; Painting Restoration Studio Collection; Humpal Collection; Lundberg Collection; Parsons Collection
Exhibits: Circle A Club (1911); Society of Oregon Artists (12, 13); Portland Art Museum; Panama Pacific International Exposition—San Francisco (15); Seattle Art Museum; Oregon Society of Artists; American Artists Professional League (32, 36–38); J.K. Gill Gallery (1PS 38); Elfstrom Gallery (1PS 1940s); Lincoln County Art Center (46–48); Oakland Museum; Chamber of Commerce—Eugene (1PS); Clatsop County Historical Society (94)
References: BI; COL; DAW; FIE; HAV; MAL; WWN; WWW; YNG; A2 (1913, 14, 19–22, 32, 40, 42); C3 (29, 30, 34, 35, 48, 49); C5; C7 (20, 22); C10; C11; C13 (46–48); C14 (46–48); ARTC; CD (14)
Media: Oil
Specialty: Landscapes (storms), seascapes (ships), Indians
See artwork in color section
See photograph of artist on p. 82

A resident of Oregon since the age of three, Cyrus Fulton was known for painting expansive views of the state. He favored eastern Oregon vistas, the rolling surf of coast towns, and the Cascade mountains. His early canvases were painted in an impressionistic style using high key, bright colors and mellow sunlight. A haberdasher by profession, Fulton began doing his own sign lettering, window painting, and ad writing. He liked this graphic artwork so much that he set up a home studio and art shop on NE Sandy Boulevard in Portland. Unfortunately, his first venture as an artist did not suceed.

Fulton worked for the WPA, completing works in Salem and Eugene. From the 1930s on he adopted a modernist style. In 1935 he built a studio in Eugene and devoted himself to painting full-time until his death. In these final years, his style became bolder and his colors even brighter. He was a good friend of the Northwest Indians and was able to converse in several of their dialects. One of his most popular subjects was a portrayal of Native Americans in natural fishing and hunting scenes.

FURUYA, Kyuzo

b. 1888 Japan

d. 1929 Mt. Shuksan, WA

Membership: Oregon Society of Artists; Arts Guild; Society of Independent Artists—New York

Collections: Portland Art Museum

Exhibits: Portland Art Museum, posthumous (1PS 1930); Society of Independent Artists—New York (24, 25, 29); Seattle Art Museum; Portland Woman's Club (26); Salons of America (26, 27); Oregon Society of Artists; Oakland Art Gallery (28); Arts Guild

References: DAV; DAW; HUG; SA; SIA; A2 (1916, 17, 19, 21, 22); A4 (29, 59); A5 (30); C3 (27, 28); C7 (25)

Media: Oil, watercolor

Specialty: Still life, landscapes (mountains)

Kyuzo Furuya came to America in 1908. He began classes at the Museum Art School in 1918 and spent eleven years as a full or part-time student. In order to pay his tuiton, Furuya worked at a variety of jobs—on a railroad section gang, as a salad maker in a restaurant, and as a reporter on the *North America Times*, a Japanese language newspaper. Every summer he took to the road and the mountains to paint. His devotion to nature had a profound influence on the young artist, Charles Heaney*. Furuya loved the mountains and spent many hours climbing them. He died in a sudden blizzard, falling into the very crevasse he had recently sketched. He left a cache of work at his base camp in care of a friend which was exhibited after his death. An oil, *Still Life*, and a watercolor, *Mountains*, are in the Portland Art Museum Collection.

G

GALAHER, Bob

b. 1919 North Andover, MA *d.*
Education: Museum Art School (1946–50); Zurich
Membership: Artists Equity; Portland Art Museum (Artist Membership)
Awards: Library of Congress
Exhibits: Portland Art Museum; Harvey Welch Gallery (1950); Eugene (51) Library of Congress
References: OET; A3 (1953, 56)
Media: Oil, prints

Bob Galaher trained at the Museum Art School and continued his studies in Zurich. He, Rick Norwood*, and George Johanson* were selected to represent Oregon in a national traveling show of outstanding student artists of 1949. In his later years, Galaher concentrated on prints. He knew and admired C. S. Price*.

GANGLE, Martina. *See* CURL, Martina

GANTENBEIN, Rhoda. *See* ADAMS, Rhoda

GARDNER, Byron J.

b. 1930 Portland, OR
d. 1992 Oregon City, OR
Education: Museum Art School: *Bunce** (1948–52); Brooklyn Art Museum (53); Mexico City College (54)
Membership: Artists Equity; Portland Art Museum (Artist Membership)
Collections: Portland Art Museum; Coos Art Museum; University of Oregon; Oregon State University; Kaiser Permanente Collection; Parsons Collection; Arlene and Harold Schnitzer Collection; Catlin Gabel School Collection
Exhibits: Portland Art Museum (AM, 1PS 1959); Oakland Art Gallery (52); Seattle Art Museum; Reed College (56, 58; 1PS 57, 58); Morrison Street Gallery (1PS 57); New Gallery of Contemporary Art (59); Oregon Centennial (59)
References: ALM; A3 (1952–54, 56–58); A4 (52, 59); C6; C7 (52, 55, 59); C17
Media: Oil, watercolor, prints (etching, lithograph, woodcut)
Specialty: Landscapes, cityscapes, figures, abstracts
See artwork in color section

An art professor at Portland State University from 1967 to 1992, Byron Gardner was known for his landscapes of the American Southwest. He used a strong, bright palette to produce work that was poetic and lyrical. He was inspired by the western landscape to seek new relationships of form, color, and shape, first in Oregon's high desert country and then in Utah, Nevada, and New Mexico. His early work was figurative; later Gardner was one of Oregon's foremost abstract expressionist painters. In his middle years, his interest and proficiency in falconry was evidenced by the theme of flight expressed in his paintings.

Byron Gardner was one of the founding artists of the Portland Art Museum's Rental Sales Gallery in 1959. He maintained an affiliation with the gallery throughout his life.

GATCH, Helen (Nellie) Plummer

b. 1861 Alton, IL

d. 1942 Oakland, CA
Awards: Oregon State Fairs
Exhibits: Portland Mechanics Fairs; Oregon State Fairs; Oregon Historical Society (1990)
References: C4 (1879, 83); C9; OSF (85, 87–97, 1900, 03, 04, 09); M2; M3
Media: Oil, watercolor, and crayon
Specialty: Portraits, landscapes, seascapes

Nellie Gatch lived in Portland from 1864 to 1885. She married and moved to Salem, where she lived until 1912. She was a frequent exhibitor at the Portland Mechanics Fairs and the Oregon State Fairs. Her husband, Claude, was Mayor of Salem from 1893 to 1897. They moved to Berkeley, California in 1912.

She became interested in photography and won over eighty awards for her work, vying with Myra Wiggins* in both art and photography, locally and nationally. A photograph of her son, taken in 1900, inspired John Trullinger's* painting, *Sarah MacGregor West Removing Splinter from Tom Gatch's Foot.* Gatch was a member of the Salon Club of America, a photographic group that opposed the Photo-Secessionists, to which Wiggins* belonged.

GATENS, Helengray. *See* O'BRIEN, Helengray

GEER, Isabelle Trullinger

b. 1861 Oswego, OR
d. 1947 Portland, OR
Education: Museum Art School (1910); San Francisco
Membership: Oregon Art Association; Oregon Society of Artists
Awards: Oregon State Fairs
Collections: Oregon Historical Society
Exhibits: Oregon Art Association (1896); Oregon State Fairs; Oregon Society of Artists; Oregon Historical Society (1990)
References: C3 (1936); C9; ARTC; CD (1898); OSF (1900–06); M2; M3
Media: Watercolor
Spec Florals, landscapes

Isabelle Geer was a member of the first class of the Museum Art School. She was the sister of artists Paul and John Trullinger* and was married to T. T. Geer, Governor of Oregon.

GÉGOUX, Théodore

b. 1850 St. Louis de Gonzaque, Quebec, Montreal, Canada
d. 1931 Downey, CA
Education: Paris, France
Collections: Oregon Historical Society; Booth Collection; Champoeg Visitor's Center; Jefferson County Historical Society, Public Library—Watertown, New York; Keewaydin State Park—Alexandria Bay, New York
Exhibits: Carnegie Exhibition—Pittsburgh (1896); Oregon Historical Society (1917)
References: DAV; GER; M1
Media: Oil, crayon, pastel
Specialty: Portraits, still life, seascapes, landscapes, florals
See artwork in color section

Canadian by birth, Théodore Gégoux trained in Paris by studying and copying the French masters. He returned to America in 1879 and set up a studio in Watertown, New York, where he specialized in portraits. He exhibited his work, *A Young Paganini,* at the first Carnegie Exhibition in Pittsburgh, Pennsylvania in November 1896. Gégoux moved to Portland in 1909 and opened a studio in the Gleall Castle the following year. His most renowned work from this period was *The Portland Rose,* completed in 1911, featuring a woman arranging roses in the foreground and a view of Mt. Hood in the distance. By 1913 he had moved to Santa Monica, California. There he continued painting portraits and began a series on the mayors of Portland, aided by photos supplied by the Oregon Historical Society. Gégoux returned to Portland with the completed series of twenty-nine portraits of the early mayors and consigned them to George Himes at the Historical Society, where they remain.

In 1916 Gégoux established a studio in Aurora, Oregon at the Old Jette Saloon. He began sketches of what was to be his masterpiece, *The Inception of the Birth of Oregon.* It depicted the historic vote to form Oregon's first provisional government in Champoeg, 1843. Again, aided by photographs of some of the participants, he was able to recreate the original occasion with a large degree of realism. Surviving a near disaster when his studio burned, Gégoux rescued the painting and moved to the Memorial House at Champoeg, where he exchanged caretaking duties for the right to exhibit his paintings. *The Inception of the Birth of Oregon* was completed in 1923 and a year later the artist and his son, Frank, completed the frame. Frustrated at not finding a buyer for the painting, Gégoux moved to Highland Park, California in late 1924. His son Frank continued efforts to sell the work with an unveiling at the Governor's office in 1925, followed by viewings at the US Bank and the Library Association. It was warehoused for over forty years before finally being sold and hung in its rightful place in Champoeg in 1979. Gégoux died in July 1931, penniless and without the fame he had sought and deserved.

GEISER, Bernard F., Rev.

b. 1887 Geuda Springs, KS

d. 1965 Portland, OR

Education: Pennsylvania Academy of Fine Art—Philadelphia; University of Oregon: *A. Vincent**; Museum Art School: *W. Givler**

Membership: American Artists Professional League; Artists Equity; Oregon Society of Artists; Oregon Guild of Painters and Sculptors; Portland Art Museum (Artist Membership)

Collections: Portland Art Museum; Powell Collection; Seattle Art Museum; Pathways Collection; Riley Collection

Exhibits: American Artists Professional League (1936); Portland Art Museum; National Exhibition of American Art (38); Seattle Art Museum; Oregon Guild of Painters and Sculptors (48); Henry Art Gallery—University of Washington (51); Denver Art Museum; Oregon Centennial (59); Clatsop County Historical Society (94)

References: ALM; COL; DAV; DAW; HAV; MAL SUP; WWN; WWW; A2 (1940, 42, 44, 46); A3 (36, 39, 49, 51, 53); C6; C7 (46, 47, 49; 52); C11; C15 (46); C30 (46)

Media: Oil, tempera, watercolor

Specialty: Landscapes, religious murals

See artwork in color section

Bernard Geiser was a professional artist before his ordination as an Episcopal priest in 1924. He had attended the Pennsylvania Academy of Fine Arts and, while in France in World War I, painted murals in the base hospital in Périgueux. He later headed the art department at Western State College in Colorado. He arrived in Portland in 1931. While assigned to St. Marks Church, he completed a series of eleven murals and exhibited paintings there. Geiser commented, "I gave up art for the Church and somehow the Church gave it back." He attended the University of Oregon in 1939 on a Carnegie Scholarship. He exchanged ideas and paintings with friends Charles Heaney* and Hank Kowert* over the years. They attended his memorial exhibition at Forest Grove's Valley Art Association. He was active in local art circles from his arrival in the 1930s until his death.

GELLERT, Samuel M., M.D.

b. 1884 Concord, CA
d. 1951 Portland, OR
Membership: Oregon Society of Artists; American Physician's Art Association
Awards: San Francisco Museum of Art (1938)
Exhibits: Oregon Society of Artists; American Artists Professional League (1933, 34); San Francisco Museum of Art (38)
References: ALM; COL; DAV; DAW; HUG; WWN; C3 (1932)
Media: Oil

Samuel Gellert lived in the Irvington neighborhood of Portland. He was a former officer of the American Physicians Art Association. He painted in his leisure time, depicting a variety of subjects. He instituted art classes at the Neighborhood House, a community center in Portland.

GERLACH, Albert Antony

b. 1884 Chicago, IL
d. 1974 Portland, OR
Education: Art Institute of Chicago
Membership: Oregon Society of Artists; American Artists Professional League
Collections: Powell Collection; Lundberg Collection
Exhibits: Oregon Society of Artists; American Artists Professional League (1932)
References: ALM; BEN; BI; COL; DAV; DAW; HAV; HUG; MAL; OET; WWN; WWW; YNG; C3 (1928–34, 46)
Media: Oil, watercolor, stained glass
Specialty: Landscapes, portraits

Albert Gerlach was best known for his stained glass work in Portland churches and Temple Beth Israel. After arriving in Portland, Gerlach worked for Povey Glass for two years and W.P. Fuller Glass for the next twenty-three years. Upon retirement in 1950, Gerlach worked from his home. He was president of the Oregon Society of Artists in 1933 and 1955.

GERMAIN, Harriet Meyer

b. 1909 Portland, OR ***d.***
Education: Mills College—Oakland; University of Oregon (1931)
Membership: American Artists Professional League; University Alumni Art League, University of Oregon
Exhibits: University of Oregon (1931); American Artists Professional League (32, 33); Portland Art Museum; University Alumni Art League
References: A2 (1933); C25 (36)
Media: Oil
Specialty: Portraits

Under her maiden name, Harriet Meyer taught privately and maintained a gallery on SW Summit Drive in Portland. She exhibited at the University of Oregon and the Portland Art Museum. She moved to California after 1936 and began to specialize in sculpture.

GIBBS, Katherine A.

b. d.
Membership: Oregon Art Association
Exhibits: Portland Mechanics Fair; North Pacific Industrial Exposition (1889); Portland Industrial Exposition (91); Oregon Art Association (96)
References: C2 (1889, 91); C4 (85); ARTC; CD (1898–1903); M2; M3
Media: Oil
Specialty: Still life, florals

Katherine Gibbs had a studio in Portland from 1889 to 1906. Her work was shown in the Portland Mechanics Fair and the Industrial Expositions. She signed her work *Kate Gibbs.*

GILBERT, Carrie Monroe

b. d.
Awards: Oregon State Fair
Collections: Oregon Historical Society;

Oregon State University
Exhibits: Oregon State Fair
References: OSF (1889); M2
Media: Oil, watercolor
Specialty: Portraits

Carrie Gilbert was known for oil portraits of Indian chiefs painted on rawhide. She illustrated her husband's book, *The Way of the Indian*, copyrighted in 1902. The J.C. Gilberts lived in Salem.

GILBERT, Ralph

b. 1884 Salem, OR
d. 1965 Salem, OR
Education: *Myers*
Membership: Oregon Society of Artists; Rembrandt Artists Guild
Awards: Oregon State Fair (1937)
Exhibits: Portland Art Museum; Carmel Art Gallery (1927); Seattle Art Museum; Salem Library (1PS 35); Oregon State Fair (37); Salem Federal Art Center (1PS 40)
References: COL; DAV; DAW; WWN; A2 (1919, 21, 22, 40); C7 (28, 29)
Media: Oil
Specialty: Landscapes

Ralph Gilbert came from a family of artists, including brother Roman Monroe Gilbert*. He exhibited his oil paintings at the Portland and Seattle Art Museums, the Oregon State Fair, in Salem at the Library and Art Center, and the Carmel Art Gallery in California. He was a member of the Rembrandt Artists Guild in Salem.

GILBERT, Roman Monroe

b. 1876 Salem, OR
d. 1959 Salem, OR
Membership: Salem Art League
Exhibits: Portland Art Museum; Seattle Art Museum; Oregon State Fair
References: A2 (1920); C7 (22)
Media: Oil
Specialty: Landscapes

Roman Monroe Gilbert owned an art shop in Salem. He and his wife, Myrtle, helped found the Salem Art League. Gilbert produced a book of pen and ink drawings during the Spanish-American War. He often signed his work *R. Monroe Gilbert*. His brother was Ralph Gilbert*.

GILBERT, Warren H.

b. Salem, OR *d.*
Education: Willamette University
Membership: Oregon Society of Artists
Awards: Oregon State Fairs
Exhibits: Oregon State Fairs; Oregon Society of Artists
References: C3 (1928–30); OSF (1888, 90, 92, 94, 95)
Media: Oil, watercolor, prints (etching)
Specialty: Landscapes, seascapes, portraits, history

After working as a cartoonist for the *Kansas City Post* and the *Denver Post*, Warren Gilbert returned to live and work in Eugene. His oils and watercolors were exhibited in the Oregon State Fairs and with the Oregon Society of Artists.

GILBERT, Dorothy. *See* WILSON, Dorothy

GILL, John

b. 1851 Holmfirth, England
d. 1929 Portland, OR
Membership: Portland Art Club; Portland Sketch Club
Exhibits: Portland Art Club (1886); Portland Sketch Club (99)
References: ARTC; M1

At age three John Gill arrived in America with his family. They settled on the East Coast, where he later served as a printer's apprentice. He came to Portland and was one of the founders of the J.K. Gill Stationers Stores, where art exhibition space was made available. In addition to his art work, Gill was a talented amateur musician and well known as an expert fisherman.

GILL, Margaret

b. d.
Education: Willamette University: *M. LeGall** (1905); Cooper Union—New York City; Pratt Institute; Art Students League (12)
Awards: Oregon State Fairs
Collections: Oregon Historical Society
Exhibits: Oregon State Fairs
References: OSF (1904, 08, 09)
Media: Oil, watercolor, china painting
Specialty: Landscape

Margaret Gill began her art training at Willamette University under Marie Craig LeGall* and continued in New York City at Cooper Union, the Pratt Institute, and the Art Students League. While Gill did make use of more traditional media, she was known for her china painting. She was listed in the artist section of the Salem City Directory in 1909 and served as teacher at Willamette University from 1910 to 1912. There may have been another artist named Margaret Gill living in Salem at about the same time; one of them was known as Greta Gill.

GILMORE, Norma Driscoll

b. 1927 Great Falls, MT ***d.***
Education: University of Oregon: *J. Wilkinson*, D. McCosh*, A. Vincent** (1950); San Francisco
Membership: Portland Art Museum (Artist Membership)
Exhibits: Maryhill Museum—Goldendale, Washington; California Palace of the Legion of Honor—San Francisco (1947); University of Oregon; Seattle Art Museum; Pepsi Cola International
References: C7 (1947, 53, 54)

Norma Driscoll lived in Eugene and married artist Robert Gilmore*. They were friends of artist Vernon Witham* and lived and worked together in San Francisco in the early 1950s. She was influenced by cave paintings, Cézanne, and the logic of the ancient Greek philosophers. She painted in a cubist style and, with Vernon Witham* and Paul Georges, was one of three Oregon artists to appear in a juried show at the California Palace of the Legion of Honor in 1947.

GILMORE, Robert

b. 1923 Pocatello, ID ***d.***
Education: University of Oregon: *J. Wilkinson*, D. McCosh*, A. Vincent** (1946–54)
Exhibits: Portland Art Museum
References: A3 (1950, 53); C7 (54)
Media: Oil

Robert Gilmore began his artistic career after brief stays in Mexico and California. His work was influenced, he said, by classical and modern thought. "Built on a tradition of beauty...he paints in the style of Picasso, Cézanne and Titian". He showed his oil paintings at the Portland and Seattle Art Museums and presented gift paintings to Dwight Eisenhower, John Kennedy, and Igor Stravinsky. Gilmore was married to artist Norma Driscoll*.

GIVLER, William Hubert

b. 1908 Omaha, NE ***d.***
Education: Museum Art School; Art Students League
Membership: Artists Equity; American Artists' Congress; Oregon Guild of Painters and Sculptors; Arts Guild; Portland Art Museum (Artist Membership)
Awards: Portland Art Museum (1938); Seattle Art Museum (39)
Collections: IBM; Portland Art Museum; Seattle Art Museum; Philadelphia Art Museum; Reed College; Oregon State University; Museum of Modern Art; Victoria and Albert Museum—London; Bibliothèque

Nationale—Paris; University of Oregon; Hallie Ford Museum of Art—Willamette University; Mills College—Oakland; Kaiser Permanente Collection; Booth Collection; Timberline Lodge Collection; Huntington Collection; Riley Collection

Exhibits: Portland Art Museum (3PS 1936; AM, 1PS 57); Creative Art Gallery (33); Arts Guild; Seattle Art Museum (4PS 53); American Artists' Congress (37); Golden Gate International Exposition—San Francisco (39–40); New York World's Fair (39); Salem Federal Art Center; Pennsylvania Academy of Fine Art—Philadelphia (41); San Francisco Museum of Art (43); Western Washington Fair; Oregon Guild of Painters and Sculptors (1PS 48); Henry Art Gallery—University of Washington (51); Reed College (1PS 52); Kharouba Gallery (1PS 52); Portland State University (58); Victoria and Albert Museum—London; National Academy of Design; Metropolitan Museum of Art; Whitney Museum of Art; Oregon Centennial (59); Oregon Historical Society (90)

References: ALM; COL; DAV; HAV; OET; WWN; WWW; A2 (1932–34, 40, 42, 44, 46); A3 (35, 36, 38, 39, 49–56); A4 (59); A5 (33); C6; C7 (34–36, 39, 40, 46, 47, 52, 54); C8; C9; C10; C15 (34, 46); C27; C30 (46); CD (40)

Media: Oil, tempera, pastel, prints (lithograph, etching)

Specialty: Landscapes (coastal scenes)

See artwork in color section

William Givler was one of the most influential artists and teachers in Oregon. He devoted forty-two years to the Museum Art School, beginning in 1931 as an instructor, interrupted by service as a forester during World War II, and then as dean from 1944 until his retirement in 1973. He established the four-year degree program and secured accreditation for the school. In 1949 Givler inaugurated the first Print Annual at the Portland Art Museum.

In 1953 Givler, Carl Hall*, Louis Bunce*, and Carl Morris* exhibited in a four-person show at the Seattle Art Museum. He had many one-person shows throughout the United States during his long career: Seattle Art Museum, Portland Art Museum, Santa Barbara Museum of Art, University of Virginia, and others. In 1959 Givler painted an oil, *Mt. Hood,* for Timberline Lodge.

Givler's work was rooted in nature, primarily dealing with landscapes or figures in environments. His canvases were comparatively small in scale and contemplative in nature. He was sensitive to the essential forms of his chosen visual subjects and composed and organized his work carefully. Many paintings were romantic in feeling, filled with the brooding blues and greens of the Oregon Coast. The freedom and vitality of his brushwork helped convey the drama he saw in the forms of the Northwest landscape. In later years he developed an interest in printmaking and achieved further success in that medium.

GLEASON, Clifford Leon

b. 1913 Portland, OR

d. 1978 Portland, OR

Education: Salem Federal Art Center: *L. Bunce**; University of Oregon Extension: *A. Vincent**; Museum Art School (1939–41); Paris: *Léger* (53–54)

Membership: Artists Equity; Oregon Guild of Painters and Sculptors; Portland Art Museum (Artist Membership)

Collections: Portland Art Museum; Lewis and Clark College; University of Oregon; Hallie Ford Museum of

Art—Willamette University; Parsons Collection

Exhibits: Salem Federal Art Center (1938); Portland Art Museum (AM, 1PS 55); Oregon Guild of Painters and Sculptors (48; 2PS 48); Kharouba Gallery (49); Harvey Welch Gallery; Capitol building—Salem; Oregon Centennial (59)

References: A2 (1940, 42, 46); A3 (54, 58); C6

Media: Oil, watercolor

Specialty: Nature, landscape

See artwork in color section

As a WPA artist, Clifford Gleason worked with Louis Bunce* to create a mural for the Bush Elementary School in Salem. His study with Bunce at the Salem Federal Art Center helped orient him to Modernism. He owned the Clifford Gleason Studio and Art Gallery in Salem in the mid 1950s. He displayed his work in the Marion County Health Building. Gleason had three one-person shows at the Portland Art Museum. He exhibited widely in Oregon and his works were housed in more than fifty public and private collections.

Gleason was one of Oregon's true Modernists. He was a gifted colorist, whose abstractions were based on nature. His surfaces were softly textured, the simple forms often isolated in empty space. Although he used muted color early in his career, later works showed more brilliant color.

GOODWIN, Richard LaBarre

b. 1840 Albany, NY

d. 1910 Orange, NJ

Education: Rhode Island School of Design; Art Students League

Collections: National Museum of American Art; Stanford University

Exhibits: Lewis and Clark Centennial Exposition (1905); Oregon State Fair; Commercial Club—Portland (08)

References: BI; DAV; DAW; FIE; GER; GW; HUG; SAM; SMI; WWW; YNG; OSF (1907)

Media: Oil

Specialty: Still life (game, fish), portraits, landscapes

Richard Goodwin was an itinerent portrait painter from the East. His most famous work was *Theodore Roosevelt's Cabin Door*, a widely exhibited piece. Goodwin was known for his technical skill and his harmonious landscapes. He painted views of the autumn woods of Oregon and the mill race at Eugene.

GORDON, Charles S.

b. 1879 Cincinnati, OH

d. 1965 Portland, OR

Membership: Oregon Society of Artists; American Artists Professional League; Attic Club

Awards: American Artists Professional League (1932); Oregon Society of Artists (33, 38)

Collections: Oregon Historical Society; Portland Customs House

Exhibits: Seattle Art Museum; Oregon Society of Artists; Portland Art Museum; American Artists Professional League (1932, 33, 37, 39)

References: COL; OET; WWN; A2 (1932, 40, 46); A3 (53); C3 (29–31, 33, 34, 36, 38, 45–51); C7 (27); C10; CD (16, 18)

Media: Oil, watercolor

Specialty: Portraits, landscapes

Charles S. Gordon was a WPA painter and, later, a commercial artist. He was a member of the Oregon Society of Artists, the Attic Club, and the American Artists Professional League, whose paintings were shown at the Portland and Seattle Art Museums. He won many awards at Oregon State and County Fairs. Gordon's illustrations were used by H. L. Mencken in his poetry collection, *Ventures in Verse.*

GORHAM, Aimee Spencer

b. 1883 St. Paul, MN
d. 1974 Seattle, WA
Education: Pratt Institute: *Parsons* (1912); University of Oregon
Membership: Society of Oregon Artists; Oregon Society of Artists; American Artists Professional League; Skidmore Fountain Art Center, Inc.
Exhibits: Society of Oregon Artists (1913); Portland Art Museum; Panama Pacific International Exposition—San Francisco (15); Oregon Society of Artists; Oregon Historical Society (90)
References: ALM; COL; OET; WWN; A2 (1914, 21, 33); C3 (27); C5; C9; C10; ARTC; CD (43–44); M2
Media: Oil, stained glass, wood, mosaic

In addition to painting, WPA artist Aimee Gorham worked as a book illustrator, mural artist, and sculptor. She was known for her marquetry, which she exhibited at the 1939 New York World's Fair and the 1939 Golden Gate Exposition. Examples of her marquetry can be seen at Timberline Lodge, Oregon State University, the Chapman School, and various churches and schools in Portland. Many sources state the date and place of Gorham's death as Portland in 1974, but Kovinick (see Ref. KOV) refers to Seattle in 1973.

GRAFSTROM, Jonas Olof

b. 1855 Attmar, Sweden
d. 1933 Stockholm, Sweden
Education: Academy of Fine Arts—Stockholm (1882)
Awards: Portland Mechanics Fair (1887)
Collections: M.H. DeYoung Museum—San Francisco; Painting Restoration Studio Collection; King Oscar II—Norway-Sweden
Exhibits: Portland Mechanics Fairs; North Pacific Industrial Exposition (1889)
References: BEN; BI; DAV; DAW; GER; THI; C2 (1889); C4 (87, 89)
Media: Oil
Specialty: Landscapes, portraits, religious, fresco

Olof Grafstrom's father wanted him to remain in Sweden and become a farmer, but the Stockholm-trained artist came to Portland in 1886 to pursue his art career. There was a large Scandinavian community in Portland and he found the local scenery to be much like that of his homeland. He had exhibited successfully in Sweden, producing several hundred altar pieces, and one of his paintings was in the collection of the royal family of Norway-Sweden.

Grafstrom exhibited in the Portland Mechanics Fair of 1887, where he won an award. He also exhibited in the Industrial Fair of 1889. His oil paintings evidenced a link between his old-world aesthetics and the artistic tastes of the people of the American Northwest. He also painted frescoes in local saloons. In 1890 he moved to Spokane, Washington and then to San Francisco in 1891.

Grafstrom began his teaching career at Bethany College in Kansas in the 1890s. He then moved to Rock Island, Illinois, where he became head of the art department at Augustana (Swedish-American) College for twenty-nine years. During this time he produced oil paintings and executed many commissions for church altar pieces. He retired in 1926 at age 71 and returned to Sweden for his remaining years.

Grafstrom maintained his close ties to the Scandinavian communities which continued to offer him friendship and financial support through art commissions for portraits and religious pieces. One good example was the altar piece for the Bethany Lutheran Church in Warren, Oregon, commissioned in the early 1920s.

GRELLERT, Paul J.

b. 1916 Breslau, Germany ***d.***
Education: Museum Art School
Membership: Portland Art Museum (Artist Membership)
Collections: Medical Service Club—Manila, Philippines
Exhibits: Portland Art Museum
References: COL; DAV; HAV; MAL SUP; WWN; WWW; A2 (1940); A3 (54); CD (40)
Media: Oil, prints (etching)

Paul Grellert's work appears in the collection of the Manila Medical Service Club in the Philippines. As a WPA artist he produced a mural for the East Portland Post Office entitled *Post Rider.* Grellert was also a sculptor.

GRIER, Auda Fay

b. 1898 Geary, MI ***d.***
Education: University of Oregon; *M. Wanker**
Membership: Oregon Society of Artists; American Artists Professional League
Awards: Oregon Society of Artists (1938)
Exhibits: Portland Art Museum; Oregon Society of Artists
References: COL; DAV; DAW; WWN; A2 (1933, 40); C3 (34, 38)
Media: Oil

Auda Grier studied at the University of Oregon and privately with Maude Wanker*. Her oil paintings were displayed at the Portland Art Museum and with the Oregon Society of Artists.

GRIFFIN, Rachael Smith

b. 1906 Portland, OR
d. 1983 Portland, OR
Education: Museum Art School; University of Oregon: *Pelton, Steinhof;* Reed College
Membership: Artists Equity; Arts Guild
Awards: Artists Equity (1959)
Collections: Oregon Historical Society
Exhibits: Portland Art Museum; Arts Guild; Creative Art Gallery (1933); Dekum Gallery; Oregon Historical Society (90)
References: WWN; A2 (1930, 32, 33); A3 (36); A4 (36, 59); A5 (30, 33); C9; C10; M2
Media: Watercolor, oil
Specialty: Portraits, florals

For forty-one years Rachael Griffin had a strong association with the Portland Art Museum. She hosted a Sunday morning radio program, *At the Art Museum*, for twenty years. It was credited with increasing the awareness of the Museum, its art, and artists for more than one generation. She joined the Museum staff in 1950 as an information assistant, edited art catalogues, and wrote about northwest artists. Her essay in the catalogue *Art of the Pacific Northwest from the 30's to the Present* is the major document on artists of that period. She remained on staff as curator until her retirement in 1974.

Griffin exhibited watercolors and sculpture at the Museum, the Creative Art Gallery, and the Dekum Gallery in the early 1930s. Her portrait of George Himes, founding director of the Oregon Historical Society, remains in their collection. She curated exhibitions and collections and helped secure the Gebauer Collection of Cameroon Art for the Portland Art Museum. Her main interest was in contemporary art in all forms. She worked to publicize and encourage younger Oregon artists.

She was active in the restoration project of Timberline Lodge, serving as chairman of their art committee. In this capacity she was instrumental in the renovation and acquisition of art in this historic WPA lodge on the western slopes of Mt. Hood.

GRISWOLD, Jennie Montague

b. d.
Membership: Oregon Art Association
Exhibits: Oregon Industrial Exposition (1895); Oregon Art Association (96)
References: DAV; HUG; PET; C2 (1895); ARTC; CD (1895–1900)
Specialty: Portraits

Jennie Griswold had an art studio in the Marquam Building. One of her paintings, *Cup of Tea*, received favorable notices when exhibited in the 1895 Industrial Exposition. She moved to Los Angeles in 1903. Petteys (see Ref. PET) lists an artist by the same name who was active in Washington D.C. from 1908 to 1914, exhibiting with the Society of Washington Artists and the Cosmos Club. It could possibly be the same person.

GROTHJEAN, Francesca C.R.

b. 1865 Hamburg, Germany
d. 1945 Portland, OR
Education: Paris: *Courtois, Girard;* Denmark
Membership: Society of Oregon Artists
Awards: Portland Mechanics Fair (1883); Oregon State Fair; Paris Exposition Universelle (1915)
Collections: Jake's Famous Crawfish Restaurant—Portland
Exhibits: Portland Mechanics Fairs; Paris Salons; Oregon State Fair; World Columbian Exposition—Chicago (1893); Portland Art Museum; National Academy of Design
References: BEN; DAV; DAW; FI (1893); GER; KOV; PET; THI; WWW; A1 (1902, 06); C4 (1882, 85); CD (89, 1903–13, 15–18, 40, 41, 43–4); OSF (1893); M1; M2
Media: Oil
Specialty: Portraits, marines, landscapes
See artwork in color section

Francesca Grothjean was one of the notable women artists of Oregon at the turn of the century. Accounts differ as to whether she was born in Denmark or Germany, and whether the year was 1863 or 1865. She came to Portland as a young child and began her education there before traveling to Paris to complete her studies. She exhibited at the Paris Salons of 1893 and 1900 and received a special award at the Paris Exposition in 1915. Grothjean's best-known works included portraits, marine oils, and landscapes. She completed the *Portland Hotel Under Construction* when she was quite young. The painting is now owned by and proudly displayed in Jake's Famous Crawfish Restaurant in Portland. Grothjean devoted her final years to a project that her brother Edward had started—artwork illustrating the principles for which America stands. They developed posters to be displayed in city schools and to be given to newly naturalized citizens.

GROVER, John Cuvier

b. 1865 Portland, OR
d. 1930 Pendleton, OR
Education: Paris: *Grutheirn, Laurens* (1887–92)
Membership: Oregon Art Association; Portland Sketch Club
Exhibits: Portland Industrial Exposition (1892); Oregon Industrial Exposition (95); Oregon Art Association (96); Portland Sketch Club (99)
References: C2 (1892, 95); ARTC; CD (1899–1904, 11–18)
Media: Oil
Specialty: Portraits

John Grover received his art education in Paris. He was best known for a portrait of his father, a former Governor of Oregon. Grover was also a sculptor. The Oregon Historical Society has one of his sculptures (a medallion) of his father in its collection. He exhibited in the Industrial Expositions and with the

Oregon Artists Association and the Portland Sketch Club in the 1890s. Grover became mentally ill and lived in Portland, as a recluse, with his mother. He developed a fear of people viewing his work and painted over a canvas as soon as he completed it. As a result, most of his work was lost. After his mother's death, it appears he may have been committed to a mental hospital in Pendleton, where he died.

GROVER, Ruth Dennis

b. 1912 Portland, OR ***d.***
Education: University of Michigan; Detroit Institute of the Arts
Membership: Oregon Society of Artists; Cascade Artists Group; Oregon Amateur Watercolor Society; Master Watercolor Society of Oregon
Collections: Oregon Historical Society; Coos Art Museum; Goodman Collection; University of Oregon; Haseltine Collection; Hallie Ford Museum of Art—Willamette University
Exhibits: Portland Art Museum; Oregon Society of Artists; Lincoln County Art Center (1948, 49); Cascade Artists Group; Master Watercolor Society of Oregon (58); Seattle Art Museum; Dekum Gallery; University of Oregon (75)
References: A2 (1944, 46, 48); C3 (48, 49); C7 (59); C14; C22; ARTC; M2
Media: Watercolor, acrylic, encaustic
Specialty: Birds, landscapes (coastal scenes)
See artwork in color section

Ruth Grover, a fifth generation Oregonian, was born in Portland and grew up in Detroit, Michigan, where she studied at the Detroit Institute of Art. She settled on the Oregon Coast in 1940. There she began teaching at the Lincoln County Art Center, which she and Maude Wanker* established. She also taught at DeLake Grade School in Lincoln City. A watercolorist, she was a member of the Oregon Amateur Watercolor Society and the Master Watercolor Society of Oregon.

In 1952 Grover established the Cascade Artists Group, a cooperative that organized exhibitions of members' work. This group sponsored shows at their gallery as well as traveling exhibitions along the West Coast. She served as director of the Cascade Art Gallery. Later in her career, Grover became interested in the media of encaustic. Most of these works were abstractions based on natural patterns and forms, including those of rocks she had collected and polished over the years. Grover's papers are housed at the Hallie Ford Museum of Art archive at Willamette University.

GRUHLER, Jesse

b. d.
Membership: American Artists Professional League; Oregon Society of Artists
Awards: Oregon Society of Artists (1932, 34)
Exhibits: Oregon Society of Artists; American Artists Professional League (1932, 33); Seattle Art Museum; Portland Art Museum; Oakland Art Gallery (40)
References: DAV; HUG; A2 (1933); C3 (27, 32, 33, 35); C7 (32)
Media: Oil
Specialty: Landscapes, portraits, genre

Jesse Gruhler, a member of the American Artists Professional League and the Oregon Society of Artists, exhibited in Oregon and Washington in the 1930s. She showed at the Oakland Art Gallery after her move to Oakland in 1940.

GUNN, Paul James

b. 1922 Guys Mills, PA ***d.***
Education: Edinboro State Teachers

College—Pennsylvania (1947); California College of Arts and Crafts (48)
Membership: Portland Art Museum (Artist Membership)
Awards: Spokane (1954, 56); Seattle Art Museum (54)
Collections: Portland Art Museum; Seattle Art Museum; Cheney Cowles Museum—Spokane, Washington; Victoria and Albert Museum—London; Oregon State University
Exhibits: Seattle Art Museum; Portland Art Museum (AM, 1PS 1953); Oakland Museum (51, 56); Spokane (54, 56); Albany (IPS 58); Oregon Centennial (59)
References: HAV; WWAA; A3 (1951–56, 58); C6; C7 (51, 54, 56, 59)
Media: Watercolor, oil, prints
Specialty: Northwest landscapes, seascapes

After serving in the Navy from 1943 to 1946, Paul Gunn completed his education and art training at Edinboro State Teacher's College in Pennsylvania and the California College of Arts and Crafts. He came to Oregon to teach art at Oregon State College (now Oregon State University), where he became chairman of the art department in 1964. Gunn exhibited frequently at the Portland and Seattle Art Museums. In 1948 he began to concentrate on printmaking. He received several awards at the annual Northwest Artist Exhibits from 1950 to 1956.

GUSTAFSON, Vesta Lorene Wells

b. 1901 Russell, IA
d. 1982 Portland, OR
Education: Museum Art School
Membership: Oregon Society of Artists; Arts Guild
Awards: Oregon Society of Artists (1931, 37)
Collections: Medford High School
Exhibits: Oregon Society of Artists; Seattle Art Museum; Portland Art Museum; Arts Guild;
References: COL; WWN; A2 (1930, 33); A3 (35–37); A5 (30, 33); C3 (27–33); C7 (29); C10; C11; M2
Media: Oil, watercolor
Specialty: Florals, landscapes

Vesta Gustafson was a scholarship student at the Museum Art School in Portland from 1927 to 1929. She was a poet, WPA artist, and worked as a tinter for a photography shop. She was a member of the Arts Guild and the Oregon Society of Artists. Gustafson exhibited at the Portland and Seattle Art Museums.

H

HABERSHAM, Richard P.

b. 1859 Atkin, SC
d. 1933 Portland, OR
Education: U.S. Naval Academy (1873)
Membership: Portland Art Club
Collections: Painting Restoration Studio Collection; Parsons Collection
Exhibits: Portland Art Club (1885, 86); Oregon Industrial Expositions (95, 96); Washington State Capitol Museum (1988); Maryhill Museum—Goldendale, Washington (93)
References: DAV; C2 (1895, 96); C24; ARTC; CD (86); MYH
Media: Oil
Specialty: Landscapes (mountains), genre, still life

Richard Habersham was a civil engineer, working with the railroads as early as 1888. He was a charter member of the Portland Art Club. Habersham exhibited at the Oregon Industrial Expositions.

HAGERUP, Nielson (Nels) J.

b. 1864 Christiana, Norway
d. 1922 San Francisco, CA
Education: Christiana Art School—Norway; Royal Academy of Arts—Berlin
Membership: Oregon Art Association
Awards: Lewis and Clark Centennial Exposition (1905); Alaska-Yukon Pacific Exposition (09)
Collections: Oregon Historical Society; M.H. DeYoung Museum—San Francisco; Oakland Museum; California Historical Society; Public Library—San Bruno, California; Painting Restoration Studio Collection
Exhibits: North Pacific Industrial Exposition (1889, 90); Portland Industrial Exposition (92); Oregon Art Association (96); Lewis and Clark Centennial Exposition (1905); Alaska-Yukon Pacific Exposition; Oregon Historical Society (90)
References: DAV; DAW; GER; HUG; BI; C2 (1889, 90, 92); C9; ARTC; CD (89, 91, 93–97)
Media: Oil, prints (engraving)
Specialty: Marines (boats), seascapes (harbors), landscapes, cityscapes, florals, portraits, still life

Nels Hagerup, a merchant seaman, settled in Portland in 1882. He became an instructor of drawing at Bishop Scott Academy from the late 1880s until 1892. He was one of the founding members of the Oregon Art Association in 1895. Two years later he moved to San Francisco, where he worked as a stevedore and established a home and studio in that city's Sunset district. Hagerup painted nearly six thousand oils of ship and marine scenes. Hughes (see Ref. HUG) calls him "a master of atmospheric seascapes." Reproductions of his work appear in *Oregon The Picturesque* by Thomas Murphy. He signed his work *Nels* or *Nils Hagerup.*

HAINES, Mabel. *See* OSTER, Mabel

HALEY, Sally

b. 1908 Bridgeport, CN *d.*
Education: Yale (1931); Munich: *Maxon* (33–34)
Membership: Artists Equity; Portland Art Museum (Artist Membership)
Collections: Portland Civic Auditorium;

Portland Art Museum; Oregon Historical Society; Multnomah Athletic Club Collection; Booth Collection; Tonkon Torp Collection; Kaiser Permanente Collection; Capitol Collection—Salem; Hallie Ford Museum of Art—Willamette University; Oregon State University; Arlene and Harold Schnitzer Collection; Hurst Collection; Huntington Collection; Riley Collection

Exhibits: Harvey Welch Gallery (1PS 1947, 52, 59); San Francisco Museum of Art (49); Portland Art Museum; Denver Art Museum (52, 56, 57); Walker Art Center—Minneapolis (54); Portland State University; University of Portland; Ruthermore Gallery—San Francisco (59); Oregon Centennial (59); Oregon Historical Society (90)

References: ALM; DAV; HAV; WWW; A3 (1949, 51, 53, 58); A4 (59); C6; C9

Media: Tempera; acrylic

Specialty: Still life, portraits

See artwork in color section

Sally Haley received her art education at Yale. While there she studied with Daniel Thompson, who taught her the application of egg tempera, a technique which leaves a flat, brushless surface. She also had private art instruction in Munich. While participating in the WPA, she completed a mural project for the post office in McConnelsville, Ohio titled *Mail—The Connecting Link.* This twelve-foot-long painting is Haley's largest work. While living in Connecticut during World War II, she completed some paintings of the outdoors, but this was unusual subject matter for her. She preferred domestic subjects and interior spaces with hints of the indoor or outdoor space that lay beyond. Starting in the mid 1940s, her theatrical use of space and scale marked the influence of Italian painter Giorgio de Chirico.

She arrived in Portland in 1947 with her husband, Michele Russo*, who had accepted a position at the Museum Art School. Paintings from this period continued to show her interest in surrealistic space, and her experimentation with placement of objects in a manipulated environment. Starting with the mid-1950s, however, the objects themselves became the subject; her treatment of them changed as the space became more minimal and related to the objects in a new way. The *Oregonian* commented on her 1959 one-person show at Harvey Welch's Gallery: "Set against almost stark backgrounds, each item can be fully enjoyed for its beauty of form and color and texture without the distraction which a more complicated composition would provide."

In the early 1960s she ceased using oil paint, continuing instead with acrylic and egg tempera. Her work continues to be varied in dimension and subject matter, gaining inspiration from "the environment which provides so many opportunities."

HALL, Carl A.

b. 1921 Washington, DC

d. 1996 Salem, OR

Education: Meinzinger Art School—Detroit: *Lopez*

Membership: Artists Equity; Master Watercolor Society of Oregon; Portland Art Museum (Artist Membership)

Awards: Detroit Institute of the Arts (1940, 41); Portland Art Museum (49); National Institute of Arts and Letters

Collections: Hallie Ford Museum of Art—Willamette University; Portland Art Museum; Coos Art Museum; Detroit Institute of the Arts; Boston Museum of Fine Arts; Whitney Museum of Art; Eastern Oregon College; Corcoran Gallery of Art—Washington, D.C.; Oregon State

University; Swope Art Museum—Terre Haute, Indiana

Exhibits: Detroit Institute of the Arts (1940, 41); Corcoran Gallery of Art—Washington, D.C.(41); Art Institute of Chicago (41, 46, 47); Whitney Museum of Art (43); Levy Gallery—New York (1PS 47); University of Illinois (48, 50, 51); California Palace of the Legion of Honor—San Francisco (48–51); Elfstrom Gallery (48); Portland Art Museum (1PS 50; AM, 1PS 56); Metropolitan Museum of Art (50); Western Oregon State College (1PS 52); Seattle Art Museum (4PS 53); Master Watercolor Society of Oregon (58); Oregon Centennial (59); Oregon Historical Society (90)

References: HAV; OET; A3 (1949–51, 54–58); A4 (59); C6; C7 (52, 53, 56, 58, 59); C9; C13 (48)

Media: Oil, watercolor

Specialty: Landscapes

See artwork in color section

Carl Hall was the student of Carlos Lopez at the Meinzinger School and a promising artist in Detroit when he interrupted his career to join the army. He came to Oregon as an infantryman during World War II in 1942, fell under the spell of the local landscape, and returned permanently in 1946. He began teaching in the art department at Willamette University in 1947 when Professor Esther Huffman discovered his work and offered him a part-time teaching position. Soon he was full-time artist-in-residence at Willamette and eventually attained regular faculty status. He received national recognition in March of 1948 when *Life* magazine featured an article about his work, calling him a "magic realist." One year later he received a grant from the National Institute of Arts and Letters. In spite of all the national attention, Hall made the decision to stay in Salem, continuing to show his work in juried national exhibitions while also establishing an important regional career in the Northwest. In 1953 William Givler*, Louis Bunce*, Carl Morris*, and Hall exhibited in a four-person show at the Seattle Art Museum. In 1959, he was a member of the advisory committee for Oregon's Centennial Art Exhibition. In the early 1960's, he painted a mural (now destroyed) for the Commercial Bank in Salem.

Hall is fondly remembered by students, whom he led on expeditions to the coast, the mountains, to his home, and on prowls all over to see the country in a creative way. He reminded them that knowing their environment is part of education. He felt that "arts exist because someone has to tell the truth about life...the arts remind us...that we are not a crowd. We're individuals. Art teaches awareness...it's a way of exploring the world and yourself." He admired Emerson and Thoreau and was a writer himself, a part-time poet, and art critic. John Casey, in a review of Hall's work at Willamette University, described his style as "a blend of realism and formalism of abstraction...suggestive...thus engaging the imagination of the viewer."

Hall was noted for his paintings of the Willamette Valley, the Oregon Coast, the female figure, and (in the 1970's) Alaska. He retired from Willamette in 1986. The Pacific Northwest Gallery of the Hallie Ford Museum of Art at Willamette University is named the Carl Hall Gallery.

HALL, Cyrennius

b. 1830

d. 1904

Education: Munich

Collections: National Portrait Gallery; Oregon Historical Society; Lewis and Clark College

Exhibits: Portland Art Museum; Oregon Centennial (1959)
References: BI; DAV; DAW; GER; HAV; SAM
Media: Oil
Specialty: Portraits, landscapes

An itinerant painter, Cyrennius Hall first came to Portland in 1853 and 1854. He studied in Europe, painted in South America, and returned to Portland in the late 1860s and in the 1880s. Hall painted in a luministic style. He executed views of Mt. Hood and Mt. Rainier as well as a portrait of Chief Joseph in 1878 which hung in the National Gallery in Washington, D.C.

HALL, Howard A.

b. 1923 Eugene, OR ***d.***
Education: University of Oregon: *D. McCosh*, A.Vincent*, J. Wilkinson** (1942–43, 46–51)
Membership: Portland Art Museum (Artist Membership)
Awards: Spokane (1951)
Collections: Coos Art Museum; University of Oregon
Exhibits: Portland Art Museum (AM, 2PS 1953; 1PS 58); Seattle Art Museum; Spokane (50, 51); Eugene Art League (1PS 1953); Southern Oregon College—Ashland; Artists Equity (58); New York (58); Denver Art Museum (58); University of Oregon (58); Oregon Centennial (59)
References: A3 (1950–56, 58); C1; C6; C7 (51, 52, 55–57, 59)
Media: Oil

Howard Hall received his art training at the University of Oregon. He exhibited his paintings at the Portland and Seattle Art Museums, Spokane, Southern Oregon College, and at *Art USA:58* in New York. He was head of the art department of Klamath Falls High School from 1954 to 1964 and was associated with the Maude Kerns Art Center in Eugene. In 1964 he became professor of art at Southwestern Oregon Community college.

HALL, Mabel. *See* OSTER, Mabel Haines

HALL, Norma Bassett

b. 1891 Halsey, OR
d. 1957 Santa Fe, NM
Education: Museum Art School (1910–14); Art Institute of Chicago (15–18)
Membership: Arts Guild
Collections: Smithsonian Institution; Brooklyn Library; Bibliothèque Nationale
Exhibits: Portland Art Museum; Arts Guild
References: DAV; DAW; FIE; HAV; KOV; MAL; PET; WWW; A2 (1914); A5 (33)
Media: Watercolor, prints (woodcuts, block)
Specialty: Landscapes, nature

Norma Hall was a 1910 scholarship student in the first class of the Museum Art School in Portland. She taught in a small school in Milwaukee in 1915 and then went to Chicago. She married and settled in Kansas, where she became interested in color block prints. Norma Hall continued her studies in Edinburgh, Scotland from 1925 to 1929. She returned to Kansas to live and work, moving to Virginia in 1943, and finally settling in New Mexico. Her watercolors were painted in a realistic style, but she was more interested in printmaking, especially woodcuts. After Hall left the state, she returned frequently for vacations, painting many views of Oregon. Dawdy and Petteys (see Ref. DAW, PET) lists her birthdate as 1889.

HALVORSEN, Ruth Elise

b. 1896 Camas, WA
d. 1993 Portland, OR
Education: Museum Art School

(1915–17); Pratt Institute (20–21); University of Oregon (33–35); Columbia University (36–38); *E. Wuest**

Membership: American Artists Professional League; Oregon Society of Artists; Oregon Guild of Painters and Sculptors; Master Watercolor Society of Oregon; Portland Art Museum (Artist Membership)

Collections: Oregon Historical Society; Portland Art Museum; Lincoln County Art Center; University of Oregon; Reed College; Gerber Collection; Pacific University

Exhibits: Oakland Art Gallery (1938, 40); San Francisco Museum of Art (39); Golden Gate International Exposition—San Francisco (39–40); Portland Art Museum (1PS 47); Henry Art Gallery—University of Washington (1PS 43, 48); University of Oregon (1PS 47); Reed College (1PS 48); Oregon Guild of Painters and Sculptors (48, 52; 1PS 49); Elfstrom Gallery (1PS 51); Coos Art Museum (54); Astoria (55); Salem (1PS 55); Master Watercolor Society of Oregon (58); Lincoln County Art Center (48, 59); Klamath Falls (59); Oregon Centennial (59); Oregon Historical Society (90)

References: ALM; COL; DAV; HAV; KOV; WWN; WWW; A2 (1940, 42); C9; C14; C17; M2; M3

Media: Oil, watercolor

Specialty: Landscapes, cityscapes, florals

See artwork in color section

See photograph of artist on p. 81

Ruth Halvorsen had a long and busy career as an exhibiting artist and art educator. Her oils and watercolors were exhibited widely in California, Oregon, and Washington. She was featured in many one-person shows in museums and galleries throughout the Northwest. She was a member of many professional arts organizations and held the vice-presidency and presidency of the National Art Education Association. Halvorsen taught art at Lincoln High School in Portland from 1922 to 1943, was supervisor of art in the Portland Public Schools from 1944 to 1962, and was an instructor of art at the University of Oregon.

In 1937 Halvorsen was active in the formation of the Contemporary Crafts Gallery. She authored many articles on art education and received the Theta Sigma Phi Woman of the Year Award in 1948. In 1947 she established the annual Oregon Scholastic Arts Award Exhibition.

HAMMACK, John (Jack)

b. 1925 Portland, OR ***d.***

Education: Museum Art School

Exhibits: Portland Art Museum; Kharouba Gallery (1952); Seattle Art Museum; Reed College

References: A2 (1948); A3 (50, 51, 53); C7 (47)

Media: Oil

Jack Hammack was a student of the Museum Art School in Portland. He became a teacher at the school's Saturday children's classes. His work was shown at the Portland and Seattle Art Museums, Reed College, and the Kharouba Gallery.

HANSON, Hazel. *See* CHILSTROM, Hazel

HARRIS, Levina. *See* STREIF, Levina

HART, Lance Wood

b. 1891 Aberdeen, WA

d. 1941 Portland, OR

Education: Art Institute of Chicago; Royal Academy of Arts—Stockholm; University of Oregon

Membership: American Artists Professional League; Oregon Society of Artists; University Alumni Art

League, University of Oregon
Collections: University of Oregon; Reed College; Parsons Collection; Martin-Zambito Collection
Exhibits: Seattle Art Museum; Portland Art Museum; American Artists Professional League (1933); University Alumni Art League; Oregon Society of Artists; University of Oregon (1PS 38); Philadelphia Art Museum;
References: COL; DAV; DAW; HAV; MAL SUP; WWN; WWW; A2 (1920, 40); C3 (34); C7 (19–22, 25, 28, 30, 38); C25 (35, 36)
Media: Watercolor, oil
Specialty: Landscapes, figures
See artwork in color section

Lance Hart showed his art ability at an early age. In 1908 the *Grays Harbor Post* mentioned him as "possessing exceptional skill and abilities." In high school he was also acclaimed for his oratory and acting prowess. While attending the Art Institute of Chicago he received newspaper attention for his art and his involvement in regional theater productions as an actor and stage designer. After his tour in the U.S. Army Ambulance Corps during World War I, Hart returned to Aberdeen, Washington, where he continued painting and directing local community theater productions. The paintings from his time in Aberdeen show Hart's attachment to the landscape of his hometown area.

Prior to, and for ten years after World War I, Hart's works showed the influence of French impressionism and post-impressionism in his approach to color, concept, and design. By 1922 Hart had established his artistic reputation in the Northwest and was exhibiting with the Seattle Fine Arts Society, forerunner to the Seattle Art Museum. He went to Sweden for further study and returned to Aberdeen about 1926.

In 1931 Hart became assistant professor of drawing and painting at the University of Oregon. He exhibited regionally and nationally, experimenting with cubism and expressionism while retaining his figurative base. He was a WPA artist and executed a mural at the Snohomish Washington Post Office.

HART, Ruth Patterson

b. 1910 Seattle, WA
d. 1991 Portland, OR
Education: Art Students League; Florence—Italy; Colorado Springs Fine Arts Center; Mills College—Oakland
Membership: Oregon Guild of Painters and Sculptors; American Artists' Congress
Awards: Honolulu Artists Society (1935)
Collections: Catlin Gabel School Collection
Exhibits: Creative Art Gallery (1933); Seattle Art Museum (34); Honolulu Artists Society (35); Honolulu Academy of Art; Portland Art Museum (3PS 36); American Artists' Congress (37); Oregon Guild of Painters and Sculptors (48)
References: COL; MAL SUP; SAM; WWN; A2 (1942); A3 (35, 36); C7 (35, 36, 41); CD (34); M2; M3
Media: Oil, watercolor
Specialty: Landscapes, genre

Ruth Hart received her art training at New York's Art Students League, the Colorado Fine Arts Academy, Mills College in California, and Florence, Italy. She exhibited in Hawaii, Oregon, and Washington. She was one of the organizers of the cooperative Creative Art Gallery. Hart was also a teacher at Riverdale School in Portland.

HART, Sarah (Sally)

b. 1891 Portland, OR
d. 1959 Bellingham, WA

Education: Portland Academy; Museum Art School; Columbia University; Académie de Colarossi
Membership: Oregon Society of Artists; American Artists Professional League; Arts Guild
Exhibits: Portland Art Museum; Oregon Society of Artists; Arts Guild; American Artists Professional League (1933)
References: COL; DAV; DAW; WWN; A2 (1917, 30, 32, 33); A3 (37, 38); A5 (30); C3 (27)
Media: Watercolor, tempera
Specialty: Landscapes, marines, florals

Sally Hart came from an old and prominent Portland family and was the niece of Henry Pittock, the *Oregonian* publisher. Dawdy (see Ref. DAW) states that Hart exhibited mainly in Portland but had at least one exhibit in New York City.

HASELTINE, James

b. 1924 Portland, OR ***d.***
Education: Reed College (1946–47); Museum Art School (47, 49); Art Institute of Chicago (47–48); Brooklyn Art Museum (50–51)
Membership: Artists Equity; Portland Art Museum (Artist Membership)
Awards: University of Washington (1951); Portland Art Museum (53); Seattle Art Museum (57, 59)
Collections: Portland Art Museum; University of Oregon
Exhibits: Portland Art Museum (AM, 2PS 1953); Library of Congress (50); Kharouba Gallery (50, 2PS 51); Reed College (50, 51, 2PS 52); Brooklyn Art Museum (51, 52); The Contemporaries Gallery—New York (51); Seattle Art Museum (57, 58); San Francisco Museum of Art (53, 54); Oakland Museum (54); Coos Art Museum (57); Oregon Centennial (59); University of Oregon (75)
References: ALM; HAV; WWAA; A3 (1950–56, 58); C6; C7 (52, 53, 56, 59); C22
Media: Oil, enamel, casein, prints
Specialty: Abstracts, landscapes

James Haseltine was educated at Reed College and the Museum Art School in Portland, the Art Institute of Chicago, and the Brooklyn Art Museum School. He was a reporter for the *Stars and Stripes* during World War II. Although Haseltine was in the wholesale hardware and industrial supply business in Portland, he pursued an active career in art. He exhibited at the Brooklyn, Portland, Seattle, San Francisco, and Oakland Museums, the Library of Congress in Washington, D.C., and in private galleries.

Haseltine was extremely involved in the Artists Equity movement and devoted much of his time to that organization. He was president of the Oregon chapter from 1953 to 1954 and national director of Artists Equity from 1955 to 1958. From 1954 to 1956 he was vice-president of the Oregon Art Alliance, a state-wide organization of museums, art centers, and art schools. Haseltine worked in art development for Reed College and was the chairman of the painting exhibition for the Oregon Centennial of 1959. His wife, Maury Haseltine*, was also an artist.

HASELTINE, Maury Janney

b. 1925 Portland, OR
d. 1998 Olympia, WA
Education: Reed College (1942–46); Museum Art School (45–46, 49–50); Eastern New Mexico University (52–53)
Membership: Artists Equity; Portland Art Museum (Artist Membership)
Collections: Coos Art Museum; University of Oregon; First Interstate Bank; U.S. Bank; Washington State Capitol Museum; Kaiser Permanente Collection; Oregon Historical Society; Tacoma Art Museum; Portland Art Museum

Exhibits: Portland Art Museum (2PS 1953; 4PS 55); Harvey Welch Gallery (1PS 50); Reed College (50); Eastern New Mexico University (1PS 52); Seattle Art Museum; Coos Bay Art Festival (57); Oregon Centennial (59); University of Oregon (75); Oregon Historical Society (90)
References: HAV; WWAA; A2 (1948); A3 (53–56, 58); A4 (55); C6; C7 (53, 57, 59); C9; C22
Media: Oil, prints
Specialty: Landscapes, abstracts

Maury Haseltine attended Portland's Reed College, the Museum Art School, and Eastern New Mexico University. She was a craftsperson as well as a painter. She was an art administrator in Salt Lake City. From 1947 to 1955 she painted under the name Maury Janney. In 1955 she was one of four women artists featured in a show at the Portland Art Museum. Her painting displayed at the Oregon Centennial Show is in the collection of the Oregon Historical Society. The Haseltines moved to Olympia, Washington.

HASSAM, Childe B.

b. 1859 Dorchester, MA
d. 1935 Easthampton, NY
Education: Académie Julian: *Boulanger, LeFebre;* Boston
Membership: American Watercolor Society; Society of Independent Artists—New York
Awards: Paris Salon (1889); Munich (92); World Columbian Exposition—Chicago (93); Pan American Exposition—Buffalo (1901); St. Louis Universal Exposition (04)
Collections: Portland Art Museum; Metropolitan Museum of Art; Corcoran Gallery of Art—Washington, D.C.; National Museum of American Art; Museum of Modern Art
Exhibits: Paris Salons; World Columbian Exposition—Chicago (1893); Pan American Exposition—Buffalo (1901); St. Louis Universal Exposition (04); Lewis and Clark Centennial Exposition (05); Alaska-Yukon Pacific Exposition—Seattle (09); Panama Pacific International Exposition—San Francisco (15); Portland Art Museum (1PS 19, 53; 3PS 25); Society of Independent Artists—New York (17, 20); Oregon Historical Society (90)
References: BEN; BI; DAV; DAW; FI (1887–90, 97, 98); FIE; GER; HAV; HUG; MAL; OET; SAM; THI; WWW; YNG; A1 (1902, 06, 09, 15, 20, 33); A4 (11, 14, 16); C9; C21
Media: Oil, prints (lithograph, etching)
Specialty: Landscapes, portraits, genre, murals

Childe Hassam, a member of the group known as "Ten American Painters" organized in 1898, was one of the leading American adapters of French impressionism. He was best known for paintings of his native New England. Hassam made two trips to Oregon to visit his friend, fellow artist, C.E.S. Wood*. In 1904 Hassam arrived in Portland to install a mural he had created for the Wood home, and stayed through the summer. He spent his time painting still lifes and landscapes, including Oregon Coast scenes from Ecola and Mt. Hood. He also painted the Cascades from Cloud Cap Inn on the eastern slopes of the mountain. Hassam returned to Oregon in 1908, this time to accompany Wood on a trip to Harney County in southeastern Oregon. In September they were guests at the P-Ranch of William Hanley, where both artists painted the landscapes of Harney and Malheur counties. After their return to Portland in late October, over thirty of Hassam's paintings from the trip were placed on exhibit at the Portland Art

Museum. One of these, *Afternoon Sky, Harney Desert*, was purchased by a group of art patrons as the first oil painting for the fledgling Portland Art Museum. Another work from that expedition, *Golden Afternoon, Oregon*, is in the collection of the Metropolitan Museum of Art in New York City. In 1909 the Montross Gallery of New York had an exhibition of Hassam's Harney county paintings and in 1953 twenty-nine of his works were featured at the Portland Art Museum in an exhibit entitled *Childe Hassam in Oregon*.

HATHAWAY, Ella C.

b. Hungary ***d.***
Education: Art Institute of Chicago; Chicago Academy of Fine Arts; University of Oregon
Membership: American Artists Professional League; Rembrandt Artists Guild
Exhibits: National Exhibition of American Art (1936, 38); American Arists Professional League (38); Portland Art Museum; Oregon State Fair
References: COL; WWN; A2 (1940)
Media: Oil

Ella Hathaway received her art education at the Art Institute of Chicago, the Chicago Academy of Fine Arts, and the University of Oregon. She was a member of the American Artists Professional League and the Rembrandt Artists Guild of Salem. She exhibited at the Oregon State Fair and the Portland Art Museum. She was also the director of the Salem Art Center.

HAYES, William P. (W.P.)

b. 1885 Dubuque, IA
d. 1974 Portland, OR
Education: *G. O'Brien*; Currie*
Collections: Parsons Collection; Huntington Collection
Exhibits: Portland Art Museum; Seattle Art Museum; University of Portland
References: C7 (1937); C10
Media: Oil
Specialty: Portland scenes, shipyards
See artwork in color section

This WPA painter came to Oregon with his family in 1896, settling in Hubbard. He sketched farm animals and landscapes at an early age and was mostly self-taught, except for some instruction from George O'Brien* and a Miss Currie of Portland. His early work was as a free-lance commercial artist producing ad layouts. During World War II he worked with many of the local artists at the shipyards.

He was an eccentric who never married and lived with his sister, Frances. He showed his work rarely, and while he would occasionally offer his paintings as gifts, there is no evidence that he ever sold a piece of art. Upon the death of his sister, despondent over medical bills and the uncertainty of his future, he started burning his life's output. Close to five hundred pieces were destroyed in the fire. At his death in 1974 it was believed that only 150 pieces remained.

Throughout his life the prevailing theme of his artwork was local subject matter and, because he never drove a car, his world was relatively limited. He developed friendships with other artists, especially C.S. Price*, who became a mentor. This friendship lasted over thirty years and his influence on Hayes' work is often apparent. In style, Hayes was surprisingly diverse. There is evidence of impressionism, realism, and an extension of pointillism, which he adapted to make uniquely his own by using wavy or jerky lines instead of fine points of color. Light appears to penetrate the painting, giving an overall effect of depth and movement. He used a strong and extensive color palette and signed his work *W.P. Hayes*. Though relatively unknown and possessing little formal training, W.P. Hayes exerted a strong, regional influence that deserves more attention.

HAYNE, Josephine Jane (Jennie)

b. 1856 Oregon City, OR
d. 1938 Portland, OR
Education: San Francisco School of Design: *A. Chittenden, W. Keith*, R. Yelland**
Membership: Portland Sketch Club; Oregon Art Association
Awards: Oregon State Fair; Portland Mechanics Fair (1885); North Pacific Industrial Exposition (89); Oregon Art Association (96); Lewis and Clark Centennial Exposition (1905)
Collections: Oregon Historical Society
Exhibits: Portland Mechanics Fair; Oregon State Fair; North Pacific Industrial Exposition (1889, 90); Portland Industrial Exposition (91); Oregon Art Association (96); National Academy of Design (97); Portland Sketch Club (1PS 98); Lewis and Clark Centennial Exposition (1905); Oregon Historical Society (90)
References: C2 (1889, 90, 91); C4 (85); C9; ARTC; CD (86–88, 90–92, 96, 97, 1903–05, 17); OSF (1885); M2; M3
Media: Oil, watercolor
Specialty: Florals, still life
See artwork in color section

Born on an 1847 Oregon donation land claim, Jennie Hayne attended the Oregon City Seminary until age 15. She married Joseph T. Hayne, a printer who worked for newspapers in Portland and San Francisco. They returned to Portland, where she advertised as an artist and private teacher of oil and watercolor painting. She was an exhibiting member of the Portland Sketch Club and the Oregon Art Association. Hayne was featured in a one-person show of her oil paintings in the 1891 Portland Industrial Exposition. She is probably the Mrs. J.T. Hayne who exhibited at the National Academy of Design, New York in 1897. One of her paintings, *Caroline Testout Roses*, features the official Portland flower, which was planted in abundance during the 1905 Lewis & Clark Exposition. Her paintings were signed *J.T. Hayne.*

HEANEY, Charles Edward

b. 1897 Oconto Falls, WI
d. 1981 Portland, OR
Education: Museum Art School: *H. Wentz**; University of Oregon
Membership: Oregon Society of Artists; American Artists Professional League; American Artists' Congress; Oregon Guild of Painters and Sculptors; Arts Guild; Portland Art Museum (Artist Membership)
Award: Seattle Art Museum (1942); Denver Art Museum; Portland Art Museum
Collections: National Museum of American Art; Clatsop County Historical Society; Seattle Art Museum; Portland Art Museum; Oregon Historical Society; Goodman Collection; Booth Collection; University of Oregon; Reed College; Kaiser Permanente Collection; Parsons Collection; Arlene and Harold Schnitzer Collection; Pathways Collection; Huntington Collection; Riley Collection; Capitol Collection—Salem; Pacific University; Hallie Ford Museum of Art—Willamette University
Exhibits: Oregon Society of Artists; Portland Art Museum (1PS 1946, retrospective 52, 1PS 59); Arts Guild; University of Oregon (32, 75); Seattle Art Museum (33, 35; 4PS 54); Salem Federal Art Center (38); New York World's Fair (39); San Francisco Museum of Art (39, 43); Western Washington Fair; Whitney

Museum of Art (47, 51); Oregon Guild of Painters and Sculptors (48); Harvey Welch Gallery (48); Reed College (1PS 48); Metropolitan Museum of Art (50); Denver Art Museum (50); Henry Art Gallery—University of Washington (51); Kharouba Gallery (51); Kraushaar Galleries—New York (52); Sao Paulo Biennial III—Brazil (55); M.H. DeYoung Museum—San Francisco; Art Institute of Chicago; Corcoran Gallery of Art—Washington, D.C.; Oregon Centennial (59); Oregon Historical Society (90); Clatsop County Historical Society (94)

References: ALM; COL; DAV; DAW; HAV; MAL; OET; SAM; WWW; A2 (1930, 32–34, 40, 42, 44, 46, 48); A3 (37, 49–51, 53–56, 58); A4 (52, 59); A5 (30, 33); C3 (27); C6; C7 (37, 40–43, 45, 46, 47, 49); C8; C9; C11; C15 (46); C18; C22; C27; C30 (46)

Media: Prints (etching), oil, watercolor; tempera

Specialty: Landscapes (Eastern Oregon, John Day), Indians

See artwork in color section

See photograph of artist on p. 83

If ever an artist exhibited a strong sense of what Oregon Country represents, it was Charles Heaney. He arrived in Portland as a teenager with his mother and sister in 1913 after his father died. His first job as an apprentice to a jewelry engraver was a stepping stone to his real art education that began at the Museum Art School. It was there he began to discover the talent that allowed him to express himself. At first, his interest was in prints, woodcuts, and linoleum blocks. It would be some years before he turned to painting. He painted only as long as it held his interest; sometimes he would put a piece aside for as long as ten years, then take it up again as a fresh outlook spurred his interest. He worked in many media, mastering one and then turning to something different. He returned to the School in 1937 to study engraving, leading to his innovative fossil paintings with relief surfaces. The Portland Art Museum honored him in 1952 with a retrospective of his work.

Like so many others, he came to revere C.S. Price*. He adopted Price's ideal of the simple life with almost obsessive dedication to his art. There are occasional similarities in their brushwork and color palette, but Heaney's work shows a more personal, intimate touch. Heaney loved eastern Oregon, where he traveled extensively throughout the area and, with camera in hand, took photos that would jog his memory when he returned to the studio. He loved geological formations; the space, color, and textures of the desert challenged him as a painter. He also made frequent trips to Nevada for this same reason—the stark colors of the earth, the textural surfaces of the sand, and the play of light on the surfaces. Another artist who made a profound impression on Heaney was Kyuzo Furuya*, whom he met in 1915. It was Furuya's devotion to nature that impressed Heaney, and brought him a renewed appreciation for the natural world.

Rachael Griffin*, in her article, "Heaney's Landscape," summarized the essence of his work: [his landscapes] "capture the *spirit* of the scene ... they are landscapes of the mind or of the *soul* for each of us there are discoveries to be made in Heaney's landscapes ... subtle, layered, *deeper* ... than their familiar topical features might suggest."

HECKBERT, Georgia Richardson

b. 1878 Woburn, MA

d. 1964 Portland, OR

Education: Boston

Membership: Oregon Society of Artists
Awards: Oregon Society of Artists (1928)
Collections: Oregon Historical Society
Exhibits: Oregon Society of Artists; Portland Art Museum; Seattle Art Museum
References: A2 (1932, 34, 40, 42, 44, 46, 48); A3 (36, 38); C3 (27–32); C7 (37)
Media: Watercolor, oil
Specialty: Florals

Georgia Heckbert exhibited at the Portland and Seattle Art Museums. She was well known for her miniature paintings on ivory.

HEDRICK, Mary S.

b. Illinois, 1869
d. 1956 Portland, OR
Education: Art Institute of Chicago
Membership: Attic Club; American Artists Professional League; Oregon Society of Artists
Awards: American Artists Professional League (1936); Oregon Society of Artists (39, 43)
Collections: Miranda Collection
Exhibits: Oregon Society of Artists; Portland Art Museum; American Artists Professional League (1932–34, 36–38)
References: COL; DAW; WWN; A2 (1932, 40, 42, 44, 48); C3 (27–31, 33, 36, 43, 45–47, 49, 50); C10; ARTC; M2; M3
Media: Watercolor, oil
Specialty: Landscapes, nature, florals
See artwork in color section

Mary Hedrick was educated at the Art Institute of Chicago. She moved to Portland in 1916, where she became a member of the Attic Club, the American Artists Professional League, and a founding member of the Oregon Society of Artists. Hedrick was a WPA artist actively exhibiting her oils and watercolors in Oregon from the 1920s to 1950s.

HEIDEL, Florence Saltzman

b. 1917 Winnipeg, Canada
d. 1972 Portland, OR
Education: Art Institute of Chicago; Académie de la Grande Chaumière
Membership: California Watercolor Society; Portland Art Museum (Artist Membership)
Awards: Henry Art Gallery—University of Washington; U.S.A. Watercolor Show—Springfield, Illinois
Collections: Victoria and Albert Museum—London; Bibliothèque Nationale—Paris; University of California Berkeley; Henry Art Gallery—University of Washington; Portland Art Museum; Coos Art Museum; Tonkon Torp Collection
Exhibits: M.H. DeYoung Museum—San Francisco; Metropolitan Museum of Art; Los Angeles County Museum of Art (1945, 46); Andover (1PS 48); San Francisco Museum of Art (49); Portland Art Museum; Santa Barbara Museum of Art (1PS); Portland State University (1PS 52); Sao Paulo Biennial III—Brazil (55); Seattle Art Museum; Oregon Centennial (59)
References: A3 (1950, 51, 53, 54, 56–58); C6; C7 (55)
Media: Watercolor
Specialty: Portraits, landscapes

Florence Heidel, married to artist Frederick Heidel*, taught at Long Beach City College, the University of Southern California, and Portland State University. She came to Oregon in 1949, moving to Portland in 1953. She felt an artist must learn to talk with brush and color; painting was, for her, an entire language with an unlimited vocabulary—a language to learn and love. She considered her landscapes to be portraits of the land. Her earlier work can be found under the signature *Florence Saltzman.*

HEIDEL, Frederick H.

b. 1915 Corvallis, OR ***d.***
Education: University of Oregon: *D. McCosh**, *A. Vincent** (1938); Art Institute of Chicago (41, 56)
Membership: California Watercolor Society; Portland Art Museum (Artist Membership)
Awards: California Watercolor Society (1947); San Francisco Museum of Art (48); Oakland Museum (50); Portland Art Museum (52); Oregon State Fairs (54, 57–59); Oregon Centennial (59)
Collections: Portland Art Museum; Portland State University; Coos Art Museum; University of Oregon; Arlene and Harold Schnitzer Collection
Exhibits: Portland Art Museum (AM, 1PS 1953); Los Angeles County Museum of Art (46–49); Pepsi Cola Annual (47); San Francisco Museum of Art (47, 48, 52, 1PS 49); Oakland Museum (50–55); University of Oregon (1PS 50, 55, 75); Metropolitan Museum of Art (51); Seattle Art Museum; Marylhurst College (1PS 54); Oregon State Fairs (54, 57–59); Sao Paulo Biennial III—Brazil (55); Bush Barn—Salem (1PS 57); Santa Barbara Museum of Art (57); Portland State University (58); Denver Art Museum (58); Smithsonian Institution Traveling Exhibits (58); Eastern Oregon College (1PS 59); Oregon Centennial (59)
References: HAV; WWAA; A2 (1946); A3 (50–58); A4 (46, 59); C6; C7 (51, 52, 55–59); C20; C22
Media: Oil
Specialty: Landscapes, murals
See artwork in color section
See photograph of artist on p. 83

Frederick Heidel began teaching art at Biarritz American University, Biarritz, France in 1945. Later he taught at Long Beach City College in California and became professor of art at University of Oregon in 1949. In 1951 Heidel began his long association with Portland State University where he was both professor and chairman of the department of art and architecture until 1980.

Heidel's subjects were mostly landscapes, painted with a warm palette. His paintings were interpretive of, and inspired by, the visual world; subject matter was secondary to patterning. His later works were characterized by intense color and expressive form. Heidel has stated that he felt most akin to the Expressionists; he painted to express ideas and feelings relating to people and things, in time and place. By 1968 Heidel had made a marked departure from painting and turned to laminated constructions in glass.

Heidel exhibited nationally and internationally and was featured in numerous one-person shows. His work can be found in Oregon in the collections of the Portland Art Museum, Portland State University, the Coos Art Museum, and the University of Oregon. There is a mural by Frederick Heidel at the Lane County Courthouse in Eugene.

HELM, Myra Sager

b. 1869 Linn Co., OR
d. 1959 Portland, OR
Education: *C. Keller*; E. Quigley**
Membership: Society of Oregon Artists; Mutual Art Association; Oregon Society of Artists
Collections: Oregon Historical Society; Powell Collection; Counting Eagles Collection
Exhibits: Society of Oregon Artists (1913); Portland Art Museum; Oregon Society of Artists; Clatsop County Historical Society (94)
References: A2 (1940, 44, 46); C3 (45, 46); C11; ARTC; CD (1899, 1900, 03–06, 09–11, 13–16, 33, 40, 41, 43–4, 51, 53–4); M2; M3

Media: Oil
Specialty: Florals, landscapes, miniatures

Myra Helm was a painter, photographer, illustrator, and author. She was a member of the early Society of Oregon Artists, the Mutual Art Association, and the Oregon Society of Artists. She studied with Clyde Keller* and Ed Quigley*. Her oils were exhibited at the Portland Art Museum. Helm earned her living as a practicing artist and ran a School of Decorative Arts in Portland. Her mother, Elizabeth Sager Helm, orphaned on the Oregon Trail, was one of seven children adopted by missionaries Marcus and Narcissa Whitman. Later, Elizabeth Helm survived what came to be known as the Whitman Massacre. In 1952 Myra Helm wrote and illustrated an account of her mother's experiences, *Lorinda Bailey and the Whitman Massacre.*

HELSER, Margot G.

b. d.
Education: University of Portland: *E. Jacques**; New York
Membership: Oregon Society of Artists; American Artists Professional League
Exhibits: Oregon Society of Artists; Portland Art Museum; American Artists Professional League (1932–34); Seattle Art Museum; National Exhibition of American Art (36)
References: A2 (1932, 33, 34); C3 (27, 30, 31); C7 (34); C10
Media: Watercolor, oil
Specialty: Fantasy, portraits

Margot Helser was already known as an illustrator of children's books when she married Darrel Austin*. Through the WPA, Helser executed a series of watercolor paintings for Doernbecher Children's Hospital, including two intricate illustrations of fairy tales, which disappeared in 1950. Although commercially unsuccessful in Portland, their move to Hollywood later brought financial and critical success to both artists. Eventually they moved to New York City to live and work.

HENDRICK, Marian

b. d.
Membership: Oregon Society of Artists; Portland Art Museum (Artist Membership)
Exhibits: Portland Art Museum; Lincoln County Art Center (1948); Oregon Society of Artists
References: A2 (1948); C3 (51); C14
Media: Watercolor

Marian Hendrick lived and worked in Nelscott. She was a member of, and exhibited with, the Oregon Society of Artists. She also showed her watercolors in Portland and Lincoln City. Her name is sometimes spelled *Hendricks.*

HERMANN, Darle Ann

b. 1929 Astoria, OR ***d.***
Education: Stanford University: *Faulkner* (1947–50); Cranbrook Academy—Bloomfield Hills, Michigan: *Mitchell* (54–55); Museum Art School: *Reynolds*
Membership: Artists Equity; Portland Art Museum (Artist Membership)
Awards: Oregon State Fair (1953)
Exhibits: Portland Art Museum; Oregon State Fair (1953); Reed College (55)
References: A3 (1953–55)
Media: Oil, casein

Darle Hermann was an art teacher at Grant High School in Portland. She attended Syracuse University, Cranbrook Academy, and Portland's Museum Art School. She exhibited her paintings at the Oregon State Fair, the Portland Art Museum, and Reed College.

HETROVO, Nicolai Sergei

b. 1896 Petrograd, Russia
d. 1956 San Francisco, CA
Collections: Oregon Historical Society

Exhibits: Portland Art Museum; M.H. DeYoung Museum—San Francisco (1PS 1949)
References: DAV; DAW; HUG; WWN; A3 (1936–38); C10
Media: Watercolor
Specialty: Landscapes, portraits

Nicolai Hetrovo was an architect and WPA artist who lived in Portland from 1931 to 1936. He moved to San Francisco in the late 1930s. One of his watercolor street scenes is housed in the collection of the Oregon Historical Society. Hetrovo produced representational and nonobjective paintings. He apparently suffered mental problems in later life and died in a mental institution. Hughes (see Ref. HUG) gives his birthdate as 1892.

HEYSER, Norma. *See* PETERSON, Norma

HEYWOOD, Herbert

b. 1893 Portland, OR
d. 1969 Portland, OR
Education: University of Oregon (1918); Oregon State University; Museum Art School
Membership: Arts Guild; University Alumni Art League, University of Oregon
Collections: University of Oregon
Exhibits: Arts Guild; Portland Art Museum; University Alumni Art League
References: COL; DAV; DAW; WWN; A2 (1934); A3 (35, 37, 38); A5 (33); C25 (35); CD (21–22, 23–32)
Media: Oil, tempera, watercolor
Specialty: Landscapes, seascapes, murals

Herbert Heywood, a WPA artist, was also a commercial artist and taught art appreciation at the University of Portland. He was a muralist, with work at the University of Portland and Peninsula Park. Heywood was educated at the University of Oregon, Oregon State University, and the Museum Art School.

HILL, Edward

b. 1843 England
d. 1923 Hood River, OR
Membership: Mutual Art Association
Collections: Denver Art Museum; Oregon Historical Society; Painting Restoration Studio Collection; Counting Eagles Collection; Le Meitour Collection
Exhibits: Mutual Art Association (1914, 15)
References: BI; DAV; HUG; ARTC; CD (1915, 17, 18)
Media: Oil
Specialty: Landscapes
See artwork in color section

Edward Hill arrived in the United States in 1844 and came to Portland about 1880. Later he went to San Francisco to share a studio with his brother Thomas, a well-known California artist. Edward Hill returned to Portland in 1911, living and painting there until he moved to Hood River, where he maintained a residence for the remainder of his life. He was the uncle of Edward Rufus Hill*.

HILL, Edward Rufus

b. 1851 Taunton, MA
d. 1908 Oakland, CA
Education: *T. Hill*
Awards: Portland Mechanics Fairs
Collections: Oregon Historical Society; Stenzel Collection
Exhibits: Portland Mechanics Fairs; Portland Art Museum; Oregon Historical Society (1990)
References: BI; DAV; HUG; WWW; A2 (1914); C4 (1879–86); C9; C16; CD (80, 81)
Media: Oil
Specialty: Landscapes (river scenes)

Edward Rufus Hill was the son of artist Thomas Hill and nephew of artist Edward Hill*. He frequently painted small landscapes on cigar boxes. Hill exhibited in the Portland Mechanics

Fairs from 1879 to 1886. His works are signed *E.R. Hill.* The *Bicentennial Inventory* gives his birthdate as 1852.

HILLYER, Mary

b. d.
Exhibits: Portland Art Museum
References: A2 (1913, 15, 19, 20, 22)

Mary Hillyer exhibited at the Portland Art Museum from 1913 to 1922.

HINSHAW, John Bernard

b. 1903 Mackinaw, IL
d. 1981 Portland, OR
Education: Wesleyan—Illinois; University of Chicago (1943)
Membership: Oregon Society of Artists; American Artists Professional League
Exhibits: American Artists Professional League (1936–38); Portland Art Museum; Seattle Art Museum (40, 44)
References: ALM; COL; WWAA; WWN; A2 (1940); C7 (41)
Media: Watercolor, oil
Specialty: Cityscapes

Bernard Hinshaw was a teacher at the Art Institute of Chicago and Lewis and Clark College in Portland, where he became chairman of the art department in 1946. He was a member of the American Artists Professional League and the Oregon Society of Artists. His work was shown at the Portland and Seattle Art Museums. The Oregon Historical Society has some Hinshaw drawings in its collection. His wife, Kathryn, was also an artist and her work is in the Oregon Historical Society collection.

HIXSON, William J.

b. 1922 Shawnee, OK ***d.***
Education: University of Oregon (1948, 50); Académie de la Grande Chaumière (49)
Membership: Artists Equity; Portland Art Museum (Artist Membership)
Awards: Seattle Art Museum (1946); Western Washington Fair (58)
Collections: University of Oregon; Corcoran Gallery of Art—Washington, D.C.; Tupperware Museum—Orlando, Florida
Exhibits: Seattle Art Museum (4PS 1955); University of Oregon (1PS 50); Henry Art Gallery—University of Washington (1PS 50, 51); Portland Art Museum; Denver Art Museum (51, 52); Western Washington Fair; Australia (55); Santa Barbara Museum of Art (57)
References: HAV; A3 (1950, 53, 55); C7 (46, 51, 52, 54–59); C20; C30 (51–59)
Media: Oil
Specialty: Portraits

William Hixson served in the U.S. Infantry during World War II. He lived in Eugene while attending the University of Oregon in the late 1940s and early 50s. He was featured in shows at the University of Oregon, the Seattle Art Museum, the Henry Gallery of the University of Washington, and the Denver Art Museum. In 1953 he moved to Seattle to teach painting at the University of Washington. He continued to teach, paint, and exhibit actively in Colorado and Washington.

HOFER, Winona

b. McGregor, IA
d. 1941 Portland, OR
Awards: Oregon State Fairs
Exhibits: Oregon State Fairs
References: OSF (1891, 97, 98, 1900)
Media: Oil
Specialty: Florals, seascapes

In 1881 Winona McKinnie married Ernst Hofer, her high school classmate, in McGregor, Iowa. They came to Oregon in 1890, where he became editor of the Salem *Capitol Journal.* They lived in Salem during the time she exhibited at the Oregon State Fairs. She was known for her florals and seascapes. She and Colonel Hofer moved to Portland, where he built two mansions in the southwest area for his family. Winona Hofer remained reticent, while her outspoken husband dominated the literary scene, being especially interested in poetry.

HOFFMAN, Julia Christianson

b. 1856 Gunnison, UT
d. 1934 Portland, OR
Education: Salt Lake City—Utah; Portland: *F. DuMond**
Membership: Oregon Society of Artists
Exhibits: Oregon Society of Artists
References: C3 (1927); M2
Media: Oil

In addition to painting, Julia Hoffman worked in ceramic, metal, photography, and sculpture. She lived in Portland throughout her adult life. Hoffman founded the Arts and Crafts Society in 1907 (later the Oregon College of Arts and Crafts). In 1902 she became the first lifetime member of the Portland Art Association, forerunner of the Portland Art Museum. Hoffman helped found the Museum Art School and underwrote the salary of the first instructor of design. She studied with Frank DuMond*, who gave classes in the attic of Hoffman's home. Her daughter, Marjorie Hoffman Smith*, supervised the production of decorative arts for the WPA project at Timberline Lodge. Hoffman died as a result of injuries suffered in an auto accident.

HOGAN, Mamie

b. d.
Awards: Oregon State Fairs
Exhibits: Oregon State Fairs
References: OSF (1891–94)
Media: Oil
Specialty: Florals

Mamie Hogan gave a Salem address for her Oregon State Fair entries from 1891 to 1894.

HOLDREDGE, Ransome Gillette

b. 1836 England
d. 1899 San Francisco, CA
Education: Europe
Collections: Oakland Museum; Oregon Historical Society; Stenzel Collection
Exhibits: Portland Mechanics Fair; University of Oregon (1959); Oregon Historical Society (90)
References: DAV; DAW; HUG; SAM; WWW; C4 (1880); C9; C12; C16

Ransome Holdredge served as head draftsman at the Mare Island Naval Yard in the 1860s. He left the Navy and became an itinerant painter who traveled the Northwest and lived with the Indians. In the 1870s he studied in Europe and, upon his return, was employed by *Scribners* magazine. Holdredge helped found the San Francisco Art Association. It was said he died in poverty as an alcoholic.

HOLLAND, Alice. *See* HUTCHINSON, Alice Holland

HOLLISTER, Anna Maud Sutherlin

b. 1873 Oakland, OR
d. 1965 Portland, OR
Membership: Attic Club; American Artists Professional League; Oregon Society of Artists
Awards: American Artists Professional League (1932); Multnomah County Fair (42)
Collections: Oregon Historical Society

Exhibits: Second Eastern Oregon District Agricultural Fair (1891); Portland Art Museum; Oregon Society of Artists; American Artists Professional League (1932–34); Multnomah County Fair (42); Lincoln County Art Center (48)
References: KOV; A2 (1932, 40, 42, 46, 48); C3 (32, 33, 45–51); C10; C14; ARTC; SEO (1891); M2; M3
Media: Oil
Specialty: Landscapes (historic houses, landmarks); florals; china painting
See artwork in color section

Maud Sutherlin Hollister was a member of a prominent Oregon pioneer family, for whom the town of Sutherlin is named. In her youth she was known as Anna, Annie, or Anne, but later dropped the first name in favor of Maud. She moved to Portland in the early 1890s, remaining there until her death seventy-four years later.

Hollister was interested in documenting landmarks and historic houses. She was a charter member of the Oregon Society of Artists and, during the Depression, was a WPA artist. At the 1942 Multnomah County Fair her oil painting won first prize.

HOLMAN, Mary. *See* ALBERT, Mary

HORSFALL, Robert Bruce

b. 1868 Clinton, IA
d. 1948 Venice, CA
Education: Bavaria Konig Art Academy—Munich; Cincinnati Art Academy: *Lutz, Noble* (1886–89); Académie de Colarossi (89–93)
Membership: Oregon Society of Artists
Collections: New York City: American Museum of Natural History, Zoological Society; Oregon Historical Society
Exhibits: Art Institute of Chicago (1886); Académie de Colarossi (89–93); San Francisco (93–94); World Columbian Exposition—Chicago (93); Portland Art Museum; Audubon Society (1919, 22); Salem Art League (20); Oregon Society of Artists; Oregon Historical Society (90)
References: ALM; BEN; BI; DAV; DAW; FIE; HAV; MAL; OET; SAM; SMI; THI; WWW; YNG; A2 (1916, 17, 19, 20, 40); C3 (27); C9; CD (15–18, 20, 23)
Media: Watercolor, oil, pastel
Specialty: Nature

Robert Horsfall grew up in the Midwest. At age seventeen he sent a painting of ducks alighting on a slough to the Art Institute of Chicago. It was accepted for exhibition and he continued to be a regular contributor there for several years. He drew pastels in order to earn money to pay for his training at the Cincinnati Art School. He later won a two-year scholarship to Munich and Paris.

In 1904 Horsfall accompanied, and did the illustrations for, the Princeton Expedition to Patagonia. He illustrated more than twenty books, including a children's book, and assisted with many others. In 1902 he painted background scenery for exhibits at the American Museum of Natural History in New York. In 1914 the artist came to Oregon, where he studied and painted wild birds, produced a handbook of Oregon birds, and, in 1919 and 1922, exhibited in the Audubon shows. He taught at Reed College in Portland and moved to New York in 1923.

Horsfall was considered by many to be America's greatest painter of birds and flowers. He did many works for the National Association of Audubon Societies and was on the staff of *Nature* magazine. Sometimes his signature is found as *R. Bruce Horsfall.*

HOTKA, Ray

b. 1913 IA *d.*
Education: University of Iowa; *P. Manser**; *C. Mulvey**; *P. Tyler**
Membership: Oregon Amateur Watercolor Society; The Dalles Art Club
Awards: Wasco County Fair
Exhibits: Wasco County Fair
References: OR (The Dalles Art Club)
Media: Watercolor
Specialty: Still life, old buildings

Ray Hotka has been a long-time resident of The Dalles, a leader of the local art association, an art teacher, and a member of the Oregon Amateur Watercolor Society. He studied with Percy Manser*, Charles Mulvey*, and Phil Tyler. He was influenced by Grant Wood, Georgia O'Keeffe, Thomas Hart Benton, Cézanne, and Van Gogh. Hotka won many awards from the Wasco County Fairs, where he exhibited his paintings.

HOUSE, Howard Elmer

b. 1877 Manhattan, KS
d. 1969 Portland, OR
Education: Art Institute of Chicago; Chicago Academy of Fine Arts
Membership: American Artists Professional League; Oregon Society of Artists; Skidmore Fountain Art Center, Inc.
Awards: American Artists Professional League (1936, 38, 40)
Collections: Powell Collection; Oregon Historical Society; Lundberg Collection; Cofield Collection
Exhibits: American Artists Professional League (1935–40); National Exhibition of American Art (36); First National Bank (1PS 36); Portland Art Museum; Oregon Society of Artists; Citizens for Art Group (59); Oregon Centennial (59); Clatsop County Historical Society (94)
References: DAV; DAW; HAV; MAL SUP; WWW; A2 (1940, 44, 48); C3 (49–51); C11; CD (55)
Media: Oil
Specialty: Landscapes, portraits, seascapes
See artwork in color section

H. Elmer House was educated at the Art Institute of Chicago and the Chicago Academy of Fine Arts. He came to Portland in the 1930s and was associated with the Mid West Studios. He was a member of, and exhibited with, the American Artists Professional League and the Oregon Society of Artists. House painted portraits of many prominent Portland people; the Oregon Historical Society has four of his portraits in its collection. He was one of six artists representing Oregon in the 1936 National Exhibition of American Art in New York. His painting of *John Fitzgerald Kennedy* hung in the Kennedy Library. He signed his paintings *H.E. House*, *H. Elmer House*, or *House*.

HUBER, Bernice M.

b. d.
Education: Chouinard Art Institute
Membership: Oregon Society of Artists; Northwest Watercolor Society
Awards: Oregon Society of Artists (1943, 47)
Exhibits: Portland Art Museum; Oregon Society of Artists; Seattle Art Museum; Northwest Watercolor Society; Elfstrom Gallery (2PS 1947)
References: A2 (1940, 42, 44, 46); C3 (43, 45–49); C29 (48, 52)
Media: Watercolor
Specialty: Landscapes

Bernice Huber lived and exhibited in Oregon during the 1940s. She was a member of the Oregon Society of Artists. She and Nancie Confer* held a two-person show at the Elfstrom Gallery in Salem in 1947. She moved to Seattle in the 1950s and exhibited with the Northwest Watercolor Society.

Huber was featured in their 1948 show at the Riverside Museum in New York.

HUCK, Robert Emerson

b. 1923 Kalispell, MT
d. 1961 Corvallis, OR
Education: University of Montana (1946); Colorado Springs Fine Arts Center (46–50); University of Colorado (50–52)
Membership: Master Watercolor Society of Oregon; American Watercolor Society; Portland Art Museum (Artist Membership)
Awards: Seattle Art Museum (1948); Spokane (48); Jocelyn Art Museum—Omaha (50); Portland Art Museum (55); Henry Art Gallery—University of Washington (56)
Collections: Portland Art Museum; University of Oregon; University of Washington; Seattle Art Museum; Victoria and Albert Museum—London; Coos Art Museum; Oregon State University
Exhibits: Seattle Art Museum (1948, 55–59); Denver Art Museum (50–52, 56, 57); Omaha, Nebraska (50–52); Corcoran Gallery of Art—Washington, D.C. (51); Oregon State University (1PS 55–57, 59); Portland Art Museum (AM, 1PS 57); Duveen Gallery—New York (58); Master Watercolor Society of Oregon (58); Chehalis Public Library—Washington (1PS 59); Oregon Centennial (59); University of Oregon (75)
References: HAV; WWAA; A3 (1956, 58); A4 (59); C6; C7 (55–57, 59); C22
Media: Watercolor, graphics
Specialty: Landscapes, murals

Robert Huck served in the U.S. Signal Corps from 1942 to 1945. Pursuing his art education, Huck traveled to Italy on a Fulbright Fellowship from 1954 to 1955. He exhibited nationally in group and one-person shows. His landscapes often contain the image of a hunter. The Henry Gallery in Seattle has a print by Huck in its collection.

Robert Huck said that, for him, painting was a basic problem of stating an experience; he was not interested in qualities of paint and arrangement of forms. Huck said that he must begin with a concrete idea. Much of his work related to the warmer Northwest colors of gold and russet. He painted a mural at the Portland Airport Sheraton.

Huck was on the art faculty of Oregon State College (now Oregon State University) from 1955 until his death in an auto accident in 1961.

HUFFMAN, Robert B.

b. d.
Exhibits: Portland Art Museum; Town Art Gallery (1947); Lincoln County Art Center (48)
References: A2 (1942, 44, 48); C14
Media: Oil, watercolor

Robert Huffman was the owner of the Towne Gallery in Portland and showed his watercolors there, at the Portland Art Museum, and at the Lincoln County Art Center on the Oregon Coast.

HUKARI, Oscar

b. 1878 Finland
d. 1962 Hood River, OR
Education: University of North Dakota; *C. Keller**
Membership: Oregon Society of Artists; American Artists Professional League
Awards: Oregon Society of Artists (1932)
Collections: Tofthagen Museum Library—Lakota, North Dakota
Exhibits: Oregon Society of Artists; American Artists Professional League (1932–34, 36–8); Portland Art Museum
References: COL; DAV; DAW; WWN;

A2 (1933, 34); C3 (32–36, 46, 47, 49, 50)
Media: Oil, pastel
Specialty: Landscapes

When Oscar Hukari moved to Oregon he studied painting with Clyde Keller*. He was a member of, and exhibited with, the American Artists Professional League, the Oregon Society of Artists, and the Portland Art Museum. Hukari won prizes at the Gresham Fair and the Multnomah County Fair. He was an orchardist in Hood River.

HULME, Harold

b. 1882 Birmingham, England
d. 1970 Clackamas, OR
Education: Birmingham Academy of Art—England; Paris
Membership: Oregon Society of Artists
Exhibits: Birmingham, England (1899); Securities Building—Seattle (1PS 1926); Oregon Society of Artists; Portland Art Museum
References: ALM; COL; DAV; DAW; WWN; A2 (1940); C3 (36)
Media: Oil

Harold Hulme received his art education in Birmingham, England, and Paris. He lived and worked in Oregon for much of his adult life. Hulme was listed in the Seattle City Directory of 1930. He presented one of his paintings to President Franklin Roosevelt in October of 1933. Hulme signed his paintings *Emluh*, which was Hulme spelled backwards.

HURGREN, Esther Robbins

b. 1839 NY ***d.***
Awards: Oregon State Fairs; Portland Mechanics Fairs (1881, 82)
Exhibits: Oregon State Fairs; Portland Mechanics Fairs
References: C4 (1879–82); OSF (70–72; 79); M2; M3
Media: Oil
Specialty: Still life, florals, china painting

Esther Robbins was a teacher of drawing and music at Spencer Hall (later St. Helen's Hall) in 1864. She was known for her china painting and flower panels.

HUSSEY, Rhoda C.

b. d.
Membership: Oregon Society of Artists; American Artists Professional League
Awards: Oregon Society of Artists (1933)
Exhibits: Portland Art Museum; American Artists Professional League (1933); Oregon Society of Artists; Lincoln County Art Center (48)
References: A2 (1932, 48); C3 (33, 47); C14
Media: Oil
Specialty: Landscapes

Rhoda Hussey was active in Oregon from 1930 to 1950. She exhibited with the American Artists Professional League and the Oregon Society of Artists. She participated in shows at the Portland Art Museum and the Lincoln County Art Center.

HUTCHINSON, Alice Holland

b. d.
Education: *S. Bell**
Membership: Oregon Society of Artists
Exhibits: Oregon Society of Artists; Portland Art Museum; Elfstrom Gallery; Citizens for Art Group (1959)
References: A2 (1948); A3 (54); C3 (46–50); C13 (47); CD (51)
Media: Oil

Alice Hutchinson studied with local artist Sidney Bell*. She exhibited in Portland and Salem during the 1940s and 50s and was represented by the Patecky Studio Gallery in Portland.

J

JACQUES, Emile

b. 1874 Moorslede, Flanders
d. 1937 Belaire, MI
Education: Ecole des Beaux Arts—Antwerp
Membership: Oregon Society of Artists; Society of Independent Artists—New York
Awards: Antwerp
Collections: University of Portland
Exhibits: Portland Art Museum (1PS 1923); Portland Woman's Club (26); Seattle Art Museum; Society of Independent Artists—New York (27); Oregon Society of Artists; Art Institute of Chicago (29); New York City (35); National Gallery of Art (35)
References: DAV; DAW; HAV; HUG; MAL; OET; WWW; C3 (1928); C7 (26, 27); CD (25–29)
Media: Oil, prints (lithograph, mezzotint)
Specialty: Landscapes, religious paintings, murals

A Flemish painter in the tradition of the Dutch and Flemish schools, Jacques taught in The Hague from 1919 to 1923. His reputation had already been established in Europe when his family near Portland drew him to Oregon. In 1923 he created an art department at Columbia University (now the University of Portland) and was dean until 1929, when he left to teach art at the University of Notre Dame.

Within a few months of his arrival in Portland he had a one-person show at the Portland Art Museum. He opened a studio in the Ainsworth Building, where Darrel Austin* and Margot Helser* became his students. Jacques loved Oregon scenery and painted many views from life. During his time in Portland, Jacques exhibited nationwide to excellent critical reviews.

He was a muralist whose work adorned public spaces and private homes. Jacques painted murals in Antwerp, for the University of Notre Dame, the chapel at the University of Portland, and St. Mary's Cathedral in Portland. Darrel Austin* was the model for several angels in some of Jacques' murals. Emile Jacques drowned while on vacation in Michigan.

JAMES, Jimmie

b. 1883 Woodston, KS
d. 1969 Portland, OR
Education: Art Institute of Chicago; Metro Art Institute—New York
Membership: American Artists Professional League; Oregon Society of Artists; Silver Palette Club
Exhibits: Oregon Society of Artists
References: COL; DAV; DAW; WWN; C3 (1929, 31); CD (31)
Media: Oil, etching, charcoal
Specialty: Landscapes

Jimmie James received his formal training at the Art Institute of Chicago and in New York. He was a veteran of World War I, arriving in Oregon in 1919. He developed a technique of charcoal drawing influenced by nature, his part-Cherokee heritage, and early American Indian art and artifacts. He had a large personal collection of Indian artifacts. One of his best-known paintings was a view of the Bridge of the Gods, which spans the Columbia River.

James was an activist who worked unsuccessfully to save Celilo Falls on the Columbia River from being flooded by the dam built at The Dalles in 1957.

JAMESON, Demetrios George

b. 1919 St. Louis, MO
d. 1996 Corvallis, OR
Education: Washington University—St. Louis, Missouri: *Beckmann* (1949); University of Illinois (50)
Membership: Artists Equity; Master Watercolor Society of Oregon; Portland Art Museum (Artist Membership)
Awards: St. Louis (1947); Denver Art Museum (51); Portland Art Museum (51, 52, 54); Seattle Art Museum (54); Oregon State Fair (57)
Collections: Portland Art Museum; Coos Art Museum; Goodman Collection; Salishan Lodge Collection; Seattle Art Museum; Victoria and Albert Museum—London; Oregon State University; Tacoma Art Museum; Hallie Ford Museum of Art—Willamette University; University of Oregon; Oregon State University
Exhibits: Seattle Art Museum; Denver Art Museum (1951, 53); Oakland Art Gallery (51); Portland Art Museum (AM, 1PS 52); Library of Congress (52); Willamette University (1PS 52, 55); Kraushaar Galleries—New York City (52); Corcoran Gallery of Art—Washington, D.C.(53); Kharouba Gallery (53); Guggenheim Museum (54); Oregon State Fair (57); Oregon State University (1PS 57); Master Watercolor Society of Oregon (58); Oregon Centennial (59)
References: DAV; WWAA; A3 (1951–56, 58); A4 (52, 59); C6; C7 (46, 51–59)
Media: Oil, watercolor, prints
Specialty: Figures, landscapes
See artwork in color section

A Navy combat artist during World War II, Demetrios Jameson came to Oregon in 1950. He was an assistant professor of art at Oregon State College (now Oregon State University) from 1950 until his retirement in 1982. Jameson exhibited throughout the United States and won awards in St. Louis, Denver, Seattle, and Portland.

Jameson's earlier works were almost exclusively figures. The female figure was used as a symbol of strength and creation; children seemed caught on canvas at a significant moment in a complex game. His treatment was formal and linear, with jewel-like colors. When Jamison moved into landscapes he retained a similar palette. He sought to express the purity and essence of an idea in a simple form.

"Art," Jamison said, "is a document of the personality of the artist: his soul, mind, sensitivity and his temperament. It is a constant search for his own true self. It becomes his way of life, his document of the century in which he lives."

JAMIESON, Agnes D.

b. d.
Education: School of Design—Pittsburgh, Pennsylvania; New York: *Dewey*
Membership: Oregon Art Association
Exhibits: Oregon Art Association (1896); Portland Art Museum
References: DAV; DAW; PET; WWW; A2 (1911, 13, 15); A4 (11); ARTC; CD (1900–02, 14–17)
Media: Oil
Specialty: Miniatures

Agnes Jamieson was a member of the Oregon Artists Association and exhibited with them in 1896. An article in the Portland *Spectator* of February 26, 1910 stated that Agnes Jamieson was a talented miniature artist.

JANNEY, Maury. *See* HASELTINE, Maury

JANSON, Ronald Tore

b. 1935 Klamath Falls, OR ***d.***
Education: Museum Art School (1953–57); University of Oregon (57–59)
Collections: University of Oregon; Pacific Northwest College of Art
Exhibits: Klamath Falls Art Association (1957); Portland Art Museum; Oregon Centennial (59)
References: A3 (1958); A4 (59); C6
Media: Oil, pencil, acrylic
Specialty: Figures

Ron Janson graduated from Klamath Union High School in 1953 and came to Portland to attend the four-year program at the Museum Art School. He continued his education at the University of Oregon and Portland State University, where he added a teaching certificate to his other degrees. Most of Janson's exhibitions took place after 1959 when his work was shown in Seattle, San Francisco, Goteborg, Sweden, and throughout Oregon. He signed his work *Tore Janson.*

JARDON, L.E.

b. d.
Education: Ecole des Beaux Arts—Paris
Collections: Oregon Historical Society
Exhibits: Portland Industrial Exposition (1891); Paris; Oregon Historical Society (1990)
References: BEN; DAV; GER; C2 (1891); C9
Media: Oil
Specialty: Portraits, still life

L.E. Jardon, a well-known Parisian artist, came to Portland in the late 1880s for a lengthy visit. He was in demand in Portland as a portrait artist. His name is sometimes spelled L.E. Jourdan, L.E. Jardin or Le Jardon.

JEFFERY, George

b. 1864 Derbyshire, England
d. 1940 Portland, OR
Education: George Stephenson Memorial Hall—Chesterfield, England
Membership: Oregon Society of Artists
Awards: Lewis and Clark Centennial Exposition (1905)
Collections: Nottingham Castle—England; Oregon Historical Society
Exhibits: Lewis and Clark Centennial Exposition (1905); Seattle Art Museum; Oregon Society of Artists; Portland Art Museum
References: DAV; C3 (1928, 31); C7 (27); C10; CD (1899–1915, 18)
Media: Oil
Specialty: China painting, miniatures

George Jeffery was apprenticed to the Crown Derby China Works in England. He painted the dinnerware presented to Prime Minister Gladstone. Jeffery was an art teacher in Chesterfield, England and New York. He moved to Portland, where he lived for fifty years. Jeffery was a WPA artist who exhibited at the Portland and Seattle Art Museums. The Oregon Historical Society has Jeffery's hand-painted punch bowl and cups in its collection. His last name is sometimes spelled *Jeffrey*.

JENSEN, Eunice. *See* PARSONS, Eunice

JOHANSON, George

b. 1928 Seattle, WA ***d.***
Education: Museum Art School: *L. Bunce*, W. Givler*, J. McLarty*, M. Russo** (1946–50); Atelier 17—New York City: *Schrag* (51); Mexico
Membership: Portland Art Museum (Artist Membership); Artists Equity
Awards: Western Washington Fair (1955)
Collections: Portland Art Museum; Henry Art Gallery—University of Wash-

ington; Art Institute of Chicago; Lewis and Clark College; University of Oregon; Reed College; Seattle Art Museum; Oregon State University; National Museum of American Art; Goodman Collection; Kaiser Permanente Collection; Arlene and Harold Schnitzer Collection; Capitol Collection—Salem; Hallie Ford Museum of Art—Willamette Universtiy; Pacific Northwest College of Art; Parsons Collection

Exhibits: Portland Art Museum (AM, 1PS 1957); Kharouba Gallery (50); Wittenborn Gallery—New York (52); Western Washington Fair (55); Morrison Street Gallery (56); Santa Barbara Museum of Art (57); Portland State University (58); Reed College (58, 59); Ruthermore Gallery—San Francisco (59); Oregon Centennial (59); University of Oregon (75)

References: OET; WWAA; A3 (1949, 50, 54, 56–59); A4 (59); C6; C7 (53, 54); C20; C22; C27; C30 (53–55)

Media: Prints (etching), oil

Specialty: Portraits, murals, animals

See artwork in color section

See photograph of artist on p. 84

A *Scholastic Magazine* scholarship brought George Johanson to Portland from Seattle in 1946 to attend the Museum Art School. It was his first acquaintance with fine art and it also introduced him to printmaking. He joined fellow artists Rick Norwood* and Bob Galaher* in a traveling exhibition of best student artists in 1949. He assisted artist Lucia Wiley* with the murals she completed in Tillamook in 1950. In 1951 he traveled to New York to study etching at Atelier 17. He spent two years as a volunteer in rural Mexico and then returned to Portland in 1955. Soon after his return he joined the faculty of the Museum Art School and remained there for twenty-five years until his retirement in 1980, serving as head of the printmaking department for fifteen years. Johanson received the Governor's Award for the Arts in 1992.

Working out of a studio in his home, Johanson always divided his time between painting and printmaking. His subject matter often included figures in interior spaces with the cityscape in the distance. Strong surrealist tones, underlying mystery with colors that evoke another time or place, figures caught up in situations that are fascinating to observe and yet distanced from the observer are all characteristics of his work. The omnipresent cat is also a feature. Little affected by the landscape of the region, Johanson's studies grew out of of his own invention and originality.

JOHN, Margaret Sawyer

b. 1885 Patoka, IL ***d.***

Education: Art Institute of Chicago

Membership: Oregon Society of Artists; American Artists Professional League

Awards: American Artists Professional League (1932, 34, 36); Seattle Art Museum (32); Oregon State Fair; Oregon Society of Artists (35); Multnomah County Fair

Exhibits: Seattle Art Museum; Oregon Society of Artists; American Artists Professional League (1932–37); Portland Art Museum; Corvallis Art Center (1PS 38); Oregon State Fair; Multnomah County Fair

References: ALM; COL; DAV; DAW; HAV; MAL; PET; WWN; WWW; A2 (1933, 44, 46); C3 (28, 29, 32–35, 45); C7 (27, 32)

Media: Oil

Specialty: Still life, florals, landscapes

Margaret John was a member of, and exhibited with, the Oregon Society of Artists and the American Artists Professional League. She won prizes at the Multnomah County Fair, the Oregon State Fair, the American Artists Professional League, the Oregon Society of Artists, and the Seattle Art Museum shows. She lived in Corvallis from 1928 to 1936.

JOHNSON, Anne Michalov

b. 1904 Chicago, IL ***d.***
Education: Art Institute of Chicago (1937)
Membership: Oregon Art Alliance; Portland Art Museum (Artist Membership)
Collections: Parsons Collection; Sylvia Beach Hotel—Newport
Exhibits: Panama Pacific International Exposition—San Francisco (1915); New York World's Fair (39); Portland Art Museum; Seattle Art Museum; Oregon Centennial (59)
References: KOV; A3 (1954)
Media: Watercolor, oil, tempera, prints (etching, lithograph, murals)
Specialty: Landscape, still life, murals

Anne Michalov Johnson studied at the Art Institute of Chicago, graduating in 1937. She worked under the WPA and created murals for Chicago schools. Johnson exhibited at the New York World's Fair in 1939. She taught at the Spokane Art Center for the WPA. She later moved to Oregon with her husband, Willard Johnson*. Favored subject matter included Idaho's mining towns and Oregon's coastal scenes. Kovinick (see Ref. KOV) lists her birth place as Coal City, West Virginia.

JOHNSON, Clara M.

b. d.
Awards: Oregon State Fairs
Exhibits: Oregon State Fairs; North Pacific Industrial Exposition (1889)
References: C2 (1889); CD (90–92, 94); OSF (84, 89)
Media: Oil
Specialty: Marines

Clara Johnson lived in Portland and Oregon City. She exhibited oil paintings at the Industrial Exposition and the Oregon State Fairs.

JOHNSON, Doro H.

b. d.
Membership: Artists Equity; Oregon Society of Artists; Portland Art Museum (Artist Membership)
Exhibits: Oregon Society of Artists; Portland Art Museum; Oregon Centennial (1959)
References: A3 (1954–56); C3 (49, 50); C6; CD (50, 53–4, 55)
Media: Oil, casein, prints
Specialty: Abstracts

Doro Johnson, a member of Artists Equity and the Oregon Society of Artists, exhibited in Portland during the 1950s.

JOHNSON, Halley Phillip

b. d.
Education: University of Oregon (1935)
Membership: American Artists Professional League; University Alumni Art League, University of Oregon
Awards: American Artists Professional League (1932)
Collections: University of Oregon
Exhibits: American Artists Professional League (1932–34); University of Oregon (33); University Alumni Art League; Portland Art Museum
References: A2 (1946, 48); C25 (35, 36)
Media: Oil

Halley Johnson was a WPA artist. An oil painting entitled, *Forestry*, which he produced under the WPA in 1941, is in the University of Oregon collection. He was also known as Phillip Johnson. He left a bequest to create a scholarship in his name for a fine arts student. It was first awarded in 1972–73.

JOHNSON, Jeannette D.

b. 1909 Warrenton, MO ***d.***

Education: Museum Art School
Membership: Arts Guild
Awards: Portland Art Museum (1937); Oregon State Fair (35)
Collections: Portland Art Museum
Exhibits: Portland Art Museum; Creative Art Gallery (1933); Arts Guild; Oregon State Fair (35)
References: COL; WWN; A2 (1932–34, 40); A3 (35, 37); A4 (36); A5 (33); C10
Media: Oil, watercolor, prints (etching)
Specialty: Genre, landscapes

Jeannette Johnson was a scholarship student at Portland's Museum Art School from 1934 to 1936. She was a member of the Arts Guild, with whom she exhibited in 1933. Johnson won the Carey Prize for drawing in 1934 and 1936. She was a WPA artist, a printmaker, and craftsperson.

JOHNSON, Josephine Devore (Josie)

b. 1845 IL
d. 1927 Portland, OR
Education: Willamette University (1868)
Awards: Oregon State Fairs
Exhibits: Oregon State Fairs; Portland Mechanics Fairs; Oregon Historical Society (1990)
References: C4 (1878, 80); C9; OSF (72–78); M2; M3
Media: Watercolor, pencil, crayon
Specialty: Nature

Josephine Johnson arrived in Oregon in 1852. She lived in Salem and Oregon City, studied literature and art at Willamette University, and was the first woman on the Pacific Coast to be awarded the degrees of B.A. and M.A. She exhibited at Oregon State Fairs and the Portland Mechanics Fairs. Johnson was a leader in the Oregon women's sufferage movement. Her son, Merle Johnson, born in 1874, became a noted New York illustrator and cartoonist.

JOHNSON, Lorraine DeYoung

b. d.
Education: Museum Art School
Membership: Arts Guild; Klamath Falls Art Association
Exhibits: Arts Guild; Portland Art Museum
References: A2 (1932, 33); A4 (72); A5 (30); CD (32)
Media: Watercolor
Specialty: Genre

A graduate of the Museum Art School and member of the Arts Guild, Lorraine De Young exhibited at the Portland Art Museum during the 1930s. She was a member and president of the Klamath Falls Art Association in southern Oregon.

JOHNSON, Willard C.

b. 1902 Minneapolis, MN
d. 1990 Portland, OR
Education: Chicago Academy of Fine Arts (1926); Art Institute of Chicago (27–31); Museum Art School (53)
Membership: Artists Equity; Portland Art Museum (Artist Membership)
Collections: Portland Art Museum; U.S. Marine Hospital—Lexington, Kentucky; Sylvia Beach Hotel—Newport
Exhibits: Finley Gallery, American Fore Gallery—Chicago (1939); University of Michigan (40); Portland Art Museum (AM, 54); Dekum Gallery; Elfstrom Gallery (52); Oregon Centennial (59)
References: DAV; A3 (1950–52, 55, 56)
Media: Watercolor, oil, prints (lithograph)
Specialty: Landscapes (mountains, ocean), nature

A position as an artist for the Bonneville Power Administration brought Willard Johnson to Oregon in 1948. He painted many Northwest scenes with a strong, forceful technique and a free-flowing style. His work was exhibited at the Portland Art Museum, the Dekum Gallery, and the Elfstrom Gallery. His wife, Ann Michalov Johnson*, was an artist specializing in printmaking and watercolors.

JOSEPH, Julius

b. 1867
d. 1901 Albany, OR
Membership: Portland Sketch Club
Exhibits: Portland Sketch Club (1900); Lewis and Clark Centennial Exposition (05)
References: C21; ARTC

Julius Joseph was a member of the Portland Sketch Club and exhibited with them in 1900. He also exhibited at the Lewis and Clark Exposition in 1905.

JOURDAN, Alda Burke Peasley

b. 1889 Salem, OR
d. 1962 Portland, OR
Education: Art Institute of Chicago
Membership: American Artists Professional League; Oregon Society of Artists; Society of Independent Artists—New York
Awards: Seattle Art Museum (1929)
Collections: Los Angeles County Museum of Art; Painting Restoration Studio Collection; Oregon Historical Society
Exhibits: Portland Woman's Club (1926); Oregon Society of Artists; Society of Independent Artists—New York (27); Seattle Art Museum; American Artists Professional League (32); Portland Art Museum; San Francisco Art Association
References: BI; COL; DAV; DAW; SIA; WWN; A2 (1932, 33); C3 (27–31); C7 (29, 30); M2; M3
Media: Watercolor
Specialty: Landscapes, botanicals, florals

Alda Jourdan was a skilled photographer, author, and teacher as well as an accomplished painter. As Alda Peasley, she and her husband shared a photographic studio from 1914 to 1925. With her second husband Albert Jourdan, also a photographer, she exhibited their realistic photographic art nationally and internationally. Alda Jourdan wrote many articles on art and photography.

JUNK, Anna

b. 1847 NE
d. 1934 Salem, OR
Awards: Oregon State Fairs
Collections: Bush House Museum—Salem
Exhibits: Oregon State Fairs; World Columbian Exposition—Chicago (1893)
References: SI; OR (Salem Art Association); OSF (1894–97, 1902, 08); M2
Media: Oil, pastel
Specialty: Still life, florals, wildlife, china painting
See artwork in color section

Anna Junk had the first china-firing kiln in Salem. She sold her china and paintings from her studio, where she also taught. The Salem Art Association recommended this artist, whose name can be found in the artist section of the Salem City Directory in 1909. Her still life, *Pumpkins and Apples*, an Oregon State Fair award winner, is on view at the Bush House Museum in Salem.

K

KAFOURY, Eleanor Patten

b. 1909 Minneapolis, MN *d.*
Education: Minneapolis School of Art; University of Oregon (1927–32)
Membership: University Alumni Art League, University of Oregon
Exhibits: Portland Art Museum; University Alumni Art League
References: COL; WWN; A2 (1933, 34, 38); C10; C25 (35, 36)
Media: Oil, watercolor, acrylic, mixed media
Specialty: Nature

Eleanor Kafoury was a WPA painter who preferred nature-related subjects. Her later work became abstract. Kafoury was an art teacher at Jefferson High School in Portland for nine years. The Rental Sales Gallery at the Portland Art Museum has represented her.

KAMEI, Yasuo

b. d.
Membership: Oregon Society of Artists
Exhibits: Oregon Society of Artists; Portland Art Museum
References: COL; WWN; A2 (1940); A3 (37, 38); C3 (27); CD (24, 25)
Media: Oil
Specialty: Landscapes, portraits, genre

Yasuo Kamei exhibited at the Portland Art Museum and with the Oregon Society of Artists from the 1920s to the 1940s.

KARL, Margaret (Maggie)

b. 1921 Ft. Collins, CO *d.*
Education: University of Oregon; Oregon State University; Kansas State University
Collections: Coos Art Museum
Exhibits: University of Oregon; Oregon State Fair; Coos Art Museum; Master Watercolor Society of Oregon (1958)
References: OR (Coos Art Museum)
Media: Encaustic, watercolor, oil

Margaret Karl taught adult art courses at S.W. Oregon Community College. She was an early director of the Coos Bay Museum, the Corvallis Art Center, and the Eugene Art Center.

KEE, Bue

b. 1893 Portland, OR
d. 1985 Multnomah County, OR
Education: Museum Art School; Arts and Crafts Society
Membership: American Artists Professional League; Arts Guild
Collections: Portland Art Museum
Exhibits: Portland Art Museum; Arts Guild; American Artists Professional League (1937, 38); Meier and Frank Co. (40)
References: COL; WWN; A2 (1930, 40, 42, 44, 46, 48); A3 (36–39); A4 (59); A5 (30)
Media: Oil, watercolor, pastel
Specialty: Landscapes

Bue Kee was a WPA artist who worked in oil, watercolor, and pastel, but mainly in ceramics. Some of Kee's ceramic pieces are displayed at Timberline Lodge on Mt. Hood.

KEITH, William

b. 1839 Old Meldrum, Scotland
d. 1911 San Francisco
Education: Dusseldorf (1868); Munich (83–86)

Awards: Pan American Exposition—Buffalo (1901)
Collections: Brooklyn Art Museum; Corcoran Gallery of Art—Washington, D.C.; Los Angeles County Museum of Art; Portland Art Museum; University of Oregon; Stenzel Collection
Exhibits: Portland Mechanics Fair; World Columbian Exposition—Chicago (1893); Pan American Exposition—Buffalo (1901); Portland Art Museum (1PS 11); Lewis and Clark Centennial Exposition (05); Mark Hopkins Institute (1PS 08); Alaska-Yukon Pacific Exposition—Seattle (09); University of Oregon (59); Washington State Historical Society—Tacoma (85)
References: BEN; BI; DAV; DAW; FIE; HUG; MAL; GER; GW; SAM; SM; THI; WWW; YNG; A1 (1902, 06, 08, 09); C4 (1883); C13; C21; C28
Media: Oil
Specialty: Landscapes

William Keith arrived in America in 1851 and made his way to California. Later he was hired by the Oregon Navigation and Railroad Company to paint the Northwest country. He pursued art studies in Dusseldorf in 1868 and Munich from 1883 to 1886. In the winter of 1869 Keith sketched along the Columbia River, then climbed and painted views of Mt. Hood. He painted a series of views along an Oregon stagecoach route which were used as engravings for business advertisements. In 1887 Keith and John Muir passed through Oregon on a painting trip from Lake Tahoe to British Columbia. He had a painting in the 1908 opening show of the Shop of Fine Arts and Industries in Portland.

Keith was a reknowned teacher. He accepted more women than men as students at a time when this was uncommon. He achieved a reputation as a California artist and became a leader in the art community.

KELLER, Clyde Leon

b. 1872 Salem, OR
d. 1962 Cannon Beach, OR
Education: Willamette University: *M. Bridges,* M. LeGall*; Knowles; Christmas*
Membership: Mutual Art Association; Society of Oregon Artists; Oregon Society of Artists; American Artists Professional League
Awards: Oregon State Fair; Seattle Art Museum (1923); American Artists Professional League (32); Oregon Society of Artists (33, 35, 37, 39, 43)
Collections: Oregon Historical Society; Powell Collection; Miranda Collection; Painting Restoration Studio Collection; Parsons Collection; Counting Eagles Collection; Lundberg Collection; Pathways Collection; Cofield Collection; Slippery Slope Historical Collection
Exhibits: Portland Art Museum; Society of Oregon Artists (1913); Mutual Art Association (14, 15); Panama Pacific International Exposition—San Francisco (15); Seattle Art Museum; Great Crystal Palace—New York City (24); Portland Woman's Club (26); Oregon Society of Artists (39); American Artists Professional League (32, 33, 37–39); Elfstrom Gallery; Lincoln County Art Center (48, 49); Oregon Historical Society (90); Clatsop County Historical Society (94); Oregon State Fair
References: ALM; BEN; BI; COL; DAV; DAW; FIE; GER; HAV; HUG; MAL; OET; SAM; THI; WWN; WWW; YNG; A2 (1912–14, 16, 17, 19, 21, 22, 33, 34, 40, 42, 44, 46); A4 (29); C3 (27–29, 32–36, 43, 45–51); C5; C7 (19–23,

25– 30); C9; C11; C13 (46–48); C14; ARTC; CD (40, 41, 43–4, 50, 52)
Media: Oil; watercolor
Specialty: Landscapes, seascapes, portraits
See artwork in color section
See photograph of artist on p. 84

In 1884, at the age of 12, Clyde Leon Keller was enrolled at Willamette University, attending the drawing class taught by Mary Bridges*. He later studied there under Marie LeGall*. By 1893 he had an artist listing in the Salem City Directory and in 1894, under the influence of Homer Davenport, he began his career as a cartoonist for the *San Francisco Examiner.* Keller began by painting landscapes and portraits but his teacher, E. W. Christmas, advised him to concentrate on landscapes. While in San Francisco he opened an art shop but lost everything in the 1906 earthquake.

Keller returned to his native Oregon and opened an art and frame shop in Portland from 1907 to 1936, where he taught, painted, and held exhibitions. He was a founding member of the Society of Oregon Artists and, later, a founding member of the Oregon Society of Artists, for which he served as president in 1931. His son, Clyde Keller Jr., a well-known watercolor artist, was also president of the Oregon Society of Artists.

When Keller was eighty-three he presented a painting, *The North Fork of the Santiam,* to his childhood friend, President Herbert Hoover. A painting of the Bonneville Dam by Keller hung behind Franklin D. Roosevelt's desk in the White House.

Keller was a prolific artist whose works were present in every state, thirteen European countries, and South America. He won over 275 prizes during his lifetime.

KELLER, Paul

b. 1902 Fremont, OH
d. 1976 Portland, OR
Education: Oregon State University; Chicago Academy of Fine Arts
Membership: Attic Club; Oregon Society of Artists; Portland Art Museum (Artist Membership)
Awards: Oregon Society of Artists (1933, 43)
Collections: Oregon Historical Society; Powell Collection; Painting Restoration Studio Collection; Lundberg Collection
Exhibits: Portland Art Museum; Oregon Society of Artists; Salons of America (1934) Oregon Historical Society (90); Clatsop County Historical Society (94)
References: COL; DAV; SA; WWN; A2 (1932, 33); A4 (46); C3 (32, 33, 43); C9; C11; ARTC
Media: Watercolor, oil, crayon, pen and ink
Specialty: Landscapes, genre, marines

Paul Keller came to Oregon with his family and grew up in Klamath Falls. He began his newspaper career with the *Portland News,* followed by the *San Francisco Chronicle.* In 1926 he returned to Portland and joined the *Oregon Journal* as a staff artist. While he also taught at the Portland Academy of Art from 1929 to 1931, his focus was on newspaper illustration. He later became head of the art department for the *Oregon Journal* until he left for military service during World War II. From 1934 to 1939, Keller drew a weekly series of Oregon vignettes for the newspaper. Two hundred of his sketches of Oregon were later reprinted as a book.

During the war, Keller was head of the art department for the Office of War Information in Calcutta. There he produced marine drawings and illustrated propaganda leaflets directed against the Burmese, Thai, Chinese, and Japanese. After the war, Keller returned to the

Oregon Journal and remained until his retirement in 1946. He then worked for an insurance agency until his death, doing promotional work on the side. He was a charter member, and later president, of the Oregon Society of Artists.

KEMP, Margaret Stark

b. 1925 Orlando, FL ***d.***
Education: Rollins College—Florida; Professional Institute—Richmond, Virginia (1942–46); University of Oregon: *D. McCosh** (46–49); Museum Art School
Membership: Artists Equity; Portland Art Museum (Artist Membership)
Exhibits: Art Museum—Richmond, Virginia; Spokane (1947); Klamath Falls (1PS 50); 12th Street Gallery—Eugene; Portland Art Museum (AM, 54; 1PS 55)
References: A3 (1950, 51, 53)
Media: Oil, watercolor, acrylic, pastels, prints (lithograph, etching)
Specialty: Landscapes, figures, portraits

Margaret Kemp was active as an artist in Oregon during the 1950s. She taught at the Maude Kerns Art Center in Eugene.

KENNEDY, Leta Marietta

b. 1895 Pendleton, OR
d. 1986 Portland, OR
Education: Museum Art School: *A. Crocker** (1917, 18); Columbia University; Colorado Springs Fine Arts Center: *Barrett, Robinson; Hofmann*
Membership: Oregon Society of Artists; Arts Guild; Portland Art Museum (Artist Membership)
Collections: Portland Art Museum; Pacific Northwest College of Art
Exhibits: Portland Art Museum; Arts Guild; Seattle Art Museum; Oregon Society of Artists; University of Oregon; Philadelphia Art Alliance (1939)
References: ALM; COL; DAV; DAW; HAV; PET; WWN; WWW; A2 (1920, 22, 30, 33); A3 (35); A5 (30); C3 (27, 28)
Media: Watercolor, oil, prints (etching)
Specialty: Landscapes
See photograph of artist on p. 84

Leta Kennedy was born on a farm near Pendleton and, in 1909, moved to Portland, where she attended Jefferson High School. She received her teaching certificate from Columbia University and returned to Oregon in 1922 to assume a faculty position at Portland's Museum Art School, remaining there for forty-nine years. Kennedy taught the full spectrum of art media with strengths in design and ceramics. William Givler*, former dean, said, "Many, many young artists in the area shared in what she had to give." Her main interest was in teaching, although she exhibited watercolors and oils at the Philadelphia Art Alliance and other venues. She worked in ceramics, crafts, and was also a designer.

KENNEDY, Richard H.

b. 1917 Portland, OR
d. 1998 Milwaukie, OR
Education: *P. Sheffers*, C. Keller*;* Art Students League: *Brackman;* National Academy of Design
Membership: Oregon Society of Artists
Awards: Oregon Society of Artists (1943)
Collections: Arlene and Harold Schnitzer Collection; Parsons Collection
Exhibits: Oregon Society of Artists; Portland Art Museum
References: A2 (1944); C3 (43, 45)
Media: Oil
Specialty: Landscapes

Richard Kennedy began experimenting with oil paint while at a dude ranch in eastern Oregon. In 1939 he was introduced to Peter Sheffers*, who encouraged him to develop his talent. Then Kennedy's abilities began to be recognized. After studying at the Art Students League he returned to

Portland, showing the impressionist influence of his teacher, Robert Brachman. Richard Kennedy depicted the lights and shadows of the Pacific landscape, urban and rural. He was a friend of Clyde Keller* and accompanied him on painting trips to Sauvie Island.

Kennedy retired from his position as a graphic artist in the early 1980s. He then devoted his time to painting and sketching Oregon scenery and taught at Clackamas Community College.

KENNELLY, Rosemarie

b. d.

Membership: Oregon Society of Artists

Awards: Oregon Society of Artists (1943)

Exhibits: Oregon Society of Artists; Portland Art Museum; Fole-Myers Gallery; J.K. Gill Gallery (2PS 1947)

References: A2 (1944); C3 (43, 46, 47, 49)

Media: Oil

Rosemarie Kennelly was a member of, and exhibited with, the Oregon Society of Artists in Portland in the 1940s. She exhibited with artist Anna Kirwan* in a two-person show at the J.K. Gill Gallery in 1947.

KENSLER, Barbara Sampson

b. 1927 ***d.***

Education: Art Institute of Chicago

Memberships: Klamath Falls Art Association

Collections: University of Oregon

Exhibits: Portland Art Museum; Fole-Myers Gallery (1957); Oregon Centennial (59)

References: A3 (1956); C6

Media: Casein, acrylic

Specialty: Murals

Barbara Kensler lived and painted in Hawaii, where she won many awards. She then moved to Klamath Falls, where she was a member of the Klamath Falls Art Association and created murals for the public schools of that community. Her husband, Gordon*, was also an artist.

KENSLER, Gordon L.

b. 1924 ***d.***

Education: University of Oregon; Art Institute of Chicago

Exhibits: Art Institute of Chicago; Portland Art Museum; Seattle Art Museum; Fole-Myers Gallery (1957); Oregon Centennial (59)

References: A3 (1953); C6; C7 (56, 59)

Media: Oil

Specialty: Landscapes, murals

Gordon Kensler was an assistant professor of art education at the University of Oregon. At one time he was art supervisor of Klamath Falls Public Schools and, with his wife Barbara*, painted murals in the schools. His oil paintings were shown at the Art Institute of Chicago, the Portland and Seattle Art Museums, and the Oregon Centennial exhibition.

KERNS, Maude Irvine

b. 1876 Portland, OR

d. 1965 Eugene, OR

Education: University of Oregon (1899); Mark Hopkins Institute; Columbia University: *Dow* (1904–06); New York: *Johnnot, Chase*; Art Institute of Chicago: *Wessels;* Académie Moderne—Paris; Japan

Membership: Oregon Society of Artists; American Artists Professional League; Oregon Guild of Painters and Sculptors; University Alumni Art League, University of Oregon, American Federation of Arts; California Watercolor Society; Kansas Print Society

Awards: Oregon State Fair; Alaska-Yukon Pacific Exposition—Seattle (1909); American Artists Professional League (34, 36); Pen and Brush Club (54)

Collections: University of Oregon; Portland Art Museum; Seattle Art Museum; Guggenheim Museum; Haseltine Collection; Painting Restoration Studio Collection; Maude Kerns Art Center

Exhibits: Oregon State Fair; Alaska-Yukon Pacific Exposition—Seattle (1909); Seattle Art Museum (1PS 46); Oregon Society of Artists; American Artists Professional League (32, 33, 34, 36); Portland Art Museum (1PS 47); Los Angeles County Museum of Art (34–36); University Alumni Art League; National Exhibition of American Art (36); Studio Guild—NewYork (1PS 39); Guggenheim Museum (41–52); Denver Art Museum (45); Oregon Guild of Painters and Sculptors (48; 1PS 49); Paris Salon—des Réalités Nouvelles (48); National Gallery of Art (1PS 54); Pen and Brush Club (54); National Association of Women Artists (55); University of Oregon (75); Oregon Historical Society (90); Autry Museum—Los Angeles (95)

References: ALM; COL; DAV; DAW; GER; HUG; KOV; MAL; PET; WWN; WWW; A2 (1932, 33, 40); A3 (35, 36); C3 (31); C7 (25, 26, 28a, 31, 34, 44–48, 51); C9; C18; C22; C23; C25 (35); OSF (02); M2; M3

Media: Oil, watercolor, tempera, prints

Specialty: Landscapes, portraits, abstracts

See artwork in color section

Maude Kerns met and studied with Arthur Wesley Dow in 1904 when she went to Columbia University Teachers College in New York. After her graduation in 1906 she moved to Seattle, where she taught art in high schools and, for two summers, at the University of Washington. During those years she continued to paint and exhibit. In 1913, due in no small part to the international perspective that Dow had introduced to his classes, Kerns traveled through Europe to study the modern art movements of futurism, cubism, expressionism and early abstraction. There she was exposed to, and influenced by, the works of Mondrian and Kandinsky. Dow had a lasting effect on the course of Kerns' artistic career. Their friendship continued until his death in 1922.

She came to the University of Oregon as the head of the new normal arts department (art education), remaining in that position until her retirement in 1947. A fire in the art school in 1922 destroyed her art collection and materials, so few early examples of her work exist.

In addition to the demands of teaching, Kerns continued what she called her own "independent painting career." She continued her art education, spending summers studying at the Art Institute of Chicago and in New York with Chase and Junnot. In the Northwest she was known primarily for her watercolor landscapes. At the same time, although few in the Northwest were aware, she was experimenting with abstractionism. By 1934 she had exhibited a completely abstract work in Los Angeles. She spent summers studying with Hans Hofmann and Alexander Archipenko and, in 1940, began her affiliation with the Museum of Non-Objective Art in New York (now the Guggenheim Museum). Kerns continued to exhibit there on a regular basis throughout the decade, sometimes with another Oregon artist, Albert Patecky.* She was an Oregon pioneer in the non-objective style, which placed her at odds with most of the Oregon art community. Kerns later became influenced by the simplification and spiritualism she found in Asian art and by similar trends in the European modern art movement. Her artistic development evolved from realistic landscapes and portraits to an emphasis on color and form, in a life-long process of moving away from the world of the physical toward the world of the spiritual. Kerns' early works, which reveal the underlying forms of nature and architecture as well as surface patterns, laid a foundation for her later abstractions. Subject matter became increasingly secondary to the combination of flat design, structural forms, and textural application of paint. Maude Kerns enjoyed a strong reputation in the East but was not as well known in her home state of Oregon.

After retiring from academic life, Kerns founded the Eugene Art Center in 1951, which was renamed the Maude Kerns Art Center in 1961. A retrospective of her artwork was held there in 1994.

KIMBRELL, Leonard Buell

b. 1922 Archibald, LA ***d.***
Education: University of Oregon (1949–54); University of Iowa (56–65)
Membership: Portland Art Museum (Artist Membership)
Collections: University of Oregon
Exhibits: Portland Art Museum (AM, 4PS 1959)
References: A3 (1954, 55, 57, 58)
Media: Watercolor, prints (lithograph)

Leonard Kimbrell taught art history and printmaking at Eastern Oregon State College in La Grande from 1958 to 1959. He moved to Portland State University in 1962, where he taught art history and became head of the art department in 1977. In 1959 he was part of a four-person show sponsored by the Artist Membership of the Portland Art Museum with Pattie Dodd*, Nelson Sandgren*, and Richard Newstrum*. Kimbrell was also an art critic, lecturer, and writer on art history.

KING, Kenneth L.

b. 1891 Sodus, MI ***d.***
Education: Chicago Academy of Fine Arts
Exhibits: Elfstrom Gallery; Lincoln County Art Center (1948)
References: C13 (1948); C14; CD (09–12, 15, 40, 41, 43–44)

Kenneth King divided his time between commercial and fine art. He worked for advertising agencies and eventually became an art director. He was a teacher at the Lincoln County Art Center in Lincoln City and lived at Wecoma Beach on the central Oregon Coast.

KIRWAN, Anna Mae

b. 1889 Richland, MO
d. 1985 Coos County, OR
Education: Museum Art School: *P. Sheffers*, S. Bell**
Membership: Oregon Society of Artists
Exhibits: Oregon Society of Artists; Portland Art Museum; J.K. Gill Gallery (2PS 1947); Citizens for Art Group (59); Oregon Centennial (59)
References: A2 (1946, 48); C3 (45–51)
Media: Oil
Specialty: Florals, landscapes, portraits

Anna Kirwan's impressionist paintings won awards at Gresham and Salem Fairs. She and artist Rosemary Kennelly* exhibited in a two-person show at the J.K.Gill Gallery in 1947. She lived for a time in Lake Oswego before moving to the southern Oregon Coast.

KLEIN, Lilly Veatch O'Ryan

b. ca. 1880 Sillery, Quebec, Canada ***d.***
Education: Cooper Union—New York City; New York City: *Brush, Chase, Metcalf, Cox;* Cowles Art School—Boston
Awards: New York University; World Columbian Exposition—Chicago (1893); Alaska-Yukon Pacific Exposition—Seattle (1909)
Collections: Oakland Museum; Yale University

Exhibits: World Columbian Exposition—Chicago (1893); New York University; Alaska-Yukon Pacific Exposition—Seattle (1909); Panama Pacific International Exposition—San Francisco (15); San Francisco Art Association

References: BI; DAV; DAW; GER; HUG; PET; WWW; C5; CD (1907–18); M2

Media: Oil, watercolor, pastel

Specialty: Portraits, miniatures

Lilly Klein was born around the 1880s. During her four years at the Cooper Union in New York City, she won first prize for antique, life, and portrait classes each year. She also took top prize for portraiture at New York University. At that time she was known as O'Ryan.

She moved to San Francisco in 1900 and lived there until 1906, when she lost most of her work in the earthquake. She then established a studio in Portland about 1907, where she was a portraitist until 1924. Klein received an award at the Alaska-Yukon Exposition in 1909. She also exhibited at the Panama Pacific International Exposition, San Francisco in 1915.

Klein depicted many personages, including a famous painting of Archbishop Christie of Oregon. She also received acclaim for her work as a sculptor, and her clay figures, busts and figurines she called "humoresques," sold well.

Klein and her husband moved to San Francisco in 1924 and lived there until his death in 1933.

KLEP, Rolf

b. 1904 Portland, OR

d. 1981 Portland, OR

Education: University of Oregon; Art Institute of Chicago; Art Students League

Membership: Pacific Arts Guild

Collections: University of Oregon; Mariner's Museum, Library, City Hall—Astoria; Haseltine Collection

Exhibits: University of Oregon (1975)

References: ALM; DAV; WWW; C22

Media: Oil, watercolor

Specialty: Marines, seascapes

From his childhood in Astoria, at the mouth of the Columbia River, Rolf Klep acquired a love of ships and the sea. He pursued his art studies at the University of Oregon, the Art Institute of Chicago, and the Art Students League. In New York he became a commercial artist who adapted the photo airbrush to advertising illustration techniques. He was also an author and illustrator of books and magazines. Klep returned to the Oregon Coast in 1956, living in Surf Pines, Gearhart. He did much of the research and all the drawings for the reconstruction of historic Fort Clatsop on the northern Oregon Coast.

KNOWLES, W.L. Everett

b. Clinton, CT *d.*

Membership: Society of Oregon Artists; Mutual Art Association

Collections: Counting Eagles Collection

Exhibits: Society of Oregon Artists; Mutual Art Association (1914, 15)

References: ARTC; CD (1917, 18)

Media: Watercolor

Specialty: Landscapes, marines, portraits

Everett Knowles was president of the Mutual Art Association in Portland from 1914 to 1916. He exhibited at Clyde Keller's* gallery in 1911. His paintings were relatively small in size and often rendered on cardboard. Knowles was known as a lecturer and writer on the arts. Drawings by Knowles are in the collection of the Oregon Historical Society. He signed his work *W.L.E. Knowles.*

KOCH, Karl F.

b. 1888 Sandusky, OH

d. 1975 Portland, OR
Education: Minneapolis School of Art; New York School of Art: *Henri*
Membership: Oregon Society of Artists; Portland Art Museum (Artist Membership)
Awards: Oregon Society of Artists
Collections: Oregon Historical Society
Exhibits: Oregon Society of Artists; Portland Art Museum; Seattle Art Museum
References: COL; DAV; DAW; WWN; A2 (1934, 40, 42, 46); A3 (35, 36); C3 (32–34); C7 (38)
Media: Oil, tempera, watercolor
Specialty: Landscapes

Karl Koch studied at the Minneapolis School of Art and the New York School of Art. He was art director for the Foster & Kleiser Advertising Agency in Portland. Koch exhibited at the Portland and Seattle Art Museums in the 1930s and 1940s.

KOLLOCK, Mary

b. 1832 Norfolk, VA
d. 1911 New York City, NY
Education: Pennsylvania Academy of Fine Art—Philadelphia; Art Students League: *Wylie, Bristol, Wyatt;* Académie Julian; Académie Delecluse
Membership: Oregon Art Association
Exhibits: Pennsylvania Academy of Fine Art—Philadelphia (1864, 76–87); Philadelphia Centennial Exposition; National Academy of Design (1866–87); Oregon Industrial Exposition (95); Oregon Art Association (96)
References: BEN; BI; DAV; GW; KOV; PET; THI; WWW; YNG; A1 (1895, 96); C2 (95); CD (95, 96); M2; M3
Media: Oil
Specialty: Landscapes, still life, portraits

Mary Kollock was a well-trained artist who was brought to Portland to head the art department of St. Helen's Hall from 1895 to 1897. She exhibited in Philadelphia, New York City, and in Oregon at the Industrial Exposition and the Oregon Art Association. Petteys (see Ref. PET) gives a birth date of 1840.

KOWERT, Henry (Hank) John

b. 1924 Chicago, IL
d. 1977 McMinnville, OR
Education: Cranbrook Academy—Bloomfield Hills, Michigan: *Sepesky* (1948–51); Haystack Mountain School (55)
Membership: Portland Art Museum (Artist Membership)
Awards: Oregon Centennial (1959)
Collections: Pacific University; Eastern Oregon College; Salem Art Association; Sunriver Lodge; Salishan Lodge Collection; University of Oregon; Portland Art Museum; Goodman Collection; Reed College; Kaiser Permanente Collection; Parsons Collection; Catlin Gabel School Collection; Capitol Collection—Salem; Hallie Ford Museum of Art—Willamette University
Exhibits: Portland Art Museum (AM, 1PS 1954); Eastern Oregon College; Pacific University; Denver Art Museum; Seattle Art Museum (58); Bush Barn—Salem; Cafe Espresso Gallery (59); Oregon Centennial (59); University of Oregon (75)
References: A3 (1953, 54, 57, 58); C6; C7 (58, 59); C22
Media: Oil, watercolor, prints (serigraph)
Specialty: Landscapes (Oregon), still life
See artwork in color section

Hank Kowert arrived in Oregon in the early 1950s. His work was a distillation of his vision of nature through the perception of changes in light, atmosphere, and the passage of the seasons. Kowert used a very distinctive palette, described as tawny, golden, earthy shades, burning reds, acidic greens, and almost transparent blues. He was well known for his silk-screen calendars.

Kowert produced a small body of work because he was particular about what he released. He rarely allowed sketches or unfinished pieces to be seen, even by close friends. He had many one-person shows and received numerous awards after 1959. Kowert appeared to be recovering from injuries he suffered in an auto accident when he died suddenly in 1977.

KRAUSE, LaVerne Irene Erickson

b. 1924 Portland, OR
d. 1987 Eugene, OR
Education: University of Oregon: *J. Wilkinson** (1946); Museum Art School (52–58)
Membership: Artists Equity; Portland Art Museum (Artist Membership)
Awards: Oregon Centennial (1959)
Collections: Portland Art Museum; Seattle Art Museum; Henry Art Gallery—University of Washington; First National Bank; Portland State University; Reed College; Oregon Historical Society; University of Oregon; Salishan Lodge Collection; Haseltine Collection; Coos Art Museum; Kaiser Permanente Collection; Booth Collection; Tonkon Torp Collection; Painting Restoration Studio Collection; Parsons Collection; Arlene and Harold Schnitzer Collection; Hurst Collection; Huntington Collection; Capitol Collection—Salem; Pacific University; Lundberg Collection
Exhibits: Portland Art Museum (1PS 1952; 3PS 52, AM, 1PS 58); Seattle Art Museum (47, 55, 58, 59); Kharouba Gallery (1PS 51, 54); Adele's Restaurant (1PS 54); Wichita Art Association Annual (54, 58, 59); University of Oregon (55, 56, 58, 75); Marylhurst College (55); Bush Barn—Salem; Linfield College; Oregon State University; Smithsonian Institution; 12th Ave. Gallery—Eugene (58); Chehalis Public Library—Washington (1PS 58); Cafe Espresso Gallery (59); Philadelphia Sketch Club (59); Oregon Centennial (59)
References: WWAA; A2 (1946); A3 (49–56, 58); C6; C7 (47, 55, 58, 59); C10; C22
Media: Oil, watercolor, acrylic, prints
Specialty: Landscapes, seascapes
See artwork in color section
See photograph of artist on p. 85

LaVerne Krause was orphaned as a child. She later won an art scholarship to the University of Oregon. While there she considered Jack Wilkinson* to be her greatest teacher. She married and, when her children were small, painted from her home. When they were old enough to attend school, she began taking classes at the Museum Art School. Included in her exhibitions during this time was a four-woman show at the Kharouba Gallery with LaVon Lucas*, Amanda Snyder*, and Jolan Torok*.

In 1959 Krause's style moved toward abstract expressionism. Her palette ranged from hot purple, red, and turquoise to cool pastels, with the color applied in repeating bands. She believed light and color were central to conveying the mood of what was experienced. Form was conveyed through a tension between positive and negative, frontality and deep space, and between paint and the raw linen that was her canvas of choice. Her early paintings showed bridges, cities, and architecture—used for their structural qualities as well as their evocative powers. As her painting matured, she stripped them down to the simplest forms, using color and light to develop her vision.

Krause was instrumental in founding the Oregon Artists Equity. In 1959 she began teaching at the Museum Art School and later at the Arts and Crafts Society and the University of Oregon. As her interest in printmaking increased, she helped to establish the Northwest Print Council. Krause was the founder of the printmaking program at the University of Oregon.

In her lifetime she produced over ten thousand prints and paintings. In 1980 LaVerne Krause was recognized with the Oregon Governor's Art Award, the highest honor an Oregon artist can receive.

KREPS, Helen. *See* TRAYLE, Helen

KUNZ, Don

b. 1932 Portland, OR ***d.***
Education: Art Institute of Chicago; Museum Art School
Membership: Artists Equity; Oregon Society of Artists; Portland Art Museum (Artist Membership)
Collections: Reed College; Kaiser Permanente Collection
Exhibits: Portland Art Museum (AM, 1PS 1959); Oregon Society of Artists; Lipman Little Gallery; Lewis and Clark College (1PS 55); Friendship House (3PS 57); Oregon Centennial (59); Seattle Art Museum
References: A3 (1956, 58); C6; C7 (59)
Media: Watercolor, oil

Don Kunz was an art teacher at Grant High School in Portland. He trained at the Art Institute of Chicago and Portland's Museum Art School. During the 1950s Kunz's paintings were shown at the Portland and Seattle Art Museums and at galleries in Portland. He participated in a three-person show with Albert Patecky* and Chester Murphy* at the Friendship House in 1957. His work was described as canvases filled with rich color and texture.

KUTKA, Anne. *See* McCOSH, Anne

L

LACY, Hammett, Mrs.

b. d.

Awards: Oregon State Fairs

Exhibits: Oregon State Fairs

References: OSF (1899, 1900, 03)

Media: Oil, watercolor

Specialty: Landscapes, marines, florals

Mrs. Lacy won an award at the Scarrett Collegiate Institute of Neusbo, Missouri as a young girl. She was a member of the early Salem art community and took several first prizes at Oregon State Fairs between 1899 and 1903.

LAMADE, Erich

b. 1894 Braunsweig, Germany

d. 1969 Portland, OR

Education: John Herron Art Institute—Indianapolis (1917); Museum Art School: *H. Wentz** (22–24); Art Students League (24–27)

Membership: American Artists Professional League; Arts Guild; American Artists' Congress

Collections: Marine Hospital—Seattle; Timberline Lodge Collection; Parsons Collection

Exhibits: Arts Guild; Portland Art Museum; California Palace of the Legion of Honor—San Francisco (1934); Corcoran Gallery of Art—Washington, D.C. (36, 39); American Artists Professional League (37, 38, 39); University of Portland (1PS 38); West Shore (41); American Artists' Congress (41); Seattle Art Museum (42); Portland State University (1PS)

References: ALM; COL; DAW; HAV; MAL SUP; OET; WWN; WWW; A2 (1933, 34, 42); A3 (35, 38, 41); A5 (30); C10; C15 (34); CD (30–40)

Media: Oil, watercolor, tempera, fresco

Little of Erich Lamade's work exists today. By his wife's admission, much was destroyed at his own hand and much by the "vagaries of bureaucracy." He traveled to the United States with his parents at age eleven. He began school in 1917 at the John Herron Art Institute in Indianapolis, but left to volunteer in the war effort as a draftsman. At a friend's urging, he settled in Portland in 1919 and became a commercial artist. He attended the Museum Art School and in 1924 went to New York to study at the Art Students League. Upon graduation he secured a job as art director for a New York ad agency. Lamade was paid well in this new position and invested heavily in the stock market, but after the fateful crash in 1929 he returned to Portland. His concern for the independence of artists led him to attempt to set up a co-op gallery in Portland. It was to have been artist-operated and controlled, but it never materialized because other artists failed to support it. He then discovered the small town of Mosier, where he could live frugally. The distinctive quality of the landscape pleased him—the graceful cliff formations and dry, grassy terrain reminded him of the work of Cézanne, the artist he admired above all others. He spent two summers in Mosier.

Lamade doubted he could maintain his artistic independence during the Depression, as artists were required to meet federal art project criteria. He had difficulty working within this bureaucratic system while assigned to the Public Works of Art Project and the Federal Arts Project (also known as the WPA) from 1935 to 1937. Visitors to Timberline Lodge can see his carvings over the dining room fireplace. Various other commissions followed: he completed a mural for the Grants Pass Post Office entitled *Present Industry* (1937) with Louis Bunce* and a mural for the St. Johns Post Office, *Early History*, with John Ballator* and Bunce.

By 1940 he was discouraged with the work that was assigned and moved to Seattle, where disaster struck. In 1941 a fire destroyed his studio with his paintings and art materials. After some travel, including a brief time in New York, he returned to Oregon in the early 1950s. By this time, his health was beginning to decline, requiring a change in media from oil to pastels and finally to black and white sketches.

Erich Lamade was a meticulous craftsman. He wrote a book, *The Craft of the Artist*, to fill a gap in the information needed for fine art painting classes and reading materials. No publishing house would produce his book so he mimeographed it and offered it by direct mail. It became a text at the University of New Mexico, the University of Arizona, Hofstra, and Syracuse University, but eventually was too expensive for him to continue to produce in such a limited way. Lamade was an intense, serious artist who died bitter and discouraged by what he saw as life's unfairness.

LANE, Frances (Fannie)

b. d.
Awards: Oregon State Fairs
Exhibits: Oregon State Fairs
References: BI; DAV; OSF (1895–98)
Media: Oil
Specialty: Landscapes, florals, marines

Fannie Lane lived in Salem and was an Oregon State Fair entrant from 1895 to 1898.

LARSEN, Benjamin Daniel

b. 1892 Cedar Falls, IA
d. 1970 Madrid, Spain
Education: Chicago Academy of Fine Arts
Membership: Oregon Society of Artists; American Artists Professional League
Awards: Oregon Society of Artists (1932, 34)
Collections: Lundberg Collection
Exhibits: Oregon Society of Artists; Plaza Hotel—New York City (1930); American Artists Professional League (32, 38); Meier and Frank Co. (1PS 33); Portland Art Museum
References: COL; DAV; DAW; WWN; A2 (1933); C3 (28, 29, 31–35, 47); CD (16, 17, 43, 44)
Media: Oil, watercolor, pastel, prints
Specialty: Landscapes, florals

Educated at the Chicago Academy of Fine Arts, Ben Larsen traveled abroad extensively after 1930. A Meier and Frank Co. exhibition in 1933 displayed fifty oils and pastels from his trips, as well as his examples of Oregon scenery and historic Portland landmarks. Throughout many of his years of travel, he maintained an address and studio in Portland. Larsen served as president of the Oregon Society of Artists in 1932, 1938, and for two consecutive terms in 1965 and 1966.

LAUGHLIN, Lillian C.

b. Toronto, IA
d. 1967 Salem, OR
Education: Art Institute of Chicago
Membership: American Artists Professional League; Rembrandt Artists Guild
Awards: American Artists Professional League (1937)
Exhibits: Texas (1914); American Artists Professional League (34–39); Rembrandt Artists Guild (38); National

Exhibition of American Art (38); Oregon State Fair; Portland Art Museum

References: A2 (1940, 42, 44, 46, 48); A3 (38)

Lillian Laughlin came to Oregon in 1923. She lived in Salem and participated in the Rembrandt Artists Guild. She also used the name Mrs. S.B. Laughlin.

LAURITZ, Paul

b. 1889 Larvik, Norway

d. 1976 Glendale, CA

Education: Norway

Membership: Mutual Art Association; American Artists Professional League; Oregon Society of Artists

Awards: Golden Gate International Exposition—San Francisco (1939–40); California Palace of the Legion of Honor—San Francisco (1942, 45); Oakland Art Gallery (43, 44)

Collections: San Diego Museum; UCLA; University of Chicago; Jocelyn Art Museum—Omaha; University of Portland Library

Exhibits: Mutual Art Association (1914, 15); Portland Art Museum; Los Angeles County Museum of Art (20, 32); Art Institute of Chicago (22); Seattle Art Museum; American Artists Professional League (33, 37); Golden Gate International Exposition—San Francisco (39–40); Oregon Society of Artists; California Palace of the Legion of Honor—San Francisco; Oakland Art Gallery; Art Institute of Chicago; Pennsylvania Academy of Fine Art—Philadelphia; San Francisco Museum of Art

References: BI; DAV; DAW; HUG; SAM; WWW; A2 (1920); C3 (51); C7 (29); ARTC

Media: Watercolor, oil, prints (etching)

Specialty: Landscapes (mountains, deserts), portraits, marines, plein-air paintings

Born in Norway, Paul Lauritz worked his way west to Canada in 1905. He traveled to Portland in 1912, where he lived with his brother and worked as a commercial artist. Lured north by the gold rush, he journeyed to Vancouver, Canada, and then Alaska. A painting excursion on the Columbia River brought him back to Oregon in 1924. A year later he returned to his place of birth, but finally settled in Los Angeles, where he was active in the art community. He set up a studio and taught for many years, first at the Chouinard Art Institute and then at the Otis Art Institute.

His painting technique related to the phenomenon of color vibration. He arranged complementary colors side by side, a technique used by the French Impressionists. His scene of the Vista House on the Columbia River demonstrated his interest in showing the clear atmosphere after a heavy rain.

LEAVSTRAND, Pete

b. d.

Membership: American Artists' Congress; Arts Guild

Awards: Portland Art Museum (1937)

Exhibits: Portland Art Museum (3PS 1936); Creative Art Gallery (33); Arts Guild; Lipman Little Gallery (36); American Artists' Congress (37)

References: A2 (1933); A3 (35, 36, 37); A5 (33); C10

Pete Leavstrand lived in Milwaukie in 1936. He was a member of the American Artists' Congress of New York and a participant in the WPA. He worked in Oregon during the 1930s.

LeFEVER, Albertina Bird Pruden

b. 1885 Portland, OR

d. 1977 Portland, OR
Education: *C. Keller**
Membership: American Artists Professional League; Attic Club; Oregon Society of Artists
Awards: American Artists Professional League (1932); Oregon Society of Artists (37, 43)
Collections: Powell Collection; Oregon Historical Society; Lundberg Collection
Exhibits: Oregon Society of Artists; American Artists Professional League (1932–38); Portland Art Museum; Clatsop County Historical Society (94)
References: COL; WWN; A2 (1934, 40, 42); A4 (32); C3 (27, 32, 34, 37, 43); C11; ARTC; M2; M3
Specialty: Landscapes, seascapes
Media: Oil
See artwork in color section

Bird LeFever studied with Clyde Leon Keller* and accompanied him on many painting trips to Sauvie Island. She was a member of the Attic Club, the American Artists Professional League, and a charter member of the Oregon Society of Artists. She painted in and around the Monterey Peninsula in California and published her work in Eastern magazines. Her last name is also spelled Lefevre and Lefebre.

LeGALL, Marie Craig

b. 1860
d. 1944 Salem, OR
Education: Pennsylvania Academy of Fine Art—Philadelphia; Philadelphia School of Design
Awards: Oregon State Fairs; Philadelphia School of Design
Collections: Bush House Museum—Salem; Hallie Ford Museum of Art—Willamette University
Exhibits: Oregon State Fairs; Oregon Historical Society (1990)
References: C9; OSF (1885, 90, 91, 95, 97, 99, 1900); M2; M3
Media: Oil, crayon, watercolor
Specialty: Portraits, landscapes
See artwork in color section

Educated in the East, Marie Craig won the first gold medal for illustration at the Philadelphia School of Design. She came west to teach at Willamette University and joined the faculty there in 1886, staying until 1908. During this time she was a frequent contributor to Oregon State Fair exhibitions. For most of the years she taught at Willamette University she was the only art teacher, and depended on the tuition of students for her salary. Some of her more well-known students were Mamie Parvin Brown*, Clyde Leon Keller*, Myra Wiggins*, and Melville Wire*. In 1905 she married art student Victor LeGall, but the marriage was short-lived. Examples of her work are rare; the Bush House Museum collection in Salem contains her portrait of *Asahel Bush IV* completed in 1890. After her retirement from Willamette she developed an interest in poetry, some of which was published in *Sunset Trails* in 1933.

LeMON, John

b. Belfast, Ireland
d. 1941 Portland, OR
Membership: American Artists Professional League
Exhibits: American Artists Professional League (1935)
References: BI; HUG; CD (1932–39)
Media: Pastel, oil
Specialty: Landscapes, portraits, seascapes

John LeMon was born in Belfast, Ireland. He served as Headmaster of Crescent Academy, Belfast, for many years. In 1898 he came to America, spending a brief time in Philadelphia before moving west. References list a San Francisco address for him in 1917. During the 1930s John LeMon had a studio and home on Hawthorne Boulevard in Portland. He invented the Romney Pastel and was known for his use of pastels with rich warm brown tones. LeMon signed works with his last name only.

LEVINE, Shepard (Shep)

b. 1922 New York City, NY ***d.***

Education: University of New Mexico (1946–50); L'Université de Toulouse—France (52)

Membership: Portland Art Museum (Artist Membership)

Collections: Salishan Lodge Collection; University of Oregon; Oregon State University

Exhibits: University of New Mexico; (50, 51); New Mexico Museum (1951); Toulouse, France (52, 1PS 53); University of Oregon (53, 54); Western Washington Fair; Oregon Society of Artists; Portland Art Museum (1PS 57); Henry Art Gallery—University of Washington (54); Spokane Art Museum (54–58); Seattle Art Museum (55); Oregon State University (lPS 55, 57, 59); San Francisco Museum of Art (58); Willamette University (58); Oregon Centennial (59)

References: HAV; WWAA; A3 (1955, 58); C6; C7 (56–58); C30 (53)

Media: Oil, watercolor, prints (lithograph)

Specialty: Religious themes

Shep Levine studied in southern France in 1952. He had a one-person show in Toulouse, France the following year. Levine became a professor at the University of Oregon in 1953 and joined the faculty of Oregon State College (now Oregon State University) in 1954. He has exhibited widely in the Northwest, and lectured on Jewish symbolism and art motifs.

LEVRA, Ray E.

b. 1929 Redlodge, MT ***d.***

Membership: Master Watercolor Society of Oregon; Portland Art Museum (Artist Membership)

Awards: Oregon State Fairs (1958, 59); Master Watercolor Society of Oregon

Exhibits: Portland Art Museum; Oregon State Fairs (1958, 59); Eastern Montana College (1PS); Montana State College (1PS); University of Oregon (1PS); Master Watercolor Society of Oregon (58); University of Washington; Oregon Centennial (59)

References: A3 (1956); C6

Ray Levra was active in Oregon during the mid to late 1950s. He showed work at Oregon State Fairs and *The Oregon Scene* exhibition in the Centennial celebration.

LEWIS, Henry

b. 1915 Lynch, NE

d. 1958

Education: University of Oregon: *D. McCosh*, J. Wilkinson*, A. Vincent**; Chicago

Membership: Portland Art Museum (Artist Membership)

Collections: Portland Art Museum; University of Oregon; Pacific University

Exhibits: Portland Art Museum (AM, 1954); Eugene Art Center (1PS 52); Seattle Art Museum (55)

References: A3 (1950–52, 55, 56); A4 (41); C7 (51)

Henry Lewis studied commercial art in Chicago before moving to Oregon in 1937. He taught art for many years at Parkrose High School and exhibited at the Portland and Seattle Art Museums. Lewis had a one-person show at the Eugene Art Center in 1952.

LIBERTY, Dorothy

b. 1920 Marquette, MI ***d.***

Education: Carleton College—Minnesota (1937–39); Art Institute of Chicago (43–45); Saugatuck Summer Art Colony—Michigan (45)
Membership: National Watercolor Society; Northwest Watercolor Society; Portland Art Museum (Artist Membership)
Collections: County Historical Society—Marquette, Michigan
Exhibits: Detroit Institute of the Arts (1947); Western Washington Fair; Seattle Art Museum; Northwest Watercolor Society; Spokane (49); Lincoln County Art Center (50); Henry Art Gallery—University of Washington (51); Portland Art Museum (AM, 54); Oregon Centennial (59)
References: A3 (1953, 55, 58); C6; C7 (49, 51, 54); C29 (49, 50); C30 (48–51)
Media: Watercolor
Specialty: Florals, landscapes, seascapes

Dorothy Liberty exhibited at the Portland Art Museum's juried shows of the 1950s, and participated in the Centennial show, *The Oregon Scene*. She taught adult art education classes and exhibited in Washington state.

LOGAN, Thayne J.

b. 1900 Joplin, MO
d. 1990 Portland, OR
Education: University of Oregon; *S. Bell*; C.Keller**
Membership: Oregon Society of Artists; American Artists Professional League
Awards: Oregon Society of Artists (1933, 36, 37, 39, 43, 44); Oregon State Fair (34)
Collections: Oregon Historical Society; Miranda Collection; Painting Restoration Studio Collection; Counting Eagles Collection; Parsons Collection; Lundberg Collection; Cofield Collection
Exhibits: Portland Art Museum; Oregon State Fairs (1927–30, 34); Oregon Society of Artists; American Artists Professional League (33); Citizens for Art Group (59); Oregon Centennial (59); Oregon Historical Society (90); Clatsop County Historical Society (94)
References: COL; DAV; WWN; A2 (1922, 40); C3 (28–31, 33, 34–37, 43, 46–51); C9; C11
Media: Watercolor, oil, pastel
Specialty: Landscapes, seascapes
See artwork in color section

Thayne Logan came to the Northwest from Missouri in 1907. Painting interested him from an early age but, since he felt the life of an artist would mean many sacrifices, he turned to architecture as a career. His building designs are present everywhere in the Willamette Valley: Mt. Angel Abbey, University of Portland, many churches, banks, and Safeway stores. Logan worked as a designer for the Carl Linde firm and his rendering for Portland's Shemanski Fountain appeared in the *Oregon Journal* in December, 1925. The fountain is located in the South Park blocks.

His early paintings of the 1920s and 1930s are closely observed regional landscapes. During the 1930s, when business was slow, Logan oversaw a WPA project in The Dalles. He joined the Oregon Society of Artists as a charter member and served as president four times (1934, 1939, 1941, and 1967). The design for the present Society building, erected in 1954, was also his.

He had no interest in selling his work, and kept no records of who bought them or how much was paid. He traveled extensively with his sketch book by his side. After his retirement in 1966, he continued to paint, remaining active in the Oregon Society of Artists until his death. He wrote a history of the Society and worked to keep its tradition of conservative art alive.

LOVE, Fanchon (Fannie) McDowell

b. Beulah, OR
d. 1913 Jacksonville, OR
Exhibits: Southern Oregon Agricultural Fair; First Southern Oregon District Agricultural Fair; Southern Oregon County Fair
References: SO (1890); FSO (98); SOCF (99)
Media: Oil, china painting
Specialty: Florals

Fannie Love was born in Harney County. She and her husband, George Love, traveled to Alaska, then owned a hotel in Sumpter, Oregon before finally settling in Jacksonville. She was active in art circles in southern Oregon.

LOWDEN, Adelaide Archibald

b. d.
Membership: Mutual Art Association; Oregon Society of Artists
Exhibits: Mutual Art Association (1915); Oregon Society of Artists
References: C3 (1927, 28); CD (16); ARTC

Adelaide Lowden appeared in the 1916 Portland City Directory artist listing. She was also a member of the Mutual Art Association and exhibited with them in 1915. One of the charter members of the Oregon Society of Artists, she participated in their first show in 1927.

LOWNSDALE, Gertrude Grey

b. 1853 Lansing, IA
d. 1927 Portland, OR
Education: Willamette University: *M. LeGall**
Awards: Oregon State Fair
Collections: Oregon Historical Society
Exhibits: Oregon State Fair; Oregon Historical Society (1990)
References: C9; OSF (1871); M2; M3
Media: Oil, pencil
Specialty: Animals

Settling in Oregon in 1865 with her family, Gertrude Lownsdale attended Willamette University in Salem. The Oregon Historical Society collection contains her drawing of a setter dog and bird that won first prize at the 1871 Oregon State Fair. She exhibited and lived in eastern Washington.

LUCAS, LaVon Salmela

b. 1926 Hockinson, WA ***d.***
Education: Chouinard Art Institute—Los Angeles (1945–46), Jeppson Art School—Los Angeles (47); Museum Art School: *H. Wentz**, *L. Bunce**, *J. McLarty**, *M. Russo**, *C. Voorhies** (48–54)
Membership: Portland Art Museum (Artist Membership); Washington Art Association; Artists Equity
Awards: Washington Art Association (1949, 53)
Collections: Washington Art Association; U.S. Bank; Hallie Ford Museum of Art—Willamette University
Exhibits: Washington Art Association—Vancouver (1949, 53); Portland Art Museum (AM, 3PS 52); Vancouver Art Association (51); Seattle Art Museum; Oakland Art Gallery (52); Art League of Bellingham (53); San Francisco Museum of Art; Kharouba Gallery (4PS 54); Harvey Welch Gallery (1PS 55); Oregon Centennial (59)
References: A3 (1950, 52, 54, 55); A4 (59); C7 (51, 53, 54)
Media: Oil, gouache, watercolor, charcoal, ink, prints (lithograph, wood block)

Specialty: Portraits, still life, florals, figures

LaVon Lucas received her art education in Los Angeles at the Chouinard Institute School and the Jeppson Art School. She continued her studies at the Museum Art School in Portland under Louis Bunce*, Harry Wentz*, and others. In Oregon she frequently exhibited in regional shows at the Art Museum. Her early style, concentrating on portraits and figurative elements, evolved into a more abstract one; colors that had been soft became stronger in later exhibitions. At the Kharouba Gallery she exhibited her art with three other women: Amanda Snyder*, Jolan Torok*, and LaVerne Krause*. The Lincoln County Art Center and Harvey Welch's Gallery also exhibited her work. A 1957 show at Welch's featured her Venetian and Greco-Roman motifs in gouache. Many branches of the U.S. National Bank of Portland exhibited her work.

LaVon Lucas has lived in Vancouver, Washington for most of her career. She has exhibited in Oregon, Washington, and California. Her artist husband, Jack, was also a student at the Museum Art School. He owned the Restoration Studio in Vancouver, where he restored paintings and produced hand-crafted frames.

LYNCH, Douglas

b. 1913 La Grande, OR ***d.***

Education: Museum Art School (1932–38); Chouinard Art Institute—Los Angeles (36)

Exhibits: Portland Art Museum

References: COL; WWN; C10; CD (1939, 50)

Media: Oil, watercolor

Specialty: Graphics, murals

In the 1930s Douglas Lynch was the first commercial artist to respond to the Bauhaus idea that painters and commercial artists shared a common ground. During World War II, the *Oregonian* published Lynch's paintings in order to promote the northwest timber and shipbuilding industries. He was also a participant in the WPA and crafted much of the wood sculpture at Timberline Lodge. He joined the Museum Art School faculty in 1947; their Fall 1952 newsletter listed him as a book jacket designer for Beacon Press. In 1960 the Portland Art Museum honored him with a retrospective. Lynch was a friend of C.S. Price*, who had a major influence on him.

Light Through
Old Growth Forest
(n.d.)
Hamilton Aaris
Parsons Collection

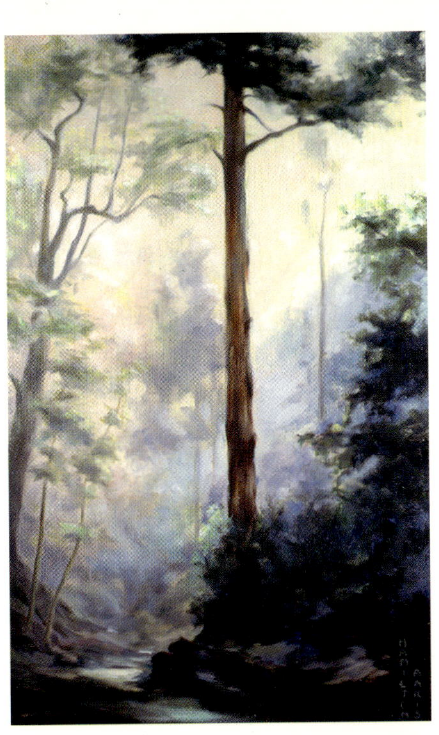

The Skier
(1936)
Darrel Austin
Timberline Lodge
WPA Project
Mt. Hood National Forest

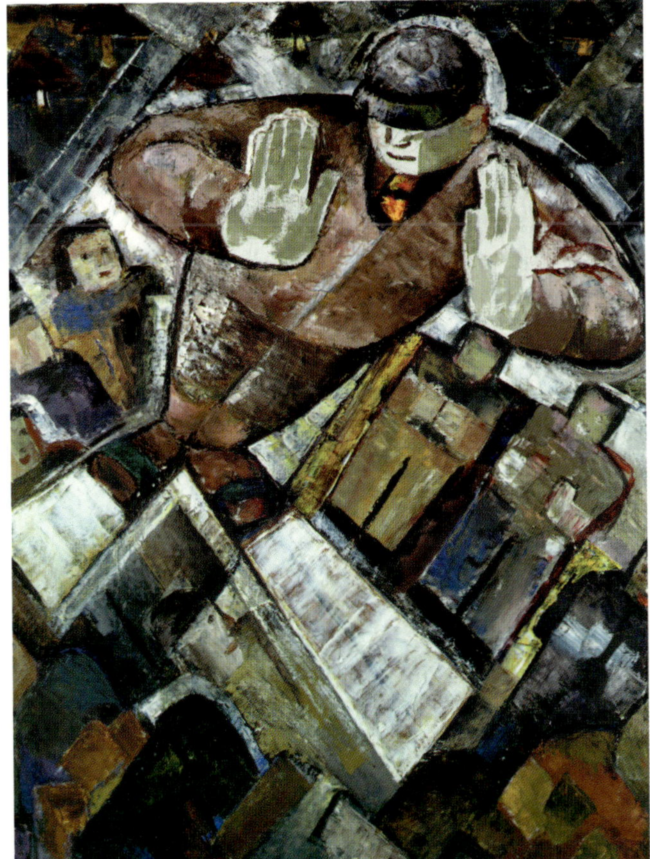

Multnomah Falls
(ca.1880)
Eliza Barchus
Miranda Collection

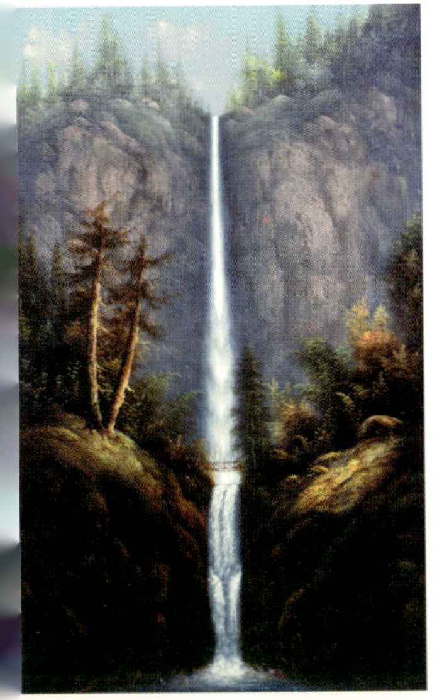

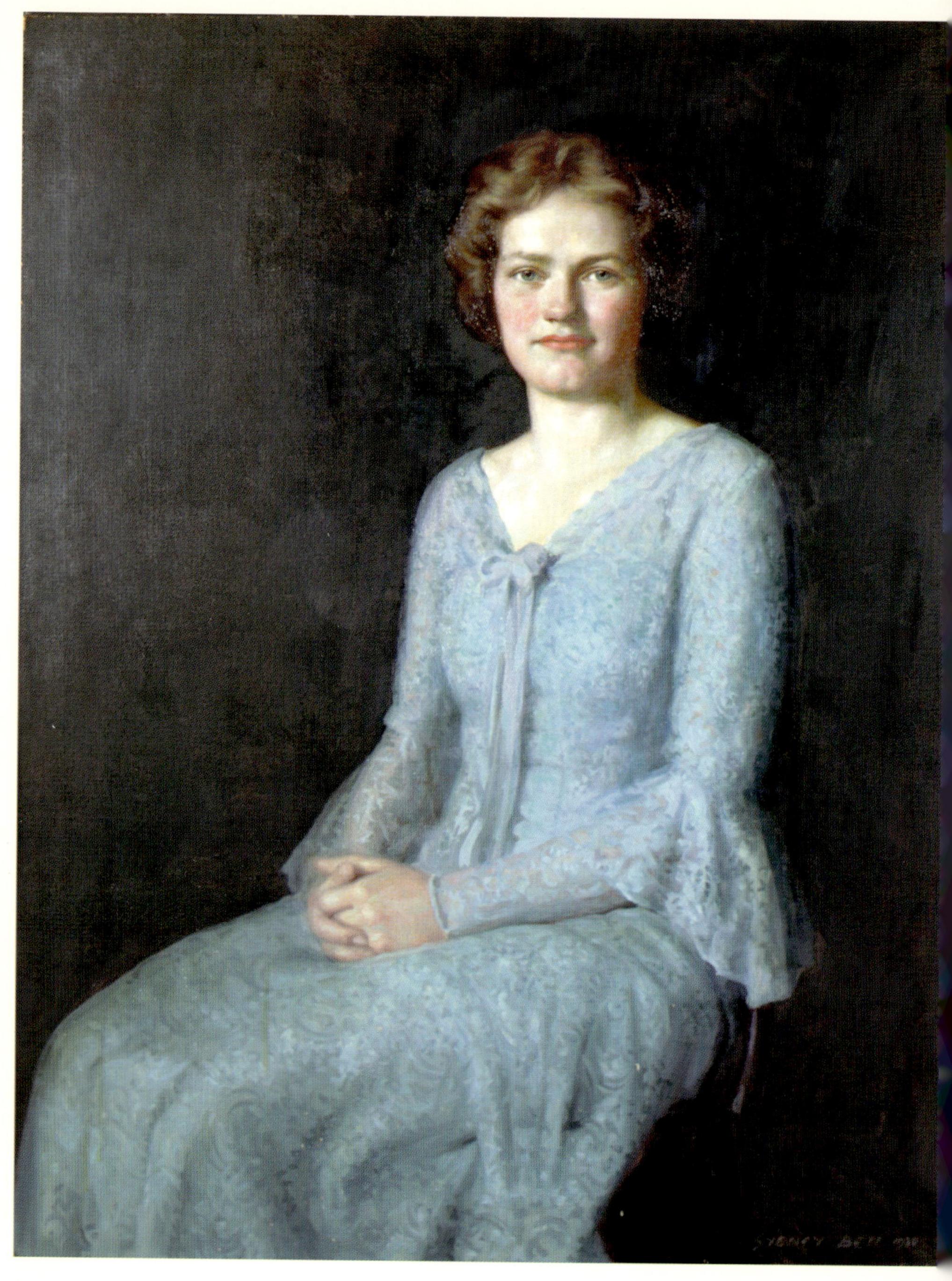

Portrait of Miss Catlin
(ca.1930)
Sidney Bell
Sovereign Collection

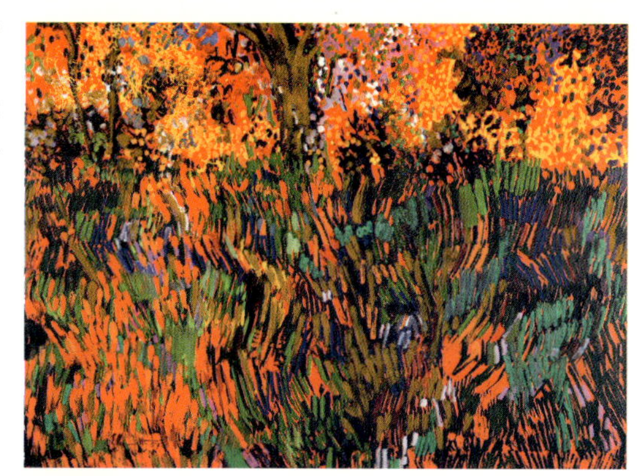

Fall '57
(1957)
Eugene Bennett
Collection of U.S. Bank

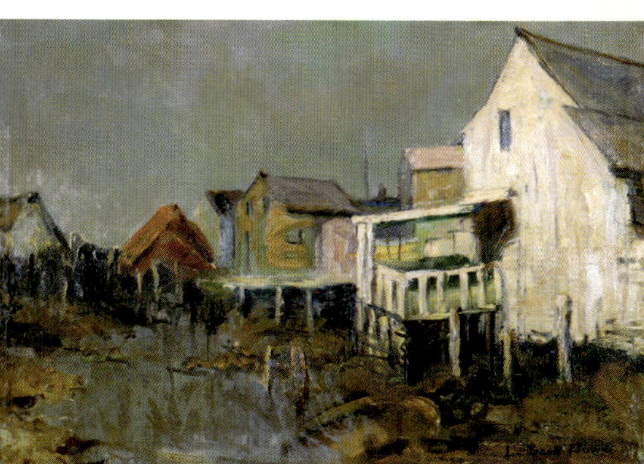

Astoria Houses
(n.d.)
Lucy Scott Bower
Lundberg Collection

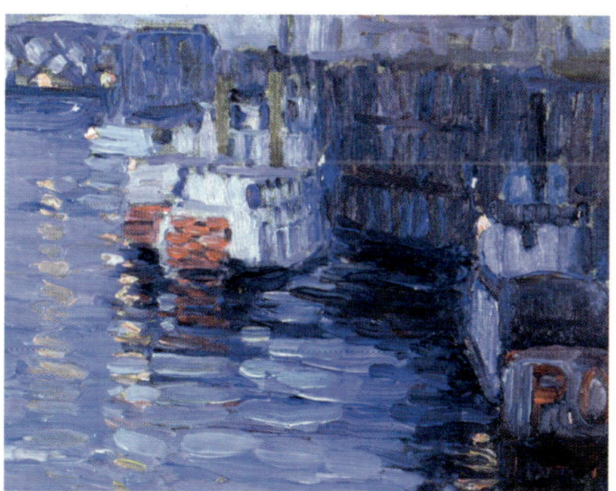

Old Boats Near Steel Bridge
(n.d.)
Edna Cranston Breyman
Parsons Collection

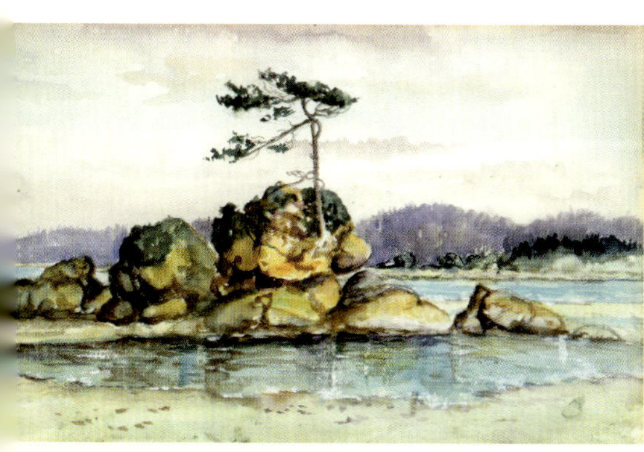

Rock-Away-Beach
(1910)
Mamie Parvin Brown
Oregon Historical Society
97-36.2.1, .2

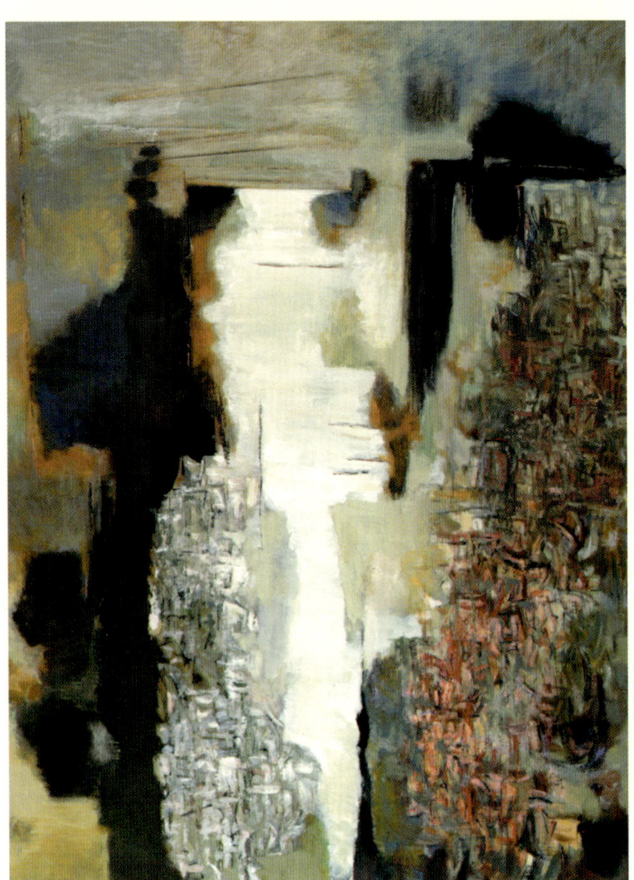

Beach, Low Tide #2
(1954)
Louis Bunce
Collection of Arlene
and Harold Schnitzer

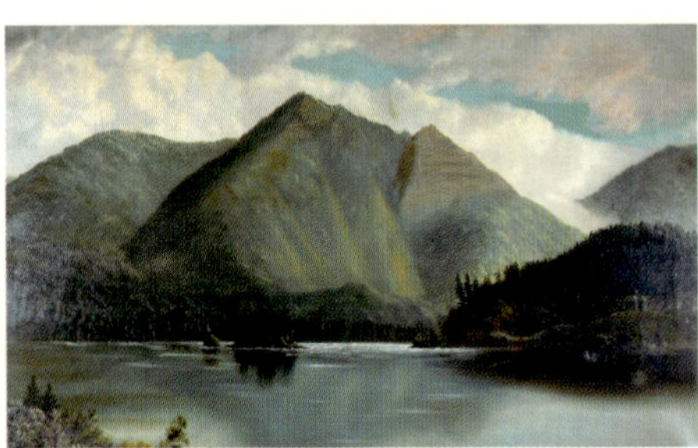

Blockhouse and Upper Cascades
(1879)
Clyde Cooke
Oregon Historical Society
84-141.1, .2

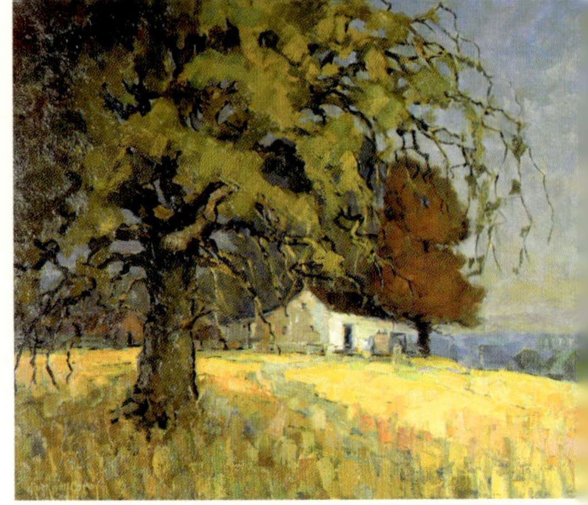

Deserted Farmhou
(193
Rockwell Care
Oregon Historical Socie
69-40

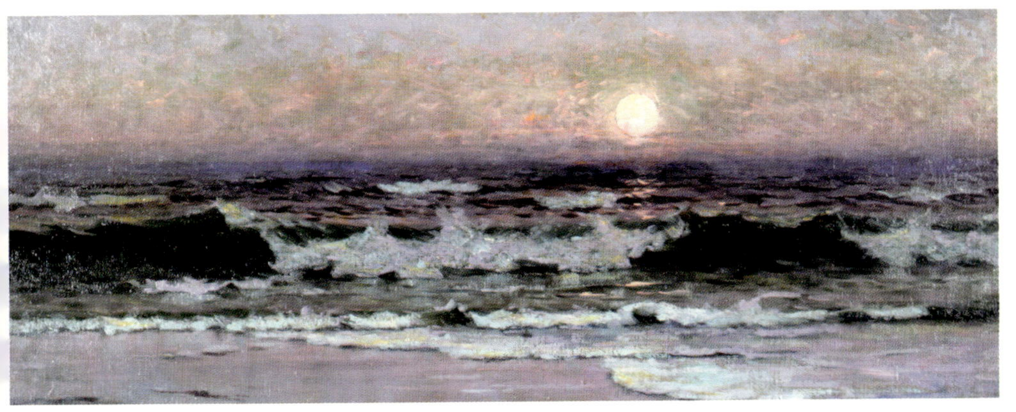

Sunset
(1887)
Edward Espey
Sovereign Collection

Sailing Xmas Day
(1907)
John Marion Crook
Miranda Collection

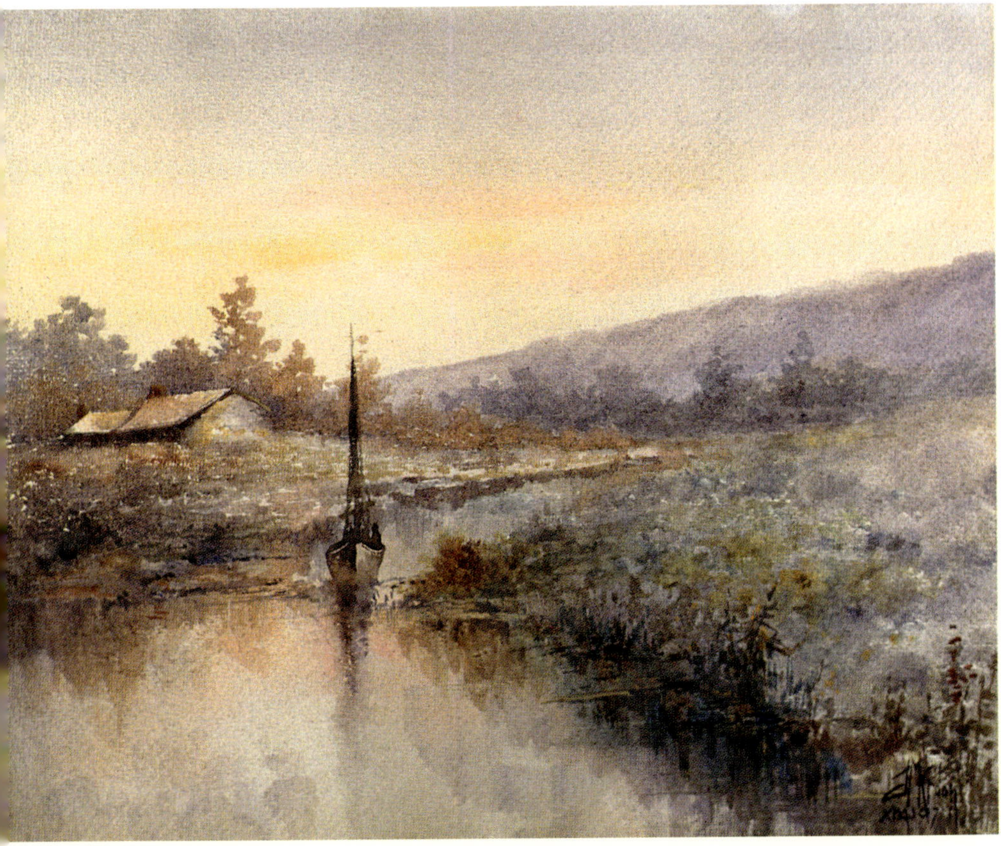

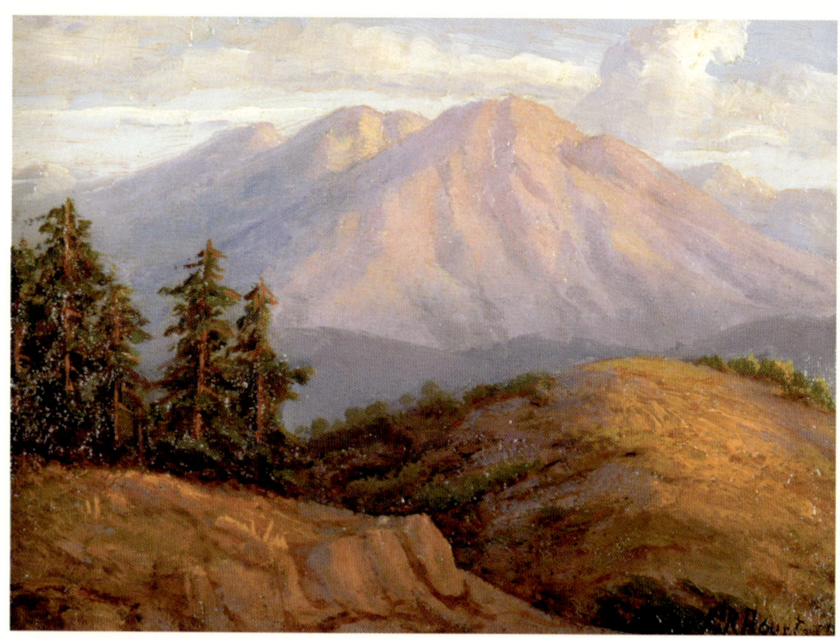

Siskiyou Afternoon
(n.d.)
Grace Fountain
Lundberg Collection

Golden Oregon Sunset
(ca.1920)
Anthony Euwer
Miranda Collection

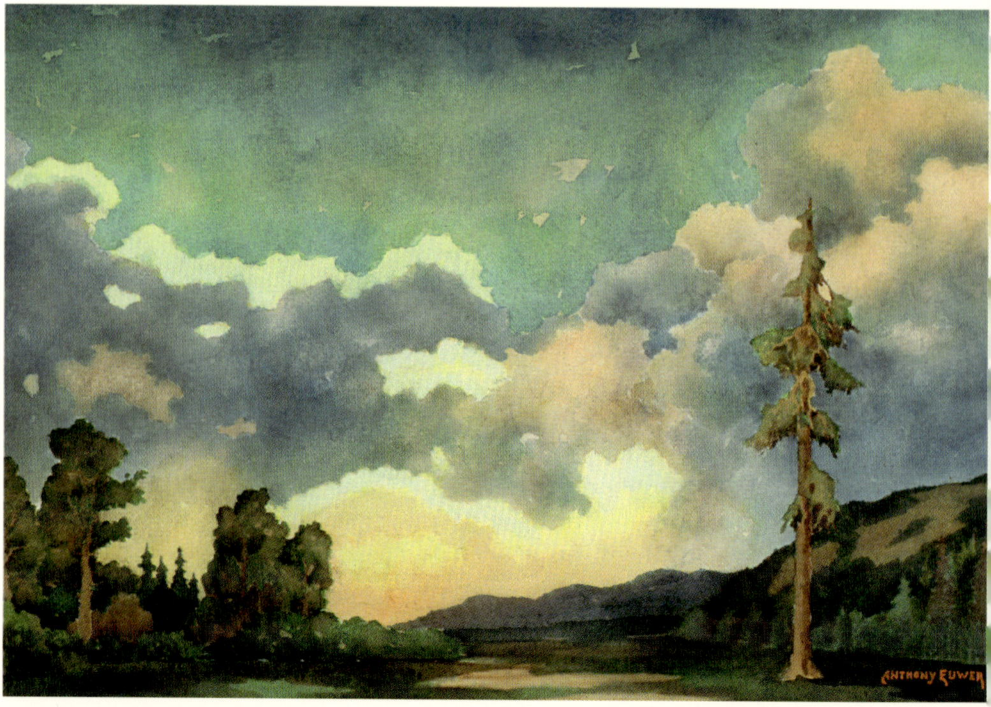

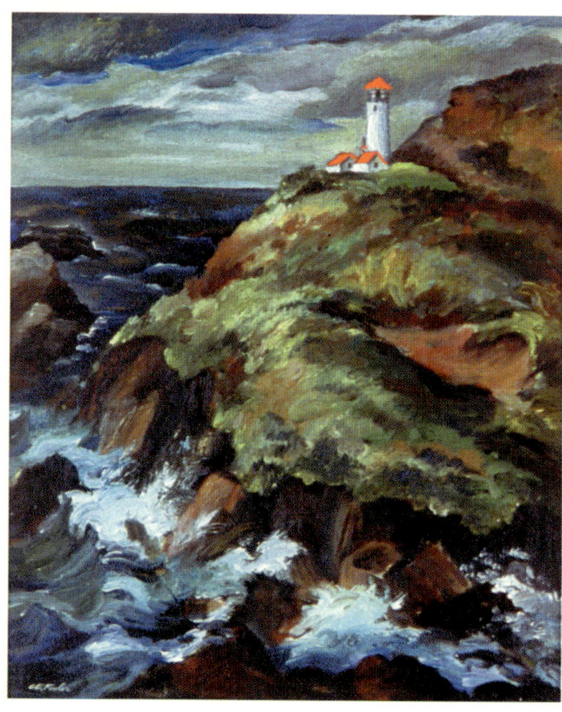

Heceta Lighthouse
(1937)
Constance Fowler
Hallie Ford Museum of Art,
Willamette University, Salem
Gift of Connie Bataille

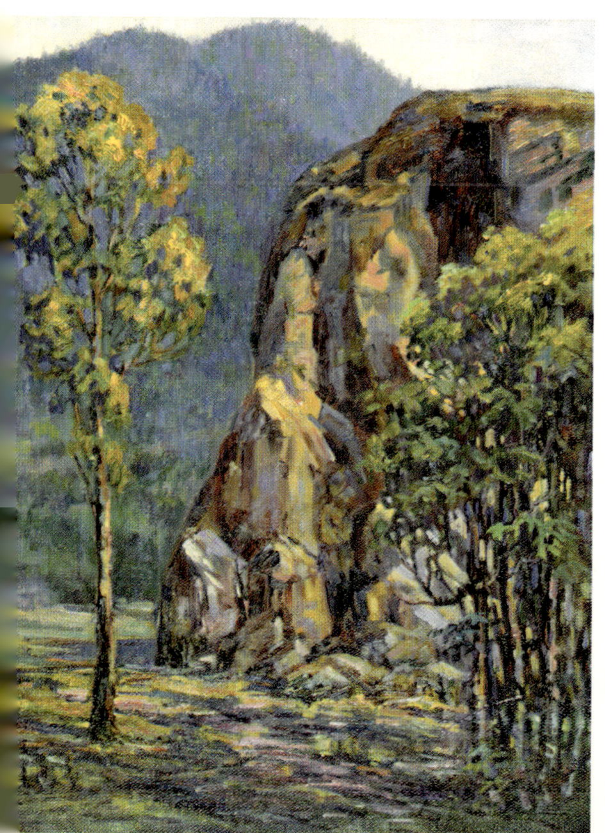

Columbia Gorge
(1915)
E.D.M. Fowle
Lundberg Collection

Hendricks Park
(1921)
C.J. Fulton
Humpal Collection

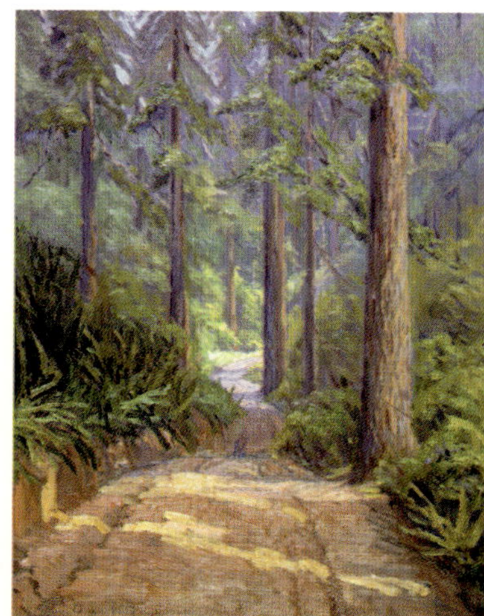

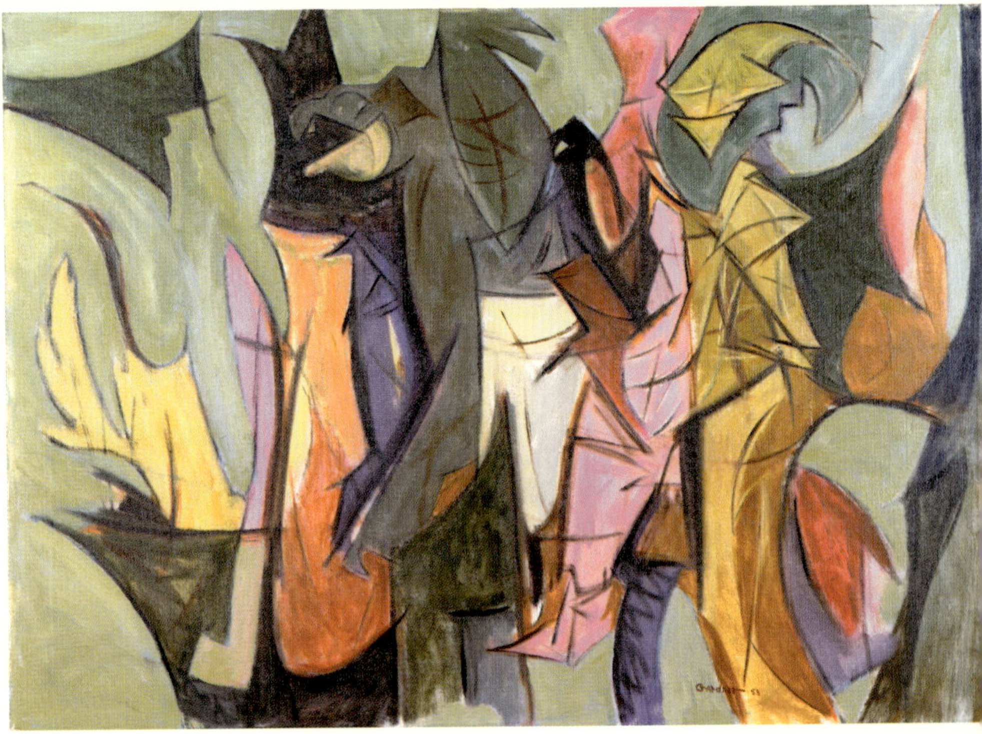

Mounted Knight
(1953)
Byron Gardner
Catlin Gabel School Collection

Still-Life with Jelly Ja
(1911
Théodore Gégou
Booth Collectio

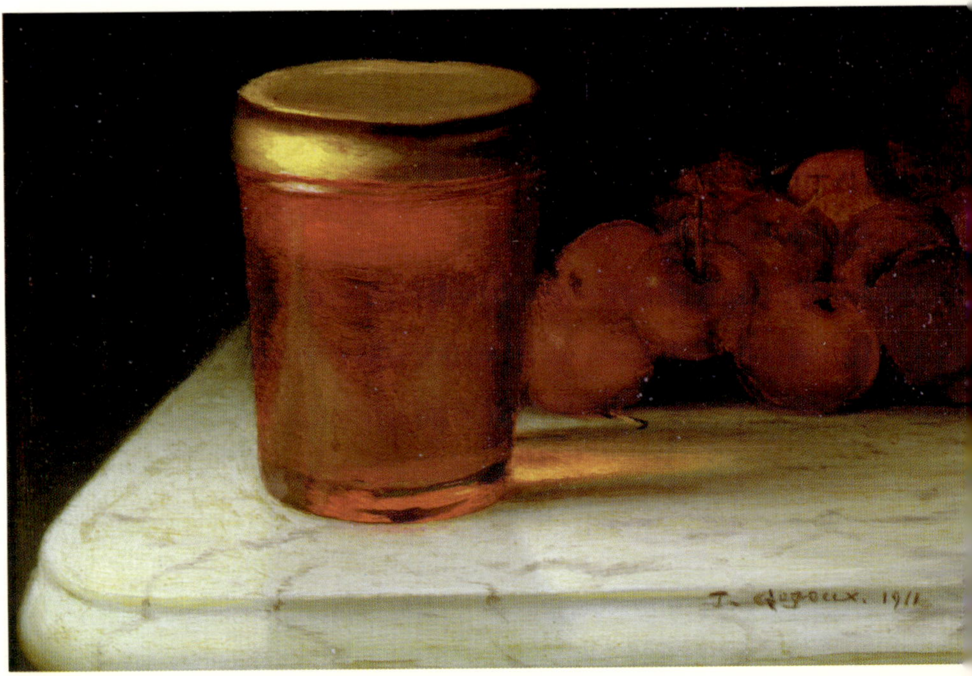

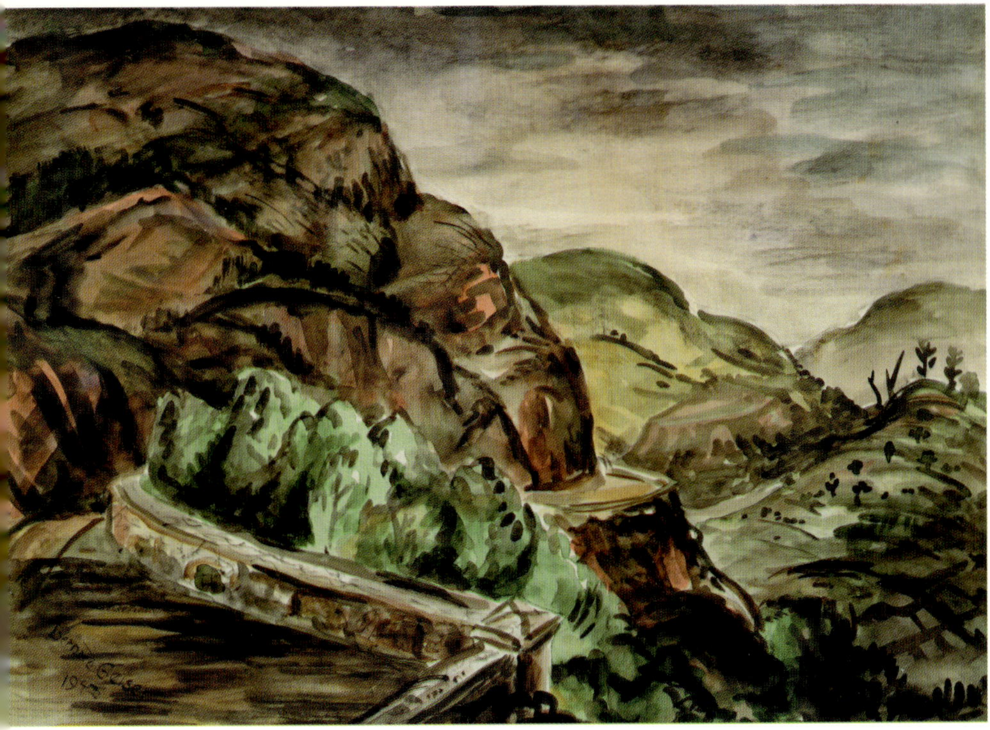

Columbia River Highway
(1941)
Bernard Geiser
Pathways/OI Partners Collection

The Cove
(n.d.)
William Givler
Portland Art Museum
Helen Thurston Ayer Fund
45.9

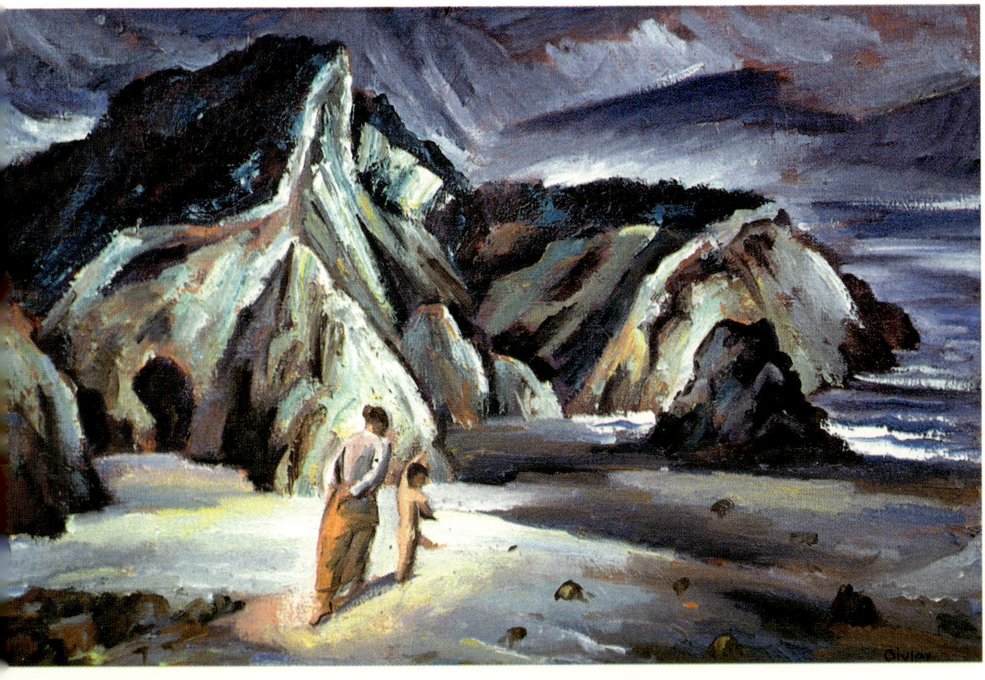

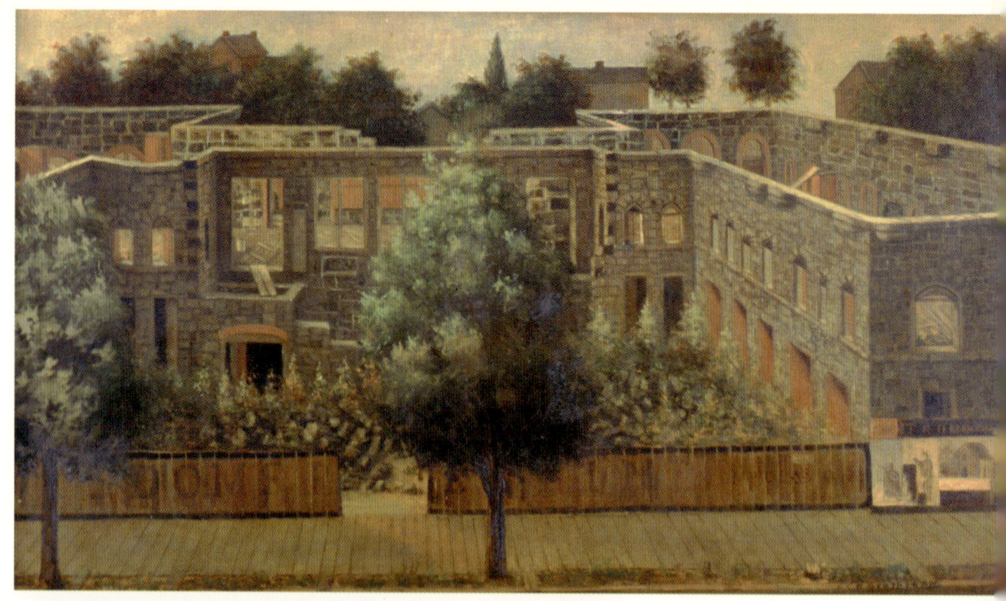

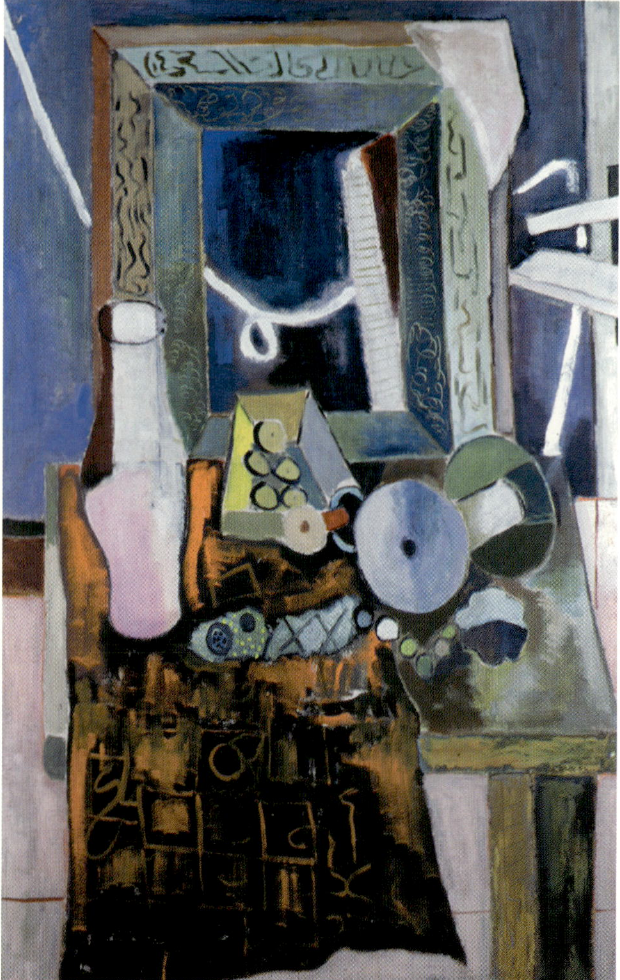

Portland Hotel Under Construction
(ca.1883)
Francesca Grothjean
Jake's Famous Crawfish
Restaurant

Spools
(ca.1940)
Clifford Gleason
Hallie Ford Museum of Art,
Willamette University, Salem
Maribeth Collins Art
Acquisition Fund

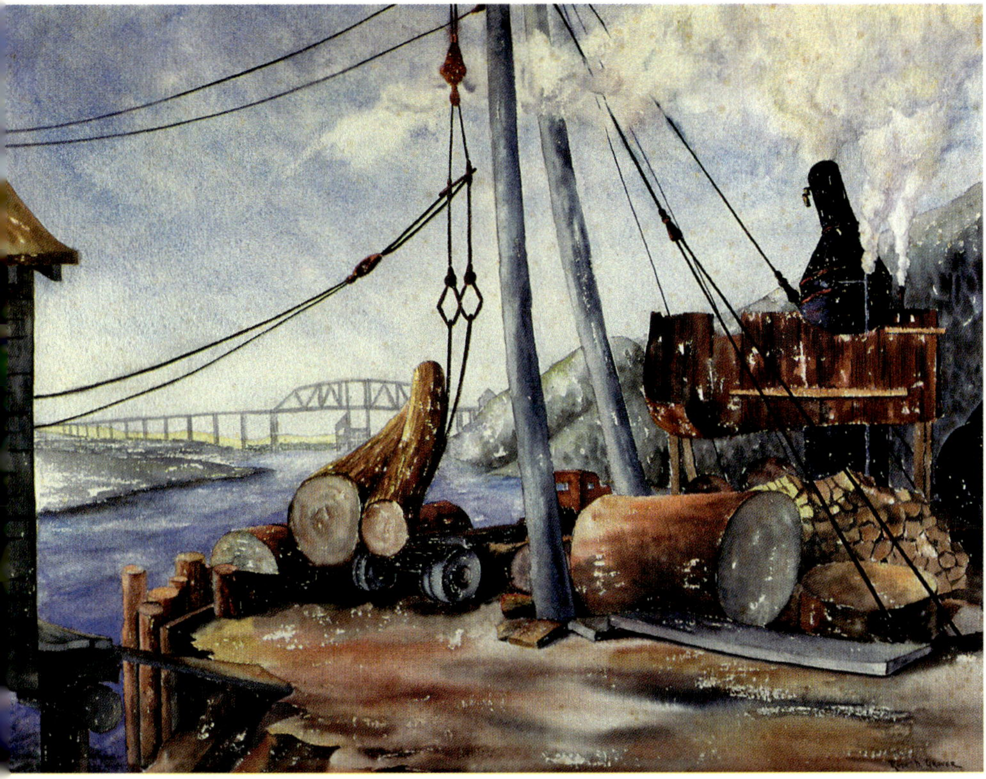

Donkey Engine, Siletz River
(ca.1956)
Ruth Grover
Hallie Ford Museum of Art,
Willamette University, Salem
Elmer Young Purchase Fund

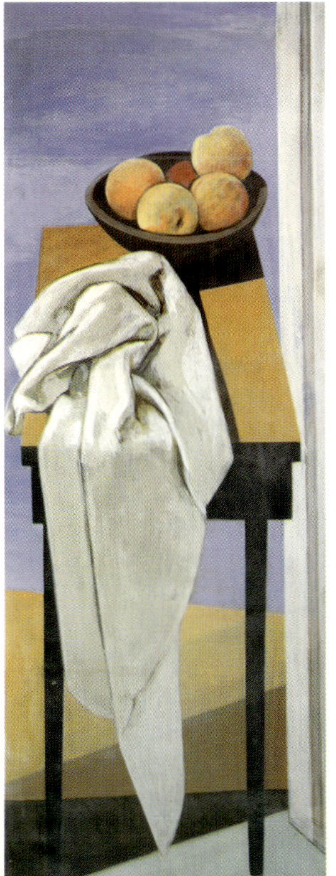

Still Life with Peaches
(n.d.)
Sally Haley
Hurst Collection

Earth, That is Sufficient
(1950)
Carl Hall
Hallie Ford Museum of Art, Willamette University, Salem
Purchased by Willamette University on the occasion of Professor Hall's retirement in 1986.

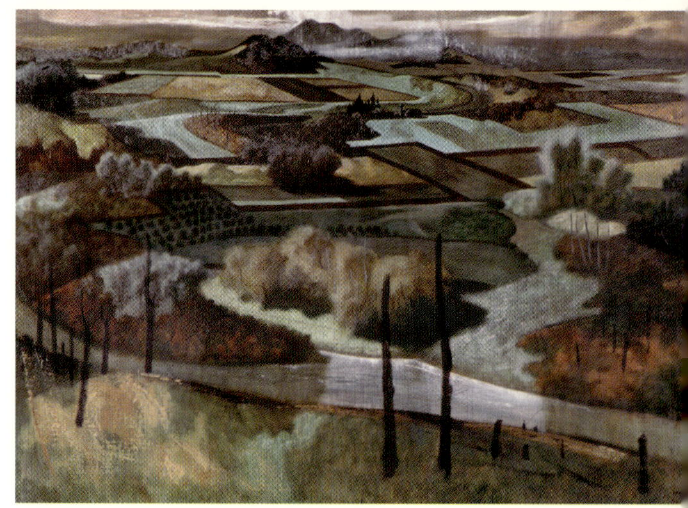

Farmhouse
(ca.1942)
Ruth Halvorsen
Oregon Historical Society
95-131.1.1, .2

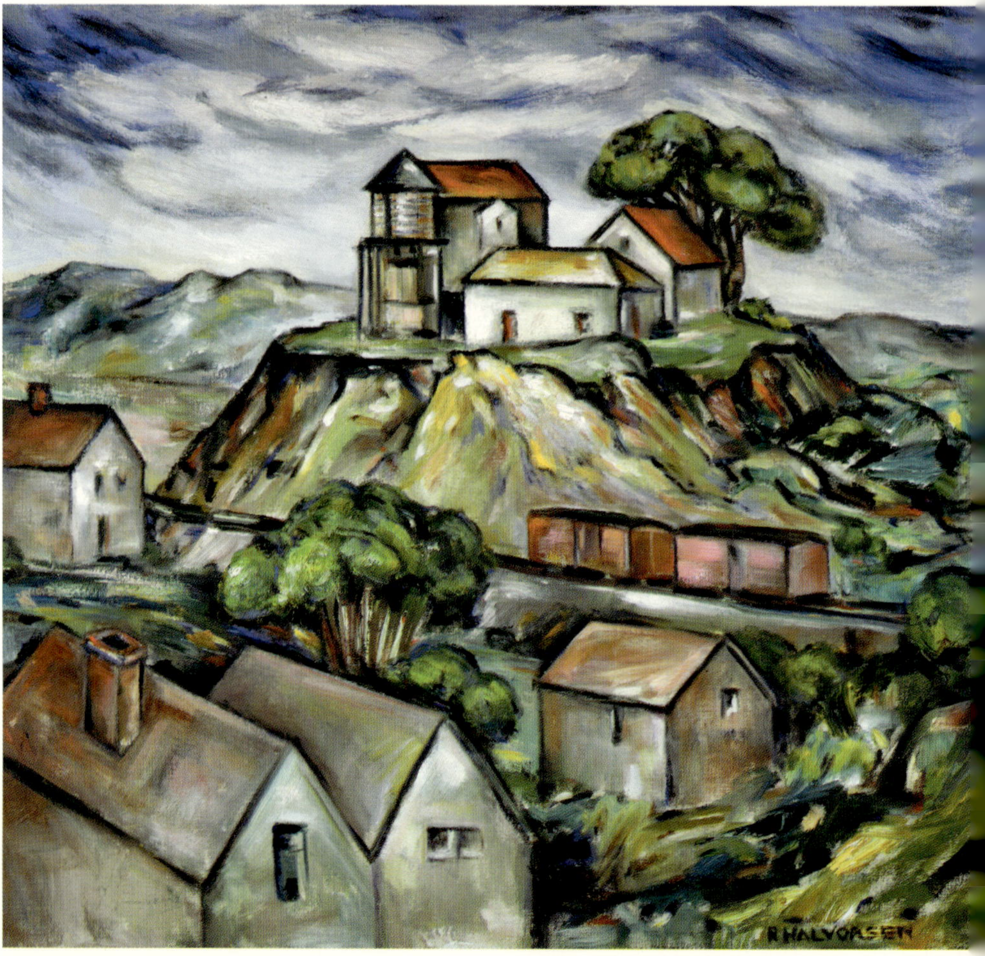

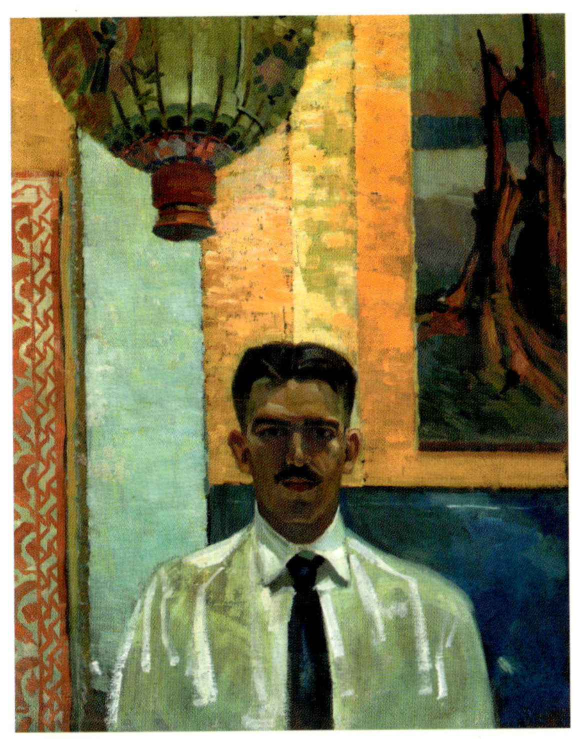

Self Portrait
(1919)
Lance Wood Hart
Martin-Zambito
Fine Art, Seattle

Jennings Lodge
(n.d.)
William P. Hayes
Allen Collection

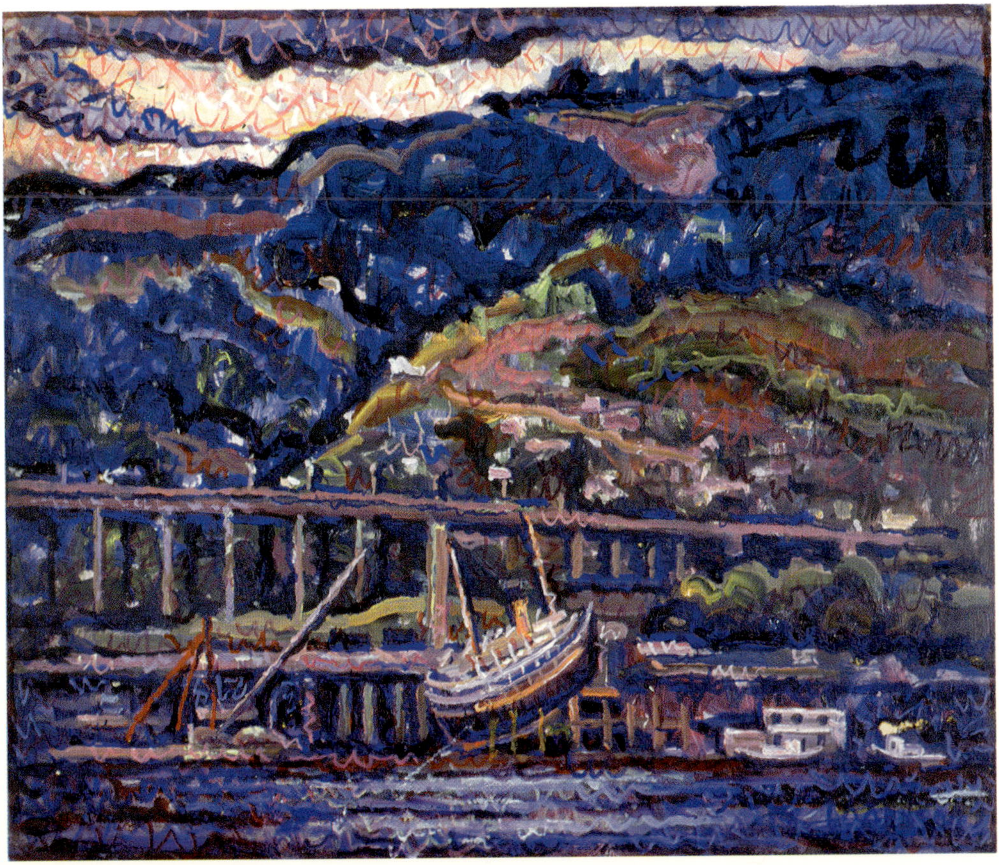

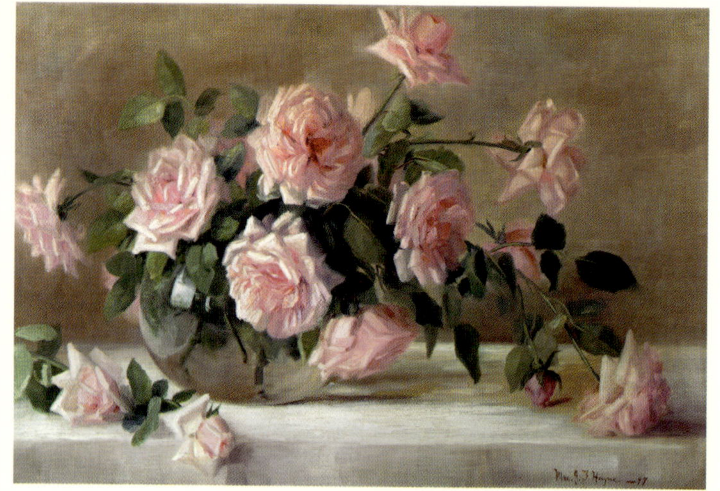

Caroline Testout Roses
(1897)
Josephine T. Hayne
Oregon Historical Society
95-118.1.1, .2

Branching Road
(n.d.)
Charles Heaney
Booth Collection

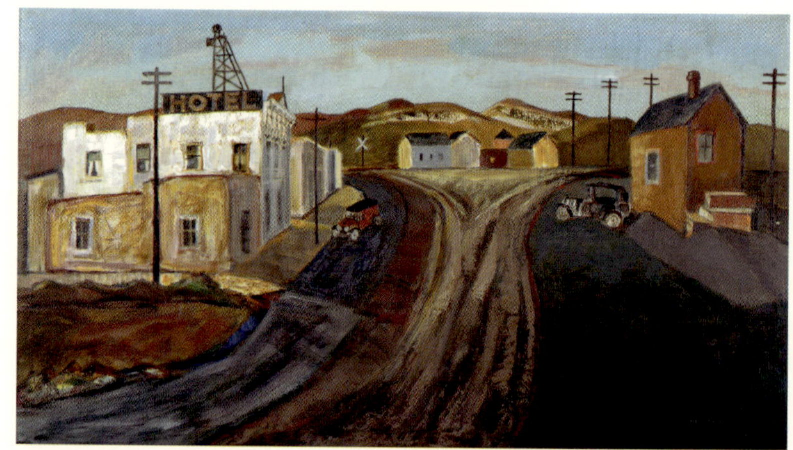

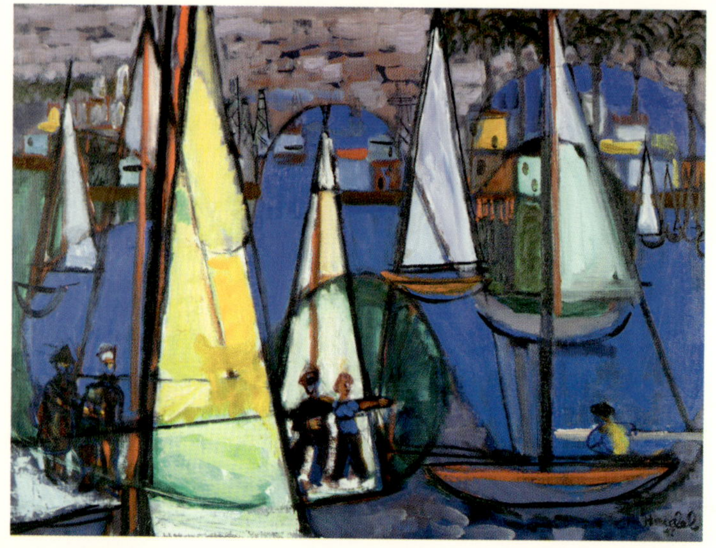

Boats
Frederick Heidel
(ca.1950)
Artist's Collection

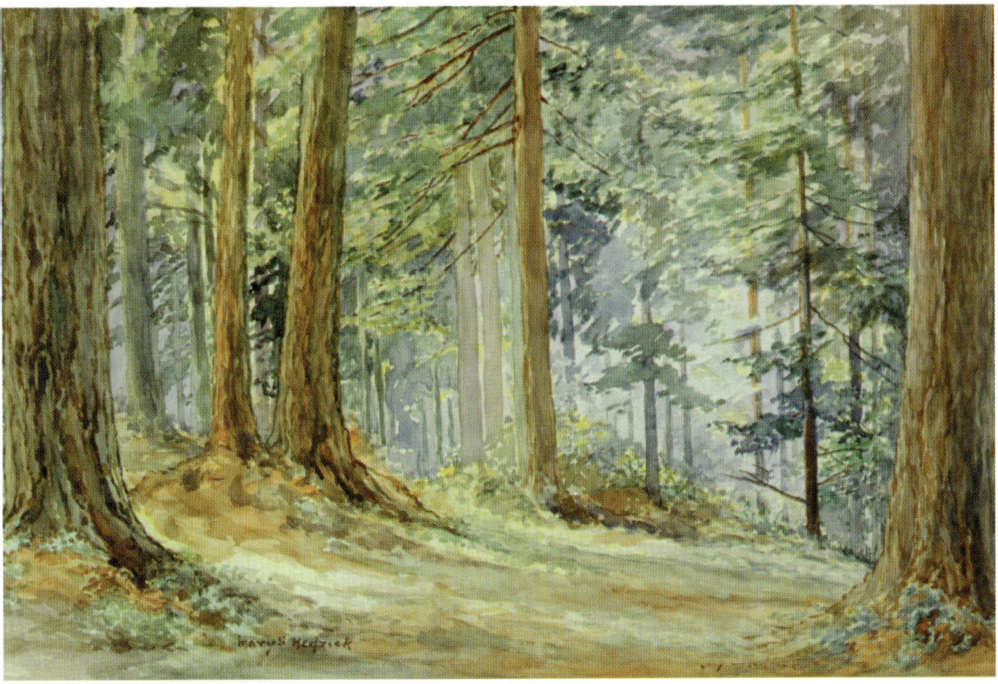

Untitled
(n.d.)
Mary Hedrick
Private Collection

Clearing the Forest near Hood River
(1914)
Edward Hill
Le Meitour Gallery

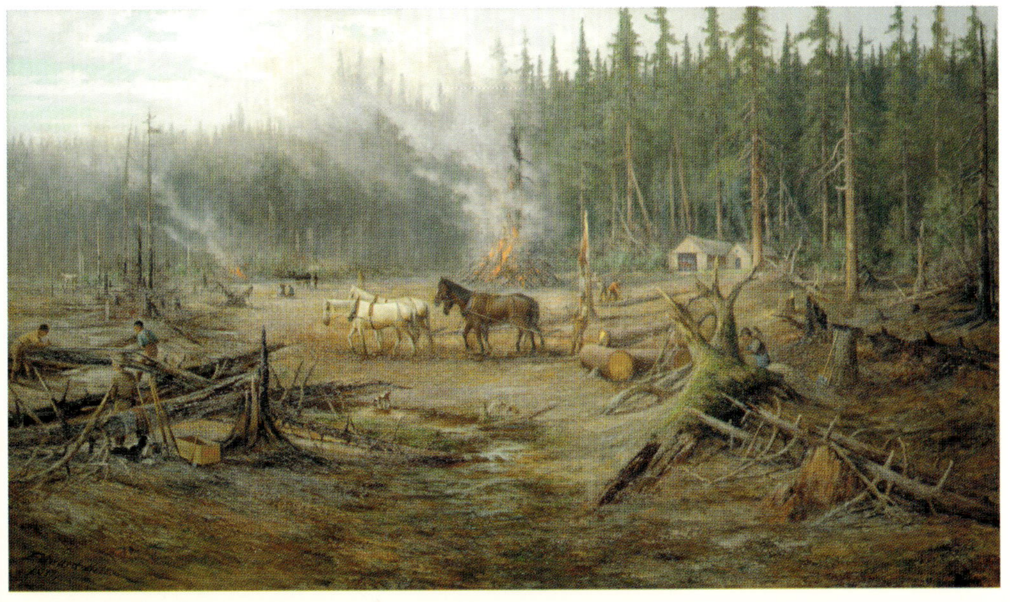

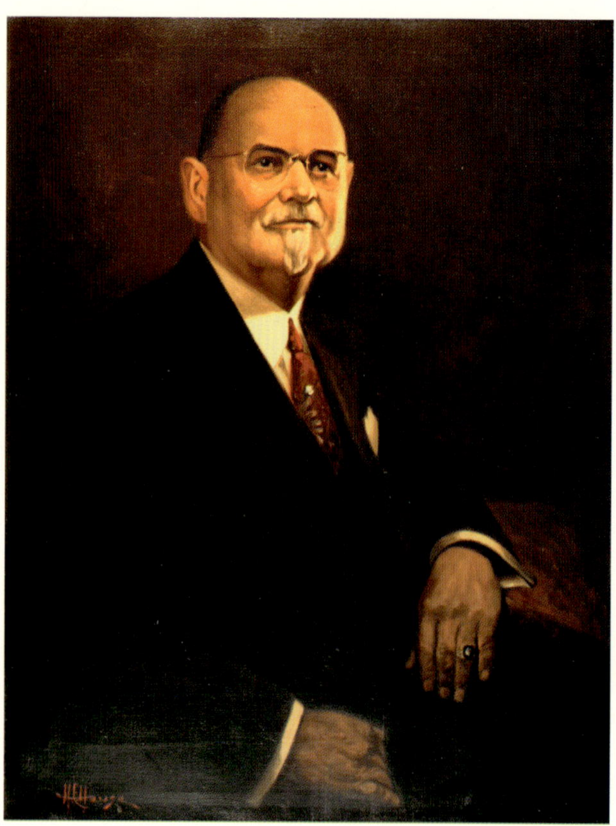

Henry Thiele
(1950)
H. Elmer House
Oregon Historical Society
86-214.1, .2

Koukla
(n.d.)
Demetrios Jameson
Portland Art Museum
Helen Thurston Ayer Fund
52.50

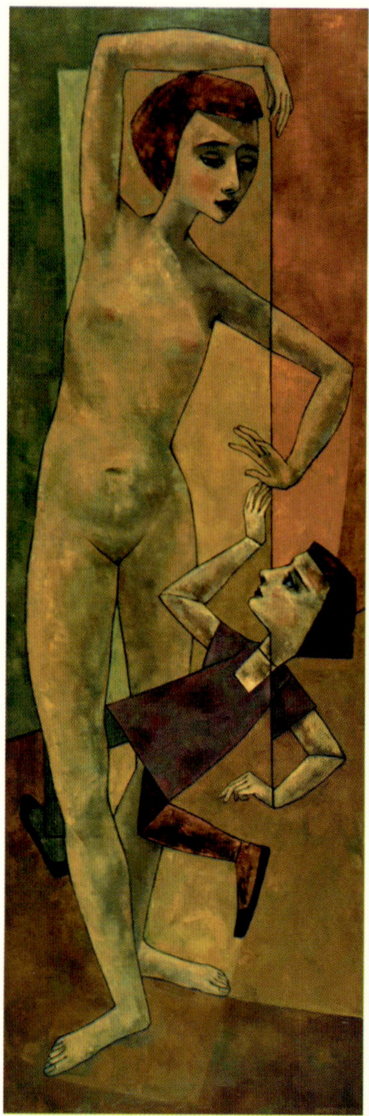

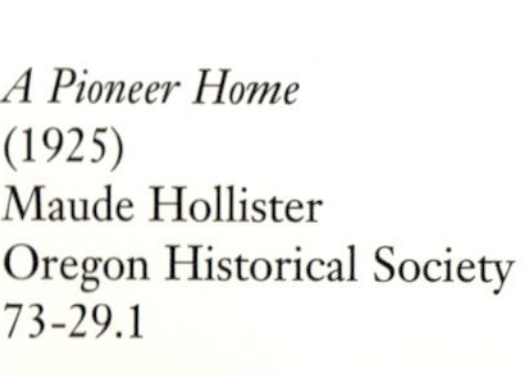

A Pioneer Home
(1925)
Maude Hollister
Oregon Historical Society
73-29.1

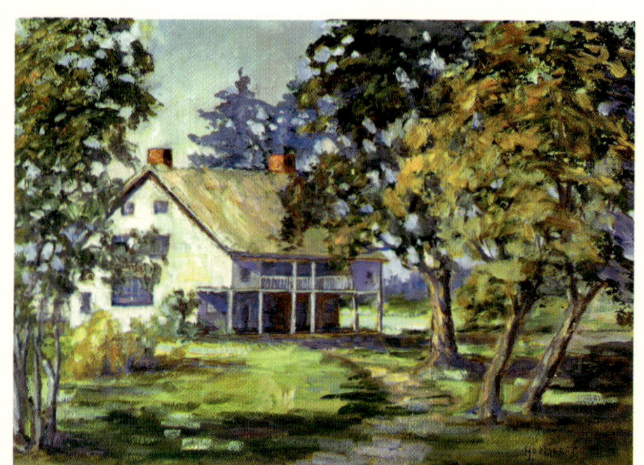

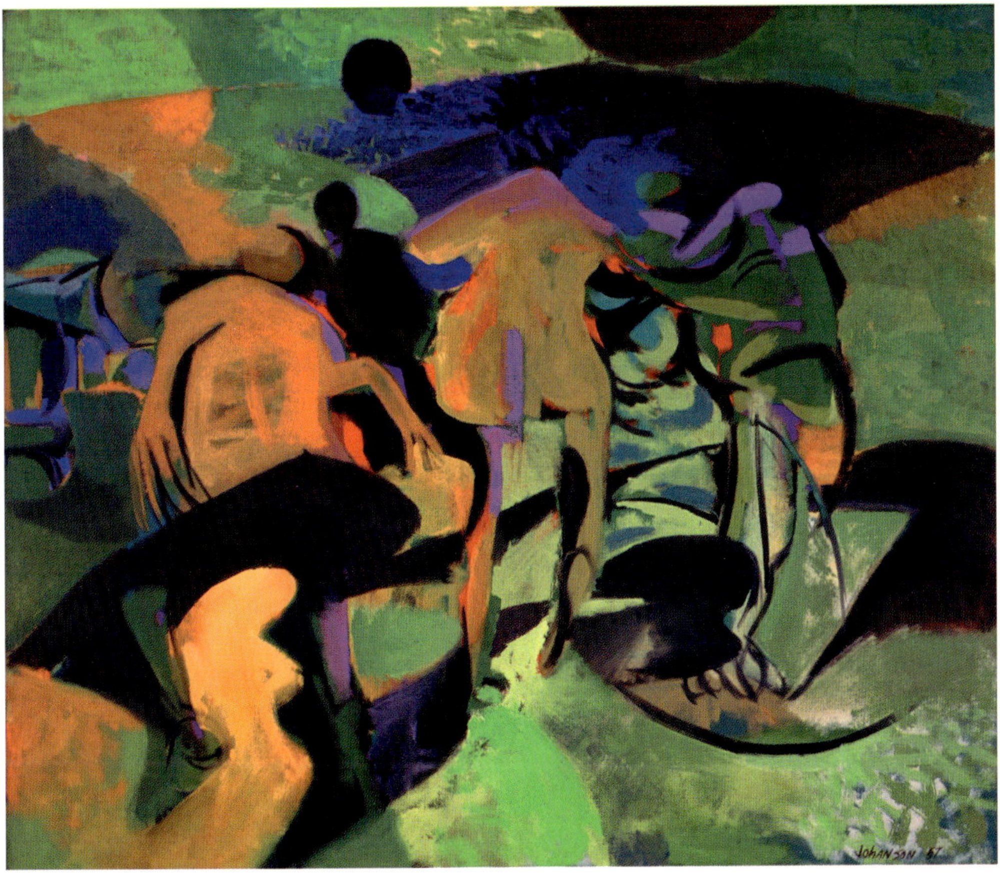

Running Figures
(1957)
George Johanson
Artist's Collection

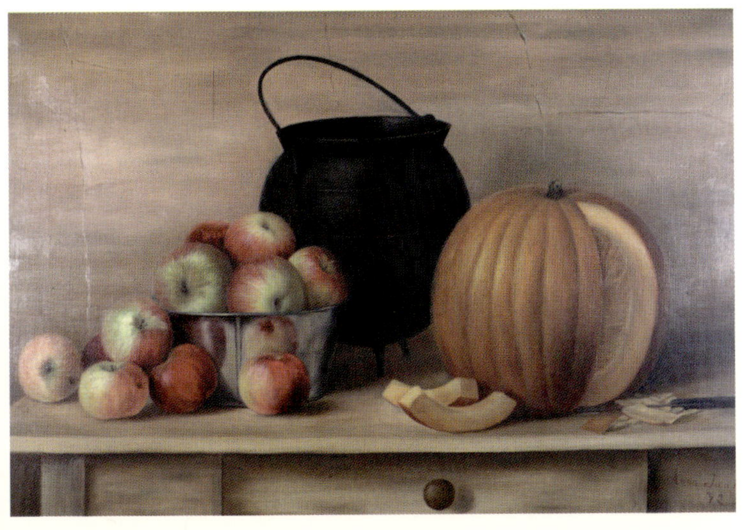

Pumpkins and Apples
(1892)
Anna Junk
Bush House Museum, Salem

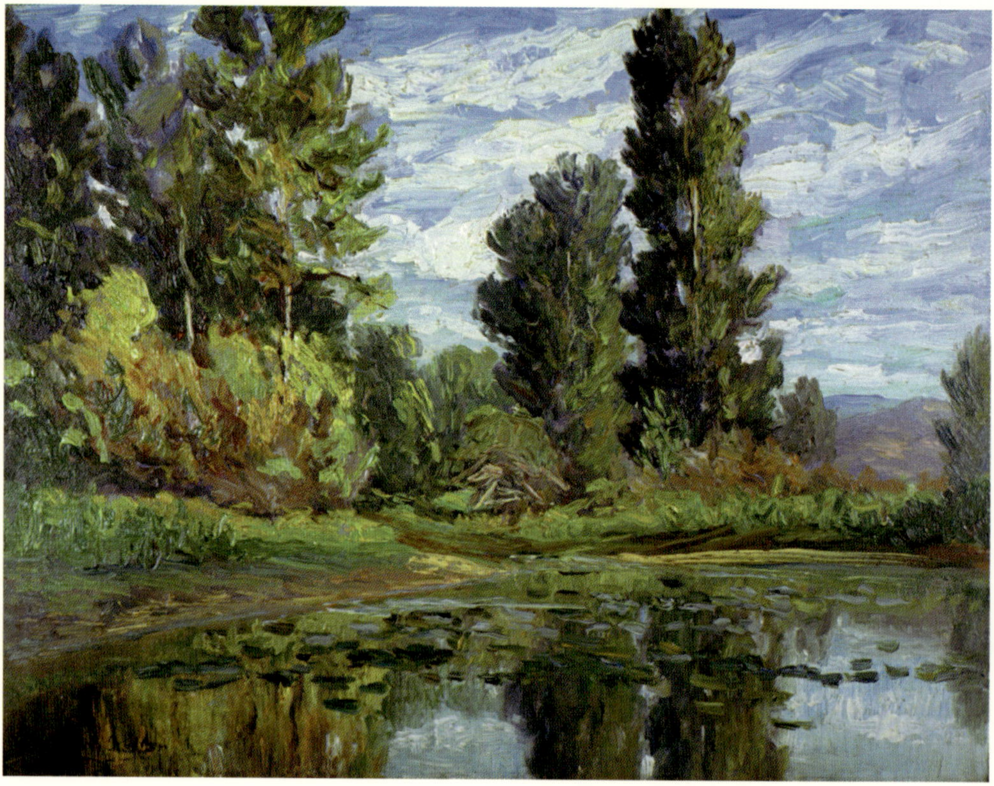

Water Lily Pond
(1917)
Clyde Leon Keller
Miranda Colleciton

Composition #26
(1944)
Maude Kerns
University of Oregon
Museum of Art, Eugene
Gift of the Estate of
Maude Kerns

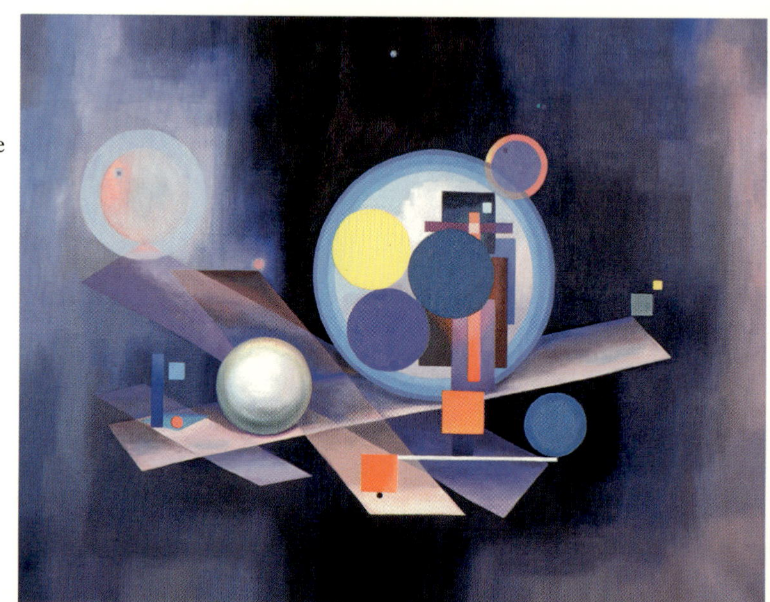

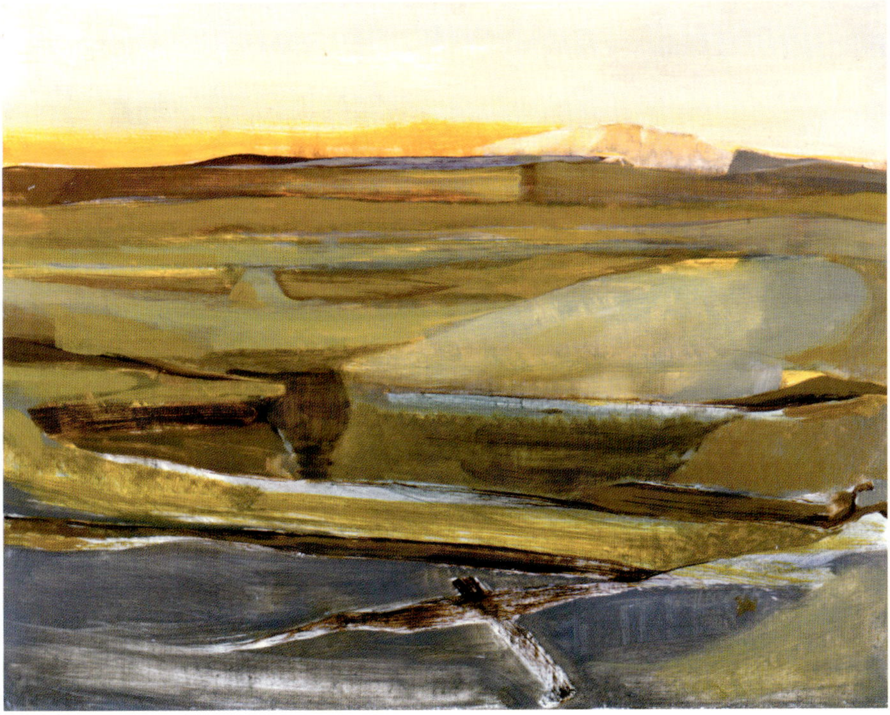

First View of the Western Mountains
(n.d.)
Hank Kowert
Parsons Collection

Storm Over Willamette
(ca.1959)
LaVerne Krause
Painting Restoration Studio

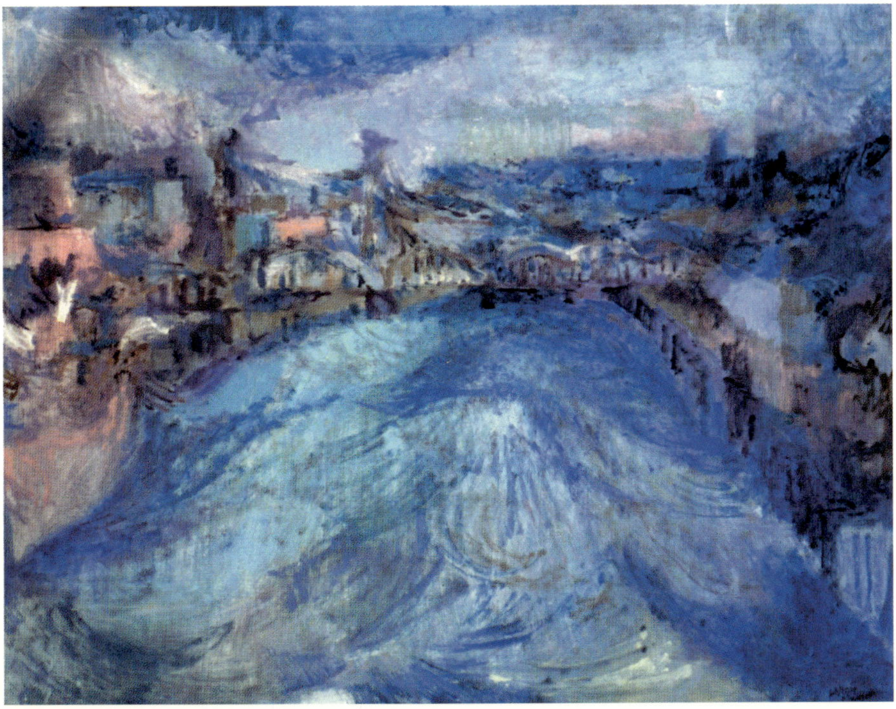

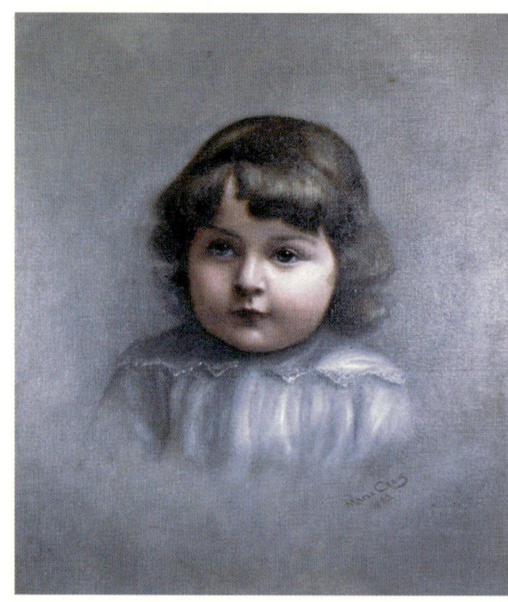

Asahel Bush IV
(1890)
Marie Craig (LeGall)
Bush House Museum,
Salem

Sauvie Island
(n.d.)
Bird LeFever
Lundberg Collection

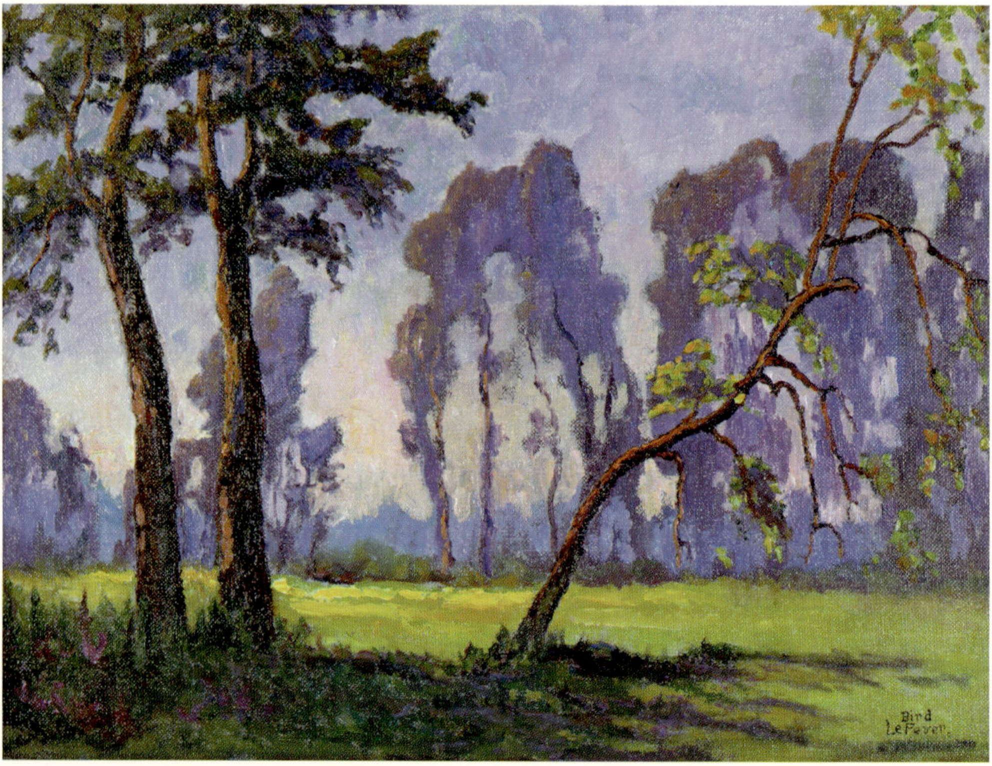

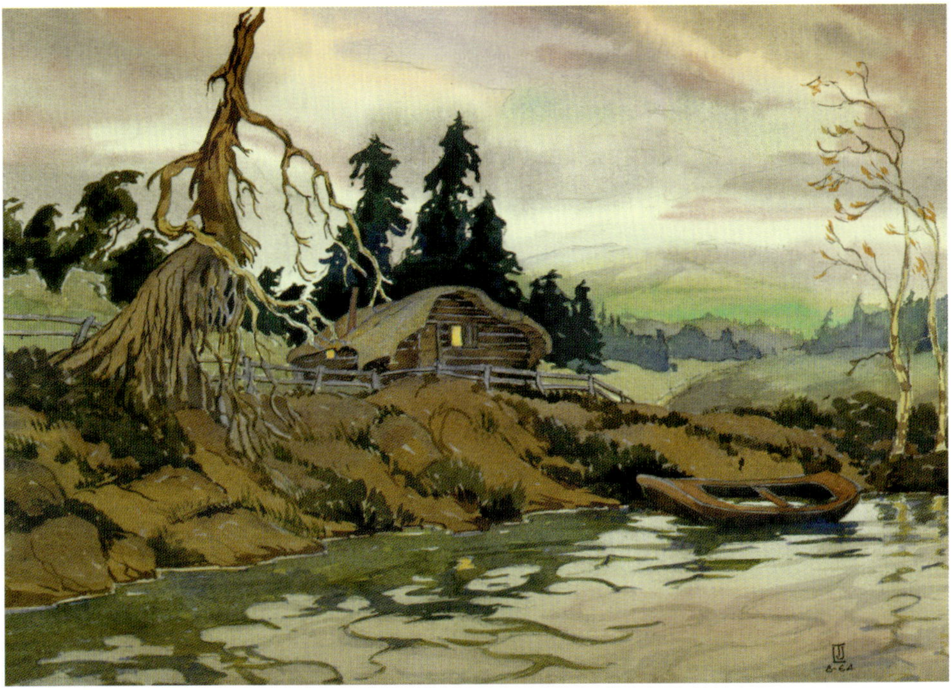

Untitled
(c. 1930, dated 1964)
Thayne Logan
Klevit Collection

The Sunlit Valley
(1924)
Percy Manser
Miranda Collection

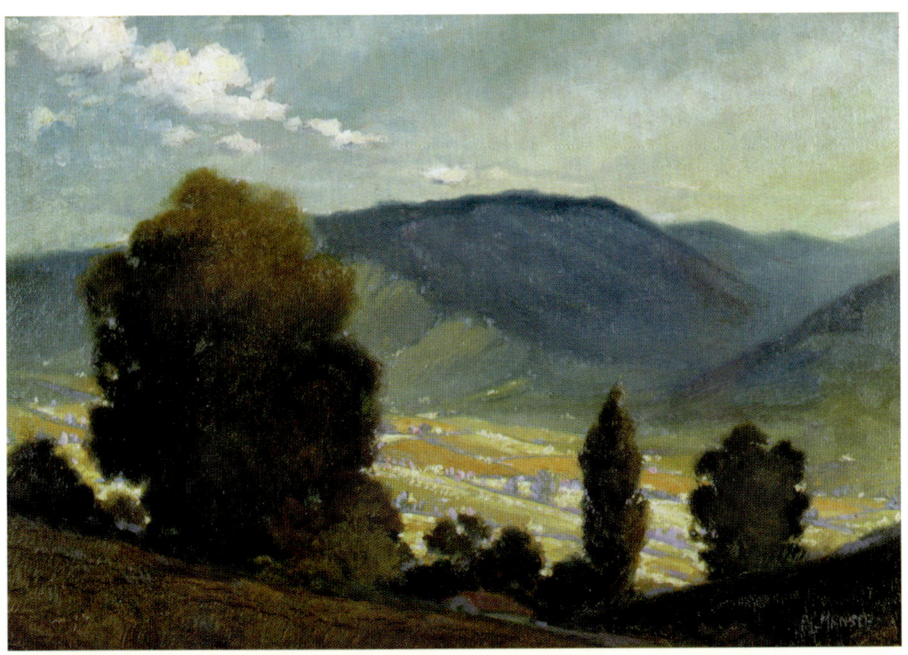

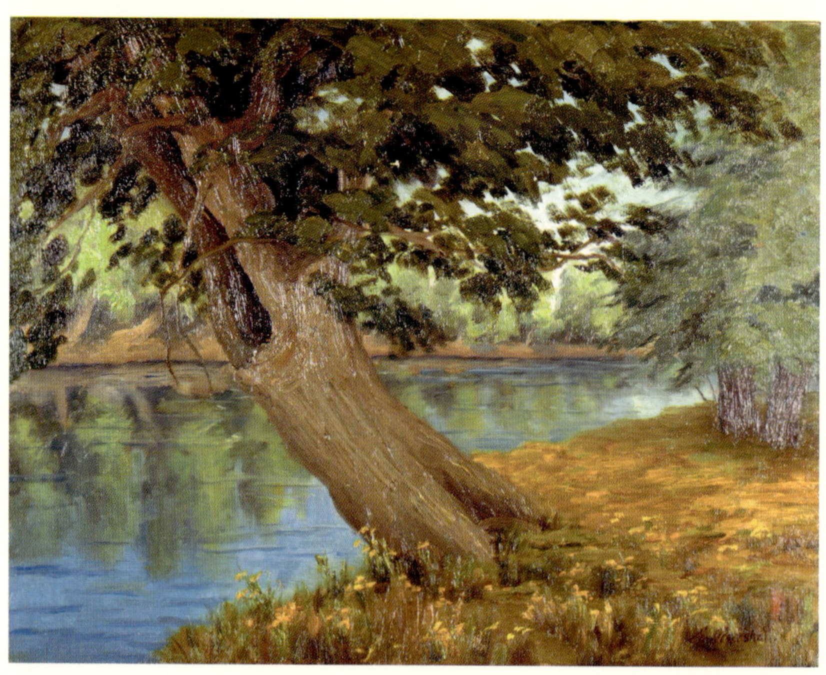

Columbia Slough
(n.d.)
Augusta Marshall
Painting Restoration Studio

Gangster's Funeral
(1928)
David McCosh
University of Oregon
Museum of Art, Eugene
Gift of Anne McCosh

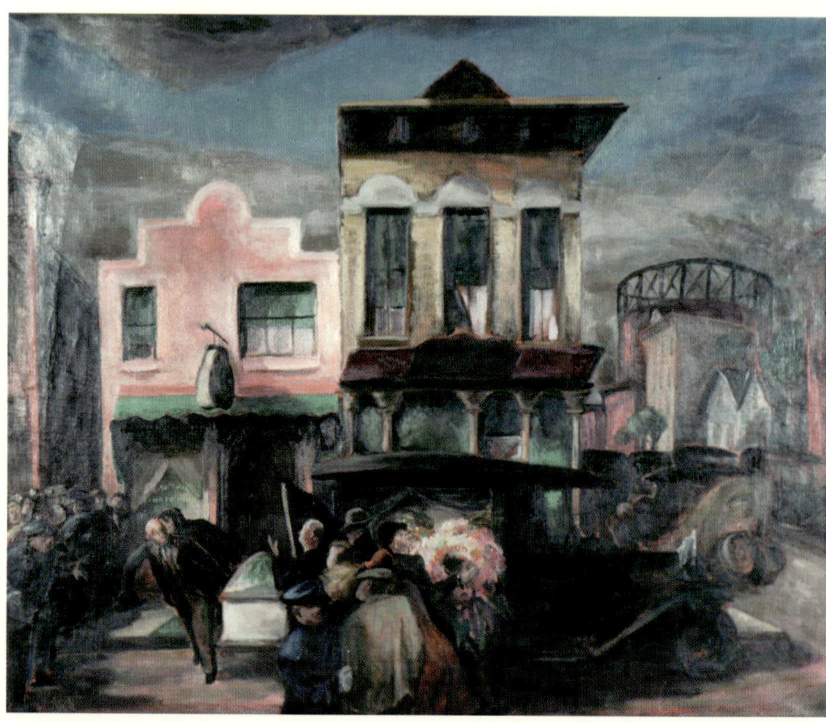

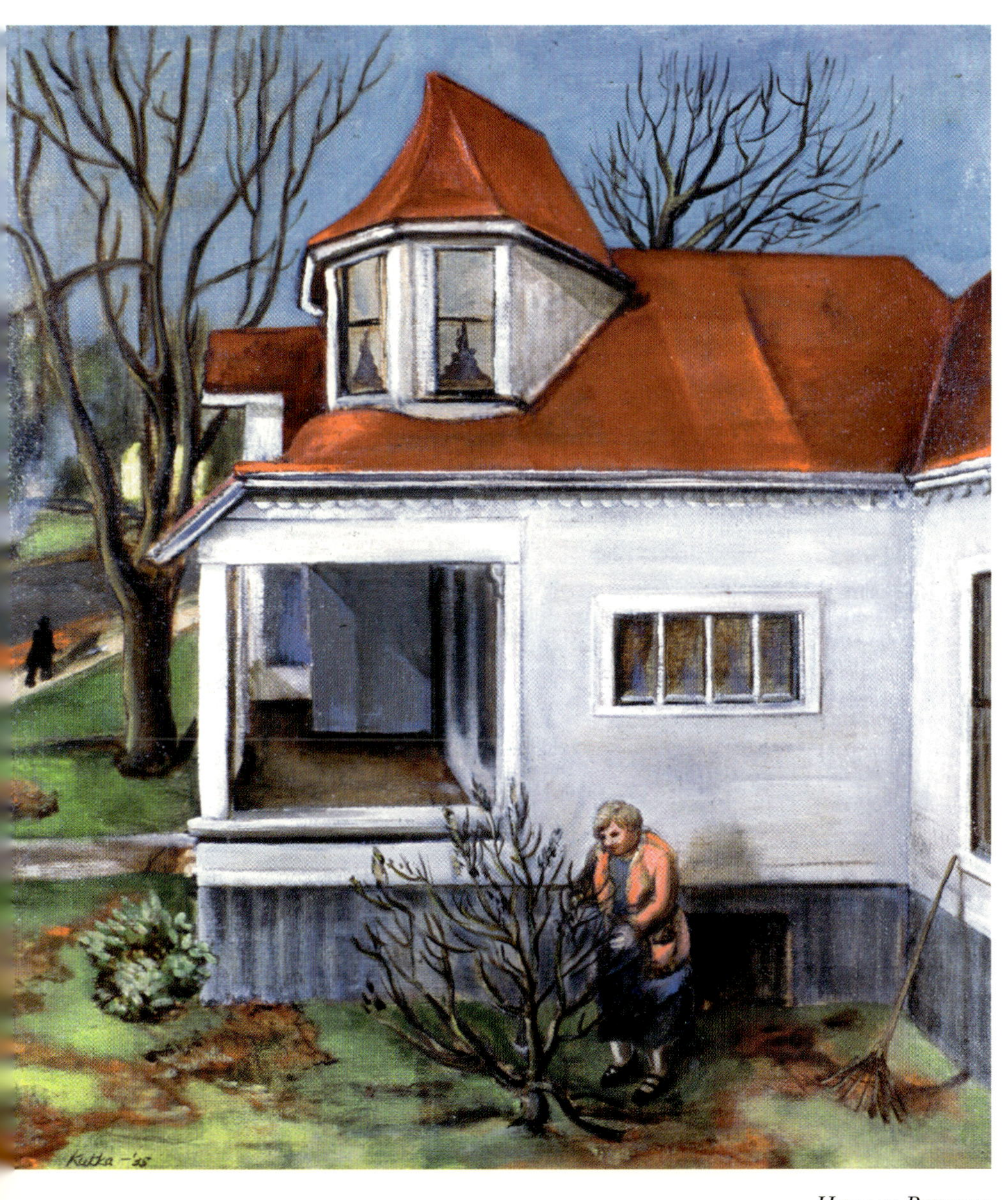

House on Patterson
(1935)
Anne Kutka McCosh
Parsons Collection

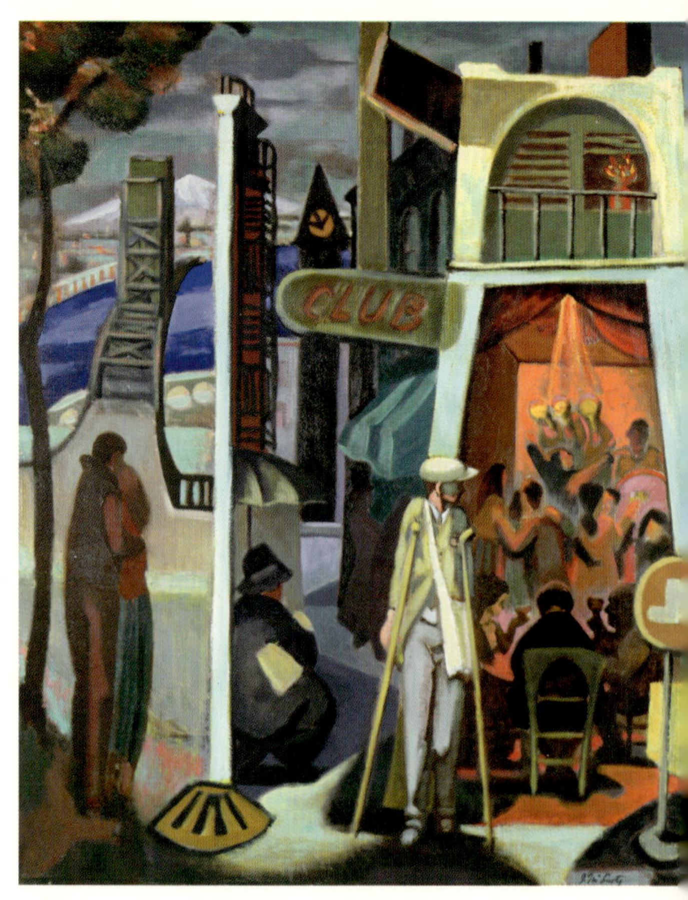

The Bystander
(1944)
Jack McLarty
Portland Art Museum
Caroline Ladd Pratt Fund
64.8

Mt. Hood from a Marsh
(1911)
Charles C. McKim
Miranda Collection

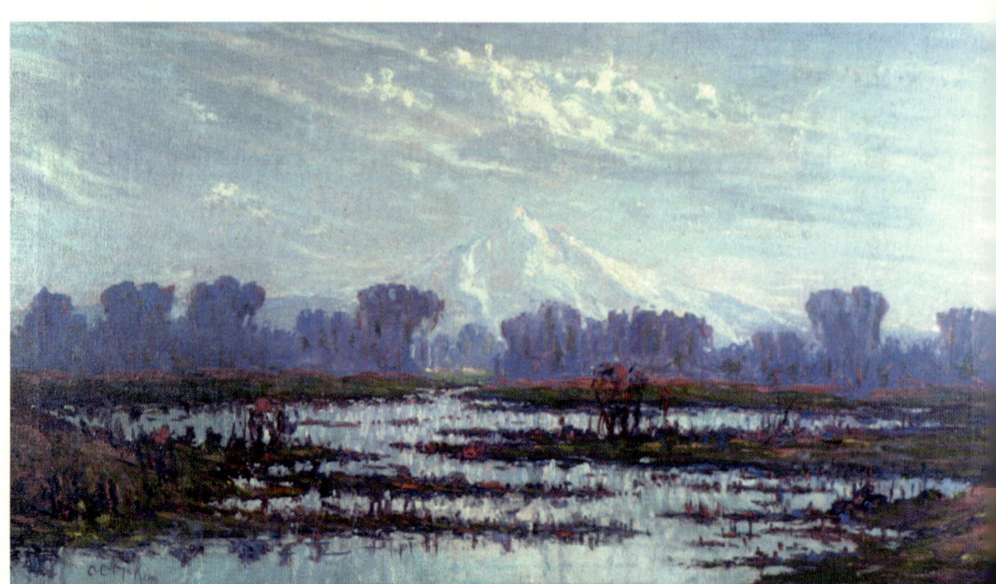

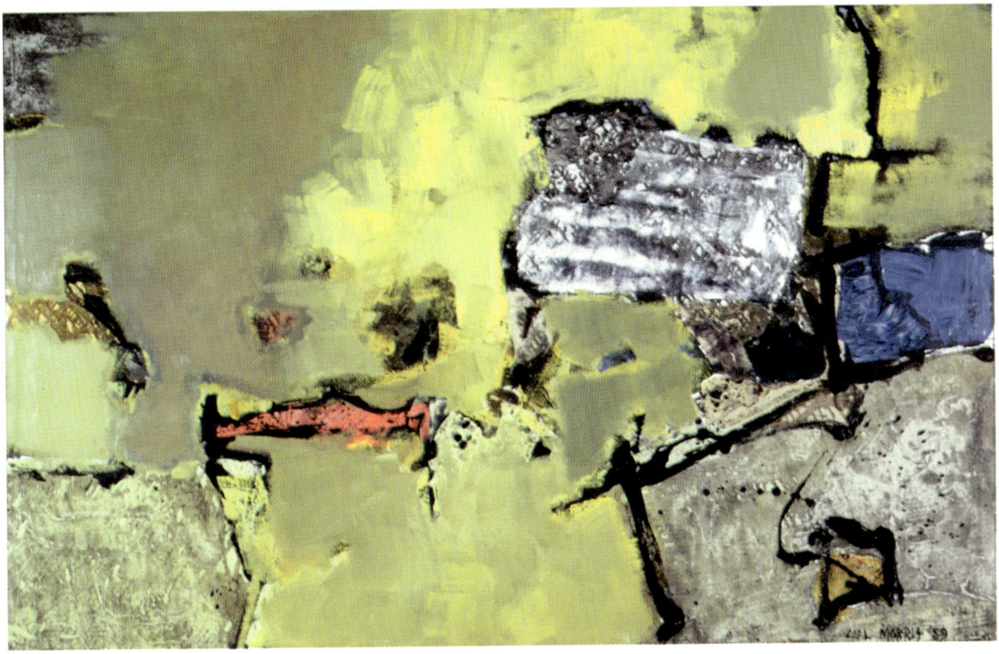

Light and Rock
(1959)
Carl Morris
Collection of Arlene
and Harold Schnitzer

Visitor from London
(ca.1930)
Charlotte Roberta Mish
Miranda Collection

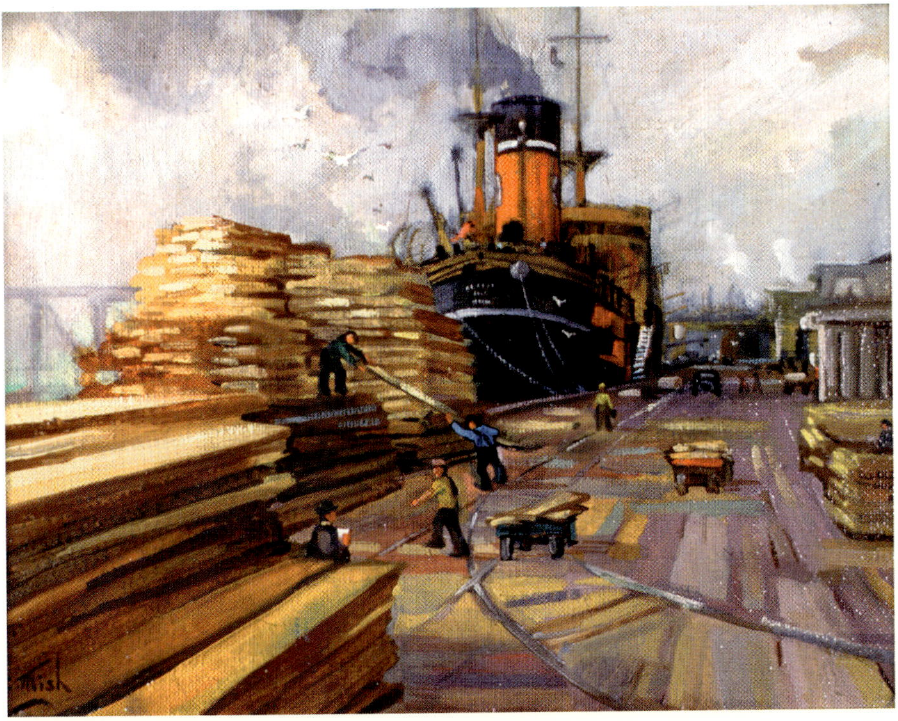

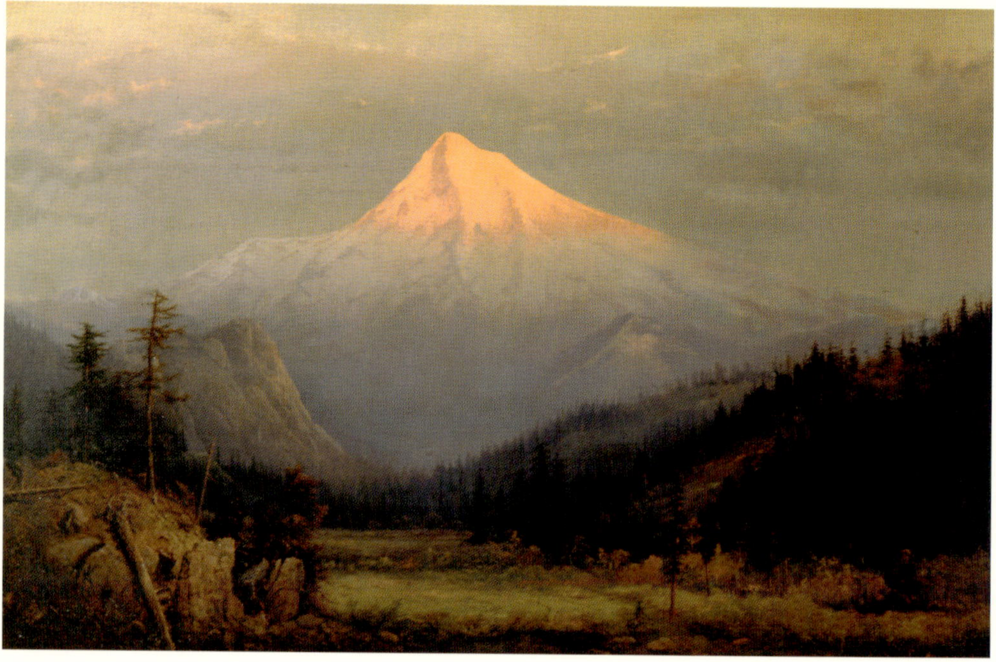

Mt. Hood
(n.d.)
William S. Parrott
Lewis and Clark College

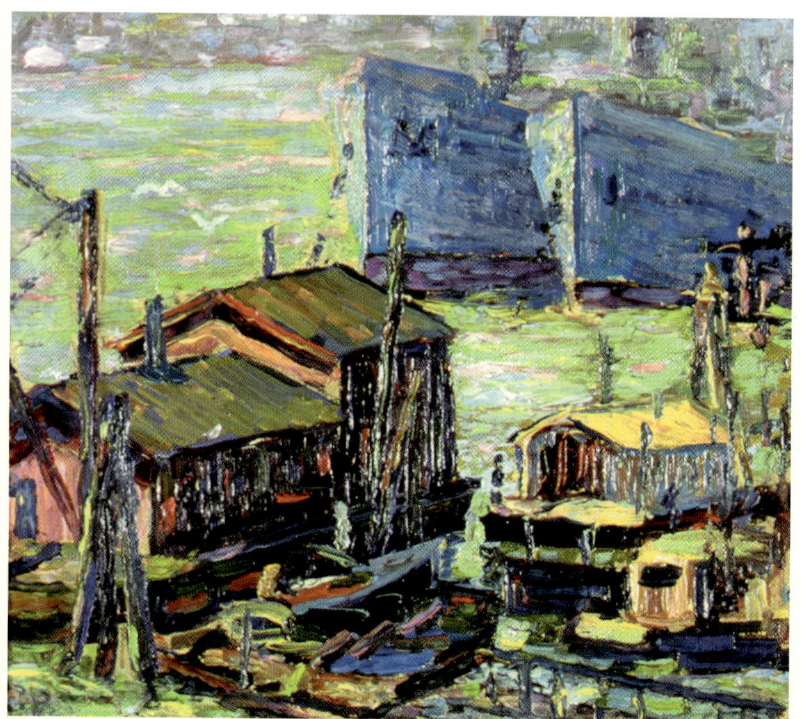

Looking West from the Steel Bridge
(1916)
Conrad Pedersen
Collection of
Brooks and
Dorothy Cofield

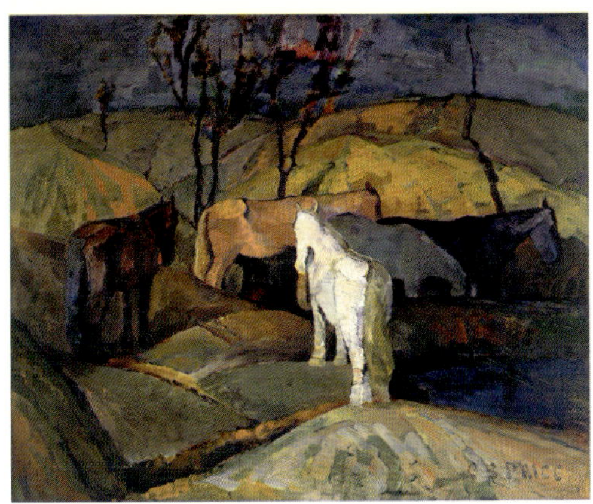

By the River
(1927)
C.S. Price
Collection of Arlene
and Harold Schnitzer

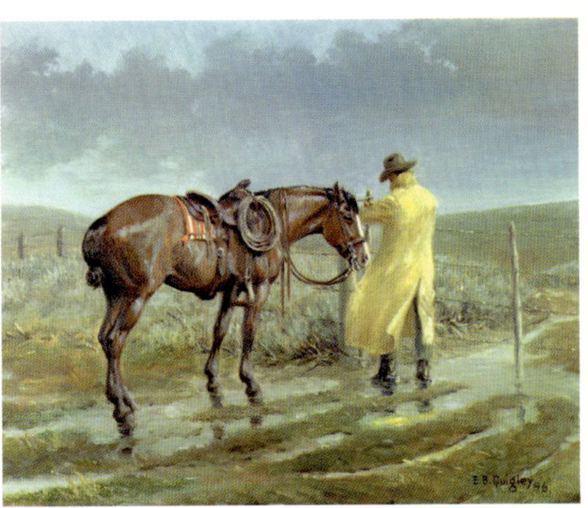

Yellow Slicker
(1946)
Ed Quigley
Oregon Historical Society
83-71.1.1, .2

Abstraction (Composition) #51
(ca.1949)
Albert Patecky
Hallie Ford Museum of Art
Willamette University, Salem
Maribeth Collins Acquisition Fund

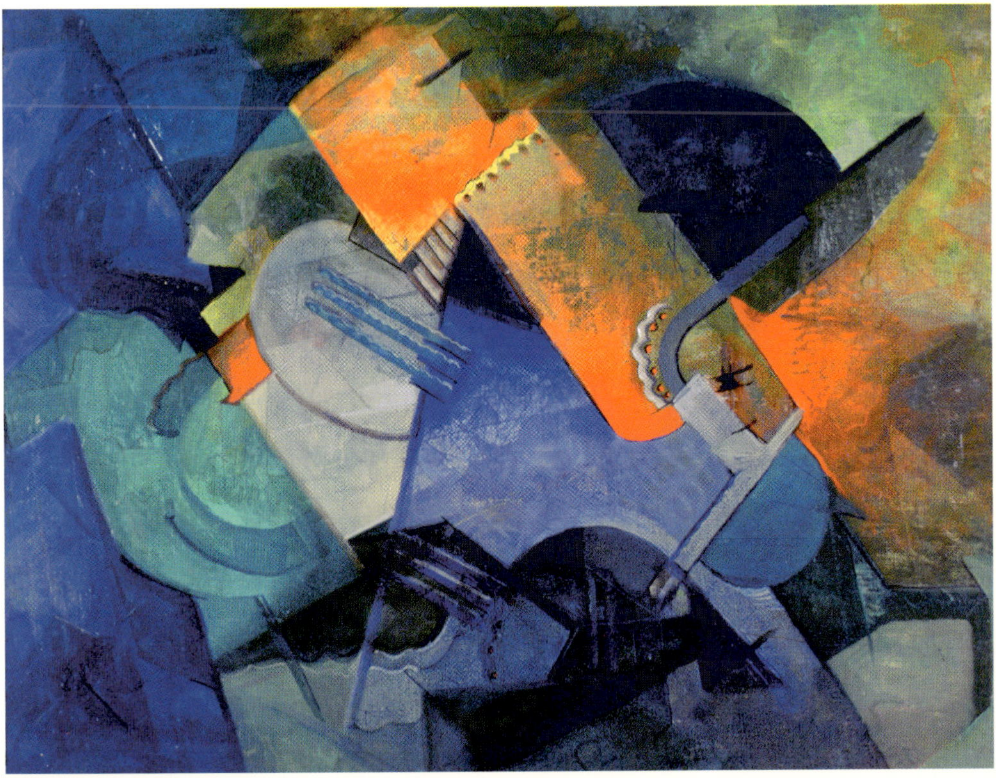

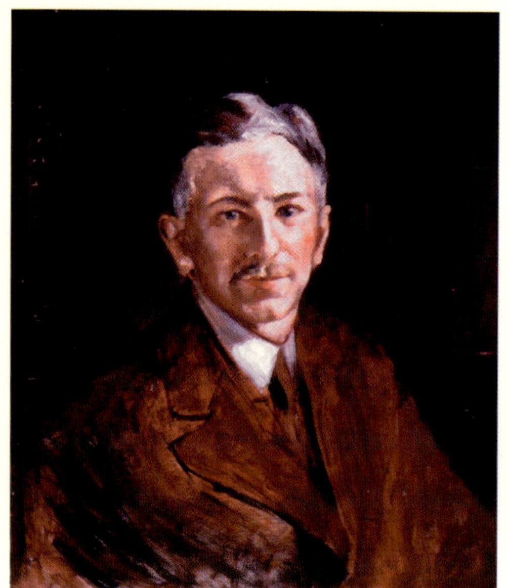

Richard Frederick Scholz
(ca.1922)
Lucy Dodd Ramberg
Reed College

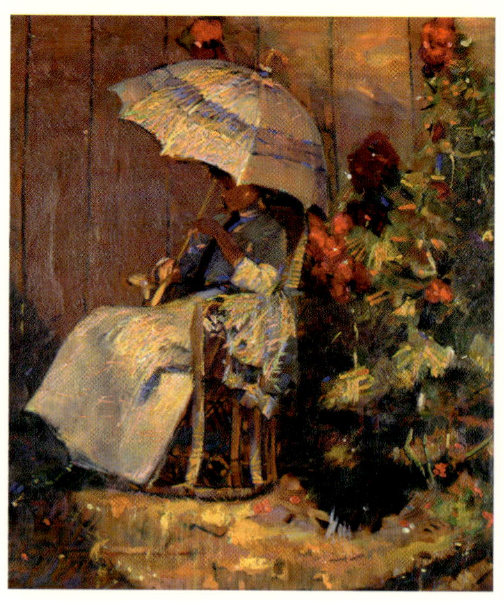

Woman With Umbrella
Regina Dorland Robinson
Southern Oregon Historical Society, Medford
B-301

Early Salmon Canneries, Mid-Columbia River Near Crown Point
(n.d.)
Cleveland Rockwell
Oregon Historical Society
80-51.9.5.1,.2

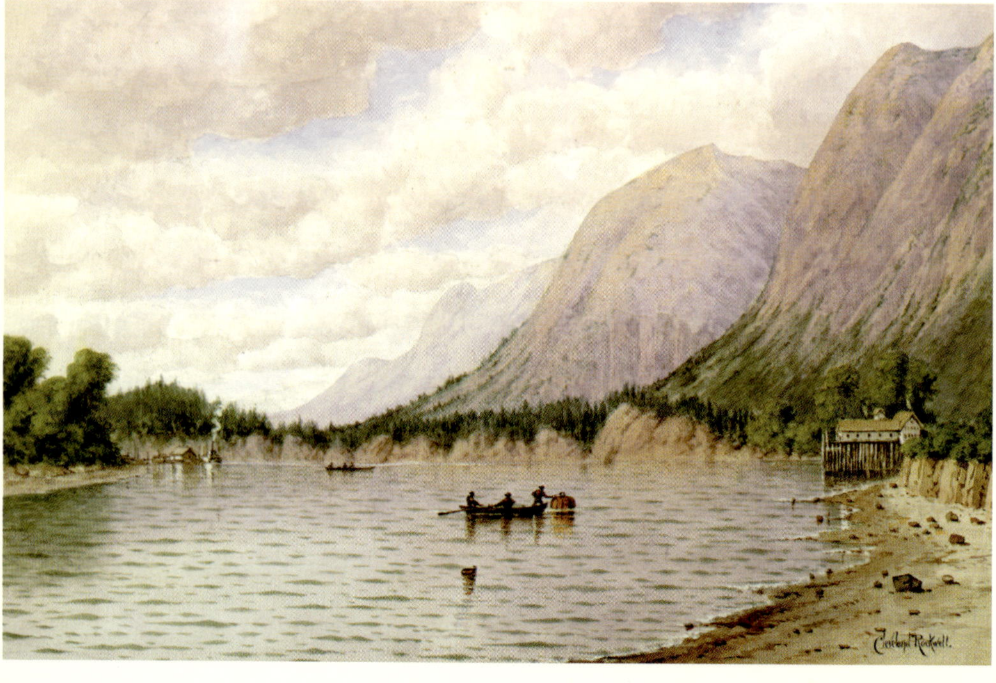

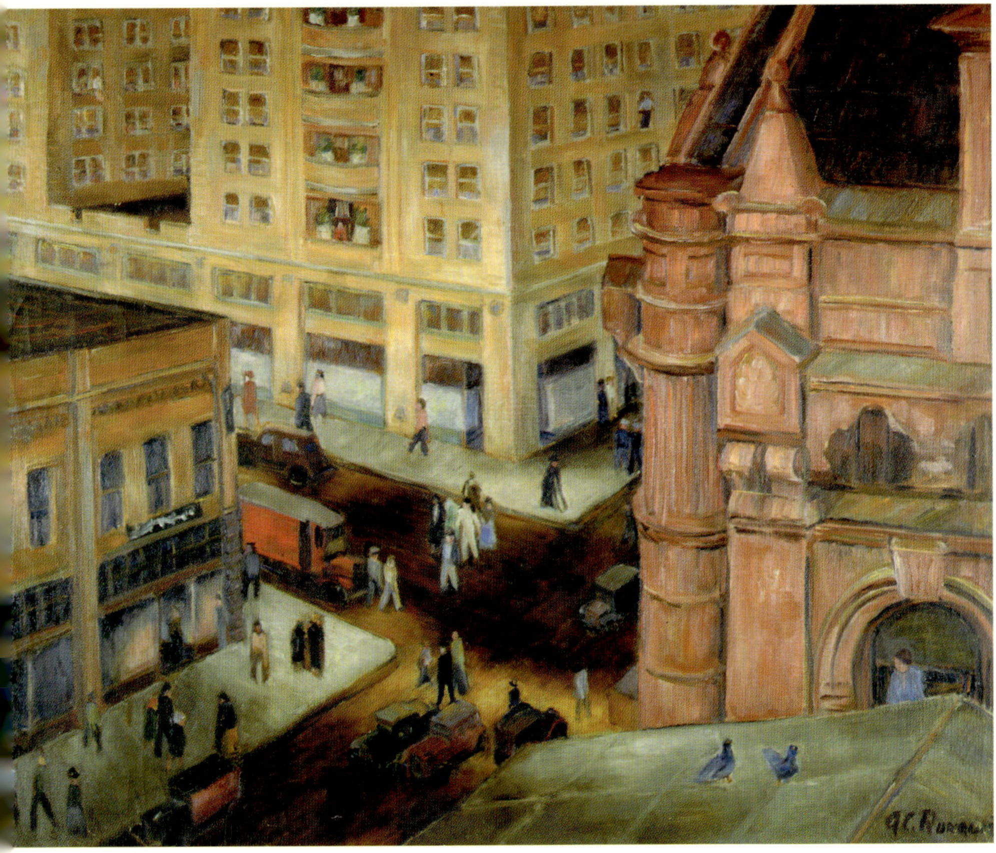

View of Multnomah Hotel, Portland
(ca. 1935)
Albert C. Runquist
Oregon Historical Society
89-221.2.1, .2

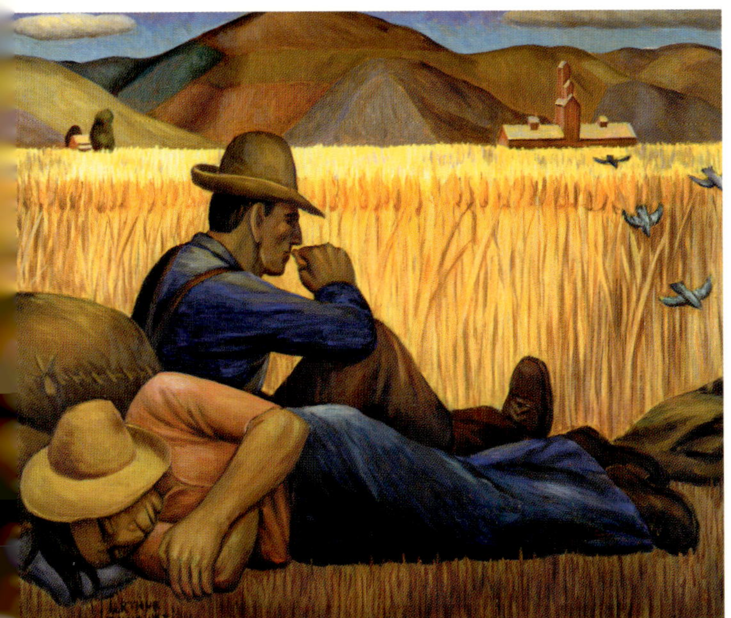

Lunch
(1939)
Arthur Runquist
Portland Art Museum
Courtesy of Public Building Service, General Services Administration
L45.3.7

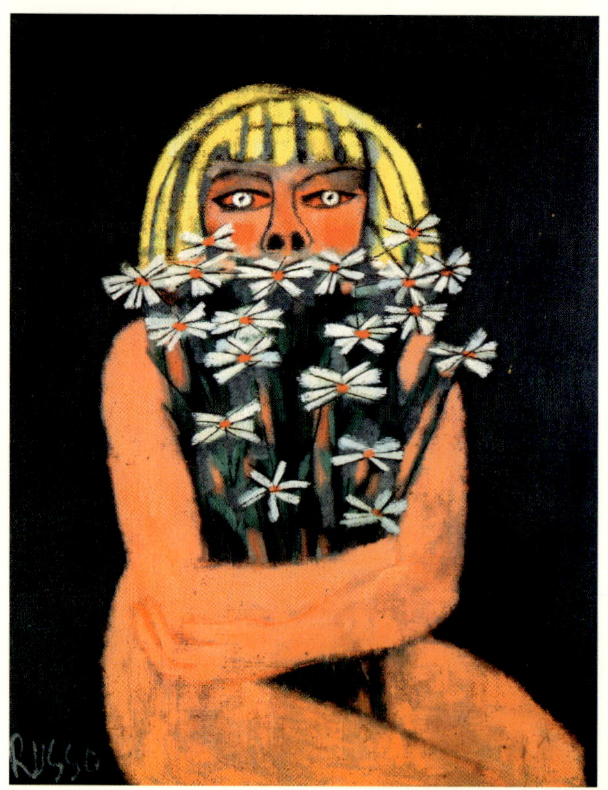

Girl With Daisies
(ca. mid 1950s)
Michele Russo
Collection of Arlene
and Harold Schnitzer

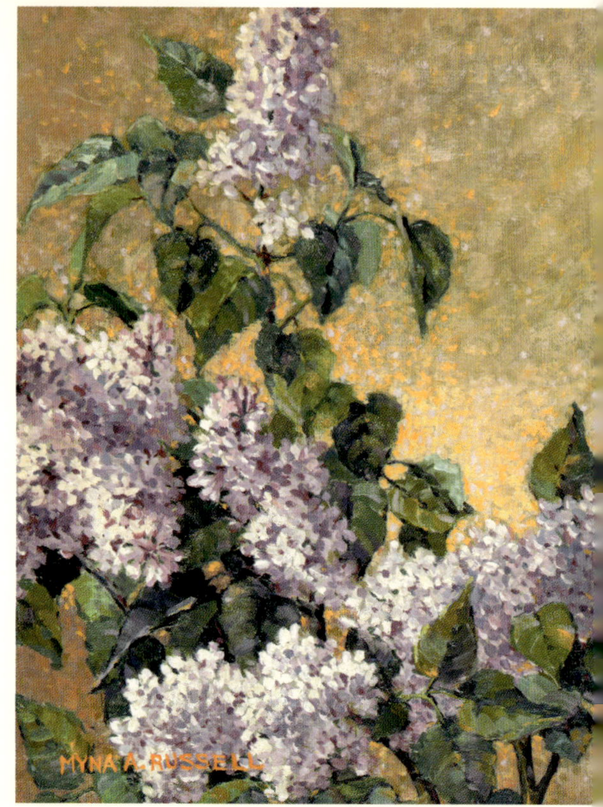

Lilacs
(ca.1920)
Myna Russell
Miranda Collection

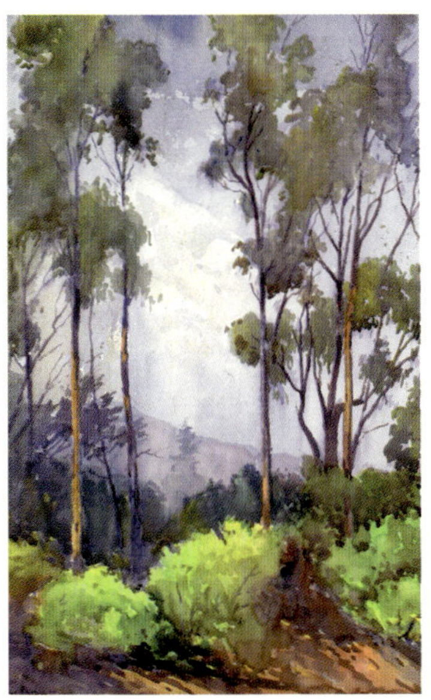

Summer Landscape
(1936)
Alfred Schroff
Miranda Collection

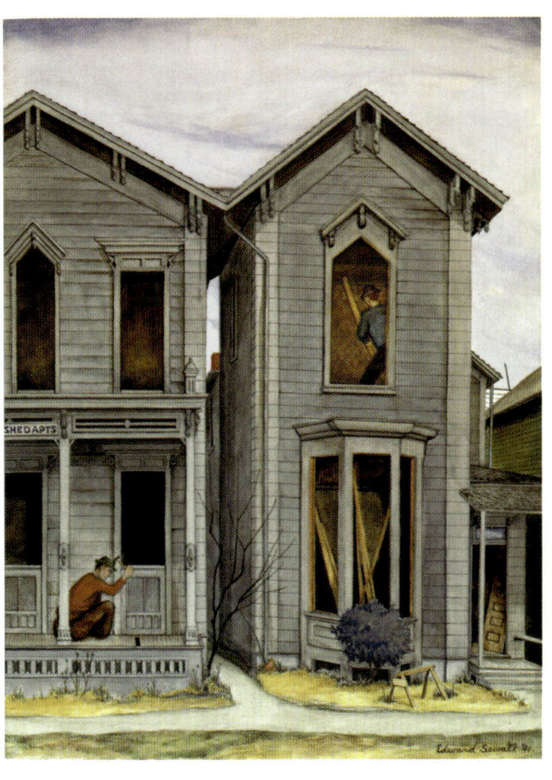

Death of A House
(n.d.)
Edward Sewall
Portland Art Museum
Helen Thurston
Ayer Fund
41.16

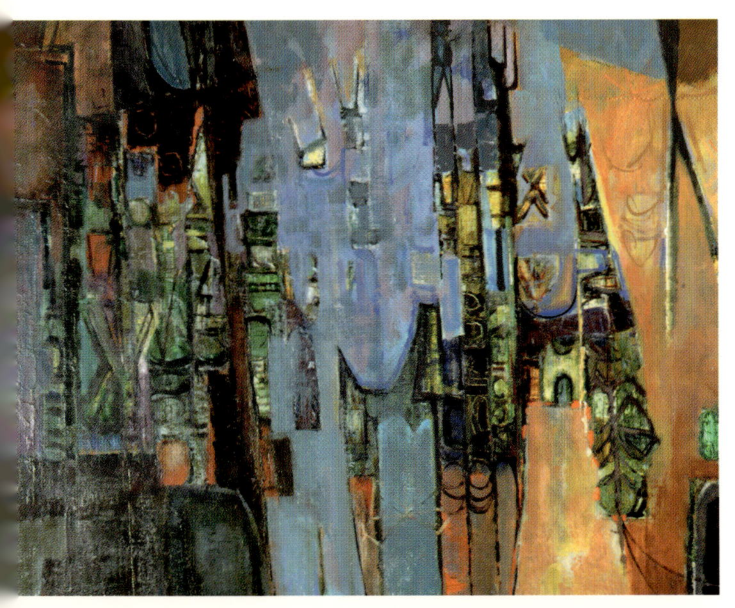

Upper Forest Fantasy
(1959)
Nels Sandgren
Portland Art Museum
Gift of Carol Norton
Yates and Richard C.
Yates in memory of
Agnes and Marion Yates
92.7

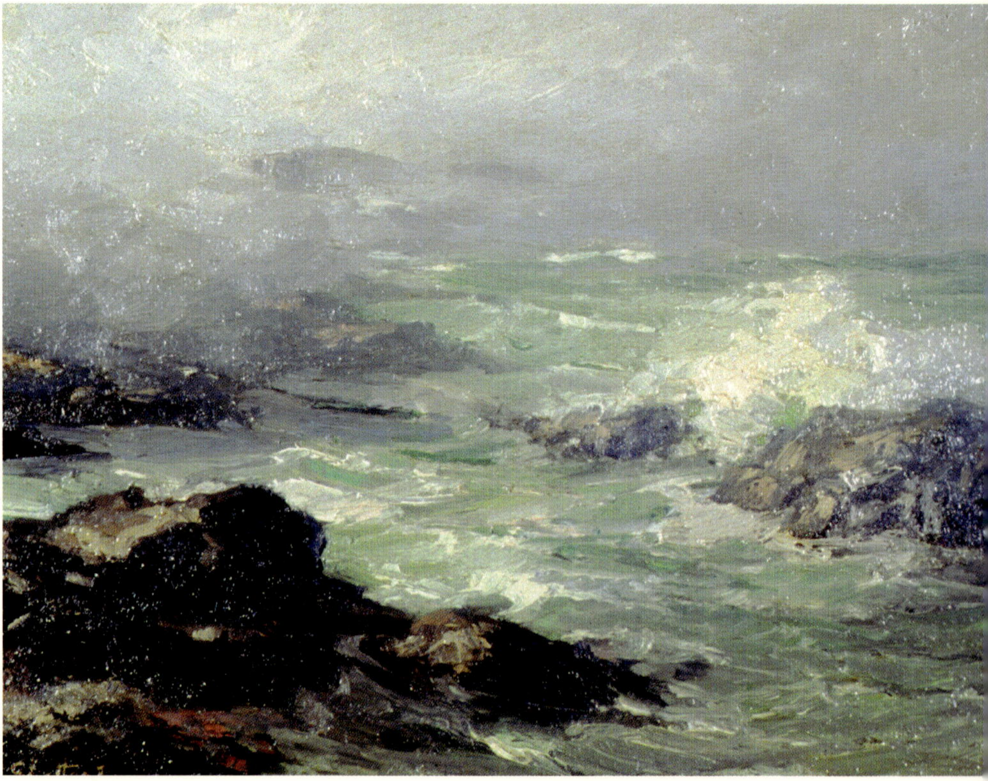

Foggy Morning on the Coast
(1942)
Peter Sheffers
Parsons Collection

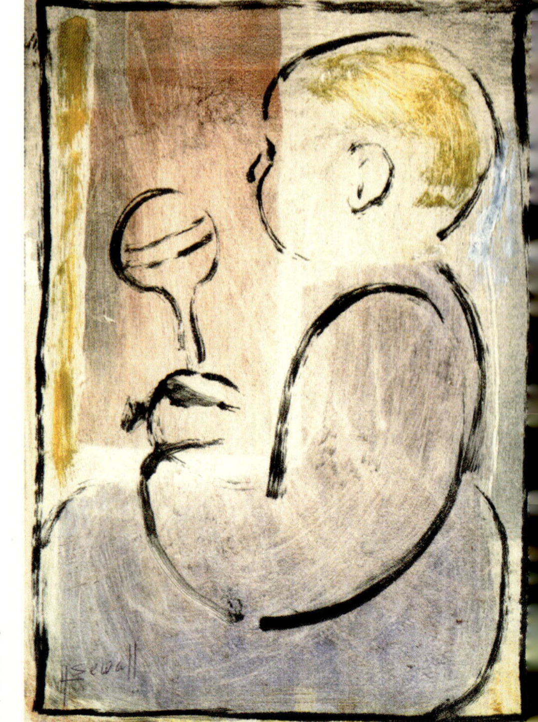

Seated Baby
(n.d.)
Howard Sewall
Booth Collection

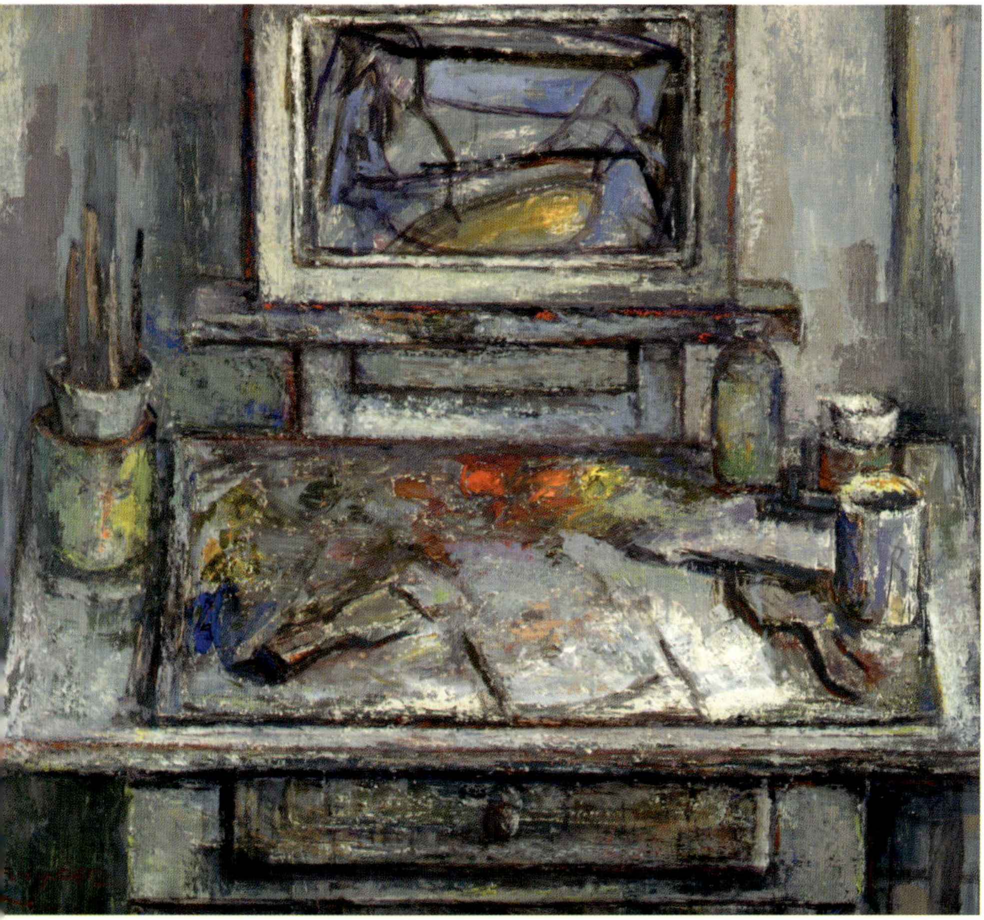

Price's Work Table
(n.d.)
Amanda Snyder
Portland Art Musuem
Gift of the Artist
64.34

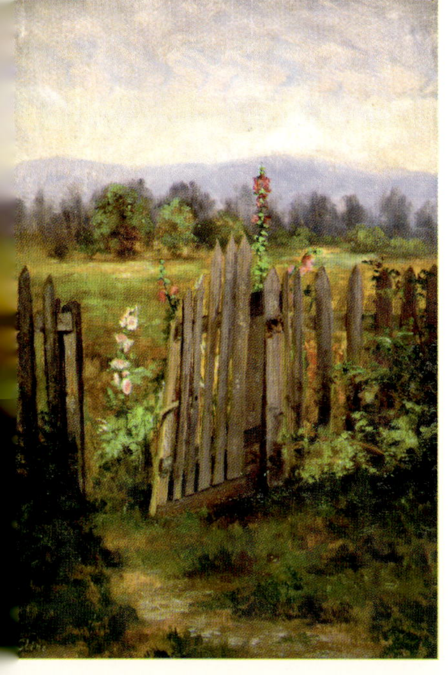

Hollyhocks on Garden Gate
(1891)
Eva Cline Smith
Painting Restoration Studio

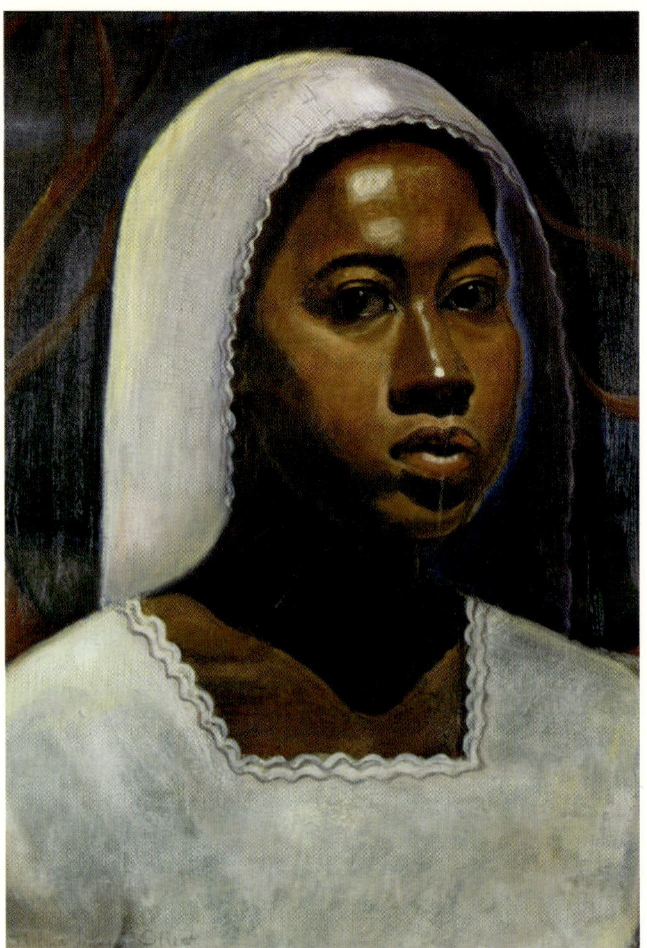

Black Virgin
(n.d.)
Thelma Johnson Streat
Reed College

Mt. Hood
(n.d.)
Nellie Starr
Painting Restoration Studio

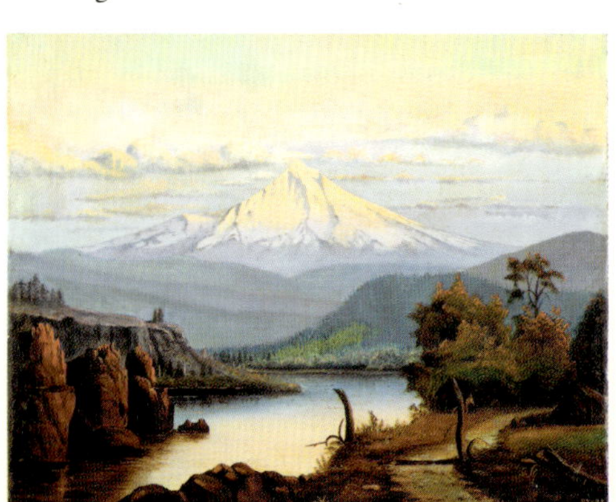

New Bridge at Oregon Ci
(192
Clara Jane Stephe
Powell Collectio

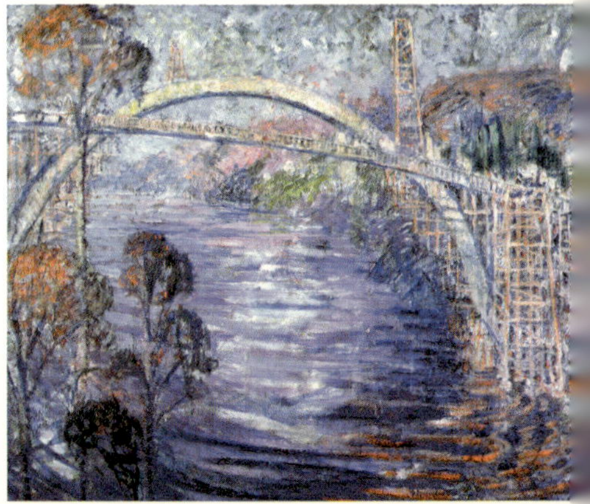

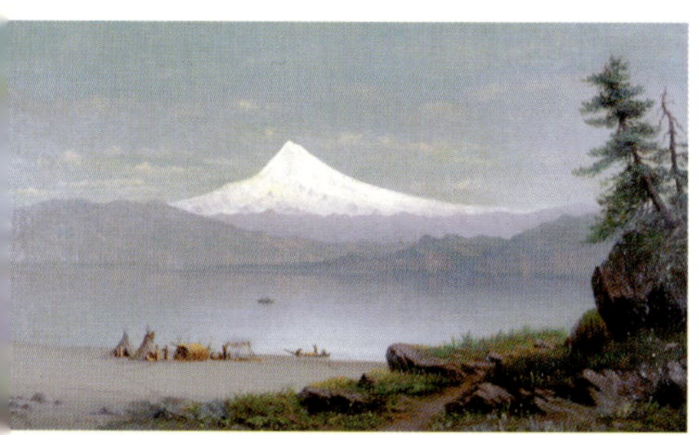

ıdians on The Bank of the Columbia River
ı883)
ımes Everett Stuart
Iarquard Collection

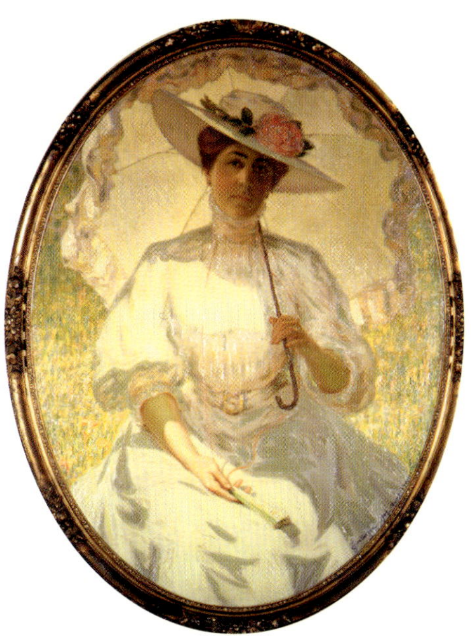

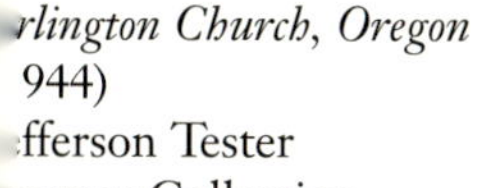

rlington Church, Oregon
944)
ıfferson Tester
ırsons Collection

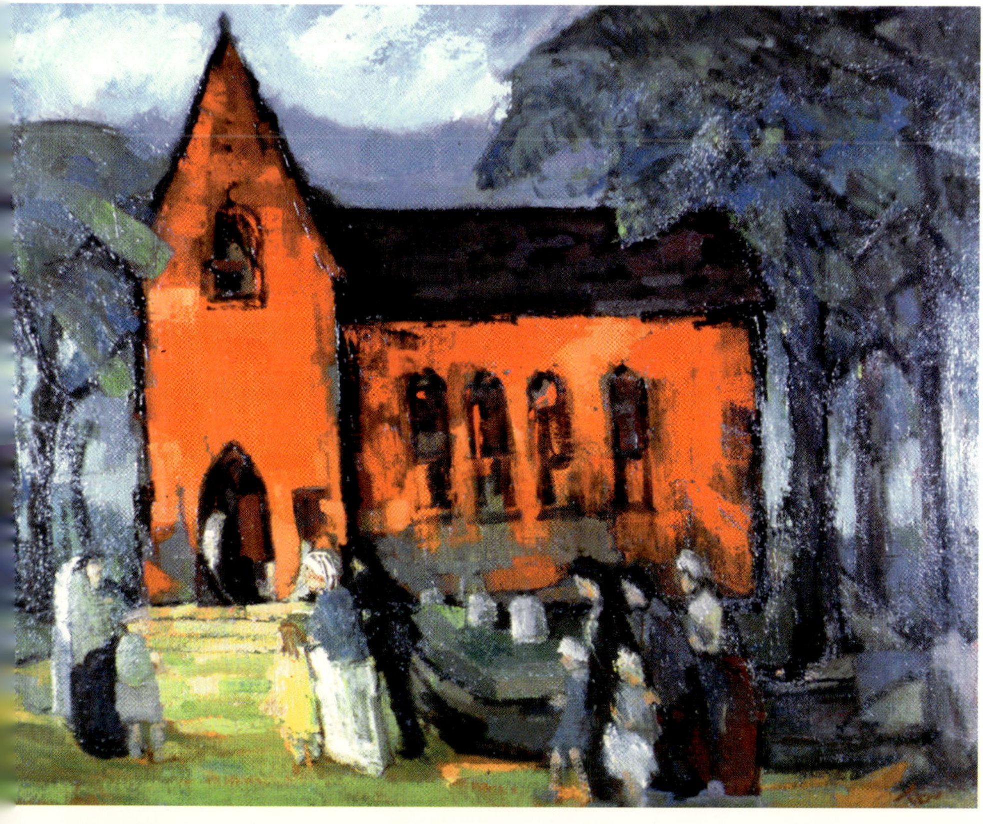

Woman with Parasol
(1909)
John Trullinger
Clatsop County Historical Society, Astoria

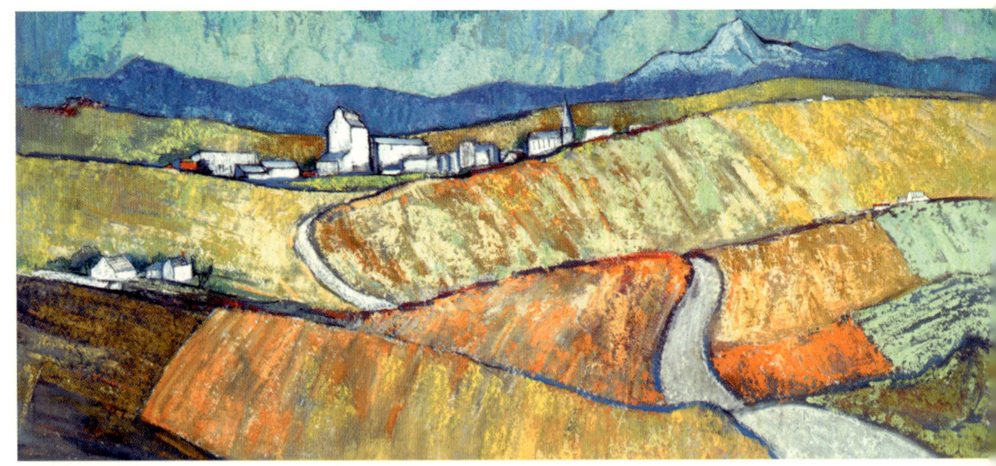

East of Hood
(ca. 1959)
Charles Voorhies
Breithaupt Collection

Coast Cotta
(ca. 195
Andrew Vince
Painting Restoration Stud

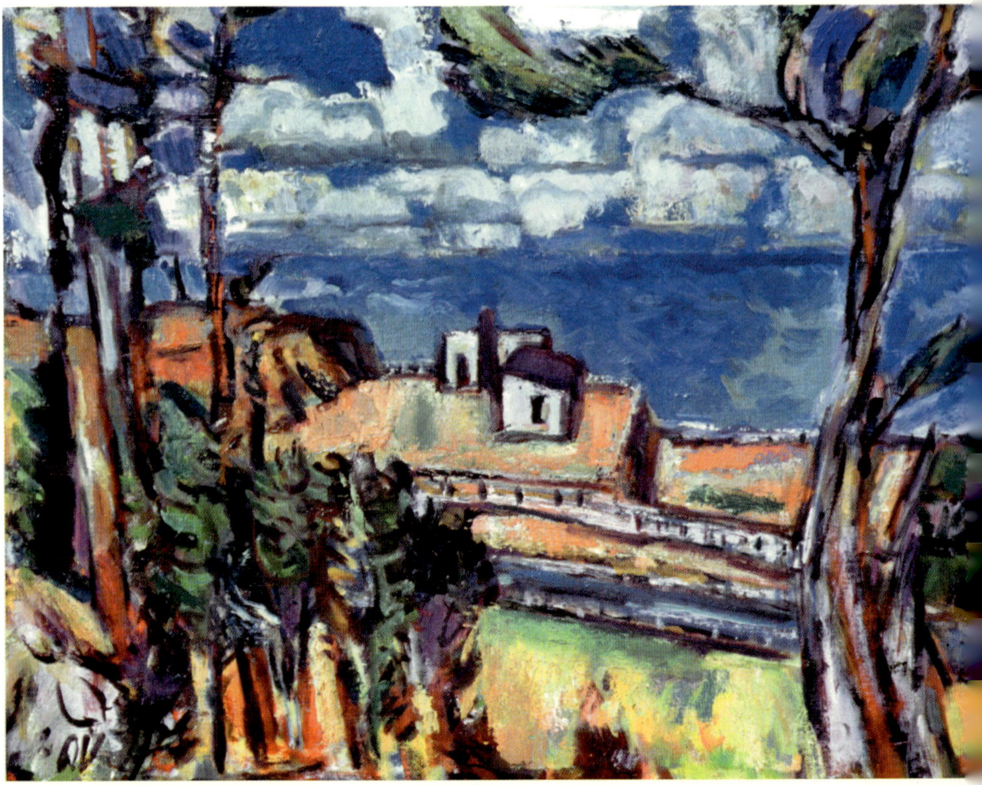

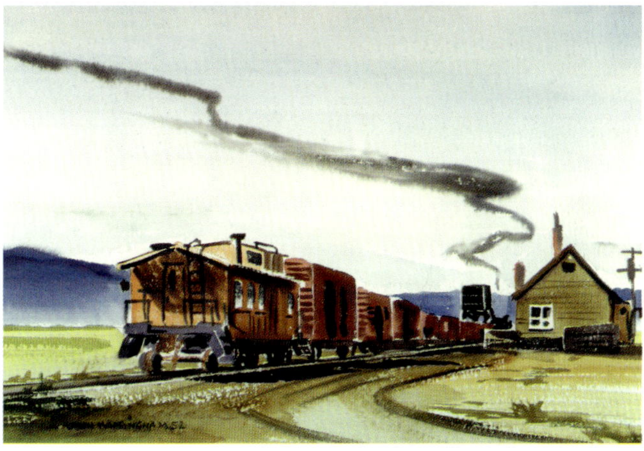

Whistle Stop
(1951)
John Waddingham
Artist's Collection

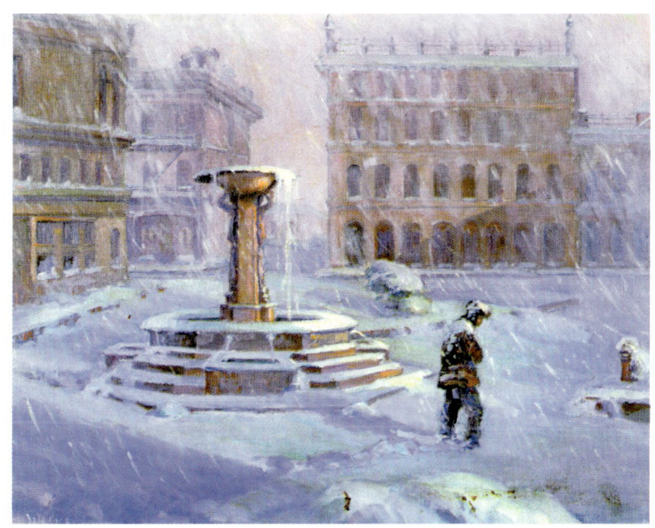

Skidmore Fountain, Winter
(ca.1935)
Maude Wanker
Oregon Historical Society
90-185.2.1, .2

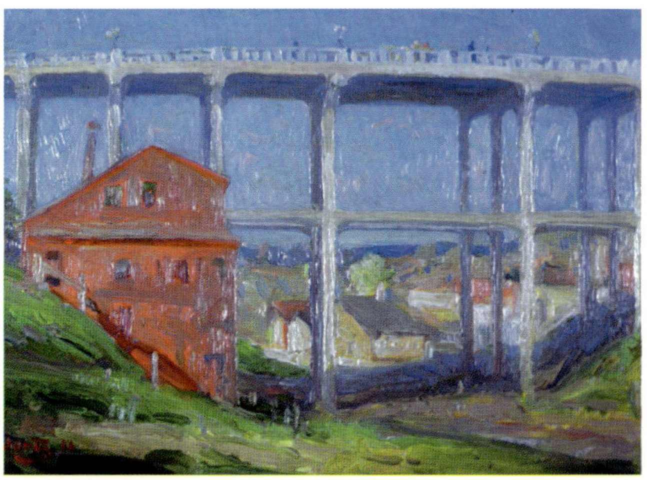

Sullivan's Gulch Bridge
(1913)
Harry Wentz
Miranda Collection

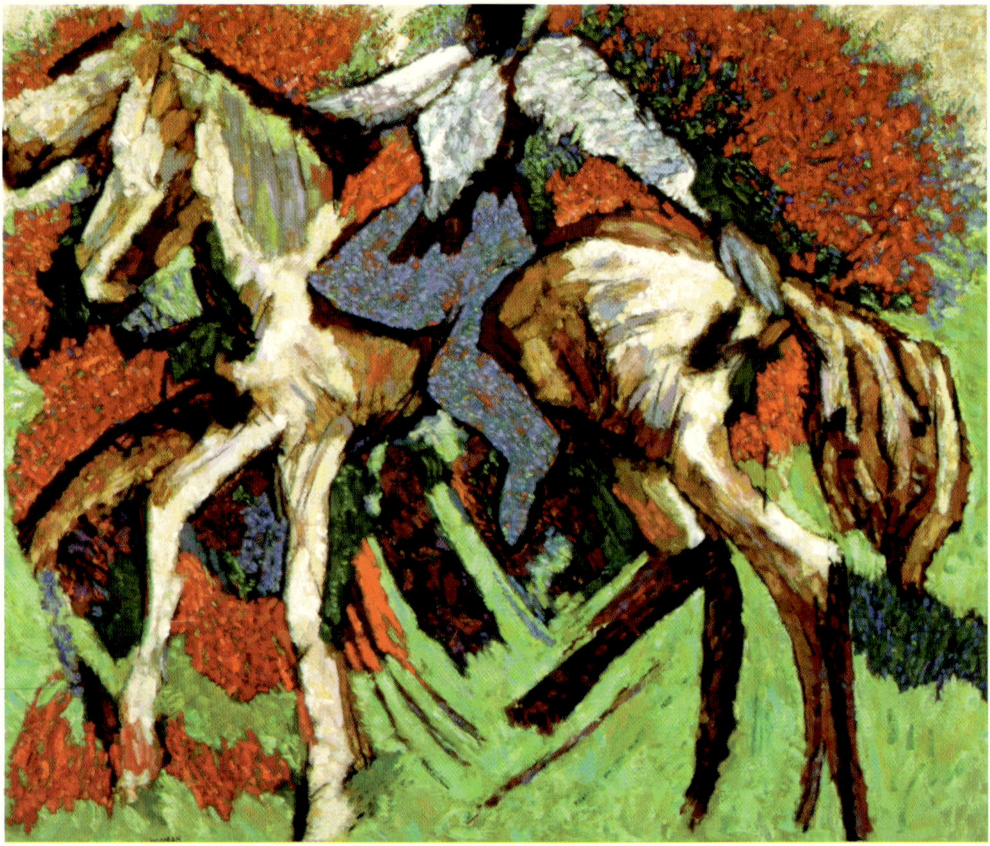

Horse and Rider
(1958)
Harry Widman
Artist's Collection

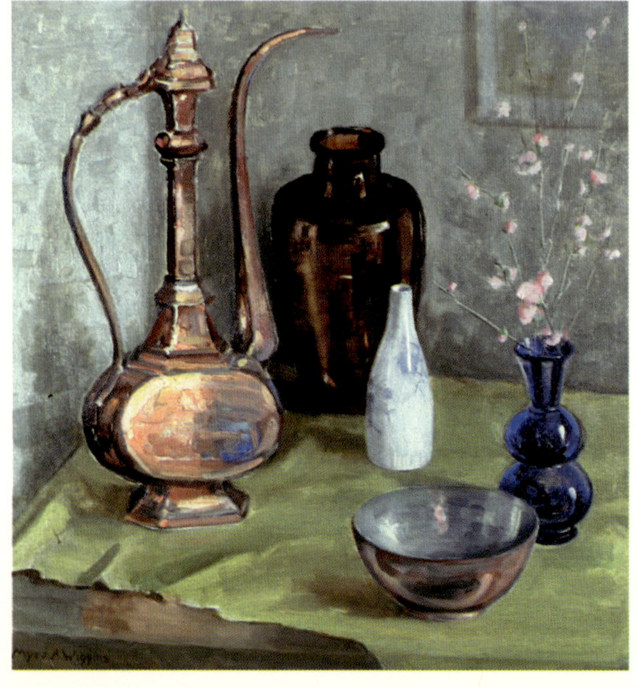

Metals With Glass and Porcelain
(1915)
Myra Albert Wiggins
Parsons Collection

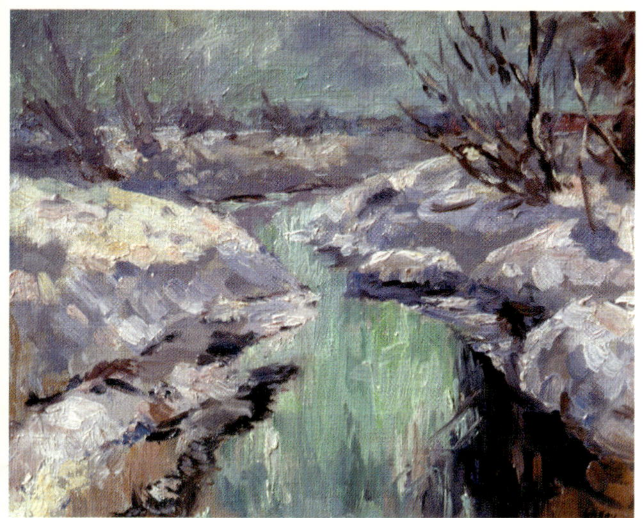

Winter on Beaver Creek
(n.d.)
Lucia Wiley
Painting Restoration Studio

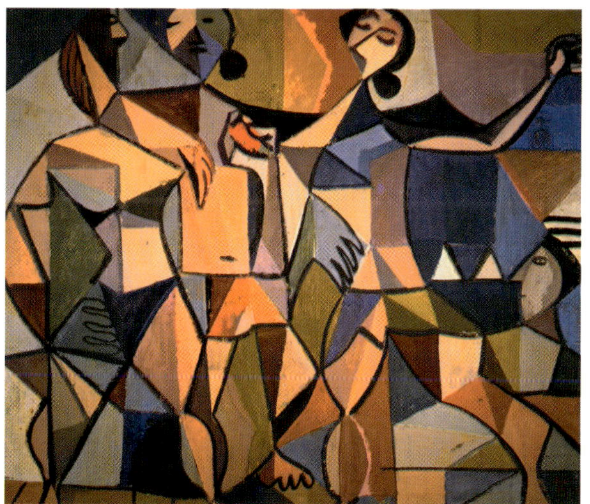

Carnival Dancers
(1949)
Jack Wilkinson
Witham Collection

Untitled
(n.d.)
Milton Wilson
Reed College

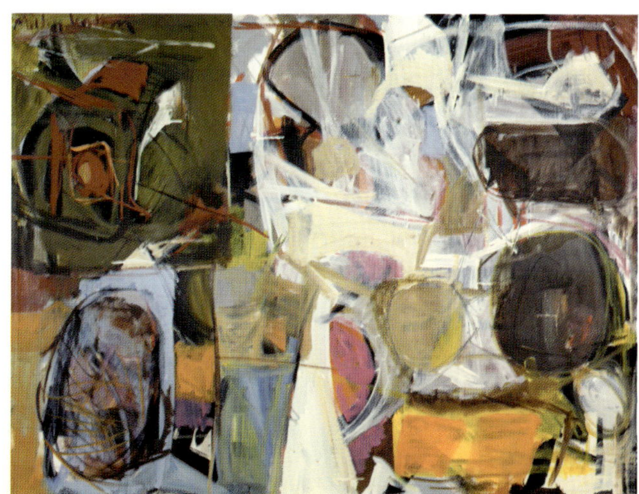

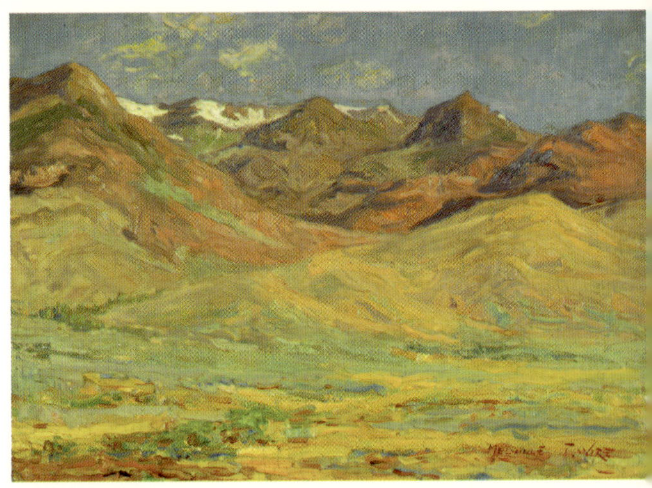

Steens Mountain/Alvord Ranch
(1928)
Melville T. Wire
Painting Restoration Studio

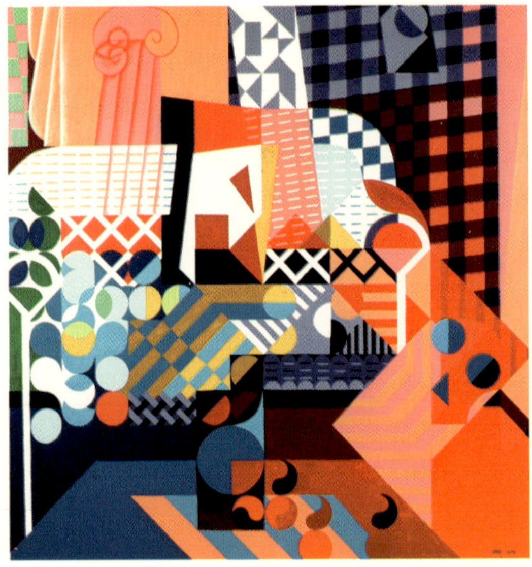

Sunlit Studio Interior
(1948, 1970)
Vernon Witham
University of Oregon, Museum of Art, Eugene

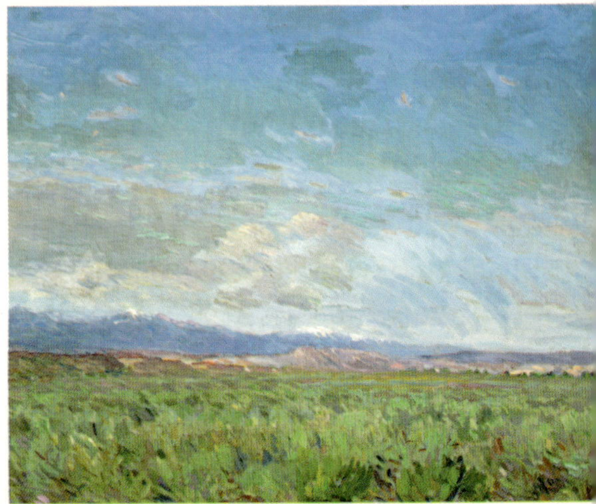

Eastern Oregon Desert
(ca. 1915)
C.E.S. Wood
Sovereign Collection

M

MacKENZIE, Catherine DeWitt

b. 1896 Portland, OR
d. 1960, Ojai, CA
Education: Museum Art School; Art Students League
Membership: Arts Guild; Oregon Society of Artists
Collections: Portland Art Museum; Reed College; Multnomah County Library Collection
Exhibits: Portland Art Museum (1PS 1935); Oregon Society of Artists; Arts Guild; Reed College (1PS 49); Harvey Welch Gallery (1PS 59)
References: DAV; DAW; MAL SUP; A2 (1919–22, 30, 33); A3 (35, 39); A5 (30); C3 (27); CD (32–35)
Media: Watercolor, oil, pastel, charcoal
Specialty: Landscapes, Western genre

Catherine MacKenzie was a graduate of the Museum Art School. She participated in the WPA and had a studio in Portland. Her watercolor, *Mt. Hood*, in the Multnomah County Library Collection was acquired in 1935. MacKenzie had one-person shows at Reed College in 1949 and at Harvey Welch's Gallery in 1959 as part of the Oregon Centennial celebration.

MACKLIN, Eliza (Lida) Allen

b. 1870 Story City, IA
d. 1961 West Linn, OR
Education: Museum Art School; University of Oregon; *C. Keller**; *C. McKim**
Membership: Oregon Society of Artists; American Artists Professional League
Awards: Oregon State Fair
Collections: Oregon Historical Society; Humpal Collection
Exhibits: Oregon Society of Artists; Portland Art Museum; Oregon State Fair; American Artists Professional League (1933)
References: COL; DAV; DAW; WWN; A2 (1940, 42, 44, 46); C3 (28–30, 32–38, 43, 45–47, 49)
Media: Oil, watercolor
Specialty: Landscapes, still life

Lida Macklin lived in Tacoma and San Francisco before 1910. According to her granddaughter's memoirs, on file at the Oregon Historical Society, the Macklins owned a cabin on Mt. Hood. On family outings, she would set up her paints and record the scenery while her husband fished and their children played nearby. Records also list her name as Mrs. Sylvanus G. Macklin.

MAGNER, Adelaide

b. 1881 Brooklyn, N.Y. ***d.***
Membership: Society of Oregon Artists; Society of Independent Artists—New York
Exhibits: Portland Art Museum (1PS 1911); Society of Independent Artists—New York (17, 20, 23, 25–44)
References: DAV; SIA; PET; WWW; A2 (1911–13); ARTC
Specialty: Portraits, landscapes

Adelaide Magner exhibited at the Portland Art Museum from 1911 to 1913. Her one-person show in 1911 featured scenes of Holland, Italy, and New York. She was a charter member of the Society of Oregon

Artists, established in 1912, and was the first vice-president, listed as Miss Adelaide in subsequent records. She taught at Willamette University from 1912 to 1913. Davenport (see Ref. DAV) lists a Winona, Minnesota address for her in 1915. Magner moved to Jamesville, New York and exhibited with the Society of Independent Artists from 1925 to 1944.

MANSER, Percy L.

b. 1886 Tunbridge Wells, England
d. 1973 Hood River, OR
Education: King Charles School—England: *Waters* (1896–1901); Pratt Institute—Ashland
Membership: American Artists Professional League; Master Watercolor Society of Oregon; American Watercolor Society; Oregon Society of Artists; Society of Western Artists; The Dalles Art Club
Awards: Oregon State Fair (1925); American Artists Professional League (32, 34, 36, 38, 40); Oregon Society of Artists (31–35, 37–47)
Collections: Portland Art Museum; Oregon Historical Society; Powell Collection; Painting Restoration Studio Collection; Miranda Collection; University of Oregon; University of Idaho; Lincoln County Art Center; Maryhill Museum—Goldendale, Washington; U.S. Bank; Parsons Collection; Gerber Collection; Humpal Collection; Huntington Collection; Lundberg Collection; Cofield Collection
Exhibits: Oregon State Fair (1925); Hood River Library (25; 1PS 56); Oregon Society of Artists; Seattle Art Museum; Portland Art Museum; American Artists Professional League (32–36, 38, 40); National Exhibition of American Art (36, 38); Congress Hotel—Portland (1PS 37); Lincoln County Art Center, (retrospective 38, 48); Circle A Club (1PS 38, 48); Elfstrom Gallery; Maryhill Museum—Goldendale, Washington (1PS 48, 54); Fole-Myers Gallery—Portland (51); Washington State Capitol Museum (1PS 56); Astoria (1PS 56); Artists Equity (58); Coquille Art Association (56, 58); Master Watercolor Society of Oregon (58); Medford (58); Frye Museum—Seattle; Oregon Centennial (59); Oregon Historical Society (90); Clatsop County Historical Society (94)
References: ALM; COL; DAV; DAW; OET; WWN; A2 (1932, 34, 40, 42, 48); A3 (58); C1; C3 (27–33, 35–38, 45–51); C6; C7 (27, 28a, 29, 38, 44); C9; C10; C11; C13 (46, 47, 48); C14; MYH
Media: Watercolor, oil
Specialty: Landscapes, seascapes, murals
See artwork in color section
See photograph of artist on p. 86

Percy Manser lived in Hood River from 1917 until his death. In 1925, twenty-two oil paintings, mostly landscapes, were displayed at the Hood River Library as a benefit for the community hospital. Eleven years later, he was one of six Oregon artists to represent the state in the National Exhibit of American Art in New York City. About this time he completed a seventy-foot long mural for the local high school. Manser's Hood River murals are also located at the local Courthouse, the Hospital, and the Elks Building. His painting, *The Edge of the Desert*, was voted the most popular entry in the Oregon Society of Artists Show in 1941 held at the Meier and Frank Co. in Portland. He developed a close working relationship with the director of Maryhill Museum in Washington state, where he had one-person shows in 1948 and 1954.

Manser's academic British training was evident in his early landscapes. His style of bold, wide brushstrokes, where light and shadows set the mood, brought him fame as one of the outstanding regionalists of his day. During the 1930s and 1940s, Manser painted the region around Hood River in the *plein air* tradition. Historian Keith McCoy says, "No artist has better captured the grandeur of the Columbia River Gorge or of the snow-capped sentinels that guard it ... his eminent place in Northwest art will grow with the years." From the 1950s on, he began to experiment with geometric abstractions, his style changing noticeably as he explored new trends. His entry in the Oregon Centennial Exhibition, *The Oregon Scene*, is an example of this new direction. His career spanned sixty years. He was a noted teacher at Crook County's Juniper Art Guild and elsewhere. Manser was also a WPA artist. Sometimes his signature contained the initials of the British Watercolor Society. Scholars consider him the major Oregon landscape artist of his period.

MARSH, Alice Randall

b. 1869 Coldwater, MI
d. 1929 NY
Education: Art Institute of Chicago; Paris: *Merson, Collin, Whistler, MacMonnies*
Membership: Oregon Art Association; American Society of Miniature Painters
Exhibits: Paris Salons (1895, 99); Oregon Art Association (96)
References: BI; DAV; FI (1895, 99); FIE; MAL;PET; WWW; YNG; CD (87); ARTC
Media: Oil, watercolor
Specialty: Miniatures

Alice Randall was born in Coldwater, Michigan and educated at the Art Institute of Chicago. She also studied in France, where she exhibited at the Paris Salon of 1895. Oregon records show she joined the Oregon Art Association and exhibited with them in 1896. Randall married artist Fred Dana Marsh. There is an additional Paris Salon exhibition record in 1899 under her married name. Marsh was a miniature painter and a member of the national American Society of Miniature Painters. References list a Nutley, New Jersey address for the Marshes in 1926 and a later address in New Rochelle, New York.

MARSH, Elaine Cornford

b. 1914 Portland, OR ***d.***
Education: Museum Art School (1924–25, 37); Chouinard Art Institute—Los Angeles (35–37); *Sheets; Jepson*
Membership: American Artists Professional League; Oregon Society of Artists; Portland Art Museum (Artist Membership)
Awards: Oregon State Fairs (1929, 37, 39, 40, 46); American Artists Professional League (40–42); Multnomah County Fair (39–42, 46)
Exhibits: Oregon State Fairs (1929, 37–40, 46); Portland Art Museum (AM, 1PS 50; 1PS 51); Multnomah County Fair (39–42, 46); American Artists Professional League (40); Paul Elders Gallery—San Francisco (1PS 42); Western Washington Fair; J.K. Gill Gallery (1PS 48); Rubin Gallery—Longview, Washington (49); Southwest Washington Fine Arts Exhibit (49)
References: COL; WWN; A2 (1940, 42, 46, 48); C3 (50, 51); C15 (46); C30 (46, 48); M2
Media: Oil, watercolor, prints
Specialty: Portraits, landscapes

Elaine Armstrong Cornford attended the Museum Art School in Portland followed by study in California. She exhibited at Oregon State Fairs and won awards at the American Artists Professional League shows of 1940 and 1942. She later married Max Marsh and moved to Castle Rock, Washington. She was active in the Oregon Art Educators group, serving as an officer in 1959 and 1960. In addition to painting, Marsh was a decorator and sculptor. She painted under the names *Cornford* and *Marsh*.

MARSH, Florence E.

b. 1887 Minneapolis, MN
d. 1936 Portland, OR
Education: University of Oregon
Membership: American Artists Professional League; Oregon Society of Artists; Skidmore Fountain Art Center Inc.
Awards: Oregon Society of Artists, posthumous (1938)
Exhibits: Oregon Society of Artists
References: DAV; HAV; MAL; WWW; C3 (1930, 31); M2

Florence Marsh introduced the idea of sponsoring an Annual Art Week under the auspices of the American Artists Professional League. This became a reality for the first time with the Portland Chapter in 1932, nationally in 1934, and finally internationally, with the first one held in Paris. It was also her idea to circulate art through libraries. She was an officer of the Oregon Society of Artists, exhibiting with them in 1930 and 1931, then receiving a posthumous award for her entry of 1938. Marsh was the wife of artist and architect, Harold Dickson Marsh*. Two years after her death, her husband agreed to buy an oil painting by an Oregon artist each year. These paintings would then be given to the National Council of the American Artists Professional League, who would in turn award it as their prize. The award was named the Florence Marsh Memorial Award.

MARSH, Harold Dickson

b. 1889 Portland, OR ***d.***
Education: Oregon State University
Membership: Society of Oregon Artists; Oregon Society of Artists; American Artists Professional League
Awards: American Artists Professional League (1932); Portland Art Museum (33)
Collections: La Grande Library; Capitol Collection—Salem; Water Works Bureau—Portland
Exhibits: Oregon State Fair; Oregon Society of Artists; Portland Art Museum; American Artists Professional League (1932–34)
References: DAV; DAW; HAV; MAL; WWW; A2 (1933); C3 (30–32); C10
Media: Oil
Specialty: Landscape

Primarily an architect, Harold Marsh also participated as a painter in the WPA. He was the husband of Florence Marsh*.

MARSHALL, Augusta (Gussie) A.

b. d.
Membership: Portland Sketch Club
Collections: Painting Restoration Studio Collection
Exhibits: Portland Mechanics Fair; North Pacific Industrial Exposition (1890); Portland Sketch Club (96)
References: C4 (1883); C2 (90); ARTC
Media: Oil
Specialty: Landscapes
See artwork in color section

A member of the Portland Sketch Club, Gussie Marshall exhibited at the Portland Mechanics Fair and Industrial Fair.

MATSEN, Ida M.

b. Bickleton, WA ***d.***
Education: Washington State University; University of Washington; Art Institute of Chicago; Pratt Institute; Columbia University;

University of Oregon
Membership: American Artists Professional League; Oregon Society of Artists
Awards: Seattle Art Museum (1921, 23); Seattle Fine Art Society
Exhibits: Seattle Art Museum; Oregon Society of Artists; American Artists Professional League (1933, 34); Portland Art Museum; Seattle Fine Art Society
References: DAV; COL; WWN; WWW; A2 (1940); C3 (33–35); C7 (21–23, 25, 27–29, 28, 28a, 32, 34); M2; M3
Media: Watercolor, oil, prints
Specialty: Still life

Ida Matsen was educated at the Art Institute of Chicago, the Pratt Institute, the University of Oregon, and in Washington state. She became a teacher at Oregon State University from 1927 to 1948. Matsen was also a member of the American Artists Professional League and the Oregon Society of Artists. Matsen was a Corvallis resident at least through 1948.

MATTER, Frank Louis

b. 1891 St. Paul, MN
d. 1979 Portland, OR
Collections: Humpal Collection; Lundberg Collection
Exhibits: Portland Art Museum
References: DAV; A2 (1942); CD (12, 13, 15, 17, 18, 20, 34)
Media: Watercolor
Specialty: Still life, florals, fruit, landscapes

Frank Matter was a commercial artist for twenty-five years. His style was impressionistic. After retirement, he became fascinated by objects in miniature and developed small tools and lathes, which he sold all over the world. Matter was listed in the artist section of the Seaside City Directory in 1959.

McBRIDE, George M.

b. 1876 Portland, OR
d. 1953 Portland, OR
Membership: Oregon Society of Artists
Awards: Oregon Society of Artists (1939)
Collections: Oregon Historical Society
Exhibits: Oregon Society of Artists; Portland Art Museum
References: A2 (1940, 48); C3 (36, 39, 46–50)
Media: Oil
Specialty: Marines, landscapes, portraits

George McBride was an attorney who specialized in admiralty law. This career prompted a passionate interest in painting marine and seascape subject matter. While he also painted landscapes and portraits, his most memorable works were misty, impressionistic coastlines. McBride was a member of the Oregon Society of Artists and served as president of that organization in 1937. He exhibited frequently with them and won an award in 1939. He had an art studio in the Selling-Hirsch Building in the 1940s.

McCALL, Alice Howe

b. 1872 Exeter, Devonshire, England
d. 1956 Portland, OR
Education: London; Canada; University of Oregon; Ashland: *Young*
Membership: Oregon Society of Artists
Awards: Oregon Society of Artists
Collections: Powell Collection
Exhibits: Oregon Society of Artists; Art Institute of Chicago (1934); Portland Art Museum; Oregon State University; Oregon State Fair; Clatsop County Historical Society (94)
References: COL; DAW; WWN; A2 (1940, 42, 44, 46); C3 (30–32, 35, 36, 44); C11; M2; M3
Media: Oil, watercolor

Also known as Mrs. Frank J. McCall, Alice McCall moved from Canada to

Salem in 1887. She was a charter member of the Oregon Society of Artists. Her artwork was exhibited at the Art Institute of Chicago in 1934 and the Portland Art Museum in the 1940s.

McCOSH, Anne Kutka

b. 1902 Danbury, CN
d. 1994 Eugene, OR
Education: Yonkers School of Design—New York (1916); Art Students League: *Nicolaides, Fitsch, Miller, Benton* (23–30); Mexico
Membership: American Artists Professional League; Oregon Guild of Painters and Sculptors; Art Students League; Portland Art Museum (Artist Membership)
Awards: American Artists Professional League (1937)
Collections: University of Oregon; Parsons Collection; Capitol Collection—Salem; Hallie Ford Museum of Art—Willamette University
Exhibits: Salons of America (1925); Pennsylvania Academy of Fine Art—Philadelphia (32, 34); Portland Art Museum (1PS 48); Art Institute of Chicago (35); Seattle Art Museum; American Artists Professional League; Denver Art Museum (38); New York World's Fair (39); University of Oregon (44, 47); Elfstrom Gallery; Western Washington Fair; Oregon Guild of Painters and Sculptors (48); Museum of Modern Art (53); Metropolitan Museum of Art; Willamette University (1PS 57); Autry Museum—Los Angeles (95)
References: ALM; COL; DAV; HAV; KOV; OET; SA; WWN; WWW; A2 (1938, 40, 42, 44, 46, 48); A3 (35, 37, 39, 51); C7 (36–39, 41, 45, 46, 48); C13 (46); C15 (46); C23; C30 (46); CD (39); M2; M3
Media: Oil, watercolor, prints (lithograph)
Specialty: Portraits, New York urban life, landscapes
See artwork in color section

Anne Kutka studied and worked at the Art Students League in New York. *The Van Courtland Express*, painted in 1933, portrayed the subway she rode to art classes. The humorous *Dressing Room, Klein's Department Store* shows yet another aspect of the life she experienced in New York. When she married David McCosh* in 1934 and moved to Eugene, she brought an East Coast urban perspective. Soon she was painting her new environment "shoulder to shoulder with the cornerstones of the regionalist movement." She stressed the characteristic features of the people and events of this college town.

In 1991 the University of Oregon sponsored a lifetime retrospective of her work. The catalog stated: "The art ... is a sensitive documentary of her life and times that spanned the burgeoning development of regionalism ...(It) draws us into her enthusiasm and admiration for life." Her painting, *Leaving the Lecture, Faculty Wives*, shows how she drew on real-life experiences for inspiration. Its formal composition with underpainting, modeling, and glazing is striking, but her emphasis is on the inner thoughts of the subjects, rather than their outward appearance. She created more than 650 oils, drawings, watercolors, and prints. She taught in her home studio and at the Maude Kerns Art Center for more than twenty years.

McCOSH, David John

b. 1903 Cedar Rapids, IA
d. 1981 Eugene, OR
Education: Art Institute of Chicago; Coe College—Iowa
Membership: American Watercolor

Society; Portland Art Museum (Artist Membership)
Awards: Seattle Art Museum (1936, 48, 55)
Collections: U.S. Bank; University of Oregon; Portland Art Museum; Seattle Art Museum; Whitney Museum of Art; National Museum of American Art; IBM; Coos Art Museum; Salishan Lodge Collection; Hallie Ford Museum of Art—Willamette University; Booth Collection; Tonkon Torp Collection; Parsons Collection; Huntington Collection; Capitol Collection—Salem
Exhibits: Art Institute of Chicago (1931; 1PS 32, 34); Portland Art Museum (AM, 1PS 52); Colorado Springs Fine Arts Center (35–38, 45); Seattle Art Museum; Golden Gate International Exposition—San Francisco (39–40); Pennsylvania Academy of Fine Art—Philadelphia (40); San Francisco Museum of Art (43); Western Washington Fair; Museum of Modern Art; Kharouba Gallery; University of Washington; Willamette University; Marylhurst College; Elfstrom Gallery; Oregon Guild of Painters and Sculptors (48); Oregon Centennial (59); University of Oregon (75); Oregon Historical Society (90)
References: ALM; COL; DAV; FIE; HAV; MAL; OET; WWN; WWW; A2 (1940, 42, 44, 46, 48); A3 (35, 37, 51, 52, 54–56); A4 (59); C6; C7 (35–37, 40, 45, 47, 48, 54, 55); C8; C9; C13 (46); C15 (46); C17; C22; C27; C30 (46)
Media: Oil, watercolor, prints (lithograph)
Specialty: Figures, murals
See artwork in color section

David McCosh began his academic career as a teacher at the Art Institute of Chicago from 1931 to 1933. He was commissioned to paint a mural for the Chicago World's Fair Century of Progress. As a WPA artist, he also created murals for the Department of the Interior in Washington, D.C., the Post Office in Beresford, South Dakota, and the Post Office in Kelso, Washington. He arrived at the University of Oregon to teach art in 1934 and remained there until his retirement in 1972. McCosh had great importance as a teacher and influenced many young artists during his tenure. Leonard Kimbrell* said of him, "McCosh leads one to look and teaches one to see."

David McCosh's paintings from the 1920s and early 30s were influenced by American Regionalist painters such as Grant Wood and Thomas Hart Benton as well as members of the Ashcan School. After he won a European Travel Scholarship in 1927 and a Tiffany Foundation Fellowship from 1929 to 1930, his work showed the influence of Cézanne and Matisse. In the 1930s social realism was his subject, painted in a realistic and individualistic style; later works became more abstract. Until the mid-1950s McCosh's paintings were in a somber key, supported by black. He turned to brilliant color, using deep violets, greens, and reds in his earlier works, giving way to the bright yellows and blues of his later years. He suffered a mid-life crisis which was resolved with a sabbatical year painting along the coast near Cohasset, Washington. There he painted without brushes, applying paint directly from the tube to the canvas. He later returned to using his brushes.

The 1940s and 50s showed a major shift in his style from the figurative or primarily representational view of the world to one progressively more abstract, with a strong, almost calligraphic component. In his later style he continued to work with the relationship between figure and ground, shape and surroundings. McCosh was an artist who steadily grew and evolved as he traveled, painted, and experienced life. He developed new ways of looking at things; his work bore little relationship to the art trends of his day. David McCosh said, "I believe that learning to paint is learning to see."

McCOY, Wirth Vaughan

b. 1913 Duluth, MN ***d.***

Education: University of Iowa (1948); Académie de la Grande Chaumière (50–55); California School of Fine Arts; *Zadkine; Léger; Lachay; Rothko*

Membership: Portland Art Museum (Artist Membership)

Awards: Duluth Art Institute (1946, 47)

Collections: University of Iowa; Spokane Art Center; University of Minnesota

Exhibits: Portland Art Museum; Seattle Art Museum; Henry Art Gallery—University of Washington (1954, 55); Western Washington Fair; San Francisco Museum of Art (56); Washington State College; Oregon State University; University of Iowa

References: HAV; WWAA; A3 (1949, 50, 53); C7 (49, 55–57, 59); C30 (55, 56)

Wirth McCoy was a teacher in the art department at Oregon Agricultural College (now Oregon State University) from 1948 to 1953 and at Washington State College from 1953 to 1958. He was director of the Spokane Art Center in 1953, with a Spokane address after that date. McCoy participated in the Washington State Faculty Exhibition at the Henry Gallery in 1955, the Portland and Seattle Art Museums, and the San Francisco Museum of Art among others.

McGARRELL, James

b. 1930 Indianapolis, IN ***d.***

Education: University of Indiana: *Pickens* (1948–53); UCLA: *Jones* (53–55); Stuttgart (55–56); *Steppart; Nunes*

Membership: Artists Equity; Portland Art Museum (Artist Membership)

Awards: Brooklyn Art Museum (1954–55); Santa Barbara Museum of Art

Collections: Art Institute of Chicago; Museum of Modern Art; National Museum of American Art; Portland Art Museum; San Francisco Institute of Art; University of Oregon; University of Indiana; Metropolitan Museum of Art; Whitney Museum of Art; Reed College; Pennsylvania Academy of Fine Art—Philadelphia; Brooklyn Art Museum; Parsons Collection; Arlene and Harold Schnitzer Collection

Exhibits: Brooklyn Art Museum (1954–55); Philadelphia Art Museum (55); Art Institute of Chicago (56); Whitney Museum of Art (57, 59); Santa Barbara Museum of Art (57); Jocelyn Art Museum—Omaha (58); Paris; Portland Art Museum (AM, 1PS 58); Henry Art Gallery—University of Washington (3PS 59); Museum of Modern Art (59); Ruthermore Gallery—San Francisco (59); Smithsonian Institution Traveling Exhibits (59); Oregon Centennial (59); University of Oregon (75)

References: ALM; DAV; HAV; WWW; A3 (1958); A4 (59); C6; C7 (58); C20; C22

Media: Oil, pencil, prints (etching)

James McGarrell was an artist-in-residence at Reed College from 1956 to 1959 and served on the faculty at Indiana University. A Fulbright fellowship in 1955 allowed him to study in Stuttgart.

Art News of December, 1955 called him a "pictorial dramatist of decay and physical corruption...a painter trying to come to grips with imagery stated in twentieth century terms." McGarrell says there are no symbols in his painting, only visual metaphors. He did contemporary, representational painting that did not "hand everything over to the viewer." He had many one-person shows in California, New York, Illinois, and Europe. Later in his career he joined the faculty at Washington University in St. Louis, Missouri.

McGRAW, Claude Edward

b. 1919 Birmingham, AL
d. 1979 Portland, OR
Education: Colorado Springs Fine Arts Center: *Charlot, Britten, Tilley* (1947–49); Museum Art School (50–52)
Membership: Artists Equity; Portland Art Museum (Artist Membership)
Collections: Portland Art Museum; University of Oregon; Parsons Collection
Exhibits: Colorado Springs Fine Arts Center (1948, 49); Kharouba Gallery (IPS 52); Seattle Art Museum (52); University of Portland (1PS); Denver Art Museum; Portland Art Museum (AM, 1PS 59); Oregon Centennial (59)
References: A3 (1951–56, 58); C7 (51)
Media: Oil
Specialty: Western scenes, landscapes, mountains

In Portland since 1950, Claude McGraw was an instructor for the Parks Department, an assistant director of the Junior Museum from 1953 to 1967, and the director of Portland Parks Art Center until his retirement in 1978. He had one-person shows at Louis Bunce's* Kharouba Gallery in 1952, the University of Portland, and the Portland Art Museum in 1959.

Western landscapes, particularly the mountains of Oregon and Washington, dominated his work. The Museum's Rental Sales Gallery represented him. Besides painting he had an interest in photography.

McILWRAITH, William Forsyth

b. 1867 Gault, Ontario, Canada
d. 1940 Fishkill, NY
Education: Art Students League
Membership: Oregon Society of Artists
Collections: University of Oregon; Stenzel Collection; Lundberg Collection
Exhibits: Oregon Society of Artists; Portland Art Museum
References: ALM; BI; DAV; DAW; MAL SUP; OET; SAM; WWN; WWW; A2 (1933); C3 (27–31, 33–36)
Media: Watercolor, oil, prints (etching)
Specialty: Landscapes (Celilo Falls, river shipping), Indians, history

A successful commercial artist in New York, William McIlwraith moved to Hood River to farm in 1911. Around 1919 he had a Portland address, where he worked as a commercial artist and illustrator. His work was important for its documentation of the fishing and shipping activity on the Columbia and Willamette Rivers. He avoided exhibitions and sold mainly to friends. After living twenty years in Portland, where he was known as one of the leading etchers on the Pacific Coast, he returned to New York in 1939 in ill health. His series of calendars reflected his affection for many of the local sights: the Burnside Bridge, the Skidmore Fountain, the Battleship Oregon, Timberline Lodge, the McLoughlin House, and more. McIlwraith was also a participant in the WPA and a close friend of Charles Heaney.*

McKIM, Charles C.

b. 1872 Bristol, ME
d. 1939 Portland, OR
Education: Maine: *Homer*; Boston
Membership: Circle A Club; Society of Oregon Artists; Oregon Society of Artists; American Artists Professional League
Awards: Oregon Society of Artists (1938)
Collections: Powell Collection; Miranda Collection; Painting Restoration Studio Collection; Parsons Collection; Humpal Collection; Lundberg Collection; Huntington Collection; Oregon State University; Cofield Collection
Exhibits: Circle A Club; Portland Art Museum; Society of Oregon Artists (1912, 13); Christiansen Gallery (16); Portland Woman's Club (26); American Artists Professional League (33–35); Oregon Society of Artists; Oregon Historical Society (90); Clatsop County Historical Society (94)
References: DAV; DAW; OET; WWN; A2 (1912); C3 (35, 38); C9; C10; C11; ARTC; CD (13, 14, 18, 26, 28)
Media: Oil, watercolor
Specialty: Seascapes, landscapes (snow, Willamette Valley)
See artwork in color section

Charles C. McKim was strongly influenced by artist Winslow Homer. McKim wrote about his summer camp experiences with Homer for the *Spectator* in 1922. Eventually McKim went to Boston to study and opened a studio in Portland, Maine. He next lived in New York and later came to Portland, Oregon in 1911, where his uncle Charles Follen McKim was a successful architect. He opened a studio in the Labbe Building at Second and Washington Streets. McKim had one of his first exhibitions at the Portland Press Club in the Elk's Building. Included were scenes of Siletz Bay, Salmon River Bay, Cascade Head, and sketches of sunsets and opalescent mornings. This early show provided an interesting comparison between the Atlantic Coast paintings he brought with him and the work he was producing at that time.

One year after his arrival in Portland, he was instrumental in forming the short-lived Society of Oregon Artists, for which he served as the first president. Their mission was: "to seek to interest buyers of works of art of Oregonians and to encourage the work of artists; ... and bring into prominence latent talent." This group enjoyed the participation of prominent artists of the day, boasting a membership of forty-five and sponsoring four exhibits before disbanding in 1913. McKim also wrote a column on art and its value in society in the *Spectator* in the 1920s.

McKim spent his summers at Crater Lake or at Yachats on the coast, where he filled many sketch books. His choice of subject was sometimes unusual: the chill of fog which all but obscured the subject matter, sunlight dancing over the violet waters of Crater Lake, or the sluggish Columbia Slough portrayed in a romantic way. He said in an interview in 1922 that he was in Oregon now because "he is in love with the scenery." When the snow fell he took his easel outdoors and painted until every flake disappeared; he filled his studio with snow scenes. Oregon scenery is the constant theme of his work. He was an artist of clear and sensitive vision, Oregon's quintessential impressionist. He signed his work *C.C. McKim*.

McLARTY, William James (Jack)

b. 1919 Seattle, WA ***d.***
Education: Museum Art School: *C. Stephens** (1937–39); American Artists School: *Refregier, Solman* (40)

Membership: Artists Equity; Oregon Guild of Painters and Sculptors; Portland Art Museum (Artist Membership)

Awards: Seattle Art Museum (1946, 49); Portland Art Museum (53, 56); Oregon Art Association (58); Oregon Centennial (59)

Collections: Portland Art Museum; University of Oregon; Seattle Art Museum; Lewis and Clark College; Reed College; Tonkon Torp Collection; Library of Congress; Pacific University; Portland State University; University of Portland; Multnomah Athletic Club; Henry Art Gallery—University of Washington; Kaiser Permanente Collection; Multnomah County Library Collection; Parsons Collection; Oregon Historical Society; Arlene and Harold Schnitzer Collection; Portland Community College; Portland Civic Auditorium; Salem Art Association; Capitol Collection— Salem; Huntington Collection; Lundberg Collection; Hallie Ford Museum of Art—Willamette University; Pacific Northwest College of Art

Exhibits: Portland Art Museum (1PS 1945, 48, 50, 57; retrospective, 63); Seattle Art Museum; Oregon Guild of Painters and Sculptors (45, 47, 48); Pasadena Art Institute (46); Western Washington Fair; Denver Art Museum (47); Henry Art Gallery—University of Washington (51); Santa Barbara Museum of Art (57); Portland State University (58); Ruthermore Gallery—San Francisco (59); Reed College; Oregon State University; Kharouba Gallery; Philadelphia Art Museum; Oregon Centennial (59); University of Oregon (75); Oregon Historical Society (90)

References: ALM; DAV; HAV; OET; WWW; A2 (1940, 42, 44, 46, 48); A3 (49–58); A4 (59); C6; C7 (44, 46–49; 50–56, 59); C9; C15 (46); C20; C22; C27; C30 (46)

Media: Oil, acrylic, prints (lithograph, serigraph, wood cut, wood engraving, etching)

Specialty: Portland city life, murals

See artwork in color section
See photograph of artist on p. 85

Jack McLarty moved from Seattle to Portland in 1921. He studied at the Museum Art School from 1936 to 1939 then attended the American Artists School in New York. He joined the Museum Art School faculty in 1946, serving as acting dean from 1958 to 1959, remaining until his retirement in 1981. McLarty and friend, Louis Bunce*, also an instructor at the Museum Art School, moved to Newport during the vacation periods from 1948 to 1950 to establish an outdoor art school on the beach.

In *Oregon Artist*, the fall 1953 Museum Art School newsletter, William Givler* editorialized about the opportunities for artists and architects to collaborate, citing Jack McLarty's mural in the library at Laurelhurst Elementary School. He is also known for serigraphs, lithography, and wood cuts, which he claimed helped with his painting in that the limitations imposed a "sort of discipline." McLarty described his work as "surrealistic" and he felt the artistic atmosphere in Portland helped him develop in his own independent fashion, "Portland has too few painters for groups of any kind."

His early themes, from 1950 to 1952, included the city of Portland at night and the 1948 Vanport flood, with lurid colors and imminent dangers. In the mid-50s his canvases displayed a less vibrant color palette, less outlining and shading. Themes of sports and games appeared in the late 1950s and a change to a lighter, brighter palette. McLarty has continued to change style and technique as social and environmental problems engaged his interest and concern. Along with his wife, Barbara, he opened the Image Gallery in 1961, which continued to be a mainstay of the gallery scene in Portland for more than thirty years. Some of the artists represented there were: Byron Gardner*, William Givler*, Charles Heaney*, Frederick Heidel*, George Johanson*, Hank Kowert*, Richard Muller*, Albert and Arthur Runquist*, Charles Voorhies* and Harry Widman*. The McLartys have published a retrospective book titled *Worldwatcher: Jack McLarty, Fifty Years 1943-1993*.

Rachael Griffin*, in an essay in the 1963 Portland Art Museum catalog retrospective, said McLarty's painting is "independent and personal, making almost no contact with the work done around him. He draws his subjects from urban scenes and rituals. He is an astute and sensitive observer of all that passes daily before our unseeing eyes. He is interested in forms of things and he understands what they reveal."

McMAHON, Harold(e) A.R.

b. 1889 Dubuque, IA
d. 1941 Portland, OR
Education: *C. Keller**; University of Oregon Extension; *M. Oster**
Membership: Oregon Society of Artists; Skidmore Fountain Art Association
Awards: Multnomah County Fairs
Exhibits: Portland Art Museum; Oregon Society of Artists; American Federation of Arts (1937–44); Multnomah County Fairs
References: COL; DAV; DAW; WWN; A2 (1933, 34, 42); C3 (33–36)
Media: Oil, watercolor, pencil
Specialty: Seasonal

Harold McMahon was an active member and president of the Oregon Society of Artists. He received many awards at Multnomah County Fairs.

MEACHAM, Nellie F.

b. d.
Awards: Oregon State Fairs
Exhibits: Oregon State Fairs
References: OSF (1874–77)
Media: Oil
Specialty: Landscapes

An Oregon State Fair entrant, Nellie Meacham was presumably a member of the early Salem art community.

MERITT, Margaret

b. 1912 Clackamas, OR ***d.***
Membership: Oregon Amateur Watercolor Society; The Sagebrushers
Exhibits: Southern Oregon Art Exhibit
References: C26 (1956, 58)
Media: Oil, watercolor
Specialty: Landscapes (desert, juniper trees)

In 1950 Margaret Meritt opened a gallery in Bend; "Margaret's Studio" existed for forty years. She was always fascinated by the vegetation of the desert area around Bend, painting the landscape and making her frames from the weathered wood of abandoned homesteads. Her work can be found in corporate offices and professional buildings. She was one of the founders of the Sagebrushers, an artists organization in Bend.

MERRIAM, Irma Seavey

b. d.
Exhibits: Portland Art Museum; Seattle Art Museum; Portland Woman's Club (1926)
References: DAV; WWW; A2 (1912, 13, 15, 16, 17); C7 (20–23)
Specialty: Landscapes

Irma Merriam participated in many shows at the Portland Art Museum during the 1910s. Her residence in 1925 was Seattle.

MEYER, Harriet. *See* GERMAIN, Harriet

MEYER, Louis Richard Max

b. 1856 Berlin, Germany
d. 1912 Portland, OR
Education: Berlin; Munich; Dresden
Awards: Oregon State Fairs
Collections: Stenzel Collection; Oregon Historical Society; Painting Restoration Studio Collection
Exhibits: Oregon State Fairs; Washington State Historical Society—Tacoma (1985); Washington State Capitol Museum (88)
References: BI; DAV; DAW; SAM; C24; C28; CD (1903–12); OSF (06, 07)
Media: Oil, watercolor
Specialty: Portraits, landscapes, florals, fruit, animals

Richard Meyer left Germany in 1892 and arrived in Washington state, where he headed the art department at the University of Puget Sound until 1900. Following his arrival in Portland he became known for his fine portrait work, established a studio, and taught at the Art Emporium on Alder Street. This studio was open from 1900 until he moved to larger quarters at 433 Stark Street, shortly before his death. He also exhibited under the name *Max Meyer.*

MICHALOV, Anne. *See* JOHNSON, Anne

MIETTUNEN, Paul A.

b. d.
Membership: Portland Art Museum (Artist Membership)
Exhibits: Portland Art Museum
References: A2 (1946, 48); A3 (52); A4 (59)
Media: Oil, prints (engravings)
Specialty: Landscapes, seascapes

Paul Miettunen resided in Colton, Oregon. Although an accomplished engraver, the exhibitions at the Portland Art Museum in 1946, 1948, and 1952 showed examples of his painting. He was part of the group Centennial show held at the Portland Art Museum in 1959.

MILBANK, Dorothy K.

b. 1905 Seattle, WA ***d.***
Education: University of California (1923); Kahn Art Institute (51); *L. Bunce**; *J. Mclarty**
Membership: Portland Art Museum (Artist Membership); Southern Oregon Art Association
Awards: Southern Oregon Art Association (1949, 51, 53–55)
Exhibits: Southern Oregon Art Association (1949, 51, 53–55); Art News Amateur (53); Southern Oregon Art Exhibit; Portland Art Museum
References: A3 (1955); C26 (53, 54, 55)

Dorothy Milbank participated in exhibitions of the Southern Oregon Art Association in Medford and also showed work at the Portland Art Museum during the 1950s. She lived in Grants Pass and was active in the southern Oregon art community.

MILLER, Robert Aubrey

b. 1854 Eugene, OR
d. 1941 Forest Grove, OR
Membership: Society of Oregon Artists; Mutual Art Association; Oregon Society of Artists; American Artists Professional League
Awards: Oregon Society of Artists (1932)
Collections: University of Oregon; Hallie Ford Museum of Art—Willamette University; Oregon Historical Society; Painting Restoration Studio Collection
Exhibits: Society of Oregon Artists (1912); Mutual Art Association (14, 15); Portland Woman's Club (26);

Oregon Society of Artists (1PS); American Artists Professional League (32–34)
References: C3 (1928, 32, 34); ARTC
Media: Watercolor, oil
Specialty: Landscapes, marines

After receiving his law degree from Willamette University, Robert Miller joined Judge Robert Bybee's office as collection clerk, but had other interests such as poetry and writing. He also worked as a newspaperman for the *Salem Statesman* and the *Hesperian*. His interest in art surfaced early, after an encounter with artist James Sutton. Young Miller, after observing Sutton working on a picture of the Rogue River, hurried home to announce to his mother that he was going to be a painter. She found some watercolor paints and he immediately started to copy the Sutton picture from memory. Miller's father showed the effort to Sutton and he invited the young student to visit, which was the beginning of some early lessons. He devoted spare moments to sketching and his office in the Worcester Building in Portland contained dozens of his watercolor landscapes and marines. He was proud of his technique to "combine the strength of oil with the brilliancy of watercolor in using the latter."

Affectionately known as Colonel Bob because of his service in the militia, he was also a legislator and candidate for Senate. A member of a well-known pioneer family in southern Oregon, he is buried in the Jacksonville cemetery.

MISH, Charlotte Roberta

b. 1896 Lebanon, PA
d. 1974 Portland, OR
Education: University of Southern California: *Judson* (1919); Art Students League: *F. DuMond** (24); Paris; England; *S. Bell*; H. Wentz**
Membership: American Artists Professional League; Oregon Society of Artists; Art Students League
Collections: Oregon Historical Society; Powell Collection; Miranda Collection; Painting Restoration Studio Collection; Capitol Collection—Salem; Parsons Collection; Lundberg Collection; Cofield Collection
Exhibits: Portland Art Museum; Seattle Art Museum; Portland Woman's Club (1926); Oregon Society of Artists; American Artists Professional League (33, 34, 37); Cup that Cheers Restaurant—Portland (33); Portland Chamber of Commerce (1PS 36); Meier and Frank Co. (1PS 55); Boston; New York; USSR; Clatsop County Historical Society (94)
References: DAV; FIE; HAV; KOV; MAL; OET; WWW; A2 (1920, 22); C3 (27, 28, 55); C7 (21–23, 25, 27); C11; CD (20–23, 57–59); M2; M3
Media: Oil
Specialty: Marines, landscapes, animals, portraits, murals, posters
See artwork in color section

Charlotte Roberta Mish was born in Pennsylvania and moved to Portland with her parents as a small child. Portland City Directories first list her as an artist from 1920 to 1923. She left in 1924 to study with Frank DuMond* at New York's Art Students League. Returning to Portland, Mish gained national attention for her poetry, published in the *Forum*. She participated in the annual art exhibitions at the Seattle Art Museum. She became a charter member of the Oregon Society of Artists and exhibited with them in their first two shows.

In 1928 Mish held a benefit for the Fine Arts Building at the University of Oregon. Two of her best-known portraits to date, *St. Francis* and *Abraham Lincoln* were on view. Naming the fundraiser "Charlotte Mish Day", fellow artists Alice Weister* and Graziella Boucher arranged for paintings, poetry, and a piano recital as part of the celebration. In the decade that followed she continued to travel and exhibit widely throughout the United States and abroad. Twenty-five of the works exhibited in Boston and New York went on display in Portland at The Cup That Cheers restaurant. This show featured landscapes, marines, and portraits, including those of animals, which she favored. She and close friend Boucher were co-founders of the Animal Defenders League of Oregon, an effort she pursued with tireless energy.

Mish was also known for her murals. In Seattle, she decorated the Music Box Theater and The Blue Mouse. In 1947 she completed a series of murals for Portland's Congress Hotel, using a blue heron motif. The Oregon State Library featured her mural map of the state's flora. Later she finished a fifteen-foot-long mural, depicting the landing operation of ships in Albina shipyards. This painting hung in the lobby of the United Seaman's Service Recreation Center. The shipyards and maritime themes are probably the work for which Mish is most famous. An editorial in the *Journal on Art and Industry* describes her technique: "faithful portrayal of shipping scenes, hull and mast and beautiful, clear balanced color. Her skill enables her to use much detail without disturbing the demands of simplicity ... (she) puts on canvas the beauty that is to be found in steel, wood and the majesty and dignity of labor." She also painted in an impressionistic style. Her documentary and industrial paintings were owned by President Franklin Roosevelt and Henry J. Kaiser. Her painting *Maiden Voyage*, caused much comment in the 1933 show at the Cup That Cheers and was purchased by a shipowner in Bergen, Norway. She sometimes signed her work on the front and back, with title or description added.

Widely traveled and educated, Charlotte Mish gained international fame, but today remains little known in her adopted state of Oregon.

MITCHELL, Olive

b. d.
Awards: Oregon State Fairs (1900–03)
Exhibits: Oregon State Fairs
References: OSF (1900–03)
Media: Oil
Specialty: Animals, history

Olive Mitchell was living in Salem at the time of her State Fair entries.

MITCHELL, Patricia Carter

b. Oakland, CA ***d.***
Education: Museum Art School
Membership: Arts Guild
Exhibits: Arts Guild; Portland Art Museum
References: COL; WWN; A2 (1930, 32, 33); A3 (36); A5 (30, 33)
Media: Watercolor

Exhibiting in Oregon in the 1930s, watercolorist Patricia Mitchell was a member of the Arts Guild.

MITCHELL, W. E.

b. d.
Awards: Oregon State Fairs
Exhibits: Oregon State Fairs
References: OSF (1884, 85, 87)
Media: Oil, china painting
Specialty: Landscapes, marines

W. E. Mitchell listed a Salem address for the Oregon State Fair entries.

MIZUNO, Sadao

b. 1873 Japan
d. 1948 Vanport, OR
Education: Museum Art School (1916–21)
Membership: Oregon Society of Artists
Awards: Seattle Art Museum (1921)

Collections: Oregon Historical Society
Exhibits: Portland Art Museum; Seattle Art Museum; Oregon Society of Artists; Oregon Historical Society (1990)
References: COL; DAV; WWN; WWW; A2 (1915–17, 19–22, 33, 42, 46); A3 (35, 36, 37); C3 (27); C7 (19, 20–23, 27; 28, 31, 32); C9
Media: Oil, watercolor
Specialty: Landscapes, portraits

Originally from Kumamoto, Japan, Sadao Mizuno pursued a career as a painter and photographer in Portland. He illustrated a story for *McCall's* magazine in 1924. His portrait, *Captain W.H. Hardy*, is in the Oregon Historical Society collection. Mizuno was well known for formal, photographic portraits of prominent Japanese families. He owned the Rose City Photographic Studio in Portland from 1912 until 1941, when he was sent to one of the internment camps during World War II. He drowned in the Vanport flood in May of 1948, after having moved there only two and a half years before.

MOMENT, Jeanne

b. 1901
d. 1984 Portland, OR
Education: University of California Berkeley (1921); Columbia University (28); California School of Fine Arts; Museum Art School: *W. Givler** (44–54)
Membership: Artists Equity; Portland Art Museum (Artist Membership)
Collections: Portland Art Museum; Reed College; Portland State University; Sunriver Lodge; Salishan Lodge Collection; U.S. Bank; First National Bank; Goodman Collection; Hallie Ford Museum of Art—Willamette University; Oregon Historical Society; Parsons Collection; Lundberg Collection
Exhibits: Portland Art Museum; Reed College (1958); University of Oregon; Lewis and Clark College; Oregon Centennial (59)
References: A3 (1958); C6
Media: Oil, watercolor, sumi, prints (etching, lithograph)
Specialty: Nature, landscapes

Jeanne Moment was a Los Angeles high school teacher for twenty-five years before she and her family came to Oregon in 1940. She fell in love with Oregon's outdoor experience—skiing, hiking, and camping. This sense of nature and the environment was to be present in all her future works, and was the inspiration for the 1952 national "Keep America Beautiful" campaign.

Many of her landscapes showed the influence of J.M.W. Turner, a nineteenth-century English artist. She employed color to illuminate the subtleties of nature. In her later years Moment turned to graphics, which appeared in many shows after 1960. Although her style continued to evolve and change, her subject matter—nature—remained the same.

MOORE, Elbridge Willis

b. 1857 Gardiner, ME
d. 1938 Tracy, CA
Membership: Portland Art Club
Awards: Portland Mechanics Fair (1887)
Collections: Haseltine Collection; Oregon Historical Society
Exhibits: Portland Mechanics Fairs; Portland Art Club (1886); North Pacific Industrial Exposition (89); Oregon Industrial Exposition (95); Elk's Carnival (1901); Portland Art Museum
References: GER; A2 (1916); C2 (1889, 95); C4 (83, 85, 87, 90); ARTC; CD (84, 89–93, 95, 97, 1902, 09, 17, 18); M1
Media: Oil, watercolor, pastel, crayon

Specialty: Portraits

Elbridge Moore had a photography studio and gallery in the Dekum Building in downtown Portland in 1883. His photographs appeared in *The West Shore* magazine, which also featured his prize-winning paintings. His paintings and photographs were exhibited at the Portland Mechanics Fairs, Industrial Expositions, and the Portland Art Museum. Moore executed a celebrated portrait of Chief Joseph. He painted portraits of five Oregon governors. Unfortunately, all five paintings were lost in a fire at the State Capitol in 1938.

MORRIS, Carl A.

b. 1911 Yorba Linda, CA
d. 1993 Portland, OR
Education: Art Institute of Chicago; Paris; Vienna
Membership: Oregon Guild of Painters and Sculptors; American Artists' Congress; Portland Art Museum (Artist Membership)
Awards: San Francisco Museum of Art; Seattle Art Museum (1943, 46, 47); Denver Art Museum; Pepsi Cola Annual (48)
Collections: Whitney Museum of Art; Guggenheim Museum; Metropolitan Museum of Art; Portland Art Museum; Smithsonian Institution; California Palace of the Legion of Honor—San Francisco; Sao Paulo Museum—Brazil; Tacoma Art Gallery; Seattle Art Museum; Reed College; Goodman Collection; Salishan Lodge Collection; Skamania Lodge Collection; University of Oregon; Museum of Modern Art; Multnomah Athletic Club Collection; San Francisco Museum of Art; Seattle Art Museum; Booth Collection; Swedish Medical Center—Seattle; Arlene and Harold Schnitzer Collection; Catlin Gabel School Collection; Huntington Collection
Exhibits: Paris (1PS 1935); San Francisco (1PS 37); Golden Gate International Exposition—San Francisco (39–40); Seattle Art Museum (1PS 40, 46, 4PS 53); Art Institute of Chicago (41, 42); Western Washington Fair; Portland Art Museum (1PS 46, 52; AM, 1PS 55); San Francisco Museum of Art (43, 44, 46); Oregon Guild of Painters and Sculptors (45); California Palace of the Legion of Honor—San Francisco (46); Oregon Society of Artists; Kraushaar Galleries—New York (52; 1PS 56, 58); Sao Paulo Biennial III—Brazil (55); Seligman Gallery—Seattle (2PS 57); Oakland Museum; Reed College; Santa Barbara Museum of Art (57); Ruthermore Gallery—San Francisco (59); Oregon Centennial (59); Smithsonian Institution Traveling Exhibits (59); Ford Foundation (59); Whitney Museum of Art; Guggenheim Museum; Metropolitan Museum of Art; University of Oregon (75); Oregon Historical Society (90)
References: ALM; DAV; HAV; HUG; MAL SUP; OET; WWN; WWW; A2 (1942, 44, 46, 48); A3 (49–58); A4 (59); C3 (49); C6; C7 (39, 40, 42–48, 51–53, 58); C8; C9; C15 (46); C18; C20; C22; C27; C30 (41, 46)
Media: Oil
Specialty: Abstract landscapes, murals
See artwork in color section
See photograph of artist on p. 86

Carl Morris grew up in California, the son of citrus farmers. He was influenced during high school by the ceramicist, Glenn Lukins. In 1935, after an art education in the United States and Europe, he returned to a job at Universal Studios in California. He left there for San Francisco and a teaching position at the Art Institute.

In 1938 the Federal Art Project

recruited him to found an arts center in Spokane, Washington. His program, considered one of the best of the Federal Art Projects, attracted many artists, including the one who would become his wife, Hilda* Deutsch. It was here that he also met the artists who would come to be known as the "Northwest School": Guy Anderson, Morris Graves, Kenneth Callahan, and Mark Tobey. Because the center was so successful, Morris was sent to Seattle to head a similar project there. After the closure of the Federal Art Project, Morris remained in Seattle and joined Tobey and his fellow artists. Poor group dynamics and a basic difference in orientation eventually led to Morris' departure.

In 1941 Carl and Hilda Morris moved to Oregon, where they spent the rest of their lives. During that year he was commissioned to paint a mural for the Eugene Post Office. He worked in Portland during World War II and did camouflage painting, which had an influence on his later abstract work.

Morris' art was permeated by the colors and landscape of Oregon. Nature provided the structure and visual stimulus for his work. Many of his early figurative pieces are set in the Palouse and Eastern Oregon, an area of high deserts, plains, and mountains. He was an ardent fisherman and went to that region often, absorbing its color and light. Morris received great praise and respect for his command of the figure; but he tired of that subject and wanted to convey mood, thought, and feeling. He felt this could best be achieved by turning to abstraction. He was in sympathy with the goals, ideals, and energies of the abstractionists and had a network of New York abstract painters as close friends. Morris based his abstract expressionist work on nature, poetry, scenery, and his own restless inquiring mind. He constantly explored new material and at the end of his career still produced work that showed growth and change. His canvases have an inner light source, a glow from within—possibly something spiritual, although not overtly so, which became more subtle over time.

In 1957 Carl Morris departed for a summer teaching position at the University of Colorado. There he found a new approach to painting—inspired, perhaps, by the brilliant light, clear air, open spaces, and arid landscape. When he returned to Oregon the muted light, semi-abstraction, dense color, heavily defined shapes, and block figures were gone. These were replaced by dazzling light, the timeless, colorful vastness of mountains and desert, with mysterious fissures, fractures, and eruptions in a more abstract manner.

Carl Morris, many critics agree, was Oregon's most historically important painter—a man who chose to pursue his art far from the limelight of the major art centers of the country, but who, nevertheless, achieved national stature. In 1985 Carl and Hilda Morris* were honored with the Governor's Art Award, the most prestigious in Oregon.

MORRIS, Hilda

b. 1911 New York, NY

d. 1991 Portland, OR

Education: Hunter College—New York; Cooper Union—New York City; Art Students League; Detroit Students League

Membership: Portland Art Museum (Artist Membership)

Collections: Portland Art Museum; Seattle Art Museum; San Francisco Museum of Art; University of Oregon; Tacoma Art Museum; Reed College; Arlene and Harold Schnitzer Collection

Exhibits: Museum of Modern Art;

Metropolitan Museum of Art; Reed College; Portland Art Museum (1PS 46; 55); Sao Paulo Biennial III—Brazil (1955); Denver Art Museum; Oregon Centennial (59); Autry Museum—Los Angeles (95)
References: DAV; FIE; HAV; A3 (1957); A4 (52, 59); C6; C23; C27
Media: Watercolor, sumi ink
See photograph of artist on p. 86

In 1938 Hilda Morris moved to Spokane to work in the sculpture department of the WPA Art Center. It was here she met her future husband, Carl. She then worked on the Federal Art Project in Seattle from 1940 to 1941. By this time she had gained international fame as a sculptor. They moved to Portland in 1941 and she joined the staff of the Museum Art School, where she taught until 1943. She began exhibiting paintings, including watercolors, that served as studies for sculpture. The importance of angle and stroke was demonstrated both in her sculpture and her painting. Her later sumi ink work shows a strong Asian influence: "What counts is the initial gesture." She favored root-like shapes and the circle as subjects. Titles "ancient" and "primal" often appear. She and her husband, Carl*, won the Governor's Award for the Arts in 1985.

MORRISON, Monte Boyde

b. 1928 Spokane, WA ***d.***
Education: Whitman College—Washington (1948–52); University of Oregon (52, 55); Ruskin School—Oxford, England
Membership: Portland Art Museum (Artist Membership)
Collections: University of Oregon
Exhibits: Portland Art Museum
References: DAV; HAV; WWAA; A3 (1954–56, 58)
Media: Plastic-based painting

An educator and painter, Monte Morrison was chairman of the art department at the University of Puget Sound. He was also a teacher at Wesleyan College in Macon, Georgia.

MUELLER, Michael J.

b. 1893 Durand, WI
d. 1931 Bend, OR
Education: Yale University: *Kendall, Winter, Savage*; American Academy—Rome, Italy
Membership: Oregon Society of Artists
Awards: Seattle Art Museum (1930)
Exhibits: University of Oregon; Oregon Society of Artists; Seattle Art Museum
References: DAV; DAW; FIE; MAL; SAM; WWW; C3 (1929, 30); C7 (30)
Media: Oil
Specialty: Northwest landscapes (John Day, Fossil, Bend), murals

During World War I Michael Mueller worked for the Navy observation balloon division. He studied art at Yale University and then at Rome's American Academy in Italy for three years. He was gaining a favorable reputation as an artist in the East in 1929 when he was appointed the head of the art department at University of Oregon. Mueller had just completed three murals at the Pennsylvania Academy of Fine Arts before coming west. Although his portraits are rare, an award-winning portrait at the Seattle Art Museum exhibition of 1930 received extensive press attention. He enjoyed experimenting in all art forms and subject matter. His career was tragically cut short when he died from appendicitis in Bend in 1931.

MUIRDEN, Phyllis. *See* RYDER, Phyllis

MULLER, Richard Arthur

b. 1928 Morristown, NJ

d. 1991 Multnomah Co., OR
Education: Syracuse University (1947–51); University of Oregon (54–56)
Collections: Portland Art Museum; Salishan Lodge Collection; University of Oregon; Huntington Collection
Exhibits: Portland Art Museum; Santa Barbara Museum of Art (1955); Oakland Museum (57); Locke Galleries—San Francisco (1PS 58); Seattle Art Museum; University of Oregon (75)
References: A3 (1955, 56); C7 (59); C22
Media: Oil, tempera, acrylic, pen and ink
Specialty: Landscapes

Richard Muller joined the Army after graduating from Syracuse University. When he continued his art education at the University of Oregon in 1954, he shared an apartment with Harry Widman*. His paintings are landscape oriented with many levels of meaning, all relating to nature. With a cool, muted palette, Muller captured the "essence of wildness." He joined the art faculty at Portland State University in 1959 to replace Frederick Heidel* who was on sabbatical leave.

MULVEY, Charles

b. 1918 Oregon City, OR ***d.***
Education: Art Center School of Design—Los Angeles; University of Portland: *Lowe;* Washington D.C.: *O'Hara;* Art Institute of Chicago; Museum Art School; Cornish College of the Arts—Seattle
Awards: Craftsman Press (1957)
Collections: Publishers Paper Co.—Oregon City; U.S. Bank
Exhibits: Seattle (1PS); Tacoma (1PS); Walla Walla (1PS); Olympia (1PS); Astoria (1PS); University of Portland (1PS); Lincoln County Art Center (1PS); San Diego; Australia; South America
Media: Watercolor
Specialty: Seascapes (harbor scenes)

Charles Mulvey taught watercolor techniques and presented workshop demonstrations in thirty-eight cities in Oregon, Washington, and California. He was a member of many watercolor societies. Mulvey's home and gallery, The Sea Chest, has been located in Seaview, Washington since 1954. The artist stated that he preferred a realistic approach, though he considered his work to be "impressionistic." "I change and move and leave out and recompose. I don't paint exactly what is there." His favorite subject was the beach rather than the sea. Using sweeping strokes he was able to suggest the feeling of sand. His palette captured the elusive colors of nature. He said his greatest test and accomplishment was a yearly demonstration to sixth graders at Ilwaco Elementary School in Washington.

MURPHY, Chester (Chet) Glenn

b. 1907 Harper, KS
d. 1997 Portland, OR
Education: *C. Keller**
Membership: Oregon Society of Artists; American Artists Professional League; American Artists' Congress
Collections: Lundberg Collection
Exhibits: Oregon Society of Artists; Citizens for Art Group (1959); Maryhill Museum—Goldendale, Washington; Oregon Centennial (59)
References: DAV; C3 (1951)
Media: Oil
Specialty: Landscape, seascapes, murals

Chester Murphy taught at the Juniper Art Guild in Crook County. He moved to Portland in 1927 and was exhibiting with the Oregon Society of Artists by 1951, later serving as their president. His visits to foreign countries, including Mexico and the Philippines, provided themes for his illustrated books. He received many awards for juried shows after 1959.

MURPHY, Miriam Clare

b. 1904 Anoka, MN
d. 1984 Clackamas County, OR
Education: University of Oregon (1936); Art Students League: *Sternberg* (36); University of Washington; *B. Hinshaw**
Membership: Portland Art Museum (Artist Membership)
Collections: University of Washington; University of Oregon
Exhibits: Portland Art Museum (AM, 1954; 1PS 55); Henry Art Gallery—University of Washington (50); Friendship House—Portland (3PS 57); Oregon Centennial (59)
References: A2 (1948); A3 (38, 49, 51, 58); C6
Specialty: Portraits

Also known as Sister Miriam Clare, Miriam Murphy came to Portland in 1920 and became a nun three years later at the age of 19. Her art teacher and mentor, Bernard Hinshaw*, encouraged her to pursue painting. Murphy had a one-person show at the Portland Art Museum in 1955 and a three-person show with Jan Kunz and Albert Patecky* in 1957 at the Friendship House in Portland. She became a teacher at Marylhurst College.

MURRAY, Colista. *See* DOWLING, Colista

N

NASH, Louisa A'hmuty

b. 1838 Greenwich, England
d. 1922 Nashville, OR
Education: England, Germany, France, Switzerland
Collections: Oregon Historical Society; Oregon State University
Exhibits: Oregon Historical Society (1973, 86, 96)
References: DAV; DAW
Media: Watercolor, oil
Specialty: Landscapes

In 1879 Louisa Nash and her husband, Wallis*, moved to Oregon from their native England. They settled on a farm outside of Corvallis, known today as the town of Nashville. Her work provided an interesting documentary record of early Oregon: towns, buildings, and mining camps on the Oregon Coast. Other subjects included the family farm, the city of Portland between the years 1880 and 1905, and oils of the Lewis and Clark Exposition. In addition, Nash wrote and illustrated magazine articles. Their daughter, Dorothea, was a gifted musician and artist who taught art at Oregon Agricultural College (now Oregon State University), and Oregon State Normal School (now Western Oregon State College). She signed her work *L.A.N.*

NASH, Wallis

b. 1837 London, England
d. 1926 Lincoln Co., OR
Collections: Oregon Historical Society
Exhibits: Oregon Historical Society (1990)
References: DAV; DAW; C9
Media: Watercolor, prints (engraving)
Specialty: Illustrations

Wallis Nash, a London attorney, first came to Oregon in 1877. There was interest in building a railroad from Yaquina, on the coast, inland to Mill City and Nash represented the potential investors. He returned two years later with his family and twenty-six emigrants. Nash was actively involved with the Oregon Pacific Railroad until its failure. He authored many books, two containing engravings after his sketches. *Two Years in Oregon*, written in 1882, showed early views of Astoria, Willamette's falls, Yaquina Bay, and the Oregon Coast. Nash continued practicing law and was one of the founders of Oregon State University. The town of Nashville was named for him. Among other well-known family members, his wife, Louisa*, was an artist who worked in oil and watercolor. Their daughter, Dorothea, was also an artist and a musician. Nash signed his work *W.N.*

NASTASIA, James Emmet

b. 1922 New Jersey ***d.***
Education: Cornell; University of Southern California
Membership: Artists Equity; Portland Art Museum (Artist Membership)
Collections: Reed College; Marylhurst College; University of Oregon; Seattle Art Museum; Los Angeles County Museum of Art; San Diego Museum
Exhibits: Portland Art Museum; Seattle Art Museum

References: A3 (1952–56); C7 (55)
Media: Watercolor, oil

James Nastasia was a teacher at the University of Southern California. After his exhibit at the Portland Art Museum in 1956, he traveled extensively in the Yucatan for one year. He developed a watercolor painting technique that is dryer than usual and delivers a more pronounced color effect.

NEPERUD, Ronald W.

b. 1929 La Crosse, WI ***d.***
Education: Eastern Washington State College—Cheney, Washington; Willamette University: *C. Hall** (1952, 54); University of Washington: *Alps* (54); University of Oregon: *D. McCosh**, *J. Wilkinson** (64)
Membership: Portland Art Museum (Artist Membership)
Collections: University of Oregon
Awards: University of Oregon (1959)
Exhibits: Portland Art Museum; University of Oregon; Cheney Cowles Museum—Spokane, Washington; San Jose State College
References: A3 (1951)
Media: Watercolor; prints (wood block)
Specialty: Landscape

A teacher in Salem Public Schools, Ron Neperud later became an art professor at Eastern Washington State College, the University of Oregon, and the University of Wisconsin. He remained at the University of Wisconsin-Madison until his retirement twenty-eight years later. Neperud edited the art section of the *Northwest Review* from 1959 to 1961 and has served as co-editor or contributor to texts on art. He published numerous articles on the perception and valuing of art in various publications. In 1959 he was honored with a one-person print exhibit at the University of Oregon.

In an artist statement Neperud writes: "Working in the broad context of landscapes, I am particularly interested in edges created by juxtaposing fluid areas of watercolor and by the quality of light struggling to be revealed through foliage."

NEWSTRUM, Dick C.

b. 1931 Portland, OR ***d.***
Education: University of Oregon (1949–53, 57–58)
Membership: Portland Art Museum (Artist Membership)
Exhibits: Portland Art Museum (AM, 4PS 1959); Seattle Art Museum; Oregon Centennial (59)
References: A3 (1957, 58); C7 (57)
Media: Watercolor

Though Dick Newstrum was just beginning his art career in the late 1950s, he had a group watercolor show with fellow artists Patti Beaton Dodd*, Leonard Kimbrell*, and Nelson Sandgren* sponsored by the Artist Membership of the Portland Art Museum. He also participated in the Centennial exhibition organized by Frederick Heidel* at Portland State University.

NICKLIN, Lydia (Lida) S.

b. 1849 Clackamas Co., OR
d. 1900 Salem, OR
Education: Willamette University; San Francisco; Portland
Awards: Oregon State Fairs
Exhibits: Oregon State Fairs; Portland Mechanics Fair; North Pacific Industrial Exposition (1890); Portland Industrial Exposition (91)
References: C2 (1890, 91); C4 (87); CD (89, 90); OSF (72, 94–98); M2; M3
Media: Oil, crayon
Specialty: Florals, still life, landscapes, animals

Lydia Nicklin moved to Salem with her family as a young girl. She received her art education at Willamette University and in San Francisco. By 1887 she had moved to Portland and was exhibiting in the Portland Mechanics Fair and the Industrial Fairs. After many years in Portland, she returned to Salem in 1894, six years before her death. Her name appears in the artist listing of the Salem City Directory in 1896. Sometimes she is listed as Lida or as Mrs. T. L. Nicklin.

NIEDERER, Carl L.

b. Portland, OR ***d.***
Education: University of Oregon: *J. Wilkinson** (1949); Paris: *Léger* (51–52); *R. Halvorsen**
Exhibits: Portland Art Museum; University of Oregon; Kharouba Gallery
References: A2 (1948)
Media: Watercolor

Carl Niederer grew up in Southwest Portland, attended Lincoln High School and studied art with Ruth Halvorsen*. After World War II he returned from the Navy to continue his education at the University of Oregon and then at the Atelier Fernand Léger in Paris. Niederer's varied career included advertising, cinematographic design, and chairmanship of the art department at the University of Wyoming for four and a half years. He completed many watercolors while traveling in Australia and England. His art gallery in Eugene was called Gallery 720. He also had a studio in San Francisco for nineteen years. He was a good friend of artist Otto Fried*.

NORRBO, Bennet

b. 1930 Minneapolis, MN ***d.***
Education: Museum Art School (1947–49); San Francisco
Membership: National Watercolor Society; Artists Equity; Portland Art Museum (Artist Membership)
Collections: University of Oregon; First National Bank; Multnomah Athletic Club Collection; Portland: Benson Hotel, University Club, Providence Hospital, Bank of California, Pacific NW Bell
Exhibits: Portland Art Museum
References: A2 (1946)
Media: Watercolor, oil, acrylic, mixed media (wood, terra-cotta)
Specialty: Fanciful subjects; animals

Bennet Norrbo was one of Oregon's most prolific artists. His work can be found in many collections, both private and public. He had a career as a successful commercial artist for fifteen years before devoting himself to painting full-time. Most of his exhibitions were after 1959, when he frequently worked on shows that could be grouped together. Norrbo's work was sometimes exceptionally small and detailed with sophisticated color combinations. Animals and fanciful subject matter interested him, something a friend referred to as a "satire on art itself." The Portland Rental Sales Gallery has represented him. He also enjoyed filmmaking, with special attention to the details of creating models of ruins and creatures.

NORTON, Mary I.

b. d.
Exhibits: Portland Mechanics Fairs; North Pacific Industrial Exposition (1889)
References: C2 (1889); C4 (83, 86); CD (96, 97, 1899–1902); M2

A teacher at St. Helens Hall, from 1886 to 1896, Mary Norton's name was listed as Mrs. F.B. Norton in a Mechanics Fair Entry of 1883.

NORWOOD, James Richard

b. 1922 Rainier, OR ***d.***
Education: Art Center School of Design—Los Angeles (1942); Museum Art School (46–51); Reed College (48–50); California School of Fine Arts (49)

Membership: Portland Art Museum (Artist Membership)
Exhibits: Addison Gallery at Phillips Academy—Andover, Massachussetts (1949, 54); Portland Art Museum (AM, 1PS 55); Kharouba Gallery (1PS 52); Adele's Restaurant—Portland; Oakland Art Gallery (1PS); Reed College (1PS); Seattle Art Museum
References: A3 (1950, 53–56); C7 (53)
Specialty: Murals

Rick Norwood was attending the Museum Art School in 1949 when his work, along with that of George Johanson* and Bob Gallaher*, was selected for a traveling exhibition of outstanding student art. He taught summer school at the Museum Art School in 1952 and 1953 as well as Saturday children's classes. He completed murals for the Oregon Centennial Exposition, and for St. Paul's Lutheran Church in Vancouver, Washington. He is also known as Richard James Norwood.

O

O'BRIEN, George McNeil

b. St. Paul, MN
d. 1914 Rochester, MN
Membership: Society of Oregon Artists
Awards: Oregon State Fair (1912)
Collections: Oregon Historical Society
Exhibits: Oregon State Fair (1912); Society of Oregon Artists (13); Portland Art Museum
References: SI; A2 (1914); ARTC; CD (10, 11, 14, 15)
Specialty: Pioneer portraits

George O'Brien was born and raised in St. Paul, Minnesota. In the early part of the century, he brought his family to southern Oregon and then to Portland. He had studios in Portland in the Dekum Building in 1910 and the Labbe Building in 1911. O'Brien taught aspiring artist W. P. Hayes* and others. His portraits included pioneer *John Minto*, a prize-winner at the Oregon State Fair of 1912. This painting and his *Jason Lee* are now in the Oregon Historical Society collection. By 1914 he was painting portraits of the Doctors Mayo at their Clinic in Rochester, Minnesota, where he died of cancer.

O'BRIEN, Helengray Gatens

b. d.
Education: University of Oregon
Membership: University Alumni Art League, University of Oregon
Exhibits: University Alumni Art League; Portland Art Museum; Oregon Society of Artists; J.K. Gill Gallery (1PS)
References: A2 (1942, 44); C3 (43, 46, 48–50); C25 (35, 36)
Media: Oil, watercolor

Helengray O'Brien was an artist and poet who exhibited her work at the Portland Art Museum and the Oregon Society of Artists. She also had a one-person show at the J.K.Gill Gallery.

O'RYAN, Lilly. *See* KLEIN, Lilly

OSENBRUGGE, Margaret P.

b. d.
Membership: Southern Oregon Art Association
Exhibits: Grants Pass Museum of Art; Southern Oregon Art Association; Southern Oregon Art Exhibit
References: C26 (1958); OR (Grants Pass Museum of Art)

Margaret Osenbrugge was active in the southern Oregon art community and was recommended by the Grants Pass Museum of Art. She lived in Medford and Gold Hill.

OSTER, Mabel Haines Hall

b. 1886 Portland, OR
d. 1975 Newberg, OR
Education: *N. Zane**; *J. Fairbanks**; *E. Wuest**; *P. Sheffers**; *Erhman*
Membership: Oregon Society of Artists
Awards: Oregon Society of Artists (1947)
Exhibits: Oregon Society of Artists; Portland Art Museum
References: A2 (1948); C3 (29, 39, 46–51); CD (30–33, 43, 44)
Media: Oil, watercolor, pastel

Mabel Haines Oster was raised in

California, but returned to Portland, her birthplace, in 1902. She studied with several outstanding Oregon artists: Nowland Zane*, J. Leo Fairbanks*, Esther Wuest*, and Peter Sheffers*. Oster was a charter member of the Oregon Society of Artists and had a studio in Portland for thirteen years. She then traveled to San Francisco, where she successfully sold her art at Gump's Galleries. On her return to Portland in 1940, she opened a studio in the Selling-Hirsch Building, where she worked and taught until 1946. Winsor and Newton, Inc., a long-established English art supply company, asked her to write descriptive accounting of "her colors" for their new American market. Her exhibit of 1939 was listed under the name Hall.

P

PARROTT, Sue

b. d.
Collections: Powell Collection
Exhibits: Elks Carnival (1901); Clatsop County Historical Society (94)
References: BI; DAV; C11; CD (1890–93, 1896–1903); M2; M3
Media: China painting, oil
Specialty: Landscape

Sue Parrott was active in Portland from 1889 to 1904. Known for her china painting, she was an instructor in that field. There is evidence to suggest she may be Sue Hendershott Parrott, wife of the artist William Samuel Parrott*.

PARROTT, William Samuel

b. 1843 MO
d. 1915 Goldendale, WA
Education: San Francisco Museum of Art
Awards: Oregon State Fair
Collections: San Francisco Museum of Art; Oregon Historical Society; Painting Restoration Studio Collection; Portland Art Museum; Brooklyn Art Museum; Stenzel Collection; Counting Eagles Collection; Huntington Collection; Slippery Slope Historical Collection
Exhibits: Oregon State Fair; Portland Mechanics Fairs; C. C. Morse; Shanahan Gallery; Washington State Capitol Museum (88); Oregon Historical Society (90)
References: BEN; BI; DAV; DAW; FIE; GER; HUG; MAL; SAM; SMI; THI; VOL; WWN; WWW; YNG; C1; C4 (1878–80, 83, 85); C9; C16; C24; CD (81, 1886–1902); MYH; OSF (1875); M1
Media: Oil
Specialty: Landscapes (mountains, lakes)
See artwork in color section

Born in Missouri, William Samuel Parrott arrived in Oregon with his family in 1847. He had a natural talent for drawing and as a child had a strong desire to reproduce scenes in color. At first he used wildflowers for paint pigment, cloth or bark for canvas, and strands of his sister Jane's hair for brushes. He opened his first studio in the old National Bank Building in Portland in 1867. Students who claimed to have studied with him, often just observed him at work; while there are artists who paint in his style, the so-called "Parrott School" probably does not exist.

Parrott closed his Portland studio in 1887 to travel the wilds of Oregon, Washington, and California. His years of solitude in the mountains made him something of a recluse, often moody and temperamental. It was rumored that he would not sign any paintings he gave as gifts, to insure they would not achieve the commercial value of his signed works. According to family records, he eventually settled in Oakland, California with his second wife, Sue Hendershott Parrott, also a painter of some renown. When his health began to fail in 1911, he returned to the Northwest, where he spent the years until his death with his sister Jane in Goldendale, Washington. Another sister, Elizabeth Parrott Pond, was a well-known Washington state artist.

Parrott's mountain landscapes were very popular and were commissioned more than any other subject. Variations of *Sunrise over Mt. Hood from Lost Lake*, with his recognizable atmospheric effects, appear in many collections. One of his paintings of Mt. Hood hung in the Louvre. Many of his other mountain canvases can be found in museums and collections worldwide.

PARSONS, Eunice Jensen

b. Loma, CO ***d.***
Education: Art Institute of Chicago; Museum Art School (1950–54)
Membership: Artists Equity; Portland Art Museum (Artist Membership)
Collections: University of Oregon; Kaiser Permanente Collection
Exhibits: Oregon Society of Artists; Portland Art Museum; Seattle Art Museum; Cafe Espresso Gallery (1959); Marylhurst College (1PS 59); Ruthermore Gallery—San Francisco (59); Oregon Centennial (59)
References: COL; WWN; A2 (1940); A3 (53–56); C3 (31); C6; C7 (54, 55, 58, 59)
Media: Oil, gouache, prints, collage
Specialty: Florals, still life, street scenes

An art teacher at Portland State University and the Museum Art School, Eunice Parsons was mainly a printmaker. The exhibitions listed above include her paintings.

PATECKY, Albert

b. 1906 Mancolona, MI
d. 1994 Tigard, OR
Education: Chicago Academy of Fine Arts (1925–28); Art Students League (45); Museum Art School: *W. Givler*, H. Wentz*, C. Voorhies*; S. Bell*; P. Sheffers**
Membership: Artists Equity; Oregon Society of Artists; American Artists Professional League; Attic Club; Art Students League; Portland Art Museum (Artist Membership)
Awards: Oregon Society of Artists (1942, 44, 46, 47, 49); Oregon State Fairs (43, 46, 47); Multnomah County Fair (42, 44, 47, 49)
Collections: Oregon Historical Society; University of Oregon; Parsons Collection; Hallie Ford Museum of Art—Willamette University; Gerber Collection; Lundberg Collection
Exhibits: Oregon Society of Artists; Multnomah County Fairs (1942, 44, 45, 47, 49); Oregon State Fairs (43, 46, 47, 49); J.K. Gill Gallery (2PS 44); Portland Art Museum (1PS 49, 50); Clark County Art Center—Washington (46, 1PS 49); Oakland Art Gallery (46, 48); Portland Children's Museum (1PS 46, 50); Seattle Art Museum; Western Washington Fair; Elfstrom Gallery; Lincoln County Art Center (48, IPS 50, 1PS 54); Guggenheim Museum (49–53); Corvallis Arts Guild (49); Gump's Galleries—San Francisco (1PS 50, 53, 54); Paris Salon—des Réalitiés Nouvelles (50, 52, 53); Fole-Myers Gallery (51); Coos Artist League (1PS 53); Lewis and Clark College (IPS 53); Reed College (2PS 53; 1PS 54); Hood River Art Association (1PS 53, 56); American Artists Professional League (54); Public Library—Longview, Washington (55); Meier and Frank Co. (1PS 55, 58); Marylhurst College (1PS 55); Klamath Falls Art Association (1PS 55); Friendship House—Portland (3PS 57); Artists Equity (58); University of Portland (59); Chehalis Public Library—Chehalis, Washington (1PS 59); National Academy of Design; Cologne; Art Students League; Bush Barn—Salem; Dekum Gallery; Oregon Centennial (59); University of Oregon (75); Oregon

Historical Society (90); Clatsop County Historical Society (94)

References: BEN; COL; DAV; OET; WWN; A1 (1953); A2 (44, 46, 48); A3 (53, 54); A4 (52); C1; C3 (43, 45–50); C7 (46, 48); C9; C11; C13 (46, 47, 48); C14; C15 (46); C22; C30 (46); ARTC; CD (51, 53–4, 56–59)

Media: Oil, watercolor, prints (monoprint)

Specialty: Still life, landscapes, marines, circus, ballet

See artwork in color section

See photograph of artist on p. 87

Born and educated in the Midwest, Albert Patecky arrived in Portland in 1928. He studied with local artist Sidney Bell* in the early 1930s and then worked as a cartoonist and illustrator for Pacific Telephone and Telegraph during the Depression and war years. His work received attention when he began studying with Peter Sheffers* in 1939. J.D. Cleaver in *The Artists Patecky: A Place in History*, recounts fifty awards at various exhibits between 1942 and 1948. His landscape and marine work after 1940 showed new clarity and confidence as a result of his association with Sheffers. An active participant with the Oregon Society of Artists, he served as president in the mid-1940s. Patecky's entry in one of the Oregon Society of Artists's shows, *Oregon Shipyard Shanty*, shows grim times near the St. Johns community outside Portland. Other entries featured circus sketches and rural subject matter.

In 1945 Patecky studied at the Art Students League in New York. Here his traditional schooling gave way to experimentation with cubism and abstraction. When he returned to Portland, he opened a studio and shared quarters with the Attic Sketch group. In 1948 he opened the Patecky Studio Gallery that represented many of the well-known painters of the time: Sidney Bell*, Louis Bunce*, Ted Christensen Jr.*, Bernard Geiser*, William Givler*, Charles Heaney*, Alice Hutchinson*, Clyde Keller*, Percy Manser*, C.S. Price*, Ed Quigley*, Howard Sewall*, Menalkas Selander*, Amanda Snyder*, and Mildred Warner* among others.

The decade of the 1950s was very productive: he gained an international reputation in the Non-Objective movement and appeared in over one hundred exhibitions nationally and world-wide. It was at this time that he began teaching, and joined in a partnership with artist Viktor Von Pribosic* as founder and director of the Creative Art Workshop. He later taught in Portland and Vancouver, Washington schools and privately. Patecky was in demand as a lecturer and juror of exhibitions. In Oregon he was best known for his monoprints.

In 1952 Patecky and Maude Kerns*, who had also exhibited at the Museum of Non-Objective Painting (later the Guggenheim), collaborated in an unusual experimental performance of *Hear the Painting*. It featured visual images on stage with musicians and singers behind curtains. The interest in music could be attributed to his long marriage to and partnership with his wife, Blanche*, a noted musician and artist. Their son, Ken, was also a noted sculptor. Patecky's work reflected Oregon's people, climate, and landscape over a long period that saw his style change from realistic to non-objective.

PATECKY, Blanche

b. 1904 Chicago, IL

d. 1996, Tigard, OR

Education: *N. Zane** (1919); Museum Art School (28); *A. Patecky**; University of Oregon Extension: *B. Hinshaw** (31–32)

Membership: Oregon Society of

Artists; Portland Art Museum (Artist Membership)
Awards: Oregon State Fair (1947)
Collections: Oregon Historical Society; Gerber Collection
Exhibits: Portland Art Museum; Oregon State Fair (1947); Bush Barn—Salem; Henry Art Gallery —University of Washington; Dekum Gallery
References: A2 (1946)
Media: Watercolor, oil
Specialty: Florals

Blanche Patecky moved from Chicago to Seattle in 1907 and then came to Portland in 1910. She had two careers: art and music. She painted with a semi-abstract technique, enhanced by her use of the palette knife. Patecky painted murals for the Elks Temple in Portland. Governor Tom McCall chose her painting *Blue Lilies* to tour New Mexico as one of the representative art pieces from Oregon in 1968. She was equally famous as a talented composer and teacher. In the 1920s she appeared in piano performances on the Chautauqua circuit. She was the wife of Albert Patecky*.

PATTEN, Eleanor. *See* KAFOURY, Eleanor

PATTERSON, Ruth. *See* HART, Ruth

PEARSON, Thelma Forsythe

b. 1910 Indiana, PA ***d.***
Education: John Herron Art Institute—Indianapolis (1930); Washington School of Art—Washington, D.C. (50); Portland State University; Oregon State University
Membership: Oregon Society of Artists; Northwest Watercolor Society; Oakland Art Gallery
Awards: John Herron Art Institute —Indianapolis; Northwest Watercolor Society
Collections: Oregon Historical Society
Exhibits: Lincoln County Art Center (1PS); Northwest Watercolor Society; Allied Arts—Richland, Washington (1PS); Bellevue, Washington; Seattle Art Museum (1955); Frye Museum—Seattle; University of Oregon; Coos Art Museum; Bush Barn—Salem; Evansville Museum of Arts and Sciences—Evansville, Indiana
References: COL; C29 (1952, 53)
Media: Watercolor, oil, encaustic, enamel
Specialty: Landscapes, seascapes, marines

A teacher at Central Washington College in Ellensburg, Linn-Benton College, and Clackamas Community College in Oregon, Thelma Pearson also gave private watercolor lessons for twenty-five years. The Thelma Pearson Gallery at Lincoln City was a famous landmark for coast visitors. She said: "The colors and forms of the ocean and nearby land ... provide so much inspiration for the arts." The Portland Art Museum Rental Sales Gallery featured her in a one-person exhibition.

PEASE, Lute (Lucius) Curtis

b. 1869 Winnemucca, NV
d. 1963 Maplewood, NJ
Education: Franklin Academy—New York: *Malone* (1887); Museum Art School (1910)
Membership: Circle A Club; Oregon Art Association; American Artists Professional League
Awards: Pulitzer Prize (Illustration, 1949)
Collections: Smithsonian Institution; Stenzel Collection
Exhibits: Portland Art Museum;

National Academy of Design; Oregon Historical Society (1990)
References: BI; DAV; DAW; MAL; HAV; SAM; WWW; C9; C16; ARTC; CD (1904, 12, 13)
Media: Oil
Specialty: Genre, portraits, landscapes

Lute Pease, while trying to earn money to study art in Paris, was working at a bicycle shop in Portland when he witnessed a murder-suicide. He sketched the tragic event and sold it to the *Oregonian* for ten dollars and a job. He was the first reporter and editorial cartoonist for the *Oregonian* from 1895 to 1897. He interviewed Mark Twain and sketched him for the newspaper when Twain stopped in Portland at the beginning of his 1895 world tour.

In 1897 Pease left for Alaska and a life of adventure for the next five years. He mined for gold, drove an ox team, and acted as Yukon and Nome correspondent for the *Seattle Post Intelligencer* and the *Oregonian.* In later years he said that the time spent in Alaska was the high point of his life.

In 1902 he returned to Portland and the *Oregonian.* Pease was one of the cartoonists who contributed to the *As We See 'Em* book of Portland caricatures published by Edward Thomson. In 1906 he became the editor of *The Pacific Monthly* and did many illustrations and covers for the magazine before leaving for Newark, New Jersey in 1914. It was there, as a political cartoonist, that he won the Pulitzer Prize in 1949. Pease retired in 1952. Pease once said ruefully that he never made it to Paris. He was married to artist Nell Pease*.

PEASE, Nell Christmas McMullen

b. 1883 Steubenville, OH
d. 1958 Maplewood, NJ
Education: Corcoran Gallery of Art School—Washington, D.C.: *Helmick*; Museum Art School (1910)
Collections: Oregon Historical Society; Stenzel Collection
Exhibits: National Academy of Design
References: BI; DAV; DAW; HAV; KOV; MAL SUP; PET; SAM; WWW; C16; M2; M3
Media: Oil
Specialty: Portraits, genre, landscapes

Nell Pease was in the first class of the Museum Art School of the Portland Art Museum. Later she was an illustrator for *The Pacific Monthly*, edited by her husband, Lute Pease*. Nell and Lute Pease operated the Pease School of Instruction in her studio in Portland from 1905 to 1910. She depicted views of Oregon and lumber scenes of the Northwest. She was also active in Washington, D.C. and Maplewood and Newark, New Jersey. Kovinick (see Ref. KOV) gives her deathplace as Cedar Grove, New Jersey.

PEDERSEN, Conrad Georg

b. 1887 Denmark ***d.***
Education: Denmark: *Pedersen; C. McKim**
Membership: Society of Oregon Artists; Oregon Society of Artists
Collections: University of Oregon; Oregon State University; Humpal Collection; Portland Courthouse; Coos County Courthouse; Pendleton Hospital; Lundberg Collection; Cofield Collection
Exhibits: Society of Oregon Artists (1913); Portland Art Museum; Corcoran Gallery of Art—Washington, D.C.; Christiansen Gallery
References: COL; DAV; DAW; WWN; A2 (1915, 20, 22, 33); C10; ARTC; CD (18, 52)
Media: Oil, watercolor, pastel
Specialty: Landscapes (Columbia River), seascapes, portraits

See artwork in color section

Conrad Pedersen painted in an impressionistic style. He was a charter member of the Oregon Society of Artists and participated in the WPA. His subject matter demonstrated an interest in the landscape around Portland, especially the waterfront, and the Columbia Gorge.

PERKINS, Grace Whitman Gray

b. 1884 Vancouver, WA
d. 1949 Milwaukie, OR
Education: Art Students League (1901–02); University of Oregon (03–06); *Pyle*
Exhibits: Portland Art Museum
References: A2 (1919, 21)
Media: Oil, charcoal, watercolor, pen, pencil
Specialty: Landscapes, portraits

Grace Perkins spent her early years in Vancouver, Washington and Portland. She attended the Art Students League in New York and then returned home to Oregon to complete her art education. The illustrator, Howard Pyle, praised her work. Others commented on her ability to capture exact likenesses of subjects through subtle facial expressions. She continued to paint as she raised her family, until multiple sclerosis limited her. Around 1930 she turned her attention to sculpture and weaving, skills more compatible with her disability. Perkins died in a house fire in 1949 with her husband, who attempted to save her life. Most of her work was destroyed at this time.

PETERSON, Norma Heyser

b. 1933 Portland, OR ***d.***
Education: University of Oregon (1951–53); Museum Art School (53–56)
Awards: Oregon Centennial (1959)
Exhibits: Portland Art Museum; Seattle Art Museum; New Gallery of Contemporary Art (1959); Oregon Centennial (59)
References: ALM; A3 (1955, 58); C6; C7 (57)

Norma Heyser taught children's classes while she was a student at the Museum Art School in 1955. She graduated in 1956. A year later she taught children's classes at the Museum of Modern Art in New York City. In 1958 she co-founded the New Gallery of Contemporary Art in Portland with her husband, Ron. The gallery was short lived, closing in 1962, but represented several promising contemporary artists: The Petersons, Byron Gardner*, Duane Zaloudek*, Bonnie Bronson, Milton Wilson*, Lee Kelly, Marlene Gabel (sculptor), and Joyce Britton* (textiles). In 1967 she developed interests in film and environmental concerns.

PICKETT, James Tilton

b. 1857 Bellingham, WA Territory
d. 1889 Portland, OR
Education: California
Membership: Portland Art Club
Awards: Portland Mechanics Fair (1888)
Collections: Washington State Historical Society—Tacoma
Exhibits: Portland Mechanics Fairs; Portland Art Club (1886); Washington State Capitol Museum (1988)
References: DAV; DAW; GER; C4 (1883, 86, 88); C24; ARTC; M1
Media: Oil, prints (lithograph)
Specialty: Landscape (rivers, houses, steamer boats)

James Tilton Pickett was the son of George Edward Pickett, who led the famous Civil War charge, and a Haida Indian woman who died shortly after his birth. As an infant, he was left with friends of his father in Washington state. He loved to paint at a very early age, and used chunks of charcoal to sketch, coloring his works with berry juice and green leaves. Both a painter and a lithographer, his work appeared in the *Oregonian* and other newspapers. His illustrations in D.D. Fagan's *History of Benton County* (1885) reflect his keen observation while traveling the County, inland to the coast. James Pickett died of tuberculosis at age thirty-two in Portland.

PIERS, Anton. *See* FABRICK, Anton

PILADAKIS, Imanuel (Manolis)

b. 1927 Alexandria, Egypt ***d.***
Education: Oregon State University (1955–58); University of Oregon (59–60); *D. Jameson*; N. Sandgren**
Membership: Master Watercolor Society of Oregon; Portland Art Museum (Artist Membership)
Collections: Portland Art Museum; University of Oregon; Oregon State University; Hallie Ford Museum of Art—Willamette University
Exhibits: Master Watercolor Society of Oregon (1958); Seattle Art Museum; San Francisco Museum of Art; Oregon Centennial (59); Greece; University of Oregon (75)
References: A3 (1958); C6; C7 (58, 59); C22
Media: Oil, watercolor, prints
Specialty: Landscapes, marines

Imanuel Piladakis was a member of the Oregon State College (now University) faculty from 1961-63. He was an instructor of art in Athens, Greece, exhibiting his work in Italy, France, and England. References sometimes list his first name as Manolis or Emmanuel.

PLATZ, Clifford A.

b. 1892 Erie Co., PA
d. 1983 Portland, OR
Education: *S. Bayless*; F. Wertz**
Membership: Oregon Society of Artists; Southern Oregon Society of Artists; Society of Western Artists; Laguna Beach Art Association—California; Yakima Valley Art Association—Washington; Rogue Valley Art Association
Awards: Southern Oregon Art Exhibit (1955, 57)
Exhibits: Southern Oregon Art Exhibit; Oregon Society of Artists; J.K. Gill Gallery (2PS 1949); Laguna Beach Art Association—California (1PS 49); Rubin Gallery—Longview, Washington (1PS 50); Yakima Valley Art Association—Yakima, Washington (1PS 50); Society of Western Artists (50); Jacksonville Gold Rush Jubilee (51); Southern Oregon Society of Artists (51, 52, 55)
References: C3 (1949, 50); C26 (48, 54–56, 58)
Media: Oil, watercolor, acrylic, tempera
Specialty: Landscapes, marines, desert scenes

Clifford Platz began his art career late in life. A painting contractor by profession, he suffered a heart attack at age fifty-five and began painting as therapy. He discovered a latent talent and, with lots of time on his hands, began reading about painting techniques, putting it all to practice. Almost entirely self-taught, he sought the guidance of many local painters in the Medford area: Stephen Bayless*, Fritz Wertz*, and Eugene Bennett* among others. His application to the Portland-based Oregon Society of Artists was accepted in 1949 and upgraded to active status in 1951. He exhibited at the Laguna Beach Art Association in California in 1949. Other venues followed in San Francisco and

Washington state, often as two-person shows with fellow southern Oregon artist Vola Tolman.

Platz's interest in painting continued on the organizational side as well. He was instrumental in setting up the Southern Oregon Artists Association in 1951 and was honored by that group with an exhibition in 1970 on their nineteenth anniversary. He served as regional representative for the Society of Western Artists, based in San Francisco. Platz was also an active part of the organization of the Rogue Valley Art Association in 1957. He later moved to Portland.

By his own admission his style was traditional and he valued the term "amateur". He painted the landscapes of the Medford area from notes and quick sketches and is remembered for his desert scenes. He said: "Since my desire has been...the achievement of serious work, I have painted constantly, with many misgivings and fears; over sensitive and over anxious, I have, however worked hard to achieve my present ability to express myself."

PLUMMER, Helen (Nellie). *See* GATCH, Helen (Nellie)

POGUE, M.E. Mrs.

b. d.
Awards: Oregon State Fairs
Exhibits: Oregon State Fairs
References: OSF (1899, 1904, 06–08)
Media: Oil
Specialty: Marines, landscapes

Another of the early Oregon State Fair contributors, Mrs. Pogue lived in Salem.

PORTAL, Joseph M.

b. 1908 Chicago, IL
d. 1988 McMinnville, OR
Education: Art Institute of Chicago; Kansas City
Membership: American Artists Professional League; Oregon Society of Artists
Exhibits: Young's Gallery—Chicago (1928); American Artists Professional League (37); Salem Federal Art Center (37, 38); St. Benedict's Abbey—Mt. Angel (37); Sacred Heart Academy—Salem (38); Portland Art Museum
References: ALM; COL; WWN; A2 (1940)
Media: Oil, tempera, watercolor, pastel, pen and ink
Specialty: Religious subject matter

Trained at the Art Institute of Chicago, Joseph Portal was a member of the American Artists Professional League and participated in the WPA. He traveled and studied in Europe, Africa, Canada, and Mexico. He also served in the Coast Guard. Later a professor at public and Roman Catholic Colleges, Portal decorated interiors with religious subject matter. St. Joseph's Church in Salem showed evidence of his medieval European influences. He lived in Salem in the 1940s.

POST, Charles W.

b. 1857 Gallon, OH
d. 1922 Troutdale, OR
Education: Royal Academy—Munich: *Piloty;* Ecole des Beaux Arts; Rome; Florence, Italy: *Dannar*
Membership: Mutual Art Association
Collections: Baldwin Saloon Collection
Exhibits: Mutual Art Association (1914, 15)
References: ARTC
Media: Oil, prints (etching)
Specialty: Landscapes, portraits, animals

Trained in the classical European art tradition, Charles Post began a teaching career after he returned to America. He came west in 1908 at age fifty and bought ten acres of land in Corbett,

Oregon, where the scenic beauty reminded him of Switzerland. He built a studio at Chanticleer Point overlooking the Columbia River on the site where the Women's Forum State Park (Crown Point) stands today. From this vantage point he was able to paint incredible vistas of the Columbia Gorge. He believed that the river and hills portrayed the ultimate scenic value. In 1919 he spent several months in the hills above Mosier, converting a homesteader's cabin into a studio. His regard for animals was demonstrated in the painting of a Jersey cow, exhibited at the Pacific International Livestock Exposition. He also had an interest in photography and was working on a book of etchings at the time of his death.

PRASCH, Richard (Dick) John

b. 1918 Seattle, WA
d. 1986 Portland, OR
Education: California Institute of Fine Arts (1937–38); Art Center School of Design—Los Angeles (39–41); University of Washington (48); University of Oregon (51)
Membership: Artists Equity; Portland Art Museum (Artist Membership); Northwest Watercolor Society
Awards: Seattle Art Museum (1953, 56); Northwest Watercolor Society (54); Oregon Centennial (59)
Collections: University of Oregon; Seattle Art Museum; Portland Art Museum; Marylhurst College; Oregon Historical Society; Portland State University; Pacific University
Exhibits: Seattle Art Museum (4PS 1954); Northwest Watercolor Society; Portland Art Museum; Henry Art Gallery—University of Washington (51, 55); Western Washington Fair; Santa Barbara Museum of Art (57); Portland State University (58); Marylhurst College (IPS 58); Harvey Welch Gallery (59); Willamette University; Denver Art Museum (1PS); Oregon Centennial (59); Oregon Historical Society (90)
References: COL; A3 (1950, 56–58); C6; C7 (44–46, 47, 50–59); C9; C20; C27; C29 (46, 52–54); C30 (53, 54)
Media: Oil, watercolor, prints
Specialty: Landscapes, cityscapes

Richard Prasch was an art instructor first at Seattle University in 1955, the University of Oklahoma, the University of Oregon, and then at Portland State College (now Portland State University). His exhibit at the Henry Gallery in 1955 featured watercolors that had been on view in Oakland, California. A review of his exhibition at Harvey Welch's in 1959 describes Portland as seen through the artist's eyes, "the relationship of colors, shapes ... the city in a reflective mood after hours." His style was impressionistic in the early years, later becoming more abstract. The Portland Art Museum's Rental Sales Gallery represented him.

PRICE, Clayton Sumner (C.S.)

b. 1874 Bedford, IA
d. 1950 Portland, OR
Education: St. Louis School of Fine Arts: *Russell*
Membership: American Artists Professional League; Oregon Society of Artists; Society of Independent Artists—New York
Awards: Seattle Art Museum (1929); American Artists Professional League (32); Portland Art Museum (50)
Collections: National Museum of American Art; Portland Art Museum; Oregon Historical Society; Seattle Art Museum; Metropolitan Museum of Art; Timberline Lodge

Collection; Oakland Museum; Multnomah County Library Collection; Goodman Collection; Stenzel Collection; University of Oregon; Reed College; Museum of Modern Art; Detroit Institute of the Arts; Los Angeles County Museum of Art; Arlene and Harold Schnitzer Collection; Riley Collection

Exhibits: Beaux Art Gallery—San Francisco (1PS 1925); League of Fine Arts—Berkeley (1PS 27); Oregon Society of Artists (1PS 29); Portland Art Museum (1PS 42, 50, 51); Seattle Art Museum; American Artists Professional League (32, 33, 37); San Francisco Museum of Art (43); Detroit Institute of the Arts (44); Valentine Gallery—New York (1PS 45); Western Washington Fair; Museum of Modern Art (46); Reed College (1PS 48, 50); Oregon Journal (1PS 50); Los Angeles County Museum of Art; Oakland Museum; Henry Art Gallery—University of Washington (51); Walker Art Center—Minneapolis (51); Corcoran Gallery of Art—Washington, D.C.; Metropolitan Museum of Art; California Palace of the Legion of Honor—San Francisco; Oregon Centennial (59); Oregon Historical Society (90)

References: ALM; ART; BI; COL; DAV; DAW; FIE; HAV; HUG; MAL SUP; OET; SAM; SIA; WWN; WWW; A1 (1953); A2 (40, 42, 44, 46, 48); A3 (37, 49, 50); A4 (29, 52, 59); C3 (29, 32, 49); C6; C7 (29); C8; C9; C10; C15 (46); C18; C30 (46); CD (40, 41, 43–4); MYH; M2

Media: Oil

Specialty: Landscapes (ranches), portraits, birds, animals, murals

See artwork in color section

See photograph of artist on p. 87

C.S. Price was a gentle man, reclusive by nature, who had an immeasurable effect on the artists of his time and on the tradition of western art. Born the third of thirteen children in Bedford, Iowa in 1874, Price's family progressively moved west, buying and tending range cattle. As a young man, his ability to draw and carve attracted the attention of a wealthy cattleman who agreed to finance a year of art school in St. Louis. After this training, Price returned to Wyoming, repaid the debt, and homesteaded. By 1908 his mother had died and he joined his father and family in Alberta, Canada. Having decided to pursue an artistic career, in 1909 Price moved to Portland and became an illustrator for *The Pacific Monthly*, which later merged with *Sunset*. His years of experience on the range gave him first-hand knowledge of the horse and cowboy subjects that he helped popularize.

A trip to California in 1915, including a visit to the Panama-Pacific Exposition in San Francisco, was his first exposure to Modern Art. He decided this was what he wanted to do. He moved to Monterey, California, rented space in the Stevenson House, and sold his paintings. He became known as one of the early modernists and experimented with innovative ways to paint. He was often dissatisfied with much of his work; for each canvas completed, five or six were painted over or scraped off. In 1928 he returned to Portland and remained there until his death in 1950.

During the decade of the 1930s Price was an active participant in the Government's Federal Art Project. He was the first artist on the rolls in Region 16 (Portland). In less than a year he had completed eight large paintings, and later, murals. Timberline Lodge displays the murals, *Huckleberry Pickers* and *Pack Train*. The Multnomah County Library in Portland includes *Indians* and

Pioneers in its collection.

Around 1940, when Price was sixty-six, there was a change in his style and motivation. The artist searched for a way to use increasingly abstract painting as a vehicle for spiritual development. Animal subjects remained, but they became translucent to allow the spirit to appear from behind the form. Where details were lacking, the essence remained.

His national reputation continued to grow, but Price avoided the limelight. He refused exhibition commitments and insisted that he should be allowed to sell works to friends. He never accepted students, but greatly influenced other artists: Rockwell Carey*, William Hayes*, Charles Heaney*, Howard Sewall*, and Amanda Snyder* among many others. Snyder's son, Eugene, wrote a poignant account of his impressions of Price. His death in 1950 prompted the Portland Art Museum and the Walker Art Museum in Minneapolis to mount a joint exhibition and publish a catalog of C.S. Price's work. It brought together 543 works from 117 owners. Since there was little documentation during Price's life, this was finally an opportunity to date and catalog the work; many friends and family members assisted in the process. One of Oregon's most significant artists, his view of the West helped shape America's view of the West as well.

PRUITT, Ida Bessie

b. 1905 Kalispell, MT
d. 1991 Springfield, OR
Education: Bible University—Eugene: *Dunn, Elkins* (1923–25); University of Oregon (23–24); Springfield: *Swank*
Membership: Springfield Art League; Oregon Society of Artists; National Museum of Women in the Arts
Collections: Favell's Museum of Western Art and Artifacts—Klamath Falls; Willamalane Memorial Building—Springfield
Exhibits: Meier and Frank Co. (1PS 1959)
References: KOV
Media: Oil, pen and pencil, colored pencil, pastel, prints (etching)
Specialty: Landscapes, western, religious, nature

Ida Pruitt had some formal art training but was mainly self-taught. She was president of The Puyallup High School Art Club in Washington in 1923. Her first commission was an illustrated volume of poems by Elmore Gilstrap published in 1929. She then completed etchings for a book by Mary Dunn. She worked for several magazines through 1946. Pruitt's first exhibit was a display in the Old Lamp Bookstore in Eugene in 1953, which won the first award during that city's Fall Opening Festival. By 1958 she began to do serious work in oil and completed an exhibit of twenty paintings at the Meier and Frank Co. the following year. She served as a judge in the traditional art category of the Oregon Centennial (1959) and at a later Oregon State Fair painting exhibit.

Pruitt often sketched and painted in eastern Oregon's Steens Mountain area while accompanying her husband, Veltie. Aided by her daughter, Janice Gutenberg, she later produced a book of her paintings, *Steens Mountain Heritage Scrapbook* (1982). Credited with more than 300 major oil paintings and many miniatures and drawings, she received the statewide honor of Oregon Artist of the year in 1985. Kovinick (see Ref. KOV) gives her first name as *Ina* and a birthdate of 1904.

Q

QUIGLEY, Edward Burns

b. 1895 Park River, ND
d. 1984 Portland, OR
Education: Chicago Academy of Fine Arts; Art Institute of Chicago
Membership: American Artists Professional League; Oregon Society of Artists; Attic Club
Awards: Oregon Society of Artists (1936, 37, 43, 44)
Collections: Oregon Historical Society; Maryhill Museum—Goldendale, Washington; Stenzel Collection; Hallie Ford Museum of Art—Willamette University; Lundberg Collection; Huntington Collection; Burns Courthouse; Capitol Collection—Salem; Cowboy Hall of Fame—Oklahoma
Exhibits: Oregon Society of Artists; American Artists Professional League (1938); Portland Art Museum; Kharouba Gallery (46); J.K. Gill Gallery (46); Elfstrom Gallery; Lincoln County Art Center (48); Western Washington Fair; Maryhill Museum—Goldendale, Washington (49); Graves Gallery—San Francisco (1PS); Oregon State Fair; Oregon Centennial (59); Oregon Historical Society (90); Clatsop County Historical Society (94)
References: ALM; COL; DAV; DAW; SAM; OET; WWN; WWW; A2 (1940); C3 (34, 36, 43, 46–51); C9; C11; C13 (46–48); C14; C30 (49); CD (31)
Media: Oil, watercolor
Specialty: Western scenery, animals, murals
See artwork in color section
See photograph of artist on p. 88

Ed Quigley had a keen fascination with horses from his childhood days in Spokane, Washington. It was said that as a toddler he bit cookies into the shape of horses. Quigley's penchant for drawing was encouraged by his family and teachers. In second grade he won his first art competition for his drawing of a group of pigs. He served in World War I, then settled in the Midwest to attend art school and pursue a career as a commercial artist.

In 1930 Quigley returned to the Northwest, living in a cabin at the base of Mt. Hood and maintaining a small studio in Portland. During the Depression he painted murals for public buildings and private homes. A meeting with the Yakama Indians, who kept large herds of horses, led to a new direction in his work. Quigley helped run the wild horses and worked on trail drives and round-ups. These experiences led him to paint intensely personal visions of the Oregon High Desert, often picturing bunch grass and horses against the rimrock.

Quigley was also a wood-carver, a skill he learned as a child. He produced circus animals and trains which, along with some of his paintings, are in the collection of the Oregon Historical Society. During his WPA years he painted full-wall murals at the Irvington School in Portland. It took him four months to complete the commission, for which he was paid forty dollars a month and was "doggoned glad to get it." He used only eight colors on his palette, saying this was to avoid being restricted by details.

Quigley received the Governor's Arts Award in 1982 and was a life member of the Oregon Society of Artists. In 1984 he was inducted into the National Cowboy Hall of Fame in Oklahoma City for "his paintings and carvings that depict life in the Old West." A Quigley painting and a carving are in their collection. He signed his works *E. B. Quigley* or *Quig*.

R

RAMBERG, Lucy Dodd

b. 1876 Portland, OR
d. 1929 Florence, Italy
Education: Berlin; Munich (1896); Paris: *Collin* (98); Rome (1901)
Membership: Mutual Art Association
Collections: Reed College; Oregon Historical Society
Exhibits: Florence (1912); Munich (15); Mutual Art Association (15); Meier and Frank Co. (21–22); Portland Art Museum (1PS 22)
References: ALM; BI; DAV; PET; WWW; ARTC
Specialty: Portraits, still life, landscapes
See artwork in color section

Born in Portland, Lucy Ramberg studied in Europe and married a German art critic, who died during World War I. She established a studio in Munich in 1918, but post-War problems forced her to return to Portland in 1920. She enjoyed a brief success there, including a one-person show of her portraits at the Portland Art Museum. Ramberg desired to return to Italy, where she had a villa and some property. There she arranged classes and European art tours for students at her home, the Lucy Dodd Ramberg School for American Girls. She died of blood poisoning in Florence in 1929.

RANDALL, Alice. *See* MARSH, Alice

RAVENSCROFT, Ellen

b. 1885 Jackson, MS
d. 1949 New York City, NY
Education: New York: *Chase, Henri;* National Academy of Design; Paris
Membership: Society of Oregon Artists; Society of Independent Artists—New York; New York Society of Women Artists
Collections: Oregon Historical Society
Awards: C.L. Wolfe Art Club (1908, 15); Kansas City Art Institute—Kansas City, Missouri (23)
Exhibits: Portland Art Museum; Paris Salon—d'Automne (1912); Society of Oregon Artists (13); Society of Independent Artists—New York (17, 22, 24–27, 30, 35, 36, 40)); Salons of America (22–24, 34); Kansas City Art Institute—Kansas City, Missouri (23)
References: BEN; BI; DAV; FIE; HAV; MAL; SA; SIA; PET; THI; WWW; YNG; A2 (1912–14); M2; M3
Media: Oil, prints (lithograph)
Specialty: Landscapes, portraits, still life

Ellen Ravenscroft was living in Portland by 1912. A *Spectator* article recounts her return after spending the summer in New York City, where the purpose of the trip was to paint and live in an "art atmosphere." She exhibited a portrait and other works in New York and Paris later in the year. Ravenscroft was one of the founders and officers of the Society of Oregon Artists in 1913. She was a teacher at St. Helen's Hall from 1911 to 1914, painting in her studio at the school. She lectured on the importance of art training and exhibiting in the United States, emphasizing that a European education was no longer necessary. In her case she had studied abroad, but had come home to paint. As late as 1917, a *Spectator* article tells of her recognition in the East and comments on the work to be exhibited at the Society of Independent Artists later that year. In 1917 Ravenscroft moved to New York City.

RAYMOND, Kate Cordon

b. 1888 Cuero, TX
d. 1961 Portland, OR
Education: *C. McKim**
Membership: Oregon Society of Artists
Collections: Humpal Collection
Awards: Multnomah County Fair (1937, 38); Oregon State Fairs (37, 38); Oregon Society of Artists (36, 38, 39, 44)
Exhibits: Oregon Society of Artists; Oregon State Fairs (1937, 38); Multnomah County Fairs (37, 38); Portland Art Museum; Citizens for Art Group (59); Oregon Centennial (59)
References: COL; DAV; DAW; WWN; A2 (1942, 44, 46); C3 (27, 28, 45–51)
Media: Oil, watercolor
Specialty: Landscapes, portraits

Kate Raymond studied under the Oregon artist C. C. McKim*. She was a charter member of the Oregon Society of Artists and was active in Oregon from the 1920s to the 50s. Raymond's paintings won awards at County and State Fairs and the Oregon Society of Artists shows.

REED, Cyrus A.

b. 1825 Grafton Co., NH
d. 1910 Portland, OR
Education: Union Academy
Collections: Oregon Historical Society
Exhibits: U.S. Centennial Exhibition —Philadelphia (1876); France; Germany
References: CD (1894, 1896–1910)
Media: Oil
Specialty: Landscapes, panorama

Cyrus Reed arrived in California in 1849 and settled in Oregon a few months later. He supported himself in Portland as a signpainter then moved to Salem, where he helped found the Willamette Woolen Mills. Painting was always a strong interest and he pursued it as an avocation. Reed was appointed the state's first adjutant general in 1852 and was elected to the state legislature in 1862, where he served four terms. Reed also taught art and his students received favorable newspaper coverage for their 1874 entries in the Oregon State Fair. When he returned to Portland to live, he supported himself by selling real estate, but continued to paint. Reed is listed in the artist section of the Portland City Directory in 1894 and later in 1896 through 1910.

Reed's most memorable work was a substantial three foot by seven foot panorama depicting an elevated river view of Oregon City. This work may have been the *Panorama of Oregon* that was shown at the United States Centennial Exhibition in Philadelphia and then later featured in exhibitions in France and Germany.

RICEN, Stanley

b. 1909 Portland, OR
d. 1977 Multnomah Co., OR
Education: Museum Art School
Membership: Attic Club
Exhibits: Portland Art Museum
References: COL; WWN; A2 (1932, 33, 46, 48); C10; ARTC
Media: Oil, watercolor, tempera
Specialty: Landscape

After studying at the Museum Art School, Stanley Ricen became a commercial artist. He was associated with the Attic Club as a member and manager. He participated in the 1934 WPA exhibit at the Portland Art Museum.

RICHARDSON, Ernest C.

b. 1900 Millnocket, ME
d. 1981 Portland, OR
Education: Académie de Colarossi

(1920); Académie Julian; Art Institute of Chicago; Smith School —Los Angeles; Museum Art School

Membership: Attic Club; Portland Art Museum (Artist Membership)

Collections: Ford Motor Company Collection—Dearborn, Michigan; Library of Congress

Exhibits: Portland Art Museum; Pennsylvania Academy of Fine Art—Philadelphia (1947); Lincoln County Art Center

References: A2 (1919, 21, 41); A3 (50, 51, 53, 54); ARTC

Media: Watercolor, prints

Specialty: History

Ernest Richardson achieved fame for his illustrations of the books by noted Oregon writer, Stewart Holbrook. He worked in the *Oregonian* art department from 1941 until he retired in 1972. During that period he was a frequent exhibitor at the Portland Art Museum and was a founding member of the Attic Club. He also enjoyed a career as designer of scenic Hollywood movie sets. His design decorates the bookplate for special gifts to the Multnomah County Library.

RICHARDSON, Francis (Fanny) Boyd

b. 1853 McMinnville, OR

d. 1931 Portland, OR

Education: Willamette University

Awards: Oregon State Fairs

Collections: Oregon Historical Society

Exhibits: Oregon State Fairs

References: OSF (1890, 93, 1896–1900, 06); M2; M3

Media: Oil

Specialty: China painting, marines, seascapes

Fanny Boyd married a physician from Salem, where they both lived before moving to The Dalles. In 1910 she and her husband settled in Portland. She was an Oregon State Fair entrant at the turn of the century. The Oregon Historical Society has examples of her china painting and a marine.

RICHARDSON, Harley

b. 1893 La Grande, OR

d. 1947 La Grande, OR

Education: University of Oregon

References: OR (Eastern Oregon College)

Media: Watercolor

Specialty: Landscapes

Harley Richardson spent his whole life in La Grande. A simple coin toss determined that he would buy an art shop instead of dispensing medicine, thus Harris' Art Shop became Richardson's Art and Gift Shop in the 1920s and 1930s. He was a well-known photographer who produced picture post cards and tinted photos of this historic region. He devoted much of his life to a study of the Grand Ronde Valley and the Old Oregon Trail. Richardson later sold the art shop and became business manager of the La Grande Hospital.

ROBBINS, Esther. *See* HURGREN, Esther

ROBINSON, Amy Margaret

b. 1896

d. 1989 Douglas Co., OR

Membership: Southern Oregon Art Association

Collections: Douglas County Museum

Exhibits: Southern Oregon Art Association (1947, 48, 52); Southern Oregon Art Exhibit

References: C26 (1954); OR (Douglas County Museum)

Media: Watercolor

According to the Douglas County Museum, Amy Robinson painted in the Roseburg area. She was a member of the Southern Oregon Art Association and exhibited with them and at the Southern Oregon Art Exhibit in 1954.

ROBINSON, Regina Dorland

b. 1891 Jacksonville, OR
d. 1917 San Mateo, CA
Education: Jacksonville: *P. Britt**; Portland (1907–08); Pennsylvania Academy of Fine Art—Philadelphia: *Chase* (11), San Francisco: *Chittenden*
Membership: San Francisco Sketch Club
Awards: Rogue River Fair (1907)
Collections: Southern Oregon Historical Society; Jacksonville Museum
Exhibits: Portland Art Museum; Portland Hotel (1916); Holland Hotel—Medford (16); San Francisco (16)
References: KOV; A2 (1916); OR (Southern Oregon Historical Society)
Media: Oil, watercolor, charcoal, pastel, gouache
Specialty: Portraits, landscapes (southern Oregon)
See artwork in color section

When Dorland Robinson began showing artistic promise at the age of five, her parents built a studio in the family home in Jacksonville. In elementary school she did portraits and sepia pencil sketches of her friends. In 1905 she was greatly impressed by the art at the Lewis and Clark Centennial Exposition in Portland. Upon her return home she became more serious than ever about becoming an artist. Her portrait of Portland mayor *George Williams* was displayed at Portland City Hall. All her entries at the Rogue River Fair in Grants Pass won first prizes.

Her doting father decided his talented daughter deserved an eastern art education; she accompanied him on a visit to Philadelphia where she was enrolled at the Pennsylvania Academy of Fine Art. Her studies continued in Oregon, then in California, where she joined the San Francisco Sketch Club. In 1916 she had five works, in a variety of media, on display at the Portland Art Museum. There were plans for a one-person show at the Museum the following year that never took place due to her untimely death. The circumstances surrounding her death were unclear: a hasty marriage, a rumored pregnancy, a divorce. A breakdown followed and suicide ended a promising career in 1917.

ROCKWELL, Cleveland Salter

b. 1837 Youngstown, OH
d. 1907 Portland, OR
Education: New York University (1856); Europe; England
Membership: Portland Art Club; Oregon Art Association; Portland Sketch Club
Awards: Portland Mechanics Fair (1887)
Collections: Oregon Historical Society; Powell Collection; Stenzel Collection; Miranda Collection; Clatsop County Historical Society; Counting Eagles Collection; Maritime Museum, Flavel House—Astoria
Exhibits: San Francisco Art Association (1873, 74, 77, 83); Portland Art Club (86); Portland Mechanics Fairs; North Pacific Industrial Exposition (89, 90); Portland Industrial Expositions (91, 92, 93); Oregon Industrial Exposition (95); Oregon Art Association (96); Portland Sketch Club (98); Bernstein's Art Shop (99); Philadelphia (1908); University of Oregon (59); Washington State Capitol Museum (88); Oregon Historical Society (90); Clatsop County Historical Society (94)
References: DAV; DAW; GER; HUG;

OET; WWW; C2 (1889–93, 95); C4 (79, 83, 85–87); C9; C11; C12; C16; C24; ARTC; CD (86, 89, 1896–1906); M1
Media: Watercolor, oil
Specialty: Marines, landscapes
See artwork in color section

Cleveland Rockwell was a direct descendant of William Bradford, the Puritan Governor of Massachusetts. An engineer by profession, Rockwell worked for the U.S. Coast and Geodetic Survey from 1857 to 1892. During the Civil War he was employed by the War Department, taking part in the Union Army's march through Georgia. The military maps he drew were considered the most accurate ever made to that time. He was appointed Chief of the U.S. Coast and Geodetic Survey in the Northwest, living in San Francisco from 1867 to 1878, then in Portland, where he remained until his death. He mapped the Oregon Coast and the Columbia and Willamette Rivers, thereby promoting navigation and economic development in the region.

He painted—an avocation throughout his professional career—in the style of the English Romantic painters. His scientific knowledge of the subjects made his canvases historically accurate as well as aesthetically pleasing. Rockwell's works were filled with such detail that one could experience, for instance, the reality of a floating cannery or a fishing fleet at the mouth of the Columbia. Having worked outdoors for many years, he painted nature as he saw it, without embellishments. In contrast to Bierstadt's* romantic approach, Rockwell did not exaggerate the mountains or rearrange scenery to improve upon nature. When he added figures to his paintings, they appeared only in their natural environments.

Rockwell was vice-president of the Portland Art Club and president of the Oregon Artists Association. His work was exhibited in 1899 at Bernstein's Art Shop in Portland. He is considered by many to be Oregon's best nineteenth-century painter. He sometimes signed his work using the initials *C.R.*

ROLLINS, Warren Eliphalet

b. 1861 Carson City, NV
d. 1962 Winslow, AZ
Education: San Francisco School of Design: *Williams* (1878)
Membership: Oregon Art Association; Portland Sketch Club
Awards: San Francisco School of Design (1878–81); Pan-California Exposition—San Diego (1915)
Collections: Huntington Library—San Marino, California; Stenzel Collection; University of Oregon; Oakland Museum; San Francisco Museum of Art; Santa Fe Railroad; Post Office, Harvey House—Gallup, New Mexico; Hubbell Trading Post—Ganado, Arizona
Exhibits: Portland Industrial Expositions (1892, 95); Oregon Industrial Exposition (95); Oregon Art Association (96); Bernstein's Art Shop (99); Pan-California Exposition—San Diego (1915); Washington State Historical Society—Tacoma (85)
References: BI; DAV; DAW; HAV; MAL; SAM; WWW; C2 (1892, 95); C16; C28; ARTC; CD (92–94, 1896–1902)
Media: Oil, watercolor, gouache, pastel, crayon
Specialty: Landscapes, portraits, marines, Indians

Warren Eliphalet Rollins was born in Nevada and educated in California and the East before coming to Tacoma, Washington. He operated an art school there for two years, then headed for Portland in 1892. He was a regular contributor to the Industrial Fairs, one of the earliest venues for artists to exhibit their work. He also was a member of, and instructor at, the Portland Sketch Club and a Board member of the Oregon Art Association. His work was featured in their 1896 exhibition.

The Columbia River was one of his favorite subjects. He also spent time along the coast, including one summer in Newport. His illustrations appeared in *The Pacific Monthly*, and he wrote articles on art. It was Rollins who called for a permanent building to house the work of local artists after seeing Frank DuMond's* exhibit at Bernstein's Gallery. Shortly thereafter, the Portland Art Museum opened its doors. Rollins may have played an important role in promoting its establishment.

A newspaper article titled "Artist to Leave West", written around 1903 identified Warren Rollins as planning to travel to Boston to study with a noted colorist and landscapist. He was then to travel to Europe for an extended period before returning to Portland and participating in the Lewis and Clark Centennial Exposition. There is no record that he took this trip, nor is there any record that he exhibited at the Lewis and Clark Exposition in 1905. He was living in Southern California by 1910, and his friend, E.I. Couse*, residing in Taos by this time, encouraged him to visit. Rollins' career continued in the Southwest, furthering his interest in the landscape and Indians of the area. He was one of the first painters to live among the residents of the Pueblo villages of Arizona and New Mexico. From the mid-1940s until his death he lived in Arizona, where he was regarded as "dean" of the Taos and Santa Fe art colonies. His wife, Birdella Bracken Rollins, was also an artist and member of the Oregon Art Association, where she exhibited in 1896.

ROSINA, Mary (Sister)

b. 1888 Pueblo, CO

d. 1977 Portland, OR

Education: St. Mary's Academy; University of Washington; Museum Art School; University of Oregon, Extension; College of Arts and Crafts—Oakland

Membership: American Artists Professional League; Oregon Society of Artists

Awards: American Artists Professional League (1937, 38); Oregon State Fair (27)

Collections: St. Mary's Academy

Exhibits: Oregon State Fair (1927); Portland Art Museum; American Artists Professional League (37, 38); J.K. Gill Gallery (37, 38); Oregon Society of Artists

References: ALM; COL; WWN; A2 (1938, 40, 42, 44); C3 (38)

Media: Oil, watercolor, pastel

Specialty: Still life, landscapes, florals

Sister Mary Rosina taught studio art at St. Mary's Academy during a distinguished career that lasted from 1924 to 1977. Highly respected by Portland's art community, she signed her artwork with initials.

ROTHSTEIN, Theresa M.

b. 1893 Richmond, MN ***d.***

Education: Museum Art School; *C. Keller**

Membership: Oregon Society of Artists; American Artists Professional League

Awards: Oregon Society of Artists (1932, 38, 39); American Artists Professional League (34, 36)

Collections: Portland Woman's Club

Exhibits: Oregon Society of Artists;

Portland Art Museum; American Artists Professional League (1934–38); Salem (35, 36); Lincoln County Art Center (48)
References: DAV; DAW; HAV; MAL SUP; PET; WWW; A2 (1933, 34, 42, 46, 48); C3 (28–36, 38, 39, 45–51); C14
Media: Oil
Specialty: Landscape

Theresa Rothstein exhibited at the Portland Art Museum in the 1930s and 1940s. Her prize-winning painting from the American Artists Professional League competition of 1934 now hangs in the dining room of the Portland Woman's Club. Rothstein also participated in Salem exhibitions in 1935 and 1936 as well as the Lincoln County Art Center show featuring Oregon artists in 1948. References listed a Vancouver, Washington address.

ROUTLEDGE, Frederick A.

b. 1871 Abilene, KS
d. 1936 Portland, OR
Membership: Circle A Club; Society of Oregon Artists; Oregon Art Association
Exhibits: Portland Art Museum; Society of Oregon Artists (1913)
References: DAV; HUG; A2 (1912); ARTC; CD (1893, 95, 1909, 10, 12, 14–18)
Media: Oil, watercolor, prints (lithograph, engraving)
Specialty: Pictorial maps, portraits, genre, caricatures

Fred Routledge was a commercial artist who was also well known for his pictorial maps and contour map drawings. His first artwork in Portland was for *The West Shore* magazine; he later joined the *Oregonian* and became head of their art department from 1895 to 1906. Routledge and Rollin Caughey designed and worked together on the engravings for the front page of the Lewis and Clark Centennial Exposition official publication as well as a poster featuring a bird's eye view of the Exposition grounds. In 1906 Routledge joined artists A. Burr*, C. Murray (Dowling)*, C. Chapin, C. L. Smith*, and L. Pease* in contributing to Edward Thomson's book of caricatures of Portland citizens titled *As We See 'Em*. He also had his own commercial art studio until his death in 1936. Locations for his studio varied: the McKay Building in 1910, the Henry Building from 1911 to 1912, the Northwest Bank Building from 1914 to 1928, the American Bank Building from 1929 to 1932, and finally the Gerlinger Building until 1936.

Routlege was instrumental in helping organize the Circle A Art Club in 1911, for "men actively engaged in occupations which require a knowledge of art." A charter member of the early Society of Oregon Artists in 1913, he was also working in Los Angeles in pictorial advertising that same year. His wife, Lydia, was a teacher and china painter.

RUMSEY, Sarah Jane

b. ca. 1830 New York City *d.*
Awards: Oregon State Fairs
Collections: Oregon Historical Society
Exhibits: Oregon State Fairs; Oregon Historical Society (1990); Autry Museum—Los Angeles (95)
References: C9; C23; CD (1871, 73, 74); OSF (66, 70, 73); M2; M3
Media: Oil, watercolor, pastel
Specialty: Landscapes, portraits

Sarah Jane Rumsey's exact birth and death dates are unavailable. Educated by some of the best teachers in the eastern United States, she received a great deal of press attention when she arrived in Oregon. Rumsey lived in Oregon only ten years, from 1865 to 1870 in Salem and from 1870 to 1875 in Portland, where she had a studio in the Corbett Building. Two of her portraits, completed in 1870, are in the Oregon Historical Society Collections: *Mrs Matthew P. Deady*, watercolor and pastel, and *Judge Riley Evans*, pastel. She worked as a photographer and photo-colorist for the leading photographer of the time, Joseph Buchtel, whose studio was adjacent to hers. Sarah Jane Rumsey was the first known female professional artist in the state and the first to advertise, announcing landscape painting lessons in Salem's *Oregon Statesman* in the mid 1860s.

RUNQUIST, Albert Clarence

b. 1894 Aberdeen, WA
d. 1971 Portland, OR
Education: University of Oregon (1920); Museum Art School; Art Students League (29–32)
Membership: Oregon Guild of Painters and Sculptors; American Artists' Congress
Awards: Portland Art Museum (1938); Oregon Centennial (59); U.S. Treasury Department Post Office Competition
Collections: Portland Art Museum; Oregon Historical Society; Powell Collection; Goodman Collection; Booth Collection; Tonkon Torp Collection; University of Oregon Library; Parsons Collection; Huntington Collection; Pathways Collection; Capitol Collection—Salem; Cofield Collection; Pacific University; Hallie Ford Museum of Art—Willamette University
Exhibits: Portland Art Museum (2PS 1957); American Artists' Congress (37, 39); New York World's Fair (39); San Francisco Museum of Art (40, 43); Western Washington Fair; Oregon Society of Artists; Oregon Guild of Painters and Sculptors (48); Oregon Centennial (59); University of Oregon (75); Oregon Historical Society (90); Clatsop County Historical Society (94)
References: ALM; COL; DAV; DAW; HAV; WWN; WWW; A2 (1933, 34, 38, 40–42, 46, 48); A3 (37, 39, 51); A4 (59); C6; C8; C9; C10; C11; C15 (46); C22; C27; C30 (46)
Media: Oil, tempera, prints
Specialty: Seascapes (beach, coast), murals
See artwork in color section

The younger of the Runquist brothers by three years, Albert was born in Aberdeen, Washington and educated at the University of Oregon, the Museum Art School, and the Art Students League in New York. He exhibited at the New York World's Fair in 1939 and at the San Francisco Museum of Art the following year. He worked on the WPA Post Office project in Sedro Wooley, Washington in 1940, but left to be a shipbuilder for Willamette Iron and Steel. He continued at the Kaiser Shipyards in Vancouver, Washington until 1945 and the end of World War II.

In 1946 the Runquist brothers, Albert and Arthur, moved into the Harry Wentz* house at Neahkahnie on the Oregon Coast. They lived and worked there for eighteen years. Albert commuted to Portland in 1946 to teach at the Museum Art School. The years on the Coast were productive; they lived in relative isolation and devoted their lives to painting. A Portland Art Museum catalog states: "Working within a limited range of color he achieves canvases which are genuinely poetic interpretations of the coastal scenes he knows so intimately. Driftwood, fishermen, boats, surf dunes and meadows, expressed with a light, nervous brushstroke, exist in a cool, silvery light." Albert's work appeals to the eye and emotions. He painted at the scene and worked quickly to capture the light before it disappeared. "Nature does not sit still to have her portrait painted," Runquist stated.

The two brothers returned to Portland in 1963. Albert continued to paint until 1970 and died the following year. There was an original quality about the work of the Runquist brothers, and many times they were thought of as one. It is often difficult to distinguish the difference in style between the two. They felt signatures were not important and left many works unsigned. When Albert developed medical problems, Arthur signed his paintings for him.

RUNQUIST, Arthur

b. 1891 South Bend, WA
d. 1971 Portland, OR
Education: University of Oregon; Art Students League (1920); Museum Art School
Membership: Oregon Guild of Painters and Sculptors; Oregon Society of Artists; American Artists Professional League; American Artists' Congress
Awards: Portland Art Museum (1938); Oregon Centennial (59)
Collections: Portland Art Museum; Oregon Historical Society; Powell Collection; Goodman Collection; Booth Collection; Tonkon Torp Collection; University of Oregon Library; Kaiser Permanente Collection; Parsons Collection; Arlene and Harold Schnitzer Collection; Huntington Collection; Pathways Collection; Riley Collection; Capitol Collection—Salem; Cofield Collection; Pacific University; Hallie Ford Museum of Art—Willamette University
Exhibits: Oregon Society of Artists; Portland Art Museum (2PS 1957); American Artists' Congress (37, 40); New York World's Fair (39); Golden Gate International Exposition—San Francisco (39–40); Oregon Guild of Painters and Sculptors (48); American Artists Professional League; Seattle Art Museum; Oregon Centennial (59); University of Oregon (75); Oregon Historical Society (90); Clatsop County Historical Society (94)
References: ALM; COL; DAV; DAW; HAV; MAL SUP; WWN; WWW; A2 (1932, 34, 38–41, 48); A3 (49, 51–53); A4 (59); C3 (27); C6; C7 (28); C9; C10; C11; C22; CD (40, 41, 43–4)
Media: Oil, tempera, prints (lithograph, etching)
Specialty: Seascapes (beach, coast), murals
See artwork in color section

Arthur Runquist, the elder of the two Runquist brothers, was born in South Bend, Washington in 1891 and educated at the University of Oregon. He was Alfred Schroff's* assistant there until he left in 1920 to study at the Art Students League. Like his brother, Albert*, he exhibited at the New York World's Fair in 1939 and the American Artists' Congress in New York a year later. In addition, Arthur showed paintings at the Golden Gate International Exposition in 1939. Working for the WPA, he completed two murals with the theme, *Tree of Life* painted in 1938 at the University of Oregon. Albert also assisted on this project, as did Martina Gangle Curl*. Murals for Pendleton High School in Eastern Oregon were completed in 1941.

Arthur worked at the Kaiser Shipyards in Vancouver, Washington from 1942 to 1945. His painted documentation of the workers gained him a reputation for social commentary. Figures are more prominent in his work than in the work of his brother, Albert. Even landscapes were secondary in importance to the people appearing in them. Like his brother, he recorded life on the Oregon Coast with sensitivity. In their early paintings it is often difficult to distinguish one brother's work from the other. It was only later that their styles began to differ. Arthur's style was somewhat tighter, more linear and figure centered, while Albert's was looser, more painterly, showing atmosphere and effects of light.

In 1963 the brothers returned to Portland and continued painting until shortly before Arthur died in 1971. Albert died later the same year. Often thought of as one person because they lived their lives in parallel, the Runquist brothers played an important role as social critics of life in the 1930s and 1940s. They are also remembered as important chroniclers of life on the Oregon Coast.

RUSCO, Bessie A.

b. d.
Exhibits: Portland Art Museum
References: DAV; HUG; A2 (1917, 19–22); A3 (35)
Specialty: Landscape

Davenport and Hughes (see Ref. DAV, HUG) both listed a San Diego address for Bessie Rusco in the 1930s.

RUSSELL, Myna Ayers

b. 1884 Sioux City, IA
d. 1975 Portland, OR
Education: Morningside College Academy—Iowa; Chicago Academy of Fine Arts (1907)
Membership: American Artists Professional League; Oregon Society of Artists
Awards: American Artists Professional League (1936, 37); Oregon Society of Artists (32, 37); Oregon State Fair
Collections: Oregon Historical Society; Miranda Collection; Gerber Collection; Parsons Collection; Cofield Collection
Exhibits: Oregon State Fair; Oregon Society of Artists; American Artists Professional League (1933–38); Portland Art Museum; Capitol building—Salem (35)
References: A2 (1933, 34); C3 (29–37, 45, 46); M2; M3
Media: Oil
Specialty: Landscapes, florals, portraits
See artwork in color section

Myna Russell was awarded a scholarship to the Chicago Academy of Fine Arts. She established art and photography studios in Sioux City, Iowa and Chicago, Illinois before moving to Portland in 1920.

In 1927 she was a charter member of the Oregon Society of Artists, exhibiting with them and the American Artists Professional League. She painted landscapes and florals in an impressionistic manner. Russell was also a published poet. Her prize-winning painting, *Mountain Ash and Hydrangeas*, exhibited at American Artists Professional League Art Week, is in the Oregon Historical Society Collection.

RUSSELL, Robert Ashley

b. 1922 Yreka, CA
d. 1944 Normandy, France
Education: Museum Art School (1942); *E. Quigley**, *P. Keller**
Membership: Oregon Society of Artists
Awards: Portland Public Schools
Collections: Oregon Historical Society; Parsons Collection
Exhibits: Portland Art Museum; Trenton, New Jersey (1943, 44); Gimbel Auditorium—Philadelphia (44); Oregon Society of Artists
References: A2 (1942, 44); A4 (46)
Media: Oil, watercolor, gouache, pen and ink
Specialty: Landscapes, figures

Robert Ashley Russell's promising career ended in an early death. Educated at the Museum Art School in Portland, through a Portland Public School scholarship, and at the University of Oregon, he was represented in a Museum show in 1943. He sketched visitors to the Museum art galleries as well as famous jazz musicians and big band personalities. After he entered the military, his work was part of the *Art of the Armed Forces* shows of 1943 and 1944 in Trenton, New Jersey. Russell was also a skilled sculptor and ceramicist before losing his life in France during World War II. Most recently his work was featured in the 1995 Oregon Historical Society Exhibition, *Home From the War* and the 1989 retrospective, *I Hear Music*. The Russell family produced many artists: his father, Ashley Howard, was a commercial artist who lived in Oregon; his aunts, Grace Russell Fountain* and Mabel Russell Lowther, were also very accomplished, as was his grandmother, Jane H. Russell.

RUSSO, Michele

b. 1909 Waterbury, CN ***d.***
Education: Yale University (1934); Colorado Springs Fine Arts Center: *Robinson* (37)
Membership: Artists Equity
Awards: Frye Museum—Seattle (1959)
Collections: Portland Art Museum; University of Oregon; Seattle Art Museum; Reed College; Hilton Hotel; Equitable Center—Portland; Goodman Collection; Hallie Ford Museum of Art—Willamette University; Kaiser Permanente Collection; Multnomah Athletic Club Collection; Tonkon Torp Collection; Arlene and Harold Schnitzer Collection; Catlin Gabel School Collection; Huntington Collection
Exhibits: Colorado Springs Fine Arts Center (1936); A.C.A. Gallery—New York (40–41); Washington (1PS); Mattatuck Historical Society—Waterbury, Connecticut (47); Denver Art Museum; Portland Art Museum (1PS 53); Reed College (1PS 51, 52, 59); Kraushaar Gallery—New York (52); Seattle Art Museum; Dallas Museum of Fine Arts (54); National Museum of American Art; Reed College (59); Frye Museum—Seattle (59); Henry Art Gallery—University of Washington (3PS 59); Ruthermore Gallery—San Francisco (59); Oregon Centennial (59); University of Oregon (75); Oregon Historical Society (90)
References: ALM; BI; A3 (1950, 51, 53–58); A4 (52, 59); C2; C6; C7 (53, 54, 59); C9; C22; C27
Media: Oil
Specialty: Figures, still life
See artwork in color section
See photograph of artist on p. 88

When Michele Russo was five years old his mother took him to Italy for a visit that became a prolonged stay in a community threatened by World War I. Because he could not speak Italian and attend public school, Russo became the charge of a Catholic priest. This man became a surrogate father to the boy, teaching him the Italian language and culture, and introducing him to the priest's own enthusiasm for birds, gardens, art, and humanistic values. It was through this mentor that Russo's interest in art was cultivated by trips to art galleries. When the time came for the boy to leave Italy, the priest painted a canvas for him, which he kept as a reminder of the man and his influence. Russo was ten years old when his family returned to the United States, and Italian enough to feel like a misfit among his peers. Although he was an excellent student, he worked as a laborer after high school until he entered Yale in 1930. There he found the academically conservative approach to art frustrating, especially the rejection of Modern Art. After graduation he became a political activist, although this was not reflected in his paintings.

He met fellow artist Sally Haley* in 1934 and they wed in 1935. Russo was awarded WPA mural projects in Connecticut at Nathan Hale School in Hamden and Columbus School in New Haven. After attending the Colorado School of Fine Arts, Russo returned to New Haven and taught art and history in a Federal Education Program. During World War II, he was employed as a technician with the U.S. Rubber Company.

The Russos moved to Oregon in 1947. He began teaching art history, painting, and drawing at Portland's Museum Art School in 1948, remaining there until 1974. During this time he was sent, by the Museum Art School, to teach at venues throughout the state. He introduced academic subjects in art programs statewide. The Museum and the School were important advocates of Modern Art at that time.

Russo considered his early paintings allegorical and mysterious. His palette was dominated by dark blues, browns, and black. He was chided at Yale and again in Colorado for his generous use of black, but it remained an important part of his work. He said he sought clarity, not complexity, in his paintings. The formal aspects of art—the structure of a painting, the composition of the forms, as well as the simplicity and monumentality of shapes—were problems that continued to occupy him. He tried to avoid specific references in his work and used the figure as a symbol of universality. His simple, powerful style and strong colors lend themselves to the large scale of his canvases. One critic remarked that his work was "classical and abstract, simple and complex, provocative and staid, reserved and confrontational." Art critic Rachael Griffin* wrote of Russo: "If the design, the treatment of images in the canvas reassure us with their simplicity, the total import of the work does not." It was a paradox of his work that the apparent lightheartedness was undone by the "lurking, furtive and menacing" implications felt but not seen.

Michele Russo has been a tireless advocate for the rights of artists, earning him a position as a leading figure on the visual arts scene. He was one of the founders of Artists Equity, considering it a vehicle for uniting artists and the community. Later he helped found the Portland Center for the Visual Arts. In 1977 he was the first artist appointed to the Metropolitan Arts Commission in Portland, continuing his advocacy of artist and community unity, and in 1979 was presented the Governor's Award for the Arts.

RYAN, Charles Bryan

b. 1910 Fort Jones, CA ***d.***

Education: University of Oregon (1939, 40); Italy

Membership: Portland Art Museum (Artist Membership)

Collections: University of Oregon

Exhibits: Seattle Art Museum; Portland Art Museum (AM, 1PS 1954); Eugene; Lincoln County Art Center; San Francisco; University of Oregon (75)

References: A3 (1950, 51, 53, 55, 58); C7 (48); C22

Charles Ryan exhibited work at the Seattle Art Museum, the Lincoln County Art Center, and in San Francisco. The Portland Art Museum honored him with a one-person show in 1954. He listed a Eugene address in 1948, beginning a teaching career at the University of Oregon that spanned the years from 1951 to 1989.

RYDER, Phyllis Muirden

b. 1890
d. 1976 Portland, OR
Education: Glasgow School of Art —Scotland; Paris
Membership: American Artists Professional League
Exhibits: Portland Art Museum; Panama Pacific International Exposition—San Francisco (1915); American Artists Professional League (37); Oregon Centennial (59)
References: OET; A2 (1914); C5; CD (37–40)
Media: Watercolor
Specialty: Figures

Phyllis Muirden studied at the Glasgow School of Art for six years before coming to the United States in 1913. She became head of the art department at Commerce High School in Portland and was also a book illustrator. Muirden was the winner of the *Spectator* magazine cover contests in December of 1922, 1925, 1926, and 1927.

S

SALTZMAN, Florence. *See* HEIDEL, Florence

SANDGREN, Nelson (Nels) Ernest

b. 1917 Dauphin, Manitoba, Canada ***d.***

Education: Chicago Institute of Design; University of Oregon (1947); University of Michoacan —Mexico (48, 50, 51)

Membership: Master Watercolor Society of Oregon; Northwest Watercolor Society; Portland Art Museum (Artist Membership)

Awards: Northwest Watercolor Society (1955, 56); Seattle Art Museum (55); Oregon Centennial (59)

Collections: Portland Art Museum; Coos Art Museum; Salishan Lodge Collection; University of Oregon; Hallie Ford Museum of Art—Willamette University; Victoria and Albert Museum—London; Ford Motor Company—Dearborn, Michigan; Georgia Pacific; Kaiser Permanente Collection; Hurst Collection; Pathways Collection; Oregon State University

Exhibits: Klamath Falls Art Center (1940, 58); Portland Art Museum (AM, 1PS 52; 3PS 52; 1PS 57; 4PS 59); Stanford University (52); Northwest Watercolor Society (52, 55, 56, 57); Seattle Art Museum; Cheney Cowles Museum—Spokane; Santa Barbara Museum of Art (57); California Palace of the Legion of Honor—San Francisco; Reed College (1PS); Oregon State University (1PS); Master Watercolor Society of Oregon (58); Denver Art Museum; London; Oregon Centennial (59)

References: A2 (1942); A3 (49–58); C6; C7 (53–58); C20; C29 (52, 55–57)

Media: Oil, watercolor, prints (lithograph), collage

Specialty: Landscape, seascape (coast), murals

See artwork in color section

A Canadian by birth, Nelson Sandgren received his art education at the Chicago Institute of Design and then attended the University of Oregon. After his graduation in 1947, he joined the faculty of Oregon State College (now Oregon State University) in Corvallis and taught drawing and painting there for thirty-eight years. He continued to teach at the University of Oregon and offered workshops. His long exhibition history included shows in California, Colorado, and England, as well as Seattle and Portland. The Portland Art Museum honored him with one-person shows in 1952 and 1957. His murals are in the Lane County Courthouse in Eugene and the Oregon State University Library in Corvallis. The Portland Art Museum's Rental Sales Gallery has represented him.

Though he traveled widely, the Oregon Coast has been his main source of interest. He has been a keen observer of landscape and the sea. Stylistically he condensed the essence of the environment into simplified, dynamic strokes. Critics often described Sandgren as having "a light touch." He expressed his feelings thus: "Whether work appears abstract or literal in imagery is of no real importance. The final stylistic appearance will alter with one's own reaction and work almost always stems from the nature motif. I find in nature, particularly the Northwest, an endless array of exciting symbols to express my painting desires and necessities."

SAWARD, Virginia

b. d.

Membership: Artists Equity; Portland Art Museum (Artist Membership)

Awards: Washington Art Association (1949, 50, 53); Oregon Centennial (59)

Collections: Portland Art Museum; Kaiser Permanente Collection

Exhibits: Washington Art Association (1949, 50, 53); Portland Art Museum; Oregon Centennial (59)

References: A3 (1951, 55–58); C6

Media: Watercolor, prints

Virginia Saward was curator of the Kaiser Permanente Collection. She exhibited with the Washington Art Association and was a resident of Vancouver, Washington.

SCHAEFER, Harry

b. 1891 Lockhaven, PA

d. 1944 Portland, OR

Education: Chicago: *Aylward, Lydendecker brothers*

Membership: Oregon Society of Artists; Portland Art Museum (Artist Membership)

Collections: Painting Restoration Studio Collection; Humpal Collection

Exhibits: Oregon Society of Artists; Portland Art Museum; J.K. Gill Gallery (1PS 1932)

References: DAV; DAW; A2 (1932); C3 (30, 31); C16; CD (21–2, 23)

Media: Oil, watercolor, tempera, gouache

Specialty: Portraits

Harry Schaefer was a Portland commercial artist from 1918 through the mid 1930s. He spent six years living in Spokane, Washington. Schaefer had a printing shop in Portland and produced work for Eliza Barchus* and Samuel Parrott*, among others. He was a friend of artist Thayne Logan*. Schaefer was known for his portraits, which included one of Portland Mayor George L. Baker. The Northwest National Bank acquired a collection of his work. It was thought that Schaefer was an alcoholic. He died at the Multnomah County Poor Farm.

SCHLEY, Robert C.

b. 1902 Grand Rapids, MI

d. 1964 Portland, OR

Education: Art Institute of Chicago; Pennsylvania Academy of Fine Art—Philadelphia; National Academy of Design

Membership: Oregon Society of Artists; Attic Club; Portland Art Museum (Artist Membership)

Collections: Oregon Historical Society

Exhibits: Portland Art Museum

References: COL; WWN; A2 (1940); A3 (35, 36, 39, 52); ARTC; CD (35)

Media: Watercolor, oil, pen and ink, pastel

Specialty: Landscapes, portraits, genre

Originally an interior decorator and furniture designer, Robert Schley later worked for the U.S. Army Corps of Engineers as a draftsman from 1949 to 1964. He was an active participant in the Attic Club.

SCHROFF, Alfred Herman

b. 1863 Springfield, MA

d. 1939 Eugene, OR

Education: Ecole des Beaux Arts—Fontainebleau, Paris (1924); Cowles Art School: *Chominski, Major, DeCamp*

Membership: Oregon Society of Artists; American Artists Professional League
Awards: Annual National Competition—Springville, Utah (1922, 23); Seattle Art Museum (23); Oregon Society of Artists (28, 34, 35)
Collections: University of Oregon; Miranda Collection; Painting Restoration Studio Collection; Counting Eagles Collection; Lundberg Collection; Oregon State University; Cofield Collection
Exhibits: University of Oregon (1918, 21, 22, 25); Portland Art Museum; Seattle Art Museum; Oregon Society of Artists; American Artists Professional League (33, 34)
References: COL; DAV; DAW; FIE; HAV; HUG; MAL; WWN; WWW; A2 (1920, 33); A4 (29); C3 (28, 31, 33, 35); C7 (20, 23, 28a)
Media: Watercolor, oil, prints (lithograph, etching)
Specialty: Landscapes, seascapes
See artwork in color section

In 1915 Alfred Schroff moved from Boston to Eugene to become professor of painting at the University of Oregon and, in 1923, chairman of the fine arts department. He built a studio in Carmel, California, where he spent summers producing art and teaching at the University of California.

He went from Alaska to Mexico along the West Coast, painting as he traveled. He worked in the *plein air* tradition for his land and seascapes. He was more interested in the spirit of things than in a literal description of nature. His moods varied from bright and open to dark and somber. Schroff had a vigorous, vibrant technique with sweeping lines and was greatly admired for his use of color. Unfortunately, in 1927 Schroff suffered a nervous breakdown and never returned to teaching. His wife Lucy*, also an artist, was an art teacher at the University of Oregon.

SCHROFF, Louise (Lucy) Barrows

b. 1863 Sturgis, MI
d. 1946
Education: Boston Museum of Fine Arts; Fontainebleau, France (1924)
Membership: Oregon Society of Artists
Collections: University of Oregon
Exhibits: Portland Art Museum; Oregon Society of Artists
References: BIN: COL; WWN; A2 (1920, 40); C3 (34)
Media: Watercolor
Specialty: Portraits, seascapes, miniatures

Louise Schroff came to Eugene with her husband Alfred Schroff* in 1917. She assumed his teaching position at the University of Oregon after 1927. Her specialty was pottery and sculpture.

SCOTT, Lucy. *See* BOWER, Lucy

SELANDER, Arthur Ale

b. 1885 Marshfield, OR
d. 1978 Washington County, OR
Education: *P. Sheffers**
Membership: American Artists Professional League; Oregon Society of Artists
Awards: Oregon Society of Artists (1941–43)
Collections: Coos Art Museum; Oregon Historical Society; Parsons Collection; Counting Eagles Collection
Exhibits: Portland Art Museum; Oregon Society of Artists; Elfstrom Gallery; Dekum Gallery; Oregon Centennial (1959)
References: OET; A2 (1942); C3 (45–51); C13 (46–48)
Media: Oil, drawings
Specialty: Landscape

Arthur Selander took an art course from the International Correspondence School in 1905 and worked for the

Oregonian as a cartoonist in 1907 and 1908. He was an accomplished draftsman and his drawings showed exceptional skill. Later in life he taught for the Juniper Art Guild in Crook County. He had a one-person exhibition in Virginia. Some critics admired his keen ability to depict the wonders of nature on canvas. Selander was president of the Oregon Society of Artists in 1952 and a member of the American Artists Professional League. He exhibited in the Oregon Society of Artists Centennial Group Show in 1959.

SELANDER, Menalkas

b. 1913 Coquille, OR ***d.***
Education: Art Institute of Chicago (1937)
Membership: Oregon Society of Artists; Master Watercolor Society of Oregon
Collections: Maryhill Museum—Goldendale, Washington; Oregon Historical Society
Exhibits: Elfstrom Gallery; Oregon Society of Artists; Dekum Gallery; Master Watercolor Society of Oregon (1958)
References: ALM; OET; C3 (1947–51); C13 (46–48)
Media: Watercolor, pencil
Specialty: Oregon landscape

Son of Oregon artist Arthur Selander*, Menalkas worked as a commercial artist before turning to the fine arts later in his career. In 1950 Selander completed a large map mural that was featured in Portland traveler information centers and is now in the Oregon Historical Society collection. Since his retirement in the early 1970s he has taken up woodcarving.

SEWALL, Edward G.

b. 1905 Portland, OR ***d.***
Education: Museum Art School (1927–32); Art Students League: *Brook* (31–34)
Membership: Oregon Guild of Painters and Sculptors; American Artists Professional League; Oregon Society of Artists; Arts Guild
Awards: Art Students League (1930); College Art Exhibition—New York (35)
Collections: Portland Art Museum; Oregon Historical Society; Capital Collection—Salem; Booth Collection; Marine Hospital—Carville, Louisianna; Parsons Collection
Exhibits: Art Students League (1930); Portland Art Museum; Oregon Society of Artists; Arts Guild; John Herron Art Institute—Indianapolis (33); Seattle Art Museum (33); Creative Art Gallery (33, 34); Los Angeles County Museum of Art (33, 35); Art Institute of Chicago (34, 41); Golden Gate International Exposition—San Francisco (39–40); San Francisco Museum of Art (40); California Watercolor Society (40); National Gallery of Art (41); Oregon Guild of Painters and Sculptors (45, 48)
References: ALM; COL; MAL SUP; OET; WWN; A2 (1930, 32–34, 40, 42, 44, 46); A3 (35–37, 39); A4 (36); A5 (30, 33); C3 (30, 31); C7 (34, 35, 37, 40, 44); C10; CD (43–4, 52, 57)
Media: Watercolor, oil
Specialty: Portraits, landscape, still life
See artwork in color section

Edward Sewall was awarded the first Carey Prize, which included a scholarship to the Portland Museum Art School. In 1930, as a student, he received honorable mention for work sent to the Art Students League exhibit in New York. Some of his early work was done as a WPA artist. He was the only Oregon representative in the 1933 annual exhibit of American Contemporary Artists at the

John Herron Art Institute in Indiana. In 1935 he was awarded second prize for a watercolor at the College Art Association exhibit in New York.

After attending the Art Students League from 1931 to 1934, Sewall returned from New York in 1935 and opened the Barn Studio in Portland at SW Broadway and Columbia. He was well known for portraiture and in 1935 was commissioned for a painting of Governor Julius Meier, which is now in the State of Oregon collection. He painted a series of watercolors of old Portland houses, some of which were exhibited. One of his watercolors, *Woodland Arrangement*, was part of an exhibition at the National Gallery of Art in 1941 and was selected for the Marine Hospital in Carville, Louisiana. He helped organize the Creative Arts Gallery in Portland in 1933. In 1936 he took part in an exhibition sponsored by that gallery, held at the Portland Art Museum. In 1950, partly because his work was receiving little notice, Sewall gave up painting for photography.

SEWALL, Howard Stoyell

b. 1899 Minneapolis, MI
d. 1975 Portland, OR
Education: *E. Barchus** (1920–21); *C. Keller** (25–26); *S. Bell** (27–28); *C. Price**; University of Oregon (29–30)
Membership: American Artists Professional League; American Artists' Congress; Oregon Society of Artists; Portland Art Museum (Artist Membership)
Awards: Architectural League—New York (1938)
Collections: Powell Collection; Multnomah County Library Collection; Pacific University; Parsons Collection
Exhibits: American Artists Professional League (1937–39); Salem Federal Art Center (39, 40); Portland Art Museum; J.K. Gill Gallery (44); Dekum Gallery; Smith Tower—Seattle
References: ALM; COL; DAV; DAW; HAV; MAL SUP; OET; WWN; WWW; A2 (1940, 44, 46); A3 (51, 53, 54); C11; CD (39–41, 43–44, 50)
Media: Watercolor, oil, tempera, prints (serigraph, blockprint, monoprint)
Specialty: Murals, zoo animals, people
See artwork in color section

Howard Sewall was a founder and member of the Washington School of Art in Washington, D.C. in 1915. He arrived in Portland in 1920. His friend Ruby Hammill recalled that he worked as a WPA artist from 1935 to 1942. She also related that in 1940 he taught at the Salem Art Center. For most of his career he was a commercial artist who worked and taught in downtown studios. During the 1930s he was in the Worcester Building with a studio adjoining C.S. Price's*. During the 1940s his studio was located in the Kramer Building. In the 1950s he moved to the Selling-Hirsch building and, in the decade of the 1960s, he relocated to the McKay building. He deplored the destruction of several of these buildings and made numerous sketches of their demolition. Sewall was complex, unpredictable, and emotional, yet had a fine sense of humor, which often shows in his work. He had several years of formal art training and studied with some of Oregon's prominent artists, though he considered himself to be self-taught.

Murals that he completed in the 1930s and 1940s received much recognition. *Stonecutters* was honored by the Architectural League of New York in 1938. Two large murals depicting iron and wood workers are in the Timberline Lodge collection. In 1932 he completed eleven murals for the Imperial Hotel in

Portland. Unfortunately the owners painted over them. Sewall experimented with a single line design technique using candid sketches of people, animals, and buildings as subjects. His forty-two sketches depicting people in the Central Library in Portland remain in the Library's collection and have been prominently displayed. He also was adept with watercolor and preferred painting outdoors.

The Oregon City High School commissioned him to paint ten murals for their auditorium and six for the library, featuring themes from Elizabethan drama and figures from the arts. He taught and painted through the 1950s and 1960s in a style that grew increasingly abstract. Cancer finally forced him to quit painting in 1970. Besides painting, he also produced textiles and hand loomed rugs, was a professional Spanish dancer, a singer, and an impersonator. Sewall's comment "Experimentation is the most remarkable teacher" was an apt summation of his accomplishments. He signed his work *H. Sewall* or *H.S.*

SEWELL, Alice E.

b. 1883 Hillsboro, OR
d. 1973 Hillsboro, OR
Education: Art Students League: *Chase, F. DuMond**; University of Oregon; Museum Art School; Pacific University: *L. Bain**; Vienna: *Steinhof*; Paris (1927)
Membership: Oregon Society of Artists; American Artists Professional League; Arts Guild
Awards: Oregon Society of Artists (1932, 38)
Collections: Timberline Lodge Collection; Pacific University; Parsons Collection
Exhibits: Portland Art Museum; Buffalo, New York (1925); Portland Woman's Club (26); Oregon Society of Artists; Arts Guild; American Artists Professional League (32);
References: ALM; DAV; HAV; KOV; MAL; WWN; WWW; A2 (1912, 20, 22, 30, 32, 40, 46); A3 (33, 35); A5 (30); C3 (27–32, 36); C10; CD (23–25); M2
Media: Oil, prints (etching)
Specialty: Portraits, landscape

Alice Sewell was educated at the Art Students League, the University of Oregon, the Museum Art School, Pacific University, and in Vienna and Paris. She was a painter, printmaker, sculptor, art lecturer, and art educator as well as an accomplished pianist. Sewell taught at Brandon Hall in Portland and exhibited her paintings frequently in the Portland area. As part of her work for the WPA, she painted a mural for the Hillsboro High School. Sewell was known as a good colorist.

SHEFFERS, Peter Winthrop

b. 1893 San Antonio, TX
d. 1949 Bremerton, WA
Education: Royal Academy of Arts—Berlin; Paris: *Lecompte*; London: *Jarosy*
Membership: American Artists Professional League; Oregon Society of Artists; American Federation of Arts
Awards: All Illinois Fine Arts Society (1940)
Collections: Powell Collection; YMCA—Salem; Peoria Library—Illinois; Parsons Collection; Humpal Collection; Slippery Slope Historical Collection
Exhibits: Drake Hotel—Chicago (1PS); All Illinois Fine Arts Society (1940); San Francisco Art Association; Portland Art Museum; Maryhill Museum—Goldendale, Washington (46); Elfstrom Gallery; Oregon Society of Artists (1PS 49); Clatsop County Historical Society (94)

References: BI; DAV; DAW; HAV; MAL SUP; OET; WWW; A2 (1942, 44, 46); C11; C13 (46, 47); CD (43–4)
Media: Oil, watercolor
Specialty: Marines, landscapes (mountains, rivers, Yosemite)
See artwork in color section

Born in San Antonio, Texas Peter Sheffers had a rocky beginning as a starving artist in Paris in 1916. During World War I, when painting sales were scarce, he enlisted in the French army as an interpreter. Wounded by a German shell, he recovered and went to London, where he painted and sold with more success than in France. He eventually returned to New York in 1922. In Europe he had received strong, academic art training, and had several exhibitions to his credit before settling in New York for eight years, then in the Chicago area for ten.

His initial visit to Portland in 1941 was to have been a short one, but he decided to remain because of the "unending inspiration of the Northwest." He won the acclaim of Gump's Galleries in San Francisco as the artist who was able to do justice to the different aspects of the Northwest, emphasizing its coast. They had been searching for such an artist to promote for years, and this association was a springboard for Sheffers' steady success in the Northwest. He was a member of the Oregon Society of Artists, the American Artists Professional League, and the American Federation of Arts. Peter Sheffers was also a teacher, with a studio in his home on SW Montgomery Drive. He died in an automobile accident in Bremerton, Washington while driving a friend home.

The notes from a 1946 exhibition catalog at Maryhill Museum in Goldendale, Washington stated that in addition to the "fine rendering of the thing seen," Sheffers also conveyed the colors of nature with subtle transitions of tone, while maintaining their relationship to the broader color masses of the whole. His paintings in many Northwest collections convey his love of the region.

SHEPARD, Olivia. *See* BARBER, Olivia

SHIRLEY, Lily

b. d.
Awards: Oregon State Fairs
Exhibits: Oregon State Fairs
References: OSF (1892, 93, 97–99)
Media: Oil
Specialty: Florals, marines, animals

Lily Shirley, also known as Mrs. George Shirley, listed a Salem address for her Oregon State Fair entries of the latter part of the nineteenth century.

SIMMONS, Kate Cameron

b. d.
Education: Columbia University: *Dow*; Pratt Institute
Exhibits: Portland Art Museum
References: GER; WWW; A2 (1911, 14); A3 (11); CD (10); M2; M3
Media: Oil
Specialty: Landscape

Prior to her arrival in Oregon, Kate Simmons was supervisor of drawing in Middleton, New York and supervisor of drawing and art in a New York high school. She was the first art instructor employed by the Portland Museum Art School from 1909 to 1910 and taught a comprehensive art course. Simmons painted at least one landscape of Mt. Hood, receiving praise for "one of the best views of this towering peak."

SISSON, Nellie Stowell

b. 1871 La Prairie Center, IL
d. 1945 Carmel, CA
Education: Art Institute of Chicago; Berlin: *Erneke*

Membership: American Artists Professional League; Oregon Society of Artists; Society of Oregon Artists
Awards: American Artists Professional League (1936)
Collections: Oregon Historical Society; Reed College
Exhibits: Portland Art Museum; Society of Oregon Artists (1913); Portland Woman's Club (26); Oregon Society of Artists; American Artists Professional League (33, 34, 36, 37)
References: DAV; KOV: WWN; WWW; A2 (1913, 14, 21, 32–34); A3 (35, 36); A4 (29); C3 (28–36); C10; ARTC; M2; M3
Media: Watercolor
Specialty: Landscapes (northwest, California), wildflowers

Trained at the Art Institute of Chicago and in Berlin, Nellie Sisson became an art teacher. She taught at Bradley Polytechnic Institute in 1899. A member of the early Society of Oregon Artists, she exhibited with them in 1913. That same year she was an active participant in early shows at the Portland Art Museum. She was a member of the later Oregon Society of Artists and participated in their shows starting in 1928. Sisson was also a WPA artist. She was married to Edward O. Sisson, Professor of Philosophy at Reed College. Davenport (see Ref. DAV) lists a Missoula, Montana address for her before her death in Carmel, California in 1945.

SKINNER, Charlotte Butler

b. 1879 San Francisco, CA
d. 1963 Morro Bay, CA
Education: California School of Fine Arts; Mark Hopkins Institute: *Matthews*; California School of Design (1900–02)
Membership: American Artists Professional League; San Francisco Society of Women Artists
Awards: American Artists Professional League (1934)
Collections: Capitol Collection—Salem
Exhibits: Oakland Art Gallery (1928); San Francisco Art Association (30); Portland Art Museum; American Artists Professional League (1PS 33; 34)
References: DAV; FIE; HAV; HUG; KOV; MAL; PET; SAM; WWW; A2 (1933); C10
Media: Oil, watercolor, prints (etchings)
Specialty: Landscapes (mountains), portraits

Charlotte Butler Skinner grew up in San Francisco and attended the California School of Design. Around 1910 she settled in Lone Pine and by the early 1930s she had moved to Eugene. The location of her one-person show, sponsored by the American Artists Professional League in 1933, was the Portland Art Museum. It contained forty oils and several watercolors of the California High Sierras, for which she was best known. She participated in the WPA. In 1935 she moved to Morro Bay, California and helped found its local art association in the early 1950s.

SMITH, Amanda Jennie

b. d.
Membership: Oregon Art Association
Exhibits: North Pacific Industrial Exposition (1890); Oregon Industrial Exposition (95); Oregon Art Association (96)
References: C2 (1890, 95); ARTC; CD (89–92, 94–97, 1901, 02); M2
Media: Oil
Specialty: Fruit

Amanda Smith operated an art school in partnership with artist Lottie C. Young in Portland from 1889 to 1897, after which Young moved to Los Angeles. Smith then maintained studios in the Washington and Marquam Buildings from 1897 to 1902. She was also a member, treasurer, and exhibitor at the Oregon Art Association.

SMITH, Armista Roselle Morgan

b. 1850 Rochelle, IL
d. 1929 Portland, OR
Membership: Oregon Art Association; Oregon Society of Artists
Awards: Oregon State Fair
Exhibits: Oregon State Fair; North Pacific Industrial Exposition (1889); Oregon Industrial Exposition (94); Oregon Art Association (96); Portland Art Museum; Oregon Society of Artists
References: A2 (1920, 22); C2 (1889, 94); C3 (1927, 28); ARTC; OSF (1881); M2
Media: Oil, oil on ivory
Specialty: Miniatures, portraits, florals

Armista Smith, wife of *The West Shore* art editor, C. L. Smith*, lived in San Francisco in 1876 and settled in Portland after 1882. She was an active participant in the early Portland Mechanics and Industrial Fairs. She separated from Smith and remained in Portland until her death in 1929.

SMITH, Clarence L.

b. 1851 Elgin, IL
d. 1934 Portland, OR
Membership: Portland Art Club
Collections: Oregon Historical Society
Exhibits: Portland Art Club (1886)
References: DAV; HUG; A4 (1929); ARTC; CD (1889); M1
Media: Prints (lithograph), oil
Specialty: Caricature

Clarence Smith began as a watchmaker in Elgin, Illinois who sketched while at his workbench. He then served as head of the lithograph and art department of *The West Shore* publication in Portland from 1882 to 1892. When *The West Shore* failed he returned to Chicago, then to San Francisco, where he worked for the *San Francisco Examiner*. He finally came back to Portland and joined the *Oregonian* in 1905. He headed their art department from 1924 until his retirement in 1931. Smith was one of the artists who contributed to the *As We See 'Em* book of caricatures published by Edward Thomson in 1906.

SMITH, Eva Augusta Ford Cline

b. Northfield, VT *d.*
Education: Art Students League: *Walcott, F. DuMond**; Munich: *C.Cooke**
Membership: Portland Sketch Club; Oregon Art Association
Awards: Portland Art Museum (1900)
Collections: Painting Restoration Studio Collection; Cofield Collection
Exhibits: Oregon Art Association (1896); American Watercolor Society (98); Portland Sketch Club (1900); Portland Art Museum (00)
References: PET; ARTC; CD (1893, 1896–1900, 02–09, 12, 13, 16, 17, 25); M2; M3
Media: Oil, pen and ink
Specialty: Landscapes, animals, still life
See artwork in color section

Educated at the Art Students League in New York City, Eva Ford taught painting and drawing at her studio in Portland. She was a book illustrator as well as a painter. Although married to John P. Cline in 1874, she chose to exhibit under the name Ford at the 1893 Portland International Exposition and with the Portland Sketch Club in 1900. She lived in North Albina, which had a City Directory listing separate from Portland around the turn of the century. A widow in 1907, she married A.O. Smith in 1909. Davenport (see Ref. DAV) mentions that Melville Wire* was one of her students.

Smith signed her work in a variety of ways: *Ford*, *Cline*, and *Cline-Smith*.

SMITH, Fern Thatcher

b. 1908 ND ***d.***
Education: *F. Smith*; T. Pearson*; N. Sandgren*; Vip; Hamilton*
Awards: Oregon State Fair
Collections: Oregon Historical Society
Exhibits: Oregon State Fair
Media: Watercolor
Specialty: Landscapes, florals

Fern Smith exhibited in two-person invitational shows that toured the western United States in partnership with husband, Fred*, who was her teacher and professional colleague. She served as judge of state and county fair art competitions.

SMITH, Frederick Wilson

b. 1903 OR
d. 1990 Salem, OR
Education: *Vip; Hamilton; C. Mulvey**
Membership: Oregon Society of Artists
Awards: Oregon State Fair
Collections: Oregon Historical Society
Exhibits: Portland Art Museum; Oregon Society of Artists; Oregon State Fair
References: A2 (1938, 42)
Media: Watercolor
Specialty: Landscapes, seascapes, old buildings

Fred Smith started out as a commercial artist after high school in 1922, but changed careers to become a retail lumberman. It was not until his retirement in 1959 that he returned to his love of art and resumed painting. Known for his bold strokes of color, he produced over one thousand paintings in his lifetime, averaging one a week. He was a founder of the Watercolor Society of Oregon in 1966 and served as their first president. Along with his wife, Fern*, he participated in invitational watercolor shows that toured most of the western United States.

SMITH, Margery Hoffman

b. 1888 Portland, OR
d. 1981 San Francisco, CA
Education: Art Students League; Museum Art School: *H. Wentz*; Dow; Miller; Rosse*
Membership: Arts Guild; Oregon Society of Artists; San Francisco Society of Women Artists
Awards: Seattle Art Museum (1923)
Collections: Portland Art Museum; Oregon Historical Society; Lundberg Collection
Exhibits: Portland Art Museum; Seattle Art Museum; Oregon Society of Artists; Arts Guild
References: ALM; COL; DAV; DAW; FIE; HAV; MAL; PET; WWN; WWW; A2 (1916, 19, 20, 21, 22, 30); A4 (29); A5 (30); C3 (27–29); C7 (22, 23, 28, 28a, 30, 31); C15 (22)
Media: Oil
Specialty: Portraits, florals, still life, decorative panels

Although known primarily as an interior designer who managed the Timberline project from 1936 to 1937, Margery Hoffman Smith was also a painter. Trained at the Art Students League in New York and at the Museum Art School in Portland, she exhibited in shows at the Portland Art Museum beginning in 1916 and continuing through the 1920s. She was also a charter member of the Oregon Society of Artists. Her entry in the Seattle Art Museum's 1923 annual exhibition garnered a prize.

Born and reared in Portland, her family's art legacy is strong. Her mother, Julia Hoffman*, founded the Portland Arts and Crafts Society in 1907. Margery Smith's association with the Portland Art Museum prompted her to donate the Asian art pieces that became the foundation of the Museum's Asian collection, as well as a purchase fund to accompany it. After a long residency in Portland, she eventually moved to San Francisco, with frequent return trips to Oregon.

SMITH, Mattie Ellis

b. 1860 Decatur Co., IA
d. 1892 Salem, OR
Awards: Oregon State Fairs
Exhibits: Oregon State Fairs
References: OSF (1888–91); M2; M3
Media: Oil, watercolor
Specialty: Marines, landscapes

Also known as Mrs. John Newton Smith, wife of a prominent physician in Salem, Mattie Smith painted under both names. She died at the age of thirty-two from complications of childbirth.

SMITH, Rachael. *See* GRIFFIN, Rachael

SNYDER, Amanda Tester

b. 1894 Neva, TN
d. 1980 Portland, OR
Education: Museum Art School: *S. Bell*, Abbott* (1917)
Membership: Oregon Society of Artists; American Artists Professional League; Portland Art Museum (Artist Membership)
Awards: Oregon Society of Artists (1932, 34, 37, 43, 44); American Artists Professional League (32, 36)
Collections: Oregon Historical Society; Portland Art Museum; Reed College; Goodman Collection; Salishan Lodge Collection; Skamania Lodge Collection; University of Oregon; Seattle Art Museum; First National Bank; Coos Art Museum; Multnomah Athletic Club Collection; Booth Collection; Miranda Collection; Parsons Collection; Gerber Collection; Pathways Collection; Huntington Collection; Cofield Collection; Hallie Ford Museum of Art—Willamette University
Exhibits: Oregon Society of Artists; American Artists Professional League (32–35); Portland Art Museum (1PS 49); Seattle Art Museum; Kharouba Gallery (1PS 49, 54); Willamette University; Reed College (1PS 50, 54, 57); Henry Art Gallery—University of Washington (51); Harvey Welch Gallery; Ruthermore Gallery—San Francisco (59); Oregon Centennial (59); University of Oregon (75); Oregon Historical Society (90)
References: DAV; DAW; MAL SUP; OET; A2 (1932, 33, 34, 40, 48); A3 (49–56, 58); C3 (29–32, 34, 36, 43); C6; C7 (35, 37, 52–55, 58); C9; C22; M2; M3
Media: Oil, watercolor, encaustic, prints (linocut, woodcut), collage
Specialty: Birds, circus, clowns, portraits, still life
See artwork in color section
See photograph of artist on p. 88

Amanda Tester Snyder's family—which included her brother, artist Jefferson Tester*—moved from Tennessee to Oregon when she was nine years old. In 1916, at the age of twenty-two, she married and moved to Portland with her husband.

Snyder liked the rough texture of many layers of paint softened by scumbling—and used that technique to great effect. In 1929 she met and befriended C. S. Price* at one of his gallery shows. On a visit to her studio he mentioned that her work, especially the clowns and religious paintings, had something in common with the French painter Rouault. Snyder, who was not familiar with Rouault, had independently developed her use of heavy black outlines. She was, however, influenced by C.S. Price* and his circle. She made mannequins as models for her clown figures and sent one of these to Price. One can detect a wistfulness and sadness in her clown figures.

Snyder painted over one hundred portraits during her life and painted still lifes from the beginning to the end of her career. Her style moved from realistic through impressionistic to the increasingly abstract.

In discussing her work Snyder said: "My inspiration comes from shape and color. I see beauty and design in everyday things in my home and garden. My greatest pleasure is to produce paintings which communicate a love of simple life."

She had thirty-two one-person shows, including two at the Portland Art Museum and three at Reed College. In 1954 Snyder exhibited with LaVerne Krause*, LaVon Lucas*, and Jolan Torak* in a four-woman show at the Kharouba Gallery in Portland.

SORENSON, Don Eldon

b. 1927 Astoria, OR
d. 1994 Portland, OR
Education: Museum Art School (1947–49)
Membership: Artists Equity; Portland Art Museum (Artist Membership)
Awards: Portland Art Museum (1949); Oregon State Fair (50)
Collections: Portland Art Museum; Vancouver Public School; Washington Art Association
Exhibits: Portland Art Museum (AM, 2PS 1953); Seattle Art Museum (50); Oregon State Fair (50); Harvey Welch Gallery (1PS 52, 57); Washington Art Association (53); Santa Barbara Museum of Art (55); Reed College (59); Ruthermore Gallery—San Francisco (59); California Palace of the Legion of Honor—San Francisco; Henry Art Gallery—University of Washington; Bush House Museum—Salem; Oregon Centennial (59); New Gallery of Contemporary Art (59)
References: ALM; A3 (1950, 52, 53, 55–58); C6; C7 (52, 59)
Media: Oil, prints

Don Sorenson grew up in logging camps, roaming the forest and exploring the world of nature around him. He had a special love of birds and pursued the sport of falconry. This interest is reflected in many of his works. A teacher in the art departments at Portland State University and the University of Portland, Sorenson had abilities in many media. He completed a glass mosaic mural in Portland's Lloyd Center Sheraton Hotel in 1959. His steel sculpture entrance to the Exhibition Hall at the Oregon Centennial Exhibition was a memorable landmark for that show. He worked in oil and printmaking in a style that became more and more abstract.

SPALDING, Eliza Hart

b. 1807 Kensington, CN
d. 1851 Brownsville, OR
Education: Chipman Female Academy—Clinton, New York
Collections: Oregon Historical Society
References: DAV; DAW; PET; M1; M2
Media: Natural pigments and dyes, watercolor
Specialty: Religious

Eliza Spalding made the overland journey to the West in 1836, and was one of six women in the Oregon mission, settling at Lapwai, Idaho from 1836 to 1847. She and her husband worked with Marcus Whitman and others to place teachers and establish missions in the Pacific Northwest. She produced the first-known artwork by a woman in the Oregon Territory. Her subject matter was religious. One of her most significant pieces was *The Protestant Ladder*. She did several of these "ladders," which were used as teaching tools for the native Indians. The example in the Oregon Historical Society collection is the only one known to survive. It was a visual aid, representing Biblical scenes of Christ's time painted in a fashion similar to the ones the Catholic Church was using. Natural dyes and pigments were the materials that were available to her.

SPAUGH, Sara

b. 1917 Coos Bay, OR ***d.***
Education: California School of Fine Arts: *Albertson, Poole, Mackey* (1939–40); *H. Widman**; *P. Gunn**; *N. Sandgren**; *D. McCosh**; *B. Hinshaw**; *W. Wolf**
Membership: Oregon Amateur Watercolor Society; Portland Art Museum (Artist Membership); Coos Art League
Awards: Oregon State Fair (1958)
Collections: Larvik, Norway; International Paper Co.—Reedsport
Exhibits: Southwest Oregon Annual (1955–59); Oregon State Fairs (56–59); Oregon Amateur Watercolor Society (57–59); Southern Oregon Art Exhibit; Oregon Centennial (59)
References: C6; C26 (1958)

Sara Spaugh was a member of the Oregon Amateur Watercolor Society and also exhibited in the Southern Oregon Art Exhibit of 1958. Active in the southern Oregon art community, she taught at Southwest Oregon Community College. Spaugh listed a Coos Bay address.

SPENCER, Aimee. *See* GORHAM, Aimee

SPIEGEL, Richard

b. 1903 Bochum, Westfalia, Germany
d. 1985 Portland, OR
Education: Germany: *Herwig* (1913, 20), *Treskow* (18–21); Portland State University
Membership: Oregon Society of Artists; American Artists Professional League; American Federation of Arts; Portland Art Museum (Artist Membership)
Collections: Oregon Historical Society
Exhibits: Germany; Dekum Gallery; American Artists Professional League (1941, 44); Meier and Frank Co. (41); Zell Bros. (41); J.K. Gill Gallery (2PS 44); Portland Art Museum; Oregon Society of Artists
References: COL; A2 (1944); C3 (46)
Media: Watercolor, oil, tempera, casein
Specialty: Still life, seascapes

Richard Spiegel was a colorist, impressionist, expressionist and a fauvist, strongly influenced by Matisse. Escaping Nazi Germany during World War II, he came to Portland in 1940 and remained there until his death in 1985. He was also quite well known for creating fashion jewelry. His work is in private collections in Germany, Uruguay, Spain, Oregon, and Washington. The Portland Art Museum's Rental Sales Gallery represented him. In addition to his art career, he was a practicing attorney.

SPRINGER, Isabel. *See* EDINA, Sister Mary

STAMPS, Nancie. *See* CONFER, Nancie

STANLEY, John Mix

b. 1814 Canandaigua, NY
d. 1872 Detroit, MI
Collections: Detroit Institute of the Arts; Metropolitan Museum of Art; Smithsonian Institution; Phoenix Art Museum; Buffalo Historical Society—New York; Stenzel Collection; Amon Carter Museum —Ft. Worth, Texas
Exhibits: Washington Art Association (1957, 59); Oregon Historical Society (90)

References: BEN; BI; DAV; DAW; GER; GW; HUG; OET; SAM; THI; YNG; C9; M1
Media: Watercolor, oil, prints (lithograph)
Specialty: Portraits, landscapes, Indians

A sign and coach painter in Detroit in 1842, John Mix Stanley traveled west to Santa Fe in 1846. His love of travel brought him to California and Oregon in the late 1840s. Employed as chief artist with the Isaac Stevens Survey for the proposed transcontinental railroad in 1854, he and fellow artists created drawings and watercolor paintings that recorded the progress of the expedition. Scenes of the Indians en route, river and mountain passes, and other natural formations of the Pacific Coast were turned into engravings in the final report. Tragically, the Smithsonian Institution fire of 1865 destroyed over 150 of his works. Among his most memorable surviving paintings are his panoramas—such as *Oregon City* in the Amon Carter Museum in Ft. Worth, Texas, and a *Mt. Hood.*

STAPRANS, Raimonds

b. 1926 Riga, Latvia *d.*
Education: Stuttgart; University of Washington: *Melcarth, Archipenko* (1952); University of California
Membership: Portland Art Museum (Artist Membership)
Exhibits: Portland Art Museum (AM,1PS 1955); Maxwell Gallery —San Francisco (1PS)
References: DAV; HAV; A3 (1951, 54, 55)
Specialty: Coast scenes, boats

Primarily known as a California artist, Raimonds Staprans studied in the Northwest and spent some time here in the mid 1950s. In 1955 he had a one-person show at the Portland Art Museum. He was also a sculptor.

STARR, Nellie S.

b. 1869 IL
d. 1953 Portland, OR
Membership: American Artists Professional League; Oregon Society of Artists
Awards: Oregon Society of Artists
Collections: Painting Restoration Studio Collection
Exhibits: Oregon Society of Artists; American Artists Professional League (1933); Portland Art Museum; Oregon State Fairs; Multnomah County Fairs
References: COL; DAV; DAW; WWN; A2 (1942, 44, 46); C3 (32, 34, 35); CD (37)
Media: Watercolors, pastels, oils
Speciality: Mountains
See artwork in color section

A member of the American Artists Professional League and the Oregon Society of Artists, Nellie Starr was an active artist in Oregon during the 1930s and the early 1940s. She exhibited at the Oregon State Fairs and Multnomah County Fairs.

STEPHENS, Clara Jane

b. 1877 near Land's End, England
d. 1952 Portland, OR
Education: Art Students League: *Cox, F. DuMond** (1904–05); Italy: *Chase* (13); Museum Art School (10); *E. Woolfolk**
Membership: Portland Sketch Club; American Artists Professional League; Society of Independent Artists—New York; Oregon Society of Artists
Awards: Lewis and Clark Centennial Exposition (1905); Seattle Fine Art Society (20, 22, 25); Salt Lake City (23)
Collections: Oregon Historical Society; Powell Collection; Portland Art Museum; Parsons Collection; Lundberg Collection

Exhibits: Portland Sketch Club (1894); Oregon Art Association (96); Lewis and Clark Centennial Exposition (1905); Portland Art Museum (1PS 14, 19); Panama Pacific International Exposition—San Francisco (15); Seattle Art Museum; San Francisco Art Association (18); National Academy of Design (20); Society of Independent Artists—New York (21, 22, 24, 25, 27, 31); Salons of America (22, 25–27, 29, 30, 31); Salt Lake City (23); Ainslie Galleries —New York (1PS 25); Portland Woman's Club (26); Oregon Society of Artists; Oakland Art Gallery (28); Frances Webb Galleries—Hollywood (1PS 48); Oregon Historical Society (90); Clatsop County Historical Society (94); Autry Museum—Los Angeles (95)

References: BEN; DAV; DAW; FIE; GER; HAV; HUG; KOV; MAL; PET; SA; SIA; WWW; YNG; A1 (1920, 24); A2 (11–17, 19, 20–22, 32, 33); A4 (11, 29); C3 (27); C5; C7 (15, 17–18, 20, 22, 23, 25–29); C9; C11; C15 (22); C21; C23; ARTC; CD (12, 15, 18, 19, 29, 33, 38–9, 41, 43–4); M2; M3

Media: Oil, watercolor, charcoal

Specialty: Portraits, landscapes, still life

See artwork in color section

Born near Land's End, England in 1877, Clara Jane Stephens arrived in Portland in 1894. She studied with artist Eva Woolfolk* before attending Frank DuMond* and Kenyon Cox's classes at the Art Students League in New York. She continued her art education with a summer course in Italy from William Merritt Chase. Chase painted her portrait and presented it to her as was his custom to honor his outstanding pupil. She was one of the early women to be associated with the Portland Sketch Club, exhibiting there in 1894. She also had an affiliation with the Oregon Artist Association, which had an exhibition in 1896 to benefit the Library.

Stephens received an honorable mention at the Lewis and Clark Exposition in 1905 for "her artistic feeling and exquisite coloring." At the time she was teaching at both the Portland Academy and the Allen Preparatory School, positions she held until 1916 when they closed. She was an exhibitor at the Panama Pacific International Exposition held in San Francisco in 1915. She taught children's classes at the Portland Art Museum in 1916 and joined the faculty of the Museum Art School in 1917, remaining there until her retirement in 1938. An article in the *Spectator* newspaper included comments on those Saturday children's classes: [The children] "would eagerly gather under the skillful and intelligent guidance of their beloved teacher, Clara Jane Stephens. Problems, which are fundamental to all good work in arts, are simply and fascinatingly presented." In addition to teaching in the School, she exhibited frequently at the Portland Art Museum starting in 1911. She had one-person shows in 1914 and again in 1919. Oils, watercolors, and charcoal drawings, including several Venetian sketches, were described as "full of color and originality."

A devoted teacher, she continued to exhibit her work. In 1920 she was featured in a one-person show at the Seattle Art Museum sponsored by the Fine Art Society. *Jack O'Lantern Makers* received much favorable comment and was widely reproduced. In 1923 she had an exhibition at the Artcraft and Curio Shop on Morrison Street in Portland. Among her landscapes and portraits, a Mt. Hood was singled out because of its unusual color and viewpoint from the upper valley. It was exhibited in 1922 at the Anderson Galleries in New York and also appeared at the Waldorf Astoria Hotel in a Society of Independent Artists Exhibition. Stephens was a member of this group.

In 1925 Stephens had an important exhibit in New York at the Ainslie Galleries on Fifth Avenue. A New York review was very favorable and it even impressed French art critic, Comte Chabrier. He submitted a review to his Parisian magazine, *La Revue du Vrai et du Beau*, calling her paintings "modern works without exaggeration, which separate themselves from the ordinary by their sense of color and spiritual realism of (the) person depicted."

News of her acclaim in New York and Paris reached Portland, and the newspapers at home boasted of her acceptance on a national and international level. At this time she won a second award at the Seattle Art Museum. Her exhibit on view at the University of Oregon circa 1925 elicited the following review: "Techniques vary as do subjects ... sometimes smooth strokes, sometimes long, quick . . . often short dabs that appear as a mass of color close-up but (are really) the Oregon City Bridge...when viewed from a distance."

In 1927 she became one of the charter members of the Society of Oregon Artists and exhibited with them in their first annual show. Her piece, *Over Mantel*, evoked much comment at the time. In 1948 an exhibition at the Frances Webb Galleries in Hollywood, California presented Miss Stephens as "one of the outstanding artists of the Pacific Coast." She never married and died in 1952 as the result of a fall. Highly underrated in recent history, Clara Jane Stephens was one of Oregon's outstanding women painters.

STEWART, Pernot. *See* DUFF, Aimee L. Pernot

STONE, Margaret Anthony

b. 1910 Providence, RI ***d.***
Education: Art Center School of Design—Los Angeles; *Rindgel; Chatterton; Reckless*
Membership: American Artists Professional League
Awards: American Artists Professional League (1937, 38, 39)
Collections: Lewis and Clark High School, City Hall—Spokane, Washington
Exhibits: National Exhibition of American Art (1936); American Artists Professional League (37–39); Portland Art Museum; National Academy of Design (43, 45); San Francisco; Philadelphia; Chicago; Seattle
References: ALM; COL; DAV; HAV; MAL SUP; WWN; WWW; A2 (1942)
Specialty: Portraits

Records show that Margaret Stone lived in Portland in the late 1930s and was a designer who gained fame as the "Rose Queen" portrait artist. She lived in Larchmont, New York after 1947.

STOUT, Ella Jackson

b. 1875 Napa, CA
d. 1965 Portland, OR
Education: Museum Art School
Membership: Arts Guild; American Artists' Congress
Awards: Portland Art Museum (1938)
Exhibits: Arts Guild; Portland Art Museum; Creative Art Gallery (1933); Lipman Little Gallery (36); Seattle Art Museum; American Artists' Congress (37)
References: COL; DAV; DAW; MAL SUP; WWN; A2 (1930, 33, 42); A3 (35–38); A4 (36); A5 (30, 33); C7 (36, 38, 39, 45)
Media: Oil

Educated at the Museum Art School, Ella Stout exhibited work at the Portland

Art Museum, the Seattle Art Museum, the Circle A Gallery, and the Lipman Little Gallery in Portland. In addition to painting, she was a wood carver and sculptor. Stout lived in Newberg.

STOVER, Allan James

b. 1887 West Point, MS
d. 1967 San Diego, CA
Education: Cleveland School of Art
Collections: Oregon State University
Exhibits: Portland Art Museum
References: DAV; DAW; FIE; HAV; HUG; MAL; WWW; YNG; A2 (1913, 14, 16, 17, 19–21)
Media: Pen and ink, oil
Specialty: Landscapes (rivers, bridges), portraits

Allan Stover was an illustrator, commercial artist, and participant in the WPA. In 1924 he worked as an illustrator for Oregon Agricultural College (now Oregon State University) and submitted a panoramic drawing characterizing the look of buildings of the future. He produced pen and ink drawings of prominent Oregonians, decorated the Masonic Temple in Corvallis, and illustrated the book, *Oregon Commercial Forests.*

STRANGE, Mildred Holmes

b. 1897 Oakland, CA *d.*
Education: University of Oregon; California College of Arts and Crafts; Oregon State University
Membership: American Artists Professional League
Exhibits: Meier and Frank Co.; American Artists Professional League (1935); Grumbacher, traveling exhibition (35); Oregon State University (38)
References: COL; DAW; WWN
Media: Oil, pastel
Specialty: Landscapes

Mildred Strange was a member of the American Artists Professional League, with whom she exhibited in 1935. She was state director of their American Art Week in 1938. She worked in both Corvallis and Salem as an art teacher and writer.

STREAT, Thelma Johnson

b. 1912 Yakima, WA
d. 1959 Los Angeles, CA
Education: Museum Art School (1934–35)
Collections: San Francisco Museum of Art; Museum of Modern Art; Mills College—Oakland, California; Reed College; Honolulu Academy of Arts
Exhibits: YWCA—Portland (1934); J.K. Gill Gallery (38); City of Paris—San Francisco (39); Museum of Modern Art (42); Art Institute of Chicago (43); New York Public Library (44); San Francisco Museum of Art (46); Portland Art Museum; M.H. DeYoung Museum—San Francisco
References: DAV; HAV; HUG; MAL SUP; WWW; A2 (1948)
Media: Gouache, watercolor, oil, tempera
Specialty: Portraits, African-American themes
See artwork in color section
See photograph of artist on p. 89

Born in Yakima, Washington, Thelma Streat grew up in Portland, where she attended high school and the Museum Art School. She was multi-talented, gaining fame as a singer, dancer, artist, and graphic designer. She moved to San Francisco in 1940 and gave dance performances and art exhibitions around the world. Her specialty was African-American themes, showing an abstract-expressionist influence with simpicity of color and form. She visited the Native Americans of the Queen Charlotte Islands combining study with her love of art and dance. She traveled to Hawaii in 1949 and settled there permanently in 1952; the Islands had a great influence on her subsequent work. She and husband, John Edgar, established the Children's City projects to fight intolerance in Hawaii and Canada.

STREIF, Levina Harris

b. 1899 Portland, OR *d.*
Education: Museum Art School (1921–23)
Membership: Arts Guild; Portland Art Museum (Artist Membership)
Awards: Portland Art Museum (1932)
Exhibits: Portland Art Museum; Arts Guild
References: A2 (1930, 32, 33); A3 (35, 36, 57); A5 (30); C10
Media: Oil, watercolor
Specialty: Portraits

A WPA artist, Levina Streif lived in The Dalles in 1936. Her name was listed as Harris for a Portland Art Museum exhibit in 1957. Her last name is sometimes spelled Streiff.

STRICKER, Rosamund. *See* DAY, Rosamund

STRICKLAND, Fred

b. 1880 Essex, England
d. 1956 Portland, OR
Education: England; University of Oregon (1933)
Membership: Oregon Society of Artists
Collections: Oregon Historical Society; Hopkins Art Gallery—San Francisco; Doncaster, England; Lundberg Collection
Exhibits: Portland Art Museum; J.K. Gill Gallery (1922); Diocesan Office—Ainsworth Building (22); Oregon Society of Artists
References: DAV; HUG; WWW; A2 (1917, 20–22, 44); A3 (35); C3 (28, 29)
Media: Watercolor, oils, pen and ink, prints (woodcuts)
Specialty: Landscapes (rivers, French scenes)

Fred Strickland settled in Portland in 1915. Three years later he completed a series of watercolor and pen and ink sketches of rivers and countryside in France that he had observed during World War I while serving as a member of the Canadian Engineers. These were exhibited at the J.K. Gill Gallery in 1922. He became a teacher at Benson Technical High School in 1927. Known for his religious carving, the artist donated one of his carved pieces to Portland's Trinity Episcopal Church. He also created landscapes of the Willamette Valley and participated in the WPA program. His daughter, Phyllis Melzian, was also an artist.

STRONG, Ray Stanford

b. 1905 Corvallis, OR *d.*
Education: California School of Fine Arts; Art Students League: *F. DuMond**; Art Students League —San Francisco: *Van Sloun, Dixon; C. Keller**
Membership: Oregon Society of Artists; Art Students League; National Arts Club
Awards: National Arts Club—New York (1930, 31)
Collections: Multnomah County Library Collection, Gresham branch
Exhibits: Oregon Society of Artists; Creative Art Gallery; Golden Gate International Exposition—San Francisco (1939–40); Elfstrom Gallery (47); Portland Art Museum; National Arts Club; Corcoran Gallery of Art—Washington, D.C.; Pennsylvania Academy of Fine Art—Philadelphia; Santa Barbara Museum of Art; San Francisco Museum of Art; M.H. DeYoung Museum—San Francisco; California Palace of the Legion of Honor—San Francisco
References: DAV; HAV; HUG; MAL; WWW; A3 (1950); C3 (27, 28, 31, 45–49)

Media: Oil, charcoal
Specialty: Murals, dioramas, landscapes

Although born in Corvallis, Ray Strong began painting at the age of eight while studying at the California School of Fine Arts. He continued his education in New York at the Art Students League. In 1924 he became a teacher at the College of Marin in California. Strong was a charter member of the Oregon Society of Artists and continued exhibiting with them intermittently through 1949. His oil paintings, *The Kale Patch* and *The Sandy River Gorge* are in the Multnomah County Library Collection.

Strong became involved with dioramas in the mid-1930s when the U.S. Forest Service in San Francisco searched for an artist to paint backgrounds for their Civilian Conservation Corps. He later painted dioramas at Mt. Lassen, California and in White Sands, New Mexico. The University of California exhibit at the Golden Gate International Exposition in 1939 contained six of his dioramas. "In a diorama, it's not surface facts that I'm after, but a sense of substance below, the geology of a subject."

In 1940 he became education director for the Association of Co-ops in Northern California. In Decatur, Texas he painted a Post Office mural and another in San Gabriel, California, both WPA-sponsored projects. He taught for a while in the 1950s and from 1960 to 1964 he served as artist-in-residence at the Santa Barbara Museum of Natural History. He has lived and worked there ever since.

STUART, James Everett

b. 1852 Bangor, ME
d. 1941 San Francisco, CA
Education: San Francisco School of Design: *Williams, R. Yelland*, W. Keith*, Hill* (1870); New York City
Membership: Portland Art Club; American Artists Professional League
Awards: American Art Society (1902)
Collections: Oregon Historical Society; Los Angeles County Museum of Art; The White House; M.H. DeYoung Museum—San Francisco; Washington State Historical Society—Tacoma; Smithsonian Institution; Montana Historical Society—Helena; Stenzel Collection; Jocelyn Art Museum—Omaha; University of Southern California; Marquard Collection; California State Library; Painting Restoration Studio Collection; Parsons Collection; Counting Eagles Collection; Huntington Collection
Exhibits: Portland Mechanics Fairs; Portland Art Club (1886); Washington State Historical Society—Tacoma (1985); Washington State Capitol Museum (88); Oregon Historical Society (90)
References: BEN; BI; DAV; DAW; FIE; GER; HAV; HUG; MAL; SAM; SM; WWW; YNG; C1; C4 (1883, 86); C9; C24; C28; ARTC; CD (82–86); MYH; M1
Media: Oil
Specialty: Portraits, landscapes (mountains), Indians
See artwork in color section

James Everett Stuart was the grandson of the renowned painter, Gilbert Stuart. He came to California with his parents in 1860 and studied at the San Francisco School of Design under Raymond Yelland* and William Keith*. He made his first trip to the Northwest in 1876 and established a studio in 1881 in Portland's Union Block. His paintings were occasionally published in *The West Shore* and *Pacific Monthly* publications. Stuart joined the Portland Art Club and was a member of the American Artists Professional League. He helped organize the art department of the Mechanic's Fair in 1883, where he exhibited eleven paintings. In the early 1880s he had a studio in Ashland, Oregon and by 1886 listed a New York address which he maintained until 1890. He traveled to Alaska in 1891 and later to Chicago, where he lived and worked for twenty years. During his travels he continued to return to Oregon to paint. He eventually reestablished residence in San Francisco in 1912, where he opened a large gallery on Geary Street, remaining there until his death in 1941.

Stuart had a clearly identifiable style in his early years that changed as he became progressively more influenced by the French Barbizon painters. He received recognition for paintings with sunset glows on the snow-capped peaks of Mt. Hood, Mt. Adams, Mt. Rainier, and Mt. Shasta. He was fond of the landscape of the Columbia River Gorge and documented Indian life. His studio productions were elaborate and pretentious compared to the large oil sketches he made in the field. These were fresh, spontaneous, and less labored. He was nationally famous and became a millionaire from the sale of his paintings. Although expensive, his work was very popular; he was a prolific painter and was usually able to secure the prices he demanded. His unique habit of listing the price, number, date, and geographic location on the reverse of all his paintings was an identifying characteristic. He was criticized for his innovative method of painting on aluminum, which he considered indestructible. Stuart's paintings are in museum and private collections world-wide.

SWEETSER, Carolyn K.

b. 1863 Centerville, MA
d. 1952 Eugene, OR
Collections: University of Oregon Library
Exhibits: Lewis and Clark Centennial Exposition (1905); Panama Pacific International Exposition—San Francisco (15); Audubon Society (19, 22)
References: COL; DAV; DAW; WWN
Media: Watercolors
Specialty: Still life, botanicals, wildflowers, birds

Carolyn Sweetser, who specialized in wildflower and bird studies, was probably aided by her husband, Albert, who worked in the botany department at the University of Oregon. Her watercolors were featured in two exhibitions cosponsored by the Audubon Society and the University of Oregon. The first, in 1919 at the Multnomah County Library in Portland, consisted of 150 watercolors of Oregon wildflowers; the second included birds as well. Bruce Horsfall* contributed to both exhibits and Herman T. Bohlman* to the second. Sweetser is sometimes spelled Sweetzer.

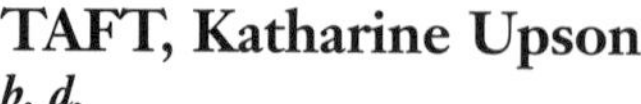

TAFT, Katharine Upson

b. d.

Membership: Oregon Art Association
Awards: Oregon State Fairs
Exhibits: Portland Industrial Exposition (1893, 96); Oregon State Fairs; Oregon Art Association (96); Oregon Industrial Exposition (96)
References: C2 (1893, 96); ARTC; CD (92–97); OSF (95, 96); M2; M3
Specialty: China painting

The first instructor in fine arts at Portland University was Katharine Upson Taft in 1891. The school closed after a short time. She advertised in the 1893 Portland Blue Book as a teacher in the Dekum Building, where she taught drawing, painting, and china painting.

TAPPAN, William Henry

b. 1821 Manchester, MA
d. 1907 Manchester, MA
Awards: Oregon State Fair
Collections: Oregon Historical Society; Wisconsin Historical Society; Amon Carter Museum—Ft. Worth, Texas
Exhibits: Oregon State Fair; Oregon Historical Society (1990)
References: BEN; DAV; DAW; FIE; GER; GW; SAM; SMI; WWW; YNG; C9; CD (1863); MYH; OSF (62); M1
Media: Oil, prints (engraving)
Specialty: Maps, landscape

Cartographer, engraver, and itinerant artist, William Henry Tappan was sent to Oregon in 1849 with the U.S. Mounted Rifle Regiment that took possession of the new Army post at Fort Vancouver. His sketches were used for the engravings of the Expedition Report; fifty sketches produced along the way survived and were reproduced by the Wisconsin Historical Society in 1931. These, and the ones by Joseph G. Bruff, are the primary sources for views along the early route. Tappan lived in Clark County territory for two decades. He appears to be the region's earliest resident professional artist. He designed and engraved the state seal of Washington and painted much of the local scenery, including the *Methodist Mission at The Dalles*. Tappan exhibited work in the Oregon State Fair of 1862, winning a first place award. In his varied career, besides being an accomplished artist, he helped lay out the town of St. Helens and served as a legislator in Washington and Massachusetts. Following his return to Manchester, Massachusetts in 1876, he wrote an account of its history.

TARPLEY, Bessie

b. d.

Awards: Oregon State Fairs
Exhibits: Oregon State Fairs
References: OSF (1896, 97); M2
Media: Watercolor, oil
Specialty: Marines, portraits

Birth and death information is unavailable for Bessie Tarpley. She won awards for her oil and watercolor entries at the Oregon State Fairs. Tarpley organized an art class and study group at the Portland Art Museum in 1898; many of the first docents at the Museum came from this group. Records show a Salem address for her in 1896.

TAYLOR, Mary. *See* BARRIER, Mary

TESTER, Jefferson

b. 1900 Mountain City, TN
d. 1972 Portland, OR
Education: Art Institute of Chicago (1926); *S. Bell**
Membership: Attic Club; Oregon Society of Artists
Awards: Critic's Choice Show—New York (1945)
Collections: Oregon Historical Society; Powell Collection; Goodman Collection; Booth Collection; Parsons Collection; Gerber Collection; Pathways Collection; Huntington Collection; Hallie Ford Museum of Art—Willamette University
Exhibits: Oregon Society of Artists; Babcock Gallery—New York (1PS 1944); Art Institute of Chicago (45); Armory Show—New York (45); National Academy of Design (45); Paris (1PS 52); Dekum Gallery; Oregon Historical Society (90); Clatsop County Historical Society (94)
References: DAV; HAV; WWW; C9; C11
Media: Oil
Specialty: Portraits, landscapes, genre
See artwork in color section

Jefferson Tester grew up in Roseburg, Oregon with his sister, Amanda Tester Snyder*. As a youth, he rode a freight train to San Francisco to attend art school there. In the early 1920s, after working on a Bay Area newspaper, he returned to Oregon and joined the art department of the *Oregonian*. He was one of the founders of the Attic Club in 1925.

Tester moved to Chicago, where he studied at the Art Institute. He then went to New York to enter the commercial art field. After twenty years with some of the largest New York advertising agencies, Tester left to pursue a career in the fine arts. He traveled and had solo shows in Mexico, the West Indies, Italy, and Paris. These shows received wide critical acclaim. He eventually settled in southern Europe

In the late 1940s Tester created seven covers for *Time* magazine as well as illustrations for *The New Yorker*, *Saturday Evening Post*, *Colliers*, and other national magazines. He was selected to show his work in the "Critics Choice of the Contempory," a 1945 exhibit at the New York Armory. His painting, *Umbrellas*, was chosen by Devree, a *New York Times* art critic, as one of the ten leading canvases of the show. After a visit to New Orleans, he did a series on jazz musicians. His landscapes, circus pictures, and portraits were also well received. His works reflect an individual, energetic style, solid composition, and a brilliant sense of color and rhythm—all executed in a disciplined manner. Tester considered himself an abstract impressionist but, as one critic wrote, was less concerned with objective reality or abstract form than with mood and atmosphere.

In 1963 Tester returned to Portland, married his fifth wife, a childhood sweetheart, and lived in Lake Oswego until his death.

THOMSON, Louise A.M.

b. 1864 London, England
d. 1966 Portland, OR
Education: South Kensington School of Art—London
Membership: Oregon Society of Artists
Awards: Oregon Society of Artists (1935)
Collections: Oregon Historical Society
Exhibits: Oregon Society of Artists; Portland Art Museum
References: COL; WWN; A2 (1942); C3 (27–32–36); M2; M3

Media: Oil, watercolor
Specialty: Landscapes, church interiors

Louise Thomson was a music teacher in India from 1895 to 1900. She arrived in Portland in 1910 and taught music and art to the students of St. Helens Hall from 1921 to 1931. A charter member of the Oregon Society of Artists in 1927, she continued to teach art privately for many years and produced illustrations after leaving St. Helens Hall.

THORNTON, Nancy Mickey Huston

b. 1811 Carlisle, PA
d. 1889 Salem, OR
Education: Pennsylvania
Awards: Benton County Fair (1859)
Exhibits: Benton County Fair (1859); Autry Museum—Los Angeles (1995)
References: C23; M2; M3
Media: Watercolor

Educated in Pennsylvania, Nancy Thornton and her husband came to Oregon from Illinois. She established and taught in the first art school in Oregon, the Oregon City Seminary in 1847, which was renamed the Female School for Instruction of Young Ladies and Misses. Thornton was winner of one of the first art awards reported in Oregon at the 1859 Benton County Fair and was the first-known artist to take up residence in Oregon. It is possible that some of her sketches were the basis for the illustrations in husband J. Quinn Thornton's book, *Oregon and California in 1848.* The Thorntons later moved to Salem.

TOFFT, Peter Peterson

b. 1825 Kolding, Denmark
d. 1901 London, England
Education: Denmark
Collections: Oakland Museum; Bancroft Library—University of California Berkeley; Oregon Historical Society; Stenzel Collection; Montana Historical Society—Helena; Boston Museum of Fine Arts
Exhibits: 4th Industrial Exposition —San Francisco (1864); Royal Academy—London; University of Oregon (1959); Oregon Historical Society (90)
References: BEN; BI; DAV; DAW; GER; HAV; HUG; MAL; SAM; THI; C9; C12
Media: Watercolor, oil
Specialty: Landscapes, marines

Peter Tofft left home as a sailor, but ended this career in San Francisco in 1849. The allure of gold and promise of an easy fortune brought him to the Oregon territory in 1852, there he sketched while he panned for gold. He traveled the western United States and Canada, where his legacy of sketches and watercolors today remain as valuable historic documents. An 1866 horseback accident in Yellowstone territory caused him to abandon his life as an adventurer and follow the pursuit of art. Watercolors of the Flathead Reservation, Ft. Owens, and the area around Virginia City and Helena, Montana produced during his recuperation period show impressive attention to detail. He worked his way east, with brief stops in St. Louis and Rochester, New York, before sailing for England in 1867. It was in this year that he gained national attention when his work appeared in *Harpers* magazine.

Tofft was described as very intelligent, difficult to get along with, often arrogant, and irritable. A mining magnate and his wife became his patrons and helped support him by acting as his agents in the United States. He earned an amount sufficent to make his last years in England comfortable, with enough remaining in his estate to will to the poor children of his hometown, Kolding, Denmark. He signed his work *Tofft*, *Toft*, *Tofts*, *Toffts*, or with the monogram letter "*t*" encircled around the stem.

TOMLINSON, Henry Mulford

b. 1875 Bridgeton, NJ
d. 1967 Portland, OR
Education: Rhode Island School of Design; Cornell University; Brown University; *P. Sheffers**
Membership: Oregon Society of Artists; American Artists Professional League
Exhibits: Oregon Society of Artists; American Artists Professional League (1933); Portland Art Museum
References: BI; COL; DAW; WWN; A2 (1942, 44, 46, 48); C3 (29–31, 34, 35, 45–49)

Henry Tomlinson was an attorney who taught at the Northwest College of Law and retired as a municipal judge. He was a charter member and former president of the Oregon Society of Artists and participated in a group show there in 1936, as well as in many of their regular exhibitions. At age eighty-two he continued to paint outdoors.

TOROK, Jolan

b. 1886 Lippa, Hungary
d. 1962 Portland, OR
Membership: Artists Equity; Portland Art Museum (Artist Membership)
Collections: Portland Art Museum; Reed College
Exhibits: Reed College (1PS 1950); Kharouba Gallery (1PS 50; 4PS 54); Lincoln County Art Center; Salem (51); Portland Art Museum; Artists Equity (58); Oregon Centennial (59)
References: A3 (1953–55); C1; C6; C16

Jolan Torok began painting in 1948 and had one-person shows at Reed College and the Kharouba Gallery in 1950. She also contributed works to juried shows at the Portland Art Museum from 1953 to 1955. Torok was one of four women artists featured at the Kharouba Gallery exhibition in 1954. She was the mother of sculptor Frederic Littman.

TOWER, James Lynn

b. 1909 ***d.***
Education: American Academy of Art—Chicago: *Lowes*; Chouinard Art Institute—Los Angeles
Collections: Oregon Historical Society; Ninth Circuit Court of Appeals—Portland
Exhibits: Portland Art Museum
References: A4 (1946); CD (40)
Media: Watercolor, oil, pencil, pen and ink
Specialty: Landscapes (lighthouses), western genre

James Lynn Tower worked for the *Oregonian* newspaper art department and was best known for his series of nine Oregon lighthouses in watercolor. The Portland Art Museum's 1946 exhibit, *War Time People and Places* featured his watercolors. Tower also worked in photo-engraving and illustrated books and magazines.

TOWER, Minnie Burrell

b. 1852
d. 1934
Collections: Coos County Historical Society
References: OR (Coos County Historical Society)
Media: Oil

According to the Coos County Historical Society, Minnie Tower was an artist who worked primarily in oil. She listed a Marshfield, Oregon address.

TRAYLE, Helen

b. 1917 Portland, OR ***d.***
Education: Museum Art School: *P. Sheffers**, *A. Patecky**; Lincoln

County Art Center; University of Oregon Extension
Membership: Oregon Society of Artists
Exhibits: Portland Art Museum; Oregon Society of Artists; Lincoln County Art Center
References: A2 (1944, 46, 48), C3 (50)
Media: Oil, watercolor, and pastels
Specialty: Portraiture, still life

Helen Trayle taught life drawing and portraiture at the Lincoln County Art Center, also known as the Gallery by the Sea. At that time she lived in Lincoln City on the Oregon Coast. In 1954 she moved to Portland. She also signed her name *Helen Kreps*.

TREVETT, Katherine Lucy

b. 1866
d. 1955 Portland, OR
Education: Weimar, Germany: *Struys* (1882)
Exhibits: Portland Mechanics Fair
References: C4 (1885); M2; M3
Media: Watercolor

Lucy Trevett was one of the few Oregon women who studied in Europe prior to 1900. She studied in Germany with Alexandre Struys, whose portrait of her is in the collection of the Oregon Historical Society. She had a studio in Portland in the early 1890s and taught at the Portland Academy from 1890 to 1912.

TRULLINGER, Isabella. *See* GEER, Isabella

TRULLINGER, John Henry

b. 1870 Forest Grove, OR
d. 1960 Portland, OR
Education: Newlyn School—Cornwall, England; Academy of Stanhope Forbes—England; Académie Julian; Académie de Colarossi; Académie de la Grande Chaumière
Membership: Society of Oregon Artists; American Artists Professional League
Collections: Clatsop County Historical Society; Bush House Museum—Salem; Powell Collection; Portland Art Museum; Booth Collection; Painting Restoration Studio Collection; Parsons Collection; Lundberg Collection; Cofield Collection
Exhibits: Paris Salon—Société des Artistes Français (1909); Portland Art Museum (1PS 10); Society of Oregon Artists (13); Corcoran Gallery of Art—Washington, D.C. (34); American Artists Professional League (38); Clatsop County Historical Society (89–90; retrospective 94)
References: COL; DAV; DAW; WWN; WWW; A2 (1912, 34, 40, 42); A3 (35, 36); C10; C11; CD (11, 13, 16, 18)
Media: Oil, watercolor, pastel
Specialty: Portraits, landscape
See artwork in color section

John Trullinger was born to pioneer businessman/inventer John C. Trullinger and Hannah Boyle. At age five his family moved to Astoria, where they owned and operated a sawmill and box factory. In 1885 John and his brothers became electricians and stockholders in their father's electric company, producing the first electric light system on the North coast. From 1886 to 1888 Trullinger was a member of the Oregon National Guard, listing his profession as musician and fireman. By 1895 he was producing portraits, including a likeness of his future wife, Sadie Gilbert.

In 1902 Trullinger decided, "Even to be a poor artist would be more pleasurable than to be a successful businessman" and left for England with his wife. He attended art school there and continued his studies in Paris from 1904 to 1909. In 1909 his painting, *Lady with a Parasol*, a portrait of his wife, was accepted for exhibition at the Paris Salon by the Société des Artistes

Français. He was the only resident Oregon painter of his day to have been so honored. The Trullinger family returned to Portland in 1910 to a one-person exhibit of his paintings at the Portland Art Museum. Soon after his return he opened a studio in the Commonwealth Building in Portland and began executing portrait commissions. He painted a commissioned portrait of Louise Bryant, at that time married to his cousin Paul. After a divorce in 1912 he met and established residence with Edna Goodhue in 1916, with whom he spent the next forty years. Trullinger participated in the WPA exhibit of paintings at the Corcoran Gallery in Washington, D.C. in 1934.

Trullinger's figures painted indoors were solidly constructed, academic and somewhat conservative. In contrast, his landscapes displayed a mosaic of pigment and tactile surfaces in an impressionistic style. To Trullinger's dismay he discovered it was very difficult for a practicing artist to find sufficient patronage to enable him to live comfortably; he addressed this problem in an article in the *Oregonian* shortly after his return from Europe. His sister, Isabelle Trullinger Geer*, was also an artist.

TURNER, Ralph James

b. 1935 Ashland, OR ***d.***
Education: Reed College (1958); Museum Art School: *J. McLarty**, *L. Bunce**, *M. Russo** (58); Portland State University (59)
Exhibits: Portland Art Museum; Cafe Espresso Gallery (1959); Oregon Centennial (59)
References: A3 (1958); C6
Media: Prints (lithograph)

Ralph Turner was a sculptor and printmaker as well as a painter. He also studied calligraphy with the well-known Lloyd Reynolds. He became a teacher in Alaska in 1959.

TYLER, Phil

b. 1914 Mobile, AL
d. 1983 Hood River, OR
Education: Art Center School of Design—Los Angeles
Membership: National Watercolor Society; American Artists Professional League
Collections: Capitol Collection—Salem
Exhibits: New York; Washington, D.C.; San Diego, Los Angeles; Keller's Gallery—Salem; Dark Horse Gallery—Beaverton (1953)
Media: Watercolor, prints (engraving)
Specialty: Western genre, landscapes (mountains)

Phil Tyler moved to the upper Hood River Valley from California in 1948. He left his position as staff artist for an engraving firm in San Francisco because of deadline pressure, which may have contributed to a stomach ulcer. It was fitting that he located near the mountain that would figure so prominently in his paintings. His goal was to document life on the western cattle ranch; he traveled thousands of miles throughout the Northwest researching and photographing the spirit of the contemporary West. In the studio he translated these scenes into a series of atmospheric watercolor washes. He experimented with other media but watercolor remained his favorite because of its flexibility and unpredictable qualities. His work was featured in calendars and the *American Artist* magazine. Tyler was paired with Ed Quigley* in a two-man exhibit that traveled the state as an outreach from the University of Oregon. He is a member of the Cowboy Hall of Fame in Oklahoma. He was also a teacher.

V

VAN HEVELINGEN, Frances Abbott

b. 1916 Juneau, AK *d.*
Education: St. Mary's Academy; University of Oregon: *A. Vincent**, *D. McCosh** (1934–38); *C. and H. Morris** (54–57)
Membership: Portland Art Museum (Artist Membership)
Awards: Seattle Art Museum; Smithsonian Institution Traveling Exhibits
Collections: Portland Art Museum; Seattle Art Museum; University of Oregon; U.S. Bank; Hilton Hotel; Pacific Power & Light Collection; Oregon Historical Society; Arlene and Harold Schnitzer Collection; Huntington Collection; Hallie Ford Museum of Art—Willamette University
Exhibits: Portland Art Museum; Denver Art Museum; San Francisco Museum of Art; Seattle Art Museum; Bush House Museum—Salem; Oregon State University; Lipman Little Gallery (1PS 1959); Smithsonian Institution Traveling Exhibits; Oregon Centennial (59); University of Oregon (75)
References: A3 (1958); C6; C7 58, 59); C22
Media: Encaustic (on silk, paper)

Frances Van Hevelingen chose the medium of encaustic because there is "complete freedom with encaustic ... (one) can get a feeling of motion into painting." She participated in museum exhibits in Portland, Seattle, Denver, and San Francisco. Van Hevelingen's work can be found in private and public collections throughout the Northwest as well as the Rental Sales Gallery of the Portland Art Museum.

VEATCH, Lilyann. *See* WINDUS, Lilyann

VINCENT, Andrew McDuffie

b. 1898 Hutchinson, KS
d. 1993 Brookings, OR
Education: Art Institute of Chicago
Membership: American Artists Professional League; Oregon Guild of Painters and Sculptors; Oregon Society of Artists; Portland Art Museum (Artist Membership); University Alumni Art League, University of Oregon
Awards: Art Institute of Chicago (1928); American Artists Professional League (34); Seattle Art Museum (35, 40)
Collections: Portland Art Museum; Powell Collection; Seattle Art Museum; University of Oregon; Coos Art Museum; Painting Restoration Studio Collection; Parsons Collection; Lundberg Collection; Huntington Collection
Exhibits: Art Institute of Chicago (1928); Oregon Society of Artists; Seattle Art Museum (53); Portland Art Museum (1PS 46, AM, 1PS 53); American Artists Professional League (33, 34); University Alumni Art League; Golden Gate International Exposition—San Francisco (39–40); San Francisco Museum of

Art (43); Elfstrom Gallery; Western Washington Fair; Oregon Guild of Painters and Sculptors (48; 1PS 48); Denver Art Museum; Spokane Museum (54, 55, 57); Salem (54, 1PS 57); Washington State University (55); Bush House Museum—Salem (1PS 56); Henry Art Gallery—University of Washington (58); University of Colorado Annual (58); California Palace of the Legion of Honor—San Francisco; Mills College—Oakland; Oregon Centennial (59); Clatsop County Historical Society (94)

References: ALM; COL; DAV; DAW; HAV; MAL SUP; OET; VOL; WWN; WWW; A2 (1932, 42, 46); A3 (35, 38, 39, 49–51, 56); A4 (59); C3 (30, 31, 34); C6; C7 (30, 31, 35, 36, 38, 40); C8; C11; C13 (46); C25 (35, 36); C30 (46)

Media: Oil, watercolor

Specialty: Landscapes, murals

See artwork in color section

Andrew Vincent and his family moved to Salem, Oregon in 1910. After graduating from Salem High School in 1917, Vincent went to France with the Signal Corps, where he recorded his World War I experiences in cartoon form. Some of these were published by the *Boston Post* in 1919.

From 1923 to 1928 Vincent studied at the Art Institute of Chicago, winning the Knapp Memorial prize in 1928. He taught there briefly before moving to a position as art instructor for painting and drawing at the University of Oregon in Eugene. By 1931 Vincent had been appointed head of the department of fine and applied arts, a position he held until his retirement in 1968. During his tenure he brought the Carnegie Program to the University in 1930. Yale University and the University of Oregon were the only schools to take part in this summer program for art teachers and art educators from all over the United States which lasted for fifteen years. He was director of the program during its last few years.

Vincent was well known for his WPA murals, such as that of the old Salem Post Office installed in 1942, now in the State Executive Building. He painted additional murals for the Toppenish, Washington Post Office in 1940, the Eugene Council Chamber, and the Sunset Inn at Gold Beach, Oregon.

His canvases were described as big, bold, and warm as evidenced by his use of light and color. His earlier works show some influence of Cézanne. He made few changes to his palette throughout his career. Andrew Vincent influenced the Oregon art scene through his painting, exhibitions, and teaching. Many practicing artists had the benefit of his long teaching career. He spent the final years of his life living and painting in Brookings, Oregon.

VOLKWINKLER, Maybelle

b. 1900 Wisconsin ***d.***

Membership: American Artists Professional League

Exhibits: Portland Art Museum

References: COL; WWN; A2 (1940, 46)

Media: Oil, watercolor

A member of the American Artists Professional League, Maybelle Volkwinkler exhibited at the Portland Art Museum in 1940 and 1946. She lived in La Grande.

VON PRIBOSIC, Viktor

b. 1909 Cleveland, OH

d. 1959 San Diego, CA

Collections: Brooklyn Art Museum; Los Angeles County Museum of Art; Library of Congress; San Francisco Museum of Art; San Diego Museum

Exhibits: San Francisco (1935); Los Angeles County Museum of Art

(1PS 37, 39); New York World's Fair (39); Borden Gallery—Los Angeles (39); Golden Gate International Exposition—San Francisco (39–40); Umatilla County Library (2PS 53); Meier and Frank Co. (53); Dark Horse Gallery—Beaverton

References: DAV; HUG; MAL SUP; WWAA

Media: Oil, watercolor, prints (woodcut, lithograph, etching)

Viktor Von Pribosic moved to Los Angeles in 1928 and to Oak Grove, Oregon in 1944. While in California, he designed theater sets and furniture and worked as a photographer. In 1939 he participated in the New York World's Fair and the Golden Gate International Exposition in San Francisco. In 1953 he joined Albert Patecky* in establishing an art studio and workshop in Oregon. They had a joint exhibition that year at the Meier and Frank Co. He later established his gallery, The Dark Horse, in Beaverton. His wife, Gerrie, was also an artist.

VOORHIES, Charles Howard

b. 1901 Portland, OR

d. 1970 Portland, OR

Education: University of California Berkeley (1926–28); *Rivera* (30); California School of Fine Arts: *Sterne* (35, 36)

Membership: Oregon Guild of Painters and Sculptors; Artists Equity; Portland Art Museum (Artist Membership)

Collections: Portland Art Museum; Powell Collection; Booth Collection; San Francisco Museum of Art; Multnomah County Library Collection; Salishan Lodge Collection; University of Oregon; Reed College; Kaiser Permanente Collection; Parsons Collection; Huntington Collection; Breithaupt Collection

Exhibits: Santa Fe Museum (1PS 1930); Arts and Crafts Society (1PS 30); Portland Art Museum (1PS 32, 34, 36, 48, 57, retrospective 72); San Francisco Art Association (38); New York World's Fair (39); Art Institute of Chicago (40); San Francisco Museum of Art (42); Oregon Guild of Painters and Sculptors (45, 46, 48; 2PS 48); Western Washington Fair; California Palace of the Legion of Honor—San Fancisco; M.H. DeYoung Museum—San Francisco; Reed College (1PS 49); Harvey Welch Gallery (1PS); Kharouba Gallery (1PS 52); Seattle Art Museum; Oregon Centennial (59); University of Oregon (75); Clatsop County Historical Society (94)

References: COL; DAV; HUG; MAL SUP; OET; WWN; A2 (1933, 42, 46, 48); A3 (39, 49–51, 53, 56); A4 (59); C7 (52); C8; C11; C15 (46); C22; C30 (46)

Media: Watercolor, oil, chalk, gouache

Specialty: Murals, landscapes (Europe), seascapes (coast)

See artwork in color section

See photograph of artist on p. 89

Charles Voorhies was born in Portland to a pioneer Oregon family. He studied architecture at the University of California from 1926 to 1928, and then worked with Diego Rivera on the San Francisco Stock Exchange murals in 1930. He assisted Maurice Sterne with murals for the Library of the Justice Department in Washington D.C. in 1937. Subsequent travel took him to France, Italy, England, Mexico, and Spain for a year. Returning to Portland in 1939, he joined the staff of the Museum Art School, where he taught drawing and painting until 1957.

His exhibition history is extensive. In California during the 1930s and 40s, he showed work at the San Francisco Museum of Art, the California Palace of the Legion of Honor, and the DeYoung Museum. Voorhies also contributed to the New York World's Fair Exhibition and to the Art Institute of Chicago. The Portland Art Museum featured him in a one-person show in 1932 and he entered work in subsequent Museum shows on a fairly regular basis.

In the 1950s the mood in his series of Willamette Valley works was somber and darker in color than his previous palette, coinciding with a period of serious health problems. In 1958 he returned to France and Spain, where he painted for nine months and produced what Rachael Griffin* termed "the tall, golden oils of the Spanish sojourn." Upon his return, he continued to offer classes at a studio in his home in Portland.

Two years after his death the Portland Art Museum held a retrospective of his work. The catalog for this exhibit contained essays by Griffin, Jack McLarty*, and Jack Wilkinson*. Griffin recalled how line and brushwork became more rapid and confident as the years passed and his view of nature broadened and deepened. Voorhies considered Cézanne and Chinese landscapists to be strong influences in his painting. His line was calligraphic and figures were rare in his work. He said, "I approached painting by way of architecture." McLarty elaborated, "Perhaps it's the line that says the most ... it points out the bony structure of the rock and cuts out the shape of the cliffs and bare hills."

W

WADDINGHAM, John Alfred

b. 1915 London, England *d.*

Education: Coronado School of Fine Arts—San Diego; Museum Art School; University of Portland; *Brandt, O'Hara, Post*

Membership: Oregon Society of Artists; Attic Club; Master Watercolor Society of Oregon; American Watercolor Society; Northwest Watercolor Society; Portland Art Museum (Artist Membership)

Awards: Oregon State Fair (1952)

Collections: Oregon Historical Society; Ford Motor Company—Dearborn, Michigan; Multnomah Athletic Club Collection; Pacific University; Hurst Collection

Exhibits: Portland Art Museum; Oregon Society of Artists; Kharouba Gallery (1950); Elfstrom Gallery (1PS 51); Oakland Art Gallery (52); Meier and Frank Co. (1PS 52, 55); Lincoln County Art Center (1PS 52, 54, 58); Maryhill Museum—Goldendale, Washington (1PS 52); Oregon State Fairs (52, 53); Seattle Art Museum; Northwest Watercolor Society; Master Watercolor Society of Oregon (58); Bush House Museum—Salem; Frye Museum—Seattle (59); Oregon Centennial (59); Oregon Historical Society (90)

References: WWAA; A2 (1940, 48); A3 (50–53, 55); C3 (50, 51, 52); C7 (54, 55, 57, 58); C9; C17; C29 (54, 55, 57); ARTC

Media: Watercolor, oil

Specialty: Historic buildings, street furniture (bridges, lampposts)

See artwork in color section

John Waddingham was born in London, England and lived with his family in India and Canada before coming to the United States at the age of eleven. He became an artist after high school. In 1946, after a brief time at the *Sacramento Bee* in California, he joined the *Oregon Journal* newspaper as the promotion art director. In 1960 he moved to the *Oregonian* to become their editorial art director, a position he held for the next twenty years. When he retired he became a freelance artist and continued to paint and travel. He is also a well-known teacher and has frequently been asked to serve as juror for exhibitions.

Waddingham has had memberships in the Oregon Society of Artists, the Attic Club, the Master Watercolor Society of Oregon, and the American Watercolor Society. The latter has twice circulated his paintings throughout the United States. His illustrations have appeared in *Ford Times*, *Kiwanas International*, *The Artist* (London), *Antwerpen* (Belgium), and he has had feature articles in *American Artist* magazine in May of 1967 as well as several northwest publications. He has a lengthy exhibition history and has received many awards.

Working in a variety of media and styles, Waddingham has preferred semi-abstract watercolors. Iron-fronted historic buildings, restaurants, and street "furniture" such as lamps, trees, and fireplugs have been subjects that he has captured well. He preferred to work outdoors and painted vertically on a French easel. Keeping his eye on the subject as he painted, he turned the work upside down occasionally to gain a fresh perspective. The Portland Art Museum's Rental Sales Gallery has represented him. He often signs his work *Wadd.*

WADE, Murray Lincoln

b. 1876 Salem, OR
d. 1961 Portland, OR
Education: Mark Hopkins Institute: *W. Keith**, (1890s); *C. Cooke**
Awards: Oregon State Fair
Collections: Oregon Historical Society
Exhibits: Oregon State Fair; Oregon Historical Society (1990)
References: COL; DAV; DAW; HUG; WWN; C9; CD (1905); OSF (1894)
Media: Oil, watercolor, pen and ink, prints (lithograph, engraving)
Specialty: Personalities (theater, legislators, vaudeville)

Murray Wade was a newspaper cartoonist and commercial artist who worked for the *San Francisco Examiner,* the *Oregonian*, the *Portland Telegram*, the *Portland News*, and Salem's *Capital Journal.* He was best known for many sketches completed during legislative sessions and published in 1923 in a booklet by the *Capital Journal.* Wade later wrote a syndicated column called "Capital Parade." In 1922 he published the *Oregon Magazine*. He later served as a WPA artist. Wade, primarily a graphic artist, was also adept at oil and watercolor.

WALPOLE, Frederick Andrews

b. 1861 Port Douglas, NY
d. 1904 Santa Barbara, CA
Education: Art Institute of Chicago; Chicago: *Sloan*
Exhibits: Portland Art Museum (1903–04); St. Louis Universal Exposition (04); Carnegie-Mellon University (73)
Media: Watercolor, pen and ink, prints (lithograph)
Specialty: Botanicals

At age ten, Frederick Walpole moved with his family from New York to Chicago. He began his art training with Chicago artist, Sloan, and at the Art Institute. Eleven years later he moved to Oregon, north of Jacksonville, and homesteaded near the Rogue River. In 1883 he moved his family to Portland and became a designer and crayon artist for Lewis and Dryden Lithographing, a position he held for ten years. Encouraged to apply for a position at the Smithsonian Institution in Washington D.C., he relocated there to begin a new career as a botanical artist for the Federal Government. Sadly his wife died there of typhoid fever. Now a widower at 35, Walpole sent his young son home to Oregon to be raised by friends and family.

Walpole produced detailed india ink and brush work, fine line drawings, and vibrant color studies. Critics consider him among the finest botanical artists of the nineteenth century. Field work took Walpole west to Alaska, Washington, and again to Oregon from 1899 to 1900. Field studies of one season were placed on view at the Portland Art Association several months before his death.

In the last eight years of his life he produced over one thousand drawings, some with lines so fine they resemble engravings and could not be reproduced with satisfaction at that time. He died of typhoid fever at age 43.

WALTERS, Carl Albert

b. 1883 Fort Madison, IA
d. 1955 Woodstock, NY
Education: Minneapolis School of Art: *Henri, Sloan*

Membership: Society of Oregon Artists; Society of Independent Artists—New York; American Society of Painters, Sculptors and Gravers
Collections: Whitney Museum of Art; Detroit Institute of the Arts
Exhibits: Portland Art Museum (2PS 1915); Society of Oregon Artists (13); Panama Pacific International Exposition—San Francisco (15); Seattle Art Museum; American Federation of Arts (16); Society of Independent Artists—New York (17); Salons of America (24, 25); Copenhagen (27); Stockholm (28); Whitney Museum of Art (29–45); Art Institute of Chicago (32–45); Pennsylvania Academy of Fine Art—Philadelphia (38–45); Jeu de Paume—Paris (38)
References: BI; DAV; DAW; FIE; HAV; MAL; SA; SIA; THI; WWW; A1 (1924); A2 (13–15, 17, 18); C5; C7 (15); ARTC; CD (15–18)
Media: Oil, watercolor, crayon, prints (lithograph)
Specialty: Landscapes, shipyards, marines

Carl Walters came to Portland in 1912, first employed as an electrician. He had painted the New England Coast and mid-west scenery with artist friend Floyd Wilson*, but finally came to Oregon "where all the beautiful scenery was at hand." He had a talent for sketching and painting and soon became known for his fine landscapes. In 1918 he secured a pass to work all hours at the shipyards, sketching to record the spirit of these western industrial plants. The publication section of the U.S. Shipping Board named him their "executive artist." He sketched on site and returned to his studio to reproduce them as lithographs for publication in the shipyard papers, *Do Your Bit* and *Over the Top*. His wharf scenes often included a human element, and conveyed his sympathy for the worker. The Portland Art Museum exhibitions included his watercolors of beach scenes. The Oregon Historical Society has many of his lithographs and the shipyard papers.

Walters left Portland in 1919 for New York, where he achieved success as a ceramist and sculptor. He was awarded a Guggenheim fellowship in 1935 and won an award at the Metropolitan Museum of Art in 1940 for his ceramics. Walters also instructed at the Art Students League shortly after his arrival there. After 1947 his address was Woodstock, New York.

WANKER, Maude Walling

b. 1881 Lake Oswego, OR
d. 1970 Lincoln City, OR
Education: Museum Art School: *C. Stephens**; Art Institute of Chicago (1936); *B. Hinshaw** (37); University of Oregon: *Steinhof* (38); Vienna
Membership: American Artists Professional League; Lincoln County Art Association; Oregon Society of Artists; Arts Guild; Oregon Amateur Watercolor Society; Master Watercolor Society of Oregon; Skidmore Fountain Art Center Inc.
Awards: Multnomah County Fair (1942)
Collections: Oregon Historical Society; Capitol Collection—Salem; La Grande Library; Hallie Ford Museum of Art—Willamette University
Exhibits: Oregon Society of Artists; Seattle Art Museum; Portland Art Museum; Arts Guild; American Artists Professional League (1933–37, 39, 53); Meier and Frank Co. (1PS 35); National Exhibition of American Art (39); Lake Oswego Country Club, retrospective; Multnomah County Fair (42); Lincoln

County Art Center (42, 48, 1PS 59); Elfstrom Gallery; Master Watercolor Society of Oregon (58); Attic Club; Oregon Centennial (59); Oregon Historical Society (90); Clatsop County Historical Society (94)

References: ALM; COL; DAV; DAW; HAV; KOV; MAL SUP; OET; PET; SAM; WWN; WWW; A2 (1932–34, 42, 44, 46, 48); A5 (33); C3 (29, 30, 33–35); C7 (30, 37, 38, 40); C9; C10; C11; C13 (46–48); C14; M2; M3

Media: Watercolor, oil

Specialty: Cityscapes, seascapes, historic sites

See artwork in color section

Maude Wanker grew up in the Tualatin Valley, where she began sketching as a child. After her marriage in 1901 and the birth of a child, she began attending the Museum Art School on an irregular basis. In 1939 she was one of three artists chosen to represent Oregon at the fourth National Exhibition of American Art, held in New York's Rockefeller Center.

Wanker moved to the Oregon Coast and devoted much of her organizational skills to the creation of the Lincoln County Art Association in 1941 and the Lincoln County Art Center in 1942. She dedicated herself to the Center for twenty-eight years. In 1945 she opened her own gallery, The Paint Box Gallery, at Wecoma Beach, now part of Lincoln City. This became a gathering place for a colony of local artists.

Between 1930 and 1940 Wanker painted almost one hundred depictions of Oregon's historical sites, traveling throughout the state to record them before they disappeared. These included the Old Methodist Church, the Old Blockhouse at The Dalles, and paintings of the Skidmore Fountain in Summer and Winter, which are in the Oregon Historical Society collection.

Wanker, who taught throughout her career, was a prolific painter. She exhibited her oils and watercolors in twenty states, had one-person shows in ten states and was awarded over four hundred prizes. She was an illustrator for the *Ford Times*. Wanker was the first president of the Master Watercolor Society of Oregon, founded in 1958. Kovinick (see Ref. KOV) gives a birthdate of 1882.

WARD, J. Stephen

b. 1876 St. Joseph, MO ***d.***

Education: San Diego: *Braun, Brewer*

Membership: Oregon Society of Artists; American Artists Professional League

Awards: Arizona State Fair (1923); Oregon State Fair (30); Oregon Society of Artists (30)

Collections: Powell Collection; Fairfax High School—Hollywood, California

Exhibits: Arizona State Fair; Witte Museum—San Antonio (1929); Medford (30); Oregon State Fair (30); Oregon Society of Artists; Jacksonville (31, 33); American Artists Professional League (35, 36); Clatsop County Historical Society (94)

References: BI; DAV; DAW; FIE; HUG; MAL; WWW; C3 (1930, 31); C11

Specialty: Landscapes (mountains, lakes)

In the 1920s J. Stephen Ward lived in Glendale, California, where he operated an art gallery with his son, Thurlow. In 1930 he came to Medford, and from 1931 to 1933 he lived in Jacksonville. Florence Marsh*, of the Oregon Society of Artists, was impressed by his art and encouraged him to exhibit in the East. He followed her advice and later developed a national reputation.

WARNER, Annie

b. d.

Awards: Oregon State Fair

Exhibits: Portland Mechanics Fairs; Oregon State Fair
References: C4 (1883, 85); OSF (85)
Specialty: Still life

Annie Warner exhibited at the Portland Mechanics Fairs of 1883 and 1885. She also had a still life entry at the Oregon State Fair in 1885.

WARNER, Mildred A.

b. d.
Membership: American Artists Professional League; Oregon Society of Artists; Master Watercolor Society of Oregon; Northwest Watercolor Society
Awards: Oregon Society of Artists (1943, 47)
Exhibits: Portland Art Museum; Oregon Society of Artists; Northwest Watercolor Society; Master Watercolor Society of Oregon (1958)
References: A2 (1940, 42, 44, 46); C3 (43, 46–49, 51); C29 (48, 52)
Media: Oil, watercolor

Mildred Warner was a member of the American Artists Professional League and the Master Watercolor Society of Oregon. During the 1940s she was an active participant in exhibitions at the Portland Art Museum and the Oregon Society of Artists. She had a studio in the same building as Albert Patecky* during the 1950s.

WATERS, Lella M.

b. d.
Awards: Oregon State Fairs
Exhibits: Oregon State Fairs
References: DAV; HUG; OSF (1884, 90, 94)
Media: Oil
Specialty: Landscapes (historical)

Lella Waters listed a Salem address in 1884. Her address in 1885 was Sacramento, California.

WATSON, Evelyn Belle Clogston

b. 1906 Pomona, CA
d. 1966 Portland, OR
Education: Los Angeles: *Donaldson, Schrader; S. Bell*; Steinhof*
Membership: American Artists Professional League; Oregon Society of Artists; Skidmore Fountain Art Center, Inc.
Awards: American Artists Professional League (1932, 36, 38); Minnesota State Fair (37, 38, 40)
Exhibits: Oregon Society of Artists; American Artists Professional League (1932–38)
References: DAV; HAV; MAL; WWW; C3 (1930–34); M2
Media: Charcoal, pen and ink, pastel
Specialty: Portraits, landscapes

Evelyn Watson moved to Oregon from Los Angeles in 1923 and worked for the advertising staff of Portland's Meier and Frank Co. The publicity for her Rivoli Prize-winning poster in 1928 stated she had a "grasp of plastic expression." There is a Minnesota address for her in the late 1930s, but she returned to Portland in 1940 and remained until her death in 1966.

WATSON, Mary Bridges

b. d. 1916 Los Angeles, CA
Awards: Oregon State Fairs
Exhibits: Oregon State Fairs
References: OSF (1880–86); M2; M3
Media: Oil, crayon, pencil, etching
Specialty: Landscapes, marines, china painting

Mary Bridges taught drawing and painting at Willamette University from 1882 to 1887 and remained a Salem resident until 1890. She and her husband, Sanford Watson, moved to Los Angeles, where she remained until her death.

WEBBER, Gloria Heisley

b. 1922 Pasadena, CA *d.*
Education: Pasadena City College: *Woodhull*; Museum Art School (1951–60); Art Center School of Design—Los Angeles
Membership: Oregon Society of Artists; American Watercolor Society
Collections: Oregon Historical Society; Pacific University; U.S. Bank; Woodland Park Hospital, Oregon Health Sciences University; Zell Bros. Jewelry—Portland
Exhibits: Pacific University (1PS); Bush Barn—Salem; Oregon Historical Society (1990)
References: C9
Media: Oil, watercolor
Specialty: Florals

Gloria Webber moved to Portland in 1951 and began classes at the Museum Art School. She taught at Portland Community College and Clackamas Community College. In 1958 she and twelve male artists joined the Design Studio 1030. Webber was a commercial artist for Zell Bros. Jewelry and Hood River Distillery. A member of the Oregon Society of Artists, she served as president and has been very active in the watercolor community with workshops, lectures, and teaching. She favored a large-image format. While she used a wide range of subject matter, florals were a favorite. Her technique employed a varied, luminous overlay of colors. Most of her exhibits occurred after 1959.

WEBSTER, Mary Hortense

b. 1881 Oberlin, OH *d.*
Education: Cincinnati Art Academy: *Barnhorn, Novottny;* Académie Julian; Académie de la Grande Chaumière; Holland: *Hitchcock*; Paris: *Verlet, Waldmann*; New York: *Beyer*; Pratt Institute; Art Institute of Chicago (1933)
Membership: Society of Oregon Artists
Exhibits: Paris Salon (1906); Portland Art Museum; Society of Oregon Artists (13); Art Institute of Chicago; Pennsylvania Academy of Fine Art—Philadelphia
References: DAV; FIE; MAL; PET; WWW; YNG; A2 (1912–14); ARTC; M2; M3
Media: Watercolor

Mary Webster's educational background included studies in the eastern United States and Europe. While in France she exhibited at the Paris Salon in 1906. She was the third art teacher at the Museum Art School, replacing Kate Simmons. Although primarily a sculptor, she taught a varied curriculum there from 1911 to 1914 before returning home to Ohio. Webster studied sculpture at the Art Institute of Chicago in 1933.

WEISTER, Alice Aubrey

b. 1862 Canada
d. 1936 Portland, OR
Education: Paris; Rome
Membership: Mutual Art Association; Oregon Art Association
Awards: Lewis and Clark Centennial Exposition (1905)
Exhibits: Oregon Art Association (1896); Lewis and Clark Centennial Exposition (1905); Mutual Art Association (14, 15); Portland Woman's Club (26); Oregon Society of Artists (29)
References: ARTC; C3 (1929); CD (95–09, 18, 32); M2; M3
Media: Oil

Alice Weister taught drawing, painting, sculpture, and decorative art at Portland University from 1894 until its closure in 1900. She was a photographer, and produced hand-tinted slides of Oregon scenery. She taught privately and headed the art department at the Oregon State Fair in 1926. A woman of many talents, she wrote poetry and taught psychology. Weister was among the few women who studied in Europe early in the twentieth century and spent seven years there in pursuit of further art education.

WELCH, Thaddeus

b. 1844 La Porte, LA
d. 1919 Santa Barbara, CA
Education: McMinnville College; San Francisco: *Williams, Ogilvy*; Royal Academy of Arts—Munich: *Dietz, Piloty;* Paris
Awards: Oregon State Fair
Collections: Oakland Museum; California Historical Society; California Palace of the Legion of Honor—San Francisco; Frye Museum—Seattle; Oregon Historical Society; San Diego Museum
Exhibits: Oregon State Fair; Portland Mechanics Fairs; Paris Salons; Bohemian Club—San Francisco; World Columbian Exposition—Chicago (1893)
References: BI; DAV; DAW; FI (1880, 81); HUG; MAL SUP; WWW; C4 (79, 80, 84); OSF (75); MI
Media: Oil, prints
Specialty: Landscapes, portraits

Thaddeus Welch crossed the plains by wagon train with his family. In 1847 they established their farm in McMinnville. By 1863 he was working for a printer in Portland. He studied art and sketched in California in 1866. Serious about his art, Welch traveled to Europe in 1874 to continue his studies in Munich. While there he met the artists Chase and Twachtman. In Paris he spent four years living on a houseboat, studying and sketching. Influenced by the Barbizon School, he changed his dark palette to a lighter one. He finally returned to America in 1881 for more study in the East, including New York City, and an apprenticeship to the Boston artist Prang. His entries in the Mechanics Fair Exhibitions were loaned during the period he was in Europe.

By 1889 Welch was painting in the Southwest, where he developed an interest in Pueblo subjects. He traveled to Australia before finally settling in California, where he enjoyed several commissions from Leland Stanford. His scenes of Marin and northern California landscapes are well known. Welch moved to Santa Barbara in 1905 and remained there until his death in 1919. A 1923 article in the *Oregon Journal* details Welch's importance as one of the region's outstanding artists.

WELLS, Vesta. *See* GUSTAFSON, Vesta

WENTZ, Henry (Harry) Frederick

b. 1875 The Dalles, OR
d. 1965 Portland, OR
Education: Art Students League: *Dow, F. DuMond**; Columbia University; Europe
Membership: Portland Sketch Club; Circle A Club; Society of Oregon Artists; Oregon Society of Artists
Collections: Portland Art Museum; Washington State University; Oregon Historical Society; Hallie Ford Museum of Art—Willamette University; Booth Collection; Tonkon Torp Collection; Miranda Collection; Painting Restoration Studio Collection; Parsons Collection; Huntington Collection; Pathways Collection; Lundberg Collection
Exhibits: Portland Sketch Club (1898, 99, 1900); Lewis and Clark Centennial Exposition (05); Portland Art Museum (1PS 14, 27, 29, 55; 3PS 20, 25); Circle A Club; Society of

Oregon Artists (13); Panama Pacific International Exposition—San Francisco (15); Seattle Art Museum; Oregon Society of Artists; University of Oregon; Oregon Guild of Painters and Sculptors (48); Oregon Historical Society (90)

References: ALM; COL; DAV; DAW; FIE; GER; HAV; MAL; OET; WWN; WWW; A1 (1920, 24, 53); A2 (11–15, 16, 17, 20–22, 32, 40); A4 (11, 29, 52, 59); C3 (27); C5; C7 (15, 22, 28a); C9; C21; ARTC; CD (30, 31)

Media: Oil, watercolor, prints

Specialty: Landscapes

See artwork in color section

Harry Wentz was a student of the Sketch Club and the Oregon Art Students League, where he studied under DuMond*. He went to New York to continue his art education and then attended the Lyme School in Lyme, Connecticut. When he returned to Portland he taught art and manual training at Washington High School before joining the staff at the Museum Art School from 1910 to 1941. He gave hundreds of students the benefit of his great talent as artist and teacher. Wentz was a man much beloved by his students and fellow artists and his impact went beyond the Museum, the School, and Oregon. Pietro Belluschi, architect of the Portland Art Museum, credited the influence of Wentz on his work: "a living example of the spirit to communicate not through words alone but through the purity of one's convictions. His greatness rests on the uncompromising integrity of his whole life, the humanity of his responses, on his intolerance of anything superficial, and his ability to detect instantly fraud or insincerity in people or their works." Wentz felt that teaching was as much a creative art as painting.

Harry Wentz and Floyd Wilson* had the distinction of being two Oregon painters who exhibited in both the Fine Arts Section and the Oregon Room at the Panama Pacific International Exposition in San Francisco in 1915.

His paintings had a lively charm with brilliant, harmonious colors. He painted the ceiling of the smoking room in the Pittock Mansion in Portland with an intricate design, incorporating glowing color. Wentz also produced mountain, coast, and farm scenes, some with figures. His watercolors showed great attention to detail, light, and composition.

The Wentz house at Neahkahnie, on the Oregon Coast, was a haven for artists. Arthur* and Albert Runquist* lived and worked there for many of their productive years. This house, by well-known architect A.E. Doyle, is listed on the National Register of Historic Places.

In 1958, Wentz was presented with a special award from the Portland Arts Commission for distinguished service to the community. The Museum Art School named an exhibition gallery in his honor. It was said that Harry Wentz was the most important influence on Portland artists during the first half of the twentieth century.

WERTZ, Fayler (Fritz) Lawrence

b. d.

Education: California College of Arts and Crafts: *Martinus*

Membership: Oregon Society of Artists

Awards: Oregon Society of Artists (1943)

Exhibits: Oregon Society of Artists; Portland Art Museum; Elfstrom Gallery; Lincoln County Art Center; J.K. Gill Gallery; Maryhill Museum—Goldendale, Washington (1PS 49, 59)

References: OET; A2 (1944, 46, 48); C3 (43, 46–50); C13 (48); C14

Media: Watercolor, pastel, pen and ink
Specialty: Marines, landscapes (Rogue River), circus, wildlife, western genre

Fritz Wertz lived in the Jacksonville, Gold Hill area and painted the scenery around the Rogue River Valley. His series of watercolor portraits of old-timers of the Rogue Valley was widely exhibited. He was a friend of Peter Sheffers* and Clifford Platz*. He was well known to the Portland art community.

WHEELER, Shannah Cumming

b. 1890
d. 1981 Multnomah Co., OR
Education: Museum Art School (1913–14)
Collections: Pacific Northwest College of Art
Exhibits: Portland Art Museum
References: A2 (1913, 14, 17, 22); A4 (59); CD (16–18)

Shannah Cumming was a scholarship student at the Museum Art School. She exhibited at the Portland Art Museum in the 1910s and 1920s. A group show at the Art Museum in 1959 included her work under her married name, Wheeler.

WHETSEL, Gertrude P.

b. 1886 McCune, KS
d. 1952 Orange Co., CA
*Education: C. Keller**
Membership: Oregon Society of Artists
Awards: Oregon State Fair (1922)
Exhibits: Oregon State Fair (1922); Portland Art Museum; Seattle Art Museum (28); Oregon Society of Artists
References: BEN; DAV; DAW; FIE; HUG; MAL; PET; THI; WWW; YNG; A2 (1922); C3 (28); C7 (23)
Specialty: Landscapes, marines

Gertrude Whetsel exhibited at the Portland Art Museum, the Seattle Art Museum, and the Oregon State Fair. She was a member of the Oregon Society of Artists. Whetsel lived in Portland from 1922 to 1931, moving to Los Angeles after 1933.

WHITE, Ruth Gould

b. 1909 Nebraska *d.*
Membership: Oregon Society of Artists
Collections: First Methodist Church—Republic, Kansas
Exhibits: Portland Art Museum; Oregon Society of Artists; Oregon State Fair
References: ALM; COL; WWN; A2 (1940, 44, 48); C3 (47–51)
Media: Watercolor, oil, pastel
Specialty: Religious

Ruth White was a teacher in the Portland Public School system and exhibited her work at the Portland Art Museum, Oregon State Fair, and the Oregon Society of Artists.

WHITTEN, Andrew T.

b. 1878 New York, NY
d. 1962 Multnomah Co., OR
Education: Art Institute of Chicago; National Academy of Design
Membership: Oregon Society of Artists
Awards: Oregon Society of Artists (1937, 39)
Exhibits: Oregon Society of Artists; Portland Art Museum
References: COL; DAV; WWN; A2 (1940, 48); C3 (37–39, 47–50)
Media: Oil, watercolor, pen and ink

Andrew Whitten was a member of the Oregon Society of Artists, exhibiting with them throughout the 1930s and the late 1940s. He listed an address in Dufur, Oregon.

WIDMAN, Harry F.

b. 1929 Englewood, NJ *d.*
Education: Colorado Springs Fine Arts Center (1950); Syracuse University (51); University of Oregon:

D. McCosh, J. Wilkinson*, A. Vincent** (56)
Membership: Portland Art Museum (Artist Membership)
Awards: Oregon Centennial (1959)
Collections: Portland Art Museum; Salishan Lodge Collection; University of Oregon; Reed College; Portland State University; Bush House Museum—Salem; Lewis and Clark College; Capitol Collection—Salem; Tonkon Torp Collection; Parsons Collection; Arlene and Harold Schnitzer Collection; Hallie Ford Museum of Art—Willamette University
Exhibits: Newark Library—New Jersey (1953); Portland Art Museum; Seattle Art Museum (55); Coos Bay Library (1PS 56); Eugene Art Center (1PS 57); University of Oregon (2PS 57, 75); North Bend Library (1PS 57); 12th Street Gallery—Eugene (2PS 58); Reed College (1PS 59); Roseburg Library (1PS 59); Frye Museum—Seattle (59); Oregon Centennial (59)
References: A3 (1955–58); C6; C7 (56); C22
Media: Oil, watercolor
See artwork in color section

After graduating from Syracuse University in New York, Harry Widman served in the Army. In 1954 he and Richard Muller* moved to Eugene to attend a graduate program at the University of Oregon. He became friendly with sculptor Tom Hardy and Louis Bunce*. Widman taught painting at the Extension Division in Coos Bay from 1956 to 1960. In 1958, after moving to Roseburg, he accepted teaching positions in Port Orford, Roseburg, and Grants Pass. Those who taught Extension classes and traveled around the state acted as "art missionaries," helping the far-flung art community interact. It was an opportunity for these communities to be introduced to modern art.

Widman, during his time at the University of Oregon, was exposed to a style later called the "Willamette Valley style," inspired by Cézanne, and based on color theory and interaction. This became an important stylistic manner during the 1960s and 1970s. Widman's earlier paintings contained biomorphic images taken from nature, which gradually evolved into central images or shapes against a color field.

Widman organized and directed the Southern Oregon Arts Festival in Roseburg in 1959. The festival hosted a juried exhibit with artists from Josephine, Coos, and Douglas counties. Later in his career Widman was a teacher, and then dean, at the Museum Art School in Portland.

WIGGINS, Myra Albert

b. 1869 Salem, OR
d. 1956 Seattle, WA
Education: Willamette University: *M. Watson*, M. LeGall**; Art Students League: *F. DuMond*, Chase, Twachtman* (1891–94); New York School of Art; Mills College—Oakland; Salem: *C. Cooke** (88–89)
Membership: National Association of Women Artists, Inc.; American Federation of Arts; American Artists Professional League; Women Painters of Washington; Pacific Coast Association of Painters and Sculptors; American Artists Group
Awards: Oregon State Fairs; National League of American Pen Women (1932, 39, 48, 51); Art Institute of Chicago (33); Golden Gate International Exposition—San Francisco (39)
Collections: Oregon Historical Society; Washington State Library—Olympia; YWCA—Yakima; Parsons Collection
Exhibits: Oregon State Fairs; Seattle Art

Museum (retrospective 1953, 1PS 55); Art Institute of Chicago (33); Portland Art Museum; Golden Gate International Exposition—San Francisco (39–40); Henry Art Gallery—University of Washington (43, 51); Vancouver Art Gallery (1PS); National League of American Pen Women (48); Elfstrom Gallery (1PS 50); YMCA, YWCA, Larson Museum—Yakima, Washington (1PS 51); M.H. DeYoung Museum—San Francisco (retrospective 54, 1PS 56); Oregon Historical Society (90)

References: BEN; DAV; DAW; FIE; GER; HAV; KOV; MAL; PET; SAM; WWN; WWW; A3 (1935); C7 (19, 22, 27, 28a, 29, 31, 32, 34–36, 38, 41, 43–45); C9; C30 (40, 46, 48,); OSF (1891–1900, 02–04); M2

Media: Oil, watercolor

Specialty: Still life, interiors, landscapes

See artwork in color section

Myra Wiggins' well-rounded art career included photography and writing as well as painting. She discovered photography by chance—through her brother's request for a picture of his sweetheart—and pursued it into the rarified atmosphere of the elite Photo-Secession group, organized by Alfred Stieglitz in 1902 in New York. Myra Wiggins joined two other Oregon women photographers, Lily White and Sarah Ladd, as members of this select group, numbering only 105 members nationally. She left Oregon in 1891 when she went to New York to attend the Art Student's League. She returned to Oregon in 1894. In spite of the enormous success she achieved in photography, Wiggins stated, in an essay written in 1939, that she considered herself "a professional painter and an amateur photographer."

In 1907 her husband's nursery business took the family to Toppenish, Washington. Wiggins turned away from photography and concentrated on painting, writing poetry, and teaching both singing and painting. The family moved to Seattle around 1933 and there she opened a painting studio. Wiggins was one of the six founding members of the Women Painters of Washington. She exhibited at the Seattle Art Museum with that group in 1955. She was also a member of the Pacific Coast Association of Painters and Sculptors and the American Artists Group of New York. This organization published and sold nationally the work of American artists each year as Christmas cards. Wiggins had four of her canvases selected, one of which generated near-record sales of ninety thousand cards.

Wiggins continued to garner awards for her achievements in the arts; newspaper articles referred to her as the "dean of pacific northwest women painters." Her paintings were exhibited in London, Paris, Vienna, Hamburg, the Hague, and Brussels. She had one-person exhibitions in New York, Chicago, New Orleans, Seattle, Yakima, and Vancouver, B.C. In 1948 the National League of American Pen Women presented Wiggins with their Achievement in Art Award. A sixty-two year retrospective of her photographs and paintings was exhibited by the Seattle Art Museum in 1953, followed by a retrospective in the De Young Museum in San Francisco the next year. A biography of Myra Wiggins by Carole Glauber was published in 1997.

WILEY, Lucia

b. 1906 Tillamook, OR

d. 1998 Harlem, N.Y.

Education: University of Minnesota (1924–28); University of Oregon (32); Minneapolis School of Art (32–33)

Membership: Oregon Guild of Painters and Sculptors; Artists Equity; Oregon Society of Artists; Portland

Art Museum (Artist Membership); University Alumni Art League, University of Oregon
Collections: Portland Art Museum; Powell Collection; Seattle Art Museum; Pathways Collection; Tillamook County Pioneer Museum
Exhibits: Oregon Society of Artists; Portland Art Museum; Grand Central Gallery—New York City (1935); Bennington College—Vermont (1PS 35); University Alumni Art League; Corcoran Gallery of Art—Washington, D.C. (39, 43); Walker Art Center—Minneapolis (39, 43); Whitney Museum of Art (40); Pennsylvania Academy of Fine Art—Philadelphia (40); National Gallery of Art (41); Guatemala National Fair (41); Art Institute of Chicago (43); Metropolitan Museum of Art (43); Jocelyn Art Museum—Omaha (43); Oregon Guild of Painters and Sculptors (45, 47, 48); Seattle Art Museum
References: ALM; DAV; HAV; KOV; MAL; MAL SUP; OET; WWW; A2 (1932, 44, 46, 48); A3 (52–55); C3 (31); C7 (46, 53); C11; C25 (36); M2; M3
Media: Watercolor, fresco, prints
Specialty: Murals
See artwork in color section

Lucia Wiley is identified with the city of Tillamook on the Oregon Coast, where she was born in 1906. She completed a mural for the Tillamook Post Office in 1943 and another, *Building of "The Morning Star"*, for the County Courthouse in 1950. The latter was selected by the Architectural League of New York as one of its finalists for their 1951 gold medal exhibition. She received her art education at the University of Oregon and then attended the Minneapolis Art School in Minnesota for one year. She then joined the faculty there. Wiley completed murals for the Minneapolis Post Office, Library, and Armory, as well as the International Falls Post Office during her stay.

Primarily known for her murals, Lucia Wiley exhibited her work as early as 1932, when her graduation thesis at the University of Oregon in Eugene consisted of four frescoes. In that year she had her first exhibit at the Portland Art Museum. She exhibited in a two-person show at a St. Paul, Minnesota gallery in 1934. Bennington College in Vermont mounted an exhibition of her work titled *Mural Painting in America in 1935*. She continued to exhibit at the Walker Galleries in Minneapolis, the Corcoran Gallery in Washington, D. C., and the Whitney Museum in New York City in their *National Mural Painters Society Exhibition* in 1940. She showed watercolors at the Pennsylvania Academy of Fine Art the same year.

Wiley gained international fame with her loan of cartoons for murals to the 1941 Guatemala National Fair. Her painting, *Buffalo Hunt*, was originally purchased by the Tate Gallery in London, but is now in the collection of the Portland Art Museum. In 1942 she returned to Tillamook to paint the Post Office mural. One year later she participated in two shows at the Metropolitan Museum in New York, titled *Artists for Victory*. Her painting, *Clam Bake*, was entered in the International Watercolor show Invitational held at the Art Institute of Chicago in 1943. She remained in Tillamook until 1947 when she took a faculty position at the Museum Art School in Portland, where she taught drawing and painting until 1955. During this time she continued to work on murals and to exhibit at the Portland and Seattle Art Museums. George Johanson*, who had recently graduated from the Museum Art School, assisted her on the 1950 mural project in

Tillamook. Public records for Lucia Wiley end in 1955, when she entered the Episcopal Convent, Holy Spirit of St. Hilda's, in New York City.

WILKINSON, Jack

b. 1913 Berkeley, CA
d. 1974 East Hampton, NY
Education: University of Oregon (1932–35); California School of Fine Arts (35–36); *Sterne* (35–37); Paris: *Léger, Gromaire* (38–39, 50–51, 57–58); Mexico (45)
Membership: Oregon Guild of Painters and Sculptors; San Francisco Art Association
Awards: Oregon Centennial (59)
Collections: San Francisco Museum of Art; University of Oregon; Eagle's Lodge—Eugene, Lane County Courthouse; University of Washington; California School of Fine Arts; Huntington Collection; Witham Collection
Exhibits: University of Oregon (1934, 50); Art Institute of Chicago (37); Couvaisier Gallery—San Francisco (38); San Francisco Museum of Art (1PS 39, 40); California Institute of Fine Arts (1PS 39); University of Oregon (41, 50; 1PS 59); Portland Art Museum (1PS 43, 45, 48, AM, 1PS 54); Kharouba Gallery (48); Oregon Guild of Painters and Sculptors (48); Musée de L'Art Moderne—Paris (51–52); Klamath Falls Art Association (IPS 53); Oregon Centennial (59)
References: ALM; DAV; HAV; MAL SUP; OET; HUG; WWW; A3 (1952–56); A4 (59); C6; C10
Media: Oil; prints (lithograph)
Specialty: Landscapes, murals, circus, dancers
See artwork in color section

Jack Wilkinson was a philosopher, teaching innovator, and an artist of international repute. Born in California, he completed undergraduate courses at the University of Oregon in Eugene before continuing at the California School of Fine Arts. He traveled to Paris to study with Fernand Léger and others. After joining the faculty at the University of Oregon in 1941, he established one of the first basic design courses in an American university. He was a legendary teacher, famous for lectures lasting longer than four hours. One student, Otto Fried*, remembered: "Since he was a man interested in all subjects, we had discussions in the fields of philosophy, psychology, mathematics, design, and of course, aesthetics. One class started at 9:00 AM and continued until 8:00 at night. Ten students started out, locations changed, and Jack was still talking and illuminating. The group narrowed to three and then two, with Jack still talking." He taught people to look for the underlying principle and basic factors in experience and to think imaginatively. He brought Buckminster Fuller to the University of Oregon campus in 1951 and helped start the Artist in Public Schools program. He encouraged mural painting and completed a large one on campus at the entrance to Lawrence Hall. He also completed murals in Burns, Oregon in the Federal Building in 1941 and in the Lane County Courthouse in Eugene.

Wilkinson participated in exhibitions worldwide. He had one-person shows at the California School of Fine Arts in 1939, the Portland Art Museum in 1954, and the University of Oregon in 1959. His many group shows included the Museum of Modern Art in Paris in 1951. Stylistically he began with an analytical approach to landscape, but by the 1950s his work became more abstract and figurative. In the 1960s he returned to landscapes and studies of the nude figure. Wilkinson's work captured a spirit of spontaneity. He preferred a cool palette with blue dominating. In 1968 he moved to Louisiana to head the department of fine arts at Louisiana State University, which presented a retrospective of his work in January of 1975.

WILSON, Dorothy Gilbert

b. d.

Education: Museum Art School (1914, 15); Art Students League

Membership: Oregon Society of Artists; Arts Guild

Exhibits: Portland Art Museum; Seattle Art Museum (1920); Oregon Society of Artists; Arts Guild

References: DAV; WWN; WWW; A2 (1914, 17, 20–22, 33); A4 (29, 59); A5 (30); C3 (27); C7 (21, 22); C15 (22); CD (27)

Media: Watercolor

Specialty: Portraits

Dorothy Gilbert studied at Portland's Museum Art School and the Art Students League in New York. She exhibited at the Portland Art Museum and the Seattle Art Museum and was a charter member of the Oregon Society of Artists. Her husband, Floyd Wilson*, accompanied her on a move to New York City. Gilbert's entry in a Portland Art Museum exhibit of contemporary American painters in 1929 occurred after their move east.

WILSON, Floyd

b. 1887 St. Peter, MN

d. 1974

Education: Minneapolis: *Henri*; Paris

Membership: Society of Oregon Artists; Arts Guild

Exhibits: Society of Oregon Artists (1913); Portland Art Museum; Panama Pacific International Exposition—San Francisco (15); Multnomah County Library Collection (15); Seattle Art Museum; Golden Gate Park Museum—San Francisco (16); Arts Guild

References: DAW; HUG; WWW; A2 (1914, 17, 20, 21); A4 (29); A5 (30); C5; C7 (15); ARTC; CD (14, 15)

Media: Oil, pastel

Floyd Wilson married artist Dorothy Gilbert Wilson* in Portland. He was a member of the early Society of Oregon Artists and exhibited at the Portland Art Museum and in San Francisco before moving to New York. Wilson and fellow artist Harry Wentz* had the distincion of being two Oregon painters who participated in the Panama Pacific International Exposition in San Francisco in 1915. Their work appeared in both the Fine Arts section and in the Oregon Room. He also exhibited in a show of contemporary American painters, which traveled to the Portland Art Museum in 1929.

WILSON, Milton

b. 1923 Portland, OR ***d.***

Education: Museum Art School; California School of Fine Arts; San Francisco Institute of Art

Membership: Artists Equity; Portland Art Museum (Artist Membership)

Awards: Seattle Art Museum (1949)

Collections: Portland Art Museum; University of Oregon; Reed College; Parsons Collection; Arlene and Harold Schnitzer Collection; Hallie Ford Museum of Art—Willamette University

Exhibits: Portland Art Museum (1PS 1950); Oregon Society of Artists; Seattle Art Museum; New Gallery of Contemporary Art (59, 1PS 59); Citizens for Art Group (59); Ruthermore Gallery—San Francisco (59); Oregon Centennial (59); University of Oregon (75)

References: ALM; COL; WWN; A2 (1944, 46, 48); A3 (49–58); A4 (59); C3 (45–47, 49); C6; C7 (49, 52, 54, 59); C22; C27

Media: Oil, watercolor
Specialty: Still life
See artwork in color section

Milton Wilson was one of the co-founders of the New Gallery for Contemporary Art, which was open from 1959 to 1962 in Portland. It was important for the time because it dealt only with contemporary art. Wilson was influenced by action painters. His style was forceful, dynamic, creative, and sometimes had a decorative quality. He had little interest in landscape, but stated that "all paintings are still lifes or landscapes." His early works were mainly still lifes, for which he used a cool palette. Later his paintings became more emotional and abstract, with an almost Mediterranean sensibility to color. He was a professor in the art department at Portland State University in 1974.

WINDUS, Lilyann Veatch

b. Portland, OR ***d.***
Education: University of Oregon (1936–40, 49)
Membership: Portland Art Museum (Artist Membership)
Exhibits: Portland Art Museum (1PS 1950); University of Oregon
References: A2 (1942, 44); A3 (49, 58)
Media: Prints

Lilyann Veatch Windus studied at the University of Oregon and exhibited at the Portland Art Museum in the 1940s. She taught in the art department at Lower Columbia College in Longview, Washington.

WIRE, Bessie Edna

b. 1885 Wauceka, WI
d. 1962 Salem, OR
Education: Southern Oregon College—Ashland; Museum Art School; *M. Wire**
Membership: American Artists Professional League; Oregon Society of Artists
Awards: American Artists Professional League (1937, 38)
Collections: Painting Restoration Studio Collection
Exhibits: Meier and Frank Co. (1914); Oregon Society of Artists; American Artists Professional League (37, 38); Hostess House Gallery
References: COL; DAW; WWN; C3 (1936, 46); M2; M3
Media: Watercolor, pastel, prints (lino-cuts)
Specialty: Landscapes, florals, still life

Bessie Wire was known primarily for her prints and drawings. Some of her lino-cuts are in the Portland Art Museum collection. She married artist Melville Wire* in 1914. In that same year, her exhibition at the Meier and Frank Co. in Portland featured her work along with that of her new husband. Wire's maiden name was Burgess.

WIRE, Melville Thomas, Rev.

b. 1877 Austin, IL
d. 1966 Salem, OR
Education: Willamette University: *M. LeGall**, *C. Cooke**; *E. Cline Smith**; University of Oregon: *E. Brown**
Membership: American Artists Professional League; Society of Oregon Artists; Oregon Society of Artists; Mutual Art Association
Awards: Oregon Society of Artists (1931, 37)
Collections: Oregon Historical Society; Powell Collection; Miranda Collection; Painting Restoration Studio Collection; Library of Congress; Humpal Collection; Centenary Wilbur Church—Portland; Hallie Ford Museum of Art—Willamette University; Cleveland Art Museum—Ohio; Parsons Collection; Lundberg Collection; Oregon State University; Cofield Collection

Exhibits: Society of Oregon Artists (1913); Mutual Art Association (14, 15); Meier and Frank Co. (14); Panama Pacific International Exposition—San Francisco (15); Seattle Art Museum; Portland Woman's Club (26); Oregon Society of Artists; American Artists Professional League (33, 37–38); Elfstrom Gallery (46); Oregon State University (55); Oregon Historical Society (90)

References: ALM; COL; DAV; DAW; HUG; WWN; WWW; A2 (1913, 14, 20–22, 30); C3 (27, 29, 30–32, 34–38); C5; C7 (21, 23, 28a); C9; C11; ARTC; MYH

Media: Oil, prints (etching), watercolor, colored pencil

Specialty: Landscapes (western), seascapes (coast)

See artwork in color section

Melville Wire was born in Illinois and came to Oregon at age seven when his father became pastor of Salem's First Methodist Church. He began art classes at Willamette University with Marie Craig LeGall* at this early age and continued until he was sixteen. It was under her influence that his love of drawing and painting began to emerge. He later studied with Eva Cline Smith*. His travels to Bend in 1896 resulted in many watercolors and sketches. Study for the ministry took him to Illinois, but upon graduation in 1902 he returned to Oregon. For sixty-one years Melville Wire was a pastor of the Methodist Church of Oregon and traveled the state painting and preaching. His lifetime artistic body of work reflects the diversity of the state.

In 1915 three of Wire's paintings were selected for exhibit at the Panama Pacific Exposition in San Francisco. He became a member of the Mutual Art Association in Portland and exhibited with them in 1914 and 1915. He was also a member of the American Artists Professional League and a charter member and active participant in the Oregon Society of Artists, garnering awards from them in 1931 and 1937. Later, encouraged by Gordon Gilkey (who became curator of prints and drawings at the Portland Art Museum) Wire began to study etching with Eyler Brown* at the University of Oregon. Wire was an outdoorsman who searched out secluded spots to sketch and paint. His preferred subject matter was the western landscape, and he was able to capture the spirit of the place in his oils, watercolors, and later etchings.

Wire retired from the ministry in 1946 and continued his art full time. The Associated American Artists of New York produced a catalog of his works for publication and national distribution. He continued to paint two hours a day when he was in his late eighties until his death in 1966. His first wife, Bess Burgess Wire,* was also an artist.

WISSENBACH, Frederick Charles, Rev.

b. 1887 Darmstadt, Germany ***d.***

Education: Frankfurt; Munich; Paris

Membership: Oregon Society of Artists

Awards: Oregon Society of Artists (1937, 38)

Collections: Vert Memorial—Pendleton

Exhibits: Oregon Society of Artists; J.K. Gill Gallery (1PS 1938); Pendleton (1PS 38)

References: COL; DAW; WWN; C3 (1936–38)

Media: Oil, watercolor, pen and ink

Specialty: Indians, portraits, landscapes (Eastern Oregon)

A review of his 1938 one-person show in Pendleton states that a collection of Frederick Wissenbach's paintings was purchased for the art memorial building in that city. His wife, Billie Berry Wissenbach, was also an artist of some note.

WITHAM, Vernon Clint

b. 1925 Eugene, OR ***d.***

Education: University of Oregon: *J. Wilkinson*, D. McCosh*, A. Vincent** (1943, 46–47, 51, 53); California School of Fine Arts (52)

Collections: IBM; U.S. Bank; Multnomah Athletic Club Collection; University of Oregon; University of Wyoming; Portland Art Museum

Exhibits: Graves Music and Art (1PS 1946), Gallery 720—Eugene (47, 1PS 48); California Palace of the Legion of Honor—San Francisco (47, 1PS 59); Reed College (1PS 49); Seligmann Gallery—New York (49, 52); Garrison Studio (1PS 52); Oakland Museum (52, 54); Portland Art Museum; San Francisco Museum of Art (55); East-West Gallery—San Francisco (55); Poor Richards Gallery—San Mateo (1PS 58)

References: WWAA; A3 (1953)

Media: Oil, watercolor, prints, ceramic, bronze sculpture

Specialty: Landscapes, missions

See artwork in color section

Vernon Witham was born and raised in Eugene where, as a high school student in 1941, he was asked to paint a mural in the school hall. He chose the history of music as his subject matter. Also in 1941 he attended the *Modern Mexican Artists* show in Portland and was very impressed with the paintings, especially their carved and painted frames. He was still in high school when he first saw the work of Jack Wilkinson*, a professor of art at the University of Oregon. Witham writes that he was "completely overwhelmed." In 1943 Witham began his study at the University of Oregon with Jack Wilkinson*, David McCosh*, and Andrew Vincent*. The following year he entered the army, running a silk screen shop at Fort Bliss, Texas. From that location he was able to continue his painting on weekends, going into Mexico or out into the desert.

After his discharge in 1946, Witham went to Mexico to absorb the culture and continue painting. With the help of the G.I. Bill, he returned to his schooling at the University of Oregon and, under Wilkinson*, began exploring structural systems and how cubism related to them. From 1946 to 1951 Witham's work was built upon the cubists and, he writes, he has gone on to invent his own structures and images. In 1947 he, Norma Driscoll*, and Paul Georges were chosen by a jury to participate in the Second Annual Exhibition of Painting at the California Palace of the Legion of Honor. Many of the leading painters of the time were invited to show at this exhibit, among them were: Milton Avery, Georgia O' Keeffe, Rufino Tamayo, and Robert Motherwell.

By 1949 Witham was in New York, where Robert Motherwell extended an invitation to him to attend Motherwell's school. Although pleased, he decided against attendance. He continued to paint until he became ill and returned to San Francisco to recover. There he shared an apartment with Driscoll* and Robert Gilmore* while he attended the California Institute of Fine Arts. He returned to Eugene and the University of Oregon, where he met fellow student James Ivory, now a well-known filmmaker. Ivory photographed many of Witham's cubist-style paintings and these works can be seen in the motion picture, *Surviving Picasso*.

Vernon Witham has painted in many styles, the result of working for over fifty years on a system of how the universe, and everything in it, operates. He left Eugene in 1960 and moved to Santa Fe.

WOLF, Warren A.

b. 1924 Payette, ID ***d.***

Education: University of Oregon: *A. Vincent*, D. McCosh*, J. Wilkinson** (1942–43, 46–49); Kansas City Art Institute—Missouri (49–50)

Membership: Portland Art Museum (Artist Membership)

Awards: Oregon State Fair (1951)

Collections: Portland Art Museum; University of Texas

Exhibits: Elfstrom Gallery (1PS 1950, 51); Harvey Welch Gallery (51); Oregon State Fairs (51, 59); Portland Art Museum (AM, 1PS 54); Southern Oregon Art Exhibit; Bush House Museum—Salem (1PS 59); Frye Museum—Seattle (59)

References: A3 (1951–54, 58); C26 (54, 55, 56)

Warren Wolf was a teacher, art school administrator, and practicing artist. He was dean of the art school at the State University College in Buffalo, New York before coming to Oregon to teach at Medford High School from 1952 to 1962. He also served as dean of Moore College of Art in Philadelphia from 1965 to 1971 and dean of the Portland Museum Art School from 1973 to 1977. Wolf taught a workshop in North Bend, sponsored by the Coos Artist League.

WOOD, Charles Erskine Scott (C.E.S.)

b. 1852 Erie, PA

d. 1944 Los Gatos, CA

Education: United States Military Academy at West Point; *Weir* (1874)

Membership: Oregon Art Association; Society of Oregon Artists

Awards: Oregon State Fair

Collections: Portland Art Museum; Art Institute of Chicago; Oregon Historical Society; Multnomah County Library Collection; Booth Collection; Parsons Collection; Lundberg Collection; Hurst Collection; Huntington Collection; Breithaupt Collection

Exhibits: Art Institute of Chicago (1895, 98, 99, 1902, 06, 10, 11); Oregon Art Association (96); Lewis and Clark Centennial Exposition (1905); Oregon State Fair; Portland Art Museum (1PS 13, 30); Society of Oregon Artists (12, 13); Panama Pacific International Exposition—San Francisco (15); University of Oregon (59); Oregon Historical Society (90); Clatsop County Historical Society (94)

References: ALM; BI; DAV; DAW; GER; HUG; OET; WWW; A1 (1908, 09); C5; C9; C11; C12; C21; ARTC; OSF (07)

Media: Watercolor, oil, pastel

Specialty: Landscapes, Indians

See artwork in color section

C.E.S. Wood was a soldier, lawyer, writer, poet, art patron, art critic, bibliophile, and artist. This man of many talents and interests was raised in the East. After graduating from West Point he was assigned to a post in the West, participating in the 1877 campaigns against the Nez Perce and the Paiute. He helped negotiate the surrender of Chief Joseph, recorded his famous speech at Bear Paw Mountain in Montana, and subsequently developed a deep friendship with him. The unjust treatment of the Native Americans was one of the reasons he resigned his commission in the military. Wood went to Columbia Law School and returned to Oregon in 1884 to establish a law practice in Portland. He specialized in maritime law, but also served clients whose cases tested civil liberties—Margaret Sanger was one. His reputation as a social activist grew as he co-authored Oregon's Initiative and Referendum Measures, the first of their kind in the nation. He lobbied for women's right to vote and became the Democratic candidate for U.S. Senator.

Wood's writing appeared in many forms. He was an art critic, whose essay, *Art a Threadbare Topic*, was published in the *Pacific Monthly*: "Art is useless except in the sense that it makes the world more beautiful, life more enjoyable ... A good landscape or portrait does not imitate, it suggests the beauty of the view, or the quality of the person and it does more. There has been put into it something of the artist's soul, something of the man himself ... art work is man's soul speaking to man's soul." His *Poet in the Desert*, about his love for the Harney Desert in eastern Oregon, is his most famous poem and Wood felt it was his major creative work. His book, *Heavenly Discourse*, is also well known. He recounted his experiences in the Indian campaigns in a publication of 1901. He was a frequent contributor to the *Spectator*. In 1911 he wrote an article calling for the public to purchase a permanent art collection. This would augment the frequent loan shows, some of which came from Wood's own collection.

Wood had developed friendships with several eastern artists. Childe Hassam* was a friend whom Wood invited to come to Oregon. On their trip to eastern Oregon in 1908, both artists produced landscapes. In some cases Wood's paintings are so similar to Hassam's that one has difficulty distinguishing them. Wood called himself an amateur painter, but his watercolors were especially good. His son, Erskine Wood wrote about his father's favorite subjects: scenes of the desert, ranches, buttes of eastern Oregon, rivers, lakes, and ocean. He also enjoyed painting the Portland harbor, grain ships, stern wheelers, the Columbia River, and duck hunting on Sauvie Island. His friendship with J. Alden Weir, who also visited him in Oregon, inspired Wood to use watercolor.

Wood was a founding member of the Portland Art Association in 1892, and a participating member in several arts organizations. He exhibited in the Fine Art Section at the Lewis and Clark Centennial Exposition in Portland in 1905. A cover for *Pacific Monthly* featured his painting, *View of Portland*, which is now in the Huntington Gallery in California. His role as art patron should not be overlooked. He was responsible for bringing Olin Warner, the sculptor, to Portland to execute the city's first public sculpture, the bronze Skidmore Fountain. Wood also participated in the early affairs of the Portland Art Museum and the Library Association.

Wood left his wife and family in 1919 to settle in Los Gatos, California with the poet Sara Bard Field. Their home became a gathering place for artists and intellectuals. Wood concentrated on his writing—revising old poems and composing new ones—until he died in that city at the age of 91. He signed works with his monogram, *CESW*.

WOODS, Mary F.

b. d.

Education: New York; Chicago; Académie Julian

Membership: Mutual Art Association

Awards: Oregon State Fairs

Exhibits: Oregon State Fairs; Mutual Art Association (1914, 15)

References: ARTC; OSF (1900, 06, 08, 09); CD (01–18, 20)

Specialty: Figures, portraits

Mary Woods was a teacher with a studio in the Marquam Building in Portland. She was a member of the early Mutual Art Association with exhibitions in 1914 and 1915. She had artist listings in the Portland City Directories from 1901 to 1918 and again in 1920. Woods also entered Oregon State Fairs in the early part of this century.

WOOLFOLK, Eva M.

b. d.
Education: Paris
Membership: Oregon Art Association; Portland Sketch Club
Exhibits: World Columbian Exposition—Chicago (1893); Portland Sketch Club; Oregon Art Association (96)
References: ARTC; CD (1895, 96, 98); M2; M3
Specialty: Children, portraits

Eva Woolfolk was one of the few women who went to Europe for art education at the turn of the century. She exhibited at the Chicago World's Fair in 1893 and taught at the Portland Sketch Club. Critics praised her atmospheric effects in *Notre Dame Cathedral*, and her "pure color and refined sentiment in portraits." She was living in New York City by 1920, where she was visited by her former student, Clara Jane Stephens*.

WRIGHT, Jennifer (Jennie) E.

b. 1838 Auburn, NY
d. 1922 Portland, OR
Education: New York
Membership: Oregon Art Association
Exhibits: North Pacific Industrial Exposition (1890); Oregon Art Association (96)
References: DAV; DAW; GER; KOV; PET; WWW; C2 (1890); ARTC; CD (93, 96, 98, 1903, 05–08, 14, 15); M2; M3
Specialty: Portraits, landscapes (mountains)

Jennie Wright traveled abroad extensively and lived in Chicago and New York before coming to Portland. Reviews noted her ability to paint Mt. Hood under every atmospheric condition. She was a strong advocate for women's rights. Kovinick (see Ref. KOV) gives a birthdate of 1837.

WUEST, Esther F.

b. 1878 Blue Island, IL
d. 1975 Portland, OR
Education: Art Institute of Chicago (1903); University of Chicago; Museum Art School (10)
Membership: Oregon Society of Artists; American Artists Professional League
Exhibits: Panama Pacific International Exposition—San Francisco (1915); Oregon Society of Artists
References: C3 (1928); C5; CD (07–8); M3

From 1916 to 1922 Esther Wuest taught with the University of Oregon Extension program in Portland. She then became supervisor of art in the Portland Public School system, a position she held from 1907 until her retirement in 1944, when she was succeeded by artist and teacher Ruth Halvorsen*. After retirement Wuest designed and published a course of study for art teachers.

Y

YELLAND, Raymond Dabb

b. 1848 London, England
d. 1900 Oakland, CA
Education: National Academy of Design: *Page, Bervoord, Wilmarth* (1869–71); Paris: *Merson*; San Francisco Art Association (74)
Membership: San Francisco Art Association
Collections: Oregon Historical Society; Oakland Museum; Bancroft Library—University of California Berkeley; Stenzel Collection; California Historical Society
Exhibits: San Francisco Art Association (1874–90); Portland Mechanics Fairs; National Academy of Design (82–88); Oregon Historical Society (1990)
References: BI; DAV; DAW; FIE; GER; HAV; HUG; MAL; SAM; THI; WWW; YNG; C4 (1881, 86); C9
Specialty: Landscapes (California, Yosemite), seascapes, marines, Indians

Raymond Dabb Yelland's first painting was of Gloucester Harbor in his native England. He came to the United States in 1851 and served in the Civil War. By 1874 he was living in San Francisco, where he became an art teacher at the California School of Design in 1877. He taught there for twenty years. Yelland also taught at the University of California Berkeley, Mills College, and the Mark Hopkins Institute. Known primarily as a California artist and teacher, he had a profound influence on his Oregon students. He painted a well-known example of *Mt. Hood* in 1883 that was exhibited at the Portland Mechanics Fair that year and is now in the collection of the Oregon Historical society. Born Raymond Dabb, he added his mother's maiden name of Yelland.

YEZERSKI, Dorothy

b. 1921 Portland, OR ***d.***
Education: Museum Art School (1942); Lewis and Clark College (52); *H. and C. Morris** (53); Reed College (54); *D. Lynch** (54–55)
Membership: Artists Equity; Portland Art Museum (Artist Membership)
Collections: Bank of Tokyo—Portland
Exhibits: Portland Art Museum (1PS 1957); Reed College (55); Seattle Art Museum; Henry Art Gallery—University of Washington (56); Portland State University (57); Oregon Centennial (59)
References: A3 (1954–58); C6; C7 (55, 56)
Media: Watercolor, oil
Specialty: Landscapes

Dorothy Yezerski taught at Riverdale Elementary School in Portland in 1954 and Pacific University in Forest Grove from 1958 to 1962. She also taught children's classes at the Museum Art School. Her penchant for painting landscape scenes as viewed from above allowed her to take advantage of the colors and patterns that exist in nature. Portland Art Museum's Rental Sales Gallery has represented her.

YOUNG, Edith J.

b. d.1946 Portland, OR
Membership: American Artists

Professional League; Oregon Society of Artists

Exhibits: Oregon Society of Artists; Portland Art Museum; American Artists Professional League (1933, 34)

References: A2 (1933, 34); C3 (28–32)

A member of both the American Artists Professional League and the Oregon Society of Artists, Edith Young exhibited with them in the late 1920s and early 1930s.

YUZURIHA, Zoichi

b. 1894 Hiroshima, Japan

d. 1975 Portland, OR

Exhibits: Portland Art Museum

References: A2 (1919–22)

Zoichi Yuzuriha exhibited at the Portland Art Museum from 1919 through 1922.

Z

ZALOUDEK, Duane

b. 1931 Enid, OK *b.*
Education: Museum Art School (1957)
Awards: Oregon Centennial (1959)
Collections: Portland Art Museum; Whitney Museum of Art; Marylhurst College; Parsons Collection; Pacific Northwest College of Art
Exhibits: Portland Art Museum; University of Portland (1PS 1954); Reed College (56, 59); New Gallery of Contemporary Art (59); Seattle Art Museum; Ruthermore Gallery —San Francisco (59); Oregon Centennial (59)
References: A3 (1954, 58); C6; C7 (59)
Media: Watercolors, oil, pencil
Specialty: Seascapes

A student at the Museum Art School in Portland, Duane Zaloudek's career was just beginning in the 1950s. While his style was "hard edge" and non-objective, he painted large, primary forms within the limited space of his canvas. Zaloudek lived in New York from 1957 to 1958.

ZANE, Nowland Brittin

b. 1885 Christiana, PA
d. 1945 Siltcoos Lake, OR
Education: Art Institute of Chicago; Pennsylvania Academy of Fine Art—Philadelphia; Drexel Institute—Philadelphia; University of Oregon
Membership: Oregon Society of Artists; American Artists Professional League; University Alumni Art League, University of Oregon
Awards: American Artists Professional League (1934)
Collections: Powell Collection
Exhibits: Portland Art Museum; Oregon Society of Artists; Seattle Art Museum; American Artists Professional League (1932–34, 39); University Alumni Art League
References: COL; DAV; DAW; WWN; A2 (1921, 22, 40); A4 (29); C3 (27–31); C7 (30); C11; C25 (36)
Media: Oil, watercolor, pastel, prints, pencil
Specialty: Murals, landscapes, seascapes

Originally from Pennsylvania, Nowland Zane arrived in Oregon in 1920. He was assistant professor of fine arts at the University of Oregon before taking a position with the Portland Public School system. Well known for his murals, he completed several for the library at the University of Oregon and one for a Salem theater. The Oregon Historical Society has Zane's prints in their collection. He was also the author of textbooks on the psychology of aesthetic appreciation.

ZINSLEY, Ann (Anna) Catherine

b. 1886 Oberweis, Germany
d. 1959 Portland, OR
Education: Salem Federal Art Center (1938–43); Museum Art School
Membership: Oregon Society of Artists; American Artists Professional League; Portland Art Museum (Artist Membership)
Exhibits: Portland Art Museum; American Artists Professional League (1939); Salem Federal Art Center (39)

References: A2 (1940, 42, 44, 46, 48); A3 (36, 37, 53)
Media: Oil, tempera, watercolor, prints (lithograph)
Specialty: Landscapes, coast scenes

Ann Zinsley lived in Portland from 1890 until her death. She was a legal stenographer, but active in the art community for many years. She was an artist member of the Portland Art Museum.

BIBLIOGRAPHY

BOOKS, PERIODICALS, MANUSCRIPTS

Allan, Lois. "Multiple Visions: Tracing Oregon's Visual Arts." *Oregon Humanities* (winter 1993): 2–10.

Appleton, Marion Beymner. *Who's Who in Northwest Art*. Seattle: Frank McCaffery, 1941.

"Artists Explore Various Media." *Oregonian*, January 15, 1963.

Baerny, Sharon Long. "Public Art, Public History." *Artifact Magazine* 1, no.1 (July/August 1995): 9–14.

Barchus, Agnes. *Eliza R. Barchus: The Oregon Artist 1857–1959*. Portland: Binford and Mort, 1974.

"Beach Artist." *Daily News* (Longview, Washington). September 9, 1984.

"Benezit, E. *Dictionnaire des Peintres, Sculpteurs, Dessinateurs & Gravures*. Nouvelle édition. Paris: Librairie Grund, 1976.

Binheim, Max. *Women of the West*. Los Angeles: Publishers Press, 1928.

Brooks, James E., ed. *Oregon Almanac and Book of Facts*. Portland: Binford and Mort, 1961.

Chamberlin, Lisa J. "Women Painters of Washington Tradition and Change." *Artifact Magazine* 1, no.3 (November/December 1995): 33–34.

Clark, Malcolm, ed. *Pharisee Among Philistines: The Diary of Judge Matthew P. Deady 1871–1892*. Portland: Oregon Historical Society Press, 1975.

Cleaver, J.D. *100 Significant Oregon Women Artists 1845–1945*. (manuscript).

———. *The Artists Patecky: A Place in History*. Portland: Oregon Historical Society Press, 1983.

———. *Oregon Women Artists 1845–1945*. (manuscript).

———. *Register of Oregon Art Chronology (1839-1989)*. (manuscript).

Colman, Roger. *Oregon Artists Source Book Circa 1941*. Portland: Portland State University, 1979.

Constance, Clifford L. *Chronology of Oregon Schools 1834–1958*. Eugene: University of Oregon Books, 1960.

Corning, Howard McKinley. *Oregon End of the Trail*. Portland: Binford and Mort, 1940; revised 1951.

Curran, Christine A. *The Role of the WPA Federal Art Projects in America and Its Influence in the Pacific Northwest*. (manuscript, spring 1987).

Davenport, R.J. *Davenport's Art Reference and Price Guide*. Marceline, Missouri: Walsworth Publishing, 1996–97.

Dawdy, Doris Ostrander. *Artists of the American West, A Biographical Dictionary*. 3 vols. Chicago: Swallow Press, 1974–85.

Directory to the Bicentennial Inventory of American Paintings Executed Before 1914. National Collection of Fine Arts, Smithsonian Institution: Arno Press, 1976.

Falk, Peter, ed. *Who Was Who in American Art*. Compiled from original 34 volumes of *American Art Annual, Who's Who in Art, and Biography of American Artists from 1898–1947*. Madison, Connecticut:

Sound View Press, 1985.

Fink, Lois Marie. *American Art of the 19th Century Paris Salons.* National Museum of American Art and The National Portrait Gallery, Smithsonian Institution. Cambridge: Cambridge University Press, 1990.

Fielding, Mantle. *Mantle Fielding's Dictionary of American Painters, Sculptors and Engravers.* Poughkeepsie, New York: Apollo, 1986.

Gerdts, William H. *Art Across America: Two Centuries of Regional Painting 1710–1920.* Vol. 3. New York: Abbeville Press, 1990.

Gilbert, Dorothy, B., ed. *Who's Who in American Art.* New York: R.R. Bowker Co., 1959.

Glauber, Carole. "A Wandering Lens. Myra Albert Wiggins: Photographer, Artist and Mentor." *Artifact Magazine* 1, no.5 (March/April 1996): 33–36.

———. *Witch of Kodakery. The Photography of Myra Albert Wiggins 1869–1956.* Pullman, Washington: Washington State University Press, 1997.

Groce, George C. and David H. Wallace. *New York Historical Society's Dictionary of Artists in America 1564–1860.* New Haven, Connecticut: Yale University Press, 1957.

Goetzmann, William H. *Looking at the Land of Promise, Pioneer Images of the Pacific Northwest.* Pullman, Washington: Washington State Press, 1988.

Griffin, Rachael. "Heaney's Landscape." *Stepping Out Northwest* (winter 1982).

Haverman, Joel. "Our Artists Reject Influence." *Oregonian*, December 12, 1965.

Havlice, Patricia P. *Index to Artistic Biography.* 2 vols. Metuchen, New Jersey: Scarecrow Press, 1973; First supplement, 1981.

Howard, Lori. "Renaissance Woman." *Old Oregon* (winter 1991).

Howes, Durwood, ed. *American Women: The Standard Biographical Dictionary of Notable Women, Vol. III (1939–40).* Los Angeles: American Publications, Inc., 1939.

Hughes, Eden M. *Artists in California 1786–1940.* 2nd ed. San Francisco, California: Hughes Publishing Co., 1989.

Hull, Roger. "Constance E. Fowler: Painter and Printmaker." *Artifact Magazine* 2, no.3 (November/December 1996): 23–24.

Kovinick, Phil and Marian Yoshiki-Kovinick. *An Encyclopedia of Women Artists of the American West.* Austin, Texas: University of Texas Press, 1998.

Kuhn, Cheryl. *Willamette Scene* (Willamette University Magazine). (Summer 1986): 12-13.

Mallett, Daniel T. *Mallett's Index of Artists, International-Biographical.* New York: Peter Smith, The Bomber Co., 1935.

———. *Supplement to Mallet's Index of Artists, International-Biographical.* New York: Peter Smith, The Bomber Co., 1948.

Marlor, Clark S. *Salons of America 1922–1936.* Madison, Connecticut: Sound View Press, 1991.

———. *SIA Exhibitiion Record 1917–1944.* Park Ridge, New Jersey: Noyes Press, 1984.

Martin, David F. "Lance Wood Hart." *Artifact Magazine* 1, no.1 (July/August 1995): 31–32.

Montgomery, Charlotte B. "Artists of Oregon Seen in New Annual." *Art Digest* 23, no. 18 (July 1, 1949): 8.

Oregon Artist. Journal of Museum Art School (Portland, September, 1954).

Oregon Spectator. (Portland, Oregon, 1846–1855). Multiple references, individually cited in text.

Petteys, Chris. *Dictionary of Women Artists: An International Dictionary of Women Artists Born Before 1900.* Boston: C.K. Hall and Co., 1985.

Portland Art Museum Handbook: Portland Art Museum Selected Works. Seattle: Marquand Books, Inc., 1996.

Rasmussen, Louise. *Art and Artists in Oregon 1500–1900* (manuscript, 1940).

Revisiting the White City: American Art at the 1893 World's Fair. National Museum of American Art and The National Portrait Gallery, Smithsonian Institution: University Press of New England, 1993.

Reyes, Karen Stoner. *Examination of the Origins of Expositions of Portland and Vicinity 1875 through 1905.* (manuscript, winter 1980).

Samuels, Peggy and Harold. *Samuels' Illustrated and Biographical Encyclopedia of the American West.* Garden City, New Jersey: Doubleday, 1976.

"Selected Meetings Attract Artist to Oregon Coast Areas." *Oregonian,* November 23, 1959.

Sheralyn, Maria. *Artists of the Pacific Northwest, a Biographical Dictionary 1600's–1994.* Jefferson, North Carolina: McFarland and Co., 1994.

Smith, Ralph C. *A Biographical Index of American Artists.* Baltimore, Maryland: The Williams & Wilkins Co., 1930.

Spectator. (Portland, Oregon, 1907–1931, 1933–1942). Multiple references, individually cited in text.

Stenzel, Franz. *James Madison Alden; Yankee Artist of the Pacific Coast.* Fort Worth, Texas: Amon Carter Museum, 1975.

———. *Cleveland Rockwell, Scientist and Artist, 1837–1907.* Portland: Oregon Historical Society Press, 1972.

Thieme, Ulrich and Felix Becker. *Allgemeines Lexicon der Bildenden Künstler.* Leipzig: E.A. Seemann, 1976.

Timberline Lodge, A Guided Tour. Portland, Oregon: Friends of Timberline, 1991.

Trenton, Patricia, ed. *Independent Spirits: Women Painters of the American West.* Autry Museum of Western Heritage in association with University of California Press, 1995.

Tripp, Dodie and F. Cook Sherburne. *Washington State Art and Artists 1850–1950.* Olympia, Washington: Sherburne Antiques, 1992.

van Gent, Ans. *History of Oregon Society of Artists* (manuscript, 1980).

Vollmer, Hans. *Allgemeines Lexicon der Bildenden Künstler: Des XX Jahrhundreds 1953–1962.* Leipzig: E.A. Seemann, 1972.

"Walters Will Depict Spirit of the Shipyards." *Telegram,* September 3, 1918.

The West Shore. (Portland, Oregon) Multiple references, individually cited in text.

Young, William. *Dictionary of American Artists, Sculptors and Engravers from the Beginnings Through the Twentieth Century.* Cambridge, Massachussetts: W. Young, 1968.

EXHIBITION CATALOGS

2nd Pacific Coast Biennial. Santa Barbara Museum of Art. Portland Art Museum (September–March 1957–58).

6th Anniversary Exhibit featuring Oregon Artists. Lincoln County Art Museum. DeLake, Oregon (1948).

A Gift of Love. Haseltine Family Collection Gift to the University of Oregon Museum of Art. Eugene, Oregon (November, 16–December 21, 1975).

Alumni Art Show. Erb Memorial Union Gallery. University of Oregon. Eugene, Oregon (October 9–November 10, 1989).

Annual Exhibition of University Alumni Art League. University of Oregon at Portland Art Museum. Portland, Oregon (1935, 36).

Artists Patecky: A Place in History. Oregon Historical Society. Portland, Oregon (May 9–July 15, 1983).

Art of the Oregon Territory, Oregon Centennial Festival of Art. University of Oregon. Eugene, Oregon (1959).

Art of the Pacific Northwest from the Thirties to the Present. National Collection of Fine Arts for the Smithsonian Institution. Washington, D.C. (1974).

Art of the Thirties: The Pacific Northwest. Portland Art Museum. Portland, Oregon (1972).

Art Room in the Oregon Building. Panama Pacific International Exposition. San Francisco, California (1915).

Art: USA: 58. Artists Equity and American Federation of Arts. New York (1958).

Bank as Art Patron. University of Oregon. Eugene, Oregon (1963).

C.S. Price (1874–1950) A Memorial Exhibition. Portland Art Musuem (March 9–April 18, 1951).

Contributing Artist: The Oregon Art Community 1839–1989. Oregon Historical Society. Portland, Oregon (1990).

Department of Fine Arts, Section B, under the Auspices of the Portland Art Association at the Museum of Art. Lewis and Clark Centennial Exposition. Portland, Oregon (1905).

Early Days in the Pacific Northwest: The Collection of Dr. and Mrs. Franz Stenzel. Portland Art Museum. Portland, Oregon (1959).

Eugene Bennett: A Retrospective. Southern Oregon Historical Society. Medford, Oregon (August 9–September 9, 1983).

Eugene Bennett: A Retrospective. Schneider Museum of Art. Southern Oregon State College. Ashland, Oregon (July 7–September 9, 1994).

Exhibition of Northwest Artists. Seattle Art Museum. Seattle, Washington (1914, 15, 17–23, 25–28, 28a, 29–32, 34–59).

The Exhibition of Work Done in Oregon Under the Public Works of Art Project. Portland Art Museum. Portland, Oregon (1934).

Fifty Years with C.S. Price: The Man, the Artist (1874–1950). Presented by the Oregon Journal. The Journal Auditorium. Portland, Oregon. (June 17–25, 1950).

Fine Arts Exhibit. Lewis and Clark Centennial Exposition. Portland, Oregon (June 1-October 15, 1905).

Independent Spirits: Women Painters of the American West. Autry Museum of Western Heritage. Los Angeles, California (1995).

Jack Wilkinson: Artist, Philosopher.

Museum of Art. University of Oregon. Eugene, Oregon (January, 21–March 4, 1990)

Legacy of John Henry Trullinger. Heritage Museum. Clatsop County Historical Society. Astoria, Oregon (September 16, 1989–March 16, 1990).

Northwest Classics: Early Paintings of the Pacific Northwest. Washington State Historical Society. Tacoma, Washington (1985).

Northwest Watercolor Society Exhibitions. Seattle, Washington (1947, 48, 52–57); New York (1948).

Oregon Artists. San Francisco Museum of Art. San Francisco, Californa (1943).

Oregon Artists Collection: First Half of the Twentieth Century. Clatsop County Historical Society. Astoria, Oregon (1994).

Oregon Professional Artists. R.F. Elfstrom Gallery. Salem, Oregon (1946, 47, 48).

The Oregon Scene. Centennial Exposition Building. Portland, Oregon (1959).

Oregon Society of Artists. Various venues. (1927–36, 45–51).

Oregon Watercolors. Anniversary Exhibition. Oregon Historical Society. Portland, Oregon. (1990).

Pacific Coast Around the World. Pacific Coast Floating Exposition Association (November–December, 1901).

Paintings and Sculptures of the Pacific Northwest: Oregon, Washington and British Columbia. Portland Art Museum. Portland, Oregon (1959).

Paintings of the American Scene: The WPA in Oregon. Portland Art Museum. Portland, Oregon (1987).

Portland Art Association Loan Exhibits:

Library Building, SW Stark (1902);

Museum Building, SW 5th and Taylor (1906, 08, 09, 20, 24);

Portland Art Museum, SW Park (1933, 53).

Portland Art Museum. Arts Guild. Portland, Oregon (1930, 33).

Portland Art Museum. Portland, Oregon (1911–15, 16, 17, 19–22, 29, 32–42, 44, 46, 48–59, 72).

Sally Haley: A Lifetime of Painting. The Art Gym. Marylhurst College. Marylhurst, Oregon (January 31–March 19, 1993).

Selected Work by Western Painters. Western Association of Art Museum Directors.

Portland Art Museum. Portland, Oregon (1922, 23);

Western Washington Fair. Puyallup, Washington (1946).

Selections from the Reed College Art Collection. Douglas F. Cooley Memorial Art Gallery. Reed College. Portland, Oregon (October 28–December 15, 1989).

Southern Oregon Art Exhibitions. American Association of University Women. Grants Pass, Oregon (1953–56, 58, 59).

Snowy Mountains: The Cascades as an Artistic Vision. Washington State Capitol Museum. Olympia, Washington (1987–88).

Watercolors by Oregon Artists. Portland Art Museum. Portland, Oregon (1953).

West to the Oregon Territory. (unpublished exhibit information). Maryhill Musuem. Goldendale, Washington (March–November, 1993).

OTHER SOURCES

Ashland City Directory (artist listing 1906).

First Eastern Oregon District Agricultural Fair, premium lists (1889, 90, 93, 96, 97).

First Southern Oregon District Agricultural Fair, premium lists (1896, 98, 99).

Museum Art School Catalogs. Portland Art Museum. Portland, Oregon (1910–59).

Mutual Art Association (exhibitions 1914, 15).

Oregon Art Association (exhibition 1896).

Oregon State Fair, premium lists (1861–81, 83, 1885–1904, 06–09).

Portland Art Club (exhibition 1886).

Portland Art Museum Annual Reports (1909–59).

Portland City Directories (artist listing 1863–65, 71, 73–76, 1880–1918, 20–41, 43–44, 50, 52–59).

Portland Industrial Exposition premium lists:

Portland Mechanics Fair, Portland, Oregon (1878–1888);

North Pacific Industrial Exposition, Portland, Oregon (1889, 90);

Portland Industrial Exposition, Portland, Oregon (1891–93);

Oregon Industrial Exposition, Portland, Oregon (1895, 96, 99).

Portland Sketch Club (exhibition 1898, 99, 1900).

Salem City Directories (artist listing 1891, 93, 96, 1902, 05, 09–10, 53–54).

Seaside City Directories (artist listing 1957, 59).

Second Eastern Oregon District Agricultural Fair, premium lists (1891–98).

Second Southern Oregon District Agricultural Fair, premium lists (1894, 96–98).

Society of Oregon Artists (exhibitions 1912–14).

Southern Oregon Agricultural Fair, premium lists (1890, 92).

Southern Oregon County Fair, premium lists (1898, 99).

Western Washington Fair. Puyallup, Washington (1940, 41, 46, 48–52, 58, 59).†

Willamette University Catalogs. Salem, Oregon (1860–1917).

Premium lists are housed in the Oregon Historical Society Archives.

† Western Washington State Fair premium lists are housed in the University of Washington library archives.

ACKNOWLEDGMENTS

There are two men who deserve credit for seeing this project through to completion. Bill Allen and Harvey Klevit not only provided moral support and encouragement but also, with endless patience, set up three databases, dragged computer illiterate wives into the Information Age, read and reread the biographies until they knew the material as if they had written it, and served as mediators when decisions seemed unattainable. The debt of gratitude owed goes beyond simple words.

Two others were also instrumental in furthering this endeavor. Robert Joki and Jack Cleaver opened up their files and then their lives to our constant inquiries and needling. They inspired us with their knowledge, humor, and patience, provided access to much of the information that appears on these pages, and reviewed our manuscript for accuracy in an attempt to make it perfect.

From its very inception, Eva Rickles' quiet encouragement and clear-headed guidance kept the project focused and moving toward reality. For these contributions we thank her.

Our thanks to the staff of the Oregon Historical Society Press: Adair Law for guiding us to the successful accomplishment of this book; Evan Schneider for his photographic expertise; Denise Bekkedahl for her insightful editorial comments; and Barbara Osborne for her layout and design.

We would like to extend very special thanks to Roger Hull at Willamette University and Kenneth O'Connell at University of Oregon.

Finally Dan Lucas, former Portland Art Museum Librarian, deserves special recognition for his encouragement, wealth of information, and endless hours of proofing to ensure that the final book would be worthy of its position on a museum reference shelf.

A large number of Pacific Northwest art groups, historical societies, universities, museums, and libraries provided invaluable research assistance. Following is a list of those most helpful:

Arts Council of Southern Oregon: Jennifer Stepanik; *Bush House Museum:*

Jennifer Hagloch (Curator); *Catlin Gabel School:* Sarah Ferguson; *Central Curry Council for the Arts and Humanities; Clatsop County Historical Society*: Karen Broenneke, Mark Talonen (Curator); *Coos Art Museum:* Helen Scully; *Coos County Historical Society:* Ann Koppy; *Corvallis Art Center; Cottage Grove Museum; Crook County Historical Society:* Gordon Gillespie; *Douglas County Museum of History and Natural History:* Irene Zenev; *Grants Pass Museum:* Hatje Joswick; *Harney County Historical Society:* Sharon M. Jones; *Jake's Famous Crawfish Restaurant:* Larry Baldwin (Manager); *Josephine County Historical Society:* Marge Porter; *Juniper Art Guild:* John M. Fagan; *Kaiser Foundation Health Plan of the Northwest:* Becky Belangy; *Lane Arts Council; Lewis and Clark College:* Donna Hawk; *Marylhurst College:* Sister Rosemary Kasper (Archivist); *Maud Kerns Art Center:* Mary-Helen Burnham; *Multnomah Country Library:* June Mikkelsen; *Multnomah Athletic Club*: Alyson Breathed, Steve Tedisch; *Northwest Watercolor Society:* Linda Lee Foster; *Oregon Historical Society Library:* Sieglinde Smith; *Oregon State University:* Elizabeth Nielsen (Archives), Doug Russell (Department of Fine Arts), Kent Sumner (Memorial Union); *Oregon Trail Regional Museum; Pacific University Archives:* Richard T. Read, Julie Holcomb, Alex Toth; *Portland Art Museum:* Barbara Anderson and Debra Royer (Rex Putnam Library), Anne Eichelberg (Registrar); *Reed College:* Susan Fillen-Yeh; *Rogue Valley Art Center:* Nancy Jo Mullen; *Sagebrushers:* Margaret Meritt; *Salem Art Association; Southern Oregon Historical Society:* Carol Harbison-Samuelson, Jacque Sundstrand (Curator); *The Dalles Art Club:* Gini Smith; *Tillamook Arts Association; Tillamook County Pioneer Museum:* Wayne Jensen; *University of Oregon:* Katherine Sterling, Jean Nattinger, Kathleen Metzger, Larry Fong (Museum staff), Keith Richards (Archives), Karen Johnson (Department of Architecture and Allied Arts); *University of Portland:* Bryan Dagle; *University of Washington:* Gary Lundell (Reference Specialist, Allen Library); *US Bank:* Jim Becker; *Washington State Historical Society:* Amy McCune; *Willamette University:* Joni Roberts (Mark O. Hatfield Library), Linda Nelson (Art Department).

Several galleries have shown special interest in this project and have been generous with information and encouragement.

Artspace: Trisha and Craig Kauffman; *Bush's Antiques:* John Bush; *Kerwin Galleries:* Mercedes Kerwin; *Laura Russo Gallery:* Laura Russo; *Martin-Zambito Gallery:* David Martin, Dominic Zambito; Matthew's Galleries: Matthew Gerber; *Painting Restoration Studio:* Steve Maker, Harvey Freer; Santos Gallery: Mark Santos; *Sovereign Collection:* Robert Joki, Bill Salvesen.

Some private collectors deserve recognition for their generosity in sharing their collections with us and allowing us to cite them in the book.

Brian and Gwyneth Booth; Henry and Mary Breithaupt; Brooks and Dorothy Cofield; Ron Ennis; Mr. and Mrs. Matthew Gerber; Doug and Lila Goodman; John Gray; Mark Humpal; Wallace K. Huntington; Peter and Lannie Hurst; Tracy Linebarger; Robert Lundberg; Steve Maker and Harvey Freer; Jim and Elizabeth Marquard; Miranda Collection; Michael Parsons and Marte Lamb; Alice and Michael Powell; Marge Riley; Arlene and Harold Schnitzer; William Stallings and Diane Cazalet

Lastly, many individuals also provided support through their knowledge and encouragement. They shared their recollections of friends or relatives who were painters, or, in some cases, are the painters themselves.

Richard Abel, Linny Adamson, Lois Allan, Barbara Altermatt, C. Bryce Anderson, Laura Ashbrenner, Eugene Bennett, Terry Jo Bonbright, Marna Broekhoff, Gail Brown, Raymond and Hazel Chilstrom, Joe Erdelac, Jack Eyerly, Otto Fried, Judy Gardner, Theodore Gégoux III, Gordon Gilkey, Bruce Hamilton, James and Maury Haseltine, William Hawkins II, Frederick and Sybil Heidel, Gerry Highsmith, Ronald Tore Janson, George Johanson, LaVon Salmela Lucas, E. Kimbark MacColl, Jack and Barbara McLarty, Charles Mulvey, Greg Nelson, Norris Perkins, M.D., Dana Platz, Charles Rhyne, Mike Russo and Sally Haley Russo, Faye Sorenson, Ans van Gent, Andrew Vincent, Douglas Vincent, John Waddingham, Gloria Heisley Webber, Harry Widman, Andy Wilder, Chris Keylock Williams, Vernon Witham.

COLOPHON

The typeface used throughout *Oregon Painters, The First Hundred Years* is Janson. Created by the Hungarian type designer, Nicholas Kis, this typeface is often incorrectly attributed to the Dutch typefounder, Anton Janson

Nicholas Kis was born in 1650 and by 1677 had completed his post graduate studies in theology. In 1680 he received a mandate from Bishop Mihály Tofeus to go to Amsterdam, get information on book publishing, and explore the possibility of printing a Hungarian Bible in Amsterdam. He left Hungary in August of 1680 and by January 1681 he reported back that he was willing to take on the challenge of the Hungarian Bible project. The *Hungarian Bible* was completed in 1685.

Nicholas Kis has been described as a scholar, type designer, a cultural visionary, but above all a pursuer of beauty with his types and the printing of books. He died in 1702.

The display typeface used throughout the Dictionary section of the book is Pablo. It is a typeface modeled on the signature of Pablo Picasso.

The production of this book was accomplished through the expertise and assistance of the following people:

Editing: Denise Bekkedahl

Design and layout: Osborne Design Associates

Color photography: Evan Schneider, Oregon Historical Society

Color scanning: Richard Jost, Oregon Historical Society

Printing: Publishers Press, Salt Lake City, Utah

Production Assistance: Bob Smith, BookPrinters Network

We would also like to thank the many private collectors, gallery owners, museums and historical societies who have generously shared their collections and their passion for Oregon art.